Melbourne & Victoria

The Murray River & Around
p281

The High Country
p256

Goldfields & the Grampians
p187

Around Melbourne
p129

Gippsland & Wilsons Promontory
p231

◉ **Melbourne**
p44

Great Ocean Road & Bellarine Peninsula
p149

Mornington Peninsula & Phillip Island
p215

THIS EDITION WRITTEN AND RESEARCHED BY

Anthony Ham,

Trent Holden, Kate Morgan

Contents

PLAN YOUR TRIP

Welcome to
Melbourne & Victoria.... 4

Melbourne
& Victoria Map 6

Melbourne
& Victoria's Top 12 8

Need to Know 14

What's New 16

If You Like.............17

Month by Month.......20

Itineraries 24

Victoria Outdoors......34

Travel with Children.... 38

Regions at a Glance.... 40

ON THE ROAD

MELBOURNE....... 44

AROUND
MELBOURNE...... 129

The Dandenongs.......131
Yarra Valley 134
Healesville & the
Lower Yarra Valley 134
Warburton & the
Upper Yarra Valley 138
Marysville 139
Lake Mountain 141
The Spa Country 141
Daylesford &
Hepburn Springs 141
Macedon Ranges
& Around 147

GREAT OCEAN ROAD &
BELLARINE
PENINSULA....... 149

Geelong 152
Bellarine Peninsula 157
Great Ocean Road 162
Torquay 162
Anglesea 164
Aireys Inlet & Around ... 165
Lorne 166
Apollo Bay 170

Cape Otway............ 173
Port Campbell
National Park 174
Port Campbell.......... 175
Warrnambool 177
Port Fairy............. 181
Portland............... 184

GOLDFIELDS &
THE GRAMPIANS...187

Ballarat 190
Bendigo 196
Kyneton 201
Castlemaine 202
Maldon...............205
Maryborough 206
The Grampians 207
Grampians National
Park (Gariwerd) 207
Halls Gap.............. 210
Dunkeld & the
Southern Grampians.... 212
Wartook Valley & the
Northern Grampians 212
Horsham 213
Mt Arapiles State Park .. 213
Little Desert
National Park 213
Dimboola.............. 214

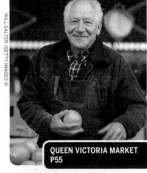

QUEEN VICTORIA MARKET
P55

MELBOURNE BARS P102

SIDNEY MYER
MUSIC BOWL P117

Contents

MORNINGTON PENINSULA & PHILLIP ISLAND... 215

Mornington Peninsula . 216

Mornington 217
Sorrento 220
Portsea 222
Point Nepean
National Park 222
Mornington Peninsula
National Park 223
Flinders 223
Red Hill & Around 224
French Island 224
Phillip Island 225

GIPPSLAND & WILSONS PROMONTORY 231

Walhalla 234
Inverloch 235
Bunurong Marine
& Coastal Park 236
Koonwarra 237
Wilsons Promontory
National Park 238
Port Albert 242
Sale 242
Ninety Mile Beach 243
Loch Sport & Lakes
National Park 244
Paynesville
& Raymond Island 244
Metung 245
Lakes Entrance 246
Buchan 249
Snowy River
National Park 249
Errinundra National Park . . . 250
Cape Conran
Coastal Park 252
Mallacoota 252
Croajingolong
National Park 254

THE HIGH COUNTRY 256

Baw Baw
National Park 257
Lake Eildon
National Park 257
Eildon 260
Jamieson 261
Mansfield 261
Mt Buller 263
King Valley
& the Snow Road 265
Beechworth 266
Yackandandah 269
Myrtleford 270
Mt Buffalo
National Park 270
Bright 271
Mt Beauty
& the Kiewa Valley 274
Falls Creek 275
Harrietville 277
Mt Hotham
& Dinner Plain 278

THE MURRAY RIVER & AROUND 281

Mildura 284
The Mallee 288
Wyperfeld
National Park 288
Murray-Sunset
National Park 288
Hattah-Kulkyne
National Park 289
Swan Hill 289
Echuca 292
Yarrawonga 298
Rutherglen 299
Chiltern 301
Benalla 302
Glenrowan 302
Wangaratta 302
Wodonga 304

UNDERSTAND

Melbourne
& Victoria Today 306
History 308
Food & Drink 318
Fashion & Shopping . . . 324
The Arts 326
Sport 334

SURVIVAL GUIDE

Directory A–Z 338
Transport 345
Index 352
Map Legend 359

SPECIAL FEATURES

Itineraries 24
Victoria Outdoors 34
Arcades & Laneways
City Walk 56

STEFANO'S RESTAURANT, MILDURA P287

Welcome to Melbourne & Victoria

Melbourne is food-obsessed, marvellously multicultural and a showpiece for Australian culture. Beyond the city limits, Victoria offers soulful history, stirring wilderness and culinary excellence.

Great Outdoors

Victorians are spoilt for wilderness choice. To the southwest, the Great Ocean Road snakes along one of the world's most spectacular coastlines, while the further east you go the wilder the coast gets, from wildlife-rich Wilsons Promontory to Gippsland's aptly named Wilderness Coast. Also east, wild rivers and epic forests of Errinundra and Snowy River yield to picturesque mountains of the High Country, where year-round activities make it an adventure destination of the highest order. Northwest, almost in the outback, desertlike national parks occupy vast swathes of the state. Opportunities to explore are endless, whether on two legs or skis, two wheels or four.

Great Indoors

In the 19th century, gold-rich Melbourne and small towns in Victoria were stamped with architectural wonders. These days many of those grand buildings survive as luxury hotels, theatres bursting with talent or colourful state-of-the-art galleries. Melbourne in particular is an art lover's smorgasbord (with signature art-strewn laneways so intimate as to feel like they're indoors), but regional Victoria holds its own when it comes to reasons to pray for a rainy day.

Food & Wine

Melbourne loves its food. A growing passion for street food has been grafted onto a long-standing multicultural culinary scene that has few peers. Throw in a highly developed cafe culture, an enduring passion for experimentation, and all manner of designer dens where serious eating is the order of the day, and you've one of Australia's true culinary capitals. Regional Victoria has a number of respected wine regions, from the Yarra Valley to King Valley, Mornington Peninsula to Rutherglen; bastions of gourmet food delights such as Milawa; and a catalogue of boutique breweries and outstanding restaurants.

History's Canvas

Victoria's history is epic, but couldn't be more accessible. The state's Indigenous story serves as a subtext throughout, but it takes centre stage with rock art and creation stories at Gariwerd (the Grampians). Fast-forward a few millennia to Victoria's 19th-century gold rush, which left behind some of Australia's most atmospheric old towns, among them Ballarat, Castlemaine, Maldon, Kyneton, Walhalla and Beechworth. And the old Murray riverboat culture of Australia's pioneering days lives on in Mildura, Swan Hill and, especially, Echuca.

Why I Love Melbourne & Victoria

By Anthony Ham, Author

I was born in Melbourne and spent my summers on Victoria's beaches. But it was only after moving overseas as an adult that I came to understand my connection with the land. In my 10 years away, I came to long for the culinary variety of Melbourne, for the forests of the far east, for the craggy Victorian coastline, for the river red gums along the Murray, for the endless horizons of the desertlike Mallee. And upon my return I discovered a city and a state that has moved forward in leaps and bounds without ever losing its soul.

For more about our authors, see page 360.

Above: Surfers at Cape Woolamai (p226), Phillip Island

Melbourne & Victoria

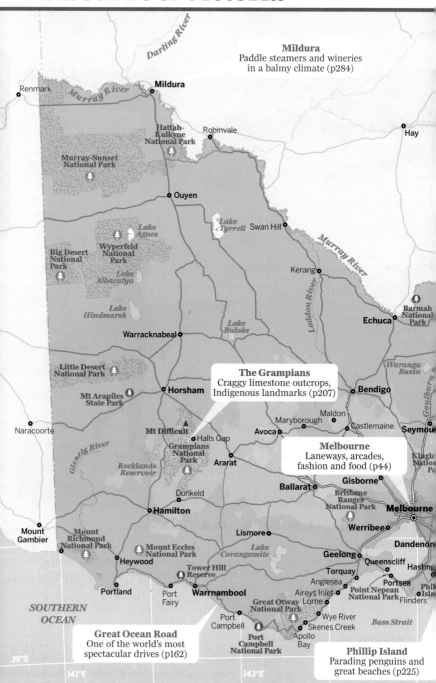

Mildura
Paddle steamers and wineries
in a balmy climate (p284)

The Grampians
Craggy limestone outcrops,
Indigenous landmarks (p207)

Melbourne
Laneways, arcades,
fashion and food (p44)

Great Ocean Road
One of the world's most
spectacular drives (p162)

Phillip Island
Parading penguins and
great beaches (p225)

N 0 — 100 km
   0 — 60 miles

ELEVATION

1200m
900m
600m
300m
0

Goulburn

Lake George

Canberra ✪

urrumbidgee River

Yarrawonga

Murray River

Rutherglen

Chiltern

Albury

Wodonga

Burrowa-Pine Mountain National Park

Hume Reservoir

Corryong

High Country Adventure
Ski in winter, stunning year-round (p256)

hepparton

Wangaratta

Yackandandah

Lake Mokoan

Beechworth

Myrtleford

Ovens River

Benalla

Mount Buffalo National Park

Mount Beauty

Bright

Harrietville

Lake Dartmouth

Mt Bogong

Falls Creek

Mt Koscuiszko

Snowy River National Park

Bega

Mansfield

Lake Eildon

Mt Buller

Mt Featherton

Mount Hotham

Omeo

Snowy River

Eildon

Jamieson

Alpine National Park

Lake Eildon National Park

Marysville

Errinundra National Park

Cooracambra National Park

ealesville

Yarra River

Baw Baw National Park

Buchan

Walhalla
Stunning and remote gold-mining hamlet (p234)

Mallacoota

Warburton

Dandenong Ranges National Park

Walhalla

Bairnsdale

Lakes Entrance

Orbost

Marlo

Cape Conran Coastal Park

Croajingolong National Park

Moe

Traralgon

Lake Wellington

Paynesville

Metung

Lake Victoria

Sale

Warragul

Morwell

Ninety Mile Beach

38°S

TASMAN SEA

ench land

Korumburra

Leongatha

Koonwarra

Tara Bulga National Park

onthaggi

Inverloch

Foster

Yarram

Port Albert

Fish Creek

Wilsons Promontory National Park

anurong Marine & Coastal Park

Tidal River

Mt Latrobe

Wilsons Promontory
Spectacular southernmost coastline (p238)

147°E

148°E

149°E

39°S

Melbourne & Victoria's
Top 12

Great Ocean Road

1 Take it slow driving along roads (p162) that curl beside spectacular beaches then whip inland through rainforests. Check out Bells Beach legendary surf, see kangaroos in Anglesea, swim at Lorne and go koala-spotting at Cape Otway. Then stand in awe at the Twelve Apostles, one of Victoria's most vivid sights. Head inland for gourmet treasures in Timboon, watch whales in Warrnambool further along the coast and discover the maritime treasure of Port Fairy. For the ultimate in slow travel, walk the Great Ocean Road (p172).
Bottom left: Twelve Apostles (p174)

Melbourne's Laneways

2 Head down the many bluestone-laden laneways (p56) in Melbourne to find hidden restaurants as well as bright, bold street art that encapsulates the alternative vibe Melburnians carry so well. In Degraves St let a local barista change the way you think about coffee. Duck in and out of boutiques on Flinders Lane before dining at one of the city's hottest restaurants. Let the evening steer you upstairs to a rooftop or down a graffiti-covered lane to find smooth drinking establishments serving up quality cocktails, wine and craft beer.
Bottom right: Centre Place (p56)

The Grampians

3 Rising up from otherwise pancake-flat countryside, the landscape of the Grampians (p207) is as timeless as it is tempting. The granite outcrops here are custom-made for rock climbing, abseiling and bushwalking. Not that adventurous? You can drive to waterfalls, stunning lookouts and bush camps carpeted in wildflowers; sample local wines; and learn stories of how Indigenous Australians lived in a place called Gariwerd. Families or couples will find just as much to do here as adventurers. Below: Aboriginal handprints, Manja Shelter (p208), Grampians National Park

Cultural & Sporting Melbourne

4 If it's footy season in Melbourne, you'll know about it. But it's not just winter that sees absolute sporting dedication (p334) from Melburnians: come spring it's the horse-racing, summer it's cricket and tennis – and everyone's invited to join in the conversation and watch the action. The arts scene (p326) is strong and highly regarded: explore Melbourne's art galleries and wear your best dark clothes to one of the many literary, comedic and musical events that pack the diaries of Melburnians. Bottom: Edge Theatre, Federation Square (p45)

DAVID HANNAH / GETTY IMAGES ©

CHRIS MELLOR / GETTY IMAGES ©

Wilsons Promontory

5 For sheer natural beauty, Wilsons Promontory (p238) has it all. Jutting out into Bass Strait, this national park is isolated but accessible, boasting sublime beaches and some of the state's best hiking. There's a well-maintained network of trails and bush-camping areas – just grab a map, strap on a pack and disappear into the wilds. The overnight walk across the Prom from Tidal River to Sealers Cove and back is a great way to get started, but serious hikers should tackle the Great Prom Walk, staying a night in the gloriously isolated lighthouse keepers' cottages. Top left: Sealers Cove Walk (p241)

St Kilda

6 It's not just the palm trees, bay vistas, briny breezes and pink-stained sunsets that give St Kilda (p71) its appeal. An eclectic cast of characters calls this place home, so it's got something for everyone. Dine at an assortment of chic eateries or indulge in one of Acland St's historical European cake shops. Up the road you can ride a rickety 1920s roller coaster while taking in the bay views, then knock back beers in a divey bar before catching a local band belting it out at the pub. Top right: Luna Park (p73)

Phillip Island & the Penguin Parade

7 Who can resist the nightly parade of cute little penguins waddling from the ocean and into their sandy burrows? Not the 3 million–plus tourists who visit Phillip Island (p225) annually, that's for sure. Luckily there's more to this little island in Western Port Bay: fabulous surf beaches, wildlife parks, a MotoGP circuit that will satisfy revheads even when there's no racing on, and loads of things to keep kids busy. For something different, make the short ferry trip to French Island (p224).

JAMES LYON / GETTY IMAGES ©

High Country Adventure

8 The mountains and valleys of the High Country (p256) are Victoria's year-round adventure playground. In the 'white season', some of the best skiing, snowboarding and après-ski in Australia can be found on the slopes of Mt Hotham, Mt Buller and Falls Creek. In the 'green season', you can make like *The Man from Snowy River* riding horses on the high plains, or dive into high-adrenalin pursuits such as mountain biking and paragliding. If all that gets too much, hit the wine-and-cheese trail in northeastern Victoria's gourmet region.
Top left: Falls Creek (p275)

Mildura

9 The riverside towns on the Murray can take you back to the days of paddle steamers, then fast-forward you to a world of houseboats, water sports and wineries. For the very best of the Murray, Mildura (p284) is an isolated oasis town with a glorious climate, a relaxed attitude, art deco architecture and some of regional Victoria's best gourmet dining. Spend the morning cruising to a winery lunch on a restored paddle steamer, the afternoon swimming, kayaking or golfing, and the evening choosing from the restaurants on 'Feast Street' – get a table at Stefano's (p287) if you can! Top right: PV *Rothbury* paddle steamer (p285)

Gippsland Lakes

10 Water, water, everywhere. Aside from the famous Ninety Mile Beach, east Gippsland's Lakes District (p242) is a glistening patchwork of waterways and inlets where boating and fishing are a way of life. Experience the coastal charm of villages such as Paynesville, Metung and gorgeous Mallacoota, cruise the lakes to wineries and waterside pubs, and gorge on the state's freshest seafood. Throw in some of Victoria's wildest coastal parks, among them World Biosphere Reserve Croajingolong, and you've a trip to remember. Above: Pier at Mallacoota Inlet (p252)

Country Charm

11 There's a lot to like about Victoria's country towns – an unhurried pace, that country air – and many are only a short drive from Melbourne. Head up the Calder Hwy to the historic goldfield towns of Kyneton, Castlemaine and Maldon (p201), where grand 19th-century buildings, galleries and markets will keep you occupied for days. Day-trip to Daylesford and Hepburn Springs (p141) for relaxing spa treatments and cafes. In the northeast, gorgeous Beechworth (p266), Yackandandah (p269) and Bright (p271) are year-round delights.

Below: Lavandula (p146), near Hepburn Springs

Walhalla

12 Caught in a time warp deep in the forests of northern Gippsland, Walhalla (p234) is arguably Victoria's most rewarding village experience. It's partly to do with its location, strung out along a forested, steep-sided valley down a road from nowhere to nowhere. But, above all, Walhalla's charm derives from its authenticity. This is no theme park, but instead a tiny hamlet where the timber houses tell a story of a mining boom that went bust, leaving the town to settle back into gentle obscurity. It's a stunning, soulful place.

Bottom: Walhalla Goldfields Railway (p234)

Need to Know

For more information, see Survival Guide (p337)

Currency
Australian dollar ($)

Language
English

Visas
Visas are required for international travellers except New Zealand passport holders; check www.immi.gov.au for information.

Money
ATMs can be found in most towns, and credit cards are widely accepted.

Mobile Phones
Local SIM cards are available and cheap. CDMA band phones don't work in Australia; other phones can be set to roaming before leaving.

Time
Australian Eastern Standard Time (GMT +10 hours; +11 hours during daylight saving)

When to Go

Warm to hot summers, mild winters

Dry climate, very hot summers, mild winters

Mildura
GO Jul–Oct

Mt Hotham
GO Jun–Sep

Ballarat
GO Mar–Jun

Cape Otway
GO Jan–Apr

High Season
(Dec–Jan)

➡ Beaches are packed with local holidaymakers soaking up the sun and enjoying school holidays.

➡ Easter and June/July school holidays are also busy times.

➡ Book months ahead for coastal accommodation, including camping.

Shoulder
(Feb–Mar)

➡ Quieter time with many more accommodation vacancies.

➡ Late-summer weather can be particularly hot.

Low Season
(Apr–Nov)

➡ Milder weather; often decent rainfall during second low season of September to November.

➡ July to September is peak whale-watching season off Warrnambool.

➡ Ski-resort high season from June to August.

Websites

Lonely Planet (www.lonely planet.com/melbourne) Destination information, hotel bookings, traveller forum and more.

Visit Victoria (www.visitvictoria. com) Official state tourism site.

Parks Victoria (www.parkweb. vic.gov.au) Profiles Victoria's national parks with details on accommodation.

Broadsheet (www.broadsheet. com.au/melbourne) Finger-on-the-pulse site devoted to getting the best out of Melbourne.

The Age (www.theage.com.au) Local news and reviews.

Bureau of Meteorology (www. bom.gov.au/weather/vic) Guidance for the weather, which can change at a moment's notice.

Important Numbers

Callers to Australia need to drop the first '0' in a mobile-phone number and the '0' of Victoria's 🖉03 area code.

Country code	🖉61
International access code	🖉00
Police, fire & ambulance	🖉000
Parks Victoria	🖉13 19 63

Exchange Rates

Canada	C$1	A$1.02
Europe	€1	A$1.53
Japan	¥100	A$1.08
New Zealand	NZ$1	A$0.94
UK	UK£1	A$1.84
US	US$1	A$1.09

For current exchange rates see www.xe.com

Daily Costs

Budget: Less than $125

➡ Dorm beds: $20–50

➡ Cheap meals and fresh food markets: $15–25

➡ Local live music: $10

➡ DIY walking tour: free

Midrange: $125–$200

➡ Hotel room: $80–100

➡ Breakfast at a quality cafe: $15–20

➡ Tapas and a couple of cocktails: $50–80

➡ A major live gig: $50–100

Top End: More than $200

➡ Hotel room: $150–300

➡ The top restaurant in town: $120-150

➡ Tickets to an event: $100-250

Opening Hours

BUSINESS	OPENING HOURS
Banks	9.30am-4pm Mon-Thu, to 5pm Fri
Post offices	9am-5pm Mon-Fri, 9am-noon Sat
Tourist offices	9am-5pm daily
Shopping centres	9am-5.30pm, often to 9pm Thu & Fri
Restaurants	lunch noon-3pm, dinner 6-10pm
Cafes	breakfast 8-11am (later on weekends), all-day lunch
Pubs	11am-1am
Bars & clubs	4pm-late (between 2am and 5am)

Arriving in Melbourne

Melbourne Airport (Tullamarine; p345)

SkyBus runs express services every 10 to 30 minutes to/from Southern Cross Station ($18), taking approximately 25 minutes. Taxis cost around $50 to the city and take around 25 minutes.

Avalon Airport (p345)

The Avalon Airport Bus meets every flight and takes passengers to Melbourne ($22, 40 to 50 minutes). Taxis cost $80 to the city (one hour), or $50 to Geelong (20 minutes).

Getting Around

Melbourne's public transport system has great coverage, but the same can't be said for public transport around the rest of the state. Buses are infrequent and the rail network is excellent but limited in its reach. Hiring a car is the ideal way to explore the state and make the most of your time here. Alternatively, consider hiring a bike at your destination or bring your own bike on the train.

Private bus tours cover many of Victoria's main sights, although they allow limited time at most stops. One way to get around this is to arrange to stay overnight near the sight and then return on the next day's tour.

Long walks are gaining popularity and shuttle-bus services are starting up to connect walkers with accommodation and public transport.

For much more on **getting around**, see p346.

What's New

Melbourne Star

Finally, the giant Melbourne Star Ferris wheel is open for business. Ride a gondola up 120m for fabulous views from its Docklands location. (p59)

Street Food

Melbourne's niche obsession with international street food has gone mainstream, with an ever-growing fleet of food trucks serving everything from Thai to Mexican, souvlaki to soup. (p94)

White Night Melbourne

Melbourne's annual all-night event sees the city illuminated in colourful projections, forming a backdrop to free art, music and film (http://whitenightmelbourne.com.au).

12 Apostles Gourmet Trail

The area's whiskey distillery, ice cream, dairy farms, wineries and Belgian chocolatier now form a tourist route for a day's indulgence on local produce. (p176)

Great Ocean Walk

This epic coastal walk from Apollo Bay to Port Campbell has recently been extended to take in spectacular views from Gibsons Steps to the Twelve Apostles. (p172)

Bellarine Taste Trail

More wineries and artisan food spots are springing up, making it harder for wine lovers and foodies to pass up this region. (p161)

Great Ocean Road National Heritage Centre

Scheduled to open in mid-2014, this modern museum in Lorne will catalogue the gruelling history of how Australia's favourite drive was built. (p166)

Yarra Valley Cider & Ale Trail

Not strictly new, but this driving route has been recently pulled together to take in microbreweries and cider houses to complement the better-known Yarra Valley wineries. (p139)

Yarra Valley Chocolaterie & Ice Creamery

Since opening its doors in late 2012, this huge complex is a sweet-tooth's paradise, with its Belgian chocolates and bowls full of free samples. (p135)

SeaWorks Maritime Complex

This historic Williamstown waterfront complex has been open since 2007, but the arrival of the Sea Shepherd conservation organisation has added considerable appeal. Tour its fleet of anti-poaching vessels and headquarters. (p76)

Bendigo Art Series Hotel

This stunning series of art hotels is heading to the country, with its first outpost due to open in Bendigo in 2014. (p199)

Port of Echuca Interpretation Centre

A fine addition to the Murray riverbank, this dazzling new visitor centre will transport you into Echuca's storied past of paddle steamers and river ports. (p293)

For more recommendations and reviews, see lonelyplanet.com/australia/melbourne

If You Like...

Wineries & Microbreweries

Victoria's wine regions and microbreweries have come into their own as traveller destinations – think cellar doors, beer on tap and fine attached restaurants.

Mountain Goat Brewery Urban Richmond brewer filled with brewing equipment offers twice-weekly tasting sessions. (p108)

Mornington Peninsula Possible as a day trip from Melbourne; begin around Red Hill and don't miss the area's pinot noir. (p224)

Yarra Valley Birthplace of Victoria's wine industry and still one of its most respected wine-producing regions. (p137)

Rutherglen Close to the Murray River, this charming area is known for its muscat and tokay. (p300)

King Valley Cool-climate wines and Italian varietals such as sangiovese, barbera, prosecco and pinot grigio among other gourmet offerings. (p265)

Bellarine Peninsula Around 50 cool-climate wineries, many award-winning; most have cellar doors offering wine tasting and artisan produce, plus coastal outlooks. (p161)

Bridge Road Brewers Beech-worth's celebrated microbrewer has nine of its brews on tap. (p268)

Jamieson Brewery Family-friendly brewery in the High Country with some unusual boutique beers. (p261)

Mildura Brewery Worth visiting for its location alone, in what was an art deco theatre. (p287)

Markets

Weekend markets are regular features across the state, from monthly food-rich farmers markets to craft markets in the small towns of Melbourne's hinterland.

Queen Victoria Market From tacky souvenirs to delightful deli produce, this the mother (and father) of all Victorian markets. (p55)

Rose Street Artists' Market Clever and crafty artists gather each weekend to sell their wares and talk shop. (p123)

Camberwell Sunday Market Where Melburnians purge their belongings, and bargain- and fashion-hunters have a field day. (p124)

St Andrews Community Market Saturday market known for its slightly alternative feel, and for food in all its forms. (p138)

Red Hill Market Monthly craft, food and tasteful bric-a-bric market that's the best of its kind around Melbourne. (p224)

Gippsland Farmers Markets Keep an eye on your calendar as you pass through the quiet towns of Southern Gippsland. (p236)

Mill Markets Former factories and mills in towns such as Ballarat (p195), Daylesford (p146) and Geelong (p156) have morphed into a chain of retro goods markets.

Live Music

Pubs around the state play host to a range of musical talents; open spaces, including wineries, clearings in rainforests and spots by the beach, also get musical, particularly in summer.

Pubs Melbourne loves its rock and roll. From the Tote to the Espy, music is in the blood. (p115)

Melbourne music fests International bands at the Big Day Out, the International Jazz Festival and a cavalcade of boutique festivals. (p20 & p329)

IF YOU LIKE... BLUES MUSIC

Book yourself a seat on the Blues Train in Queenscliff; drink local wines and listen to live blues. (p159)

Coastal fests International indie bands at the Falls Festival, folk at Port Fairy and a bit of everything at Queenscliff; look forward to sea breezes and happy festival vibes. (p20)

Regional tunes Catch big names such as the Rolling Stones at Hanging Rock (p148) and gutsy rock and roll at Castlemaine's the Bridge Hotel (p204).

Art Galleries

Victoria is home to a number of excellent galleries showcasing an impressive range of homegrown talent as well as international heavyweights. Regional Victoria has its share, too, with beautiful pieces of national importance.

Melbourne City Major galleries such as Ian Potter Centre (p45), NGV International (p57) and ACCA (p58) to smaller, impressive, contemporary spaces such as Tolarno (p55) and West Space (p55).

Out of town Spot some of Australia's best contemporary art at Healesville's Tarrawarra Museum of Art (p135) or head to Art Gallery of Ballarat (p190), the oldest and largest gallery in regional Victoria.

Collingwood Arts Precinct Great cluster of walkable galleries from Aboriginal art to contemporary works, and most at affordable prices. (p63)

Street art Melbourne's laneways serve as urban galleries flush with paste-ups, stencil art and installations by highly regarded local and international street artists. (p56)

(Top) Gourmet dining, Red Hill (p224)
(Bottom) Centre Place (p56), Melbourne

Historic Towns & Villages

Victoria's historic settlements brim with beautiful period architecture. Most owe their existence to the state's glittering goldmining heritage; signposts to bushranger exploits also survive.

Walhalla Utterly gorgeous living museum to the gold-rush days in a remote mountain valley. (p234)

Maldon Goldfields town where the past comes alive in architecture and antiques. (p205)

Kyneton Nineteenth-century bluestone buildings carry echoes of prosperous goldmining days. (p201)

Castlemaine Boom-era architecture provides a backdrop for a new boom in artistic endeavour. (p202)

Beechworth Almost uniform sandstone architecture dominates this historic settlement, which has a growing reputation for culinary excellence. (p266)

Glenrowan Scene of Ned Kelly's Last Stand; bushranger history is everywhere on show. (p302)

Yackandandah Its historic main street is the ideal setting for a slew of antique shops and associated paraphernalia. (p269)

Chiltern A main street that looks like it was built for a film set, surrounded by box-ironbark forests. (p301)

Echuca Wonderfully preserved old port that still sends paddle steamers out onto the Murray River. (p292)

Ballarat Sovereign Hill may take a theme-park approach to history but there's no finer evocation of the gold-rush days. (p190)

Wilderness & Wildlife

A fabulous destination for nature lovers, Victoria has some of eastern Australia's prime tracts of wilderness and most accessible native wildlife.

Snowy River & Errinundra National Parks Wild rivers snaking through canyons and deeply forested gorges make these parks spellbinding. (p249 & p250)

Wilsons Promontory National Park Glorious wild-coast scenery combined with bird and animal life in their natural setting. (p238)

Cape Otway One of the best places on earth to see wild koalas, just off the Great Ocean Road (p173). French Island (p224) and Raymond Island (p244) also offer top koala viewing.

Anglesea Kangaroos dodge golf balls on the fairways of the town's golf course along the Great Ocean Road. (p164)

Phillip Island The Penguin Parade gets all the headlines, and rightly so, but don't forget the fur seals at Seal Rocks. (p225)

Sorrento Swim with the dolphins in Port Phillip Bay in Victoria's premier up-close wildlife encounter. (p220)

Cape Bridgewater A seal colony, petrified forest, blowhole, dunes and white-sand beach. (p185)

Warrnambool Watch southern right whales frolic with their young off Logan's Beach from July to September. (p177)

Chiltern Box-Ironbark National Park Search for the endangered regent honeyeater in this relic forest close to Chiltern. (p301)

Healesville Sanctuary Spot native species you missed in the wild (such as platypus) in this excellent zoo close to Melbourne. (p135)

Beaches

Victoria's beaches rock, from wild coastlines with world-renowned surf where the winds whip in from Antarctica to gentle bay beaches ideal for family holidays.

Ninety Mile Beach One of the longest stretches of sand on the planet. (p243)

Squeaky Beach Wilsons Prom's most celebrated beach comes with its own sound effects. (p239)

Cape Bridgewater A near-perfect arc of white sand in the state's far west. (p185)

Bells Beach Natural amphitheatre where the surf is the stuff of legend. (p163)

Croajingolong National Park Remote and pristine beaches in the state's far east. (p254)

Cape Conran Coastal Park They don't call this the Wilderness Coast for nothing. (p252)

Port Phillip Bay Barely a ripple disturbs beaches at Mornington (p217) and Sorrento (p220), which combine proximity to Melbourne with a family vibe.

Mornington Peninsula Back Beaches Portsea, Sorrento, Gunnamatta, Cape Schanck and Flinders are close to Melbourne but as wild as they come. (p223)

PLAN YOUR TRIP IF YOU LIKE...

IF YOU LIKE... HOT SPRINGS

Head to the natural Peninsula Hot Springs (p218) for a session under the stars or indulge yourself at Hepburn Bathhouse & Spa (p142) near Daylesford.

Month by Month

TOP EVENTS

Midsumma Festival, January

White Night Melbourne, February

Melbourne International Comedy Festival, April

AFL Grand Final, September

Melbourne Cup, November

January

It can get asphalt-melting hot, with the only respite to be found in cool-water beaches or in the High Country. Beach towns are packed with local holidaymakers and their families.

☆ Australian Open

The world's top tennis players and huge crowds descend on Melbourne Park for Australia's Grand Slam championship (p335). Grab a ground pass or book ahead to see a top seed from the arena seats.

Midsumma Festival

Melbourne's gay and lesbian arts festival (p104)

features more than 150 events with a Pride March finale. Expect everything from film screenings to same-sex dance sports and massive riverside dance parties.

Big Day Out

National rock-fest Big Day Out (www.bigdayout.com) comes to town at the end of January. Big names are guaranteed, and if you miss out on the big day itself, many artists perform 'side shows' at venues around Melbourne.

Chinese New Year

Melbourne has celebrated the Chinese lunar new year since Little Bourke St became Chinatown (www.chinatownmelbourne.com.au) in the 1860s. The time to touch the dragon happens either sometime towards the end of January or early February.

February

Heatwaves are likely, but since school holidays have ended, accommodation is plentiful by the beach. City folk are still in summer mode, filling the long evenings and weekends outside.

St Kilda Festival

The week-long St Kilda Festival (www.stkildafestival.com.au) ends in a suburb-wide street party on the final Sunday (Festival Sunday). Massive crowds come for both the live music and atmosphere.

Melbourne Food & Wine Festival

Market tours, wine tastings, cooking classes and presentations by celeb chefs take place at venues across the state (www.melbournefoodandwine.com.au). Wineries and restaurants across Victoria hold events profiling local produce.

White Night Melbourne

Melbourne stays up all night (http://whitenightmelbourne.com.au) for free art, light shows and street performances. Expect throngs of people after dark.

March

Possibly the most festival-packed month of the year, March has fine weather, though everyone notices the turning leaves.

Lion dancing at Chinese New Year, Chinatown (Melbourne).

✯✯ Moomba

The action at Mooba (www.
melbourne.vic.gov.au/
moomba) is focused around
the Yarra River, where
waterskiing and the wacky
Birdman Rally (watch com-
petitors launch themselves
into the water in homemade
flying machines) take place.

✯✯ Port Fairy Folk Festival

Historic Port Fairy is
charming at any time of
year but fills with music
fans every Labour Day
long weekend for this folk
festival. Join them for
an impressive line-up of
roots acts from around the
world. (p182)

✯ Australian Formula One Grand Prix

The normally tranquil
Albert Park Lake becomes
a Formula One racetrack
and the buzz, both on the
streets and in your ears,

takes over Melbourne
for four days of rev-head
action (www.grandprix.
com.au).

✯✯ Awakening of the Dragon

Join Bendigo's Chinese
community in celebrations
(www.goldendragon
museum.org) that include
lion dancing, a costume
parade and the awakening
of Sun Loong with more
than 100,000 crackers.

✯✯ Apollo Bay Music Festival

Ocean views, a laid-back
atmosphere and a diverse
range of acts make this
festival (www.apollobay
musicfestival.com) one of
the nicest on the calendar.

April

**Mild weather and
the promise of a few
laughs and blooms give
Melbourne an April glow.**

✯✯ Melbourne International Comedy Festival

Local and international
comedians entertain Mel-
bourne with four weeks of
mostly stand-up comedy.
After the Melbourne laugh-
fest (www.comedyfestival.
com.au), comedians hit
the road to spread the love
around the state. Often
begins in March.

May

**It's time to breathe in
the last of the summer
fragrances before
shrugging on a jacket. It's
still warm in the northwest,
but nights are getting chilly.**

✯✯ St Kilda Film Festival

Australia's premier short-
film festival (www.stkilda
filmfestival.com.au) has
a grab-bag of genres and
talents on show.

June

It's getting darker earlier and people are rugging up and polishing their skis for a trip to snow-covered alpine regions.

🎷 Melbourne International Jazz Festival

International jazz cats head to Melbourne and join locals for festival gigs at venues around town (www.melbournejazz.com).

July

Though it's cold in Melbourne and icy in the alpine regions, coastal towns such as Lorne are cosy for weekend breaks.

🎿 Ski Season

It does snow in Australia! The snow zones of Mt Buller, Mt Hotham and Falls Creek are perfect for skiing and snowboarding. Mt Baw Baw suits families (and won't burn a hole in skiers' pockets).

🎬 Melbourne International Film Festival

Midwinter movie love-in brings out Melbourne's black-turtleneck-wearing cinephiles in droves. The film festival (www.miff.com.au) is held over two weeks at various cinemas across the city.

August

The region is cold and darkness continues to fall early, so it's truly time to head inside for some art- and literature-inspired enlightenment.

📚 Melbourne Writers Festival

Beginning in the last week of August, the writers festival (www.mwf.com.au) features forums and events celebrating reading, writing, books and ideas.

September

The end of September (and the AFL grand final) signals the end of rugging up on weekends and the start of sunny days.

☆ AFL Grand Final

It's not easy to get a ticket to the AFL grand final (www.afl.com.au), but it's not hard to get your share of finals fever anywhere in Melbourne. Pubs put on big screens and barbecues (often accompanied by a spot of street kick-to-kick at half-time).

🎭 Melbourne Fringe Festival

The Fringe (www.melbournefringe.com.au) has gone from alternative to relatively mainstream without losing its edge. It showcases experimental theatre, music and visual arts.

🎡 Royal Melbourne Show

The country comes to town for this school-holiday fair (www.royalshow.com.au), where carnival rides and junk-filled showbags face off against traditional farming exhibits.

🍷 Rutherglen Wine Show

The late-September Rutherglen Wine Show brings the chance to sample top wines and gourmet dishes in what is arguably Victoria's premier wine-growing region. (p299)

October

Spring has sprung; the fillies are out as Melbourne glams up for the horse races. The weather should be warming up with summer just around the corner, although cold snaps are common.

🎵 Country Music in Mildura

It may not be Tamworth, but Mildura's annual knees-up (www.milduracountrymusic.com.au) is a fabulous celebration of all things country.

🎭 Melbourne International Arts Festival

Held at various venues around the city, the arts festival (www.melbournefestival.com.au) features an always thought-provoking program of Australian and international theatre, opera, dance, visual art and music.

🎷 Wangaratta Jazz & Blues

Wangaratta hosts more than 350 national and international artists each year at Australia's most important jazz festival (www.wangarattajazz.com). The line-up is often stellar; New York greats make regular appearances.

☆ Australian Motorcycle Grand Prix

Phillip Island's Grand Prix circuit attracts the world's best motorbike riders for this three-day event (www.motogp.com.au).

November

Just when you think it's going to be hot, it's not. As with most of the year, pack for four seasons in one day. The pace in the city heats up as holiday preparations begin.

☆ Melbourne Cup

The Cup, held on the first Tuesday in November, is a horse race that 'stops the nation' and is a public holiday in Melbourne. It's all part of the fashion-conscious Spring Racing Carnival (www.spring racingcarnival.com.au).

Queenscliff Music Festival

This out-of-town music festival (www.qmf.net.au) is possible to do in a day trip, but the great range of local acts will make you want to stay for the weekend.

December

It's peak holiday time as school takes a break and offices close down until mid-January. Cricket is on the screens and streets.

☆ Boxing Day Test

Day one of the Boxing Day Test draws out the cricket fans on 26 December. Crowds are huge and excitable; expect some shenanigans from Bay 13, the infamous section of the MCG (www.mcg.org.au).

Falls Festival

The lively, traffic-jam-inducing Falls music festival (www.fallsfestival.com. au) is held in rainforest surrounds near Lorne.

(Top) Parade participants, Melbourne Fringe Festival
(Bottom) Spectators at the Melbourne Cricket Ground (MCG)

Plan Your Trip
Itineraries

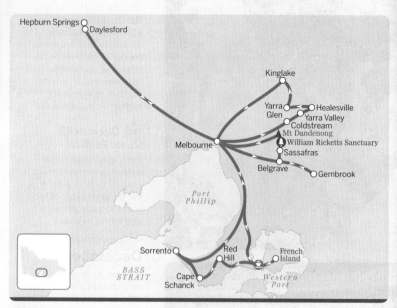

Melbourne & Around

Melbourne is the centrepiece of this itinerary, which combines day trips with some overnight stays. Dedicate at least two full days to Melbourne and then hit the road around the region, returning to Melbourne for the night between excursions.

Begin by heading southeast across the Mornington Peninsula and make for Stony Point, from where the ferry leaves for **French Island**. Stay overnight to really appreciate this special place where koalas abound and the clamour of modernity

seems a world away. The next morning, return to the mainland and journey inland to check out a couple of **Red Hill** wineries. Turn back to the coast and continue to the **Cape Schanck** lighthouse. Next stop is the refined town of **Sorrento** on your way back to Melbourne.

Early next morning, head to the Dandenongs, which offer a cool and leafy respite from the noise of the city. From the Burwood Hwy drive east to **Belgrave**, and climb aboard Puffing Billy for a steam-train journey through the mountains to **Gembrook**. Back at Belgrave, take Mon-

Alfred Nicholas Memorial Gardens, the Dandenongs (p131)

bulk Rd through the Dandenong Ranges National Park and head to **Sassafras** for its village atmosphere then past Olinda to explore **William Ricketts Sanctuary**. Round off the day by taking in the view from nearby **Mt Dandenong**, before returning to Melbourne for the night.

Start day six by heading from Melbourne along the Maroondah Hwy to antique-laden **Coldstream**. Indulge in some wine tasting in the **Yarra Valley**, before reaching **Healesville**, a lovely town with a fine animal sanctuary on the edge of the Yarra Ranges National Park. Eat at the large winery, taste a beer at the brewery and enjoy the small-town charm. In the afternoon, head directly west via **Yarra Glen** and Dixons Creek to the Melba Hwy, then turn northwest to pretty **Kinglake**. Return to Melbourne via St Andrews.

With one day left, spend it in charming **Daylesford**. A favourite weekend escape for Melburnians, it has a verdant setting, fine restaurants, shops to browse and plenty of other reasons to linger. Leave time for a spa and massage at the bathhouse and spa at **Hepburn Springs**, and head back to Melbourne in a state of bliss.

Great Ocean Road, Grampians & Goldfields

2 WEEKS

The Great Ocean Road is one of the most popular touring routes in the country. Take a week to get the best from this region, then take another week to wind down via the Grampians and goldfields.

From Melbourne, take the Princes Hwy southwest to Geelong then on to **Queenscliff**, one of the state's most appealing seaside towns and a terrific place to spend a couple of nights. The Great Ocean Road begins in earnest at **Torquay**, one of the surf capitals of the world, and gateway to the legendary swells of **Bells Beach**. Further down the coast, look for kangaroos at the golf course in family-friendly **Anglesea**. Tour the lighthouse at **Aireys Inlet** before a beach walk at **Fairhaven**, then stop for the night in **Lorne**. With its fine beach, stunning waterfall and tasty eating options, you'll want to spend at least the following morning here before heading further down the coast to **Kennett River** for koala spotting. Chances are that it's close to sunset by the time you return to the coast and **Apollo Bay** for the night. On morning five, explore the koala and lighthouse zone of **Cape Otway**, then it's on to Port Campbell National Park and its famed **Twelve Apostles** and Loch Ard Gorge; spend at least a night in nearby **Port Campbell**. Look for whales off the coast of **Warrnambool** then continue west to quaint **Port Fairy**. Stay for a couple of nights to soak up its charm before heading to tiny but fabulous **Cape Bridgewater**, then go inland via Portland.

On the way to the Grampians, stop for a meal in tiny **Dunkeld** en route to **Halls Gap**, your three-night base for your time among the granite rock formations in the **Grampians National Park**. A loop through the gold-mining towns of **Maryborough**, **Castlemaine** and **Maldon** is a rewarding journey through the terrain that formed the basis for Victoria's prosperity – this story is told in the grand old buildings that dominate streetscapes across the region. Count on at least two nights in Castlemaine. Detour north to overnight in **Bendigo**, one of Victoria's rural towns to watch, before sweeping back down through book-rich **Clunes** to **Ballarat**, with its art gallery, antique stores and world-class Sovereign Hill historic park, for the final night of your tour.

Top: Hopetoun Falls (p173), near Cape Otway
Bottom: Loch Ard Gorge (p175), Port Campbell National Park

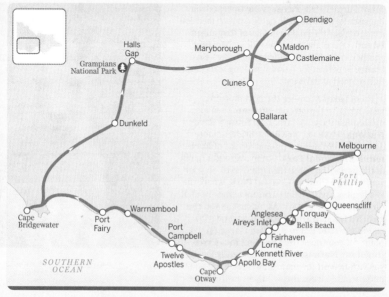

The East

2 WEEKS

Eastern Victoria combines the state's thrilling coast with a mountainous and deeply forested interior – the unifying theme wherever you go is wilderness.

From Melbourne, it's a two-hour drive down to **Phillip Island**, a place that has so much going for it – cute little penguins, seals and surf beaches, even a motorsports race track – that you'll need a couple of days here. On your way southeast, sleepy seaside **Inverloch**, historic **Korumburra**, foodie-heaven **Koonwarra** and bohemian **Fish Creek** all warrant a visit as you head for **Wilsons Promontory National Park**. The Prom is utterly spectacular, as good for pristine beaches and wandering wildlife as for remote lighthouses and fine walking trails. Spending a couple of nights in the area is essential.

If you can tear yourself away, follow the coast to **Port Albert**, then rush for the north, passing through Traralgon as fast as you're allowed en route to **Walhalla**. To truly soak up the silence and blissful isolation of this time-worn and tiny little gold-mining town, spend a couple of nights here. On your way back to the coast, pass through Sale on your way to stunning **Ninety Mile Beach**, either from Golden Beach or Seaspray. Further east, **Paynesville** (reached via Bairnsdale) is a fine little detour, not to mention a gateway for the koala colonies of **Raymond Island**. Overnight in Paynesville or **Metung**, another lovely little seaside town. **Lakes Entrance** is perfect for boat tours, long walks and fine seafood at day's end.

From Lakes Entrance the next morning, head north to the caves at **Buchan**, then loop up through the gravel tracks of **Snowy River National Park** via McKillops Bridge, before detouring into the exceptional forests of **Errinundra National Park**. Camp overnight in one of the parks, then pass through Orbost on your way to **Cape Conran Coastal Park**, where the Wilderness Coast really earns its name – soak it up over a couple of days. As far east as you can go in Victoria, **Mallacoota** has a wonderful end-of-the-road feel to it, which is true up to a point – if you travel from here out into **Croajingolong National Park**, you'll really feel like you've fallen off the map. Stay three days; you'll never want to leave this wildly beautiful place.

Top: The Pinnacles, Cape Woolamai (p226), Phillip Island
Bottom: Eastern grey kangaroo, Buchan (p249)

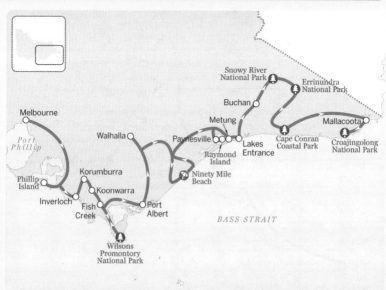

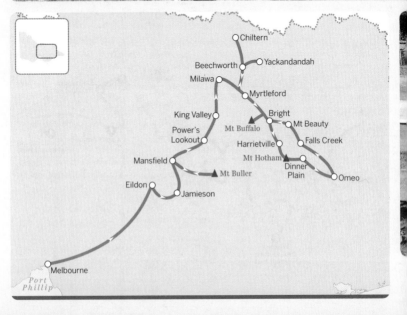

High Country

10 DAYS

Victoria's High Country is a fabulous place for car and motorcycle touring, especially outside the winter months, when even the highest roads are clear of snow. With historic towns, stirring mountain scenery and renowned gourmet regions to serve as focal points for your explorations, even 10 days may not prove sufficient.

Start your journey from Melbourne by heading up through the Yarra Valley, over the scenic Black Spur and up to **Eildon**, the base for fishing and houseboat holidays on Lake Eildon, and a good place to spend a couple of nights. From here, take the southern road around the lake to **Jamieson**, a quaint little former gold-mining town with a renowned brewery. Then it's on to the all-seasons adventure town of **Mansfield**, gateway to **Mt Buller** and a base for horse riding and mountain biking; stay a couple of nights. The utterly scenic Mansfield-Whitfield Rd winds up and over the ranges before plunging down to the King Valley – don't miss **Power's Lookout** about halfway along. Spend a few hours in the **King Valley** – an increasingly important wine region – before hitting the gourmet trail in earnest at **Milawa**, where wines, cheeses and mustards are all on offer. Nearby **Myrtleford** has a terrific butter factory in case your portable larder still has space.

As the sun nears the horizon on day five, head for gorgeous **Beechworth**, a stone-built village that glows golden close to sunset and that has wonderful restaurants, local honey and a brewery. Three nights is ideal here, with visits to the postcard-perfect towns of **Chiltern** and **Yackandandah** – both great places to nurture your love of antiques. Returning down the Great Alpine Road, detour up spectacular **Mt Buffalo**, and drop your bags off for a three-night stay in **Bright**, famous for its autumn colours and spring blossoms. From here, branch out to **Harrietville** and the winding, hairpin ascent of **Mt Hotham**. Enjoy the expansive alpine views from the summit before continuing to **Dinner Plain** and through alpine meadows to the historic town of **Omeo**. You could continue down into Gippsland, but we recommend looping up and over the mountains to **Falls Creek** on the summit and then down to **Mt Beauty** on your way back to Bright.

Top: Hut on Mt Hotham (p278)
Bottom: Rodeo at Omeo (p280)

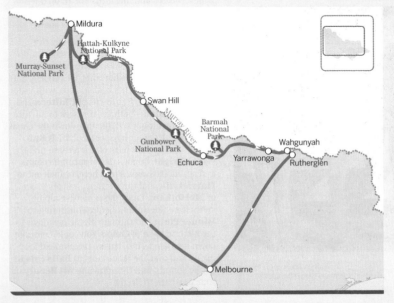

1 WEEK Murray River

Victoria's Murray River is utterly unlike anywhere else in the state: soulful riverbank towns, drowned forests of eucalypts and the semidesert Mallee region not far away. It's hard to lose your way on this route: although roads in these parts don't always follow the river, it's never far away, and sticking close to it means you can't go wrong.

Begin by flying from Melbourne to **Mildura** at the top of the Murray. Mildura is a lovely town to get acquainted with and we recommend at least two nights; its food and wine are worth the trip alone. Out here, you feel like you're on the cusp of the outback. To get a taste of what we mean, pick up your rental car and head out to **Murray-Sunset National Park** for an overnight camping trip or do the same at **Hattah-Kulkyne National Park**, where you can camp alongside one of the Murray River's beaches.

Follow the river's path through the landscape southeast to overnight in **Swan Hill**, another important provincial centre by the river. There are some great eating options here, an attractive riverside park and other important landmarks; Swan Hill's Pioneer Settlement is a wonderfully evocative place to learn about the town's past. On your way to Echuca, **Gunbower National Park** boasts some of the most beautiful river red gum forests in the state and is well worth a detour.

Echuca is arguably the pick of the Murray River towns and deserves at least two nights. Apart from being a picturesque town in its own right – its main street is quintessential rural Australia – Echuca's working paddle steamers and historic port are where the Murray's historic role as lifeblood of Victoria's north really comes alive. Consider sleeping on a houseboat.

Sticking to the river, check out the drowned river red gums of **Barmah National Park** and continue on to **Yarrawonga**. Check out Lake Mulwala, and hop on a lunch cruise around this dammed section of the river to get among the sculpture-like remains of long-dead trees. Continue to engaging little **Wahgunyah** on your way to a night in **Rutherglen**, Victoria's home of fortified wines, before joining the Hume Fwy back to Melbourne.

Top: Lake Mournpall (p289), Hattah-Kulkyne National Park
m: Pioneer statue and paddle steamer, Murray River

Plan Your Trip
Victoria Outdoors

Victoria's excellent (and really rather beautiful) network of national parks and state forests, soul-stirring mountains and meandering rivers make it a fantastic playground for outdoor enthusiasts. There are countless tracks to follow, mountains to climb, waves to surf and hills to ski, whatever the season and wherever you find yourself.

Best Outdoors

Best Walks

Great Ocean Walk Walk from Apollo Bay to Port Campbell National Park and the Twelve Apostles.

Great Prom Walk A 45km loop through spectacular Wilsons Promontory, southeast of Melbourne.

Best Fun on the Water

Yarra River Kayak along the river in Melbourne.

Murray River Hire a luxury houseboat and meander along the mighty Murray.

Best Bike Trails

High Country Mountain-bike or take the rail trails through the Alpine region when the snow dries up.

Great Ocean Road Enjoy 60km of mountain-biking tracks, inland from the stunning Great Ocean Road.

Best Adventure Activities

Snowboarding Hurtle down the slopes on a snowboard at Falls Creek and Mt Hotham.

Rock climbing Climb Mt Arapiles, Victoria's premier rock-climbing destination.

Paragliding Catch the thermals at Mystic Mountain, near Bright.

Best Surf Breaks

Bells Beach Excite your inner surfer.

Boating

You can explore Victoria's seemingly endless combination of waterways – oceans, rivers, bays and lakes – in a seemingly endless number of ways. Sailing clubs and their yachts surround Port Phillip Bay, while pleasure craft abound in the Gippsland Lakes (around Metung, for example) and low-key Mallacoota Inlet. Watersports that tend towards an adrenalin rush are particularly prevalent on Lake Eildon and in Yarrawonga. Paddle steamers are a possibility in Echuca, while cruising off into the sunset on the Murray River in Mildura and Swan Hill is a classic way to spend a holiday.

Walking

Victoria is classic bushwalking country, with countless trails leading out into the wilderness. Most trails can be found in the eastern half of the state, especially in Gippsland and the High Country, but there are some fine hikes elsewhere as well. For a serious, long-distance undertaking, the Australian Alps Walking Track is world-class, beginning in Walhalla, crossing the roof of Australia and finishing close to Canberra. Our favourite Victorian hikes include the following:

➡ **Great Ocean Road** Several wonderfully long walks that can be done as an entire leg or in separate sections.

➡ **High Country** Try Baw Baw National Park, Mt Hotham, Mt Beauty and Mt Buffalo.

➡ **Wilsons Promontory National Park** A wonderful interweaving of marked trails, stunning scenery and lovely camping spots.

➡ **Grampians National Park** More than 150km of well-marked walking tracks that pass towering waterfalls and sacred Aboriginal rock-art sites.

➡ **Croajingolong National Park** Near Mallacoota in East Gippsland, this national park offers rugged inland treks and easier coastal walks.

Canoeing & Kayaking

Victoria's waterways offer ample opportunities for paddling in a canoe or kayak. Melbourne's Yarra River is a great place to start, whether around Docklands and Melbourne's city centre or along the river's gentle lower reaches. See p75 for details.

The Glenelg River (p186), in western Victoria on the South Australian border, is a great place for multiday trips. The river works its way through deep gorges with stunning riverside wildflowers and birdlife. Best of all, it has special riverside camp sites en route, many of which are only accessible by canoe.

Apollo Bay, along the Great Ocean Road, is popular for short sea-kayaking trips.

Out in the east, kayaking and/or canoeing is possible around Wilsons Promon-tory, Port Albert, Lakes Entrance and Croajingolong National Park. Also in the east, white-water rafting down the river in Snowy River National Park could just be the most fun you can have on water.

Canoe hire costs from $40 to $75 per day, depending on the operator. Extra expenses may include equipment delivery and pick-up.

Cycling

Just about anywhere in Victoria can be good for cycling, whether you prefer long, flat tracks or winding mountain trails. The network of rail trails (www.railtrails.org) is brilliant, ranging from 134km from Tallarook to Mansfield or 116km from the Murray to the mountains, down to single-kilometre trundles around Melbourne.

Melbourne has an excellent 45km network of long urban bike trails, and scant hills. City riders take advantage of this to commute during the week, or relax on weekends – it's hard to miss the lycra-clad cafe breakfasts of the club scene. The city's Melbourne Bike Share system has just the blue beast for you to get around town on. You'll also find a huge number of shops selling bikes and accessories, as well as volunteer repair workshops at city parks such as Carlton Gardens and Ceres (p67).

RESPONSIBLE BUSHWALKING

➡ Stay on established trails, avoid cutting corners and stay on hard ground where possible.

➡ Before tackling a long or remote walk, tell someone responsible about your plans and contact them when you return. Consider carrying a personal locator beacon (PLB).

➡ Use designated camping grounds where provided. When bush camping, look for a natural clearing and avoid camping under river red gums, which have a tendency to drop their branches.

➡ Don't feed native animals.

➡ Take all your rubbish out with you – don't burn or bury it.

➡ Avoid polluting lakes and streams – don't wash yourself or your dishes in them, and keep soap and detergent at least 50m away from waterways.

➡ Use toilets where provided – otherwise, bury human waste at least 100m away from waterways (consider taking a hand trowel).

➡ Boil streamwater for 10 minutes (or purify with a filter or tablets) before drinking it.

➡ Dogs and other pets are not allowed in national parks.

➡ Use a gas or fuel stove for cooking.

➡ Don't light fires unless necessary – if you do need a fire, keep it small and use only dead, fallen wood in an existing fireplace. Make sure the fire is completely extinguished before moving on. On total-fire-ban days, don't under any circumstances light a fire – that includes fuel stoves.

Disused railway lines and riverside industrial sites have been gradually turned over to cyclists, with a number of bike paths in greater Melbourne providing excellent touring.

Out in the country the state's spectacular landscapes are the perfect backdrop for mountain bikers and road riders alike. Check Mountain Bike Victoria (www.mountainbikevictoria.com) for a list of trails and events. You'll find thousands of kilometres of diverse cycling terrain, much of it readily accessible by public transport.

The Great Ocean Road has mighty fine mountain tracks hidden in the hinterlands. During the 'green' season, there are exhilarating climbs and descents for mountain bikers in the various ski resorts and the mountains around Bright.

Events

➡ **Great Victorian Bike Ride** (www.bv.com.au; adult $895, child 13-17yr/6-12yr/under 5yr $655/330/free) A nine-day annual ride attracting more than 5000 cyclists of all ages and fitness levels. Payment for this fully supported ride includes meals, mechanical support and access to camping grounds. Hosted in different parts of the state each year – 2013 took in the Great Ocean Road.

➡ **Around the Bay in a Day** (www.bv.com.au; entry fee $180) This 250km ride attracts around 20,000 keen cyclists each year. It covers the length of Port Phillip Bay from Melbourne to Sorrento, crosses on the ferry to Queenscliff and heads back to Melbourne (or vice versa). Children over 12 years can participate in the shorter legs.

Dangers

➡ Keep an eye on surrounding cars, of course, but also on magpies: beware of the occasional dive-bombing attack by these black-and-white birds in spring.

➡ Wearing an approved bicycle helmet is compulsory in Victoria.

Fishing

Victoria has some world-class fishing, whether you want to fly fish for rainbow trout in a mountain stream, lure a yabbie out of a dam, catch a deep-river redfin or hook a yellowtail kingfish from a surf beach.

In the east, the vast Gippsland Lakes is popular for large snapper and bream, especially around Bairnsdale, Paynesville, Metung and Lakes Entrance. Further east,

Mallacoota is another favourite family fishing spot, with excellent estuary, river and ocean fishing yielding catches of bream, flathead, whiting and mulloway.

In the state's west, there are top fishing sites all along the Great Ocean Road. Apollo Bay and Port Campbell make good bases, while Warrnambool offers the chance to hook mullet, bream or garfish in the Merri and Hopkins Rivers, or whiting, Australian salmon and trevally off the wild ocean beaches.

Marine Parks

Around 5% of Victoria's coastline is protected by marine national parks and smaller marine sanctuaries, and all fishing is banned in these protected areas. For a full list of no-go zones, see the Parks Victoria website (www.parkweb.vic.gov.au).

Licence to Fish

To fish in Victoria's marine, estuarine or fresh waters that are nonprotected areas, those between the ages of 18 and 70 must purchase a Recreational Fishing Licence (RFL), which costs $6 for 48 hours, $12 for 28 days or $24.50 for a year. Licences are available online at the Department of Primary Industries (DPI) website (www.depi.vic.gov.au) – you'll need a credit card and printer to print a copy; from most tackle shops; and from DPI offices.

Horse Riding

It's impossible to watch *The Man from Snowy River*, the film about 19th-century cattlemen in Victoria's High Country, without getting the itch to go trailblazing through this stunning horse-riding terrain. Some of the state's best riding is found in these mountains; Lake Eildon and Mansfield are top horse-riding centres. Many companies offer tours in the High Country, with a choice of one-hour rides to multiday pack trips (some as long as 12 days).

For those who have dreams of cantering along a lonely windswept beach as the sun sets on the horizon, Victoria's coastline is an enticing option. Close to Melbourne, it's possible to ride through bush and beach around Gunnamatta (p223) on the Mornington Peninsula, and from Aireys Inlet on the Great Ocean Road.

Prices average $45 for a one-hour ride, $90 for a half-day ride and $200 to $225 for a full-day ride.

Skiing & Snowboarding

Victoria has three major and six minor ski resorts scattered around the high country of the Great Dividing Range. The two largest ski resorts are Mt Buller and Falls Creek. Mt Hotham is smaller, but has equally good skiing. Mt Baw Baw and Mt Buffalo are also smaller resorts, popular with families and less-experienced skiers. For day trips from Melbourne, Mt Buller and Mt Baw Baw are the closest options for downhill skiers, while cross-country skiers can choose between Lake Mountain, Mt Stirling or Mt St Gwinear.

The ski season officially commences on the first weekend of June. 'Ski-able' snow usually arrives later in the month, and there's often enough snow until the end of September. See www.snowaustraliareport.com for the latest on snow, weather and road conditions, and check the Parks Victoria website (www.parkweb.vic.gov.au) for more info on snow sports in national parks.

Costs

Rates are cheaper if you are hiring gear for longer periods. For a package deal (which can include meals and/or lessons, lift tickets, ski hire and transport), you can book directly with lodges, through travel agents or through accommodation booking services located at the major ski resorts.

The following shows what you'll pay for a day on the slopes midweek at Mt Baw Baw. Note that weekends at major resorts cost considerably more.

ITEM	COST PER DAY
snow chain rental	$25
car entry	$37
jacket & pants hire	$35
ski, poles & boot hire adult/child	$50/32
toboggan hire	$8
lift pass adult/child	$50/40
cross-country pass	$10
toboggan pass	$5

Surfing

With its exposure to the relentless Southern Ocean swell, Victoria's rugged coastline provides plenty of quality surf. But the chilly water (even in summer) has even the hardiest surfer reaching for a wetsuit. A

full-length 3mm- to 4mm-thick wetsuit is the standard for winter, and booties, helmets and even wetsuit gloves might make that extra-long session a bit easier.

Great Ocean Road

The best waves (and variety) are to be found along the Great Ocean Road. No other surf beach in Australia is more celebrated than Bells Beach. It plays host to the Rip Curl Pro (p164) every Easter, bringing an international entourage of pro surfers, sponsors and spectators. Just up the road, local and international surfers gravitate to Torquay. The town is home to legendary brands Quicksilver and Rip Curl, as well as the largest surf lifesaving club in the state. Here you'll find mega surf shops at Surf City Plaza, the Surfworld Museum and plenty of surf schools.

Further along the Great Ocean Road, the Shipwreck Coast (p175), west of Cape Otway as far as Peterborough, offers the most powerful waves in Victoria. It faces southwest and is open to the sweeping swells of the Southern Ocean. The swell is consistently up to 1m higher than elsewhere, making it the place to go if you're after big waves. Extreme care must be taken, however, as some breaks are isolated, subject to strong rips and undertows, and are generally only for the experienced surfer. It's probably best to surf with someone who knows the area.

Popular places with surf schools include Anglesea and Lorne.

South & East of Melbourne

Back beaches at Portsea, Sorrento, Blairgowrie, Rye, St Andrews, Gunnamatta, Cape Schanck and Flinders on the Mornington Peninsula are among the most popular spots, but they can be fairly wild so check with locals before heading out. The same applies to the legendary Quarantine break at Point Nepean National Park. On Phillip Island, Cape Woolamai (p226) is also popular with experienced surfers. Smiths Beach on Phillip Island, Inverloch and Lakes Entrance are good for beginners.

Plan Your Trip
Travel with Children

With its manageable distances, abundant wildlife, child-centric attractions and activities, and a tradition of family-friendly holidays, Victoria is an ideal destination for families. Melbourne is a fine place to spend time with kids, thanks to its interactive museums, City Circle tram, sweeping parkland and innovative playgrounds.

Best Regions for Kids

Mornington Peninsula & Phillip Island
Smooth bay swimming and strawberry-picking in summer, mazes, wildlife parks, a puzzle world, a chocolate factory and those mighty cute penguins.

Great Ocean Road
Warrnambool has childhood covered with its annual winter kids festival **Fun4Kids** (☎03-5562 4044; www.fun4kids.com.au; various locations), and there are few better spots to view whales and their calves.

The Murray River
Echuca has paddle steamers chugging up the Murray and kids will enjoy watching waterskiers carving up the river; book them in for a lesson.

High Country
Head here during the ski season, when Mt Baw Baw and Mt Buffalo are particularly well suited for families.

Eating Out

Families dining out together is a pretty common sight these days in Victoria, especially in Melbourne. Cafes not serving 'babycinos' (small cups of steamed milk) are few and far between, and a number of restaurants provide papers and pencils for drawing. Many restaurants have a children's menu, and even upscale restaurants can often provide an option for children, if asked (nicely).

Sleeping

Although it's rare, a few regional boutique hotels have a strict 'no children' policy, which is usually made clear at booking stage. When booking rooms through discount websites, make sure you check the 'maximum occupancy'; often the cheapest rooms are for two adults only.

Entertainment

Music festivals abound in Victoria, and children under 13 often get in free if accompanied by a paying adult. Queenscliff Music Festival (p23) has a Kids Klub that features kid-friendly acts; Apollo Bay Music Festival (p21) has a Children's Folk Circus and children's events; and Wangaratta Jazz & Blues festival (p22) runs free youth workshops.

Children's Highlights

Historic Villages

➡ Swan Hill's Pioneer Settlement (p290) has everything from horse-and-carriage rides to a sound-and-light show.

➡ Echuca's historic port (p293) is made all the more fun thanks to the frequent long-winded whistles of paddle steamers.

➡ Warrnambool's Flagstaff Hill (p177) is a maritime delight with shipwrecks and lighthouses, and its sound-and-light show is fun for older kids.

➡ Ballarat's Sovereign Hill (p190) has an exhilarating evening light show and, by day, sports an authentic gold-rush feel.

Wildlife

➡ Koalas are bountiful in the Cape Otway region of the Great Ocean Road, at Kennett River, and at Tower Hill near Warrnambool.

➡ Kangaroos can be easily spotted at Anglesea's golf course.

➡ Penguins are plentiful on Phillip Island, and St Kilda's colony shouldn't be missed.

➡ A host of native animals that the kids might have missed seeing in the wild can be found at the Healesville Sanctuary (p135).

➡ Southern right whales play offshore from Warrnambool from July to September.

Rainy-Day Activities in Melbourne

➡ The Australian Centre for the Moving Image (ACMI; p45) has age-appropriate video games and movies 'on demand'.

➡ Melbourne Museum (p65) and Scienceworks (p76) have fantastic zones for younger kids and great exhibits for older ones.

➡ The State Library of Victoria (p54) has a terrific Play Pod, and you can also show the kids Ned Kelly's armour here.

➡ Hop on the free City Circle tram (p81) or circle Melbourne on the Visitor Shuttle (p80).

Planning

Pretty much everything you'll need is available on the road in Victoria. Pharmacies may close early, so pack basic medications.

When to Go

Victoria's beach towns are hot, packed and brimful of other families during the summer school holidays. Provided you're OK with cooler and unpredictable weather, travelling in low season (out of school-holiday periods) means life is calmer, accommodation providers and restaurant staff are happy to see you, and prices are rock-bottom.

Accommodation

If you're travelling with infants, portacots are often available at an additional cost of $20 to $30. Most hotels, however, only have a limited supply, so get in early to reserve one.

In summer, caravan parks are often filled with other families, which is great for kids to socialise. Make sure, however, that you keep your kids under supervision, especially whenever there is unfenced water around.

If you're on a tight budget, YHA hostels have family rooms that sleep three to four, though motels with a double and single bed are usually cheaper. Whatever your budget, 'family room' usually means that you'll all be in the same room – if you'd prefer more space (which may be a mutual feeling if your kids are older), you can often find well-priced apartments with two bedrooms (see p339).

TRAIN JOURNEYS

The Puffing Billy (p131) steam train, which chugs along the Belgrave–Gembrook line in the Dandenongs, has long been a family favourite, while the Bellarine Peninsula Railway (p158) running the Queenscliff–Drysdale line regularly sees special visits by Thomas the Tank Engine (and friends). The Mornington Railway (p218) steam train runs most Sundays, and its special kid-friendly days include a Teddy Bears Day Out, and Easter Bunny and Santa specials.

Regions at a Glance

Melbourne

Food
Sights
Activities

Gourmet Dining

Dining out is an obsession in Melbourne. It means restaurants bursting with experimental fervour, serving up intriguing Asian-inspired dishes, Mod Oz creations and everything in between. Coffee, cocktails and even beer get the same top-class treatment.

Architecture

Federation Sq may be the contemporary showpiece, but downtown Melbourne's architecture spans the centuries, from Docklands' growing community of city-dwellers to Melbourne's gold-rush-era buildings and arcades.

Kayaking the Yarra

Drifting down the winding Yarra River under your own (paddling) steam, you'll take in the best of the Melbourne skyline, including the 88-storey Eureka Tower, without the crowds jostling around you.

p44

Around Melbourne

Relaxation
Food & Wine
Landscapes

Spa Towns

The delightful town of Daylesford and its spa-town sister Hepburn Springs lie just a short trip from Melbourne. Their easy-to-access lakes, creeks and natural mineral springs inspire indulgence and relaxation.

Local Produce

Just an hour or so from Melbourne lie two excellent wine and foodie zones: the Yarra Valley, famed for its hills, vineyards and microbreweries; and the Macedon Ranges, where you can enjoy excellent local produce at charming country eateries.

Mountains

Rise above Melbourne's eastern urban sprawl and drive through the towering forests of the Dandenong Ranges. Here, impossibly tall trees tower over quaint little settlements where garden walks and Devonshire teas draw in-the-know Melburnians.

p129

Great Ocean Road & Bellarine Peninsula

Activities
Beaches
Sights

Coastal Walks

Known as Victoria's premier driving destination, the Great Ocean Road also offers incredible walks. Long strolls along the sand between the dramatic headlands are the way to start – or you could try walking the length from Apollo Bay.

Bells Beach

Enclosed by steep cliffs, this world-famous surf beach is an intensely beautiful natural amphitheatre, and the scene of swells that draw the world's best for surf competitions and pilgrimages alike.

Twelve Apostles

The splendour of the iconic, rocky Twelve Apostles jutting out from the ocean is undeniable. The journey here, along the winding Great Ocean Road, is one of the most rewarding trips in the country.

p149

Goldfields & the Grampians

Activities
Food & Wine
Historic Sights

Hiking the Grampians

The Grampians is one of Victoria's most dramatic natural landscapes. Get up close and personal while bushwalking the endless trails that lead through fire-scarred forests and beneath (or up to the summits of) stirring rocky outcrops.

Grapes & Olives

Lesser known than other Victorian wine regions, the Grampians have numerous vineyards that are quietly gathering plaudits from critics and travelling punters. Olive farms round out the taste experience.

Goldfields Towns

Victoria's 19th-century gold-rush past lives on in the glorious streetscapes of Castlemaine, Kyneton and Bendigo. Visiting Maldon and Sovereign Hill is like time-travelling back to the state's storied past.

p187

Mornington Peninsula & Phillip Island

Activities
Wildlife
Wine

Bay & Back Beaches

Quiet bay beaches line up along the eastern shore of Port Phillip Bay like a roll call of family-friendly summer playgrounds. The peninsula's back beaches are wild and waiting for experienced surfers and lovers of a good stroll along unspoiled stretches of sand.

Penguins & Koalas

The nightly parade of little penguins along the southern shore of Phillip Island is one of Australia's greatest wildlife spectacles, while French Island is home to some of the tamest wild koalas in the country.

Red Hill Wineries

The Mornington Peninsula's premier wine region centres on Red Hill with its winning combination of picturesque countryside, cellar-door sales and restaurants. It's great for day trips or longer stays that delve into the local pinot noir in a more lingering way.

p215

Gippsland & Wilsons Promontory

Landscapes
Villages
Hiking

National Parks

From the forests of Snowy River and Errinundra, where you'll be serenaded by birdsong, to the deserted beaches of the Croajingolong Coast, Victoria's far east is wild, rugged and pristine in equal measure. It's all about wilderness in its purest form.

Walhalla

It may feel like a movie set but Walhalla, on the cusp of Victoria's High Country, is very much alive. Timbered homes all along its steepwalled valley evoke the state's mining past, while the town cemetery is poignant and beautiful.

Wilsons Prom Walks

With more than 80km of walking trails, mainland Australia's southernmost point has something for everyone. Either a short day trek or tackling the three-day Great Prom Walk immerses you in fine beaches, abundant wildlife and stirring mountains.

p231

The High Country

Activities
Food & Wine
Village Life

Winter Skiing

Mt Buller, Mt Hotham and Falls Creek promise the full range of downhill adrenalin rush on the snow and a heady mix of après-piste hedonism. Mts Baw Baw and Buffalo are perfect for more family-focused fun.

Milawa Gourmet

One of Victoria's bets regions for artisanal food experiences, Milawa and its surrounds – such as King Valley and Myrtleford – take in world-class wineries, cheese and butter factories, and a whole range of gourmet goodies.

Beautiful Beechworth

Beechworth's golden sandstone architecture ranks among the best-preserved period architecture in the state, and it provides the backdrop to a buzzing culinary and cultural life that captures the essence of regional Victoria's appeal.

p256

The Murray River & Around

Activities
Food & Wine
Historic Towns

River Fun

You could view the Murray River from the riverbank, but kayaking in Mildura or revisiting the river's history by boarding one of its grand old paddle steamers in Echuca gets you up close and personal.

Rutherglen Wines

In the Murray River's southern hinterland, Rutherglen's postcard-pretty main street serves as a gateway to the vineyards that produce the state's most celebrated fortified reds. Wine festivals in March, June and September are worth looking out for.

Chiltern

Chiltern's historic main street is beloved by film producers eager to evoke the gold-rich days of Victoria's 19th-century boom years. Antique shops, a pub or two and verandah-lined heritage buildings are essential to its charm.

p281

On the Road

**The Murray River
& Around**
p281

**Goldfields &
the Grampians**
p187

**Great Ocean Road &
Bellarine Peninsula**
p149

**Around
Melbourne**
p129

**The High
Country**
p256

**Gippsland &
Wilsons Promontory**
p231

◉**Melbourne**
p44

**Mornington Peninsula
& Phillip Island**
p215

Melbourne

POP 4,250,000

Includes ➡

Sights 45
Activities 75
Courses 79
Tours............................80
Sleeping 81
Eating 89
Drinking & Nightlife.... 102
Entertainment............113
Shopping....................119

Best Places to Eat

➡ Vue de Monde (p92)

➡ MoVida (p90)

➡ Attica (p101)

➡ Mamasita (p90)

➡ Cumulus Inc (p90)

Best Places to Stay

➡ Art Series (Cullen) (p87)

➡ Ovolo (p84)

➡ Nunnery (p85)

➡ Space Hotel (p81)

➡ Majorca Apartment 401 (p84)

Why Go?

Stylish, arty Melbourne is a city that's both dynamic and cosmopolitan, and proud of its place as Australia's cultural capital. Its stately gold-rush-era architecture and a multi-cultural make-up reflect the city's recent history, while edgy street art, top museums and sticky-carpeted band venues point to its present-day personality.

Melbourne is best experienced as a local would, with its character largely reliant upon its collection of inner-city neighbourhoods. Despite a long-standing north–south divide (flashy St Kilda versus hipster Fitzroy), there's a coolness about its bars, cafes, restaurants, festivals and people that transcends the borders. The city centre has meanwhile reinvented itself with chic laneway eateries and rooftop bars opening in former industrial buildings.

Sport is also crucial to the fabric of the town, taking on something of a religious nature here. Melburnians are passionate about AFL football ('footy'), cricket and horse racing, and also love their Grand Slam tennis and Formula One car racing.

When to Go
Melbourne

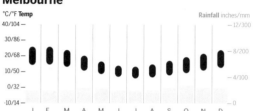

Mid-Dec–Mar Balmy nights, Grand Slam tennis and music festivals.

Apr–Sep Escape the cold with gallery-hopping, boutique shopping and warm, inviting pubs.

Sep–Nov Footy finals fever hits before the horses start cantering during Spring Racing Carnival.

⊙ Sights

Central Melbourne

Melbourne's wide main streets and legion of laneways pop and fizz day and night, seven days a week. Museums and art galleries are dotted throughout. The city's 'Little' streets (Little Bourke, etc) have attracted residents and businesses since the 1850s, a decade in which Melbourne's population quadrupled, thanks to the gold rush. City-centre living went out of favour but has since boomed in the past decade, with some 100,000 claiming CBD abodes as their own.

There are two 'big ends' of town. Skyscrapers cluster on the east and west ends of the grid – these areas are where the city does business. Southern Cross Station sits to the west, with Docklands Stadium and Docklands beyond. Opposite the central Flinders Street Station, Federation Square (better known as Fed Square) squats beside the Yarra River, and has become a favourite Melbourne gathering place. To the east is the 'top end' of the city, with its monumental gold-rush-era buildings such as Parliament House and the Treasury Building.

★ Federation Square   LANDMARK
(Map p50; www.fedsquare.com.au; cnr Flinders & Swanston Sts; 🚊 1, 3, 5, 6, 8, 16, 64, 67, 72, 🚉 Flinders St) While it's taken some time, Melburnians have finally come to embrace Federation Square, accepting it as the congregation place it was meant to be – somewhere to celebrate, protest, watch major sporting events or hang out on its deckchairs. Occupying a prominent city block, 'Fed Square' is far from square: its undulating and patterned forecourt is paved with 460,000 hand-laid cobblestones from the Kimberley region, with sight-lines to Melbourne's iconic landmarks; its buildings are clad in a fractal-patterned reptilian skin.

Within are cultural heavyweights such as the Ian Potter Centre and the Australian Centre for the Moving Image (ACMI), as well as restaurants and bars. At the square's street junction is the subterranean Melbourne Visitor Centre (p126). Highly recommended free tours of Fed Square depart Monday to Saturday at 11am; spaces are limited, so get here 10 to 15 minutes early. The square has free wi-fi, and there are always free public events going on here, particularly on weekends – as well as free daily tai chi from 7.30am, and meditation at 12.30pm on Tuesday.

★ Ian Potter Centre:
NGV Australia   GALLERY
(Map p50; ☎ 03-8620 2222; www.ngv.vic.gov.au; Federation Sq; exhibition costs vary; ⊙ 10am-5pm Tue-Sun; 🚊 1, 3, 5, 6, 8, 16, 64, 67, 72, 🚉 Flinders St) **FREE** Hidden away in the basement of Federation Square, the Ian Potter Centre is the other half of the National Gallery of Victoria (NGV), set up to showcase its impressive collection of Australian works. Set over three levels, it's a mix of permanent (free) and temporary (ticketed) exhibitions, comprising paintings, decorative arts, photography, prints, sculpture and fashion. There's also a great museum gift shop. Free tours are conducted daily at 11am, noon, 1pm and 2pm.

The Aboriginal permanent exhibition on the ground floor is stunning, and seeks to challenge ideas of the 'authentic'. There are some particularly fine examples of Papunya painting, and interesting use of mediums from bark, plus didgeridoos, contemporary sculpture and dot paintings on canvas.

Upstairs are permanent displays of paintings by artists such as Arthur Streeton and Tom Roberts, including Roberts' famous *Shearing the Rams*. There's also the work of the Heidelberg School impressionists and a fabulous collection of the work of the modernist 'Angry Penguins', including Sir Sidney Nolan, Arthur Boyd, Joy Hester and Albert Tucker. Other prominent artists on display include Fred Williams, John Brack and Howard Arkley.

Australian Centre
for the Moving Image   MUSEUM
(ACMI; Map p50; ☎ 03-8663 2200; www.acmi.net. au; Federation Sq; ⊙ 10am-6pm; 🚊 1, 3, 5, 6, 8, 16, 64, 67, 72, 🚉 Flinders St) **FREE** Managing to educate, enthral and entertain in equal parts, ACMI is a visual feast that pays homage to Australian cinema and TV, offering an insight into the modern-day Australian psyche perhaps like no other museum can. Its floating screens don't discriminate against age, with TV shows, games and movies on-call – making it a great place to waste a day watching TV and not feel guilty about it. Free tours are conducted daily at 11am and 2.30pm.

Screenworld is the main focus here, an interactive exhibition that celebrates the work of Australian cinema and TV; its exhibitions, games lab and zoetrope will interest anyone, whether they're clued in about Dexter from *Perfect Match* or not. Upstairs, you'll find the **Australian Mediatheque**, a venue set aside for the viewing of programs from the National Film and Sound Archive

MELBOURNE SIGHTS

Melbourne Highlights

❶ Discover the city centre's **laneways** and **arcades** (p56)

❷ Head to an industrial-chic cafe to quaff an artisanal **coffee** (p102)

❸ Spend the evening in the inner north experiencing its **live-music scene** (p115)

❹ **Kayak** along the city section of the Yarra (p75)

❺ Make a pilgrimage to the **MCG** (p59), one of the world's most famous sporting grounds

❻ Wander around historic **Queen Victoria Market** (p55)

See Fitzroy & Around Map (p64)

See Carlton & Around Map (p66)

Eastern Fwy

FAIRFIELD

Gatehouse St

Yarra Bend Park

Elgin St

Royal Exhibition Building & Melbourne Museum

Johnston St

Victoria Park

Abbotsford Convent

Studley Park

Grattan St

Swanston St

Inner North

Fitzroy & Collingwood

Collingwood Children's Farm

KEW

Queensberry St

Gertrude St

Collingwood

Studley Park Rd

Queen Victoria Market

La Trobe St

Langridge St

ABBOTSFORD

Carlton & United Breweries

Victoria Pde

Victoria St

Hoddle St

Barkers Rd

Lonsdale St

City Centre

Exhibition St

Treasury Gardens

RICHMOND

Church St

Bourke St

Wellington Pde

Bridge Rd

Hawthorn

Collins St

Burnley St

SOUTHBANK

Yarra River

MCG

Burnley

Swan St

BURNLEY

South Wharf

Polly Woodside

City Rd

See East Melbourne & Richmond Map (p60)

East Richmond

Royal Botanic Gardens

Herring Island Park

Alexandra Ave

Heyington

Kings Way

CityLink

South Melbourne Market

SOUTH MELBOURNE

Albert Rd

Gunn Island

Fawkner Park

Punt Rd

South Yarra

Toorak Rd

SOUTH YARRA

Williams Rd

TOORAK

Toorak Rd

Kooyong Rd

Melbourne Sports & Aquatic Centre

Albert Park Lake

Queens Rd

Commercial Rd

Hawksburn

ALBERT PARK

Albert Park

Albert Park Golf Course

Prahran

Chapel St

PRAHRAN

Malvern Rd

Toorak

Beaconsfield Pde

Windsor

WINDSOR

High St

Armadale

St Kilda Junction

See South Yarra, Prahran & Windsor Map (p68)

ARMADALE

See St Kilda & Around Map (p72)

Dandenong Rd

St Kilda Cemetery

St Kilda Pier

ST KILDA

St Kilda Rd

Alma Rd

ST KILDA EAST

Alma Rd

Orrong Rd

Carlisle St

Inkerman St

CAULFIELD NORTH

Balaclava

Balaclava Rd

BALACLAVA

for its atmosphere and fresh produce

7 Shop your way around the boutiques of **Fitzroy** and **Collingwood** (p121)

8 Explore the **Royal Exhibition Building** (p66) and neighbouring **Melbourne Museum** (p65)

9 Gallery-hop around the city centre and Collingwood to take in the **arts scene** (p55 & p63)

10 Stroll to the end of the **St Kilda Pier** (p71) to spot little penguins

and ACMI, the perfect hideaway on a rainy day. Mini-festivals of cinema classics and the occasional Pixar blockbuster are screened throughout the year; also keep an eye out for Melbourne Cinémathèque (www.melbournecinematheque.org) screenings.

★ Birrarung Marr   PARK
(Map p50; btwn Federation Sq & the Yarra River; 🚋1, 3, 5, 6, 8, 16, 64, 67, 72, 🚉Flinders St) The three-terraced Birrarung Marr is a welcome addition to Melbourne's patchwork of parks and gardens, featuring grassy knolls, river promenades, a thoughtful planting of indigenous flora and great viewpoints of the city and the river. There's also a scenic route to the Melbourne Cricket Ground (MCG; p59) via the 'talking' William Barak Bridge – listen out for songs, words and sounds representing Melbourne's cultural diversity as you walk.

The sculptural Federation Bells (www.federationbells.com.au; ☺bells 8.30-9.30am, noon-1pm & 5-6pm) perch on the park's upper level and ring out daily like a robotic orchestra, with 39 brass bells of various sizes and shapes, all with impressive acoustics, and specially commissioned contemporary compositions.

As a sign of respect to the Wurundjeri people, the traditional owners of the area (in their language, 'Birrarung Marr' means 'river of mists'), the park features a snaking eel path with Indigenous Australian art, a shield-and-spear sculpture and an audio installation outside ArtPlay that tells the story of contemporary Wurundjeri people.

Other highlights are the 10m-high, three-legged mosaic Angel, a vivid abstract sculpture by Deborah Halpern; Speakers Corner, featuring original mounds used as soapboxes in the early 20th century; and a dried riverbed lined with ghost gums and palms, giving it a tranquil billlabong feel.

Within an old railway building, ArtPlay (Map p50; ☏03-9664 7900; www.artplay.com.au; ☺Wed-Sun 10am-4pm) hosts creative workshops for two- to 13-year-olds, getting them sewing, singing, painting and puppeteering; it features a very cool playground out back.

★ Hosier Lane   STREET
(Map p50; Hosier Ln; 🚋75, 70) Melbourne's most celebrated laneway for street art, Hosier Lane's cobbled length draws camera-wielding crowds snapping edgy graffiti, stencils and art installations. Subject matter runs to the mostly political and counter-culture, spiced with irreverent humour; pieces change almost daily (not even a Banksy is safe here). Be sure to see Rutledge Lane (which horseshoes around Hosier), too.

Flinders Street Station   HISTORIC BUILDING
(Map p50; cnr Flinders & Swanston Sts) If ever there was a true symbol of the city, Flinders Street Station would have to be it. Built in 1854, it was Melbourne's first railway station, and you'd be hard-pressed to find a Melburnian who hasn't uttered the phrase 'Meet me under the clocks' at one time or another (the popular rendezvous spot is located at the front entrance of the station).

MELBOURNE IN...

Two Days

Check out the Ian Potter Centre: NGV Australia (p45) and ACMI (p45) museums, then enjoy lunch at MoVida (p90). Join a walking tour to see Melbourne's street art (p80) then chill out at a rooftop bar until it's time to join an evening kayaking tour (p75) of the Yarra River. Day two, stroll along Birrarung Marr (p48) and into the Royal Botanic Gardens (p69), then shop your way to the Queen Victoria Market (p55). Catch a tram to St Kilda (p71) and stroll along the beach. Catch a band and prop up a bar in lively Acland Street for the evening.

One Week

Spend a couple of hours at the Melbourne Museum (p65) and then revive with a coffee at DOC (p98) in Lygon St. Head to Fitzroy and Collingwood and shop along Gertrude Street before feasting at Cutler & Co (p97). Back in the city centre, wander through Chinatown (p52) and check out Ned Kelly's armour at the State Library (p54) before grabbing some dumplings for dinner. Spend the rest of the week shopping, cafe-hopping and people-watching in busy Prahran and Windsor (p69). In winter, catch a footy game at the MCG (p59) before drinks at one of the city's laneway bars. Make sure to save time to hit Mamasita (p90) for tacos and the Tote (p115) in Collingwood for live music.

Stretching along the Yarra, it's a beautiful neoclassical building topped with a striking octagonal dome.

The grand old dame's underground tendrils connect the city's north with its south, with underpasses (such as Campbell Arcade) linked to Southbank via a pedestrian bridge. Free wi-fi here.

St Paul's Cathedral   CHURCH

(Map p50; ☑ 03-9653 4333; www.stpaulscathedral. org.au; cnr Flinders & Swanston Sts; ⊘8am-6pm Sun-Fri, to 5pm Sat) Opposite Federation Sq stands the magnificent Anglican St Paul's Cathedral. Services were celebrated on this site from the city's first days. Built between 1880 and 1891, the present church is the work of distinguished ecclesiastical architect William Butterfield (a case of architecture by proxy, as he did not condescend to visit Melbourne, instead sending drawings from England). It features ornate stained-glass windows made between 1887 and 1890, and holds excellent music programs.

Young & Jackson's   HISTORIC BUILDING

(Map p50; www.youngandjacksons.com.au; cnr Flinders & Swanston Sts; ☐ Tourist Shuttle, ☐ City Circle, 1, 3, 5, 6, 8, 16, 64, 67, 72, ☐ Flinders St) Across the street from Flinders Street Station is a pub (p105) known less for its beer (served up since 1861) than its iconic nude painting of the teenaged *Chloe,* painted by Jules Joseph Lefebvre. Chloe's yearning gaze, cast over her shoulder and out of the frame, was a hit at the Paris Salon of 1875.

The painting caused an outcry in parochial, provincial Melbourne, however, and was removed from display at the National Gallery of Victoria. Eventually purchased by publican and 'art lover' Henry Figsby Young in 1909, *Chloe* found an appreciative audience and permanent home at this pub.

Melbourne Town Hall   HISTORIC BUILDING

(Map p50; ☑ 03-9658 9658; www.melbourne.vic. gov.au; cnr Collins & Swanston Sts; ⊘tour 11am & 1pm Mon-Fri) The Melbourne Town Hall has been used as a civic and entertainment venue since 1870. Queen Elizabeth II took tea here in 1954, and the Beatles waved to thousands of screaming fans from the balcony in 1964. Take the free one-hour tour to see the Grand Organ (built in 1929, and the largest grand romantic organ in the southern hemisphere), sit in the Lord Mayor's chair or tinker on the same piano Paul McCartney did. It's a busy venue during the Melbourne International Comedy Festival (p115).

Collins Street   STREET

(Map p50; btwn Spring & Elizabeth Sts) The top end of Collins St, aka the 'Paris End', is lined with plane trees, grand buildings and luxe boutiques (hence its moniker). You'll find ornate arcades leading off from Collins St. The Block network, comprising Block Pl, Block Arcade and Block Ct, was named after the 19th-century pastime of 'doing the block', which referred to walking the city's fashionable area.

Old Treasury Building   MUSEUM

(Map p50; ☑ 03-9651 2233; www.oldtreasurybuilding.org.au; Spring St; ⊘10am-4pm, closed Sat; ☐ 112, ☐ Parliament) FREE The fine neoclassical architecture of the Old Treasury (c 1862), designed by JJ Clarke, is a telling mix of hubris and functionality. The basement vaults were built to house the millions of pounds worth of loot that came from the Victorian goldfields and now feature multimedia displays telling stories from the gold rush. Also downstairs is the charmingly redolent reconstruction of the 1920s caretaker's residence, which beautifully reveals what life in Melbourne was like in the early part of last century.

The adjacent Treasury Gardens, to the south of the the building, contain the John F Kennedy Memorial.

Parliament House   HISTORIC BUILDING

(Map p50; ☑ 03-9651 8568; www.parliament. vic.gov.au; Spring St; ⊘tours 9.30am, 10.30am, 11.30am, 1.30pm, 2.30pm & 3.45pm Mon-Fri; ☐ City Circle, 86, 96, ☐ Parliament) The grand steps of Victoria's parliament (c 1856) are often dotted with slow-moving, tulle-wearing brides smiling for the camera, or placard-holding protesters doing the same. The only way to visit inside is on a tour, where you'll see exuberant use of ornamental plasterwork, stencilling and gilt full of gold-rush-era pride and optimism. Building began with the two main chambers: the lower house (now the legislative assembly) and the upper house (now the legislative council).

The library was added in 1860 and Queen's Hall in 1879. Australia's first federal parliament sat here from 1901, before moving to Canberra in 1927. Though they've never been used, gun slits are visible just below the roof, and a dungeon is now the cleaners' tearoom.

Free tours, held when parliament is in recess, take you through both houses and the library. Fascinating design features and the symbolism underlying much of the

Central Melbourne

MELBOURNE

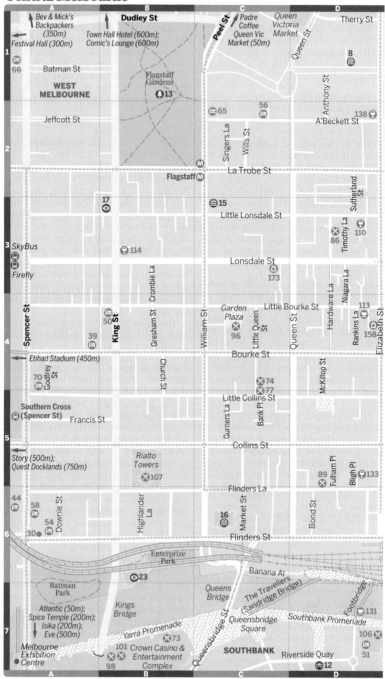

0   200 m
0   0.1 miles

Royal Melbourne Institute of Technology

Cardigan St

Earl St

Lygon St

Queensberry St

Royal Exhibition Building

33

34

Victoria St

CARLTON

Franklin St

55

Swanston St

Royal Melbourne Institute of Technology

Bowen St

19

68

Mackenzie St

Rathdowne St

Carlton Gardens South

Little La Trobe St

Melbourne Central

Melbourne Central

Melbourne Central

Melbourne Central

La Trobe St

Victoria Pde

State Library of Victoria

5

27

Davisons Pl

141

Bennetts La

Exploration La

94

Spring St

82

Little Lonsdale St

109

125

105

Red Cape La

170

QV

168   Square

Artemis La

Hayward La

Jones La

90

Lonsdale St

75

155

153

122

134

103

130

136

60

145

64

Parliament

127

78

104

CHINATOWN

10

154

91 62 42

Parliament Gardens

9

La Trobe Pl

142

Little Bourke St

Coverlid Pl

150

Exhibition St

43

85

137

97

57

151

129

102

169

120

121

163

83

146

88

118

99   128

164

166

100

21

Bourke St

40

26

115

117   22

Union La

Royal La

Russell Pl

124

63

143

126   108   49

41

Parliament

35   47

Century Building

71

Baptist Pl

Little Collins St

Alfred Pl

25

53

72

Parliament

157

111

162   87

144

18

148   139

Collins St

20

11

Manchester Unity Building

123

135

City Square

152

Regent Pl

George Pde

45

92

52

160   46

Centre Pl

165

Nicholas Building

59   31

156

6

37

Flinders La

80

93   79

116

61

81 161

119

28

24

Hosier Lane

3

95   147

Oliver La

ACDC La

76

38

84

48

Treasury Gardens

Flinders St

172

159

32

140   7

112

Wellington Pde South

Flinders St

14

2

Federation Square

167

Ian Potter Centre: NGV Australia

4

132

36

Yarra River

Princes Bridge

Southbank

St Kilda Rd

Arts Centre Melbourne (100m); NGV International (200m); Shrine of Remembrance (1km)

29

Birrarung Marr

Batman Ave

Birrarung Marr

1

149

Royal Botanic Gardens (600m)

ornamentation are illuminated by the knowledgeable guides. Ask about the mystery of the stolen ceremonial mace that disappeared from the lower house in 1891 – it's rumoured to have ended up in a brothel. Express 20-minute tours run on Monday to Fri-

day at 1pm and 4pm, and architectural tours once a month. Booking is essential.

Chinatown NEIGHBOURHOOD
(Map p50; Little Bourke St, btwn Spring & Swanston Sts; ⬜1, 3, 5, 6, 8, 16, 64, 67, 72) Chinese miners

Central Melbourne

◎ **Top Sights**
1 Birrarung Marr G7
2 Federation Square F6
3 Hosier Lane F6
4 Ian Potter Centre: NGV Australia F6
5 State Library of Victoria F2

◎ **Sights**
6 Anna Schwartz Gallery F6
7 Australian Centre for the Moving
    Image F6
8 Blender Lane D1
    Blender Studios .... (see 8)
9 Chinatown F4
10 Chinese Museum G3
11 Collins Street E5
    Dark Horse Experiment .... (see 8)
12 Eureka Skydeck D7
13 Flagstaff Gardens B1
14 Flinders Street Station E6
15 Hellenic Museum C3
16 Immigration Museum C6
17 Koorie Heritage Trust B3
18 Melbourne Town Hall E5
19 Old Melbourne Gaol F2
20 Old Treasury Building H5
21 Parliament House H4
22 Royal Arcade E4
23 Sea Life Melbourne Aquarium B6
24 St Paul's Cathedral F6
25 Tolarno Galleries G5
26 West Space F4
27 Wheeler Centre F3
28 Young & Jackson's E6

◎ **Activities, Courses & Tours**
29 ArtPlay G7
30 Bunyip Tours A6
31 Centre for Adult Education E6
    Chuan Spa .... (see 51)
32 Greeter Service F6
33 Hardrock E1
34 Melbourne City Baths F1
35 Miss Fox E5
36 Real Melbourne Bike Tours F7

◎ **Sleeping**
37 Adelphi Hotel F6
38 Adina Apartment Hotel G6
39 Alto Hotel on Bourke A4
40 Causeway Inn on the Mall E4
41 City Centre Budget Hotel H4
42 City Limits H4
43 Crossley H4

44 Grand Hotel Melbourne A6
45 Grand Hyatt Melbourne G5
46 Greenhouse Backpacker E5
47 Hotel Causeway E5
48 Hotel Lindrum H6
49 Hotel Windsor H4
50 King Street Backpackers B4
51 Langham Hotel D7
52 Majorca Apartment 401 .... E5
53 Mantra 100 Exhibition G5
54 Melbourne Central YHA A6
55 Melbourne International
    Backpackers E1
56 Nomad's Melbourne C2
57 Ovolo H4
58 Pensione Hotel A6
59 Punthill Flinders Lane E6
60 Punthill Little Bourke G3
61 Punthill Manhattan H6
62 Quest Gordon Place H4
63 Quest Hero G4
64 Quest on Lonsdale H3
65 Radisson on Flagstaff Gardens C2
66 Robinsons in the City A1
67 Sofitel H5
68 Space Hotel F2
69 United Backpackers E6
70 Vibe Savoy Hotel A4
71 Victoria Hotel F5

◎ **Eating**
72 Bar Lourinhã H5
73 Bistro Guillaume B7
74 Bistro Vue C4
75 Bomba G3
76 Bowery to Williamsburg G6
77 Café Vue C5
78 Camy Shanghai Dumpling
    Restaurant F3
79 Chin Chin G6
80 Coda F6
    Cookie .... (see 153)
81 Cumulus Inc H6
82 Don Don E3
83 Flower Drum G4
84 Gazi G6
85 Gingerboy G4
    Grossi Florentino Grill .... (see 164)
86 Hardware Societe D3
87 Hopetoun Tea Rooms E5
88 HuTong Dumpling Bar G4
89 Huxtaburger D5
90 Izakaya Chuji F3
91 Longrain H4

arrived in search of the 'new gold mountain' in the 1850s and settled in this strip of Little Bourke St, now flanked by traditional red archways. The **Chinese Museum** (Map p50; ☑ 03-9662 2888; www.chinesemuseum.com.au; 22 Cohen Pl; adult/child $8/6; ⊙10am-5pm)

here does a wonderful job of putting it into context with five floors of displays, including artefacts from the gold-rush era, dealings under the xenophobic White Australia policy, and the stunning 63m-long, 200kg Millennium Dragon that bends around the

92	Mamasita	H5
93	Meatball & Wine Bar	G6
	Mesa Verde	(see 153)
94	Misschu	G3
	Moat	(see 27)
95	MoVida	F6
96	MoVida Aqui	C4
97	Mrs Parma's	H4
	No 35 at Sofitel	(see 67)
98	Nobu	B7
	Paco's Tacos	(see 96)
99	Pellegrini's Espresso Bar	G4
100	Red Pepper	H4
101	Rockpool Bar & Grill	B7
	Seamstress	(see 136)
102	Spring St Grocer	H4
103	Stalactites	F3
104	Supper Inn	F3
105	Trunk	G3
106	Tutto Bene	D7
107	Vue de Monde	B5
108	Waiters Restaurant	H4

◉ Drinking & Nightlife
109	2 Pocket Fairtrade	E3
110	1000£Bend	D3
111	Bar Americano	E5
112	Beer DeLuxe	F6
113	Brother Baba Budan	D4
114	Brown Alley	B3
115	Carlton Hotel	F4
116	Cherry	G6
117	Chuckle Park	E4
118	Croft Institute	G4
119	Degraves Espresso	E6
120	Double Happiness	H4
121	Federal Coffee Palace	E4
122	Ferdydurke	F3
123	Hell's Kitchen	E5
	Hotel Windsor	(see 49)
124	James Squire Brewhouse	F4
125	League of Honest Coffee	G3
126	Loop	H4
127	Lounge	E3
	Lui Bar	(see 107)
128	Madame Brussels	H4
129	Melbourne Supper Club	H4
	New Gold Mountain	(see 120)
130	Nihonshu	G3
131	Ponyfish Island	D7
132	Riverland	F7
133	Robot	D5
134	Section 8	F3
135	Shebeen	E5

	Siglo	(see 129)
136	Sweatshop	G3
137	Traveller	H4
138	Workshop	D2
	Young & Jackson's	(see 28)

◉ Entertainment
139	Athenaeum	F5
140	Australian Centre for the Moving Image	F6
141	Bennetts Lane	G2
142	Billboard the Venue	F4
143	Boney	G4
144	Butterfly Club	E5
145	Comedy Theatre	G3
146	Ding Dong Lounge	G4
147	Forum Theatre	F6
148	Halftix Melbourne	E5
149	Hamer Hall	E7
150	Her Majesty's Theatre	G4
	Kino Cinemas	(see 67)
	Last Laugh at the Comedy Club	(see 139)
151	Princess Theatre	H4
152	Regent Theatre	F5
153	Rooftop Cinema	E3
154	Ticketek	G3
155	Ticketmaster	E3
	Toff in Town	(see 153)

◉ Shopping
156	Alice Euphemia	E6
157	Basement Discs	E5
	Búl	(see 153)
158	Captains of Industry	D4
159	City Hatters	E6
160	Claude Maus	E5
161	Craft Victoria Shop	H6
162	Gewürzhaus	E5
163	GPO	E4
164	Hill of Content	G4
165	Incu	E5
166	Melbournalia	H4
	Metropolis	(see 153)
167	NGV Shop At The Ian Potter Centre	F6
168	Obūs	F3
	Original & Authentic Aboriginal Art	(see 164)
169	Paperback Bookshop	H4
170	QV	F3
	Readings	(see 5)
171	Somewhere	E4
172	Sticky	E6
173	Wunderkammer	C3

building; in full flight it needs eight people just to hold up the dragon's head alone.

Here you'll find an interesting mix of Chinese and Asian restaurants; come here for yum cha (dim sum) or explore its attendant laneways for late-night dumplings or cocktails. Chinatown also hosts the city's vibrant Chinese New Year celebrations in January or February.

Royal Arcade   HISTORIC BUILDING

(Map p50; www.royalarcade.com.au; 335 Bourke St Mall; 🚊86, 96) This Parisian-style shopping arcade was built between 1869 and 1870 and is Melbourne's oldest; the upper walls retain much of the original 19th-century detail. The black-and-white chequered path leads to the mythological figures of giant brothers Gog and Magog, perched with hammers atop the arched exit to Little Collins St. They've been striking the hour here since 1892. The businesses within are an interesting mix of the classy and the common.

★ State Library of Victoria   LIBRARY

(Map p50; ☑03-8664 7000; www.slv.vic.gov.au; 328 Swanston St; ⊙10am-9pm Mon-Thu, to 6pm Fri-Sun; 🚊1, 3, 5, 6, 8, 16, 64, 67, 72, 🚇Melbourne Central) A big player in Melbourne's achievement of being named Unesco City of Literature in 2008, the State Library has been at the forefront of Melbourne's literary scene since it opened in 1854. With more than two million books in its collection, it's a great place to browse. Its epicentre, the octagonal La Trobe Reading Room, was completed in 1913; its reinforced-concrete dome was the largest of its kind in the world and its natural light illuminates the ornate plasterwork and the studious Melbourne writers who come here to pen their works.

The library has several exhibitions on display, providing a fascinating story to Melbourne's history. Its most notable item is Ned Kelly's armour, the get-up of Australia's most infamous bushranger: a menacing helmet cobbled together from a plough with a slit cut out for the eyes, and riddled with bullet dents. There's also numerous original Burke and Wills memorabilia and John Batman's controversial land treaty (read: land grab), in which he's believed to have forged signatures of the Wurundjeri people.

Bibliophiles won't want to miss the *Mirror of the World* exhibition, with a weird, wonderful collection of books through the ages, from a 4000-year-old tax receipt and rare first editions to Peter Carey's laptop and

Australian comic books (bet you never heard of Panther Man...). There's also a fine collection of Australian paintings, including the apocalyptic bushfire portrayed by William Strutt in his *Black Thursday, February 6th, 1851.*

For more information, join a free guided tour to see the library's vast collection. There's free wi-fi and internet, plus videogame consoles and a chess room.

Join locals with a takeaway lunch on the library's grassy lawn, or head down the library basement to Moat (Map p50; ☑03-9094 7820; www.themoat.com.au; Basement, 176 Little Lonsdale St, Melbourne; ⊙8am-late; 🗐), an atmospheric, European-style bistro with an appealing literary vibe.

Wheeler Centre   ARTS CENTRE

(Map p50; ☑03-9094 7800; www.wheelercentre. com; 176 Little Lonsdale St; 🚇Melbourne Central) This centre is a celebration of Unesco's 2008 acknowledgment of Melbourne as an international City of Literature, with a variety of programs and speakers (usually writers) throughout the year. Its free weekly Lunchbox/Soapbox sessions make for a great lunchtime diversion; check online for details. The centre was set up by Lonely Planet founders Tony and Maureen Wheeler.

Old Melbourne Gaol   HISTORIC BUILDING

(Map p50; ☑03-8663 7228; www.oldmelbournegaol.com.au; 337 Russell St; adult/child/family $25/14/55; ⊙9.30am-5pm; 🚊24, 30, City Circle) Built in 1841, this forbidding bluestone prison was in operation until 1929. It's now one of Melbourne's most popular museums, where you can tour the tiny, bleak cells. Around 135 people were hanged here, including Ned Kelly, Australia's most infamous bushranger, in 1880; one of his death masks is on display.

The dire social conditions that motivated criminals in 19th-century Melbourne are also highlighted, including the era's obsession with phrenology. If you're curious to see how it would feel to be an inmate here, sign up for the City Watch House Experience, where you get 'arrested' and thrown in the slammer (more fun than it sounds). During peak times you can visit the courtroom where local gangster Squizzy Taylor stood trial.

You can also join a ghost hunt or the Hangman's Night Tour (adult/concession $38/35); check the website for its schedule. Evening events are not recommended for children under 12.

CONTEMPORARY ART

Several galleries around the city centre will be of particular interest to contemporary art lovers. Once raucously bohemian, **Tolarno Galleries** (Map p50; 🖉 03-9654 6000; www.tolarnogalleries.com; 4th fl, 104 Exhibition St; ⊙10am-5pm Tue-Fri, 1-5pm Sat; 🚋 86,95,96) **FREE** is now a serious, cerebral space, with exhibitions changing monthly. **West Space** (Map p50; 🖉 03-9662 3297; www.westspace.org.au; Level 1, 225 Bourke St; ⊙noon-6pm Tue-Sat; 🚋 86, 95, 96) **FREE**, one of Melbourne's oldest nonprofit, artist-run galleries, has a varied exhibition program in a range of mediums both traditional and modern. Some of the city's most respected contemporary artists can be seen at the **Anna Schwartz Gallery** (Map p50; 🖉 03-9654 6131; www.annaschwartzgallery.com; 185 Flinders Lane; ⊙noon-6pm Tue-Fri, 1-5pm Sat) **FREE**, a standard white cube featuring often fiercely conceptual work.

⭐ **Queen Victoria Market**   MARKET

(Map p66; www.qvm.com.au; 513 Elizabeth St; ⊙6am-2pm Tue & Thu, to 5pm Fri, to 3pm Sat, 9am-4pm Sun; 🚋 Tourist Shuttle, 🚋 19, 55, 57, 59) With more than 600 traders, the Vic Market is the largest open-air market in the southern hemisphere and attracts thousands of shoppers. It's where Melburnians sniff out fresh produce among the booming cries of spruiking fishmongers and fruit-and-veg vendors. The wonderful deli hall (with art deco features) is lined with everything from soft cheeses, wines and Polish sausages to Greek dips, truffle oil and kangaroo biltong.

Saturday mornings are particularly buzzing, with marketgoers having breakfast to the sounds and shows of buskers. Clothing and knick-knack stalls dominate on Sundays; they're big on variety, but don't come looking for style. (If you're in the market for sheepskin moccasins or cheap T-shirts, you'll be in luck.)

On Wednesday evenings from mid-November to the end of February the **Summer Night Market** takes over. It's a lively social event featuring hawker-style food stalls, bars and music and dance performances. There's also a winter night market each Wednesday evening in August.

The market has been on this site for more than 130 years; before that, from 1837 to 1854, it was the old Melbourne Cemetery (remarkably, around 9000 bodies remain buried here, from underneath Shed F to the car park leading to Franklin St). There's a small memorial on the corner of Queen and Therry Sts.

A number of tours are run from the market, including heritage, cultural and foodie tours; check the website for details.

Blender Lane   GALLERY, STREET

(Map p50; 110 Franklin St; 🚋 19, 55, 57, 59) Hidden down an unsigned laneway off Franklin St en route to the Vic Market, Blender Lane features some of Melbourne's best street art. You'll also find the **Blender Studios** (Map p50; 🖉 03-9328 5556; www.theblenderstudios.com; 110 Franklin St) and **Dark Horse Experiment** (Map p50; 🖉 03-9328 5556; www.darkhorseexperiment.com; 110 Franklin St; ⊙noon-6pm Wed-Sat) galleries in an old warehouse-turned-art-studio used by underground artists. They run the highly recommended Melbourne Street Art Tours (p80). The Blender Lane Artists Market runs every Wednesday from mid-November to late February, with stalls of artists selling pieces.

Hellenic Museum   MUSEUM, ARCHITECTURE

(Map p50; 🖉 03-8615 9016; www.hellenic.org.au; 280 William St; ⊙10am-4pm; 🚋 55) **FREE** Housed in a beautiful Renaissance revival–style building that was formerly the Royal Mint, this small museum is dedicated to Greek immigrants who moved here in the 1950s, and the legacy they've left the city – the third-biggest Greek-speaking city behind Athens and Boston.

Flagstaff Gardens   PARK

(Map p50; William St, btwn La Trobe, Dudley & King Sts; 🚋 Tourist Shuttle, 🚋 24, 30, 55, City Circle, 🚇 Flagstaff) Originally known as Burial Hill, these gardens were the site of Melbourne's first cemetery, where eight of the city's early settlers were buried. Today its pleasant open lawns are popular with workers taking a lunchtime break. The gardens contain trees that are well over 100 years old, including Moreton Bay fig trees and a variety of eucalypts, including spotted, sugar gums and river red gums. There are plenty of possums about, but don't feed them.

The hill once provided one of the best views out to the bay, so a signalling station was set up here: when a ship was sighted

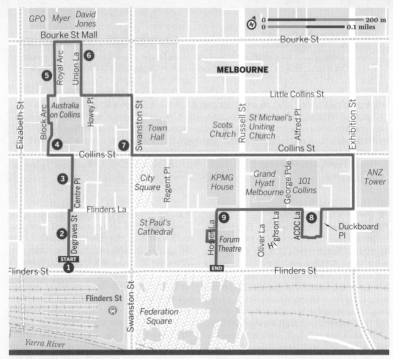

City Walk
Arcades & Laneways

START CAMPBELL ARCADE
FINISH MOVIDA
LENGTH 3KM; 2½ HOURS

Central Melbourne is a warren of 19th-century arcades and gritty-turned-hip cobbled blue-stone laneways featuring street art, basement restaurants, boutiques and bars.

Start off underground at the art deco **1 Campbell Arcade**, also known as Degraves Subway, built for the 1956 Olympics and now home to indie stores. Head upstairs to **2 Degraves St**, grab a coffee at Degraves Espresso, and then continue north, crossing over Flinders Lane to cafe-filled **3 Centre Place**, a good place to start street-art spotting.

Cross over Collins St, turn left and enter the **4 Block Arcade**; built in 1891 and featuring etched-glass ceilings and mosaic floors, it's based on Milan's Galleria Vittorio Emanuele II plaza. Ogle the window display at the Hopetoun Tea Rooms. Exit the other end of the arcade into Little Collins St and perhaps grab an afternoon cocktail at Chuckle Park.

Across Little Collins, head into **5 Royal Arcade** (p54). Wander through to Bourke St Mall, then turn right and walk until you find street-art-covered **6 Union Lane** on the right.

Follow Union Lane out and turn left onto Little Collins, then take a right on Swanston St and walk south to the **7 Manchester Unity Arcade** (1932) on the corner of Collins St. Take a look in this beautiful arcade, then go back out to Swanston and head east, up the hill, to the 'Paris End' of Collins St. Along the way, admire the 1873 Gothic Scots Church (the first Presbyterian church in Victoria) and the 1866 St Michael's Uniting Church, built in an unusual Lombardic Romanesque style.

Turn right into Exhibition St, then right into Flinders Lane, and continue until you see **8 Duckboard Place**. Head down the laneway and take your time to soak up the street art before horseshoeing around into ACDC Lane, past rock 'n' roll dive bar Cherry.

Continue on down Flinders Lane to the street-art meccas of **9 Hosier Lane** (p48) and Rutledge Lane before finishing with tapas and a drink at MoVida.

arriving from Britain, a flag was raised on the flagstaff to notify the settlers. The Wurundjeri people also found it significant for the same useful vista, which stretches as far as Mt Macedon.

Koorie Heritage Trust   CULTURAL CENTRE
(Map p50; ☎03-8622 2600; www.koorieheritagetrust.com; 295 King St; gold-coin donation, tours $15; ◉9am-5pm Mon-Fri; ☐24, 30, ☒Flagstaff) ⚑ Devoted to southeastern Aboriginal culture, this cultural centre displays interesting artefacts and oral history. Its gallery spaces show a variety of contemporary and traditional work, a model scar tree at the centre's heart, and a permanent chronological display of Victorian Koorie history. Behind the scenes, significant objects are carefully preserved; replicas that can be touched by visitors are used in the displays. It's in the process of relocating, so check the website for details.

The trust also runs highly recommended tours to Flagstaff Gardens and along the Yarra, which puts the area into context. Tours are mainly for school groups, but it's normally OK to tag along; call ahead to enquire.

Another reason to visit is its shop, which sells books on Aboriginal culture, CDs, crafts and bush-food supplies.

Immigration Museum   MUSEUM
(Map p50; ☎13 11 02; www.museumvictoria.com.au/immigrationmuseum; 400 Flinders St; adult/child $10/free; ◉10am-5pm; ☐70, 75) The Immigration Museum uses personal and community voices, images and memorabilia to tell the many stories of Australian immigration. It's symbolically housed in the old Customs House, with the restored building alone worth the visit: the Long Room is a magnificent piece of Renaissance revival architecture.

After exiting the museum, head across the river via Sandridge Bridge to check out the steel Travellers sculptures, which depict the story of arrival that belongs to many Melburnians; *Gayip,* the only sculpture to sit on land rather than on the bridge, represents Indigenous Australians from the area.

Sea Life Melbourne Aquarium   AQUARIUM
(Map p50; ☎03-9923 5999; www.melbourneaquarium.com.au; cnr Flinders & King Sts; adult/child/family $38/22/93; ◉9.30am-6pm, last entry 5pm; ☐70, 75) This aquarium is home to rays, gropers and sharks, all of which cruise around a 2.2-million-litre tank, watched closely by visitors in a see-through tunnel. See the penguins in icy 'Antarctica' or get up close to one of Australia's largest saltwater crocs in the crocodile lair. Divers are thrown to the sharks three times a day; for between $210 and $300 you can join them. Admission tickets are cheaper online.

St Patrick's Cathedral   CHURCH
(☎03-9662 2233; www.stpatrickscathedral.org.au; cnr Gisborne St & Cathedral Pl; ◉9am-5pm Mon-Fri; ☐112) Head up McArthur St (the extension of Collins St) to see one of the world's largest and finest examples of Gothic Revival architecture. Designed by William Wardell, St Patrick's was named after the patron saint of Ireland, reflecting the local Catholic community's main origin. Building began in 1863 and continued until the spires were added in 1939.

The imposing bluestone exterior and grounds are but a preview of its contents: inside are several tonnes of bells, an organ with 4500 pipes, ornate stained-glass windows and the remains of former archbishops.

◉ Southbank & Docklands

Southbank, once a gritty industrial site, sits directly across the Yarra River from Flinders St. Behind it is the city's major arts precinct, comprising the NGV International, the Arts Centre and other organisations such as the Australian Ballet. Back down by the river, the promenade stretches to the Crown Casino & Entertainment Complex, a self-proclaimed 'world of entertainment', and further on to South Wharf, the newest development of bars and restaurants. To the city's west lies the Docklands. The once working wharves of Victoria Harbour have given birth to a mini-city of apartment buildings, offices, restaurants, plazas, public art and parkland. It's early days, but its manufactured sameness has yet to be overwritten with the organic cadences and colour of neighbourhood life.

NGV International   GALLERY
(☎03-8662 1555; www.ngv.vic.gov.au; 180 St Kilda Rd; exhibition costs vary; ◉10am-5pm Wed-Mon; ☐Tourist Shuttle, ☐1, 3, 5, 6, 8, 16, 64, 67, 72) FREE Beyond the water-wall facade you'll find an expansive collection set over three levels, covering international art that runs from the ancient to the contemporary. Key works include a Rembrandt, a Tiepolo and a Bonnard. You might also bump into a Monet, a

Modigliani, or a Bacon. It's also home to Picasso's *Weeping Woman*, which was the victim of an art heist in 1986. Free 45-minute tours occur hourly from 11am to 2pm, which alternate to take in different parts of the collection.

The gallery also has an excellent decorative arts collection, and fantastic pieces in its Asia galleries from India to Japan. Its international blockbuster shows are huge, and bring with them long queues. The Australian art collection is on display at the Ian Potter Centre: NGV Australia (p45) at nearby Federation Sq.

Completed in 1967, the original NGV building itself – Roy Grounds' 'cranky icon' – is now considered one of Australia's most respected Modernist masterpieces, though it was somewhat controversial at the time.

Eureka Skydeck   LOOKOUT

(Map p50; www.eurekaskydeck.com.au; 7 Riverside Quay; adult/child/family $18.50/10/42, The Edge extra $12/8/29; ⊙10am-10pm, last entry 9.30pm; 🚌Tourist Shuttle) Melbourne's tallest building, the 297m-high Eureka Tower was built in 2006, and a wild elevator ride takes you to its 88th floor in less than 40 seconds (check out the photo on the elevator floor if there's time). The 'Edge' – a slightly sadistic glass cube – cantilevers you out of the building; you've got no choice but to look down.

Australian Centre for Contemporary Art   GALLERY

(ACCA; ☑03-9697 9999; www.accaonline.org.au; 111 Sturt St; ⊙10am-5pm Tue & Thu-Sun, 10am-8pm Wed; 🚌1) **FREE** ACCA is one of Australia's most exciting and challenging contemporary galleries, showcasing a range of local and international artists. The building is, fittingly, sculptural, with a rusted exterior evoking the factories that once stood on the site, and a soaring interior designed to house often massive installations. From Flinders St Station, walk across Princes Bridge and along St Kilda Rd. Turn right at Grant St, then left to Sturt.

Polly Woodside   MUSEUM

(☑03-9699 9760; www.pollywoodside.com.au; 2A Clarendon St; adult/child/family $16/10/43; ⊙10am-4pm Sat & Sun, daily during school holidays; 🚌96, 109, 112) The *Polly Woodside* is a restored iron-hulled merchant ship (or 'tall ship'), dating from 1885, that now rests in a pen off the Yarra River. A glimpse of the rigging makes for a tiny reminder of what the Yarra would have looked like in the 19th century, dense with ships at anchor.

Melbourne Recital Centre   ARTS CENTRE

(☑03-9699 3333; www.melbournerecital.com.au; cnr Southbank Blvd & Sturt St; ⊙box office 9am-5pm Mon-Fri; 🚌Tourist Shuttle, 🚋1) This award-winning (for its acoustics) building may look like a framed piece of giant honeycomb, but it's actually the home (or hive?) of the Melbourne Chamber Orchestra and lots of small ensembles. The program ranges from contemporary performances to classical chamber music and *Babar the Elephant*. From Flinders St Station, cross the Yarra and turn right at Southbank Blvd.

Arts Centre Melbourne   ARTS CENTRE

(☑bookings 1300 182 183; www.artscentremelbourne.com.au; 100 St Kilda Rd; ⊙box office 9am-8.30pm Mon-Fri, 10am-5pm Sat; 🚌Tourist Shuttle, 🚋1, 3, 5, 6, 8, 16, 64, 67, 72, 🚉Flinders St) The Arts Centre is made up of two separate buildings: Hamer Hall (the concert hall) and the theatres building (under the spire). Both are linked by a series of landscaped walkways. The George Adams Gallery and St Kilda Road Foyer Gallery are free gallery spaces with changing exhibitions. In the foyer of the theatres building, pick up a self-guided booklet for a tour of art commissioned for the building and including works by Arthur Boyd, Sidney Nolan and Jeffrey Smart.

The Arts Centre hosts a craft market every Sunday from 10am to 4pm. Around 80 artisans sell everything from juggling balls to photographs. Across the way in the Kings Domain is the Sidney Myer Music Bowl, a summer venue with a stage that's been graced by everyone from Dame Kiri Te Kanawa to summer dance parties.

BUNJIL

As you drive on one of the many roads surrounding Docklands, or catch a train to or from Southern Cross Station, you can't miss *Eagle*. Let's just say this bird has presence. Local sculptor Bruce Armstrong was inspired by the figure of Bunjil, the Wurundjeri creator spirit. The cast-aluminium bird rests contentedly on a mammoth jarrah perch, confidently surveying all around with a serene, glassy gaze. (Upon its unveiling, one cheeky journalist called the sculpture 'a bulked-up budgerigar'.) He's a reminder of the wordless natural world, scaled to provide a gentle parody of the surrounding cityscape's attempted domination.

LOCAL LIFE: FOOTSCRAY & THE WEST

The city's remaining working docklands divide the city from the western suburbs – which have long been proudly working class, though this has changed in the last 15 years, with many young professional families taking advantage of the area's cute cottages, close-to-city-centre location and community feel.

The area's 'capital' is the fabulously unfussy Footscray. Almost half of Footscray's population are born overseas, the majority in Vietnam, Africa, China, Italy and Greece. The **Footscray Market** (cnr Hopkins & Leeds St; ☉ 7am-4pm Tue, Wed & Sat, to 6pm Thu, to 8pm Fri; ☒ Footscray) is testament to the area's diversity, and definitely worth a visit.

The areas around Barkly St and Irving St bring those in search of Vietnamese, Ethiopian and Indian cooking and produce. Try down-to-earth **Hung Vuong** (☑ 03-9689 6002; 128 Hopkins St, Footscray; mains $9; ☉ 9am-8.30pm; ☒ 402, ☒ Footscray) for tasty Vietnamese vermicelli topped with crunchy spring rolls, **Nhu Lan** (116 Hopkins St, Footscray; rolls $4; ☉ 6am-6pm; ☒ Footscray) for fresh and tasty *bánh mì* (Vietnamese baguettes), the Ethiopian **Cafe Lalibela** (www.cafelalibela.com.au; 91 Irving St, Footscray; ☉ 11am-9pm Mon-Thu, to 10pm Fri, noon-9pm Sat & Sun; ☒ Footscray) for flavoursome dishes accompanied by injera bread, and the old-school **T Cavallaro & Sons** (www.tcavallaroandsons.com.au; 98 Hopkins St, Footscray; ☒ Footscray), an Italian cafe that's been serving strong espresso with life-changing ricotta-cream cannoli since 1956. Further afield, **Salaam Namaste Dosa Hut** (☑ 03-9687 0171; 604b Barkly St, West Footscray; ☉ 10.30am-10.30pm) serves authentic South Indian street food.

Heading south from Footscray are the fashionable residential neighbourhoods of Seddon and Yarraville. The latter centres on its train station, with a beautifully well-preserved heritage shopping area around Anderson St; it also boasts some good restaurants, bars and cafes.

For those interested in the west's unique history, head to the **Living Museum** (☑ 0419 154 265, 03-9318 3544; www.livingmuseum.org.au; Van Ness Ave, Maribyrnong; by donation; ☉ 11am-3pm Fri & Sun; ☒ 57), set in the grounds of Pipemakers Park, featuring a wetlands area and indigenous gardens. Venture further west still and you'll hit the charming maritime neighbourhood of Williamstown (p59).

Melbourne Star   FERRIS WHEEL
(☑ 03-8688 9688; www.melbournestar.com; 101 Waterfront Way, Docklands; adult/child/family $32/19/82; ☉ 10am-10pm; ☒ City Circle, 70, 86, ☒ Southern Cross) Originally erected in 2009, then disassembled due to structural problems before financial issues delayed it for several more years, the Melbourne Star ferris wheel is finally turning. Joining the London Eye and Singapore Flyer, this giant observation wheel has glass cabins that take you up 120m for 360-degree views of the city, Port Philip Bay and even further afield to Geelong and the Dandenongs. Rides last 30 minutes.

For an extra $8 you can head back for another ride at night to see the bright lights of the city.

East Melbourne & Richmond

East Melbourne's sedate, wide streets are lined with grand double-fronted Victorian terraces, Italianate mansions and art deco apartment blocks. Locals here commute to the city on foot, across the Fitzroy Gardens. During the footy season or when a cricket match is played, the roar of the crowd shatters the calm: you're in lobbing distance of the MCG.

Across perpetually clogged Punt Rd/Hoddle St is the suburb of Richmond, which stretches all the way to the Yarra. Once a ragtag collection of workers' cottages inhabited by generations of labourers who toiled in the tanneries, clothing-manufacturing and food-processing industries, it's now a rather genteel suburb, although it retains a fair swag of solid, regular pubs and is home to a thriving Vietnamese community along Victoria St. Running parallel with Victoria St are clothing-outlet-lined Bridge Rd and Swan St, a jumble of restaurants, shops and smart drinking holes. Richmond's main north–south thoroughfare is Church St.

★ **Melbourne Cricket Ground**   STADIUM
(MCG; Map p60; ☑ 03-9657 8888; www.mcg.org.au; Brunton Ave; tour adult/child/family $20/10/50; ☉ tours 10am-3pm; ☒ Tourist Shuttle, ☒ 48, 70,

East Melbourne & Richmond

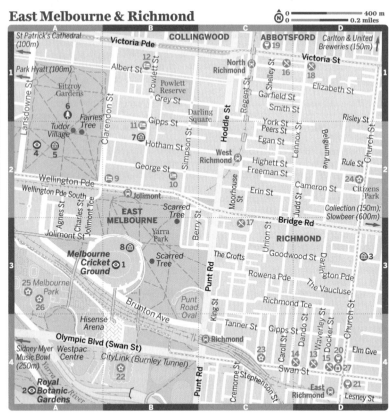

75, Jolimont) With a capacity of 100,000 people, the 'G' is one of the world's great sporting venues, hosting cricket in the summer and AFL footy in the winter – for many Australians it's considered hallowed ground. Make it to a game if you can (highly recommended), but otherwise you can still make your pilgrimage on non-match-day **tours** that take you through the stands, media and coaches' areas, change rooms and out onto the ground (though unfortunately not beyond the boundary).

In 1858 the first game of Aussie Rules football was played where the MCG and its car parks now stand, and in 1877 it was the venue for the first Test cricket match between Australia and England. The MCG was the central stadium for the 1956 Melbourne Olympics and the 2006 Commonwealth Games. It was also used as army barracks during WWII.

The MCG houses the state-of-the-art National Sports Museum.

National Sports Museum MUSEUM
(Map p60; ☎03-9657 8856; www.nsm.org.au; MCG, Olympic Stand, Gate 3; adult/concession/family $20/10/50, with MCG tour $30/15/60; ⊙10am-5pm) Hidden away in the bowels of the Melbourne Cricket Ground, this museum features five permanent exhibitions focusing on Australia's favourite sports and celebrates historic sporting moments. Kids will love the interactive section where they can test their footy, cricket or netball skills, among other activities.

There are some choice objects on display: the handwritten notes used to define the rules of Australian Rules football in 1859; a who's who of Aussie baggy green caps (including Don Bradman's) among great cricketing memorabilia; Brownlow medals; olive branches awarded to Edwin Flack, Australia's first Olympian in 1886; and Cathy Freedman's famous Sydney Olympics swift suit. The museum also incorporates the Champions horse-racing gallery.

East Melbourne & Richmond

◎ Top Sights
1 Melbourne Cricket Ground................... B3
2 Royal Botanic Gardens A4

◎ Sights
3 Charles Nodrum Gallery D3
4 Conservatory... A2
5 Cooks' Cottage A2
6 Fitzroy Gardens A1
7 Johnston Collection............................... B2
8 National Sports Museum...................... B3

⬛ Sleeping
9 Hilton on the Park B2
10 Knightsbridge Apartments................... B2
11 Magnolia Court.. B2
12 Tribeca Serviced Apartments............... B1

✖ Eating
13 Demitri's Feast....................................... D4

14 Meatball & Wine Bar D4
15 Meatmother D4
16 Minh Minh.. C1
17 Richmond Hill Cafe & Larder C3
18 Thy Thy 1... D1

◎ Drinking & Nightlife
19 Aviary C1
20 Bar Economico D4
21 Public House D4

◎ Entertainment
22 AAMI Park.. B4
23 Corner Hotel C4
24 DT's Hotel D2
25 Melbourne Park A3
26 Rod Laver Arena...................................... A3

◎ Shopping
27 Lily & The Weasel D4

Fitzroy Gardens PARK

(Map p60; www.fitzroygardens.com; Wellington Pde, btwn Lansdowne & Albert Sts; ⬛Tourist Shuttle, ⬛75, ⬛Jolimont) The city drops away suddenly just east of Spring St, giving way to Melbourne's beautiful backyard, the Fitzroy Gardens. The stately avenues lined with English elms, flowerbeds, expansive lawns, strange fountains and a creek are a short stroll from town.

The highlight is Cooks' Cottage (Map p60; ☑03-9419 5766; www.cookscottage.com.au; adult/child/family $5/2.50/13.50; ⊙9am-5pm), shipped brick by brick from Yorkshire and reconstructed in 1934 (the cottage actually belonged to the navigator's parents). It's decorated in mid-18th-century style, with an exhibition about Captain James Cook's eventful, if controversial, voyages to the Southern Ocean.

Nearby is writer Ola Cohn's kooky carved Fairies Tree, a 300-year-old stump embellished in 1932 with fairies, pixies, kangaroos, emus and possums. Between Cooks' Cottage and the Fairies Tree is the Scarred Tree: now a large stump, it was once stripped of a piece of its bark to make a canoe by Aboriginal people. In the centre of the gardens is a 'model' Tudor village. This well-meaning gift was a way of saying thanks for sending food to Britain during WWII.

The delightful 1930s Conservatory (Map p60; ⊙9am-5pm) is built in a Spanish-mission architectural style and features a range of different floral displays each year.

A new visitor centre and cafe was being constructed here at the time of research.

Johnston Collection MUSEUM

(Map p60; ☑03-9416 2515; www.johnstoncollection.org; East Melbourne; adult/concession $25/23; ⬛48, 75) Not only will you see the exquisite collection of sharp-eyed antique dealer William Johnston in his majestic East Melbourne mansion, but you'll hear his intriguing backstory. It's popular with repeat visitors as the furniture and items are changed every three months – different curators, usually an artist or designer, thematically rearrange the house from Johnston's collection. Tours depart from Hilton on the Park, leaving three times daily. Booking is required.

Charles Nodrum Gallery GALLERY

(Map p60; ☑03-9427 0140; www.charlesnodrumgallery.com.au; 267 Church St, Richmond; ⊙11am-6pm Tue-Sat; ⬛48, 75. 78) Quality gallery established in 1984, which specialises in Australian abstract and alternative art movements from the 1950s through the 1970s.

◉ Fitzroy & Around

Fitzroy, Melbourne's first suburb, long had a reputation for vice and squalor. Today, despite a long bout of gentrification, it's still where creative people meet up, though now it's more to 'do' lunch and blog about it before checking out the offerings at local 'one-off' boutiques and vintage shops. It's also home to a bunch of art galleries.

MELBOURNE SIGHTS

HEIDE MUSEUM OF MODERN ART

The former home of arts patrons John and Sunday Reed, **Heide** (☑ 03-9850 1500; www.heide.com.au; 7 Templestowe Rd, Bulleen; museum adult/child $16/free, grounds only free; ⊙ 10am-5pm Tue-Sun; ☐ 903, ⧉ Heidelberg) is a large public art gallery with wonderful grounds for exploring. It holds regularly changing exhibitions, many of which include works by the artists that called Heide home, including Sidney Nolan and Albert Tucker. See the Arts chapter (p326) for more information on the Heide artists.

Shannon Bennett's Cafe Vue does the cooking honours (Tuesday to Sunday), and you can eat in, or grab a lunch box or picnic hamper to have by the Yarra. The free tours (2pm) are a great introduction to Melbourne's early painting scene. The museum is signposted off the Eastern Fwy.

Gertrude St, where once grannies feared to tread, is Melbourne's street of the moment. Smith St in Collingwood has some rough edges, though talk is more of its smart restaurants, cafes and boutiques rather than its down-and-out days of old. As the traditional land of the Wurundjeri people, it's still a social spot for Aboriginal people. The streets behind Smith are home to what were once the southern hemisphere's largest industrial complexes. These former 'satanic mills' are now packed with million-dollar apartments. Beyond Collingwood is similarly industrial Abbotsford, bordered by a scenic stretch of the Yarra River.

Beyond Merri Creek is Northcote, one of Melbourne's fastest gentrifying suburbs, a sprawling neighbourhood of wooden Federation cottages and big backyards. Its sleepy demeanour shifts once the sun goes down and fun-seekers hit High St.

Abbotsford Convent HISTORIC SITE

(☑ 03-9415 3600; www.abbotsfordconvent.com.au; 1 St Heliers St, Abbotsford; tours $15; ⊙ 7.30am-10pm; ☐ 200, 201, 207, ⧉ Victoria Park) **FREE** The nuns are long gone at this former convent, which dates back to 1861, so don't worry, no one will ask if you've been to Mass lately. Today its rambling collection of ecclesiastic architecture is home to a thriving arts community of galleries, studios, cafes and bars, spread over nearly 7 hectares of riverside land. Tours of the complex are run at 2pm every Sunday.

There's a Slow Food Market every fourth Saturday, a clothes market (p122) every third Sunday, and during summer there's the popular Supper Market on Friday nights, featuring food stalls and live music. The offbeat Kage Physical Theatre (p118) offers modern dance performances, and the Shadow Electric open-air cinema and bar runs from

November to March. Check website the for details.

The **Convent Bakery** (www.conventbakery.com; ⊙ 7am-5pm) bakes its own pies and breads in the original 1901 wood-fired mansory ovens, while not-for-profit Lentil As Anything (p99) does delicious vegetarian dishes.

Collingwood Children's Farm FARM

(www.farm.org.au; 18 St Heliers St, Abbotsford; adult/child/family $8/4/16; ⊙ 9am-4.30pm; ☐ 200, 201, 207, ⧉ Victoria Park) The inner city melts away at this rustic riverside retreat that's beloved not just by children. There's a range of frolicking farm animals that kids can help feed, as well as rambling gardens and grounds for picnicking on warm days. The farm cafe is open early and can be visited without entering the farm itself. The monthly **farmers market** (www.mfm.com.au; 18 St Heliers St, Abbotsford; adult/child $2/free; ⊙ 8am-1pm, 2nd Sat of the month), held right by the river, is a local highlight, with everything from rabbits to roses to organic milk hoisted into baskets.

Yarra Bend Park PARK

(www.parkweb.vic.gov.au; Kew; ☐ 200, 201, 207, ⧉ Victoria Park) Escape the city without leaving town. About 5km northeast of the city centre, the Yarra River flows through bushland, an area cherished by runners, rowers, cyclists, picnickers and strollers. It's also home to two golf courses. At the end of Boathouse Rd is the **Studley Park Boathouse** (☑ 03-9853 1972; www.studleyparkboathouse.com.au), which has a kiosk and restaurant, barbecue facilities and canoes for hire.

Kane's suspension footbridge takes you across the river, from where it's about a 20-minute walk to Dights Falls, at the meeting of the Yarra River and Merri Creek. You can also walk to the falls along the southern riverbank.

Carlton & United Breweries BREWERY
(☑03-9420 6800; www.carltonbrewhouse.com.au; cnr Nelson & Thompson Sts, Abbotsford; tours adult/concession $25/20; ☑109) Foster's beer-brewing empire runs 1½-hour tours of its Abbotsford operations, where you'll encounter enormous 30m-wide vats of beer and a superfast bottling operation – and yes: samples are included in the price. Tours run from Monday to Saturday; times vary so check the website. Visitors need to be aged over 18 and wear closed-toe shoes. Bookings essential.

**Centre for
Contemporary Photography** GALLERY
(CCP; Map p64; ☑03-9417 1549; www.ccp.org.au; 404 George St, Fitzroy; ☑11am-6pm Wed-Fri, noon-5pm Sat & Sun; ☑86) FREE This not-for-profit centre has a changing schedule of photography exhibitions across a couple of galleries. Shows traverse traditional technique and the highly conceptual. There's a particular fascination with work involving video projection, including a nightly after-hours screening in a window. Also offers photography courses.

**Gertrude
Contemporary Art Space** GALLERY
(Map p64; ☑03-9419 3406; www.gertrude.org.au; 200 Gertrude St, Fitzroy; ☑11am-5.30pm Tue-Fri, 11am-4.30pm Sat; ☑86) FREE This nonprofit gallery and studio complex has been going strong for nearly 30 years; many of its alumni are now certified famous artists. The monthly openings are refreshingly come-as-you-are, with crowds often spilling onto the street, two-dollar wine in hand.

Alcaston Gallery GALLERY
(Map p64; ☑03-9418 6444; www.alcastongallery.com.au; 11 Brunswick St, Fitzroy; ☑10am-6pm Tue-Fri, 11am-5pm Sat; ☑112) FREE Set in an imposing terrace, the Alcaston's focus is on living Indigenous Australian artists. The gallery works directly with Indigenous communities and is particularly attentive to cultural sensitivities; it shows a wide range of styles from traditional to contemporary work. There's also a space dedicated to works on paper.

Collingwood Arts Precinct GALLERY
(www.collingwoodartsprecinct.com.au; ☑86) The gritty backstreets of Collingwood have long produced quality galleries, and they've now joined forces to consolidate as a precinct. It includes contemporary works

at the spacious James Makin Gallery (Map p64; www.jamesmakingallery.com; 67 Cambridge St, Collingwood; ☑11am-5pm Tue-Sun) and the intimate Kick Gallery (Map p64; www.kick-gallery.com; 4 Peel St, Collingwood), wonderful and affordable Indigenous art at Mossenson (Map p64; www.mossensongalleries.com.au; 41 Derby St, Collingwood; ☑10am-5pm Tues-Fri, 11am-5pm Sat), and a huge, varied collection at Australian Galleries (Map p64; www.australiangalleries.com.au; 28 Derby St, Collingwood; ☑10am-6pm). Most are closed Mondays and during January; visit the website for details.

On Johnston St (next door to the Tote pub) is a mural painted by the late Keith Haring, the famous New York street artist, who visited in 1984.

Gallery Gabrielle Pizzi GALLERY
(Map p64; ☑03-9416 4170; www.gabriellepizzi.com.au; 51 Victoria St, Fitzroy; ☑10am-5pm Wed-Fri, noon-6pm Sat; ☑11, 96, 112) FREE Gabrielle Pizzi, one of Australia's most respected dealers of Indigenous art, founded this gallery in the 1980s; her daughter Samantha continues to show contemporary city-based artists, as well as traditional artists from the communities of Balgo Hills, Papunya, Maningrida and the Tiwi Islands.

Sutton Gallery GALLERY
(Map p64; ☑03-9416 0727; www.suttongallery.com.au; 254 Brunswick St, Fitzroy; ☑11am-5pm Tue-Sat; ☑112) FREE Housed in a simple, unassuming warehouse space entered off Greeves St, this gallery is known for championing challenging new work.

Carlton & Around

Carlton is the traditional home of Melbourne's Italian community, so you'll see the *tricolori* unfurled with characteristic passion come soccer finals and the Grand Prix. The heady mix of intellectual activity, espresso and phenomenal food lured bohemians to the area in the 1950s; by the 1970s it was the centre of the city's bourgeoning counterculture scene and has produced some of the city's most legendary theatre, music and literature.

Lygon St reaches out through leafy North Carlton to booming Brunswick. The sprawling University of Melbourne, and its large residential colleges, takes up Carlton's western edge. Here you'll find a vibrant mix of students, long-established families,

Fitzroy & Around

N

0 — 200 m
0 — 0.12 miles

Princes St

FITZROY NORTH

Aux Batifolles
(175m)

North Fitzroy Bowls (500m);
Moroccan Soup Bar (650m);
Eureka Coffee (1.5km)

Northcote (2km)

**CLIFTON
HILL**

Alexandra Pde (Eastern Hwy)

10

Cecil St

Cecil St

Westgarth St

77

23

Westgarth St

Leicester St

68

46

George St

Gore St

CARLTON

Station St

Kay St

Rose St

70

35

Young St

Napier St

Rose St

71

40

Kerr St

49

17

26

Smith St

Keele St

69

Kerr St

3

Easey St

Spring St

Argyle St

36

15 57

28

31

50

Argyle St

33

Sackville St

Johnston St

51

ElginSt

4

42

20

60

Johnston St

Tote (150m);
Abbotsford Convent (1.5km);
Collingwood Children's Farm (2km)

24

Victoria St

Chapel St

32

Mahoney St

18

9

FITZROY

73

Bedford St

Bell St

Greeves St

64

63

58

St David St

27

Otter St

John St

Fitzroy St

47

62

41

Kent St

Brunswick St

Napier St

43

George St

Gore St

Smith St

Moor St

54

Moor St

44

Hodgson
St 22

Stanley St

29

45

Nicholson St

13

King William St

Condell St

COLLINGWOOD

Hanover St

Atherton
Reserve

Charles St

34

Little Oxford St

Oxford St

Webb St

Palmer St

Royal La

14

21

65

52

Little George St

Little Gore St

Little Smith St

39 7

Peel Hotel
(50m)

25

Peel St

75

55

72

Gertrude St

66 76

37 16

30 74 56

59

6

Cambridge St

61

19

38

5

67

53

Langridge St

2

1

Fitzroy St

Brunswick St

Young St

Napier St

George St

11

48

8

Little Victoria St

Smith St

Mason St

12

Victoria Pde

MELBOURNE

Fitzroy & Around

◉ Sights
1 Alcaston Gallery B7
2 Australian Galleries Stock Rooms D7
3 Centre for Contemporary
   Photography C3
4 Gallery Gabrielle Pizzi A3
5 Gertrude Contemporary Art Space C6
6 James Makin Gallery D6
7 Kick Gallery D6
8 Mossenson Galleries D7
9 Sutton Gallery B4

◉ Activities, Courses & Tours
10 Fitzroy Swimming Pool C1

◉ Sleeping
11 Brooklyn Arts Hotel C7
12 Home@The Mansion A7
13 Nunnery A5
14 Quest Royal Gardens A6
15 Tyrian Serviced Apartments B3

◉ Eating
16 Añada C6
17 Babka Bakery Cafe B2
18 Brunswick Street Alimentari B4
19 Charcoal Lane B6
20 Commoner B3
21 Cutler & Co A6
22 Gelato Messina D4
23 Hammer & Tong 412 .... B1
24 Horn D3
25 Huxtaburger D6
26 Ici C2
27 Jimmy Grants D4
28 Marios B3
29 Masak Masak D5
30 Moon Under Water C6
31 Pireaus Blues B3
32 Po' Boy Quarter D3
33 Robert Burns Hotel D3
34 Rosamond D5
35 Vegie Bar B2

◉ Drinking & Nightlife
36 Bar Open B3

37 De Clieu C6
38 Everleigh B6
39 Grace Darling D6
40 Industry Beans B2
41 Little Creatures Dining Hall B4
42 Naked for Satan B3
43 Napier Hotel C4
44 Panama Dining Room D5
45 Proud Mary D5
46 Rose C2
47 Standard A4
48 Storm in a Teacup D7

◉ Entertainment
49 Evelyn Hotel B2
50 Night Cat B3
51 Old Bar B3
52 Workers Club B6

◉ Shopping
53 Aesop D6
54 Alphaville B5
55 Angelucci 20th Century D6
56 Books for Cooks C6
57 Brunswick Street Bookstore B3
58 Búl B4
59 Crumpler D6
60 Das T-Shirt Automat C3
61 Ess B6
62 Fat B4
63 Gorman B4
64 Hudson D4
65 Little Salon A6
66 Mud Australia C6
67 Obüs C6
68 Poison City Records B2
69 Polyester Books B2
70 Polyester Records B2
71 Rose Street Artists' Market B2
72 Signet Bureau C6
73 Smith Street Bazaar D4
74 SpaceCraft C6
75 Third Drawer Down C6
76 Title C6
77 Tomorrow Never Knows B1

MELBOURNE SIGHTS

renovators and newly arrived migrants. The central Brunswick artery, Sydney Rd, is perpetually clogged with traffic and is packed with Middle Eastern restaurants and grocers. Lygon St in East Brunswick just keeps getting more fashionable: it has a cluster of restaurants, homeware stores and bars.

★ **Melbourne Museum**   MUSEUM
(Map p66; ☑13 11 02; www.museumvictoria.com.au; 11 Nicholson St, Carlton; adult/child & student $10/free, exhibitions extra; ☉10am-5pm; ☐Tourist Shuttle, ☐City Circle, 86, 96, ☐Parliament) This museum provides a grand sweep of Victoria's natural and cultural histories, with exhibitions covering everything from dinosaur fossils and giant squid specimens to the taxidermy hall, a 3D volcano and an open-air forest atrium of Victorian flora. Become immersed in the legend of champion racehorse and national hero Phar Lap in the Marvellous Melbourne exhibition. The

excellent **Bunjilaka**, on the ground floor, presents Indigenous Australian stories and history told through objects and Aboriginal voices with state-of-the-art technology. There's also an **IMAX cinema** on-site.

★ Royal Exhibition Building

HISTORIC BUILDING

(Map p66; ☑ 13 11 02; www.museumvictoria.com. au/reb; 9 Nicholson St, Carlton; tours adult/child $5/3.50; ☒ Tourist Shuttle, ☒ City Circle, 86, 96, ☒ Parliament) Built for the International Exhibition in 1880, and winning Unesco World Heritage status in 2004, this beautiful Victorian edifice symbolises the glory days of the Industrial Revolution, the British Empire and 19th-century Melbourne's economic supremacy. It was the first building to fly the Australian flag, and Australia's first parliament was held here in 1901; it now hosts everything from trade fairs to car shows, as well as the biennial Melbourne Art Fair.

Tours of the building leave from the Melbourne Museum at 2pm.

Ian Potter Museum of Art

GALLERY

(Map p66; www.art-museum.unimelb.edu.au; 800 Swanston St, Carlton; ☒ 10am-5pm Tue-Fri, noon-5pm Sat & Sun; ☒ 6, 8, 72) **FREE** Part of **Melbourne University**, the Ian Potter Museum of Art manages the university's extensive art collection, which ranges from antiquities to contemporary Australian work. It's a thoughtfully designed space and always has an exciting exhibition program. Pick up the *Sculpture on Campus* map here for a walking tour around Melbourne Uni's sculptures, set amid heritage-listed buildings.

Grainger Museum

MUSEUM

(Map p66; ☑ 03-8344 5270; www.grainger.unimelb. edu.au; Royal Pde, Gate 13, Melbourne Uni, Parkville; ☒ 1-4.30pm Tue-Fri & Sun, closed Jan; ☒ 19) **FREE** Percy Grainger's fascinating life is laid bare within this art deco building, in a tribute to one of Australia's great musical exports.

Carlton & Around

Leaving Australia as a nine-year-old, he became an internationally renowned composer and pianist in Europe and the USA, as well as a forerunner in experimental music. Exhibits from all points of his extraordinary life are on display, from his sound machines to a collection of fetish whips.

Royal Melbourne Zoo ZOO
(☑ 03-9285 9300; www.zoo.org.au; Elliott Ave, Parkville; adult/child $30/13.20, children free on weekends & holidays; ⊙ 9am-5pm; ☐ 505, ☐ 55, ☐ Royal Park) Established in 1861, this is the oldest zoo in Australia and the third oldest in the world. Today it's one of the city's most popular attractions. Set in spacious, prettily landscaped gardens, the zoo's enclosures aim to simulate the animals' natural habitats. Walkways pass through the enclosures: you can stroll through the bird aviary or enter a tropical hothouse full of colourful butterflies.

There's also a large collection of native animals in natural bush settings, a platypus aquarium, fur seals, lions and tigers, plenty of reptiles, and an 'Am I in Asia?' elephant enclosure.

In summer, the zoo hosts Twilight Concerts, while Roar 'n' Snore (adult/child $195/145; ⊙ Sep-May) allows you to camp at the zoo and join the keepers on their morning feeding rounds.

Melbourne General Cemetery CEMETERY
(☑ 03-9349 3014; www.mgc.smct.org.au; College Cres, Parkville; ⊙ 9am-5pm; ☐ 1, 8) Melbourne has been burying its dead in this cemetery since 1852. It's worth a stroll to see the final resting place of three Australian prime ministers, the ill-fated explorers Burke and Wills, Walter Lindrum's billiard-table tombstone and a shrine to Elvis erected by fans. Check the website for information about night tours here.

Museo Italiano MUSEUM
(Map p66; ☑ 03-9349 9000; www.museoitaliano. com.au; 199 Faraday St, Carlton; ⊙ 10am-5pm Tue-Fri, noon-5pm Sat) FREE Telling the story of Melbourne's Italian community, this museum offers a good starting point to put the history of Lygon St into both historical and contemporary context.

Ceres ENVIRONMENT PARK
(☑ 03-9389 0100; www.ceres.org.au; 8 Lee St, East Brunswick; ⊙ 9am-5pm, market 9am-2pm Wed & Sat, Thu & Fri to 5pm; ☐ 96) 🚲 FREE Ceres, the name of the Roman goddess of agriculture and fertility, also stands for Centre for Education & Research in Environmental Strategies, a two-decades-old community environment built on a former rubbish tip. Stroll around the permaculture and bushfood nursery before refuelling with an Australian-bush chai tea and cake at the pretty cafe.

There's also a community market where you can buy organic and backyard-produced goodies; the info centre here has a great bookstore on sustainability-related matter.

Carlton & Around

◎ **Top Sights**
1 Melbourne Museum D3
2 Queen Victoria Market.......................A4
3 Royal Exhibition Building D3

◎ **Sights**
4 Grainger Museum.................................A1
5 Ian Potter Museum of Art B1
6 Museo Italiano.....................................C2

🛏 **Sleeping**
7 169 Drummond C3
 Bozo Backpacker 3....................(see 24)
8 Downtowner on Lygon C4

🍴 **Eating**
9 Abla's D1
10 Café Cavallino C3
 DOC Delicatessen......................(see 11)
11 DOC Espresso......................................C2
12 DOC Pizzeria..C2
13 Epocha C4
 Miss Katie's Crab Shack ....(see 24)
14 Tiamo C2

🍷 **Drinking & Nightlife**
15 Assembly C3
16 Campos Coffee C1
17 Jimmy Watson's....................................C1
18 Seven Seeds..A3
19 Stovetop...A4

🎭 **Entertainment**
20 Cinema Nova.......................................C2
21 Imax D3
22 John Curtin Hotel...............................B4
23 La Mama C2
24 Public Bar..A4

🛍 **Shopping**
25 Eastern Market....................................C2
26 Gewürzhaus...C2
27 La Parisienne.......................................C2
28 Readings C1

South Yarra, Prahran & Windsor

N

| 0 | 400 m |
| 0 | 0.25 miles |

CREMORNE

RICHMOND

Royal Botanic
Gardens (400m);
Government
House (1km)

Yarra River

Herring
Island Park

2

Monash Fwy

12

Alexandra Ave

Punt Rd

Caroline St

Domain Rd

Como
Park

Albany (700m);
Hatton (800m);
Art Series
(The Blackman)
(1.3km)

Malcolm St

1

Lechlade Ave

Washington
St

Bruce St

South
Yarra

14   4   11
10

8

Toorak Rd

22

17

Oxford St

36

Palermo St

**SOUTH
YARRA**

TOORAK

Alexandra St

Lang St

Fawkner St

Arthur St

Fitzgerald St

Garden St

Cassell St

Albion St

Argo St

Cliff St

Grosvenor St

Hawksburn

Barry St

Chapel St

Commercial Rd

24

5   26

3

Princes
Gardens

Malvern Rd

Motherwell St

Joy St

Howitt St

McKillop St

May Rd

7

Moss St

Greville St

34

6

Clarke St

37

18   38

Lorne Rd

35

Prahran

King St

PRAHRAN

Mackay St

Murray St

Spring St
Wrights Tce

28   13

33

27   16

Victoria
Gardens

Pridham St
Bayview St
Aberdeen Rd

Andrew St

Raleigh St

20

23

High St

Green St   9

Eastbourne St

Earl St

30

21   Duke St

WINDSOR

19

Henry St

Union St

Windsor

29

Peel St

Albert St

25

15

Dandenong Rd

31

32

Wellington St

ST KILDA

South Yarra, Prahran & Windsor

◎ Sights
1 Como House...D2
2 Herring Island Park.............................D1
3 Prahran Market.....................................B4

◎ Activities, Courses & Tours
4 Aesop Spa...A3
5 Essential Ingredient...........................B4
6 Prahran Aquatic Centre B5

◎ Sleeping
7 Art Series (The Cullen) B5
8 Art Series (The Olsen) B2
9 Back Of Chapel B6
10 Hotel Claremont...................................B3
11 Punthill South Yarra Grand B3

◎ Eating
12 Baby..B1
13 Colonel Tans...B6
14 Da Noi..A3
15 Dino's B7
   HuTong Dumpling Bar ....(see 7)
16 Huxtaburger..B6
17 Misschu...B3
18 Valentino...D5

19 WoodLand House.................................D6

◎ Drinking & Nightlife
20 Borsch, Vodka & Tears.........................B6
21 Chapel St Cellars.................................B6
22 Drugstore Espresso B3
23 Dukes...B6
24 Kama Bar...A4
25 Kid Boston...B7
26 Market Lane..B4
27 Onesixone..B6
28 Revolver Upstairs B5
29 Windsor Castle Hotel...........................A7
30 Yellow Bird..B6

◎ Entertainment
31 Astor...B7
32 Red Stitch Actors Theatre B7

◎ Shopping
33 Chapel Street Bazaar B6
34 Fat...B5
35 Greville Records B5
36 Scanlan Theodore B3
37 Shelley Panton......................................C5
38 SpaceCraft D5

◎ South Yarra, Prahran & Windsor

These neighbourhoods have always been synonymous with glitz and glamour, with their elevated aspect and large allotments considered prestigious. Access from the city centre to South Yarra was by boat or punt – hence Punt Rd – before Princes Bridge was built in 1850.

South Yarra's Chapel St strip still parades itself as a must-do fashion destination, but has seen better days: it's been taken over by chain stores, tacky bars and, come sunset, doof-doof cars. But Prahran is still a gutsy and good place, with designer stores, bars and some refreshingly eclectic businesses. Chapel St continues down to Windsor, a hive of fun cafes, bars and secondhand vintage shops.

★ **Royal Botanic Gardens** GARDENS
(Map p60; www.rbg.vic.gov.au; Birdwood Ave, South Yarra; ◎ 7.30am-sunset daily year-round; ◻ Tourist Shuttle, ◻1, 3, 5, 6, 8, 16, 64, 67, 72) **FREE** One of the finest botanic gardens in the world, the Royal Botanic Gardens are one of Melbourne's most glorious attractions. Sprawling beside the Yarra River, the beautifully designed gardens feature a global selection

of plantings and specifically endemic Australian flora. Mini-ecosystems, such as a cacti and succulents area, herb garden and an indigenous rainforest, are set amid vast lawns. Take a book, picnic or Frisbee – but most importantly, take your time.

During the summer months, the gardens play host to the **Moonlight Cinema** (p114) and theatre performances. Other features include the **Observatory** for tours of the night sky, and the excellent, nature-based **Ian Potter Foundation Children's Garden** (10am-4pm Wed-Sun, daily during Victorian school holidays, closed mid-Jul–mid-Sep; ◻8), a whimsical and child-scaled place that invites kids and their parents to explore, discover and imagine.

The **visitor centre** (Observatory Gate, Birdwood Ave; ◎9am-5pm Mon-Fri, 9.30am-5.30pm Sat & Sun) is at the former centre for stargazers. A range of tours departs from here. Choose from a variety of guided walks through assorted horticultural pockets to learn a bit about history, botany and wildlife. Next to the visitor centre, the National Herbarium, established in 1853, contains 1.2 million dried botanical specimens used for identification purposes.

For visitors who can't get enough of gardens, the Royal Botanic Gardens has a

INDIGENOUS MELBOURNE

The following provide a fantastic opportunity to learn and interact with Indigenous Australian culture in Melbourne.

Sights

➡ Bunjilaka Aboriginal Cultural Centre (p65) at the Melbourne Museum

➡ Koorie Heritage Trust (p57)

➡ Aboriginal Heritage Walk (p80)

➡ Birrarung Marr (p48)

➡ Bunjil (p58)

➡ Ian Potter Centre: NGV Australia (p45)

Eating

➡ Charcoal Lane (p96)

Media

➡ Melbourne radio station 3KND (Kool n Deadly), 1503AM

➡ NITV, a nationwide TV station featuring all-Indigenous content

recently developed **Australian Garden** (www.rbg.vic.gov.au; 1000 Ballarto Rd, Cranbourne) in the outlying suburb of Cranbourne. The award-winning visitor centre was designed by local architect Kerstin Thompson.

Shrine of Remembrance MONUMENT
(www.shrine.org.au; Birdwood Ave, South Yarra; ⊙10am-5pm; 🚃 Tourist Shuttle, 🚊 1, 3, 5, 6, 8, 16, 64, 67, 72) **FREE** Beside St Kilda Rd stands the massive Shrine of Remembrance, built as a memorial to Victorians killed in WWI. It was built between 1928 and 1934, much of it with Depression-relief, or 'susso', labour. Its bombastic classical design is partly based on the Mausoleum at Halicarnassus, one of the seven ancient wonders of the world. It's visible from the other end of town; planning regulations continue to restrict any building that would obstruct the view of the Shrine from Swanston St as far back as Lonsdale St.

Thousands attend the moving Anzac Day (25 April) dawn service, while the Remembrance Day service at 11am on 11 November commemorates the signing of the 1918 Armistice marking the formal end to WWI. At this precise moment a shaft of light shines through an opening in the ceiling, passing over the Stone of Remembrance and illumi-

nating the word 'love'; all other days this effect is demonstrated using artificial lighting on the hour. The forecourt, with its cenotaph and eternal flame (lit by Queen Elizabeth II in 1954), was built as a memorial to those who died in WWII, and there are several other specific memorials that surround the Shrine. You'll get wonderful panoramic views from the Shrine's upper balcony.

The complex is under 24-hour police guard; during opening hours the police are quaintly required to wear uniforms resembling those worn by WWI lighthorsemen. Pick up the self-guided tour brochure, or otherwise join the **free guided tours** daily at 11am and 2pm, often conducted by returned soldiers. The Galleries of Remembrance will open in late 2014 for the Centenary of WWI, telling the story of Australians at war.

Government House HISTORIC BUILDING
(🗹 03-9656 9804; www.nationaltrust.org.au; Kings Domain, South Yarra; tour adult/child $18/10; 🚃 Tourist Shuttle, 🚊 1, 3, 5, 6, 8, 16, 64, 67, 72) On the outer edge of the Botanic Gardens, the Italianate-style Government House was built in 1872 and has been the residence of all serving Victorian governors since. A replica of Queen Victoria's palace on England's Isle of Wight, as well as being the royal pied-à-terre, the house and gardens are also used for an array of state functions and celebrations. Book well in advance to take the National Trust's two-hour **tour** on Monday and Thursday.

Also included in the tour is **Governor La Trobe's Cottage**, the original Victorian government house sent out from the mother country in prefabricated form in 1840.

Como House HISTORIC BUILDING
(Map p68; 🗹 03-9827 2500, tour bookings 03-8663 7260; www.comohouse.com.au; cnr Williams Rd & Lechlade Ave, South Yarra; adult/child/family $15/9/35; 🚊 8) This grand colonial residence overlooking the Yarra was begun in 1840, and since faithfully restored by the National Trust. It contains some of the belongings of the Armytage family, the last and longest owners, who lived in the house for 95 years. Opening hours are irregular, usually a few showings per month (call ahead for times and bookings), which will allow you to stroll its extensive, well-tended grounds, which are faithful to 19th-century landscaping principles and include a croquet lawn and magnificent flower walks.

The **Stables of Como** (☑03-9827 6886; www.thestablesofcomo.com.au; ☺9am-5pm Mon-Sat, 10am-5pm Sun) cafe, located in the former horse stables, can pack a picnic hamper for you to enjoy on its stately lawns; it also hosts high tea.

Herring Island Park   PARK
(Map p68; http://home.vicnet.net.au/~herring; Alexander Ave, South Yarra; ☐8, 78, ☐Burnley) Herring Island is a prelapsarian garden that seeks to preserve the original trees and grasses of the Yarra and provide a home for indigenous animals. Within the park is an impressive collection of environmental sculpture, including work by Andy Goldsworthy (UK) and locals Julie Collins, Robert Jacks and Robert Bridgewater. There are designated picnic and barbecue areas. On weekends during summer, a Parks Victoria punt operates from Como Landing on Alexandra Ave in South Yarra; other times you'll need a kayak to get here.

Prahran Market   MARKET
(Map p68; www.prahranmarket.com.au; 163 Commercial Rd, Prahran; ☺7am-5pm Tue, Thu & Sat, to 7pm Fri, 10am-3pm Sun; ☐72, 78, ☐Prahran) The Prahran Market has been an institution for more than a century and is one of the finest produce markets in the city, with numerous stalls stocking fresh seafood, deli items, fruits and vegetables. The market is also home to a culinary store, **Essential Ingredient** (☑03-9827 9047; www.theessentialingredient.com.au); check its website for details of its cooking school, featuring workshops with Melbourne's most lauded chefs.

○ St Kilda & Around

Come to St Kilda for the sea breezes, seedy history and a bit of good ol' people-watching. St Kilda was once a playground full of dance halls, a funpark, an ice-skating rink, theatres, sea baths and gardens. It got divided up (as many good things do) and now its art deco apartments are worth astronomical real-estate prices. There are still mansions dotted around, and its leafy backstreets are worth a wander (just keep in mind that its reputation as a red-light district is not unfounded). There's some great punk history here: the Boys Next Door, fronted by Nick Cave, were based here, and played gloriously chaotic gigs at the George Hotel (then known as the Crystal Ballroom).

On weekends the volume is turned up, the traffic crawls and the street-party atmosphere

sets in. It's still a neighbourhood of extreme, and often exhilarating, contrasts: backpacker hostels sit beside fine-dining restaurants, souvlaki bars next to designer shops.

Many long-time locals have turned to Carlisle St's eastern reach, traditionally a devout Jewish neighbourhood but now known for its wine bars and all-day breakfast cafes.

St Kilda Foreshore   BEACH
(Map p72; Jacka Blvd; ☐16, 96) While there are palm-fringed promenades, a parkland strand and a long stretch of sand, St Kilda's seaside appeal is more Brighton, England, than *Baywatch,* despite 20-odd years of glitzy development. The kiosk at the end of **St Kilda Pier** (an exact replica of the original, which burnt down in 2003, a year short of its centenary) is as much about the journey as the destination.

The breakwater near the pier was built in the '50s as a safe harbour for boats competing in the Olympic Games. It's now home to a colony of little penguins that have, incredibly, chosen the city's most crowded suburb in which to reside. You can also visit and learn about the penguins on an eco-themed stand-up paddleboarding tour (p80).

During summer, the **Port Phillip Eco Centre** (Map p72; ☑03-9534 0670; www.ecocentre.com; 55a Blessington St) ✎ also runs a range of tours, including guided urban wildlife walks and coastal discovery walks, and offers information on the penguin colony. Contact **Earthcare St Kilda** (www.earthcarestkilda.org.au) to get involved in penguin research.

On the foreshore south of the pier, the Moorish-style **St Kilda Sea Baths** (Map p72; ☑03-9525 4888; www.stkildaseabaths.com.au; 10-18 Jacka Blvd) has a heated indoor saltwater pool, but at $13 a dip, it's really only attractive on frosty days.

Jewish Museum of Australia   MUSEUM
(Map p72; ☑03-9834 3600; www.jewishmuseum.com.au; 26 Alma Rd, St Kilda; adult/child/family $10/5/20; ☺10am-4pm Tue-Thu, to 5pm Sun, closed Jewish holy days; ☐3, 67) Interactive displays tell the history of Australia's Jewish community from the earliest days of European settlement, while permanent exhibitions celebrate Judaism's rich cycle of festivals and holy days. The museum also has a good curatorial reputation for its contemporary art exhibitions. By car, follow St Kilda Rd from St Kilda Junction, then turn left at Alma Rd.

St Kilda & Around

MELBOURNE

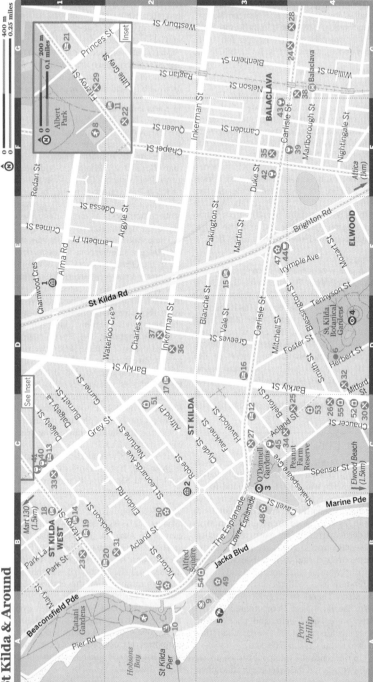

St Kilda & Around

⊙ **Sights**
1 Jewish Museum of Australia E1
2 Linden Arts Centre & Gallery C2
3 Luna Park C3
4 St Kilda Botanic Gardens...................... D4
5 St Kilda Foreshore A3

⊕ **Activities, Courses & Tours**
Aurora Spa Retreat...................... (see 20)
Kite Republic ....(see 9)
6 Port Phillip Eco Centre.......................... D4
7 Royal Melbourne Yacht
Squadron A2
8 St Kilda Bowling Club F1
9 St Kilda Sea Baths A3
10 Stand Up Paddle HQ A2
Sunset Eco Penguin Tour ....(see 9)

⊜ **Sleeping**
11 Adina Apartment Hotel St Kilda...........F2
12 Base C3
13 Coffee Palace C1
14 Easystay...B1
15 Habitat HQ E3
16 Home Travellers Motel........................... D3
17 Hotel Barkly.. D2
18 Hotel Tolarno.. B1
19 Hotel Urban B1
20 Prince B2
21 Ritz...G1

⊛ **Eating**
22 Banff F2
23 Barney Allen's B1
24 Batch Espresso G4
25 Cicciolina C4
26 Claypots.. C4
27 Galleon Cafe C3
28 Glick's.. G4

29 Golden Fields G1
30 I Carusi II...C4
31 Lau's Family Kitchen............................... B2
32 Lentil as Anything D4
Mirka's at Tolarno........................(see 18)
33 Miss Jackson.. C1
34 Monarch Cake Shop..................................C3
35 Monk Bodhi Dharma................................. F3
36 Mr Wolf... D2
37 Newmarket Hotel D2
38 Si Señor G4

⊜ **Drinking & Nightlife**
39 Carlisle Wine Bar F4
40 George Lane Bar.. C1
41 George Public Bar C1
Hotel Barkly...................................(see 17)
42 Local Taphouse F3
43 Pause Bar F3
Republica....................................... (see 9)
St Kilda Bowling Club.................... (see 8)
44 St Kilda Dispensary.................................E3
45 Vineyard...C3

⊕ **Entertainment**
46 Esplanade Hotel...B2
47 GH Hotel E3
48 Palais Theatre...B3
Prince Bandroom ....(see 20)
49 St Kilda Open Air Cinema........................B3
50 Theatreworks...B2

⊙ **Shopping**
51 Bookhouse C2
52 Dot Herbey C4
53 Eclectico C4
54 Esplanade Market B3
55 Pure Pop Records C4
Readings.. (see 25)

Linden Arts Centre & Gallery GALLERY
(Map p72; ☑ 03-9534 0099; www.lindenarts.org; 26 Acland St, St Kilda; ⊙ 1-5pm Tue-Fri, 11am-5pm Sat & Sun; ☐ 16, 96) Housed in a wrought-iron-clad 1870s mansion, Linden champions the work of emerging artists. The annual Postcard Show, which coincides with the St Kilda festival in February/March, is a highlight.

Luna Park AMUSEMENT PARK
(Map p72; ☑ 03-9525 5033; www.lunapark.com.au; 18 Lower Esplanade, St Kilda; single ride adult/child $11/9, unlimited rides $48/38; ☐ 16, 96) Luna Park opened in 1912 and still retains the feel of an old-style amusement park, with creepy Mr Moon's gaping mouth swallowing you up as you enter. There's a heritage-listed 'scenic railway' (the oldest operating roller coaster

in the world) and a beautifully baroque carousel with hand-painted horses, swans and chariots, as well as the full complement of gut-churning rides.

St Kilda Botanical Gardens GARDENS
(Map p72; ☑ 03-9209 6777; www.portphillip.vic. gov.au; cnr Blessington & Tennyson Sts, St Kilda; ⊙ sunrise-sunset; ☐ 96) Taking pride of place on the southern line of the Barkly, Carlisle and Blessington St triangle, the Botanical Gardens are an unexpected haven from the St Kilda hustle. Wide gravel paths invite a leisurely stroll, and there are plenty of shady spots to sprawl on the open lawns. There are local indigenous plants and a subtropical rainforest conservatory to ponder.

Jewish Holocaust Centre　　　　MUSEUM
(☑03-9528 1985; www.jhc.org.au; 13-15 Selwyn St,
Elsternwick; by donation; ⊙10am-4pm Mon-Thu, to
2pm Fri, noon-4pm Sun; ☑67, ☑Elsternwick) FREE
Dedicated to the memory of the six million
Jews who lost their lives during the Holocaust, this well-presented museum was set
up by survivors as a sobering reminder of
the atrocities they endured. Guided tours are
available, often led by Holocaust survivors
themselves.

Elwood Beach　　　　BEACH
(Ormond Esplanade, Elwood; ☑606) A short
drive or concerted foreshore walk will take
you to this swimming beach. It tends to be
less windswept, though often no less crowded, than St Kilda, and is surrounded by leafy
Elwood Park and Point Ormond Reserve.
There are playgrounds and kiosks. To get
here take bus 606 from St Kilda at the corner of Park and Fitzroy Sts.

Monash University Museum of Art GALLERY
(MUMA; www.monash.edu.au/muma/; 900 Dandenong Rd, Caulfield East; ⊙10am-5pm Tue-Fri, noon-
5pm Sat; ☑3, ☑Caulfield) FREE Established
during the 1960s, MUMA's art collection
has more than 1800 artworks, and they're a
great representation of Australian contemporary art.

⊙ South Melbourne, Port Melbourne & Albert Park

There's something boastful about these suburbs, and it runs along the lines of being close
to Melbourne's watery highlights: the bay, the
beach and expansive Albert Park Lake. These
are upmarket suburbs rejoicing in their
peaceful environment (though come Grand
Prix time, the noise is ramped up big-time).

Head to South Melbourne for its market, contemporary homeware shops and
top cafes (seems there's a coffee competition going on). At nearby Port Melbourne
is Station Pier, the passenger terminal for
the ferry service between Melbourne and
Tasmania.

South Melbourne Market　　　　MARKET
(www.southmelbournemarket.com.au; cnr Coventry
& Cecil Sts, South Melbourne; ⊙8am-4pm Wed, Sat
& Sun, to 5pm Fri; ☑96) The market's labyrinthine interior is packed to overflowing with
an eccentric collection of stalls ranging from
old-school to boutique. It's been on this site
since 1864 and is a neighbourhood institution, as are its famous dim sims (sold here
since 1949). There are plenty of atmospheric
eateries and a lively night market on Thursdays from November to mid-December.
There's a cooking school here, too – see the
website for details.

Albert Park Lake　　　　LAKE
(btwn Queens Rd, Fitzroy St, Aughtie Dr & Albert Rd;
☑96) Elegant black swans give their inimitable bottoms-up salute as you jog, cycle or
walk the 5km perimeter of this constructed
lake. Lakeside Dr was used as an international motor-racing circuit in the 1950s,
and since 1996 the revamped track has been

FREE FOR ALL

➡ Throw a Frisbee, read a book, sprawl on the lawn or smell the flowers at one of Melbourne's parks and gardens. Try the Royal Botanic Gardens (p69), St Kilda Botanical Gardens (p73) and Birrarung Marr (p48).

➡ Catch a free ride on the City Circle tram (p81). The wine-coloured tram, with recorded commentary, loops along Flinders St, Harbour Esplanade (Docklands), La Trobe and Spring Sts before heading back along Flinders St. It runs every 10 minutes or so between 10am and 6pm (to 9pm Thursday to Saturday during summer), and you can jump on and off at any of the frequent stops.

➡ Gallery hop: start with some conceptual art at the Australian Centre for Contemporary Art (p58), Australian works at the Ian Potter Centre: NGV Australia (p45) or the varied permanent collection of the NGV International (p57). Then browse the laneway galleries of street art in Hosier Lane (p48).

➡ Browse the Queen Victoria Market (p55) and soak up the atmosphere.

➡ Watch a 'movie on demand' at ACMI's (p45) Mediatheque.

➡ Read to your heart's content at the State Library of Victoria (p54), see Ned Kelly's armour or attend one of the fascinating free talks at the nearby Wheeler Centre (p54).

the venue for the **Australian Formula One Grand Prix** each March. Also on the periphery is the **Melbourne Sports & Aquatic Centre**, with an Olympic-size pool and child-delighting wave machine.

Gasworks Arts Park   CULTURAL BUILDING
(☑03-8606 4200; www.gasworks.org.au; cnr Graham & Pickles St, Albert Park; tours $25; ⊙tours 10.30am & 2pm Mon-Thu; ⊟1, 109) A taste of gritty Berlin in Melbourne, this former gas plant lay derelict from the 1950s before being developed into an arts precinct with red-brick galleries, a **theatre company** (check website for shows) and an ultra-dog-friendly parkland. You can meet the artists on a guided tour or come for its summer **open-air cinema** or a **farmers market** (third Saturday of each month).

Station Pier   LANDMARK
(www.portofmelbourne.com; Waterfront Pl, Port Melbourne; ⊟109) Melbourne's main sea passenger terminal, Station Pier has great sentimental associations for many migrants who arrived by ship in the 1950s and '60s, and for servicemen who used it during WWII. It has been in operation since 1854, when the first major railway in Australia ran from here to the city. It's where the *Spirit of Tasmania,* cruise ships and navy vessels dock.

🏃 Activities

Canoeing & Kayaking

Kayak Melbourne   KAYAK TOUR
(☑0418 106 427; www.kayakmelbourne.com.au; tours $72-118; ⊟11, 31, 48) ✍ Don't miss out on the chance to see Melbourne's Yarra River by kayak. These two-hour tours take you past Melbourne's newest city developments and explain the history of the older ones. Moonlight tours are most evocative and include a dinner of fish and chips. Tours usually depart from Victoria Harbour, Docklands – check the website for directions.

Studley Park Boathouse   CANOEING
(☑03-9853 1828; www.studleyparkboathouse.com.au; 1 Boathouse Rd, Kew; kayak/canoe per hr $28/36; ⊙9am-5pm) Pack a picnic and rent a two-person canoe, rowboat or kayak from the boathouse.

Cycling

Cycling maps are available from the Melbourne Visitor Centre (p126) at Federation Square and **Bicycle Victoria** (☑03-8376 8888; www.bv.com.au). The urban series includes the Main Yarra Trail (35km), off which runs the Merri Creek Trail (19km), the Outer Circle Trail (34km) and the Maribyrnong River Trail (22km). There are also paths taking you along Melbourne's beaches.

Melbourne Bike Share (☑1300 711 590; www.melbournebikeshare.com.au) began in 2010 and has had a slow start, which was mainly blamed on Victoria's compulsory helmet laws. Fortunately there's been a shift to provide free helmets (which should be left with the bike), though not all bikes have them. Otherwise, subsidised safety helmets are available at 7-Eleven and IGA stores around the city ($5 with a $3 refund on return). Once armed with a helmet, look out for one of 51 bright-blue stations. Each first half-hour of hire is free – they're ideally used for short trips and then deposited at another station – or otherwise you can rent them daily ($2.80), weekly ($8) or via a one-year membership ($56) with maximum 45-minute usage. Subscriptions require a credit card and $50 security deposit.

Humble Vintage   BICYCLE RENTAL
(☑0432 032 450; www.thehumblevintage.com) ✍ Get yourself a set of special wheels from this collection of retro racers, city bikes and ladies bikes. Rates start at $30 per day or $80 per week, and include a lock, helmet and a terrific map with plenty of ideas of what to do with your non-bike-riding hours, too. Check the website for pickup locations.

Day Spas & Relaxation

Melbourne has a number of top-notch spas and baths at which to get pampered and relax. Most of the luxury hotels have their own in-house spas, also available for use by non-guests.

Aesop Spa   DAY SPA
(Map p68; ☑03-9866 5250; www.aesop.net.au; 153 Toorak Rd, South Yarra; treatments from $120; ⊙by appointment 10am-4pm Wed-Sat; ⊟8, ⊠South Yarra) Aesop Spa takes it up a notch – you can choose from five basic treatments, and your lactate surge or detox overhaul will be further customised to your skin while you're wrapped up in a mohair blanket on a cotton futon.

Aurora Spa Retreat   DAY SPA
(Map p72; ☑03-9536 1130; www.auroraspapretreat.com; 2 Acland St, St Kilda; 1hr from $120; ⊙8.30am-8pm Mon-Fri, to 6pm Sat, 10am-7pm Sun; ⊟3a, 16, 96, 112) There's a creative menu of wellness

WILLIAMSTOWN & AROUND

A trip over the Westgate Bridge brings you to the seaside suburb of Williamstown, a yacht-filled gem with historic, salty seafaring atmosphere. It has stunning views of Melbourne and a small beach, so bring along your bathing suit on a nice day.

The **Hobsons Bay Visitor Information Centre** (☑ 03-9932 4310; www.visithobsons bay.com.au; cnr Syme St & Nelson Pl, Williamstown) on Gem Pier has plenty of info, and offers free tours Tuesday at 2.15pm and Friday 11.45am, except in winter.

Sights & Activities

A science museum that's fun? It's no wonder the interactive **Scienceworks** (☑ 13 11 02; www.museumvictoria.com.au/scienceworks; 2 Booker St, Spotswood; adult/child $10/free, Planetarium & Lightning Room additional adult/child $6/4.50; ⊙ 10am-4.30pm; ☒ Spotswood) is one of Melbourne's most popular attractions for families. It's the kind of place that's all about pushing buttons, lifting flaps and pulling levers, and while it's geared towards kids, it's fun for adults, too (afternoons are best for avoiding school groups). Displays cover the science of sport (you'll get to run against Cathy Freeman), household items and the human body. Also here is the **Melbourne Planetarium**, which recreates the night sky on a 16m-domed ceiling using a high-tech computer and projection system; you can probably guess what the **Lightning Room** involves. Ferries can drop you here, or it's a 10-minute signposted walk from Spotswood train station.

In Williamstown proper, the industrial **Seaworks** (☑ 0417 292 021; www.seaworks.com. au; 82 Nelson Pl) precinct has been redeveloped as a tourist sight, comprising historic boatsheds, a **maritime museum** (by donation; ⊙ 11am-3pm Sun) and exhibition space. It's also the headquarters for **Sea Shepherd Australia** (www.seashepherd.org.au), and on weekends you can tour their anti-poaching vessels from noon to 4.30pm (when they're out at sea tackling Japanese whalers, it's still worth dropping by to visit the centre for displays and video about their anti-whaling campaign). Seaworks also has a shipbuilding yard, a pirate-themed tavern and Victoria's oldest morgue, which you can visit on a **ghost tour** (☑ 1300 390 119; www.lanternghosttours.com).

Across from the tourist office, the large **Customs Wharf Galleria** (www.customswharf. com.au; 126 Nelson Pl; ⊙ 11am-5pm) **FREE** is worth a look for quality artwork within the historic former customs house, built in 1875.

Trainspotters should head to the **Williamstown Railway Museum** (☑ 1300 220 220; www.arhsvic.org.au/index.php/museum; Champion Rd; adult/child $8/4; ⊙ noon-5pm Sat & Sun, noon-4pm Mon-Fri during school holidays), scheduled to reopen in 2014, for a fine collection of

treatments ranging from water-based massage and full-body wraps to three- and four-hour retreat packages, all within a beautiful chic setting at the Prince hotel (p88). Good deals can be had mid week.

Chuan Spa   DAY SPA
(Map p50; ☑ 03-8696 8111; www.chuanspa.com; Langham Hotel, 1 Southgate Ave, Southbank; 1hr from $175; ⊙ 6am-8.30pm Mon-Fri, 8am-8pm Sat & Sun) A spin-off from the Hong Kong spa of the same name, Chuan has a Chinese-garden-themed ambience and focuses on the principles of traditional Chinese medicine. It offers a full range of treatments, including water-based ones, and has a steam room and swimming pool. Located in the Langham Hotel.

Japanese Bath House   BATHHOUSE
(☑ 03-9419 0268; www.japanesebathhouse.com; 59 Cromwell St, Collingwood; bath $30, shiatsu from $46; ⊙ 11am-10pm Tue-Fri, to 8pm Sat & Sun; ☒ 109) Urban as the setting may be, it's as serene as can be inside this authentic *sentō* (bathhouse). Perfect for some communal skinship (it's nude, segregated bathing), a shiatsu and a post-soak *sake* in the tatami lounge.

Isika   DAY SPA
(☑ 03-9292 8327; www.crownmetropol. au/isika; 8 Whiteman St, Southbank; 1hr from $140; ⊙ 8am-8pm; ☒ 96, 109, 112) The Crown Metropol (p84) hotel has residential rooms with staircases leading directly to its spa,

old steam locomotives, while WWII buffs can board the **HMAS Castlemaine** (www.hmas castlemaine.org.au; Gem Pier; adult/child $6/3; ⊙noon-4pm Sat & Sun), a minesweeper active in New Guinea and Northern Australia. Or else take to the skies for an aerial tour of the city with **Melbourne Seaplanes** (✆03-9547 4454; www.seaplane.com.au; Gem Pier; 15-min flight from $150), featuring take-offs and landing on the water.

Also noteworthy is **Point Gellibrand**, the site of Victoria's first white settlement, where Victoria's navy was established, and where the Timeball Tower, once used by ships to set their chronometers, was built by convict labour in 1840.

Further afield in Point Cook, **Cheetham Wetlands** is home to around 200 species of migratory and native waterbirds, viewed from an observation tower. July to November is the best time.

Sleeping & Eating

On the main strip, **Ragusa** (✆03-9399 8500; www.ragusarestaurant.com.au; 139 Nelson Pl, Williamstown; mains $17-34; ⊙noon-3pm & 6pm-late) is doing good things with its menu of modern Croatian in a beautiful heritage building. **Jimmy Grants** (www.jimmygrants.com.au; 28 Ferguson St, Williamstown), popular for its gourmet souvlakis, was also planning to open here at time of research. Williamstown has plenty of historical pubs to explore. **Quest Williamstown** (✆03-9393 5300; www.questwilliamstown.com.au; 1 Syme St; 1-bedroom apt from $199; P⊛) has self-contained apartments on the waterfront overlooking the marina.

Getting There & Away

Ferry is the most popular and undoubtedly the most scenic way to get to Williamstown – a fitting way to arrive, given the area's maritime ambience. **Williamstown Ferries** (✆03-9517 9444; www.williamstownferries.com.au; one-way Williamstown–Southbank adult/child $18/9) plies Hobsons Bay daily, stopping at Southgate and visiting a number of sites along the way, including Scienceworks and Docklands. **Melbourne River Cruises** (✆03-8610 2600; www.melbcruises.com.au; one-way Williamstown–city centre adult/child $22/11) also docks at Gem Pier.

Otherwise you can catch a train from Flinders Street Station or make the 10-minute drive from Melbourne's city centre. The other option is to cycle on the 24km Hobsons Bay Coastal Trail, which links up with the Maribyrnong Trail via the city, or the St Kilda area via the **Westgate Punt** (www.westgatepunt.com; Mon-Fri $2 one-way, weekends one-way/return $5/7; ⊙6.30am-9.30am & 4-7pm Mon-Fri, 9am-5pm Sat & Sun) ferry crossing under the Westgate Bridge.

which is warm and dimly lit and offers a couples' treatment with in-room spa.

Miss Fox   DAY SPA
(Map p50; ✆1300 64 77 36; www.missfox.com.au; Level 1-3, 285 Little Collins St; spa treatments from $175 ; ⊙11am-7pm Tue-Fri, 10am-5pm Sat; ⛼86, 96) Nineteen-fifties glamour is the name of the game at this inner-city day spa, beauty salon and hair stylist. Sip on French champagne or cocktails while you get your nails decorated and your hair spruced up, or indulge in a spa treatment with diamond-infused oils.

Golf

Some of Melbourne's golf courses are rated among the best in the world. The illustrious Sandbelt (www.thesandbelt.com) refers to eight courses stretching along the bay; they're built on a sand base, creating perfect conditions year-round. Among them are **Royal Melbourne** (✆03-9599 0500; www.royalmelbournegc.com; Cheltenham Rd, Black Rock), Australia's best and regularly rated in the world's top 10, and **Kingston Heath** (www.kingstonheath.com.au), ranked number two in Australia. To get a hit at the Sandbelt courses you'll need a letter of introduction from your own club, and often a verifiable handicap.

There are plenty of good-quality public courses, too. Green fees cost around $25 for 18 holes during the week, and all courses have clubs and buggies for hire. Visit www.publicaccessgolf.com.au/tag/melbourne for course listings.

Indoor Rock Climbing

Hardrock   ROCK CLIMBING
(Map p50; ☑ 03-9631 5300; www.hardrock.com.au; 501 Swanston St, Melbourne; adult/child incl equipment $30/14; ☺ noon-10pm Mon-Fri, 11am-7pm Sat & Sun; ☒ 1, 3, 5, 6, 8, 16, 64, 67, 72, ☒ Melbourne Central) Indoor climbing centre with naturalistic surfaces up to 18m high, and city views. There are a few storeys of glass frontage, so the city gets to view you, too.

Lawn Bowls

Formerly the domain of senior citizens, bowling clubs are now inundated by younger types – barefoot, with a cheap beer in one hand and a bowl in the other.

North Fitzroy Bowls   LAWN BOWLS
(☑ 03-9481 3137; www.barefootbowling.com.au; 578 Brunswick St, North Fitzroy; barefoot bowls $15 per person; ☺ 11am-10pm; ☒ 112) This bowls club, north of Alexandra Parade, has night bowls, barbecues, a beer garden and bistro with cheap meals. Phone to make a booking; walk-ins are accepted if it's quiet.

St Kilda Bowling Club   LAWN BOWLS
(Map p72; ☑ 03-9534 5229; www.stkildabowling club.com.au; 66 Fitzroy St, St Kilda; 2hr $20 per person; ☺ noon-sunset Tue-Sun; ☒ 16, 96) The only dress code at this popular bowling club is 'shoes off'. First-timers can get some friendly instruction. Great place for a beer (p113).

Running

The Tan   RUNNING
(Royal Botanic Gardens, Birdwood Ave, South Yarra; ☒ Tourist shuttle, ☒ 8) A 3.8km-long former horse-exercising track is now the city's most popular running spot; it surrounds the Royal Botanic Gardens and King's Domain.

Princes Park   RUNNING
(Princes Park Dr, North Carlton; ☒ 19) Joggers and walkers pound the 3.2km gravel path around the perimeter of the park, while cricket, soccer and dog-walking fill up the centre. It's the former home to the Carlton football club (and its current training ground).

Sailing

With about 20 yacht clubs around the shores of Port Phillip, plus Albert Park Lake, Melbourne has some fantastic yachting opportunities. Discover Sailing (www.discover sailing.org.au) is a good starting point for sailing centres and courses.

Royal Melbourne Yacht Squadron   SAILING
(RMYC; Map p72; ☑ 03-9534 0227; www.rmys.com. au; Pier Rd, St Kilda) Based in St Kilda. Anyone can have a go on a yacht on Wednesday nights ($20); arrive by 4pm. Wear nonmarking shoes (white soles) and take along waterproof gear, if you have it.

Swimming

In summer, do as most Melburnians do and hit the sand at one of the city's metropolitan beaches. St Kilda, Middle Park and Port Melbourne are popular patches, with suburban beaches at Brighton and Sandringham. Public pools are also well-loved.

Fitzroy Swimming Pool   SWIMMING
(Map p64; ☑ 03-9205 5180; 160 Alexandra Pde, Fitzroy; adult/child $5/3; ☺ 6am-8pm Mon-Fri, 8am-6pm Sat & Sun; ☒ 112) Between laps, locals love catching a few rays up in the bleachers or on the lawn; there are also two toddler pools.

Melbourne City Baths   SWIMMING
(Map p50; ☑ 03-9663 5888; www.melbourne.vic. gov.au/melbournecitybaths; 420 Swanston St, Melbourne; adult/child $6/3; ☺ 6am-10pm Mon-Thu, to 8pm Fri, 8am-6pm Sat & Sun; ☒ Melbourne Central) The City Baths were literally public baths when they first opened in 1860 and were intended to stop people bathing in and drinking from the seriously polluted Yarra River. They now boast the city centre's largest pool (30m), plus you can do your laps in a 1903 heritage-listed building.

In the same building is the Melbourne Bath House (☑ 03-9539 1111; www.mel bournebathhouse.com.au; from $59; ☺ 9am-6pm), where you can soak in mineral water treatments in a private clawfoot baths.

Prahran Aquatic Centre   SWIMMING
(Map p68; ☑ 03-8290 7140; 41 Essex St, Prahran; adult/child $6/3; ☺ 6am-7.45pm Mon-Fri, to 5pm Sat, 7am-5pm Sun; ☒ 72, 78, ☒ Prahran) This glam 50m heated outdoor pool is surrounded by a stretch of lawn.

Windsurfing, Kiteboarding & Stand-Up Paddleboarding

Kiteboarding has a fast-emerging scene around the St Kilda coastline and Altona beach between November and April. Elwood, just south of St Kilda, is a popular sailboarding area.

Stand Up Paddle HQ   PADDLEBOARDING
(Map p72; ☑ 0416 184 994; www.supb.com.au; St Kilda Pier; per hour $25, 2hr penguin tour $130; ☐ 96) Arrange a lesson or hire out SUP equipment from St Kilda Pier, or join one of the company's Yarra River or sunset St Kilda penguin tours (p80).

Kite Republic   KITEBOARDING
(Map p72; ☑ 03-9537 0644; www.kiterepublic.com. au; St Kilda Sea Baths, 4/10-18 Jacka Blvd, St Kilda; 1hr lesson $90; ☺ 10am-7pm) Offers kiteboarding lessons, tours and equipment; also a good source of info. In winter they can arrange snow-kiting at Mt Hotham. Also rents SUPs and Street SUPs.

RPS The Board Store   BOARD HIRE
(☑ 03-9525 6475; www.rpstheboardstore.com; 87 Ormond Rd, Elwood; 90min SUP lesson $65; ☺ 9.30am-5.30pm, to 4.30pm Sat, 11am-3pm Sun; ☒ Elsternwick) Well-established outfit that's a good all-rounder for SUP, kiteboading and windsurfing – offering lessons and equipment hire. Follow Marine Pde to Glenhuntly Rd; turn left at Ormond Rd.

Courses

Book a cooking course at the South Melbourne Market (☑ 03-9209 6887; www.southmelbournemarket.com.au/cooking-school; classes $55-125), which has everything from standard classes to masterclasses with some

---

WERRIBEE & AROUND

Those en route to the Great Ocean Road, or looking for a short trip outside Melbourne, should consider Werribee, a 30-minute drive down the Princes Hwy heading over the Westgate Bridge.

Most people visit for Werribee Open Range Zoo (☑ 03-9731 9600; www.zoo.org. au/werribee; K Rd; adult/child $30/13.20, children free weekends & holidays; ☺ 9am-5pm, last entry 3.30pm), an African-safari-style experience run by Melbourne Zoo. It's set over 225 hectares; admission includes a 45-minutes safari tour where you'll see grazing rhino, giraffe, antelope and zebra on savannah-like plains. The walking trail has enclosures for lowland gorillas, lions, hippos, cheetah and meerkats, among others. Add-ons include behind-the-scenes tours, or you can stay overnight (adult/child from $300/145) in luxury en suite tents with outlooks over the plains. If you don't have your own car, catch the train from Melbourne to Werribee train station, then bus 439 to the zoo.

Also a part of the Werribee Park complex is Shadowfax Winery (☑ 03-9731 4420; www.shadowfax.com.au; K Rd; ☺ kitchen noon-3pm, tastings 11am-5pm) (a five-minute drive from the zoo), with wine tastings and wood-fired pizzas. The Werribee Mansion (☑ 03-8734 5100; www.parkweb.vic.gov.au; Gate 2, K Rd; adult/child/family $9/6.50/28.60; ☺ 10am-5pm) is another highlight. Today serving as a museum, it was built in 1877 by prosperous farm owners and brims with colonial arriviste ambition with its Italianate edifice and Victorian period features. If you want to stay the night, the lavish Mansion Hotel & Spa (☑ 03-9731 4000; www.lancemore.com.au/mansion; rooms from $229; ☺ spa 9am-5pm Mon-Thu, to 7pm Fri & Sat, from 10am Sun; ✳ 🖥 ☒) manages to be both stylish and modern, and has a leisurely country-house ambience. Its spa is a great place to indulge with relaxation and beauty therapies.

Down the road is Point Cook, birthplace of the Royal Australian Air Force (RAAF). It's now home to the RAAF Museum (www.airforce.gov.au/raafmuseum/; Point Cook Rd, Point Cook; ☺ 10am-3pm Tue-Fri, to 5pm Sat & Sun) FREE, an essential visit for aviation fans and war buffs. There's plenty of awesome aircraft on display to enthral kids and adults alike, from flimsy box-kite planes to sleek F-111 fighters. There's also a comprehensive display on Australia at war, featuring memorabilia such as shrapnel from the Red Baron's German plane, shot down by Australians in WWI. Aim to visit 1pm Sunday, Tuesday or Thursday for flight demonstrations; though there's a good chance of seeing activity on its airfield at other times, too. It's located at the RAAF Williams base, so you'll need to bring ID.

If you don't have a car, Werribee Park Shuttle (☑ 03-9748 5094; www.werribeeparkshuttle.com.au; per person $25 return) departs from NGV International in Melbourne at 9.20am, heading to all the above sights (though if you're doing the RAAF Museum you'll only have time for one other sight) and returning to Melbourme around 2.30pm. Bookings are essential.

MELBOURNE FOR CHILDREN

➡ Ian Potter Foundation Children's Garden (p69)

➡ Collingwood Children's Farm (p62)

➡ ACMI (p45)

➡ Luna Park (p73)

➡ Scienceworks (p76)

➡ Royal Melbourne Zoo (p67)

➡ ArtPlay (p48)

➡ National Sports Museum (p60)

➡ Melbourne Museum (p65)

of Melbourne's best-known chefs; with **Essential Ingredient at the Prahran Market** (Map p68; ☑ 03-9827 9047; www.essentialingredient.com.au; classes $110-275) for subjects like pizza-making or matching food and wine; or at **Queen Victoria Market** (www.qvm.com.au; $90-160) for infrequent courses covering everything from home brewing to curing.

The **Centre for Adult Education** (CAE; Map p50; ☑ 03-9652 0611; www.cae.edu.au; 253 Flinders Lane, Melbourne) runs a wide variety of courses from cooking to language to art.

☞ Tours

Melbourne By Foot WALKING TOUR
(☑ 0418 394 000; www.melbournebyfoot.com; tours $35; 🚇 Flinders St) 🏄 Take a few hours out with Dave and experience a mellow, informative 4km walking tour that covers laneway art, politics, Melbourne's history and diversity. Tour includes a refreshment break. Highly recommended; book online.

Aboriginal Heritage Walk CULTURAL TOUR
(☑ 03-9252 2300; www.rbg.vic.gov.au; Royal Botanic Gardens, Birdwood Ave, South Yarra; adult/child $25/10; ⊙ 11am Tue-Fri and 1st Sun of the month; 🚌 Tourist Shuttle, ⑧ 8) 🏄 The Royal Botanic Gardens are on a traditional camping and meeting place of the original Indigenous owners, and this tour takes you through their story – from songlines to plant lore, all in 90 fascinating minutes. The tour departs from the gardens' visitor centre.

Melbourne Street Art Tours WALKING TOUR
(☑ 03-9328 5556; www.melbournestreettours.com; tours $69; ⊙ 1.30-5pm Tue, Thu & Sat) 🏄 Three-hour tours exploring the street-art side of Melbourne. The tour guides are street art-

ists themselves, so you'll get a good insight into this art form.

St Kilda Music Walking Tours WALKING TOUR
(SKMWT; www.skmwt.com.au; tours $40; ⊙ weekends) 'Take a walk on the wild side' with this rock 'n' roll tour that takes in the infamous bars and landmarks that played starring roles in St Kilda's underground music scene. They're led by St Kilda music icons, including Fred Negro and Fiona Lee Maynard; expect a hilarious and lewd behind-the-scenes tour of what makes St Kilda so great.

Real Melbourne Bike Tours CYCLING
(Map p50; ☑ 0417 339 203; www.rentabike.net.au/biketours; Federation Sq; 4hr-tour incl lunch adult/child $110/79; 🚇 Flinders St) 🏄 These bike tours allow you to cover more ground on a well-thought-out itinerary that provides a local's insight to Melbourne, with a foodie focus. The company rents bikes, too.

Hidden Secrets Tours WALKING TOUR
(☑ 03-9663 3358; www.hiddensecretstours.com; tours $95-195) 🏄 Offers a variety of walking tours covering subjects such as lanes and arcades, wine, architecture, coffee and cafes, and vintage Melbourne.

Walk to Art WALKING TOUR
(☑ 03-8415 0449; www.walktoart.com.au; 4hr tour $108, Fri 2hr tour $78) These walking tours take you to galleries and artist-run spaces hidden in Melbourne's buildings and laneways. The tour itinerary, around the city centre and inner neighbourhoods, is always changing, and isn't revealed until the day. The tours operate Wednesday and Saturday (four hours) or a Friday express tour (two hours). Tours include an art 'starter pack', and wine and cheese afterwards.

Sunset Eco Penguin Tour ECOTOUR
(Map p72; ☑ 0416 184 994; www.supb.com.au; 2hr penguin tour $130; 🚤 96) 🏄 See St Kilda's penguin colony from around October to April (minimum two people), while you navigate your stand-up paddleboard.

Global Ballooning SCENIC FLIGHT
(☑ 1800 627 661; www.globalballooning.com.au; from $440) Wake up at the crack of dawn to view the city from another angle on this one-hour ride.

Melbourne Visitor Shuttle BUS TOUR
(Tourist Shuttle; www.thatsmelbourne.com.au; $5 daily ticket, children under 10 free; ⊙ 9.30am-4.30pm) This bus shuttle runs a 1½-hour

round-trip with audio commentary and 13 stops that take passengers to all Melbourne's main sights.

City Circle Trams
TRAM TOUR

(Tram 35; ☑ 13 16 38; www.ptv.vic.gov.au; ⊙ 10am-6pm Sun-Wed, to 9pm Thu-Sat; ☒ 35) **FREE** Designed primarily for tourists, this free tram service travels around the city centre, passing many city sights along the way, with an audio commentary. It runs every 10 minutes or so.

Eight refurbished W-class trams operate on this route. Built in Melbourne between 1936 and 1956, they have all been painted a distinctive deep burgundy and gold. You can also dine onboard the Colonial Tramcar Restaurant (☑ 03-9695 4000; www.tramrestaurant.com.au; 3-course meal from $77) while scuttling around Melbourne's streets.

Melbourne River Cruises
CRUISE

(☑ 03-9681 3284; www.melbcruises.com.au; Federation Wharf, Melbourne; adult/child from $23/11) Take a one-hour cruise upstream or downstream along the Yarra River, or a 2½-hour return cruise, departing from a couple of locations – check the website for details. It also operates a ferry between Southgate and Gem Pier in Williamstown, sailing three to nine times daily, depending on the season.

Greeter Service
WALKING TOUR

(Map p50; ☑ 03-9658 9658; Melbourne Visitor Centre, Federation Sq; ☒ Flinders St) **FREE** Get your bearings on this free two-hour 'orientation tour', which departs Federation Square daily at 9.30am (bookings required). It's run by the city's volunteer 'greeters'.

🛏 Sleeping

While you'll have no trouble finding a place to stay that suits your taste and budget, for a city that's big on style Melbourne has only a handful of small, atmospheric hotels.

Airport & Around

Melbourne's closest airport is 25km from the city, with no direct public transport links, so odd-hour flights require taxis, a SkyBus from the city centre or a sleepover. There are three main airport hotels, ranging from bells, whistles and direct 'air bridge' access at the Parkroyal Melbourne Airport (☑ 03-8347 2000; www.parkroyalhotels.com; Arrival Dve, Melbourne Airport; r from $260; ☒ @ 🛜 ☒) and the smart but slightly further away Holiday

Inn Melbourne Airport (☑ 03-9933 5111; www.holidayinn.com; 10-14 Centre Rd, Melbourne Airport; r from $240; ☒ 🛜 ☒) to the Ibis Budget Melbourne Airport (☑ 03-8336 1811; www.ibis.com; Caldwell Dve, Melbourne Airport; r from $129; ☒ 🛜), which has basic rooms just over 600m from the terminal.

Central Melbourne

There are a lot of places across all price ranges that will put you in the heart of the action, whether you've come to town and want to shop, party, catch a match or take in some culture.

★ Space Hotel
HOSTEL, HOTEL $

(Map p50; ☑ 03-9662 3888; www.spacehotel.com.au; 380 Russell St; dm/s/d without bathroom from $28/70/99; ☒ @ 🛜 ; ☒ City Circle, 24, 30) One of Melbourne's few genuine flashpackers, this sleek, modern and immaculate hotel has something for all demographics, all at very reasonable prices. Rooms have iPod docks and flat-screen TVs, while dorms have thoughtful touches like large lockers equipped with sensor lights and lockable adapters. A few doubles have en suites and balconies. Other big ticks are its rooftop hot tub with city views, in-house cinema and social pub downstairs. Stay tuned for a new St Kilda location.

Melbourne Central YHA
HOSTEL $

(Map p50; ☑ 03-9621 2523; www.yha.com.au; 562 Flinders St; dm/d $34/100; @ 🛜 ; ☒ 70) This heritage building has been totally transformed by the YHA gang: expect a lively reception, handsome rooms, and kitchens and common areas on each of the four levels. Entertainment's high on the agenda, and there's a fab restaurant called Bertha Brown on the ground floor and a grand rooftop area.

Nomad's Melbourne
HOSTEL $

(Map p50; ☑ 03-9328 4383; www.nomadshostels.com; 198 A'Beckett St; dm $20-36, d $100-130; ☒ @ 🛜 ; ☒ Flagstaff) Flashpacking hits Melbourne's city centre with this smart hostel boasting a mix of four- to 14-bed dorms (some with en suite) and spacious doubles. There's a rooftop area with barbecue, cinema lounge, bar and plenty of gloss (especially in the females-only 'wing').

City Centre Budget Hotel
HOTEL $

(Map p50; ☑ 03-9654 5401; www.citycentrebudget hotel.com.au; 22 Little Collins St; d with shared/private bathroom $92/112; @ 🛜 ; ☒ Parliament)

Intimate, independent and inconspicuous, this 38-room budget hotel is a find. It's located at the city's prettier end, down a 'Little' street, up some stairs and inside an unassuming building. Rooms are no-frills yet neat and tidy, staff are ultra-friendly and there's free wi-fi, a laundry and communal kitchen on the pebbled rooftop.

Greenhouse Backpacker
HOSTEL $

(Map p50; ☑03-9639 6400; www.greenhouse backpacker.com.au; 6/228 Flinders Lane; dm/s/d incl breakfast $37/80/90; ❀ @ ☎; ⓐ Flinders St) Greenhouse has a fun vibe and is extremely well run – they know what keeps backpackers content. This includes: free wi-fi, free rooftop barbecues, huge communal spaces, luggage storage and activities. There's also chatty, helpful staff and spic-and-span facilities. It's a five-minute walk from Flinders St Station.

United Backpackers
HOSTEL $

(Map p50; ☑03-9654 2616; www.unitedbackpackers.com.au; 250 Flinders St; dm from $26, d with shared/private bathroom $70/90; @ ☎; ⓐ 48, 70, 75, ⓐ Flinders St) New owners have taken over to give this backpackers a total makeover, with all new fittings in its clean rooms, basement bar and modern kitchen. It's inside a historic building (c 1910) right in the heart of the action, opposite Flinders St Station, with 24-hour reception, helpful staff and free wi-fi.

Melbourne International Backpackers
HOSTEL $

(MIB; Map p50; ☑1800 557 891; www.mibp.com.au; 450 Elizabeth St; dm/d from $28/80; @ ☎; ⓐ 19, 57, 59) While the open-plan lobby at reception can be a tad overwhelming with its hive of backpackers cooking away and socialising at the cafeteria-style tables, the well-appointed rooms are away from the madness and in good condition. There are free pancakes for breakfast, and it's a handy location for the Queen Vic Market and city sightseeing.

Bozo Backpacker 3
HOSTEL $

(Map p66; ☑03-9329 9816; www.bozobackpacker.com; 238 Victoria St, North Melbourne; dm/s/d $25/60/70; ☎; ⓐ 19, 57, 59) In a stylish art deco building across from the Queen Vic Market, this grungy hostel won't suit those looking for modern digs, but rather it's a character-filled backpackers painted in vibrant yellow and reds. Reception is rarely attended, so pre-arrange your arrival. Guests get free entry to gigs at the next door Public Bar.

There are a few branches in the area, but this is the only recommendable one.

King Street Backpackers
HOSTEL $

(Map p50; ☑03-9670 1111; www.kingstreetback packers.com.au; 197-199 King St; dm/d from $25/80; @ ☎; ⓐ 86, 96, ⓐ Southern Cross) This friendly, efficient, clean and super-safe hostel (with 24-hour reception) can be a respite from the debauchery of King St, and has a handy location for Southern Cross Station. It piles on the freebies, including pancakes on Sunday, internet access and a decent feed of pasta on Wednesday nights. Dorms and private rooms are well maintained, and a step above many others.

Adina Apartment Hotel
APARTMENT $$

(Map p50; ☑03-8663 0000; www.adinahotels.com.au; 88 Flinders St; apt from $165; P ❀ ☎; ⓐ City Circle, 70, 75) Quintessential Melbourne, these designer-cool monochromatic warehouse-style loft apartments are extra large and luxurious. Ask for one at the front for amazing parkland views or get glimpses into Melbourne's lanes from the giant polished-floorboard studios, all with full kitchens. Also has apartments in St Kilda (Map p72; ☑03-9536 0000; 157 Fitzroy St, St Kilda; apt from $139) overlooking Albert Park.

Alto Hotel on Bourke
HOTEL $$

(Map p50; ☑03-8608 5500; www.altohotel.com.au; 636 Bourke St; r from $158; P ❀ @ ☎; ⓐ 86, 96) ✎ Environment-minded Alto has water-saving showers, energy-efficient lights and double-glazed windows, and in-room recycling is encouraged. Rooms are also well equipped, with good light and neutral decoration. Apartments (but not studios) have full kitchens and multiple LCD TVs, and some have spas. Freebies include organic espresso coffee, apples, and access to a massage room. Guests can use an electric car at the rate of $17 per hour.

Pensione Hotel
HOTEL $$

(Map p50; ☑03-9621 3333; www.pensione.com.au; 16 Spencer St; r from $109; P ❀ @ ☎; ⓐ 96, 109, 112) With refreshing honesty, the lovely, boutique Pensione Hotel names some rooms a 'petit double' – but what you don't get in size is more than made up for in spot-on style, room extras and super-reasonable rates.

Hotel Causeway
HOTEL $$

(Map p50; ☑03-9660 8888; www.causeway.com.au; 275 Little Collins St; r incl breakfast from $170; ❀ @ ☎; ⓐ 86, 96) With a discreet entrance in the Howey Place covered arcade, Causeway will appeal to those who've come to Melbourne to shop and bar-hop. It's intimate in scale, so don't expect the facilities of a big hotel. Rooms are boutiquey and feature luxurious linen, robes and slippers.

Robinsons in the City
BOUTIQUE HOTEL **$$**

(Map p50; ☑03-9329 2552; www.ritc.com.au; 405 Spencer St; r incl breakfast from $165; P ❋ ✱; ☒75, 96) Robinsons is a gem, with six large rooms and warm service. The building is a former bakery, dating from 1850, but it's been given a modern, eclectic look. Bathrooms are not in the rooms; each room has its own in the hall. Service is warm and personal; repeat visits are common.

Vibe Savoy Hotel
HOTEL **$$**

(Map p50; ☑03-9622 8888; www.vibehotels.com. au; 630 Little Collins St; r from $149; ❋ @ ✱; ☒Southern Cross) This lovely heritage building at Collins St's western end (opposite Southern Cross Station) has been given a bold makeover, though some rooms retain subtle period features. It's a concoction of traditional hotel comforts, bright colours and contemporary furnishings.

Quest Gordon Place
APARTMENTS **$$**

(Map p50; ☑03-9663 2888; www.questgordon place.com.au; 24 Little Bourke St; apt from $159; ✱ ✱; ☒City Circle, 86, 96, ☒Parliament) Springing up all over the city, Quest may be a chain, but each location is unique and under individual management. What they do share in common is the same quality standards, value and ideal locations across Melbourne's city centre. Gordon Place has smart apartments concealed inside a prim 1885 heritage building at the top end of town. Its outdoor pool is an unexpected bonus.

Other options are **Quest Hero** (Map p50; ☑03-8664 8500; www.questapartments.com.au; 140 Little Collins St; apt from $190; ❋ @; ☒86, 96, 109, 112), **Quest on Lonsdale** (Map p50; ☑03-9663 3317; www.questonlonsdale.com.au; 43 Lonsdale St; ☒86, 96) and **Quest Docklands** (☑03-9630 1000; www.questdocklands.com.au; 750 Bourke St, Victoria Point, Docklands; apt from $195; ❋ ✱; ☒70, ☒Southern Cross).

Mantra 100 Exhibition
APARTMENT **$$**

(Map p50; ☑03-9631 4444; www.mantra.com.au; 100 Exhibition St; apt from $149; ❋ @ ✱; ☒86, 95, 96) A great midcity location, between the bustle of Bourke St and the calm of Collins St, with streamlined apartment facilities and professional, friendly service. The floor-to-ceiling windows and the use of blonde wood, white and the odd splash of intense colour are a surprise at this price.

Causeway Inn on the Mall
HOTEL **$$**

(Map p50; ☑03-9650 0688; www.causeway. com.au; 327 Bourke St Mall; r incl breakfast $160; ❋ @ ✱; ☒86, 96) One of three Causeway hotels, the Inn is the best-value option and often full. Bonuses include helpful staff, free breakfast and a daily newspaper, and a location bang in the middle of the city. The hotel entrance is actually in the Causeway.

City Limits
APARTMENT **$$**

(Map p50; ☑03-9662 2544; www.citylimits. com.au; 20 Little Bourke St; r incl breakfast $130; ❋ @ ✱; ☒86, 96, ☒Parliament) If you can ignore the dazzling mix of decor styles (plenty of '80s aesthetics here), these apartments are excellent value. Staff are welcoming and you're in an ideal Chinatown location. The rooms have small but decently stocked kitchenettes.

Punthill Manhattan
APARTMENT **$$**

(Map p50; ☑03-9659 3788; www.punthill.com.au; 57 Flinders Lane; apt from $180; ❋ @ ✱ ✱; ☒City Circle, 48) While not quite avoiding the serviced-apartment furnishing clichés, these loft spaces are set in a former warehouse and have original industrial-age details. Large marble bathrooms, full granite-bench kitchens, a stylish muted palette and prime laneway location make this a good option. There's also a functional lap pool and gym; ask for a room at the back for an outlook.

Also has **Punthill Flinders Lane** (Map p50; ☑03-9631 1199; www.punthill.com.au; 267 Flinders Lane; ☒19, 57, 59) and **Punthill Little Bourke** (Map p50; ☑03-9631 1111; www.punthill.com.au; 11-17 Cohen Pl; apt from $160; ❋ @ ✱ ✱; ☒86, 96) city locales.

Victoria Hotel
HOTEL **$$**

(Map p50; ☑03-9669 0000; www.victoriahotel. com.au; 215 Little Collins St; s $99-110, d $125-145; P ❋ @ ✱ ✱; ☒86, 95, 96) The original Vic opened its doors in 1880, but don't worry: they've updated the plumbing since then. This city institution has around 400 rooms, and all differ slightly. Facilities include a plunge pool.

Radisson on Flagstaff Gardens
HOTEL **$$**

(Map p50; ☑03-9322 8000; www.radisson.com/ melbourneau; 380 William St; r from $189; ❋ @ ✱; ☒55) Directly opposite from the Flagstaff Gardens, this is a great option for those who enjoy a bit of greenery outside their window while being in striking distance of city sightseeing. The rooftop spa is a huge perk.

Crossley
HOTEL **$$**

(Map p50; ☑ 03-9639 1639; www.crossleyhotel.com.au; 51 Little Bourke St; r from $150; ❄ @ 🛜; 🚇 Parliament) In the heart of Chinatown, this hotel is housed in a 1930s building that provides much of its character. Rooms are nothing special, but they're modern and comfortable, and you can't fault its central location. Offers discounts to the City Baths.

★ Ovolo
BOUTIQUE HOTEL **$$$**

(Map p50; ☑ 03-8692 0777; www.ovologroup.com; 19 Little Bourke St; r incl breakfast from $209; P ❄ @ 🛜; 🚇 Parliament) Melbourne's newest boutique hotel mixes hipster chic with a funky executive vibe. It's friendly, fun and loaded with goodies – there's a free minibar in each room, and free booze downstairs at the daily happy hour. Throw in a 'goodie bag' on arrival, Nespresso coffee machine in the lobby and Le Patisserie breakfast pastries and you'll be wanting to move in permanently.

Adelphi Hotel
HOTEL **$$$**

(Map p50; ☑ 03-8080 8888; www.adelphi.com.au; 187 Flinders Lane; r from $250; ❄ @ 🛜 🏊; 🚋 3, 5, 6, 16, 64, 67, 72) Under new ownership, this discreet Flinders Lane property was one of Australia's first boutique hotels, and it's still rock 'n' roll. It's had a five-star makeover, and its cosy rooms have a distinctly glam European feel with design touches throughout. Thankfully its iconic rooftop pool, which juts out over Flinders Lane, remains.

Sweet tooths are treated with a dessert-themed restaurant and free lollies in well-stocked minibars and at reception.

Majorca Apartment 401
APARTMENT **$$$**

(Map p50; ☑ 0412 068 855; www.apartment401.com.au; 258 Flinders Lane, Majorca Building; apt from $275; ❄ 🛜; 🚋 19, 57, 59, 🚇 Flinders St) This is the ultimate in like-a-local living. The Majorca, a single apartment, is in one of the city's loveliest art deco buildings and watches over a bustling vortex of laneways. It's stylishly furnished, has timber floorboards and the windows are huge. Who needs a concierge when you're right in the centre of things already? There's a two-night minimum.

Hotel Lindrum
BOUTIQUE HOTEL **$$$**

(Map p50; ☑ 03-9668 1111; www.hotellindrum.com.au; 26 Flinders St; r from $250; P ❄ 🛜; 🚋 70, 75) One of the city's most attractive hotels, this

was once the snooker hall of the legendary and literally unbeatable Walter Lindrum. Expect rich tones, subtle lighting and tactile fabrics. Spring for a deluxe room and you'll snare either arch or bay windows and marvellous Melbourne views. And yes, there's a billiard table – one of Lindrum's originals, no less.

Crown Metropol
HOTEL **$$$**

(☑ 03-9292 6211; www.crownhotels.com.au; 8 Whiteman St, Crown Casino; r from $295; ❄ @ 🛜 🏊; 🚋 96, 109, 112) The most boutique of Crown's hotels, where guests have access to the most extraordinary infinity pool in Melbourne, with 270-degree views over the city to the Dandenongs in the distance. The beautifully appointed luxe twin rooms are the least expensive on offer and sleep four.

Hotel Windsor
HOTEL **$$$**

(Map p50; ☑ 03-9633 6000; www.thehotelwindsor.com.au; 111 Spring St; r from $175; ❄ @; 🚇 Parliament) Sparkling chandeliers and a grand piano in the lobby set the scene for this opulent, heritage-listed 1883 building that's one of Australia's most famous and self-consciously grand hotels. It was still awaiting a controversial $260 million redevelopment at time of research. Adding to its English quaintness is high tea service (p104) and the historic Cricketers Bar, decked out in cricketing memorabilia.

Grand Hyatt Melbourne
HOTEL **$$$**

(Map p50; ☑ 03-9657 1234; www.melbourne.grand.hyatt.com; 123 Collins St; r from $260; ❄ @ 🛜; 🚋 11, 31, 48, 109, 112) This famous Collins St five-star has more than 500 rooms, many with marble bathrooms, designated workspaces and grand floor-to-ceiling windows looking out to the city centre, Yarra River or the MCG.

Grand Hotel Melbourne
HOTEL **$$$**

(Map p50; ☑ 03-9611 4567; www.grandhotelmelbourne.com.au; 33 Spencer St; r $209-359; ❄ @ 🛜 🏊; 🚋 City Circle, 75, 96) Even the studios are grand in this Italianate building, which housed the Victorian Railways administration back in the days when rail ruled the world. Its self-catering rooms were originally offices, and have high ceilings with mezzanines. All vary in size and layout and are subtly furnished, some with balconies. It fills up rapidly during events at nearby Docklands Stadium.

Park Hyatt
HOTEL $$$

(✆ 03-9224 1234; www.melbourne.park.hyatt.com; 1 Parliament Sq; r from $355; ❄ ❂ ☎; ☐ 11, 31, 109, 112) Although it resembles a Californian shopping mall from the outside, the interior understands luxury to be about wood panelling, shiny surfaces and miles of marble. Rooms are elegantly subdued, and most come complete with supersized baths, clever layouts that maximise your chance of seeing natural light, and lovely treetop-level views. There's a lavish indoor pool, plus a great tennis court.

Sofitel
HOTEL $$$

(Map p50; ✆ 03-9653 0000; www.sofitel-melbourne.com; 25 Collins St; r from $280; P ❄ @ ❂ ☎; ☐ 11, 48, 109, 112, ☒ Parliament) Guestrooms at the Sofitel start on the 36th floor, so you're guaranteed views that will make you giddy. The rooms are high international style, opulent rather than minimal, and though the hotel entrance, with its superb IM Pei–designed ceiling, is relentlessly workaday, you'll soon be a world (or at least 36 floors) away.

Crown Promenade
HOTEL $$$

(✆ 03-9292 6688; www.crownpromenade.com.au; 8 Whiteman St, Crown Casino; r from $245; ❄ ❂ ☎; ☐ 55) This is Crown's 'diffusion line' hotel and linked to the mother ship (read: casino) by an air bridge. It offers large, modern and gently masculine rooms with luxurious bathrooms, big windows and flat-screen TVs.

Docklands Apartments Grand Mercure
APARTMENT $$$

(✆ 03-9641 7503; www.docklandsservicedapartments.com.au; 23 Saint Mangos Lane, New Quay, Docklands; apt from $245; P ❄ @ ❂; ☐ 35, 70) Spectacular floor-to-ceiling windows make the most of the water and city views. Apartments have balconies, full kitchens with stainless steel appliances and are furnished in a pleasing contemporary style. Free parking is a plus. There's a minimum two-night stay.

East Melbourne

East Melbourne takes you out of the action, yet is still walking distance from the city and offers ready access to the MCG.

Knightsbridge Apartments
APARTMENT $$

(Map p60; ✆ 03-9470 9100; www.knightsbridgeapartments.com.au; 101 George St; apt from $125; P ❄ @ ❂; ☐ 48, 75, ☒ Jolimont) Rejuvenated studio apartments over three floors each fea-

ture a well-equipped kitchen, plus furniture and accessories that suggest a higher price bracket. There's a chirpy welcome and the overall impression is one of 'nothing's too much trouble'. Opt for the upper floors for a better outlook and light (but note there's no lift). Call ahead to arrange parking.

Magnolia Court
HOTEL $$

(Map p60; ✆ 03-9419 4222; www.magnolia-court. com.au; 101 Powlett St; r incl breakfast from $110; ❄ ❂; ☐ 48, 75, ☒ Jolimont) Aim for the high-ceilinged apartments in this former girls' school to feel truly a part of this posh part of town. (How posh? Neighbours roared when the heritage building's fence got a fresh coat of paint.) Rooms range from standard to a fully self-contained Victorian cottage.

Hilton on the Park
HOTEL $$$

(Map p60; ✆ 03-9419 2000; www.hilton.com; 192 Wellington Pde; r from $260; ❄ @ ❂ ☎; ☐ 48, 75, ☒ Jolimont) The brown-brick Hilton building, on the verge of the gardens, is a monument to 1970s functionalism. Complete renovations of the rooms have brought in greys, wood-panelled features and simple, stylish artwork. The location is superb for those looking at an MCG-filled weekend. There's also the Hilton's riverside hotel at **South Wharf** (✆ 03-9027 2000; 2 Convention Centre Pl, South Wharf; s/d from $265/280; ❄ ❂; ☐ 96, 109, 112), on the cusp of the city centre, with dazzling views.

Fitzroy & Around

Vibrant Fitzroy hums with attractions day and night, and is a walk away from the city.

★ Nunnery
HOSTEL $

(Map p64; ✆ 03-9419 8637; www.nunnery.com.au; 116 Nicholson St, Fitzroy; dm/s/d incl breakfast from $32/90/120; @ ❂; ☐ 96) Built in 1888, the Nunnery oozes atmosphere, with sweeping staircases and many original features; the walls are dripping with religious works of art and ornate stained-glass windows. You'll be giving thanks for the big comfortable lounges and communal areas. Next door to the main building is the Nunnery Guesthouse, which has larger rooms in a private setting (from $130). It's perennially popular, so book ahead.

Home@The Mansion
HOSTEL $

(Map p64; ✆ 03-9663 4212; www.homemansion. com.au; 80 Victoria Pde, East Melbourne; dm $31-34, d $99; @ ❂; ☐ City Circle, 30, 96, ☒ Parliament) Located within a grand, heritage

Salvation Army building, this is one of Melbourne's few hostels with genuine character. It has 92 dorm beds and a couple of doubles, all of which are light and bright and have lovely high ceilings. There are two small TV areas with gaming console, a courtyard out the front and a sunny kitchen.

Travellers Trax HOSTEL $
(☑ 03-9417 1777; www.travellerstrax.com; 177 Johnston St, Collingwood; dm $18-27, d without bathroom $45; @ ᦔ; ⬚ 86, ⬚ Victoria Park) Great for those wanting to hang out in hipster-central Collingwood, this friendly, family-run hostel offers some of the best-value rooms in Melbourne. It's run like a tight ship, with a strict 'no dickhead' policy, but remains a social option up above the Barley Corn Hotel with theme nights, $4 pizzas, live music and free champagne offers on Thursday night. Also has free wi-fi.

Brooklyn Arts Hotel BOUTIQUE HOTEL $$
(Map p64; ☑ 03-9419 9328; www.brooklynarts hotel.com.au; 48-50 George St, Fitzroy; s/d incl breakfast $115/155; ᦔ; ⬚ 86) There are seven very different rooms in this character-filled and very unique hotel. Owner Maggie has put the call out for artistic people and they've responded by staying, so expect lively conversation around the continental breakfast. Rooms vary in size, but all are clean, quirky, colourful and beautifully decorated; one even houses a piano. Spacious upstairs rooms with high ceilings and street views are the pick. At time of research its future was uncertain, so call ahead first.

Tribeca Serviced Apartments APARTMENT $$
(Map p60; ☑ 03-9926 8200; www.tribecaserviced apartments.com.au; 166 Albert St, East Melbourne; 1-bedroom apt from $150; ☒ ᦔ ☒; ⬚ 24, 109) A handy inner-suburb location on the doorstep of Collingwood, East Melbourne and the city, Tribeca's apartments are generic, but get the job done as a comfy, modern base with pay TV, free wi-fi, heated pool and gym.

Quest Royal Gardens APARTMENT $$
(Map p64; ☑ 03-9419 9888; www.questroyalgar dens.com.au; 8 Royal Lane, Fitzroy; apt from $189; ☒ ᦔ ☒; ⬚ 86, 96) This rather dauntingly monumental complex of apartments is softened by hidden gardens, and has recently been updated with new furniture and full kitchens. Situated in a quiet nook of happening Fitzroy, it's so relaxed you'll feel like a local.

Tyrian Serviced Apartments APARTMENT $$$
(Map p64; ☑ 03-9415 1900; www.tyrian.com.au; 91 Johnston St, Fitzroy; r from $200; ℗ ☒ @ ᦔ; ⬚ 112) These spacious, self-contained modern apartments have a certain Fitzroy celeb appeal, which you'll feel from the moment you walk down the dimmed hallway to reception. Big couches, flat-screen TVs and balconies add to the appeal, and plenty of the neighbourhood restaurants and bars are right at your door.

Carlton & Around

Bev & Mick's Backpackers HOSTEL $
(McMahon's Hotel; ☑ 03-9328 2423; www.bevand micks.com.au; 575 Spencer St, West Melbourne; dm/d from $25/60; @ ᦔ; ⬚ North Melbourne) On the city's edge, this rough-around-the-edges backpackers is convenient for balancing sightseeing with the local life of North Melbourne. It's a solid choice, and being above a pub means it's always social, with the usual theme nights and a fantastic little beer garden. They have a few locations around town, but this is probably the best.

Downtowner on Lygon HOTEL $$
(Map p66; ☑ 03-9663 5555; www.downtowner.com. au; 66 Lygon St, Carlton; r from $174; ℗ ☒ @ ᦔ ☒; ⬚ 1, 8) The Downtowner is a surprising complex of different-sized rooms, including adjoining rooms perfect for families and couples travelling together. Ask for a light-bathed room if you can. It's perfectly placed between the city centre and Lygon St restaurants.

Vibe Hotel Carlton HOTEL $$
(☑ 03-9380 9222; www.vibehotels.com.au; 441 Royal Pde, Parkville; r from $135; @ ᦔ ☒; ⬚ 19) This early 1960s motel was once noted for its glamorous, high-Californian style; now it's more generic business hotel, but very convenient for parks and the zoo, and the city is a short tram ride away. It's a leap away from Brunswick's lively Sydney Rd.

South Yarra, Prahran & Windsor

South of the river, South Yarra has some tremendous boutique and upmarket places set in pretty, tree-lined residential streets.

Hotel Claremont GUESTHOUSE $
(Map p68; ☑ 03-9826 8000; www.hotelclaremont. com; 189 Toorak Rd, South Yarra; dm/d incl breakfast $49/89; @ ᦔ; ⬚ 8, 78, 79, ⬚ South Yarra) In a

large heritage building dating from 1868, the Claremont is good value, with comfortable rooms, high ceilings and shared bathrooms. Don't expect fancy decor: it's simply a clean and convenient cheapie.

Back Of Chapel
HOSTEL $

(Map p68; ☑03-9521 5338; www.backofchapel. com; 50 Green St, Windsor; dm incl breakfast $20-26, d $80; @; ᕫ78, 79) Literally 20 steps away from buzzing Chapel St, this clean backpackers in an old Victorian terrace has a prime location. It attracts a laid-back crew, popular with those on a working holiday. Reception closes at 5.30pm.

Punthill South Yarra Grand
APARTMENT $$

(Map p68; ☑1300 731 299; www.punthill.com.au; 7 Yarra St, South Yarra; studio/1-bedroom apt from $150/176; P✷❀❀; ᕫ8, 78, 79, ᕫSouth Yarra) It's the little things, like a blackboard and chalk in the kitchen for messages, and individually wrapped liquorice all-sorts by the bed, which make this a great choice. The bright rooms have laundry facilities and those with balconies come complete with their own (tin) dog on fake grass.

Albany
BOUTIQUE HOTEL $$

(☑03-9866 4485; www.thealbany.com.au; cnr Toorak Rd & Millswyn St, South Yarra; r $100-160; ✷@❀❀; ᕫ8) Proudly screaming fashion and rock 'n' roll, the Albany gives you the choice between fantastic refurbed rooms in an 1890s Victorian mansion, or cheap LA-style motel rooms, which are slightly shabby. There's a candy-pink rooftop pool and great location across from Fawkner Park, between the city and boutique South Yarra.

★Art Series (The Cullen)
BOUTIQUE HOTEL $$$

(Map p68; ☑03-9098 1555; www.artserieshotels. com.au/cullen; 164 Commercial Rd, Prahran; r from $209; ✷@❀; ᕫ72, 78, 79, ᕫPrahran) The edgiest of the Art Series hotels, this one's decked out by the late grunge-painter Adam Cullen, whose vibrant and often graphic works provide visions of Ned Kelly shooting you from the glam opaque room/bathroom dividers. Rooms are classic boutique – ultra comfy but not big on space.

You can borrow the keys for the hotel's Porsche Cayenne ($75 per day), smart car ($60 per day) or Kronan electric bike ($5 per hour). On the art theme, French street artist Blek le Rat contributed 17 of his signature rat stencils here, too.

Art Series (The Olsen)
BOUTIQUE HOTEL $$$

(Map p68; ☑03-9040 1222; www.artserieshotels. com.au/olsen; 637 Chapel St, South Yarra; r from $299; P✷❀❀; ᕫ8, 78, ᕫSouth Yarra) You never know who you'll bump into in the lift at this hotel honouring artist John Olsen; it's where international celebs are staying these days, and we think we know why. The staff are attentive. The modern glam foyer is beaut. The open-plan rooms are delightful. Oh, and the hotel's pool juts out over Chapel St.

Hatton
BOUTIQUE HOTEL $$$

(☑03-9868 4800; www.hatton.com.au; 65 Park St, South Yarra; r incl breakfast from $215; ✷@❀; ᕫ8) This Victorian terrace, built in 1902, is enjoying a luxurious reincarnation as a boutique hotel. Each room is uniquely styled: waxed floorboards and wooden mantels are matched with stainless steel, while antiques and contemporary local furniture are thrown effortlessly together. Its rooftop has great city views, and the location is smack-bang between the Royal Botanic Gardens and Fawkner Park.

St Kilda

St Kilda is a budget-traveller enclave but there are some stylish options a short walk from the beach, too.

Base
HOSTEL $

(Map p72; ☑03-8598 6200; www.stayatbase.com; 17 Carlisle St; dm $26-38, d $90-120; P✷@❀; ᕫ3a, 16, 79, 96) Well-run Base has streamlined dorms (each with en suite) and slick doubles. There's a floor set aside for female travellers complete with hair straighteners and champagne deals, and a bar and live-music nights to keep the good-time vibe happening.

Habitat HQ
HOSTEL $

(Map p72; ☑03-9537 3777; www.habitathq.com.au; 333 St Kilda Rd; dm/d incl breakfast from $28/89; P✷@❀; ᕫ3a, 67, 79) There's not much this clean, new hostel doesn't have. Check off open-plan communal spaces, a beer garden, free breakfast, a travel agent and a pool table, for starters. Follow Carlisle St from St Kilda to St Kilda Rd – it's on your left.

Home Travellers Motel
HOSTEL $

(Map p72; ☑03-9534 0300; www.hometravellersmotel.com.au; 32 Carlisle St; dm $25-35, d $85; @❀; ᕫ3a, 16, 79) Geared toward 'young folk', this hostel is in a former classic '70s seedy St Kilda motel. Despite its Carlisle St location remaining colourful, these days it's a professionally run place with good security and clean and simple doubles with en suites. There's a large kitchen and lounge and an outdoor barbecue.

Ritz
HOSTEL $

(Map p72; ☑ 03-9525 3501; www.ritzbackpackers.com; 169 Fitzroy St; dm/d incl breakfast from $24/68; ✳ @ ☎; ☐ 3a, 16, 79, 96, 112) Above an English pub renowned for hosting the riotously popular *Neighbours* nights, the Ritz has an excellent location, opposite an inner-city lake and park, and a five-minute walk from St Kilda's heart. It has movie nights and a free barbecue on Fridays.

Coffee Palace
HOSTEL $

(Map p72; ☑ 03-9534 5283; www.coffeepalacebackpackers.com.au; 24 Grey St; dm/d incl breakfast from $26/80; @ ☎; ☐ 3a, 16, 79, 96, 112) This rambling backpackers in a beautiful historic building has lots of rooms, lots of activities and lots of years behind it. It has a travel desk, communal kitchen, bar, pool tables, lounge and a TV room, plus a rooftop terrace. There are also private rooms with en suites ($135).

Easystay
MOTEL $

(Map p72; ☑ 03-9536 9700; www.easystay.com.au; 63 Fitzroy St; d from $80; ☐ 3a, 16, 79, 96, 112) A great choice for those who've outgrown hostels but want an affordable private room in the heart of the action. Its exterior suggests dodgy motel, but rooms are clean and comfortable within. They have serviced apartments around St Kilda, too.

Hotel Barkly
HOTEL $

(St Kilda Beach House; Map p72; ☑ 03-9525 3371; www.stkildabeachhouse.com; 109 Barkly St; dm/d incl breakfast from $29/99; ✳ @ ☎; ☐ 3, 67) Hotel Barkly is the party and you're on the guest list. Bright dorms are on the 1st floor; moody, though not luxurious, private rooms, some with balconies and views, are on the 2nd and 3rd floors. Below is a heaving pub, above is a happy, house-cranking bar. Noisy? You bet. But if you're up for it, there's definitely fun to be had.

Prince
HOTEL $$

(Map p72; ☑ 03-9536 1111; www.theprince.com.au; 2 Acland St; r incl breakfast from $185; P ✳ @ ☎ ✖; ☐ 3a, 16, 79, 96, 112) Chic Prince has a dramatic lobby while rooms feature natural materials and a pared-back aesthetic. On-site 'facilities' take in some of the neighbourhood

stars: **Aurora** (p75) day spa, **Circa** restaurant, bars and band room, and breakfast is provided by **Acland Street Cantina** downstairs. Be prepared for seepage of nightclub noise if you're staying the weekend. Free wifi is a bonus.

Hotel Tolarno
HOTEL $$

(Map p72; ☑ 03-9537 0200; www.hoteltolarno.com.au; 42 Fitzroy St; s/d/ste from $120/155/$230; ✳ @ ☎; ☐ 3a, 16, 79, 96, 112) Tolarno was once the site of Georges Mora's seminal gallery, Tolarno. The fine-dining restaurant (p100) downstairs bears the name of Georges' well-known artist wife Mirka, as well as her original paintings. A range of rooms are on offer and all come eclectically furnished with good beds, bright and bold original artworks and free wi-fi.

Those at the front of the building might get a bit noisy, but have balconies, floorboards and enormous windows overlooking Fitzroy St.

Hotel Urban
HOTEL $$

(Map p72; ☑ 03-8530 8888; www.hotelurban.com.au/melbourne; 35-37 Fitzroy St; r from $149; P ✳ @ ☎ ✖; ☐ 3a, 16, 79, 96, 112) Rooms at Hotel Urban use a lot of blonde wood and white to maximise space, and are simple, light and calming. All rooms are different: some have freestanding in-room spas while others are circular in shape. It also has a small gym.

Around St Kilda

Drop Bear Inn
HOSTEL $

(☑ 03-9690 2220; www.dropbearinn.com.au; 115 Cecil St, South Melbourne; dm/d from $26/50; @ ☎; ☐ 112) Named after Australia's legendary fearsome creature, this hostel has the advantage of being right opposite the South Melbourne Market, so it's great for fresh produce – particularly the bargains available at closing time. It's above a pub, so will suit those looking to party. Most rooms have good natural light and more charm than most hostels. Free wi-fi.

Art Series
(The Blackman)
BOUTIQUE HOTEL $$$

(☑ 1800 278 468, 03-9039 1444; www.artserieshotels.com.au/blackman; 452 St Kilda Rd, Melbourne; r from $220; ✳ ☎; ☐ 3, 5, 6, 8, 16, 64, 67, 72) While it may not have any original Charles Blackman paintings (though loads of prints and Blackman room decals), it does have superb views – aim for a corner suite for views of Albert Park Lake and the city skyline – and luxurious beds and blackout curtains for a sleep-in.

Eating

Central Melbourne

Restaurants are spread throughout the city, with many hidden down alleys, in arcades or off the 'Little' streets, particularly around Flinders Lane.

Spring Street Grocer   DELI, ICE CREAM $
(Map p50; 03-9639 0335; www.springstreetgrocer.com.au; 157 Spring St; 9am-9pm; Parliament) There are two new reasons to visit the top end of the city: gelati and cheese. Join the queue at Gelaterie Primavera for fresh gelati with a daily changing selection scooped from traditional *pozzetti* (metal tubs fitted in the counter benchtop). Or head down the winding staircase to reach the pungent 'cheese cave', an atmospheric maturation cheese cellar with an impressive selection of international cheeses.

Camy Shanghai Dumpling Restaurant   CHINESE $
(Map p50; 23-25 Tattersalls Lane; dumplings 10/20 pieces $5/7; 11.30am-3.30pm & 5-10pm Mon-Fri, noon-10pm Sat, noon-9pm Sun; 3, 5, 6, 16, 64, 67, 72) A Melbourne institution. There's nothing fancy here; pour your own plastic cup of tea from the urn, then try a variety of dumplings (steamed or fried) with some greens and BYO booze. Put up with the dismal service and you've found one of the last places in town where you can fill up for under $10.

Miss Katie's Crab Shack   AMERICAN $
(Map p66; 03-9329 9888; 238 Victoria St; dishes $8-25; 5-9pm Tue-Sun, from noon Sat; 19, 57, 59) Set up inside the Public Bar, Miss Katie's shack puts a twist on pub food through her Southern home-style cooking, using fresh produce from the Vic Market across the road and homemade hot sauces. Thank her grandma from Virginia for the signature fried chicken, and her mum from Maryland for the Chesapeake Bay–style blue swimmer crab dishes.

Misschu   SOUTHEAST ASIAN $
(Map p50; 03-9077 1097; www.misschu.com.au; 297 Exhibition St; from $7.50; 11am-10pm; City Circle, 24, 30) The self-proclaimed 'queen of rice paper rolls', Misschu continues to expand her empire of hole-in-the-wall eateries

serving cheap and tasty Laotian-Vietnamese hawker-style food and furnished in eclectic-retro design, with wooden-crate seating and 1950s retro blinds. Fill out your order form for roast-duck-and-banana-flower rice paper rolls, or beef and oxtail pho. It's in South Yarra (Map p68; 03-9041 5848; 276 Toorak Rd, South Yarra; 11am-11pm; 8, 78, 79), too.

Izakaya Chuji   JAPANESE $
(Map p50; 03-9663 8118; www.izakayachuji.com; 165 Lonsdale St; shared dishes from $7; noon-2.15pm & 6-10.15pm Mon-Fri, dinner Sat; 86, 96) One of Melbourne's most authentic izakayas, no-frills Chuji is popular for its well-priced and delicious traditional Japanese pub-style dishes, from *takoyaki* to *yakitori*. Its dark, red-lit sake bar Nihonshu (Map p50; www.nihonshu.com.au; 163 Lonsdale St; 6pm-midnight Mon-Sat) next door will instantly transport you to downtown Tokyo.

Don Don   JAPANESE $
(Map p50; 198 Little Lonsdale St; mains $6-8; 11am-9pm Mon-Sat, to 8.30pm Sun; 3, 5, 6, 16, 64, 67, 72, Melbourne Central) Due to its popularity, Don Don had to move digs to a bigger space, yet it still fills up fast. Grab a big bowl or bento box full of Japanese goodness and wolf it down indoors, or join the masses eating it on the State Library's lawns.

Bowery to Williamsburg   CAFE $
(Map p50; 16 Oliver Lane; bagels from $5; 7.30am-3pm Mon-Sat; 48, 70, 75) This basement deli is true to its NYC name, with central Melbourne's best bagels, served with schmear from traditional (caviar) to local (Vegemite). It also serves pastrami sandwiches with pretzel and pickle sides, and ice cream sandwiches for something sweet. The single-origin coffees come with a Hershey kiss.

Red Pepper   INDIAN $
(Map p50; 14-16 Bourke St; mains $10-13; 9am-3am; 86, 96, Parliament) It's mighty rare to get a decent meal for under $10, but it's possible here. The local Indian community knows it's good, and while leather-like seats feign 'upmarket' it's the fresh naan and dhal that people come here for. The mango lassis are delicious and you can rock up here any time until 3am.

Stalactites   GREEK $
(Map p50; 03-9663 3316; www.stalactites.com.au; 177-183 Lonsdale St; lamb souvlaki $10.50; 24hr; 3, 5, 6, 16, 64, 67, 72, Melbourne Central) What's not to love about a 24-hour

'souva' joint? Especially when it's been doing the best lamb souvlakis in Melbourne for more than 40 years. It's located in the heart of the Greek precinct of Melbourne, and is an absolute institution for a late-night feed.

★**Movida**   SPANISH $$
(Map p50; ☑03-9663 3038; www.movida.com.au; 1 Hosier Lane; tapas $4-6, raciones $8-28; ☺noon-late; ☒70, 75, ☒Flinders St) MoVida sits in a cobbled laneway emblazoned with one of the world's densest collections of street art – it doesn't get much more Melbourne than this. Line up along the bar, cluster around little window tables or, if you've booked, take a table in the dining area for fantastic Spanish tapas and *raciones*.

MoVida Next Door – yes, right next door – is the perfect place for a pre-show beer and tapas. Also brought to you by MoVida is **MoVida Aqui** (Map p50; ☑03-9663 3038; www.movida.com.au; 1st fl, 500 Bourke St; ☺noon-late Mon-Fri, 6pm-late Sat; ☒86, 96), a huge, open space with similar tapas menu and chargrilled cooking, while next door is its Mexican offering of **Paco's Tacos** (Map p50; ☑03-9663 3038; www.pacos tacos.com.au; 1st fl, 500 Bourke St; ☺noon-11pm; ☒86, 96). MoVida has also recently opened **Bar Pulpo** (www.movida.com.au/airport; Terminal 2 (International), Melbourne Airport; ☺8am-12.30am) at Melbourne Airport for pre-flight tapas and drinks.

Mamasita   MEXICAN $$
(Map p50; ☑03-9650 3821; www.mamasita.com. au; 1/11 Collins St; tacos from $5, shared plates from $19; ☺noon-late Mon-Sat, from 1pm Sun; ☒City Circle, 11, 31, 48, 112) The restaurant responsible for kicking off Melbourne's obsession with authentic Mexican street food, Mamasita is still one of the very best – as evidenced by the perpetual queues to get into the place. The chargrilled corn sprinkled with cheese and chipotle mayo is a legendary starter, and there's a fantastic range of corn-tortilla tacos and 180 types of tequila. No reservations, so prepare to wait.

Cumulus Inc   MODERN AUSTRALIAN $$
(Map p50; www.cumulusinc.com.au; 45 Flinders Lane; mains $21-38; ☺7am-11pm Mon-Fri, 8am-11pm Sat & Sun; ☒City Circle, 48) One of Melbourne's best for any meal; it gives you that wonderful Andrew McConnell style along with reasonable prices. The focus is on beautiful produce and simple but artful cooking: from breakfasts of sardines and smoked tomato on toast at the marble bar to suppers of freshly shucked *clair de lune* oysters tucked away on the leather banquettes. No reservations, so queues are highly probable.

It has recently opened the wine bar **Cumulus Up** upstairs; its bar menu is matched with changing regional wines.

Cookie   THAI, BAR $$
(Map p50; ☑03-9663 7660; www.cookie.net.au; 1st fl, 252 Swanston St, Curtin House; mains from $17.50; ☺noon-late; ☒3, 5, 6, 16, 64, 67, 72) Part Thai restaurant, part swanky bar, Cookie does both exceptionally well. Its all-Thai kitchen fires up authentic flavours with fusion twists to create some of the best Thai food in town. The bar is unbelievably well stocked with fine whiskies, wines and craft beers, and knows how to make a serious cocktail.

Chin Chin   ASIAN $$
(Map p50; ☑03-8663 2000; www.chinchinrestaurant.com.au; 125 Flinders Lane; mains $19-33; ☺11am-late; ☒City Circle, 70, 75) Yet another great option on Flinders Lane, Chin Chin does delicious Southeast Asian hawker-style food designed as shared plates. It's inside a busied-up shell of an old building with a real New York feel, and while there are no bookings, **Go Go Bar** downstairs will have you till there's space.

Bomba   SPANISH, TAPAS $$
(Map p50; ☑03-9077 0451; http://bombabar.com. au; 103 Lonsdale St; tapas $3.50-8, dishes $15-32; ☺noon-3pm Mon-Fri, 5pm-late daily; ☒Parliament) Reminiscent of a buzzing Spanish bodega, Bomba offers up tasty authentic tapas, *raciones* for the hungrier and Catalan stew and paellas. The wine list is predominantly Spanish, and the vermouth flows freely, as does the cold Estrella – all perfect for enjoying on the rooftop terrace to the backdrop of the St Patrick's Cathedral spire.

Bar Lourinhã   TAPAS $$
(Map p50; ☑03-9663 7890; www.barlourinha.com. au; 37 Little Collins St; tapas $4-24; ☺noon-11pm Mon-Thu, noon-1am Fri, 4pm-1am Sat; ☒Parliament) Matt McConnell's wonderful northern Spanish–Portuguese specialities have the swagger and honesty of an Iberian shepherd, but with a cluey, metropolitan touch. Start with the zingy kingfish pancetta and finish with the hearty house-made chorizo or baked *morcilla* (blood sausage). There's an intriguing wine list sourced from the region, too. Bookings only for lunch.

Waiters Restaurant ITALIAN **$$**
(Map p50; ☎03-9650 1508; 1st fl, 20 Meyers Pl; mains $15-25; ⊗noon-2.30pm Mon-Fri & 6pm-late Mon-Sat; ⧉Parliament) Head down a laneway and up some stairs to step into this restaurant – and into another era. Opened in 1947, it still bears 1950s drapes, wood panelling and Laminex tables. It was once only for Italian and Spanish waiters to unwind after work over a game of *scopa* (a card game); now everyone is welcome for its delicious, hearty plates of red-sauce pasta.

HuTong Dumpling Bar CHINESE **$$**
(Map p50; www.hutong.com.au; 14-16 Market Lane; mains $15-22; ⊗11.30am-3pm & 5.30-10.30pm; ⧉86, 96) HuTong's windows face out on the famed Flower Drum, and its reputation for divine *xiao long bao* (soupy dumplings) means getting a lunchtime seat anywhere in this three-level building isn't easy. Downstairs, watch chefs make the delicate dumplings, then hope they don't watch you make a mess eating them. There's also a branch in **Prahran** (Map p68; www.hutong.com.au; 162 Commercial Rd; ⧉72, 78, 79).

Pellegrini's Espresso Bar ITALIAN, CAFE **$$**
(Map p50; ☎03-9662 1885; 66 Bourke St; mains $16-18; ⊗8am-11.30pm Mon-Sat, noon-8pm Sun; ⧉Parliament) The iconic Italian equivalent of a classic '50s diner, Pellegrini's has remained genuinely unchanged for decades. Pick and mix from the variety of homemade pastas and sauces; from the table out the back you can watch it all being thrown together from enormous, ever-simmering pots. In summer, finish with a glass of watermelon granita.

Supper Inn CHINESE **$$**
(Map p50; ☎03-9663 4759; 15 Celestial Ave; mains $15-30; ⊗5.30pm-2.15am; ⧉1, 3, 5, 6, 8, 16, 22, 64, 67, 72) No one minds queuing on the stairs to wait for a high-turnover table in the unglamorous and dated upstairs dining room – the reward is the top-quality Cantonese food. Open until 2am, Supper Inn is a classic late-night eat.

Grossi Florentino Grill ITALIAN **$$**
(Map p50; ☎03-9662 1811; www.grossiflorentino.com; 80 Bourke St; mains $18-55; ⊗lunch & dinner Mon-Fri, dinner Sat; ⧉86, 96) Taken over by famed Melbourne chef Guy Grossi, Florentino's has long attracted rich faces taking lunchtime breaks with its authentic regional Italian menu with metropolitan flair and great produce. Next door is the more affordable **Cellar Bar**, a great place to have a quick bowl of pasta and a glass of pinot grigio, as well as breakfast. Service is snappy and professional.

If you're into grand statements (with mains hitting the $55 mark), upstairs is an opulent fine-dining stalwart.

Hardware Societe CAFE **$$**
(Map p50; 120 Hardware St; mains $13-20; ⊗7.30am-2.30pm Mon-Fri, 8.30am-2pm Sat & Sun; ⧉19, 57, 59) Expect to queue on weekends at this heaving little laneway cafe. Sit outdoors under the awnings or in the cute interior for breakfasts of baked eggs and chorizo, homemade pastries and fried brioche.

Gazi GREEK **$$**
(Map p50; ☎03-9207 7444; www.gazirestaurant.com.au; 2 Exhibition St; shared plates from $10, mains $23; ⊗11.30am-11pm; ⧉48, 70, 75) The lastest offering from George Calombaris of *MasterChef* fame, this rebadged side project to the fancier Press Club (next door) is set in a cavernous industrial space with a menu inspired by Greek street food. Select from authentic shared starters and gourmet mini souvlakis filled with prawn or duck to wood-fire-spit mains. Calombaris also owns the East Brunswick eatery **Hellenic Republic** (☎03-9381 1222; www.hellenicrepublic.com.au; 434 Lygon St, East Brunswick; mains $16-30; ⊗noon-4pm Fri, 11am-4pm Sat & Sun, 5.30pm-late Mon-Sun; ☎; ⧉1, 8).

Orient East MALAYSIAN **$$**
(www.orienteast.com.au; 348 St Kilda Rd; mains from $17; ⊗6.30am-9pm Mon-Fri, 7am-2pm & 5-9pm Sat & Sun; ⧉3, 5, 6, 16, 64, 67, 72) Convenient lunch spot for sightseers visiting the Shrine and botanic gardens, Orient East does British-colonial Malay cuisine in a get-up reminiscent of a foreign correspondent cafe circa the 1960s. It serves fantastic hawker-style food, including spicy soft-shell crab buns and yummy laksas.

Trunk AMERICAN, ITALIAN **$$**
(The Diner; Map p50; ☎03-9663 7994; www.trunktown.com.au; 275 Exhibition St; mains $18-26; ⊗7.30am-10pm Mon-Fri, from 8am Sat & Sun; ⧉City Circle, 24, 30) Trunk turns into a prime city-centre office-worker watering hole on Friday nights, but don't let Bryan from the marketing department put you off. The Italian restaurant's main building is more than a hundred years old and was once a synagogue. Next door, Trunk's diner has a busy

yet relaxed vibe serving dude food such as hot dogs, burgers and ribs.

Meatball & Wine Bar
AMERICAN, ITALIAN **$$**

(Map p50; www.meatballandwinebar.com.au; 135 Flinders Lane; meatballs $18; ⊘8am-1am Mon-Fri, from 11am weekends; ⛉City Circle, 70, 75) Banking on Melbourne's current obsession with American cuisine, this dark, smartly fitted Flinders Lane restaurant serves up the ol' American-Italian classic meatball: from your traditional beef variety to less-conventional fish or even vegetarian 'meat' balls. Choose from a selection of sauces and sides, anything from homemade pasta to creamy polenta. It has opened in **Richmond** (Map p60; 105 Swan St, Richmond; ⛉70), too.

Mesa Verde
MEXICAN, BAR **$$**

(Map p50; ☑03-9654 4417; www.mesaverde.net. au; Level 6, 252 Swanston St, Curtin House; tacos from $6; ⊘5pm-late; ⛉3, 5, 6, 16, 64, 67, 72) The latest addition to the wonderful Curtin House complex, Mesa Verde does great Mexican food to a backdrop of Sergio Leone screenings. As well as street-food dishes, there's a selection of 200 tequilas and 40 mezcals, and an exotic selection of salts for margaritas (including black truffle). Come for Taco Tuesday specials.

Hopetoun Tea Rooms
TEAROOM **$$**

(Map p50; ☑03-9650 2777; www.hopetountearooms.com.au; 282 Collins St; dishes $13-21; ⊘8am-5pm) Since 1892, patrons have been nibbling pinwheel sandwiches here, taking tea (with pinkies raised) and delicately polishing off a lamington. Hopetoun's venerable status has queues almost stretching out the entrance of Block Arcade. Salivate over the window display while you wait.

★ Vue de Monde
MODERN AUSTRALIAN **$$$**

(Map p50; ☑03-9691 3888; www.vuedemonde. com.au; Rialto, 525 Collins St; degustation $200-250; ⊘reservations from noon-2pm Tue-Fri & Sun, 6-9.15pm Mon-Sat; ⛉11, 31, 48, 109, 112, ⓡSouthern Cross) Sitting pretty in the old 'observation deck' of the Rialto building, Melbourne's favoured spot for occasion dining has views to match its name. Visionary chef Shannon Bennett has moved away from its classic French style to a subtle Modern Australian theme that runs through everything from the decor to the menu.

Stuffy tablecloths are gone and natural Australian elements are in – vases of banksia, handmade kangaroo-hide tables and cutlery holders carved from Tasmanian stone. Booking ahead is essential.

Remaining at the old barrister's chambers is the cheaper **Bistro Vue** (Map p50; ☑03-9691 3838; 430 Little Collins St; ⊘11am-late Mon-Sat; ⛉86, 96) and **Cafe Vue** (Map p50; ☑03-9691 3899; 430 Little Collins St; ⊘7am-4pm Mon-Fri; ⛉86, 96). There are also Cafe Vue branches at 401 St Kilda Rd and Melbourne Airport.

Flower Drum
CHINESE **$$$**

(Map p50; ☑03-9662 3655; www.flower-drum. com; 17 Market Lane; mains $35-55; ⊘noon-3pm & 6-11pm Mon-Sat, 6-10.30pm Sun; ☎; ⛉86, 96) The Flower Drum continues to be Melbourne's most celebrated Chinese restaurant. The finest, freshest produce prepared with absolute attention to detail keeps this Chinatown institution booked out for weeks in advance. The sumptuous, but ostensibly simple, Cantonese food (from a menu that changes daily) is delivered with the slick service you'd expect in such elegant surrounds.

Coda
MODERN AUSTRALIAN **$$$**

(Map p50; ☑03-9650 3155; www.codarestaurant. com.au; basement, 141 Flinders Lane; mains $36-38; ⊘noon-3pm & 6pm-late; ⛉11, 31, 48, 86, 112) Coda has a wonderful 'basement' ambience, with exposed lightbulbs and industrial factory-style windows. Its innovative dishes make up an eclectic menu of Asian, French and Modern Australian influences. It's a little hit-and-miss; some taste plates scream 'yes!', such as crispy prawn and tapioca betel leaf, but others don't quite hit those highs.

Longrain
THAI **$$$**

(Map p50; ☑03-9671 3151; www.longrain.com; 44 Little Bourke St; mains $31-40; ⊘noon-3pm Fri & dinner 6pm-late Mon-Thu, from 5.30pm Fri-Sun; ⓡParliament) Expect to wait up to two hours (sip a drink and relax, they suggest) before sampling Longrain's fusion-style Thai. The communal tables don't exactly work for a romantic date but they're great for checking out everyone else's meals. Dishes are designed to be shared and feed two; try the yellow curry with roasted pumpkin, fennel and pickled mustard greens; and the amazing seafood dishes.

Gingerboy
ASIAN **$$$**

(Map p50; ☑03-9662 4200; www.gingerboy. com.au; 27-29 Crossley St; shared dishes $32-50; ⊘noon-2.30pm & 5.30-10.30pm Mon-Fri, 5.30-10.30pm Sat; ⛉86, 96) Brave the aggressively trendy surrounds and weekend party scene, as talented Teague Ezard does a fine turn in flash hawker cooking. Flavours pop in dishes such as scallops with green chilli jam or coconut kingfish with peanut and tamarind dressing. There are two dinner sittings; bookings are required. Gingerboy upstairs has a long, long cocktail bar.

No 35 at Sofitel MODERN AUSTRALIAN **$$$**
(Map p50; www.no35.com.au; Level 35, Sofitel, 25 Collins St; mains from $31; ⊙lunch & dinner; 🚊11, 48, 109, 112, 🚇Parliament) Melbourne's equivalent of the *Lost in Translation* bar in Tokyo. The views of the city skyline are superb through this restaurant-bar's floor-to-ceiling windows (memorable views from its toilets, too). It's a great choice for a special occasion, and you can expect a menu of rich, delicious dishes, such as roasted sea trout and parmesan gnocchi with crab-caviar butter sauce and spinach cream.

Southbank, South Wharf & Docklands

Restaurants here come with views, though quality ranges from decent to those simply after the tourist dollar. South Wharf is a recent development still finding its feet but certainly worth a wander for some interesting dining options right on the river's edge.

Bangpop THAI **$$**
(📞03-9245 9800; www.bangpop.com.au; 35 South Wharf Promenade; mains $16-30; ⊙noon-10.30pm Mon-Thu, to 11pm Fri & Sat, to 10.30pm Sun; 🚊City Circle, 70) Sitting on the waterfront at South Wharf, Bangpop breathes a bit of colour and vibrancy into the area with its bar made from Lego, suspended bicycles hanging

from the ceiling, and dangling neon bulbs. Tasty Thai hawker-style dishes are served at communal cafe tables and accompanied by smoked margaritas.

Tutto Bene ITALIAN **$$**
(Map p50; 📞03-9696 3334; www.tuttobene.com. au; Midlevel, Southgate; mains $25-38; ⊙noon-3pm & 6-10pm; 🚇Flinders St) Across the Yarra in Southbank is this Italian restaurant that's especially known for its risotto dishes, which range from a simple Venetian *risi e bisi* (rice and peas) to some fabulously luxe options involving truffles or roast quail or aged balsamic. Don't miss its fine house-made gelato.

Bopha Devi CAMBODIAN **$$**
(📞03-9600 1887; www.bophadevi.com; 27 Rakaia Way, Docklands; mains $18-27; ⊙lunch & dinner; 🚊City Circle, 70, 86) The modern Cambodian food here is a delightful mix of novel and familiar Southeast Asian flavours and textures. Herb-strewn salads, noodles and soups manage to be both fresh and filling.

**Rockpool
Bar & Grill** STEAKHOUSE, MODERN AUSTRALIAN **$$$**
(Map p50; 📞03-8648 1900; www.rockpoolmelbourne.com; Crown Entertainment Complex; mains $20-140; ⊙lunch Sun-Fri, dinner daily; 🚊55, 🚇Flinders St) The Melbourne outpost of Neil Perry's empire offers his signature seafood raw bar, but it's really all about beef, from grass-fed to full-blood wagyu. This darkly masculine space is simple and stylish, as is the menu. The bar offers the same level of food service with the added bonus of a rather spectacular drinks menu.

JEWELS IN THE CROWN

There are several top-flight dining options in the Crown Casino complex. Well-known stayers include Neil Perry's seafood and steak star, Rockpool Bar & Grill, and global Japanese empire **Nobu** (Map p50; 📞03-9292 5777; www.noburestaurants.com; Crown Entertainment Complex; dishes $20-120; ⊙noon-2.30pm & 6-10.30pm; 🚊55, 🚇Flinders St). Other good options include:

Atlantic (📞03-9698 8888; www.theatlantic.com.au; The Riverside at Crown; dishes $18-105; ⊙noon-3pm & 6-11pm; 🚊96, 109, 112) Throw down some oysters at the oyster bar before indulging in a seafood platter.

Spice Temple (📞03-8679 1888; www.spicetemplemelbourne.com; Crown Entertainment Complex; mains $12-45; ⊙yum cha noon-3pm Thu-Sun, dinner 6pm-late daily; 🚊96, 109, 112) Another Neil Perry hit: fill up on delicious à la carte yum cha.

Bistro Guillaume (Map p50; 📞03-9292 4751; www.bistroguillaume.com.au; Crown Entertainment Complex; mains $25-120; ⊙noon-late Mon-Fri, noon-3pm & 6pm-late Sat; 🚊55, 🚇Flinders St) French bistro food with fine-dining flair.

Richmond

Richmond's main draw is restaurant-packed Victoria St, with its long strip of cheap Vietnamese and Asian eateries.

Minh Minh   VIETNAMESE, LAOTIAN $
(Map p60; ☑ 03-9427 7891; 94 Victoria St; mains $10-18; ☺ 4-10pm Tue, 11.30am-10.30pm Wed, Thu & Sun, to 11pm Fri & Sat; ☒ 109, ☒ North Richmond) Minh Minh specialises in fiery Laotian dishes – the herby green-and-red-chilli beef salad is a favourite – but does all the Vietnamese staples, too.

Thy Thy 1   VIETNAMESE $
(Map p60; ☑ 03-9429 1104; 1st fl, 142 Victoria St; mains from $9; ☺ 9am-10pm; ☒ 109, ☒ North Richmond) Head upstairs to this Victoria St original (unchanged since 1987) for cheap and delicious Vietnamese. No corkage for BYO booze.

Demitri's Feast   GREEK $
(Map p60; www.demitrisfeast.com.au; 141 Swan St mains $14-16; ☺ 7.30am-4.30pm Tue-Fri, from 8am Sat & Sun; ☒ 70, ☒ East Richmond) Warning: don't even attempt to get a seat here on a weekend; aim for a quiet weekday, when you'll have time and space to fully immerse yourself in lunches such as calamari salad with ouzo aioli.

Meatmother   AMERICAN $$
(Map p60; www.meatmother.com.au; 167 Swan St; lunch trays $14, dinner trays $19-23; ☺ 6pm-late Tue, noon-3pm & 6pm-late Wed-Sun; ☒ 70, 78, 79) Vegetarians beware; this eatery doubles as a shrine to the slaughterhouse, evident in the meat cleavers hanging on the walls and blood-dripping animal skeleton prints. All meat is smoked over oak, from the eight-hour smoked pork sandwich to the beef brisket. Messy up your chops with a dinner meat tray and a side of chipotle slaw and raise your glass of American whiskey to Meatmother.

Richmond Hill Cafe & Larder   CAFE $$
(Map p60; ☑ 03-9421 2808; www.rhcl.com.au; 48-50 Bridge Rd; lunch $12-26; ☺ 8.30am-4.30pm; ☒ 75, ☒ West Richmond) Once the domain of well-known cook Stephanie Alexander, it still boasts its lovely cheese room and simple, comforting foods such as cheesy toast. There are also breakfast cocktails for the brave.

Baby   PIZZA $$
(Map p68; ☑ 03-9421 4599; www.babypizza.com. au; 631-633 Church St; mains $17; ☺ 7am-11pm; ☒ 70, 78, ☒ East Richmond) Ignore the porno light feature (you won't notice it if you dine by day) and get into the food and vibe: delicious pizza, the occasional Aussie TV star and many, many trendy folk. It's busy, bold and run by restaurant king Christopher Lucas (Chin Chin), so it's quite brilliant. Even for a pizza joint.

MEALS ON WHEELS: MELBOURNE'S FOOD TRUCKS

Melbourne has long had an association with food vans; a game of suburban footy isn't complete without someone dishing out hot jam donuts, hot meat pies and hot chips to freezing fans over a truck counter – and what would a trip to the beach be without an ice-cream van playing its tune? But getting quality food from a van is a different matter. Taking the cue from LA's food-truck revolution, fabulous food trucks have also begun plying the streets of Melbourne in recent years. Each day the trucks post to let their Twitter and Facebook followers know where they'll be, and hungry folk dutifully respond by turning up street-side for a meal. Favourite Melbourne food trucks (and their Twitter handles) to chase down include:

Cornutopia Mexican street food (@Cornutopia)

Gumbo Kitchen New Orleans–style po' boys (@GumboKitchen)

Beatbox Kitchen Gourmet burgers and fries (@BeatboxKitchen)

Mr Burger As the name suggests (@MrBurgerTruck)

Smokin' Barry's Smoky barbecue meats (@SmokinBarrys)

GrumbleTumms Aussie bush tucker: croc or emu pies and roo burgers (@GrumbleTumms)

Also check out www.wherethetruck.at for more food trucks around town.

Fitzroy & Around

Smith St has developed an astounding amount of great new eateries in the last couple of years, while Gertrude St also packs in some winning options. Brunswick St has a few long-established favourites but the rest is a little hit-and-miss. Further along you'll hit Northcote's High St strip, which is turning into a great dining area.

Gelato Messina
ICE CREAM **$**

(Map p64; www.gelatomessina.com; 237 Smith St, Fitzroy; 1 scoop $4; ⊙noon-11pm Sun-Thu, to 11.30pm Fri & Sat; 📵86) Newly opened Messina is hyped as Melbourne's best ice-creamery. Its popularity is evident in the long queues of hipsters waiting to wrap their smackers around smooth gelato like coconut and lychee, salted caramel and white chocolate, or pear and spiced rhubarb.

Huxtaburger
BURGERS **$**

(Map p64; ☑03-9417 6328; www.huxtaburger.com. au; 106 Smith St, Collingwood; burgers from $8.50; ⊙11.30am-10pm Sun-Thu, to 11pm Fri & Sat; 📵86) This American-style burger joint is a hipster magnet for its crinkle-cut chips in old-school containers, tasty burgers (veg options available) on glazed brioche buns, and bottled craft beers. Cash only. Other branches in the City (Map p50; Fulham Pl, off Flinders Lane; ⊙11.30am-10pm Mon-Sat; 📵Flinders St) and Prahran (Map p68; 201-209 High St, Prahran; ⊙11.30am-10pm Sun-Thu, to 11pm Fri & Sat; 📵6, 78, 79).

Po' Boy Quarter
AMERICAN **$**

(Map p64; 295 Smith St, Fitzroy; rolls $10-13; ⊙11.30am-1am; 📵86) The boys behind the Gumbo Kitchen food truck have parked permanently on Smith St with this smart canteen-style eatery. Wolf down one of their rolls of pulled pork, shrimp with Louisiana hot sauce, or fried green tomatoes with Cajun slaw while people-watching out front.

Babka Bakery Cafe
BAKERY, CAFE **$**

(Map p64; 358 Brunswick St, Fitzroy; mains $10-16; ⊙7am-7pm Tue-Sun; 📵112) From borsch to dumplings, Russian flavours infuse the lovingly prepared breakfast and lunch dishes at Babka. It also has its own bakery, and the heady aroma of cinnamon and freshly baked sourdough bread, pies and cake makes even just a coffee worth queuing for. Otherwise go for the $8 champagne-cocktail Beryl Sparkles, with vodka and fresh raspberries.

Jimmy Grants
GREEK **$**

(Map p64; www.jimmygrants.com.au; 113 St David St, Fitzroy; souvlakis from $9; ⊙11am-10pm; 📵86) Set up by celebrity chef George Calombaris, this is not your ordinary souva joint – these are gourmet souvlakis, which you don't need to be plastered at 3am to enjoy. Options may include a pita stuffed with lamb, mustard aioli and chips, or honey prawn and herbs.

Gringo Vibes
MEXICAN **$**

(☑03-9044 8568; www.gringovibes.com.au; 489 High St, Northcote; 2 tacos from $11; ⊙noon-10pm Tue-Sun; 📵86, 📵Croxton) Ignore the name. Gringo Vibes does authentic Mexican, with its fantastic soft-shell corn tortillas, fine tequilas and margarita concoctions. There's a reggae playlist and courtyard seating out the back.

Brunswick Street Alimentari
CAFE **$**

(Map p64; ☑03-9416 2001; www.alimentari.com. au; 251 Brunswick St, Fitzroy; dishes $6-20; ⊙8am-6pm; 📵112) Part deli, part fuss-free cafe, popular corner local Alimentari stocks artisan bread, smallgoods and cheeses. There's a range of panini, sandwiches and wraps, and comforting staples such as meatballs with bread.

Rosamond
CAFE **$**

(Map p64; ☑03-9419 2270; 191 Smith St, Fitzroy; dishes $5-12; ⊙7.30am-3.15pm Mon-Fri, from 9am Sat; 📵86) Just off Smith St, Rosamond's tiny interior is a warm haven for the local freelance creative crew who like their daily rations simple but well considered. And that they are: free-range eggs only come scrambled, but with first-rate toast and fresh sides, and there's soup, toasties, baguettes, salads and cupcakes.

UAE
MIDDLE EASTERN **$$**

(United Arab Eatery; ☑03-9489 0703; 487 High St, Northcote; plates from $12; ⊙5.30-9.30pm Tue-Sat; 📵86, 📵Croxton) Run by a French-trained chef who did her apprenticeship under Stephanie Alexander, cafe-style UAE has delicious Middle Eastern shared plates served with an easy-going attitude. It's big on local produce and everything is homemade, from dips to its cinnamon ice cream. Also has a good selection of Lebanese and Turkish beers.

Añada
TAPAS **$$**

(Map p64; ☑03-9415 6101; www.anada.com.au; 197 Gertrude St, Fitzroy; tapas from $3.50, raciones $11-23; ⊙5pm-late Mon-Fri, from noon Sat & Sun;

(⌂86) Dishes in this lovely little restaurant are alive with hearty Spanish and Muslim-Mediterranean flavours. It has a great tapas selection, or go the nine-course banquet (chef's choice) for $50.

Hammer & Tong 412
CAFE **$$**

(Map p64; ☑03-9041 6033; www.hammerandtong.com.au; rear, 412 Brunswick St, Fitzroy; meals from $16; ⊙7am-late Tue-Sat, 8am-5pm Sun; ⌂112) Tucked down a Brunswick St side-street, Hammer & Tong's forbidding facade may have you second-guessing what kind of place this is, but within is a popular cafe set up by owners of impecable pedigree (courtesy of Vue du Monde and Jacques Reymond). Expect yabby-tail omelettes for breakfast and soft-shell-crab burgers for lunch, and elaborate mains. There's excellent coffee here, too.

Ici
CAFE **$$**

(Map p64; 359 Napier St, Fitzroy; sandwiches $12, breakfasts $12-18; ⊙7am-4pm Mon-Fri, 7.30am-4pm Sat, 8am-4pm Sun; ⌂86, 112) Meaning 'here' in French, Ici is another reason to veer off Brunswick St for this gritty Parisian-meets-backstreet-Fitzroy flavour. It's popular with locals for its strong coffee, reuben sandwiches and Vegemite brioche slices with soft-boiled eggs.

Charcoal Lane
MODERN AUSTRALIAN **$$**

(Map p64; ☑03-9418 3400; www.charcoallane.com.au; 136 Gertrude St, Fitzroy; mains $28-35; ⊙noon-3pm & 6-9pm Tue-Sat; ⌂86) ✐ Housed in an old bluestone former bank, this training restaurant for Indigenous and disadvantaged young people is one of the best places to try native flora and fauna; menu items may include kangaroo burger with bush-tomato chutney and wallaby tartare. Weekend bookings advised. It also holds cooking masterclasses using native ingredients; check the website for details.

Moroccan Soup Bar
MOROCCAN, VEGETARIAN **$$**

(☑03-9482 4240; www.moroccansoupbar.com.au; 183 St Georges Rd, North Fitzroy; banquet per person $20; ⊙6-10pm Tue-Sun; ✐; ⌂112) Prepare to queue before being seated by stalwart Hana, who will then go through the vegetarian menu verbally while you sip on mint tea (it's an alcohol-free zone). Best bet is the banquet, which, for three courses, is tremendous value. The sublime chickpea bake is a favourite, driving locals to queue with their own pots and containers for takeaway.

Vegie Bar
VEGETARIAN **$$**

(Map p64; ☑03-9417 6935; www.vegiebar.com.au; 380 Brunswick St, Fitzroy; mains $14-16; ⊙11am-10.30pm Mon-Fri, from 9am Sat & Sun; ✐; ⌂112) Its menu of delicious thin-crust pizzas, tasty curries and seasonal broths is perfectly suited to the cavernous warehouse decor with walls covered in band posters. It also has a fascinating selection of raw food dishes, and plenty of vegan choices. Its fresh juices are popular, as are its yummy, cheap and original breakfasts.

Marios
CAFE **$$**

(Map p64; www.marioscafe.com.au; 303 Brunswick St, Fitzroy; mains $17-30; ⊙7am-10.30pm Mon-Sat, 8am-10.30pm Sun; ⌂112) Mooching at Marios is part of the Melbourne 101 curriculum. Breakfasts are big and served all day, the service is swift, dishes are simple classic Italian and the coffee is old-school strong.

The Horn
AFRICAN **$$**

(Map p64; ☑03-9417 4670; www.thehorncafe.com.au; 20 Johnston St, Collingwood; mains from $17; ⊙6pm-late Wed-Sat, 3pm-10pm Sun; ⌂86) Straight outta Addis Ababa, the flavours and feel of this Ethiopian restaurant are as authentic as its homemade injera bread (prepared fresh daily). Tear it into your meal using your fingers and wash it down with Ethiopian beer. There's an attractive beer garden and jazz on Thursday evenings. Call to prearrange coffee ceremonies.

Robert Burns Hotel
SPANISH **$$**

(Map p64; www.robertburnshotel.com.au; 376 Smith St, Collingwood; mains from $20; ⊙Mon & Tue 5pm-late, Wed-Sun noon-late; ⌂86) Receiving a slick makeover meant the loss of its appealing dingy charm, but thankfully the authenticity of the Spanish flavours remain: its seafood paella is still one of Melbourne's best. The $12 lunch menu is great value.

Masak Masak
MALAYSIAN **$$**

(Map p64; 230 Smith St, Collingwood; dishes $8-21; ⊙11.30am-2.30pm & 6-10pm; ⌂86) Masak Masak is just one of many new eateries lining Smith St, but it stands out for its Malaysian hawker street food with a twist, along with its bold '80s-looking spray-art walls. The menu is divided into bites, snacks and mains with anything from sticky anchovies and buffalo wings with onion sambal to jellyfish or grilled stingray.

Aux Batifolles FRENCH $$

(📞03-9481 5015; www.auxbatifolles.com.au; 400 Nicholson St, North Fitzroy; breakfast/lunch/dinner from $7.50/12/26; 🕑cafe 8am-2.30pm Wed-Sun, restaurant 6-9.30pm Tue-Sat; 🚊96) In the evenings this atmospheric French bistro does all the classics: duck confit, *moules frites* (mussels and French fries), frog legs and steak tartare. Desserts too: crème brûlée and tarte Tatin. During the day it's a fabulous cafe that does homemade baguettes and croissants, and well-priced traditional steaks and chicken dishes for lunch.

Pireaus Blues GREEK $$

(Map p64; www.pireausblues.com.au; 310 Brunswick St, Fitzroy; mains from $15; 🕑noon-3pm & 5-10pm; 🚊112) Come for home-style oven-baked Greek dishes inspired by *yiayia's* recipes and prepared by third-generation owners. Its chargrilled calamari with feta salsa and homebaked bread is divine. There's traditional music on Monday nights.

Barry CAFE $$

(85 High St, Northcote; breakfasts from $14; 🕑7.30am-3.30pm Mon-Fri, 8am-4pm weekends; 🚊86, 🚉Westgarth) New to Northcote, Barry has the whole cafe thing down pat, with the industrial-chic warehouse interior and communal tables, but its breakfasts are what makes it stand out. Go with the summery Thai coconut sago pudding with mango, or gin-cured trout, or the don't-knock-it-till-you-try-it peanut butter and tomatoes on toast sprinkled with more salted peanuts.

Cutler & Co MODERN AUSTRALIAN $$$

(Map p64; 📞03-9419 4888; www.cutlerandco.com.au; 55 Gertrude St, Fitzroy; mains $39-47; 🕑noon-late Fri & Sun, 6pm-late Mon-Thu; 🚊86) Hyped for all the right reasons, this is another of Andrew McConnell's restaurants and though its decor might be a little over the top, its attentive, informed staff and joy-inducing dishes (roast suckling pig, Earl Grey ice-cream and Moonlight Bay oysters, to name a few) have quickly made this one of Melbourne's best.

Moon Under Water MODERN AUSTRALIAN $$$

(Map p64; 📞03-9417 7700; www.buildersarms hotel.com.au; 211 Gertrude St, Fitzroy; 4-course set menu $75 per person; 🕑6-10pm Wed-Sat, noon-3pm & 6-10pm Sun; 🚊86) Another string to Andrew McConnell's bow is this white-washed elegant dining room hidden away in the back of the Builders Arms Hotel. The

set menu changes weekly and wine pairing comes at $55 extra per head. Vegetarian menus are available. If you prefer something more casual and à la carte, check out the adjoining bistro with its daily rotisserie menu (suckling pig) from 6pm.

Bookings advised at least two weeks in advance.

Commoner MODERN BRITISH $$$

(Map p64; 📞03-9415 6876; www.thecommoner.com.au; 122 Johnston St, Fitzroy; mains from $30, 5-course $70; 🕑noon-3pm Fri-Sun, 6pm-late Wed-Sun; 🚊112) On a mission to dispel the myth that British food is dull, the Commoner succeeds with a sensational, highly seasonal menu that incorporates classic ingredients into creative dishes. Think pork belly with black pudding, broccoli and anchovy, a side of chicken-skin potatoes, and brown-ale pudding with salted-caramel sauce and cream for dessert. Sunday lunches are all about its wood-fired roast goat or beef.

Estelle MODERN AUSTRALIAN $$$

(📞03-9489 4609; www.estellebarkitchen.com.au; 243 High St, Northcote; from $25; 🕑6pm-late Tue-Thu, noon-late Fri-Sun; 🚊86, 🚉Northcote) Classy establishment where you can enjoy the elegant interior of gleaming tiled floors, or casual rear courtyard with classic Northcote backyard feel. The menu spans rich French cuisine to Asian-inspired fish dishes. The five-course tasting menus are popular, matched with wine and starting from $70.

🎋 Carlton & Around

Since the arrival of Mediterranean immigrants in the 1950s, Lygon St has been synonymous with Italian cuisine, albeit with a twist to suit the Australian palate. Avoid its spruikers and keep travelling north past Grattan St; some lovely cafes and restaurants lie here and beyond. The East Brunswick end of Lygon St is doing good things, too.

Small Block CAFE $

(📞03-9381 2244; 130 Lygon St, Brunswick East; mains $8-12; 🕑breakfast & lunch; 🚊1, 8) With salvaged service-station signage and concrete floors plus warm and efficient service, Small Block acts as a community centre with a neighbourly drop-in and stay-awhile vibe. Big, beautiful breakfasts are worth writing home about.

DON'T MISS

MIDDLE EAST UP NORTH

Sydney Rd in Brunswick is Melbourne's Middle Eastern hub. Its busy **A1 Lebanese Bakehouse** (www.a1lebanesebakery.com.au; 643-645 Sydney Rd; ⊙7am-7pm Sun-Wed, to 9pm Thu-Sat; 🚊19, 🚌Anstey) and alcohol-free **Tiba's Restaurant** (www.tibasrestaurant.com.au; 504 Sydney Rd, Brunswick; ⊙11am-11pm Sun-Thu, to midnight Fri & Sat; 🚊19, 🚌Brunswick) are worth a trip in themselves, or check out Middle Eastern–influenced Ray for more of a cafe feel.

Ray
CAFE **$**

(📞03-9380 8593; 332 Victoria St, Brunswick; meals $8-19; ⊙7.30am-4pm Mon-Fri, 8.30am-5pm Sat & Sun; 🚖; 🚊19, 🚌Brunswick) Its grafittied facade resembles an abandoned house...before opening up to reveal itself as a gleaming cavernous space with exposed brick. It has an inspired menu that reflects Brunswick by mixing Middle Eastern flavours with classic cafe fare, including fantastic breakfasts and burgers.

Sugardough Panificio & Patisserie
BAKERY **$**

(www.sugardough.com.au; 163 Lygon St, East Brunswick; mains $8; ⊙7.30am-5pm Tue-Fri, to 4pm Sat & Sun; 🚊1, 8) Sugardough does a roaring trade in homemade pies (including vegetarian ones), homebaked bread and pastries. Mismatched cutlery and cups and saucers make it rather like being at grandma's on family-reunion day.

DOC Espresso
ITALIAN **$$**

(Map p66; 📞03-9347 8482; www.docgroup.net; 326 Lygon St, Carlton; mains $12-20; ⊙7.30am-9.30pm Mon-Thu, to 10pm Fri & Sat, 8am-10pm Sun; 🚊205, 🚊1, 8, 96)   Run by third-generation Italians, DOC is bringing authenticity, and breathing new life, back into Lygon St. The espresso bar features homemade pasta specials, Italian microbrewery beers and *aperitivo* time, where you can enjoy a Negroni cocktail with complimentary nibble board (4pm to 7pm) while surrounded by dangling legs of meat and huge wheels of cheese behind glass shelves.
The **deli** (Map p66; 📞03-9347 8482; www.docgroup.net; 326 Lygon St; ⊙9am-8pm) next door does great cheese boards and panini, while around the corner is the original **pizzeria** (Map p66; 📞03-9347 2998; www.docgroup.net; 295 Drummond St; pizzas around $13-18; ⊙5.30-10.30pm Mon-Wed, noon-10.30pm Fri-Sun; 🚊205, 🚊1, 8), with excellent thin-crust pizzas and a convivial atmosphere.

Rumi
MIDDLE EASTERN **$$**

(📞03-9388 8255; www.rumirestaurant.com.au; 116 Lygon St, East Brunswick; mains $17-23; ⊙6-10pm; 🚊1, 8) A fabulously well-considered place that serves up a mix of traditional Lebanese cooking and contemporary interpretations of old Persian dishes. The *sigara boregi* (cheese and pine-nut pastries) are a local institution, and tasty mains like meatballs are balanced with a large and interesting selection of vegetable dishes (the near-caramelised cauliflower and the broad beans are standouts).

Auction Rooms
CAFE **$$**

(www.auctionroomscafe.com.au; 103-107 Errol St, North Melbourne; mains $14-20; ⊙7am-5pm Mon-Fri, from 7.30am Sat & Sun; 🚖; 🚊57) This former auction-house-turned–North Melbourne success story serves up some of Melbourne's best coffee, both espresso and filter, using ever-changing, house-roasted single-origin beans. Then there's the food, with a highly seasonal menu of creative breakfasts and lunches. From Queen Vic Market head west along Victoria St, then right at Errol St.

Epocha
EUROPEAN **$$**

(Map p66; 📞03-9036 4949; www.epocha.com.au; 49 Rathdowne St, Carlton; sharing plates small/large from $14/24; ⊙noon-2pm & 5.30-10pm Tue-Sat; 🚊City Circle, 24, 30) Set within a grand Victorian 1884 double-storey terrace, classy Epocha creates an interesting mix of Greek- and English-inspired dishes that's reflective of each of the co-owners' successes in previous restaurants. It all comes together beautifully on the $68 sharing menu. It also has fantastic cocktails at the upstairs **Hannah's Bar**.

Bar Idda
ITALIAN **$$**

(📞03-9380 5339; www.baridda.com.au; 132 Lygon St, East Brunswick; mains $15-21; ⊙6-10pm Tue-Sat; 🚊1, 8) The diner-style table coverings give little clue to the tasty morsels this Sicilian restaurant serves for dinner. Shared plates are the go, and range from pistachio-crumbed lamb loin to vegetarian layered eggplant.

Tiamo
ITALIAN **$$**

(Map p66; www.tiamo.com.au; 303 Lygon St, Carlton; mains $9-24; ⊙6.30am-11pm; 🚌Tourist Shuttle, 🚊1, 8) When you've had enough of pressed, siphoned, Slayer-machined, poured-over, filtered and plunged coffee, head here to one of Lygon St's original Italian cafe-restaurants. There's the laughter and relaxed joie de vivre that only a well-established restaurant can have. Great pastas and pizza, too. Also has the more upmarket Tiamo 2 next door.

Pope Joan
CAFE, BAR $$

(☑ 03-9388 8858; www.popejoan.com.au; 77-79 Nicholson St, East Brunswick; mains $15; ⊗ 7.30am-11pm Mon-Fri, until 5pm Sat & Sun; ☐ 96) The perfect place to drop in to cure a hangover with its menu of creative comfort food, strong coffee and 'liquid breakfasts' of Bloody Marys and spritzers. In fact, this East Brunswick fave is great any time.

Abla's
LEBANESE $$

(Map p66; ☑ 03-9347 0006; www.ablas.com.au; 109 Elgin St, Carlton; mains $27; ⊗ noon-3pm Thu & Fri, 6-11pm Mon-Sat; ☐ 205, ☐ 1, 8, 96) The kitchen here is steered by Abla Amad, whose authentic, flavour-packed food has inspired a whole generation of local Lebanese chefs. Bring a bottle of your favourite plonk and settle in for the compulsory banquet ($70) on Friday and Saturday night.

Small Victories
CAFE $$

(☑ 03-9347 4064; www.smallvictoriesrestaurant. com.au; 617 Rathdowne St, North Carlton; from $13; ⊗ 8am-5pm Mon-Sat, 9am-5pm Sun; ☐ 1, 8) Not your ordinary posh North Carlton cafe, Small Victories is big on DIY: preparing and smoking its own bacon and chorizo, churning its own butter and making pastas from scratch. It rounds it all out with single-origin coffee and craft beers.

Café Cavallino
ITALIAN $$

(Map p66; ☑ 03-9347 5520; www.cafecavallino. com.au; 181 Lygon St, Carlton; pizza from $17; ⊗ Tue-Sun 11.30am-late; ☐ 1, 8) Sure, it's your cliched Lygon St Italian trattoria, but it's also a fun, colourful choice with delicious pizzas – and it's where the Ferrari Formula One team dines come Melbourne Grand Prix (hence all the memorabilia on the walls).

✖ St Kilda & Around

Fitzroy St is a popular eating strip, and you'll find the good, the very good and the downright ugly along its length. Acland St also hums with dining options, as well as its famed cake shops. Over the Nepean Hwy, Carlisle St has more than its fair share of cute cafes and a couple of restaurants that keep the locals happy.

Monarch Cake Shop
DESSERTS, EUROPEAN $

(Map p72; ☑ 03-9534 2972; www.monarchcakes. com.au; 103 Acland St, St Kilda; slice of cake $5; ⊗ 8am-10pm; ☐ 96) St Kilda's Eastern European cake shops have long drawn crowds that come to peer at the sweetly stocked windows. Monarch is a favourite – its *kugelhopf* (marble cake), plum cake and poppy-seed cheesecake can't be beaten. It has been in business since 1934; not much has changed here with its wonderful buttery aromas and old-time atmosphere. Also does good coffee.

Si Señor
MEXICAN $

(Map p72; www.sisenor.net.au; 193 Carlisle St, Balaclava; tacos $5-7, tortas $13-15; ⊗ 11.30pm-late; ☎; ☐ 3, 16, 79) One of the latest additions to Melbourne's Mexican restaurant takeover, Si Señor is one of the most authentic. Tasty spit-and-grilled meats are heaped onto soft corn tortillas under direction of its Mexican owner. If you've overdone the hot sauce, cool it down with an authentic *horchata*, a delicious rice-milk and cinnamon drink.

Lentil as Anything
VEGETARIAN $

(Map p72; www.lentilasanything.com; 41 Blessington St, St Kilda; by donation; ⊗ 11am-9pm; ☎; ☐ 16, 96) Choosing from the organic, vegetarian menu is easy. Deciding what to pay can be hard. This unique not-for-profit operation provides training and educational opportunities for marginalised people, as well as tasty vegetarian food. Whatever you end up paying for your meal goes towards helping new migrants, refugees, people with disabilities and the long-term unemployed. Also at the **Abbotsford Convent** (www.lentilasanything.com; 1 St Heliers St, Abbotsford; by donation; ⊗ 9am-9pm; ☐ Victoria Park).

Glick's
BAGELS $

(Map p72; www.glicks.com.au; 330A Carlisle St, Balaclava; bagels $4-10; ⊗ 5.30am-8pm Mon-Fri & Sun, 7.30pm-midnight Sat; ☐ 3, 16, 79) No-frills bakery keeping the local Jewish community happy with bagels baked and boiled in-house and kosher options available. Stick with the classics and try the 'New Yorker' with cream cheese and egg salad.

Banff
PIZZA, BAR $

(Map p72; www.banffstkilda.com; 145 Fitzroy St, St Kilda; mains $9; ⊗ 8am-10pm; ☐ 3a, 16) It's not just the daily happy hour that keeps Banff's Fitzroy St–fronting chairs occupied, it's also the $9 pizzas ($5 for lunch).

Monk Bodhi Dharma
CAFE $$

(Map p72; ☑ 03-9534 7250; www.monkbodhidharma.com; Rear, 202 Carlisle St, Balaclava; breakfast $8.50-18.50; ⊙7am-5pm Mon-Fri, 8am-5pm Sat & Sun; ☑; 🖫3, 16, 79) Monk Bodhi Dharma's hidden location, down an alley off Carlisle St (next to Safeway), means it doesn't get much passing foot traffic, which is lucky given that this cosy brick cafe has enough devotees as it is. A former 1920s bakehouse, these days it's all about transcendental vegetarian food, housemade Bircher muesli and house-roasted single-estate coffee. Book ahead for Friday-night dinners.

Mirka's at Tolarno
INTERNATIONAL, ITALIAN $$

(Map p72; ☑ 03-9525 3088; www.mirkatolarnohotel.com; Tolarno Hotel, 42 Fitzroy St, St Kilda; mains $26-32; ⊙6pm-late; 🖫16, 96, 112) Murals by beloved artist Mirka Mora grace the walls in this dining room with a history (it's been delighting diners since the early '60s), part of Tolarno Hotel. The Italian menu has some rustic classics, like veal satimbocca, mixed with interesting surprises such as walnut and pear gnocchi with gorgonzola. There's also a four-course sharing menu ($60).

Cicciolina
MEDITERRANEAN $$

(Map p72; www.cicciolinastkilda.com.au; 130 Acland St, St Kilda; mains $17-43; ⊙noon-10pm; 🖫16, 96) This warm room of dark wood, subdued lighting and pencil sketches is a St Kilda institution. The inspired Modern Australian/Mediterranean menu is smart and generous, and the service warm. It only takes bookings for lunch; for dinner eat early or while away your wait in the moody little back bar.

I Carusi II
PIZZA $$

(Map p72; ☑ 03-9593 6033; 231 Barkly St, St Kilda; pizza $16-21; ⊙6-11pm; 🖫16, 96) Located beyond the Acland St chaos in this nostalgic corner shop, I Carusi pizzas have a particularly tasty dough and follow the less-is-more tenet, with top-quality mozzarella, pecorino and a small range of other toppings. Bookings advised, and don't miss the upstairs bar.

Claypots
SEAFOOD $$

(Map p72; ☑ 03-9534 1282; 213 Barkly St, St Kilda; mains $25-35; ⊙noon-3pm & 6pm-1am; 🖫96) A local favourite, Claypots serves up seafood in its namesake dish. Get in early to both get a seat and ensure the good stuff is still available, as hot items go fast. It also has a spot in the South Melbourne Market (p74).

Mr Wolf
PIZZA $$

(Map p72; ☑ 03-9534 0255; www.mrwolf.com.au; 9-15 Inkerman St, St Kilda; pizza $20-25; ⊙5pm-late Tue-Sun, from noon Fri-Sun; 🖫16) Local celeb chef Karen Martini's casual but stylish space is renowned for its crisp Roma-style pizzas. There's also a great menu of antipasti and pastas that display her flair for matching ingredients.

Lau's Family Kitchen
CHINESE $$

(Map p72; ☑ 03-8598 9880; www.lauskitchen.com.au; 4 Acland St, St Kilda; mains $25-38; ⊙dinner sittings 6pm & 8pm; 🖫16, 96) The owner's family comes with absolutely flawless pedigree (father Gilbert Lau is the former owner of famed Flower Drum) and the restaurant is in a lovely leafy location. The mainly Cantonese menu is simple, and dishes are beautifully done (if not particularly exciting), with a few surprises thrown in for more adventurous diners. Make a reservation for one of the two dinner sittings.

Newmarket Hotel
LATIN AMERICAN $$

(Map p72; ☑ 03-9537 1777; www.newmarketstkilda.com.au; 34 Inkerman St, St Kilda; meals from $15; ⊙noon-3pm & 6-10.30pm; 🖫3, 67) In typical St Kilda fashion, this historic pub has received a cosmetic enhancement, though thankfully it's been done tastefully courtesy of a modern refurb by renowned Six Degrees architects. The menu is Latin American–inspired, so expect Mexican street food, wood-barbecued meats and premium steaks. Lunch specials are excellent value, and there's a top-shelf bar, too.

Miss Jackson
CAFE $$

(Map p72; www.missjackson.com.au; 2/19 Grey St, St Kilda; mains from $15; ⊙7am-4pm Tue-Sun; 🖫16, 96) Its casual set-up and atmosphere makes it feel a bit like you've been invited around to a friend's house for brunch – a friend with good enough taste to cook things like crab scrambled eggs or panko-crumbed chicken-schnitzel burgers.

Batch Espresso
CAFE $$

(Map p72; 320 Carlisle St, Balaclava; mains $16; ⊙7am-4.30pm; 🖫3, 3a, 16, 🖫Balaclava) Its walls are decorated with bric-a-brac donated by locals who love the food on offer, friendly service and great New Zealand coffee. Good luck getting a seat during the weekend, though.

Barney Allen's   MODERN AUSTRALIAN **$$**
(Map p72; ✏03-9525 5477; www.barneyallens.com.
au; 14 Fitzroy St, St Kilda; mains from $16; ⊙3pm-
1am Mon-Thu, from noon Fri-Sun; ⛟16, 96, 112) Like
its Aussie celebrity-chef owner, Iain 'Huey'
Hewitson, there's nothing flashy about this
long-standing St Kilda local, which instead
prefers to keep things simple with a menu of
winning, comfort-food Mod Oz dishes, such
as panko-and-parmesan-crusted salmon
and its juicy Barney Allen burger.

Galleon Cafe   CAFE **$$**
(Map p72; 9 Carlisle St, St Kilda; mains from $10;
⊙7am-5pm; ⛟3a, 16, 79) Friendly folk, a decent amount of elbow room and low-key
music make this a cheery place to down a
coffee and lunch in busy St Kilda.

★Attica   MODERN AUSTRALIAN **$$$**
(✏03-9530 0111; www.attica.com.au; 74 Glen
Eira Rd, Ripponlea; 8-course tasting menu $190;
⊙6.30pm-late Wed-Sat; ⛟67, ⛟Ripponlea) Con-
sistent award-winning Attica is a suburban
restaurant that serves Ben Shewry's creative
dishes degustation-style. Many dishes are
not complete on delivery; staff perform mi-
nor miracles on cue with a sprinkle of this or
a drop of that. 'Trials' of Shewry's new ideas
take place at Tuesday night's Chef's Table
($125 per head). Booking several months
in advance is essential. Follow Brighton Rd
south to Glen Eira Rd.

Golden Fields   MODERN ASIAN **$$$**
(Map p72; ✏03-9525 4488; www.goldenfields.com.
au; 157 Fitzroy St, St Kilda; mains $32-70; ⊙noon-
midnight; ⛟16, 96) Andrew McConnell has
done it again. This chic eatery became famous for its New England lobster roll and
for good reason – it's a testament to good
things coming in small packages. Modern
Asian subtleties can be found not only in the
made-for-sharing dishes but also in the dé-
cor. Book a few weeks ahead for weekends,
or score a spot at the long (non-bookable)
bar, where you can glimpse the chefs in
action.

⛏ South Yarra, Prahran & Windsor

It's perpetual peak hour at Chapel St's many
cafes. You'll also find a few excellent dining
options in Prahran, including on Greville St
as well as at the Prahran Market. The Windsor strip keeps things cheap and cheerful.

Valentino   ITALIAN **$$**
(Map p68; ✏03-9826 8815; www.valentinorestau-
rant.com.au; 517 Malvern Rd, Hawksburn; pizzas
$20; ⊙noon-2pm Fri-Sun, 5.30-10pm Tue-Sun;
⛟72) Offering Calabrian-style dishes with a
lively welcoming atmosphere, Valentino has
a wonderful antipasto selection – but its piz-
zas are the real reason to come here. Great
aperitivi and wine list, too.

Colonel Tans   THAI **$$**
(Map p68; ✏03-9521 5985; www.coloneltans.com.
au; 229 Chapel St, Prahran; dishes $15; ⊙5-11pm
Tue-Sat, from noon Fri; ⛟6, ⛟Prahran) Set up in
the back corner of Revolver Upstairs, funky
Colonel Tans is run by the same team behind
the city centre's Cookie (p90), with similarly
yummy creative Thai fushion dishes, from
traditional curries and tangy snapper rolled
in betel leaf to kaffir-lime chicken burgers.

Dino's   SPANISH **$$**
(Map p68; ✏03-9521 3466; 34 Chapel St, Wind-
sor; mains $20-32; ⊙8am-midnight; ⛟5, 64, 78,
79, ⛟Windsor) The wine list's longer than its
food list (evidence of prior drinking lines
the walls), but it's a great spot to dine on
ex-Cumulus Inc chef's breakfast bocadillos
(sandwiches) in the early hours and Spanish
tapas flavours after dark. Opposite Windsor
station, it can get very busy.

WoodLand House   MODERN AUSTRALIAN **$$$**
(Map p68; ✏03-9525 2178; www.woodlandhouse.
com.au; 78 Williams Rd, Prahran; tasting menu
from $115; ⊙noon-3pm Thu, Fri & Sun, 6.30-9pm
Tue-Sat; ⛟6) Housed in a Victorian terrace
of ample proportions, this was the former
incarnation of Jacques Reymond, a local
pioneer of degustation dining. After 15 years
he handed over the reins to two of his sous
chefs, who learned everything they know
from the man. The tasting menu has shifted
from its original French focus to an innovative Modern Australian direction incorporating quality local produce. Sunday lunch
offers a good-value chef's set menu of four
courses for $80.

Da Noi   ITALIAN **$$**
(Map p68; ✏03-9866 5975; 95 Toorak Rd, South
Yarra; mains $35, 4-course tasting menu $93;
⊙noon-3pm & 6-10pm Mon-Sat; ⛟8, ⛟South
Yarra) Da Noi serves up beautiful Sardinian
dishes that change daily. The spontaneous
kitchen might reinterpret the chef's special
three times a night. Just go with it; it's a
unique experience and harks back to a dif-
ferent way of dining. Bookings advised.

South Melbourne, Port Melbourne & Albert Park

Andrew's Burgers   BURGERS $
(☑ 03-9690 2126; www.andrewshamburgers.com.
au; 144 Bridport St, Albert Park; burgers from $7.50;
⊙ 11am-3pm & 4.30-9pm Mon-Sat; ☐ 1) Andrew's
is a family-run burger institution that's been
around since the '50s. Walls are still wood-
panelled and now covered with photos of
local celebs who, like many, drop in for a
classic burger with the lot and a big bag of
chips to takeaway. Veg option available.

Jock's Ice-Cream   ICE CREAM $
(83 Victoria Ave, Albert Park; single cone $4; ⊙ noon-
8pm Mon-Fri, to 10.30pm Sat & Sun; ☐ 1) For more
than a decade, Jock has been scooping up
his sorbets and ice creams made on-site
(baked apple, Baci, roast almond) to baysid-
ers. Take-home tubs also available.

St Ali   CAFE $$
(☑ 03-9689 2990; www.stali.com.au; 12-18 Yarra
Pl, South Melbourne; dishes $10-28; ⊙ 7am-6pm;
☐ 112) A hideaway warehouse conversion
where the coffee is carefully sourced and
guaranteed to be good. If you can't decide
between house blend, specialty, black or
white, there's a tasting 'plate' ($18). Awarded
best food cafe in *The Age Good Cafe Guide
2013;* the corn fritters with poached eggs
and haloumi are legendary. Off Clarendon
St, between Coventry and York Sts.

Misuzu's   JAPANESE $$
(☑ 03-9699 9022; 3-7 Victoria Ave, Albert Park;
mains $18-30; ⊙ lunch & dinner; ☐ 1) Misuzu's
menu includes whopping noodle, rice and
curry dishes, tempuras and takeaway options from the neatly displayed sushi bar. Sit
outside under lantern-hung trees, or inside
surrounded by murals and dark wood.

Mart 130   CAFE $$
(☑ 03-9690 8831; 107 Canterbury Rd, Middle Park;
mains $12-20; ⊙ 7.30am-4pm; 🖰; ☐ 96) A quirky
location within the Federation-style Middle
Park tram station, Mart 130 is a cute, sun-
filled cafe that serves up corn fritters, toast-
ed pide and big salads. Its deck overlooks
the park with city views in the background.
Weekend waits can be long.

**Albert Park Hotel
Oyster Bar & Grill**   SEAFOOD, PUB $$
(www.thealbertpark.com.au; cnr Montague St &
Dundas Pl, Albert Park; mains $15-30; ☐ 1, 96)
With a focus on oysters and seafood as well
as bar food, this incarnation of the Albert
Park Hotel (thanks again to Six Degrees)
is filling seats with its promise of market-
priced fish and wood-barbecued 'big fish'
served in five different Mediterranean
styles.

🍷 Drinking & Nightlife

Melbourne's bars are legendary, from laneway hideaways to brassy corner establishments. The same goes for coffee. Out of the
city centre, shopping strips are embedded
with shopfront drinking holes: try Fitzroy,
Collingwood, Northcote, Prahran and St
Kilda. Many inner-city pubs have pushed
out the barflies, pulled up the beer-stained
carpet, polished the concrete and brought in
talented chefs and mixologists, but don't dis-
miss the character-filled oldies that still exist.

Many of Melbourne's smaller character-
filled bars and pubs double as live-music
venues, and are still great for a beer in the
fun, rowdy front bars even if you don't want
to catch a gig. See the Live Music section
(p115) for listings.

Central Melbourne

★**Bar Americano**   COCKTAIL BAR
(Map p50; www.baramericano.com; 20 Pesgrave
Pl, off Howey Pl; ⊙ 8.30am-1am; ☐ 11, 31, 48, 109,
112) A hideaway bar in a city alleyway, Bar
Americano is a standing-room-only affair
with black-and-white chequered floors complemented with classic 'do not spit' subway
tiled walls and a subtle air of speakeasy. By
day it serves excellent coffee but after dark
it's all about the cocktails; they don't come
cheap but they do come superb.

Lui Bar   COCKTAIL BAR
(Map p50; www.vuedemonde.com.au; Level 55, Rialto, 525 Collins St; ⊙ 5.30pm-midnight Mon, noon-
midnight Tue-Fri, 5.30pm-late Sat, noon-evening
Sun; ☐ 11, 31, 48, 109, 112, 🚉 Southern Cross) One
of the city's most sophisticated bars, Lui
offers the chance to sample the views and
excellent bar snacks (smoked ocean trout
jerky!) without having to indulge in the
whole Vue de Monde dining experience.
Suits and jet-setters cram in most nights so
get there early (nicely dressed), claim your
table and order drinks from the 'pop-up
book' menu containing serious drinks like
macadamia martinis – vacuum distilled at
the bar.

Melbourne Supper Club BAR
(Map p50; ☑03-9654 6300; 1st fl, 161 Spring St; ◷5pm-4am Sun-Thu, to 6am Fri & Sat; ◨95, 96, ◨Parliament) Melbourne's own Betty Ford's (the place you go when there's nowhere left to go), the Supper Club is open very late and is a favoured after-work spot for performers and hospitality types. It's entered via an unsigned wooden door, where you can leave your coat before cosying into a chesterfield. Browse the encyclopaedic wine menu and relax; the sommeliers will cater to any liquid desire.

It does good bar food too, including old-school party pies. The upstairs bar **Siglo** has wonderful views and is open to the elements for the cigar smokers, who will delight in its menu of Cuban cigars.

Madame Brussels BAR
(Map p50; www.madamebrussels.com; Level 3, 59-63 Bourke St; ◷noon-1am; ◨86, 96) Head here if you've had it with Melbourne-moody and all that dark wood. Although named for a famous 19th-century brothel owner, it feels like a camp '60s rabbit hole you've fallen into, with much Astroturfery and staff dressed à la the country club. It's just the tonic to escape the city for a jug of its Madame Brussels–style Pimms on its wonderful rooftop terrace.

Sweatshop BAR
(Map p50; www.sweatshopbar.com.au; 113 Lonsdale St; ◷Fri & Sat; ◨Parliament) There's great Cantonese cuisine and a bar upstairs at **Seamstress** (Map p50; ☑03-9663 6363; www.seamstress.com.au; mains $24-35; ◷lunch & dinner Mon-Fri, dinner Sat) that's open all week, but on weekends it's the New York–like basement dive bar that's worth squashing in for. Quaff American whiskies and craft beers to wash down inventive Asian bar food.

Brother Baba Budan CAFE
(Map p50; www.sevenseeds.com.au; 359 Little Bourke St; ◷7am-5pm Mon-Sat, 9am-5pm Sun; ◉; ◨19, 57, 59) This small city cafe by Seven Seeds, with just a few seats (most hangin' from the ceiling), does a roaring takeaway coffee trade for the inner-city workers and is a great spot for a mid-shopping caffeine buzz. Don't be put off by queues; service is fast and friendly.

Double Happiness BAR
(Map p50; ☑03-9650 4488; www.double-happiness.org; 21 Liverpool St; ◷4pm-1am Mon-Wed, to 3am Thu & Fri, 6pm-3am Sat, to 1am Sun; ◨86, 96, ◨Parliament) This stylish hole-in-the-wall is decked out in Chinese propaganda posters and Mao statues and has a range of Asian-influenced chilli- or coriander-flavoured cocktails. Upstairs is the bar **New Gold Mountain** (Map p50; ☑03-9650 8859; www.newgoldmountain.org; ◷6pm-late Tue-Thu, to 5am Fri & Sat), run by the same owners, with table service.

Croft Institute BAR
(Map p50; ☑03-9671 4399; www.thecroftinstitute.com; 21-25 Croft Alley; ◷5pm-1am Mon-Thu, to 3am Fri & Sat; ◨86, 96) Hidden in a laneway off a laneway with great grafitti, the slightly creepy Croft is a laboratory-themed bar downstairs, while upstairs on weekends it opens up the 1950s-themed gymnasium bar. There's a $10 cover charge for DJs Friday and Saturday nights.

Hell's Kitchen BAR
(Map p50; Level 1, 20 Centre Place; ◷noon-10pm Mon & Tues, noon-late Wed-Sat, to 11pm Sun; ◨Flinders St) Original hidden laneway bar located in the beautiful Centre Place Arcade, Hell's is up a narrow flight of stairs – sip on classic cocktails (Negroni, whisky sour and martinis), beer or cider and people-watch from the large windows. It attracts a young, hip crowd and also serves food.

Degraves Espresso CAFE
(Map p50; Degraves St; ◷7am-9pm Mon-Fri, 8am-9pm Sat, 8am-6pm Sun; ◨48, 70, 75, ◨Flinders St) In atmospheric Degraves St, this institution is a good spot to grab a quick takeaway coffee and then wander the laneways.

Shebeen BAR
(Map p50; www.shebeen.com.au; 36 Manchester Lane; ◷11am-late Mon-Fri, 4pm-late Sat, 4-11pm Sun; ◨11, 31, 48, 109, 112) ◢ Corrugated-iron walls and awnings give this relaxed bar a canteen-shack feel. Shebeen (the name for illegal drinking bars in South Africa during apartheid) offers a place to have a tipple without feeling too guilty about it – 100% of all drink profits go towards a charity partner overseas. At the time of research there were plans for live music and DJs.

Federal Coffee Palace CAFE
(Map p50; GPO, Elizabeth St; ◨19, 57, 59) Grab a takeaway coffee or sit among the city atmosphere, with tables beneath the colonnades of the GPO mall and space heaters to keep you toasty when the city turns chilly. At the time of research, there were plans to open a burger stand, too.

GAY & LESBIAN MELBOURNE

Melbourne's gay and lesbian community is well integrated into the general populace, but clubs and bars are found in two distinct locations: Abbotsford and Collingwood; and Prahran and South Yarra. Commercial Rd, which separates Prahran and South Yarra, is home to a couple of gay clubs, cafes and businesses. It's more glamorous than the 'northside', which has a reputation as more down-to-earth and a little less pretentious.

Plenty of Melbourne venues get into the spirit during **Midsumma Festival** (www.midsumma.org.au; ☺ Jan-Feb). It has a diverse program of cultural, community and sporting events, including the popular Midsumma Carnival at Alexandra Gardens, St Kilda's Pride March and much more. Australia's largest GLBT film festival, the **Melbourne Queer Film Festival** (www.melbournequeerfilm.com.au), screens more than 100 films from around the world each March.

For more local info, pick up a copy of the free weekly newspaper **MCV (Melbourne Community Voice)**. GLBT-community radio station **JOY 94.9FM** (www.joy.org.au) is another important resource for visitors and locals.

Drinking & Nightlife

Kama Bar (Map p68; ☑03-9804 5771; www.facebook.com/kamaclub; 119 Commercial Rd, South Yarra; ☺5pm-late; ☒72) The former Exchange Hotel, Kama Bar is one of the few remaining gay venues along Commerical Rd, with regular DJs and drag shows.

Laird (☑03-9417 2832; www.lairdhotel.com; 149 Gipps St, Collingwood; ☺5pm-late; ☒Collingwood) The Laird's been running its men-only gay hotel for more than 30 years now. It's on the Abbotsford side of Gipps St, which runs off Collingwood's Wellington St.

Chuckle Park — BAR
(Map p50; www.chucklepark.com.au; 322 Little Collins St; ☺noon-1am; ☒86, 96) The newest addition to Melbourne's creative bars, Chuckle Park uses a healthy dose of Astroturf to park its '70s caravan bar on in the narrowest of laneways. Hanging plant jars double as swaying lights and indie and rock music create the scene while the 'in the know' crowd munches on pulled-pork rolls and shares huge jars of cocktails.

Loop — BAR, CLUB
(Map p50; ☑03-9654 0500; www.looponline.com.au; 23 Meyers Pl; ☺3pm-late; ☒86, 96) Weekend DJs perform in a project space with large double screen and scattered projectors; find yourself a dark seat or a spot at the bar. It has something on every night, from beats to heartfelt docos.

Hotel Windsor — TEAROOM
(Map p50; www.thehotelwindsor.com.au; 111 Spring St; Mon-Fri $69, Sat & Sun $89; ☒Parliament) This grand hotel has been serving afternoon tea since 1883. Indulge in the delights of its three-tier platters of finger sandwiches, scones, pastries and champagne, hosted in either its front dining room or the art nouveau ballroom.

1000£Bend — BAR
(Map p50; www.thousandpoundbend.com.au; 361 Little Lonsdale St; ☺8am-11pm Mon-Wed, 8am-1am Thu, 10am-1am Sat, 10am-11pm Sun; ☎; ☒19, 57, 59) Breakfast, lunch, dinner and cruisy folk using the free wi-fi – that's not all at this mega warehouse of entertainment. It's also a whopping great venue for art shows and plays.

Section 8 — BAR
(Map p50; www.section8.com.au; 27-29 Tattersalls Lane; ☺10am-late Mon-Fri, noon-late Sat & Sun; ☒3, 5, 6, 16, 64, 67, 72) Enclosed within a cage full of shipping containers and wooden-pallet seating, Section 8 remains one of the city's hippest bars. It does great hot dogs, including vegan ones.

2 Pocket Fairtrade — CAFE
(Map p50; www.twopocket.com.au; 277 Little Lonsdale St; ☺7.30am-5pm Mon-Fri, 9.30am-5pm Sat & Sun; ☎; ☒Melbourne Central) ✔ Tucked below street level on Little Lonsdale is this part cafe, part fair-trade store. Sip on the weekly rotating single-origin coffee and snack on organic pastries while checking out the largest range of fair-trade chocolate in Australia. You can also find handmade paper from Bangladesh, cosmetics and beautiful kids' soft toys.

DT's Hotel (Map p60; ☎ 03-9428 5724; www.dtshotel.com.au; 164 Church St, Richmond; 🚊 78, 79) This small and intimate gay pub hosts some of Melbourne's best drag shows, retro nights and happy hours.

Peel Hotel (☎ 03-9419 4762; www.thepeel.com.au; 113 Wellington St, Collingwood; ⊙ 9pm-dawn Thu-Sat; 🚊 86) One of Melbourne's most famous gay venues, the Peel features a male crowd dancing to house music, retro and commercial dance. It's on Peel St, which runs east off Smith St.

Commercial Hotel (☎ 03-9689 9354; www.hotelcommercial.com.au; 238 Whitehall St, Yarraville; ⊙ Thu-Sat; 🚊 Yarraville) A friendly, low-key pub in Melbourne's inner west that presents drag shows on Saturday nights. From the city centre, follow Footscray Rd and turn left down Whitehall St.

Greyhound Hotel (Map p72; ☎ 03-9534 4189; www.ghhotel.com.au; cnr Carlisle St & Brighton Rd, St Kilda; 🚊 16, 67, 79) The old Greyhound's had a facelift; expect drag-filled evenings from Thursday to Saturday and a nightclub with a state-of-the-art sound system.

Sleeping

169 Drummond (Map p66; ☎ 03-9663 3081; www.169drummond.com.au; 169 Drummond St, Carlton; d incl breakfast $135-145; ☏; 🚊 1, 8) A privately owned guesthouse in a renovated, 19th-century terrace in the inner north, one block from vibrant Lygon St.

Ferdydurke BAR
(Map p50; ☎ 03-9639 3750; www.ferdydurke.com. au; 31 Tattersalls Lane, levels 1 & 2, cnr Lonsdale St; ⊙ noon-1am; ☏; 🚊 Melbourne Central) Run by same folks as Section 8 next door, this dive bar/art space is set over several levels. Within its gritty confines they play everything from electronic to live Polish jazz, while Wednesday nights they project computer games on the opposing giant brick wall. They also sell hot dogs.

Workshop BAR
(Map p50; www.theworkshopbar.com.au; 413 Elizabeth St; ⊙ 10am-late Mon-Fri, 1pm-late Sat & Sun; ☏; 🚊 19, 57, 59, 🚊 Melbourne Central) Popular with students and young backpackers from the smattering of nearby hostels, this industrial bar has a lively party atmosphere, with DJs playing mainly hip hop and drum 'n' bass. A good lunch spot, too, with $7 pizzas eaten on its flora-filled outdoor balcony.

Robot BAR
(Map p50; ☎ 03-9620 3646; www.robotsushi. com; 12 Bligh Pl; ⊙ 5pm-late Mon-Fri, 8pm-late Sat; 🚊 Flinders St) If neo-Tokyo is your thing or you just have a sudden urge for a sushi handroll washed down with an Asahi, check out Robot. It has an all-welcome door policy, big windows that open to the laneway and a cute mezzanine level, and attracts a laid-back young crowd.

Riverland BAR
(Map p50; ☎ 03-9662 1771; www.riverlandbar. com; Vaults 1-9 Federation Wharf, under Princes Bridge; ⊙ 10am-late Mon-Fri, 9am-late Sat & Sun; 🚊 Flinders St) Perched below Princes Bridge alongside the Yarra River, this bluestone beauty keeps things simple with good wine, beer on tap and bar snacks that hit the mark: charcuterie, cheese and barbecue sausages. Outside tables are a treat when the weather is kind. Be prepared for rowdiness pre- and post-footy matches at the nearby MCG.

Carlton Hotel BAR
(Map p50; www.thecarlton.com.au; 193 Bourke St; ⊙ 4pm-late; 🚊 86, 96) Over-the-top Melbourne rococo gets another workout here and never fails to raise a smile. Check out the rooftop **Palmz** if you're looking for some Miami-flavoured vice, or just a great view.

Young & Jackson's PUB
(Map p50; www.youngandjacksons.com.au; cnr Flinders & Swanston Sts; ⊙ 11am-late; 🚊 Flinders St) Opposite Flinders Street Station, this historical pub has been serving up beer since 1861 and makes for a popular meeting spot. Lounge on chesterfields in Chloe's Bar or head up to the rooftop cider bar, where nine Australian ciders are on tap, including the house-brewed speciality.

Lounge
BAR

(Map p50; www.lounge.com.au; 1st fl, 243 Swanston St; admission $10 after midnight Sat; ⊙ noon-late Mon-Fri, 2pm-late Sat & Sun; 🛜; 🚋 3, 5, 6, 16, 64, 67, 72) Lounge has seen a lot of years and still feels like a share house from the early '90s. Evenings are filled with the sound of DJs and live music. Escape to the big balcony with some American diner-style grub.

Cherry
BAR, LIVE MUSIC

(Map p50; www.cherrybar.com.au; ACDC Lane; ⊙ 5pm-3am Mon, 6pm-3am Tue & Wed, 5pm-5am Thu-Sat, 2pm-3am Sun; 🚋 City Circle, 70, 75) Melbourne's legendary rock 'n' roll bar is still going strong. Located down ACDC Lane (yep, named after the band, who are homegrown heroes), there's often a queue, but once inside a welcoming, slightly anarchic spirit prevails. Live music and DJs play rock 'n' roll seven nights a week, and there's a long-standing soul night on Thursdays.

It's the choice of touring bands to hang out post-gig; management made headlines by knocking back Lady Gaga to honour a local band's booking.

Alumbra
CLUB

(🗹 03-8623 9666; www.alumbra.com.au; Shed 9, Central Pier, 161 Harbour Esplanade; ⊙ 4pm-3am Fri & Sat, to 1am Sun; 🚋 Tourist Shuttle, 🚋 70, City Circle) Great music and a stunning location will impress – even if the Bali-meets-Morocco follies of the decor don't. If you're going to do one megaclub in Melbourne (and like the idea of a glass dance floor), this is going to be your best bet. It's in one of the old sheds jutting out into Docklands' Victoria Harbour.

Brown Alley
CLUB

(Colonial Hotel; Map p50; 🗹 03-9670 8599; www.brownalley.com; 585 Lonsdale St; ⊙ 10pm-7am Thu-Sun; 🚋 Flagstaff) This historical pub hides away a fully fledged nightclub with a 24-hour licence. It's enormous, with distinct rooms over three levels that can fit up to 1000 people. The sound equipment is the business and the rota of DJs includes spinners of breakbeat, psy-trance and deep house.

🛈 South Wharf & Docklands

Boatbuilders Yard
BAR

(🗹 03-9686 5088; 23 South Wharf Promenade, South Wharf; ⊙ 7am-late; 🚋 City Circle, 70, 71) Occupying a slice of South Wharf next to the historic *Polly Woodside* ship, Boatbuilders attracts a mixed crowd of office workers, travellers and Melburnians keen to discover this developing area. It's made up of 'zones' running seamlessly from the indoor cafe/bar to the outdoor barbecue and cider garden, bocce pit and soon-to-come summer gelato bar.

Story
CAFE

(700 Bourke St, Docklands; ⊙ 7am-4.30pm Mon-Fri; 🚋 Southern Cross) Another coffee spot from Dukes, this one does a roaring trade for the Docklands office workers, filling the gap for great coffee in the area. It's a short walk from Southern Cross Station along the Concourse towards Docklands Stadium.

🛈 Richmond

Bar Economico
BAR

(Map p60; 438 Church St; ⊙ 5pm-late Wed-Sat, 2pm-late Sun; 🚋 70, 79, 🚉 East Richmond) The newspapered front windows might have you turning on your heel, but rest assured you're in the right place. With its menus on ripped cardboard boxes and caged bar, Economico is a kind of Central American dive bar specialising in rum-based cocktails – Wrong Island Iced Tea sums the place up nicely. Buy your drink tickets from the booth first, then redeem them at the bar.

Public House
BAR

(Map p60; 🗹 03-9421 0187; www.publichouse.com.au; 433-435 Church St; ⊙ noon-late Tue-Sun; 🚋 70, 79, 🚉 East Richmond) Not in any way resembling a public house from any period of history, this great Six Degrees fit-out features their signature blend of found glass and earthy raw and recycled materials. There's imported beer on tap, jugs of Pimms and a short but sweet wine list. DJs set up on weekends and attract a young good-looking crowd ready to, uh, mingle.

Collection
BAR

(www.thecollectionbar.com.au; 328 Bridge Rd; ⊙ 4pm-1am Tue-Sun; 🚋 48, 75) Another bar Americana, this swampy New Orleans watering hole has big glass jars of gin and bourbon resting on its polished bar and a menu of Cajun-Creole cooking, including dishes with crocodile (no alligator, sorry), gumbo and crab sandwiches.

Touchwood
CAFE

(www.touchwoodcafe.com; 480 Bridge Rd; ⊙ 7am-4pm Mon-Fri, 7.30am-4.30pm Sat & Sun; 🚋 48, 75)

A light, airy cafe with plenty of space, both indoors and out, in its courtyard, serving single-origin coffee in a former recycled furniture store (hence: Touchwood).

Aviary BAR
(Map p60; www.theaviary.com.au; 271 Victoria St; ☺noon-1am; 🚊24,109) If you want a nightcap after your rice paper rolls, this atmospheric bluestone inner-city bar has a good range of beers and wines, or good cocktails – including by the jug.

🍷 Fitzroy & Around

Possessing the highest density of pubs of any suburb in Melbourne, Fitzroy has a big drinking scene. Neighbouring Collingwood and Northcote (along High St) also see a lot of action.

★ Naked for Satan BAR
(Map p64; ☑03-9416 2238; www.nakedforsatan. com.au; 285 Brunswick St, Fitzroy; ☺noon-midnight Sun-Thu, to 1am Fri & Sat; 🚊112) Vibrant, loud and reviving an apparent Brunswick St legend (a man nicknamed Satan who would get down and dirty, naked because of the heat, in an illegal vodka distillery under the shop), this place packs a punch both with its popular *pintxos* (Basque tapas; $2), huge range of cleverly named beverages, and unbeatable roof terrace with wraparound decked balcony.

Everleigh COCKTAIL BAR
(Map p64; www.theeverleigh.com; 150-156 Gertrude St, Fitzroy; ☺5.30pm-late; 🚊86) Sophistication and bartending standards are off the charts at this upstairs hidden nook. Settle into a leather booth in the intimate setting with a few friends for conversation and oohing-and-ahhing over classic 'golden era' cocktails like you've never tasted before.

Joe's Shoe Store BAR
(☑03-9482 7666; 233 High St, Northcote; ☺4pm-midnight Tue-Thu, 2pm-midnight Fri-Sun; 🚊86, 🚊Northcote) Someone called Joe will no longer sell you lace-up brogues but this dark, groovy drinking hole keeps the Northcote cool kids well wined and beered. Has backyard seating, and you can order pizza from next-door Pizza Meine Liebe.

Wesley Anne LIVE MUSIC, BAR
(☑03-9482 1333; www.wesleyanne.com.au; 250 High St, Northcote; ☺4pm-late Mon-Fri, 2pm-late Sat & Sun; 🚊86, 🚊Northcote) This atmospheric pub set up shop in a church mission's house

of assembly. What else can you expect when the demon drink wins out against the forces of temperance? Booze, yes, but also interesting food, live music, a big beer garden with space heaters, and a cruisy crowd who often bring their kids along in daylight hours.

Panama Dining Room BAR
(Map p64; ☑03-9417 7663; www.thepanama.com. au; 3rd fl, 231 Smith St, Fitzroy; 🚊86) Gawp at the ersatz Manhattan views in this large warehouse-style space while sipping serious cocktails and snacking on truffled polenta chips or falafel balls with tahini. The dining area gets packed around 9pm for its Mod European menu.

De Clieu CAFE
(Map p64; 187 Gertrude St, Fitzroy; ☺7am-5pm Mon-Sat, 8am-5pm Sun; 🚊86) You'll find locals spilling out the door and perched on the window-sill seats on weekends at this funky cafe (pronounced 'clue') with its polished concrete floors and excellent coffee, courtesy of Seven Seeds. The all-day brunch menu features interesting cafe fare such as miso and broadbean fritters, scrambled tofu and pork-neck roti.

Proud Mary CAFE
(Map p64; ☑03-9417 5930; 172 Oxford St, Collingwood; ☺7.30am-4pm Mon-Fri, 8.30am-4pm Sat & Sun; 🛜; 🚊86) A champion for direct trade, single-origin coffee. Caffeine is serious business here at what is your quintessential backstreet industrial Collingwood red-brick space, regularly packed out with hipsters woofing down green eggs on toast or crispy pork-belly sandwiches.

Industry Beans CAFE
(Map p64; www.industrybeans.com; cnr Fitzroy & Rose Sts, Fitzroy; ☺7am-4pm Mon-Fri, 8am-5pm Sat & Sun; 🛜; 🚊96, 112) It's all about coffee chemistry at this warehouse cafe tucked in a Fitzroy side street. The coffee guide takes you through the speciality styles on offer (roasted on-site) and helpful staff take the pressure off deciding. Pair your brew with some latte coffee pearls or coffee toffee prepared in the 'lab'. The food menu is ambitious but doesn't always hit the mark.

Napier Hotel PUB
(Map p64; ☑03-9419 4240; www.thenapierhotel. com; 210 Napier St, Fitzroy; ☺3-11pm Mon-Thu, 1pm-1am Fri & Sat, 1-11pm Sun; 🚊86, 112) The Napier has stood on this corner for over a

MELBOURNE DRINKING & NIGHTLIFE

BARS & BREWERIES FOR BEER SNOBS

Until recently, thirsty Melburnians were given the choice of only two or three main-stream beers on tap (and perhaps an interstate lager if one was feeling adventurous). But the last few years have seen the emergence of microbreweries and craft-beer bars – primed to meet the demands of beer geeks who treat their drinking more seriously.

The two biggest events on the Melbourne beer calendar are **Good Beer Week** (www.goodbeerweek.com.au) and the **Great Australasian Beer SpecTAPular** (www.gabsfestival.com.au); both held in May, they showcase local, national and foreign craft beers. **Aussie Brewery Tours** (☎1300 787 039; www.aussiebrewerytours.com.au; incl transport, lunch and tastings $150) will help you get around with a tour of several inner-city breweries and iconic pubs.

The following microbreweries in Melbourne produce their beer on-site and have a bar for sampling the goods:

Mountain Goat Brewery (www.goatbeer.com.au; cnr North & Clark Sts, Richmond; ⊙5pm-midnight Wed & Fri; ☒48, 75, 109, ☒Burnley) In Richmond's industrial backstreets, this local brewery is set in a massive beer-producing warehouse, with $11 tasting paddles, pizzas and free tours on Wednesdays. Head down Bridge Rd, turn left at Burnley St and right at North St.

Temple Brewery (☎03-9380 8999; www.templebrewing.com.au/; 122 Weston St, Brunswick East; ⊙5.30-11pm Mon-Thu, noon-11pm Fri & Sat, noon-9pm Sun; ☒1, 8) Try a seasonal craft brew at this classy brewery with a brasserie.

Matilda Bay Brewery (☎03-9673 4545; www.matildabay.com.au; 89 Bertie St, Port Melbourne; ⊙11.30am-10pm Tue-Thu, to 11pm Fri & Sat; ☒109) Great selections of beers brewed on-site, which you can sample among production equipment. Free tours on Saturdays.

James Squire Brewhouse@Portland Hotel (Map p50; ☎03-9810 0064; www.portlandhotel.com.au; 127 Russell St, Melbourne; ⊙noon-late; ☒86, 96) Brewery tours on demand (though avoid lunch and dinner rush) of this much-loved beer producer.

Carlton & United Breweries (p63) Certainly not craft beer, but a must for beer lovers.

Some bars worth checking out for their speciality beer include the following:

Local Taphouse (p112) One of St Kilda's finest establishments for craft beer.

Chapel St Cellars (Map p68; www.chapelstcellars.com.au; 89 Chapel St, Windsor; ⊙4pm-late Mon-Thu, 2-11pm Fri-Sun; ☒78, 79, ☒Windsor) This no-frills bottleshop-bar keeps things real in Chapel St. Grab a boutique beer from the fridge at cost price ($5 corkage for bottled wine) and take a seat at one of the Laminex tables. Also has craft beers on tap (takeaway fill-ups available) and BYO food.

Mrs Parma's (Map p50; www.mrsparmas.com.au; 25 Little Bourke St , Melbourne; chicken parma $25; ⊙11am-late Mon-Fri, noon-late Sat & Sun; ☒Parliament) A huge selection of Victorian craft beers to accompany its 15 different kinds of chicken parmas.

Slowbeer (☎03-9421 3838; 468 Bridge Rd, Richmond; ⊙2-8pm Mon-Wed, noon-9pm Thu-Sat, noon-8pm Sun; ☒48, 75) Part craft-beer bottleshop, part bar, Slowbeer is a great place for a casual afternoon brew. Buy a beer and enjoy it in-store (corkage fees apply) or get a takeaway growler (old-style 1.89L reusable bottle) filled with your choice of tap beer.

Alehouse Project (☎03-9387 1218; www.thealehouseproject.com.au; 98-100 Lygon St, East Brunswick; ⊙3pm-late Tue-Fri, noon-late Sat & Sun; ☎; ☒1, 8) Brunswick bar for beer snobs to convene and compare notes, or just rock up to booze on 12 craft beers on tap. Mixes beer-hall-style seating, used couches, courtyard and sports on the plasma.

Beer DeLuxe (Map p50; www.beerdeluxe.com.au; Federation Sq, Melbourne; ⊙11am-11pm Sun-Wed, 11am-late Thu-Sat; ☒Tourist Shuttle, ☒City Circle, ☒Flinders St) This Federation Square joint has a beer bible in place of a menu, with 160 selections in an attractive hall-style beer garden.

century; many pots have been pulled as the face of the neighbourhood changed, as demonstrated by the memorabilia of the sadly departed Fitzroy footy team. Worm your way around the central bar to the boisterous dining room for an iconic Bogan Burger. Head upstairs to check out its gallery, too.

The Rose PUB
(Map p64; 406 Napier St, Fitzroy; ☺ noon-midnight Sun-Wed, to 1am Thu-Sat; ☑ 86, 112) A much-loved Fitzroy backstreet local, the Rose has remained true to its roots with cheap counter meals and a non-pretentious crowd here to watch the footy.

Little Creatures Dining Hall BEER HALL
(Map p64; ☑ 03-9417 5500; www.littlecreatures. com.au; 222 Brunswick St, Fitzroy; ☺ 8am-late; ☎; ☑ 112) This vast drinking hall is the perfect place to imbibe the produce of one of Australia's most successful microbreweries, and gorge on pizzas. Also has free use of community bikes with picnic baskets, so pick up one of their beery hampers.

Grace Darling PUB
(Map p64; www.gracedarlinghotel.com.au; 114 Smith St, Collingwood; ☑ 86) Adored by Collingwood football fans as the birthplace of the club, the Grace has been given a bit of spit and polish by some well-known Melbourne foodies, and while the chicken parma remains, it is certainly not how you know it (more a terracotta bake of chargrilled chook, ham, slow-roasted tomato and parmesan). It also has live music, mainly aimed at the young indie crowd.

The Standard PUB
(Map p64; ☑ 03-9419 4793; 293 Fitzroy St, Fitzroy; ☺ 3-11pm Mon & Tue, noon-11pm Wed-Sat, noon-9pm Sun; ☑ 96, 112) Flaunting a great beer garden, the Standard is anything but its moniker. The Fitzroy backstreet local has down-to-earth bar staff and a truly eclectic crowd enhancing an atmosphere defined by live music, footy on the small screen, and loud and enthusiastic chatter.

Bar Open BAR
(Map p64; ☑ 03-9415 9601; www.baropen.com. au; 317 Brunswick St, Fitzroy; ☺ 3pm-late; ☑ 112) This long-established bar, as the name suggests, is often open when everything else is closed. The bar attracts a relaxed young local crowd ready to kick on. Bands play in the upstairs loft Tuesday to Friday and are almost always free.

Storm in a Teacup CAFE
(Map p64; ☑ 03-9415 9593; www.storminateacup. com.au; 48a Smith St, Collingwood; ☺ 10am-6pm Tue-Sun; ☎; ☑ 86) With Melbourne's infatuation with fancy coffees, it's great to see a cafe with the same devotion to tea. There's a selection of 40 different types of cuppas on offer, with black, green and white teas from around the world, including several single-origin leaves. It also does food and tea-based cocktails.

Eureka Coffee CAFE
(www.eurekacoffee.com.au; 332 St Georges Rd, North Fitzroy; ☺ 7.30am-3pm Mon-Fri, from 8am Sat; ☑ 11, 112) Specialising in Australian-grown coffee, Eureka roasts its own beans and has a great selection of single-origins, too. Come along Thursdays at 11am for free cuppings for coffee roasting and tasting.

Carlton & Around

Seven Seeds CAFE
(Map p66; www.sevenseeds.com.au; 114 Berkeley St, Carlton; ☺ 7am-5pm Mon-Sat, 8am-5pm Sun; ☑ 19, 59) The most spacious of the Seven Seeds coffee empire: there's plenty of room to store your bike and sip a splendid coffee beside the other lucky people who've found this rather out-of-the-way warehouse cafe. Public cuppings are held Wednesday (9am) and Saturday (10am). It also has standing-room-only **Traveller** (Map p50; www.sevenseeds.com. au; 2/14 Crossley St, Melbourne; ☺ 7am-5pm Mon-Fri, 10am-5pm Sat; ☑ 86, 96) and Brother Baba Budan (p103).

Assembly CAFE
(Map p66; www.assemblystore.com; 60 Pelham St, Carlton; ☺ 8am-5pm Mon-Fri, from 10am Sat & Sun; ☎; ☑ 1, 8) A far departure from what coffee once meant to Lygon St – you won't find an espresso machine here. Rather, Assembly is all about filter coffee with single-origin beans, plus an artisanal tea selection, all matched with Matt Forbes' pastries.

Campos Coffee CAFE
(Map p66; www.camposcoffee.com; 144 Elgin St, Carlton; ☺ 7am-4pm Mon-Fri, from 8am Sat; ☑ 1, 8) A Slayer espresso machine, pour-overs, aeropress, siphon, 22-hour cold-drips, on-site roasting, cupping and daily-changing single-origin African, Asia and Latin American coffees – Campos has it all covered for the modern-day caffeine freak.

Jimmy Watson's
WINE BAR

(Map p66; ☑03-9347 3985; www.jimmywatsons. com.au; 333 Lygon St, Carlton; ⊙11am-11pm; ☐1, 8) Keep it tidy at Watson's wine bar with something nice by the glass, or go a bottle of dry and dry (vermouth and ginger ale) and settle in for the afternoon and evening. If this Robyn Boyd–designed stunning mid-century building had ears, there'd be a few generations of writers, students and academics in trouble.

Mr Wilkinson
BAR

(295 Lygon St, East Brunswick; ⊙4pm-1am Mon & Wed-Fri, 2pm-1am Sat & Sun; ☐1, 8) The owners decked this place out themselves, in recycled timber, and now concentrate on keeping things mellow and their customers well watered. It's a great place for a natter to the bar staff.

Alderman
WINE BAR

(134 Lygon St, East Brunswick; ⊙5pm-late Tue-Fri, 2pm-late Sat & Sun; ☎; ☐1, 8) A classic East Brunswick local, the Alderman has an inviting traditional heavy wooden bar, open fireplace, good beer selection and cocktails by the jug. There's a small courtyard and you can order from restaurant Bar Idda (p98) next door.

Town Hall Hotel
PUB, LIVE MUSIC

(☑03-9328 1983; www.townhallhotelnorthmelbourne.com.au; 33 Errol St, North Melbourne; ⊙4pm-1am Mon-Thu, noon-1am Fri & Sat, noon-11pm Sun; ☐57) The Town Hall is an unfussy local. Live music is staged free in the front room from Thursday to Saturday, otherwise they'll be spinning some classic vinyl. There's a beer garden and pub meals, too. From the Queen Vic Market head west along Victoria St, then right at Errol St.

Stovetop
CAFE

(Map p66; www.stovetop.com.au; 100 Leicester St, Carlton; ⊙7am-5pm Mon-Fri, 8am-4pm Sat & Sun; ☎; ☐19, 57, 59) Just up from the Vic Market, Stovetop lives up to its name by preparing and serving their house blend and single-origins in stovetop espresso makers. Order from its bar set on 1970s Besser concrete blocks, and grab a gourmet sausage roll, gruyere cheese toastie with chutney or baked duck eggs for brekkie.

Gerald's Bar
WINE BAR

(386 Rathdowne St, North Carlton; ⊙5-11pm Mon-Sat; ☐253, ☐1, 8) Wine by the glass is democratically selected at Gerald's, and they spin some fine vintage vinyl from behind the curved wooden bar. Gerald himself is out the back preparing to feed you whatever he feels like on the day: goat curry, seared calamari, meatballs, trifle.

Brunswick East Project
CAFE

(☑03-9381 1881; www.padrecoffee.com.au; 483 Lygon St, East Brunswick; ⊙7am-4pm Mon-Sat, 8am-4pm Sun; ☐1, 8) Another big player in Melbourne's coffee movement, this East Brunswick warehouse-style cafe is the original roaster for Padre Coffee and brews its premium single-origins and blends. Also has **League of Honest Coffee** (Map p50; 8 Exploration Lane, Melbourne; ⊙7am-5pm Mon-Fri; ☐City Circle, 24, 30) and stalls at the **Queen Victoria Market** (String Bean Alley, M Shed near Peel St; ⊙7am-2pm Tue & Thu, to 4pm Fri-Sun; ☐55) and South Melbourne Market (p112).

Retreat
BAR, LIVE MUSIC

(☑03-9380 4090; www.retreathotelbrunswick. com.au; 280 Sydney Rd, Brunswick; ⊙noon-late; ☐19, ☐Brunswick) This pub is so big as to be a tad overwhelming. Find your habitat – garden backyard, grungy band room or intimate front bar – and relax. Sundays are very popular with locals who like to laze on the (fake) grass, and there's live music on most nights.

Brunswick Green
BAR

(313 Sydney Rd, Brunswick; ⊙4pm-midnight Tue-Thu, 2pm-1am Fri & Sat, to 11pm Sun; ☐19, ☐Brunswick) A cool Brunswick local with bohemian front bar, comfy share-house-style lounge and backyard beer garden. Wednesday nights feature the popular Variety Collective performers.

South Yarra, Prahran & Windsor

South Yarra and Windsor may be within walking distance of each other, but they're a world away in terms of their bar scenes. Windsor has a number of artfully grungy, loungey locals; South Yarra is all about shouting over the music while clutching a lurid-coloured drink. Not-so-precious Prahran is somewhere in the middle.

Yellow Bird
BAR

(Map p68; ☑03-9533 8983; www.yellowbird.com. au; 122 Chapel St, Windsor; ⊙7.30am-late; ☐78, 79, ☐Windsor) Keeps Windsor's cool kids happy with all-day drinks (including an evil coffee, sugar and beer shot) and diner-style food.

It's owned by the drummer from the band Something for Kate, so the rock 'n' roll ambience is genuine, with a passing cast of musos and a fantastic playlist of indie bands.

Borsch, Vodka & Tears BAR

(Map p68; www.borschvodkaandtears.com; 173 Chapel St, Windsor; ⊟6, ⊠Prahran) This place is *the* business for sampling vodka. The extensive list covers a range of clear, fruit-infused, oak-matured and traditional *nalewka kresowa* (made according to old Russian and Polish recipes); knowledgeable staff can help you choose your shot. Line your stomach with some excellent borsch or blintzes. There's another one in **Elsternwick** (☑03-9523 0969; www.afterthetears.net; 9b Gordon St, Elsternwick; ⊙3pm-late Mon-Thu, from 1pm Fri & Sat, from 11am Sun; ⊟67, ⊠Elsternwick), with 140 types of vodka and contemporary Eastern European dishes.

Market Lane CAFE

(Map p68; www.marketlane.com.au; Prahran Market, 163 Commercial Rd; ⊙7am-5pm Tue-Sat, 8am-5pm Sun; ⊟72, 78, 79) Market Lane is the perfect pick-me-up after poring over gourmet goodies here at the Prahran Market. All roasting is done on-site, producing some of

the best brew in the city. Come Friday and Saturday for the free cuppings (tastings) from 10am to 11am.

Windsor Castle Hotel PUB

(Map p68; 89 Albert St, Windsor; ⊙3pm-late Mon-Thu, noon-late Fri & Sun; ⊟5, 64, ⊠Windsor) This backstreet art deco building is full of cosy nooks, sunken pits, fireplaces and flocked wallpaper that all make the Windsor Castle extremely attractive...but it's the tiki-themed beer garden that makes it *great*.

Dukes CAFE

(Map p68; www.dukescoffee.com.au; 169 Chapel St, Windsor; ⊙7am-4pm Mon-Sat, 8am-4pm Sun; ⊟6, 78, 79) Exposed brick and wood beams give this Windsor cafe a warm feel and the perfect ambience for downing one of its coffees, expertly made from its own beans roasted on-site.

Kid Boston BAR

(Map p68; www.kidboston.com.au; 44 Chapel St, Windsor; ⊙5pm-late Mon-Fri, 3pm-late Sat & Sun; ⊟78, 79, ⊠Windsor) The best cocktails this side of the river. This tiny Windsor newbie has arrived in style, with top-shelf martinis, highballers, sours and apertifs to go with a delicious menu of bar food.

OPEN-AIR DRINKING

Melbourne may be home to some of the coolest bars hidden down rotten-cabbage-leaf-strewn city alleyways, but when the summer sun beats down and the evenings are long and cool, it's time for some fresh air and natural light. Whether it's riding an elevator to a secret rooftop or chugging jugs of ale at a beer garden, Melbourne has some top open-air drinking spots. Some of our favourites:

Rooftop Bars

➡ Naked for Satan (p107)

➡ Bomba (p90)

➡ Madame Brussels (p103)

➡ Palmz at the Carlton Hotel (p105)

➡ Rooftop Bar (p113)

➡ Siglo (p103)

Outdoor Bars & Beer Gardens

➡ Ponyfish Island (Map p50; www.ponyfish.com.au; under Yarra Pedestrian Bridge, Melbourne; ⊙8am-1am; ⊠Flinders St)

➡ The Standard (p109)

➡ Windsor Castle (p111)

➡ Riverland (p105)

➡ Boatbuilders Yard (p106)

➡ The Retreat (p110)

Drugstore Espresso
CAFE

(Map p68; www.drugstoreespresso.com.au; 194 Toorak Rd, South Yarra; ☺ 7am-4pm Mon-Fri, 8am-4pm Sat & Sun; 🗟; 🚊 8, 🚊 South Yarra) Just the place to re-energise from a bout of Chapel St shopping fatigue, with twice-weekly-changing single-origin coffees and a selection of hearty-sized sandwiches and wagyu beef burgers.

Onesixone
CLUB

(Map p68; ☑ 03-9533 8433; www.onesixone.com. au; 161 High St, Prahran; ☺ times vary Thu-Sat; 🚊 6, 🚊 Prahran) Front up to the peephole – if you pass muster, snaffle a couch or a pouf. A wiggle on the small dance floor is obligatory. Late-night Saturdays start at 4am and run until the rest of the world is truly up and about.

Revolver Upstairs
CLUB

(Map p68; www.revolverupstairs.com.au; 229 Chapel St, Prahran; ☺ noon-4am Tue-Fri, 24hr Sat & Sun; 🚊 6, 🚊 Prahran) Rowdy Revolver can feel like an enormous version of your lounge room, but with 54 hours of nonstop music come the weekend, you're probably glad it's not. Live music, interesting DJs and film screenings keep the mixed crowd wide awake.

South Melbourne

Clement
CAFE

(South Melbourne Market, 116-136 Cecil St, South Melbourne; ☺ 7am-5pm; 🚊 96) There's a buzz about this tiny cafe on the perimeter of the South Melbourne Market, not only for its expertly crafted brew but also for the homemade salted-caramel, jam or custard donuts. Grab a streetside stool or takeaway and wander the market.

Padre Coffee
CAFE

(www.padrecoffee.com.au; Shop 33, South Melbourne Market; ☺ 7am-4pm Wed, Sat & Sun, 7am-5pm Fri; 🚊 96) Offers a perfect (and popular) caffeine-enhanced respite from mad market shopping.

Eve
CLUB

(☑ 03-9696 7388; www.evebar.com.au; 334 City Rd, South Melbourne; ☺ dusk-late Thu-Sat; 🚊 112) Florence Broadhurst wallpapers, a black granite bar and Louis chairs set the tone, which gets rapidly lower as the night progresses. Footballers, glamour girls and the odd lost soul come for cocktails and commercial house. Expect to queue after 9pm. Spencer St becomes Clarendon; it's near the corner of City Rd.

St Kilda & Around

Carlisle Wine Bar
WINE BAR

(Map p72; ☑ 03-9531 3222; www.carlislewinebar. com.au; 137 Carlisle St, Balaclava; ☺ 3pm-1am Mon-Fri, 11am-1am Sat & Sun; 🚊 3, 16, 🚊 Balaclava) Locals love this often rowdy, wine-worshiping former butcher's shop. The staff will treat you like a regular and find you a glass of something special, or effortlessly throw together a cocktail amid the weekend rush. The rustic Italian food is good, too. Carlisle St runs east off St Kilda Rd.

George Lane Bar
BAR

(Map p72; www.georgelanebar.com.au; 1 George Lane, St Kilda; ☺ 7pm-1am Thu-Sun; 🚊 96, 16) Hidden behind the hulk of the George Hotel, tucked away off Grey St, this little bar is a good rabbit hole to dive into. Its pleasantly ad-hoc decor is a relief from the inch-of-its-life design aesthetic elsewhere. There are DJs (and queues) on the weekends.

Local Taphouse
BAR

(Map p72; www.thelocal.com.au; 184 Carlisle St, St Kilda; ☺ noon-late; 🚊 16, 78, 🚊 Balaclava) Reminiscent of an old-school Brooklyn bar. Prop up to its dark-wood polished bar and scratch your head to decide which one of its 19 craft beers on tap or its impressive bottle list to order. There's a beer garden upstairs, while downstairs has chesterfield couches, an open fire and indoor bocce pit. It's also known for its live comedy nights.

Pause Bar
BAR

(Map p72; ☑ 03-9537 0511; www.pausebar.com. au; 268 Carlisle St, Balaclava; ☺ 4pm-1am Mon-Fri, noon-1am Sat & Sun; 🚊 3, 16, 79, 🚊 Balaclava) Pause has been around for over a decade and draws a loyal local crowd who like to settle into the dim North African–inspired bar for cocktails (two for $22!) and meze. Also has live music Thursday and Friday nights, and Sunday afternoons.

George Public Bar
BAR

(Map p72; www.georgepublicbar.com.au; Basement, 127 Fitzroy St, St Kilda; ☺ 3pm-late; 🚊 3a, 96, 16) Upstairs/downstairs divisions live on, even in egalitarian St Kilda. Behind the crumbling paint and Edwardian arched windows of the George Hotel, there's the **Melbourne Wine Room** serving drinks and good-value counter meals. In the bowels of the building is the George Public Bar – formerly the infamous Snakepit – often rowdy and a good spot for a beer and a game of pool.

Republica BAR
(Map p72; www.republica.net.au; 10-18 Jacka Blvd, St Kilda Sea Baths, St Kilda; ☺ 11.30am-1am Mon-Fri, 9am-1am Sat & Sun; ☎; ☒ 3a, 16, 96) Opening right up to St Kilda Beach, Republica is the closest you'll get to a beach bar in Melbourne. It's a great spot for a sunset beer or cocktail lounging in a hanging wicker chair, but you can also start the day here by the sea with breakfast and coffee.

St Kilda Bowling Club PUB
(Map p72; www.stkildasportsclub.com.au; 66 Fitzroy St, St Kilda; ☺ noon-11pm Sun-Thu, to 1am Fri & Sat; ☒ 16, 96, 112) This fabulously intact old clubhouse is tucked behind a neatly trimmed hedge and a splendid bowling green. The long bar serves drinks at 'club prices' (ie cheap) and you'll be joined by St Kilda's hippest on Sunday afternoons. Kick off your shoes, roll a few bowls, knock back beers and watch the sun go down along with your bowling accuracy.

Hotel Barkly PUB
(Map p72; ☎ 03-9525 3354; www.hotelbarkly.com; 109 Barkly St, St Kilda; ☒ 16, 67, 79) The street-level public bar is the place to go if you're up for sinking a few pints, wiggling to whatever comes on the jukebox and snogging a stranger before last drinks are called. The rooftop bar feigns a bit of class, but things get messy up there, too. Worth it for the spectacular sunset views across St Kilda, though.

Vineyard BAR
(Map p72; www.thevineyard.com.au; 71a Acland St, St Kilda; ☺ 10.30am-3.30am Mon-Fri, 10am-3.30am Sat & Sun; ☒ 3a, 16, 96) An old favourite, the Vineyard has the perfect corner position and a courtyard barbecue that attracts crowds of backpackers and scantily clad young locals who enjoy themselves so much they drown out the neighbouring roller coaster. Sunday afternoon sessions are big here.

St Kilda Dispensary CAFE
(Map p72; 13 Brighton Rd, St Kilda; ☺ 7am-4pm Mon-Fri, 8am-4pm Sat & Sun; ☒ 16, 67, 79) What was once the first dispensary in the southern hemisphere during the 1940s, this cafe keeps with the medical theme with tiled counters, test tubes and beakers and a menu that prescribes the good stuff: organic coffees, breakfast rolls and tuna melts. Cash only.

☆ Entertainment

Cinemas

Cinema multiplexes are spread throughout central Melbourne, and there are quite a few treasured independent cinemas in both the city centre and surrounding suburbs. Outdoor cinemas are popular in the summer. Don't forget to grab a choc-top (ice-cream cone dipped in chocolate).

**Australian Centre
for the Moving Image** CINEMA
(ACMI; Map p50; ☎ 03-9663 2583; www.acmi. net.au; Federation Sq, Melbourne; ☒ 1, 48, 70, 72, 75, ⓡ Flinders St) ACMI's cinemas screen a diverse range of films. It programs regular events and festivals for film genres and audiences, as well as screening one-offs.

Cinema Nova CINEMA
(Map p66; ☎ 03-9347 5331; www.cinemanova.com. au; 380 Lygon St, Carlton; ☒ Tourist Shuttle, ☒ 1, 8) The latest in arthouse, docos and foreign films. Cheap Monday screenings.

Rooftop Cinema CINEMA
(Map p50; www.rooftopcinema.com.au; Level 6, Curtin House, 252 Swanston St, Melbourne; ⓡ Melbourne Central) This rooftop bar sits at dizzying heights on top of the happening Curtin House. In summer it transforms into an outdoor cinema with striped deckchairs and a calendar of new and classic favourite flicks.

Astor CINEMA
(Map p68; ☎ 03-9510 1414; www.astortheatre.net. au; cnr Chapel St & Dandenong Rd, Windsor; ☒ 5, 64, 78, ⓡ Windsor) See a double feature for the price of one. Screens a mix of recent releases, art-house films and classics in art deco surrounds.

Kino Cinemas CINEMA
(Map p50; ☎ 03-9650 2100; www.palacecinemas. com.au; Collins Place, 45 Collins St, Melbourne; ☒ 11, 31, 48, 109, 112) The Kino screens arthouse films in its comfy licensed cinemas. Monday is discount day.

IMAX CINEMA
(Map p66; ☎ 03-9663 5454; www.imaxmelbourne. com.au; Melbourne Museum, Rathdowne St, Carlton; ☒ Tourist Shuttle, ☒ 86, 96) Animal and adventure films in 3D screen on a grand scale here, with movies specially made for these giant screens.

MELBOURNE ENTERTAINMENT

CURTAINS UP

Blockbuster musicals have the good fortune of playing in Melbourne's graceful old city-centre theatres:

Athenaeum (Map p50; 03-9650 1500; www.athenaeumtheatre.com.au; 188 Collins St; 11, 31, 48, 112) The old dame dates back to the 1830s, with the Greek goddess of wisdom, Athena, sitting atop the facade, imbuing the theatre with classical gravitas. The theatre now hosts Melbourne Opera perfromances and the International Comedy Festival. Also a Ticketmaster box office.

Comedy Theatre (Map p50; 03-9299 9800; www.marrinertheatres.com.au; 240 Exhibition St; 86, 96) This midsize 1920s Spanish-style venue is dedicated to comedy, theatre and musicals.

Her Majesty's Theatre (Map p50; 03-8643 3300; www.hmt.com.au; 219 Exhibition St; 86, 96) On the outside Her Maj is red-brick Second Empire; on the inside it's 1930s Moderne. It's been the home of musicals and comedy since 1880 and is still going strong.

Princess Theatre (Map p50; Ticketmaster 1300 111 011; www.marrinertheatres.com.au; 163 Spring St; 86, 96) This gilded Second Empire beauty has a long and colourful history. It's reputed to have a resident ghost – that of singer Federici, who died as he descended through the stage trap in 1888 after playing Mephistopheles in the opera *Faust*. These days, shows range from *Phantom of the Opera* to *Mary Poppins*.

Regent Theatre (Map p50; 03-9299 9500; www.marrinertheatres.com.au; 191 Collins St; 11, 31, 48, 112) The opulent Regent, a rococo picture palace, was considered one of the most lavish theatres of its kind when it was built in 1929 with the advent of the talkies. Today it's used for blockbuster stage shows – still a fabulous opportunity to experience its elegant grandeur.

Moonlight Cinema   CINEMA
(www.moonlight.com.au; Gate D, Birdwood Ave, Royal Botanic Gardens, Melbourne; 8) Melbourne's original outdoor cinema, with the option of 'Gold Grass' tickets that include a glass of wine and a reserved bean-bag bed.

St Kilda Open Air Cinema   CINEMA
(Map p72; www.openaircinemas.com.au; South Beach Reserve, Jacka Blvd, St Kilda; 1-22 Dec; 79, 96) Cult classics by the sea. Rents out blankets, deckchairs ($4) and bean-bag lounges ($7).

Theatre

Melbourne's theatre district is not limited to the city centre, with individual companies and theatres spread across town. Tickets start at about $20 for independent productions and $30 for mainstream theatre. Try Halftix Melbourne (p117) for cheap tickets to the theatre, to be purchased in person on the day, with cash.

See the boxed text, above, for a listing of Melbourne's historical theatres showing blockbuster shows.

La Mama   THEATRE
(Map p66; 03-9347 6948; www.lamama.com.au; 205 Faraday St, Carlton; 1, 8) La Mama is historically significant in Melbourne's theatre scene. This tiny, intimate forum produces new Australian works and experimental theatre, and has a reputation for developing emerging playwrights. It's a ramshackle building with an open-air bar. Shows also run at its larger **Courthouse Theatre** on 349 Drummond St, Carlton, so check tickets carefully for the correct location.

Malthouse Theatre   THEATRE
(03-9685 5111; www.malthousetheatre.com.au; 113 Sturt St, Southbank; 1) The Malthouse Theatre Company often produces the most exciting theatre in Melbourne. Dedicated to promoting Australian works, the company has been housed in the atmospheric Malthouse Theatre since 1990 (when it was known as the Playbox). From Flinders Street Station walk across Princes Bridge and along St Kilda Rd. Turn right at Grant St, then left into Sturt St.

Melbourne Theatre Company THEATRE

(MTC; ☏03-8688 0800; www.mtc.com.au; 140 Southbank Blvd, Southbank; ☒1) Melbourne's major theatrical company stages around 15 productions each year, ranging from contemporary and modern (including many new Australian works) to Shakespearean and other classics. Performances take place in a brand-new, award-winning venue in Southbank.

Butterfly Club CABARET

(Map p50; ☏03-9654 4068; www.thebutterflyclub. com; Carson Pl, off Little Collins St, Melbourne; ⏱5pm-late Tue-Sun; ☒96, 112) Down a quintessential Melbourne laneway, this eccentric little cabaret club remains largely undiscovered. Expect acts that aren't really theatre, aren't quite straight comedy, and which might just throw in a song. The rooms display an extraordinary collection of kitsch, which adds to the feeling that you're never quite sure what you're in for. Has a great cocktail bar.

Red Stitch Actors Theatre THEATRE

(Map p68; ☏03-9533 8082; www.redstitch.net; Rear, 2 Chapel St, Windsor; ☒5, 64, 78, 79, ☒Windsor) This independent company of actors stages new international works that are often premieres in Australia. The tiny black-box theatre, opposite the Astor Cinema and down the end of the driveway, is a cosy, intimate space.

Theatreworks THEATRE

(Map p72; ☏03-9534 3388; www.theatreworks.org. au; 14 Acland St, St Kilda; ☒64) Theatreworks is a quality community theatre dedicated to supporting a range of arts practitioners. There's a bar for pre-show drinks.

Comedy

Held in March and April, the **Melbourne International Comedy Festival** (www. comedyfestival.com.au; Melbourne Town Hall; ⏱Mar-Apr) is a huge event, but you don't need to wait until then to have a laugh in Melbourne.

Last Laugh at the Comedy Club COMEDY

(Map p50; ☏03-9650 1977; www.thecomedy club.com.au; Athenaeum Theatre, 188 Collins St, Melbourne; show $25; ⏱Fri & Sat; ☒1, 72, 112, ☒Flinders St) The Last Laugh is open Friday and Saturday nights year-round, with additional evenings in summer. This is professional stand-up, featuring local and international artists. Dinner-show packages ($55) are available – bookings recommended. The club is also a venue for acts during the Comedy Festival.

Comic's Lounge COMEDY

(☏03-9348 9488; www.thecomicslounge.com. au; 26 Errol St, North Melbourne; ☒57) There is stand-up every night of the week here. Admission prices vary, but are usually between $15 and $25. Dinner and show nights are popular and feature Melbourne's best-known comedians (many of whom also host radio shows). Tuesday is a kind of open-mic night, where aspiring comics have their eight minutes of fame (or shame).

Live Music

Check daily papers and weekly street magazines **Beat** (www.beat.com.au) and **The Music** (www.themusic.com.au) for gig info. Radio station 3RRR (102.7FM) broadcasts a gig guide at 7pm each evening and puts it online at www.rrr.org.au.

Online **Mess+Noise** (www.messandnoise. com) is an Australian-focused music website, with an informed, irreverent chat forum. **FasterLouder** (www.fasterlouder.com.au) also has a gig guide and music news.

Esplanade Hotel LIVE MUSIC

(The Espy; Map p72; ☏03-9534 0211; www.espy. com.au; 11 The Esplanade, St Kilda; ⏱noon-1am Sun-Wed, to 3am Thu-Sat; ☒16, 96) Rock-pigs rejoice. The Espy remains gloriously shabby and welcoming to all. A mix of local and international bands play nightly, everything from rock 'n' roll to hip hop either in the legendary Gershwin Room, the front bar or down in the basement.

Even if you're not here for a gig, come for front-row seats of the pink-stained St Kilda sunset. The Espy does good pub food and the heritage-listed building itself is stunning.

The Tote LIVE MUSIC

(☏03-9419 5320; www.thetotehotel.com; cnr Johnston & Wellington Sts, Collingwood; ⏱4pm-late Tue-Sun; ☒86) One of Melbourne's most iconic live-music venues, not only does this divey Collingwood pub have a great roster of local and international underground bands, but one of the best jukeboxes in the universe. Its temporary closure in 2010 brought Melbourne to a stop, literally – people protested on the city-centre streets against the liquor licensing laws that were blamed for the closure.

Corner Hotel

LIVE MUSIC

(Map p60; ☑03-9427 9198; www.cornerhotel.com; 57 Swan St, Richmond; ⊙4pm-late Tue & Wed, noon-late Thu-Sun; ☒70, ☒Richmond) The band room here is one of Melbourne's most popular midsized venues and has seen plenty of loud and live action over the years, from Dinosaur Jr to the Buzzcocks. If your ears need a break, there's a friendly front bar. The rooftop has city views, but gets superpacked, and often with a different crowd from the music fans below.

Northcote Social Club

LIVE MUSIC

(☑03-9489 3917; www.northcotesocialclub.com; 301 High St, Northcote; ⊙4pm-late Mon & Tue, noon-late Wed-Sun; ☒86, ☒Northcote) The stage at this inner-north local has seen plenty of international folks just one album out from star status. Its homegrown line-up is also notable. If you're just after a drink, the front bar buzzes every night of the week, and there's a large deck out back for lazy afternoons.

Old Bar

LIVE MUSIC, PUB

(Map p64; ☑03-9417 4155; www.theoldbar.com. au; 74-76 Johnston St, Fitzroy; ☎; ☒96, 112) With live bands seven days a week and a licence till 3am, the Old Bar's another reason why Melbourne is the rock 'n' roll capital of Australia. It gets great local bands and a few internationals playing in its grungy band room with a house-party vibe.

Bennetts Lane

JAZZ

(Map p50; ☑03-9663 2856; www.bennettslane.com; 25 Bennetts Lane, Melbourne; ⊙9pm-late; ☒City Circle, 24, 30) Bennetts Lane has long been the boiler room of Melbourne jazz. It attracts the cream of local and international talent and an audience that knows when it's time to applaud a solo. Beyond the cosy front bar, there's another space reserved for big gigs.

Prince Bandroom

LIVE MUSIC

(Map p72; ☑03-9536 1168; www.princebandroom. com.au; 29 Fitzroy St, St Kilda; ☒16, 96, 112) The Prince is a much-loved St Kilda venue, with quality international and local rock, indie, DJs and hip-hop bands having graced its stage. Its leafy balcony and raucous downstairs bar are added attractions. These days it leans more towards dance and electropop acts.

Ding Dong Lounge

LIVE MUSIC

(Map p50; ☑03-9654 3549; www.dingdonglounge. com.au; Level 1, 18 Market Lane, Melbourne; ⊙Wed-Sun; ☒86, 96) One of the first venues that made the city cool in the early 2000s, Ding Dong has received a post-modern makeover, but remains one of the city centre's premier rock 'n' roll venues for smaller touring acts and local bands.

Public Bar

LIVE MUSIC, PUB

(Map p66; ☑03-9329 9888; www.thepublicbar. com.au; 238 Victoria St, Melbourne; ⊙2pm-late Tue-Fri, noon-late Sat & Sun; ☒19, 55, 57) This old live-music stalwart has recently been given a new lease of life, and is doing a magnificent job supporting live music with a solid line-up of rock 'n' roll Thursday to Sunday. Also has trivia on Tuesday and comedy Wednesday, and food from Miss Katie's Crab Shack (p89).

John Curtin Hotel

LIVE MUSIC, PUB

(Map p66; ☑03-9663 6350; www.johncurtinhotel. com; 29 Lygon St, Carlton; ☒1, 3, 8, 64, 72) Popular with uni students, the John Curtin is a great pub for a beer; it also hosts some great local indie and rock bands upstairs most nights.

Reverence Hotel

LIVE MUSIC, PUB

(☑03-9687 2111; www.reverencehotel.com; 28 Napier St, Footscray; ☒Footscray) Rising from the ashes of the much-loved Arthouse, the Reverence takes over as one of the city's best punk and metal venues, located in industrial Footscray (just up the road from Lonely Planet HQ). Shows a mix of Australian and internationals, from new- to old-school bands. It also does a great menu of Mexican food.

The Bendigo

LIVE MUSIC

(☑03-9417 3415; www.bendigohotel.com.au; 125 Johnston St, Collingwood; ⊙4pm-3am Tue-Sun; ☒86) The Bendigo is everything that's great about Collingwood: dark, divey and straight down the line. It's got a great roster of local and international underground bands, with a leaning towards metal and punk. Come Sunday for $10 jugs.

Boney

LIVE MUSIC, BAR

(Map p50; ☑03-9663 8268; www.boney.net.au; 68 Little Collins St, Melbourne; ⊙noon-3am Mon-Wed, to 5am Thu, to 7am Fri & Sat; ☒86, 96, 112) Taking over from one of Melbourne's most infamous rock 'n' roll bars (called Pony), this new version may be more sanitised, but the good news is it's still got the late-night 2am gigs upstairs, covering anything from fuzzed-out garage to electronica. Its American-diner-meets-Thai food is fantastic, too.

Evelyn Hotel
LIVE MUSIC, PUB

(Map p64; ☑ 03-9419 5500; www.evelynhotel.com; 351 Brunswick St, Fitzroy; ⊙ 12.30pm-1.30am; 🚇 112) Playing mostly local acts, the Evelyn also pulls the occasional international performer. The Ev doesn't discriminate by genre: if it's quality, it gets a look-in here.

Billboard the Venue
LIVE MUSIC

(Map p50; ☑ 03-9639 4000; www.billboardthevenue.com.au; 170 Russell St, Melbourne; 🚇 86, 96) Known by many Melburnians for its dodgy nightclub, these days this purpose-built entertainment venue attracts a good-quality crop of international and local bands (and it still has its famous disco).

Workers Club
LIVE MUSIC, PUB

(Map p64; ☑ 03-9415 6558; www.theworkersclub.com.au; cnr Brunswick & Gertrude Sts, Fitzroy; ⊙ 4pm-late Sun-Wed, noon-late Thu-Sat; 🚇 86, 112) The former Rob Roy has been decked out in all-retro, offering up six nights of live music, and the front bar serves up cocktails in jugs and offers cheapish mains of the rib-eye or salmon type.

Palais Theatre
CONCERT VENUE

(Map p72; ☑ 03-9525 3240, tickets 13 61 00; www.palaistheatre.net.au; Lower Esplanade, St Kilda; 🚇 3a, 16, 79, 96) Standing gracefully next to Luna Park, the heritage-listed Palais (c 1927) is a St Kilda icon. Not only is the theatre a beautiful old space, but it also stages some pretty special performances, from international bands to big-name comedians.

Night Cat
LIVE MUSIC, BAR

(Map p64; ☑ 03-9417 0090; www.thenightcat.com.au; 141 Johnston St, Fitzroy; ⊙ 9pm-3am Fri-Sat, 7pm-3am Sun; 🚇 112) The Night Cat is a barn-sized space that saw the birth of the upside-down lampshade aesthetic in the mid-'90s. There are two bars, a stage and a black-and-white chequered dance floor that sees lots of action. Music is generally in the Latin, jazz or funk vein. Offers salsa dance classes ($15) on Sunday nights.

Festival Hall
CONCERT VENUE

(☑ 03-9329 9699; www.festivalhall.com.au; 300 Dudley St, West Melbourne; 🚇 24, 30, 34, 70, 🚇 North Melbourne) This former boxing stadium – aka 'Festering Hall' (especially on hot summer nights) – is a fave for live international acts. The Beatles played here in 1964.

Toff in Town
LIVE MUSIC, BAR

(Map p50; ☑ 03-9639 8770; www.thetoffintown.com; Level 2, Curtin House, 252 Swanston St, Mel-

TICKETS

Tickets for concerts, theatre, comedy and other events are usually available from one of the agencies listed:

Moshtix (www.moshtix.com.au)

Ticketek (Map p50; http://premier.ticketek.com.au)

Ticketmaster (Map p50; www.ticketmaster.com.au)

Halftix (Map p50; www.halftixmelbourne.com; Melbourne Town Hall, 90-120 Swanston St, Melbourne; ⊙ 10am-2pm Mon, 11am-6pm Tue-Fri, 10am-4pm Sat; 🚇 Flinders St)

bourne; 5pm-late Sun-Thu, 3pm-late Fri 🚇 Melbourne Central) An atmospheric venue well suited to cabaret, but which also works for intimate gigs by rock gods and avant-folksters.

Forum Theatre
CONCERT VENUE

(Map p50; ☑ tickets 13 61 00; www.marrinertheatres.com.au; 150-152 Flinders St; 🚇 Flinders St) One of the city's most atmospheric live-music venues, it does double duty as a cinema during the Melbourne Film Festival. The Moorish exterior houses an equally interesting interior, with the southern night sky rendered on the domed ceiling.

Hamer Hall
CONCERT VENUE

(Melbourne Concert Hall; Map p50; ☑ 1300 182 183; www.artscentremelbourne.com.au; Arts Centre Melbourne, 100 St Kilda Rd; 🚇 1, 3, 16, 64, 72, 🚇 Flinders St) Having recently undergone a multi-million-dollar redevelopment, the concert hall is well known for its excellent acoustics, with a decor inspired by Australia's mineral and gemstone deposits.

Sidney Myer Music Bowl
CONCERT VENUE

(☑ 1300 182 183; www.artscentremelbourne.com.au; Linlithgow Ave, King Domain Gardens; 🚇 3, 5, 6, 8, 16, 64, 67, 72) This beautiful amphitheatre in the park is used for a variety of outdoor events, from the **Tropfest** film festival to Nick Cave and the Bad Seeds, Opera in the Bowl or the New Year's Day rave **Summerdayze**.

Rod Laver Arena
CONCERT VENUE

(Map p60; ☑ tickets 132 849; www.mopt.com.au; Batman Ave, Richmond; 🚇 70) A giant, versatile space used for headline international concerts and the Australian Open tennis, with a huge sunroof. Not the most atmospheric of venues, but then it's all about the spectacle. Ditto for the nearby **Hisense Arena**.

Dance

Melbourne's classical-dance and ballet scene has companies specialising in both traditional ballet performances and genre-busting modern pieces.

Australian Ballet   BALLET
(☏1300 369 741; www.australianballet.com.au; 2 Kavanagh St, Melbourne; ⌂1) Based in Melbourne and now more than 40 years old, the Australian Ballet performs traditional and new works at the State Theatre in the Arts Centre. You can take an hour-long Australian Ballet Centre Tour ($18; bookings essential) that includes a visit to the production and wardrobe departments as well as the studios of both the company and the school.

Chunky Move   DANCE
(☏03-9645 5188; www.chunkymove.com; 111 Sturt St, Melbourne; ⌂1) This partially government-funded contemporary dance company performs internationally acclaimed pop-inspired pieces at its sexy venue behind the Australian Centre for Contemporary Art. It also runs a variety of dance, yoga and pilates classes; check the website. From Flinders Street Station walk across Princes Bridge and along St Kilda Rd. Turn right at Grant St then left into Sturt St.

Kage Physical Theatre   DANCE
(☏03-9417 6700; www.kagephysicaltheatre.com; Abbotsford Convent, 1 St Heliers St, Abbotsford; ⌂200, 201, 207, ⌂Collingwood) This modern dance company works between theatre and dance. This is witty and innovative stuff, well worth a look if you're not after a straight narrative. Check the website for performance details.

MCG DREAMING

Where did Australian Rules football come from? There's plenty of evidence to suggest that Aboriginal men and women played a form of football (called 'marngrook') prior to white settlement. Did they play it at the MCG site pre-settlement? The MCG has two scar trees from which bark was removed by Aboriginal people to make canoes. These reminders make it clear that Melbourne's footy fans (and perhaps players) were not the first to gather at the site of the MCG – or the Melbourne Corroboree Ground, as some Indigenous Australians like to call it.

Classical Music

The following groups are a few of the city's main players, who perform at various venues across town. Check their websites or the local press for venues and concert dates. Melbourne also has a number of small, independent and often very innovative classical groups. Check the *Age* newspaper for listings.

Melbourne Symphony Orchestra   ORCHESTRA
(MSO; ☏03-9929 9600; www.mso.com.au) The MSO has a broad reach: while not afraid to be populist (it's done sell-out performances with both Burt Bacharach and the Whitlams), it can also be edgy – such as performing with Kiss – along with its performances of the great masterworks of symphony. It performs regularly at venues around the city, including Melbourne Town Hall, the Recital Centre and Hamer Hall. Also runs a summer series of free concerts at the Sidney Myer Music Bowl.

Musica Viva   ORCHESTRA
(www.musicaviva.com.au) National group Musica Viva stages 'Coffee Concerts' – morning-tea tunes (chamber music) – five times a year at the Melbourne Recital Centre.

Opera

Melbourne has nurtured internationally acclaimed opera singers and continues to stage world-class productions. People do dress up for a night at the opera, especially opening and weekend nights of Opera Australia, but no one will raise an eyebrow if you don't.

Chamber Made Opera   OPERA
(☏03-9329 7422; www.chambermadeopera.com; Arts House, Meat Market, 44 Courtney St, North Melbourne; ⌂55, 59) Founded in 1988, Chamber Made Opera showcases contemporary music and music-based performance art. Some performances are free.

Melbourne Opera   OPERA
(☏03-9614 4188; www.melbourneopera.com) A not-for-profit company that performs a classic repertoire in the stunning Athenaeum (p114). Prices are deliberately kept affordable.

Opera Australia   OPERA
(☏03-9685 3700; www.opera.org.au; cnr Fawkner & Fanning Streets, Southbank) The national opera company performs with some regularity at the Arts Centre Melbourne.

Victorian Opera   OPERA
(☏03-9001 6400; www.victorianopera.com.au) Dedicated to innovation and accessibility, its program pleasingly doesn't always play it safe.

Sport

Melbourne is a sport-obsessed city. From March to October it's all about AFL footy, while rugby league, soccer and rugby union are also very popular. In summer, cricket dominates.

Melbourne Cricket Ground　STADIUM
(☑ 03-9657 8888; www.mcg.org.au) Melbourne's sporting mecca, the 'G' hosts cricket in the summer and AFL footy in the winter. Attendance is a rite of passage for many locals. See Melbourne Cricket Ground (p59) for more information.

Etihad Stadium　STADIUM
(☑ 03-8625 7700, tours 03-8625 7277; www.etihad-stadium.com.au; Bourke St, Docklands; tours adult/child/concession/family $15/8/12/39; ☑ 70, 75, 86, 96, 109, 112, ☑ Southern Cross) Both comfortable and easy to access, this Docklands stadium seats 52,000 for regular AFL games and the odd one-day cricket match and rugby union test, with the advantage of a retractable roof to keep spectators dry. Also runs tours for sporting tragics.

AAMI Park　SOCCER, RUGBY
(Map p60; ☑ 03-9286 1600; www.aamipark.com.au; Olympic Blvd, Richmond; tickets from $30; ☑ 70, ☑ Richmond) Across from Rod Laver Arena, AAMI Park is the home of Melbourne's soccer and rugby teams. Its rectangular pitch is enclosed within a striking honeycombed-bioframe stadium, with a capacity of 30,000.

From October to May, catch Melbourne Victory or Melbourne Heart in the A-League soccer; from March to September there's rugby league, with Melbourne Storm playing in the NRL. It also hosts Melbourne Rebels in the Super Rugby league from February to August.

Melbourne Park　TENNIS, BASKETBALL
(Map p60; ☑ 03-9286 1600; www.mopt.com.au; Batman Ave, Richmond; tours adult/child/family $15/7/35; ☑ 48, 70, 75, ☑ Jolimont) Home to the **Australian Open** tennis Grand Slam held in January, Melbourne Park precinct has 34 courts including its centrepiece **Rod Laver Arena**. You can take a tour to the dressing rooms, VIP areas and superboxes. Its indoor court hire ranges from $36 to $42, and outdoor courts cost between $28 and $36, plus racquet hire.

As well as tennis, **Hisense Arena** is also home to the Melbourne Tigers basketball team in the NBL (National Basketball League), and the Melbourne Vixens

netball team. Nearby **Olympic Park** hosts athletics.

Flemington Racecourse　HORSE RACING
(☑ 1300 727 575; www.vrc.net.au; 400 Epsom Rd, Flemington; ☑ 57, ☑ Flemington Racecourse) Home of the Victoria Racing Club, Flemington has regular horserace meets, climaxing with the Spring Racing Carnival (including the Melbourne Cup) from October to November.

Shopping

Melbourne is a city of passionate, dedicated retailers catering to a broad range of tastes, whims and lifestyles. From boutique-filled city laneways to suburban shopping streets and malls, you'll find plenty of places to offload your cash and pick up something unique.

Central Melbourne

Melbourne's city centre lets you experience big-city department-store bustle as well as the thrill of finding intriguing individual shops tucked down alleys and hidden up (or down) flights of stairs. The city's main department stores, **Myer** and **David Jones**, are both on the Bourke St Mall and stock a good range of high-end local designers such as Collette Dinnigan (David Jones) and T.L. Wood (Myer), along with well-known international labels. There's a new breed of 'mini-malls' that have the convenience of lots of shops under one roof, while still retaining varying amounts of character. These include the **GPO**, the **QV** and **Melbourne Central**.

★ Craft Victoria Shop　CRAFT, DESIGN
(Map p50; ☑ 03-9650 7775; www.craft.org.au; 31 Flinders Lane; ☺ 10am-5pm Mon-Sat; ☑ City Circle, 70, 75) This retail arm of Craft Victoria showcases the best of handmade, mainly by local Victorian artists. Its range of jewellery, textiles, accessories, glass and ceramics bridges the art/craft divide and makes for some wonderful mementos of Melbourne. There are also a few galleries with changing exhibitions; admission is free.

Claude Maus　FASHION
(Map p50; ☑ 03-9654 9844; www.claudemaus.com; 19 Manchester Lane; ☺ 10am-6pm Mon-Sat, to 7pm Fri, 11am-5pm Sun; ☑ Flinders St) Subtly gothic, darkly urban and very Melbourne local label by lapsed artist Rob Maniscalco. You'll find great jeans, textural pieces and leather for

men and women in a heritage-listed shop. Other branches at 242 Brunswick St, Fitzroy, and 311 Swanston St, City.

Somewhere FASHION, ACCESSORIES
(Map p50; www.someplace.com.au; Royal Arcade, 2/314 Little Collins St; ⊘10am-6pm Mon-Sat, to 8pm Fri, 11am-5pm Sun; ⬤86, 96) Somewhere is an apt name for this hard-to-find treasure. It's located at the Little Collins St end of Royal Arcade (look for the Marais sign and take the stairs to level 2). The whitewashed warehouse space stocks predominantly Scandinavian labels, as well as local designers for men and women, along with leather tote bags, Anne Black ceramic jewellery and a good range of denim.

Incu FASHION
(Map p50; ☑03-9663 9933; www.inculclothing.com; Shop 6a, 274 Flinders Lane; ⊘10am-6pm Mon-Sat, to 8pm Fri, 11am-5pm Sun; ⬤Flinders St) Sydney retailer Incu has set up store in Melbourne and stocks a range of contemporary designers for menswear, with crisp tailored shirts from Weathered, comfy chinos, and great stuff from labels such as Vanishing Elephant and Kloke. Its women's store is in the QV building.

Captains of Industry CLOTHING, ACCESSORIES
(Map p50; ☑03-9670 4405; www.captainsofindustry.com.au; Level 1, 2 Somerset Pl; ⊘8am-5pm Mon-Thu, to 11pm Fri; ⬤19, 57, 59) Where can you get a haircut, a bespoke suit and a pair of shoes or leather wallet made in the one place? Here. The hard-working folk at spacious and industrial Captains also offer homey breakfasts and lunches; it turns into a low-key bar on Friday nights.

City Hatters ACCESSORIES
(Map p50; ☑03-9614 3294; www.cityhatters.com.au; 211 Flinders St; ⊘9.30am-6pm Mon-Fri, 9am-5pm Sat, 10am-4pm Sun; ⬤Flinders St) Located beside the main entrance to Flinders Street Station, this is the most convenient place to purchase an iconic Akubra hat, kangaroo-leather sunhat or something a little more unique.

Wunderkammer ANTIQUES
(Map p50; ☑03-9642 4694; www.wunderkammer.com.au; 439 Lonsdale St; ⊘10am-6pm Mon-Sat, to 4pm Sun; ⬤55) Surprises abound in this 'Wonder Chamber', the strangest of shops: taxidermy, bugs in jars, antique scientific tools, surgical equipment and carnivorous plants, to name a few.

Original & Authentic Aboriginal Art ARTS & CRAFTS
(Map p50; ☑03-9663 5133; www.originalandauthenticaboriginalart.com; 90 Bourke St; ⊘11am-6pm; ⬤86, 96) Open for 25 years, this centrally located gallery has a good relationship with its Indigenous artists across Australia and offers stunning and affordable pieces, all with author profiles.

Metropolis BOOKS
(Map p50; ☑03-9663 2015; www.metropolisbookshop.com.au; Level 3, Curtin House, 252 Swanston St; ⬤1, 3, 5, 6, 8, 16, 64, 67, 72) Lovely bookish eyrie with a focus on art, architecture, fashion and film.

Alice Euphemia FASHION, JEWELLERY
(Map p50; Shop 6, Cathedral Arcade, 37 Swanston St; ⊘10am-6pm Mon-Thu & Sat, to 7pm Fri, noon-5pm Sun; ⬤Flinders St) Art-school cheek abounds in the Australian-made and designed labels sold here – Romance Was Born, Karla Spetic and Kloke, to name a few. Jewellery sways between the shocking and exquisitely pretty, and its upstairs space hosts regular events and exhibitions.

Paperback Bookshop BOOKS
(Map p50; ☑03-9662 1396; www.paperbackbooks.com.au; 60 Bourke St; ⊘9.30am-10pm Mon-Thu, to 11.30pm Fri, 11am-11.30pm Sat, noon-7pm Sun; ⬤86, 96) A small space jam-packed with carefully selected titles, including a good selection of Australian literature – great when you need a novel fast.

Sticky BOOKS
(Map p50; ☑03-9654 8559; www.stickyinstitute.com; Shop 10, Campbell Arcade, Flinders Street Station; ⊘noon-6pm Mon-Fri, to 5pm Sat; ⬤Flinders St) This is a favourite haunt of those who are sick of mainstream press; you'll find hand-photocopied zines here.

GPO SHOPPING CENTRE
(Map p50; ☑03-9663 0066; www.melbournesgpo.com; cnr Elizabeth St & Bourke St Mall; ⊘10am-6pm Mon-Thu & Sat, to 8pm Fri, 11am-5pm Sun; ⬤19, 57, 59, 86, 96) This was once simply somewhere you went to buy a stamp, but a post-fire restoration has made for an atmospheric place to shop along its galleries. It houses fashion heavyweights and now hosts a three-storey concept store for European behemoth H&M.

NGV Shop at The Ian Potter Centre BOOKS, GIFTS
(Map p50; www.ngv.vic.gov.au; Federation Sq; ⬤Flinders St) This gallery shop has a wide

range of international design magazines, a kids section and the usual gallery standards. Also at NGV International (p57).

Melbournalia GIFTS, SOUVENIRS
(Map p50; www.melbournalia.com.au; Shop 5, 50 Bourke St; ⏱10am-6pm Mon-Thu, 10am-8pm Fri, 11am-5pm Sat & Sun; ☐86, 96) Pop-up store turned permanent, this is the place to stock up on interesting souvenirs by local designers – from tram tote bags and city-rooftop honey to prints of the city's icons and great books on Melbourne.

Basement Discs MUSIC
(Map p50; ✏03-9654 1110; www.basementdiscs. com.au; 24 Block Pl; ☐11, 112) Apart from a range of CD titles across all genres, Basement Discs has regular in-store performances by big-name touring and local acts. Descend the long, narrow staircase to the basement for a browse; you never know who you might find playing.

Hill of Content BOOKS
(Map p50; ✏03-9662 9472; www.hillofcontentbook shop.com; 86 Bourke St; ⏱9am-6pm Mon-Thu, to 8pm Fri, 10am-6pm Sat, 11am-5pm Sun; ☐86, 96) Melbourne's oldest bookshop (established 1922) has a range of general titles and an extensive stock of books on arts, classics and poetry.

QV SHOPPING CENTRE
(Map p50; www.qv.com.au; cnr Lonsdale & Russell Sts; ☐Melbourne Central) Taking up a whole city block, this development is on the site of the old Queen Victoria Women's Hospital and is both a parody of and homage to the city itself, with artificial laneways and arcades. It houses supermarkets, a food court, a good range of boutiques and designers, and beaut-smelling body-product stores.

Fitzroy & Around

Gertrude St has become one of Melbourne's most unique shopping strips. Smith St is decidedly vintage, with small boutique stores – though its northern end, beyond Johnston St, is jam-packed with clearance stores. Brunswick St is a mixed bag but does have some good boutique designers from Johnston St to Gertrude St. Northcote's High St has an interesting collection of homewares, vintage and young designer shops, too.

⭐**Third Drawer Down** DESIGN
(Map p64; www.thirddrawerdown.com; 93 George St, Fitzroy; ⏱11am-5pm Mon-Sat; ☐86) It all started with their signature tea-towel designs (now found in MOMA in New York) at this 'museum of art souvenirs'. Third Drawer Down makes life beautifully unusual by stocking absurdist pieces with a sense of humour, as well as high-end art by well-known designers.

Giant corn-cob stools and Rubik's cube salt grinders sit next to Rob Ryan's ceramic plates and scarves by T Wei Wei. There's a fake novelty convenience store in the back where you can pick up vegan foie gras and pizza cushions. It also has a small shop at CCP (p63).

Mud Australia CERAMICS
(Map p64; www.mudaustralia.com; 181 Gertrude St, Fitzroy; ⏱10am-6pm Mon-Fri, 11am-6pm Sat, noon-5pm Sun; ☐86) You'll find some of the most aesthetically beautiful – as well as functional – porcelainware from Australian-designed Mud. Coffee mugs, milk pourers, salad bowls and serving plates come in muted pastel colours with a raw matte finish. Prices start from $20 per piece.

Crumpler ACCESSORIES
(Map p64; ✏03-9417 5338; www.crumpler.com; 87 Smith St, cnr Gertrude St, Fitzroy; ⏱10am-6pm Mon-Sat, to 5pm Sun; ☐86) Crumpler's bike-courier bags started it all, designed by two former couriers looking for a bag they could hold their beer in while cycling home. Its durable, practical designs now extend to bags for cameras, laptops and iPods, and can be found around the world.

If you're after something more specific, hop next door to the custom store where you can have a bespoke bag whipped up in your choice of colours.

Poison City Records MUSIC
(Map p64; www.poisoncityrecords.com; 400 Brunswick St, Fitzroy; ⏱11am-6pm; ☐112) Independent record/skate shop with its own Poison City label releasing excellent indie, punk and fuzz-rock Melbourne bands, such as the Nation Blue, White Walls and Smith Street Band.

Búl FASHION
(Map p64; www.bul.com.au; 241 Brunswick St, Fitzroy; ⏱10am-6pm Mon-Thu, to 7pm Fri, to 6pm Sat, 11am-5pm Sun; ☐112) Búl offers locally designed clothes that hark back to the days of classic stylish pieces with clean lines and understated colours. Whether your eye is taken by a cream-coloured shirtdress, subtly patterned tailored pants or a burnt-orange

silk tank, you might be unable to leave empty-handed. Also in **Curtin House** (Map p50; Level 3, 252 Swanston St, Melbourne).

Little Salon
CRAFT, FASHION

(Map p64; www.littlesalon.com.au; 71 Gertrude St, Fitzroy; ☺10am-6pm Mon-Sat; ☒86, 112) Cute little store that stocks wearable art pieces from local designers, as well as decorative items for your wall or shelf.

Gorman
CLOTHING, ACCESSORIES

(Map p64; www.gormanshop.com.au; 235 Brunswick St, Fitzroy; ☺10am-6pm Mon-Thu & Sat, to 7pm Fri, 11am-5pm Sun; ☒112) Lisa Gorman makes everyday clothes that are far from ordinary: boyish, but sexy, short shapes are cut from exquisite fabrics; pretty cardigans are coupled with relaxed, organic tees. You can find other branches elsewhere around town.

Aesop
BEAUTY

(Map p64; www.aesop.com; 242 Gertrude St, Fitzroy; ☺11am-5pm Mon & Sun, 10am-6pm Tue-Fri, 10am-5pm Sat; ☒86) This homegrown empire specialises in citrus-and-botanical-based aromatic balms, hair masques, scents, cleansers and oils in beautifully simple packaging, for both men and women. There are plenty of branches around town (and plenty of opportunity to sample the products in most of Melbourne's cafe bathrooms).

Smith Street Bazaar
VINTAGE, HOMEWARES

(Map p64; 305 Smith St, Collingwood; ☺noon-6pm Mon, 11am-6pm Tue-Fri, 10.30am-5pm Sat & Sun; ☒86) A great place to find mid-century furniture (the occasional Grant Featherston chair), Danish pottery, lamps of all shades and sizes, as well as vintage clothing and shoes. Best of all, it's well organised.

Obüs
FASHION

(Map p64; www.obus.com.au; 226 Gertrude St, Fitzroy; ☺10am-6pm Mon-Sat, noon-5pm Sun; ☒86) Melbourne-based designer Kylie Zerbst set up Obüs 15 years ago with this, her first store. Known for bright geometric patterns and soft bamboo-cotton travel essentials, the clothing is sophisticated yet fun and offers pieces that get you from work to going out without a change. Other branches located at **QV** (Map p50; 10 Albert Coates Lane, QV Building; ☺10am-6pm Mon-Thu & Sat, to 8pm Fri, 11am-5pm Sun; ☒Melbourne Central) in the city and in **Northcote** (285 High St, Northcote; ☺10am-6pm Mon-Sat, noon-5pm Sun; ☒86).

Alphaville
CLOTHING

(Map p64; ☒03-9416 4296; www.alpha60.com.au; 179 Brunswick St, Fitzroy; ☺10.30am-6pm Mon-Thu, 10.30am-7pm Fri, 10am-6pm Sat & 11am-5pm Sun; ☒112) Alphaville keeps the cool kids of both genders happy with Alpha60's sharp clothes.

Angelucci 20th Century
VINTAGE, HOMEWARES

(Map p64; ☒03-9415 8001; www.angelucci.net.au; 113 Smith St, Fitzroy; ☺10am-6pm Mon-Sat, 11am-5pm Sun; ☒86) Specialising in furniture from the 1950s and '60s, Dean Angelucci's store is well known for its treasures. There are smaller pieces such as lighting and ceramics as well as the best-of-the-bunch sofas and sideboards.

Shirt & Skirt Market
CLOTHING, CRAFTS

(www.shirtandskirtmarkets.com.au; Abbotsford Convent, 1 St Heliers St, Abbotsford; ☺10am-4pm 3rd Sun of the month; ☒Collingwood) Buy limited-run clothes and accessories, for both adults and kids, from emerging designers. The Convent makes for leisurely outdoor browsing. Check the website for regular stallholder details. To get here, head east down Johnson St, turn right at Clarke St, then left.

Hudson
FASHION, ACCESSORIES

(Map p64; 291 Smith St, Fitzroy; ☺11am-5.30pm; ☒86) The St Kilda stalwart has set up shop on Smith St, showcasing its range of quirky handpicked items – mainly from Japan as well as Europe and some local designers – geometric jewellery, Post-it notes in the shape of tennis socks, clothing and accessories.

Ess
CLOTHING

(Map p64; www.ess-laboratory.com; 114 Gertrude St, Fitzroy; ☺11am-5.30pm Mon, 10.30am-6pm Tue-Fri, 10am-5.30pm Sat, 1-5pm Sun; ☒86) Japanese design duo Hoshika Oshimi and her sound-artist collaborative partner, Tatsuyoshi Kawabata, have created waves in Melbourne since Hoshika established Ess Laboratory in 2001. The National Gallery of Victoria has Ess designs in its gallery collection, but don't let that stop you claiming one for yourself.

Books for Cooks
BOOKS

(Map p64; www.booksforcooks.com.au; 233-235 Gertrude St, Fitzroy; ☺10am-6pm Mon-Sat, 11am-5pm Sun; ☒86) The breadth of this shop's new and secondhand collection is astounding, ranging from obscure gastronomic histories and books on Indigenous and bush-tucker recipes to the latest celeb-chef how-to. Extremely knowledgeable staff will help you find whatever you're after.

Polyester Books BOOKS
(Map p64; ☑03-9419 5223; www.polyester.com. au; 330 Brunswick St, Fitzroy; ⊙10am-6pm, to 9pm Fri & Sat; ☐112) This unapologetic bookstore specialises in 'seriously weird shit', including literature, magazines and DVDs on topics ranging from satanic cult sex to underground comics and everything in-between. It also stocks a great selection of music biographies and small-press zines.

Polyester Records MUSIC
(Map p64; 387 Brunswick St, Fitzroy; ⊙10am-9pm; ☐112) This great record store has been selling Melburnians independent music from around the world for decades, and also sells tickets for gigs.

Brunswick Street Bookstore BOOKS
(Map p64; ☑03-9416 1030; www.brunswickstreet bookstore.com; 305 Brunswick St, Fitzroy; ⊙10am-10pm Sun-Thu, to 11pm Fri & Sat; ☐112) Lovely store with knowledgeable staff and a good selection of children's books.

Luft HOMEWARES, ACCESSORIES
(☑03-9489 0891; www.luft.com.au; 212 St Georges Rd, North Fitzroy; ⊙10am-6pm Sat-Wed, to 7pm Thu & Fri; ☐112) A neighbourhood favourite for big-name design stars like Eva Solo, iittala and Marimekko. Good selection of Melbourne-made jewellery.

SpaceCraft HOMEWARES, FASHION
(Map p64; www.spacecraftaustralia.com; 255 Gertrude St, Fitzroy; ⊙11am-6pm Mon-Fri, 10am-6pm Sat, 11am-5pm Sun; ☐86) An excellent place to find a made-in-Melbourne souvenir that won't end up at the back of the cupboard. Textile artist Stewart Russell's botanical and architectural designs adorn everything from stools to socks to bed linens. Also in **Prahran** (Map p68; 572 Malvern Rd, Prahran; ☐72).

Rose Street Artists' Market MARKET
(Map p64; www.rosestmarket.com.au; 60 Rose St, Fitzroy; ⊙11am-5pm Sat; ☐112) One of Melbourne's most popular art-and-craft markets showcases the best of local designers, just a short stroll from Brunswick St. Here you'll find up to 70 stalls selling matte silver jewellery, clothing, milk-bottle ceramics, iconic Melbourne screen prints, wild fig candles and ugly-cute toys. Humble Vintage (p75) has bike-hire from here.

Signet Bureau CLOTHING, SHOES
(Map p64; ☑03-9415 7470; www.thesignetbureau. com; 165 Gertrude St, Fitzroy; ⊙10am-6pm Mon-

MELBOURNE'S BEST MARKETS
....

Art, Craft & Design
➡ Rose St Artists' Market (p123)
➡ St Kilda Esplanade Sunday Market (p125)
➡ Blender Lane Market (p55)

Clothing & Accessories
➡ Shirt & Skirt Market (p122)
➡ Camberwell Sunday Market (p124)

Food
➡ Prahran Market (p71)
➡ South Melbourne Market (p74)
➡ Queen Victoria Market (p55)
➡ Footscray Market (p59)

Sat, noon-5pm Sun; ☐86) This is a collaboration between cobblers Preston Zly and Munk, and also features designs by Robyn Black and MM Söhn. Go there for the amazing displays as well as for shoes, clothes and accessories.

Tomorrow Never Knows FASHION, ACCESSORIES
(Map p64; www.tomorrowneverknows.com.au; 415 Brunswick St, Fitzroy; ⊙11am-6pm Mon-Sat, noon-5pm Sun; ☐86) From the quirky T-shirts and geometric print blouses to leather belts and very Melbourne sunglasses, you'll spot something here to remind you of, well, here. Stocks all local designers, with 90% of the stock made in Melbourne.

Title MUSIC, BOOKS
(Map p64; ☑03-9417 4477; www.titlespace.com; 183 Gertrude St, Fitzroy; ⊙10am-6pm Mon-Sat, to 5pm Sun; ☐86) Equal part book-, music- and DVD store, all sourced with superb taste, from local-release vinyl, Penguin classics and art books to cult/underground film.

Das T-Shirt Automat CLOTHING
(Map p64; ☑0497 070 927; www.dastshirtautomat. com; 152 Johnston St, Fitzroy; ⊙noon-7pm Tue-Sat; ☐112) The team behind this red-and-white striped terrace-house-turned-retail-space can knock up your own customised shirt while you wait. Bring along your own design or choose from one of their ready-to-go shirts, all for about $30.

Carlton & Around

Readings BOOKS

(Map p66; www.readings.com.au; 309 Lygon St, Carlton; ⊙ 8am-11pm Mon-Fri, 9am-11pm Sat, 9am-9pm Sun; ☒ Tourist Shuttle, ☒ 1, 8) A potter around this defiantly prospering indie bookshop can occupy an entire afternoon if you're so inclined. There's a dangerously loaded (and good-value) specials table, switched-on staff and everyone from Lacan to *Charlie & Lola* on the shelves. Its exterior 'housemate wanted' board is legendary. Also in **St Kilda** (Map p72; ☑ 03-9525 3852; www.readings.com.au; 112 Acland St; ☒ 96) and the **city centre** (Map p50; State Library of Victoria, cnr La Trobe & Swanston Sts; ☒ Melbourne Central).

Gewürzhaus FOOD

(Map p66; www.gewurzhaus.com.au; 342 Lygon St, Carlton; ⊙ 10am-6pm Mon-Sat, 11am-5pm Sun; ☒ 1, 8) Set up by two enterprisng young German girls, this store is a chef's dream with its displays of spices from around the world, including Indigenous Australian blends, flavoured salts and sugars. It has high-quality cooking accessories and gifts, and cooking classes, too. There's a city store inside the **Block Arcade** (Map p50; 282 Collins St, Melbourne; ☒ 19, 57, 59).

Lab Perfumery BEAUTY

(www.thelabperfumery.com.au; 360 Rathdowne St, North Carlton; ⊙ 10am-5pm Sun-Tue, to 6pm Wed-Sat; ☒ 1, 8) Feeling right at home along this boutique stretch of Rathdowne St, the Lab has an interesting range of organic, Aussie-made skincare products, fragrances and beauty kits. Products for men, too.

La Parisienne FOOD

(Map p66; ☑ 03-9349 1852; 290 Lygon St, Carlton; ⊙ 9am-6.30pm Mon-Sat, from 10am Sun; ☒ 1, 8, 16) A French interloper in this most Italian of streets, Parisienne specialises in smallgoods and take-home dishes that are authentically Gallic. *Boudin blanc* and *noir* (white and dark pork sausage), duck confit and its famous pâtés and terrines will not disappoint. It also does a nice range of bread and little pies that are perfect for picnic provisions, and keeps a range of evocatively packaged pantry items.

Eastern Market CLOTHING

(Map p66; ☑ 03-9348 0890; www.easternmarket.com.au; 107 Grattan St, Carlton; ⊙ 11am-6pm Mon-Sat; ☒ 1, 8, 16) Fashion-maven territory with a deconstructed Euro-Tokyo edge. The

space is itself an attraction: it's a 19th-century chapel with the owner's inimitable additions.

South Yarra, Prahran & Windsor

Chapel St's South Yarra strip has both chains and smaller designer boutiques, but head into Prahran and Windsor to find a far more eclectic mix. Cute Greville St runs off Chapel, and has a good smattering of shopping opportunities, too.

Chapel Street Bazaar VINTAGE

(Map p68; ☑ 03-9521 3174; 217-223 Chapel St, Prahran; ⊙ 10am-6pm; ☒ 78, 79, ☒ Prahran) Calling this a 'permanent undercover collection of market stalls' won't give you any clue to what's tucked away here. This old arcade is a retro-obsessive riot. It doesn't matter if Italian art glass, vintage furniture or Noddy egg cups are your thing, you'll find it here. There's a mix of cluttered mayhem and well-organised boutiquey stalls.

Shelley Panton HOMEWARES, GIFTS

(Map p68; http://shop.shelleypanton.com; 440 Malvern Rd, Prahran; ⊙ 9am-7pm Mon-Wed & Fri, to 9pm Thu, 10am-5.30pm Sat & Sun; ☒ 72) Potter Shelley Panton has recently set up this beautiful store, stocking her own local wares alongside other local designers' work and imported goodies from around the world. Pick up some eco-friendly bamboo dinnerware, copper pendant lighting or Indian loom rugs.

Camberwell Sunday Market MARKET

(www.sundaymarket.com.au; Station St, Camberwell; by donation; ⊙ 6am-12.30pm Sun; ☒ 70, 72, 75, ☒ Camberwell) Filled with secondhand and handcrafted goods, this is where Melburnians come to offload their unwanted items and where antique hunters come to find them. It's great for finding pre-loved (often rarely worn) items of clothing, restocking a bookcase and finding unusual curios. It's situated behind the corner of Burke and Riversdale Rds.

Fat FASHION, ACCESSORIES

(Map p68; www.fat4.com; 272 Chapel St, Prahran; ⊙ 10am-6pm Mon-Sat, 11am-5pm Sun; ☒ 78, 79, ☒ Prahran) The Fat empire has changed the way Melbourne dresses, catapulting a fresh generation of designers into the city's consciousness, including Claude Maus, Dr Denim, Kloke and Status Anxiety. There are also branches in the GPO (p120) in the city and **Fitzroy** (Map p64; 209 Brunswick St; 🚊112).

Greville Records MUSIC
(Map p68; www.grevillerecords.com.au; 152 Greville St, Prahran; ⊘10am-6pm Mon-Sat, to 7pm Fri, noon-5pm Sun; 🚊78, 79) One of the last bastions of the 'old' Greville St, this fabulous music shop has such a loyal following that the great Neil Young invited the owners on stage during a Melbourne concert. It's now very much geared towards vinyl.

Scanlan Theodore CLOTHING, ACCESSORIES
(Map p68; www.scanlantheodore.com.au; 566 Chapel St, South Yarra; ⊘10am-6pm Mon-Thu, to 8pm Fri, to 5.30pm Sat, 11am-5pm Sun; 🚊78, 79, 🚉South Yarra) Scanlan Theodore helped define the Melbourne look back in the 1980s and is still going strong with superfeminine, beautifully tailored everyday and special-occasion wear. Although it's now considered a mature, mainstream label, its clothes always manage to make a statement.

🏛 St Kilda

As you'd expect from a suburb so dedicated to leisure, St Kilda has a slew of interesting boutiques and a rising number of antique and industrial stores.

Pure Pop Records MUSIC
(Map p72; www.purepop.com.au; 221 Barkly St; ⊘10am-6pm Mon-Wed, to 11pm Thu-Sun; 🚊96) A well-loved record store that stocks mainly independent releases and a great selection of local stuff. Also doubles as one of the most intimate live-music spaces in Melbourne; gigs are rarely advertised and, therefore, rather special. Past acts have included secret gigs by the White Stripes and Lee Ranaldo.

Dot Herbey FASHION, ACCESSORIES
(Map p72; www.dotandherbey.com; 229 Barkly St; 🚊96) Grandma Dot and Grandpa Herb smile down upon this tiny corner boutique from a mural-sized photo, right at home among the vintage floral fabrics and retro style. This is definitely not somewhere to go if you're looking for chain-store same-same; it's also a colourful departure from the Melbourne-black dictate.

Esplanade Market MARKET
(Map p72; www.esplanademarket.com; btwn Cavell & Fitzroy Sts; ⊘10am-5pm Sun; 🚊96) Fancy a Sunday stroll, shopping by the seaside? Well, here's the place, with a kilometre of trestle tables joined end-to-end carrying individually crafted products, from toys and organic soaps to large metal sculptures of fishy creatures.

Eclectico CLOTHES
(Map p72; 163a Acland St; ⊘10.30am-6.30pm; 🚊96) Your one-stop shop for all your St Kilda hippy apparel, beanies, tie-dye shirts, Indian jewellery etc. Otherwise pop in for a free chai and hang out on the rooftop patio at this funky upstairs Acland St shop. It has a good Afrobeat vinyl collection, too.

Bookhouse BOOKS
(Map p72; www.bookhousestkilda.com.au; 52 Robe St; ⊘10am-6pm Wed-Sun; 🚊3, 67) A much-loved local, Bookhouse recently relocated from Fitzroy St to this quiet backstreet shop, where you might find a quality copy of a Chomsky, Kerouac or beautiful coffee-table book on the shelves, as well as a great selection of Australiana and Melbourne-specific titles.

🏛 South Melbourne

Nest HOMEWARES
(📞03-9699 8277; www.nesthomewares.com.au; 289 Coventry St; 🚊96, 112) This light, bright homewares store stocks SpaceCraft screenprinted textiles as well as Aesop skincare. It does its own range of cotton-knit 'comfort wear' that's way too nice to hide at home in. Staff are delightful. From South Melbourne Market head along Coventry St.

🏛 Richmond

Bridge Rd is a well-known shopping precinct for its clearance stores and factory outlets. Swan St has a few good homewares and design stores.

Lily & The Weasel HOMEWARES, GIFTS
(Map p60; www.lilyandtheweasel.com.au; 173 Swan St; ⊘11am-6pm Tue-Fri, 10am-5pm Sat, 11am-4pm Sun; 🚊70, 78) Lily & the Weasel stocks a mix of beautiful things from around the globe alongside stuff from local designers. Screenprints of iconic Richmond landmarks make for great souvenirs, as do wooden children's toys, Otto & Spike scarves and Robert Gordon ceramics.

ℹ Information

DANGERS & ANNOYANCES
There are occasional reports of alcohol-fuelled violence in some parts of Melbourne's city centre late on weekend nights – King St in particular.

EMERGENCY

For police, ambulance or fire emergencies, dial ☑000.

Centre Against Sexual Assault (CASA; ☑1800 806 292)

Poisons Information Centre (☑13 11 26)

Police There's a centrally located police station at 228 Flinders Lane, Melbourne.

Translating & Interpreting Service (☑13 14 50) Available 24 hours.

INTERNET ACCESS

Wi-fi is available free at central city spots such as Federation Sq, Flinders St Station, Crown Casino and the State Library. Most accommodation options have wi-fi and computer terminals, costing anything from free to $10 per hour.

If you don't have a laptop or smartphone, there are plenty of libraries around Melbourne with terminals, though you'll need to bring ID to sign up and prebooking is recommended. Locations with free internet include **City Library** (☑9658 9500; 253 Flinders Lane; ☒Flinders St), **St Kilda** (☑9209 6655; www.library.portphillip. vic.gov.au; 150 Carlisle St; ☒3, 3a, 16), **Fitzroy** (☑1300 695 427; 128 Moor St; ☒112) and **Prahran** (☑8290 3344; 180 Greville St; ☒78). Otherwise there are plenty of internet cafes for around $2 per hour.

MEDIA

The **Age** (www.theage.com.au) covers local, national and international news. The **Herald-Sun** (www.heraldsun.com.au) does the same, only with a bit more drama). **Broadsheet** (www.broadsheet.com.au) is a great source of what's on, as well as cafe, bar, restaurant and shopping reviews. It's available from most cafes around town.

MEDICAL SERVICES

Visitors from Belgium, Finland, Italy, Ireland, Malta, the Netherlands, Norway, New Zealand, Slovenia, Sweden and the UK have reciprocal health-care agreements with Australia and can access cheaper health services through **Medicare** (☑13 20 11; www.humanservices.gov.au/customer/dhs/medicare).

Mulqueeny Midnight Pharmacy (☑03-9510 3977; 416 High St, cnr Williams Rd, Windsor; ⊙9am-midnight; ☒6)

Tambassis Pharmacy (☑03-9387 8830; cnr Brunswick & Sydney Rds, Brunswick; ⊙8am-midnight; ☒19)

Royal Children's Hospital (☑03-9345 5522; www.rch.org.au; cnr Flemington Rd & Gatehouse St, Parkville)

Royal Melbourne Hospital (☑03-9342 7000; www.rmh.mh.org.au; cnr Grattan St & Royal Pde, Parkville; ☒19, 59) Public hospital with an emergency department.

Travel Doctor (TVMC; ☑03-9935 8100; www.traveldoctor.com.au; Level 2, 393 Little Bourke St, Melbourne; ⊙9am-5pm Mon, Wed, Fri, to 8.30pm Tue & Thu, to 1pm Sat; ☒19, 57, 59) Specialises in vaccinations and health advice for overseas trips. Also at **Docklands** (TVMC; ☑03-8622 6333; Level 4, 700 Collins St, Melbourne; ⊙8.30am-5pm Mon-Fri; ☒11, 31, 48, ☒Southern Cross) and **Southgate** (☑03-9690 1433; 3 Southgate Ave, Southbank; ⊙8.30am-5.30pm Mon-Fri).

MONEY

There are ATMs throughout the city centre and in the surrounding suburbs. Bigger hotels offer a currency exchange service, as do most banks (during business hours). There are a number of foreign-exchange offices on Swanston St.

POST

Melbourne GPO (Map p50; ☑13 13 18; www.auspost.com.au; 250 Elizabeth St, cnr Little Bourke St, Melbourne; ⊙8.30am-5.30pm Mon-Fri, 9am-5pm Sat; ☒19, 57, 59) Poste restante available.

TOURIST INFORMATION

Melbourne Visitor Centre (MVC; Map p50; ☑03-9658 9658; www.melbourne.vic.gov. au/touristinformation; Federation Sq; ⊙9am-6pm; ☎; ☒Flinders St) Located at Federation Square, the centre has comprehensive tourist information on Melbourne and regional Victoria, including excellent resources for mobility-impaired travellers, and a travel desk for accommodation and tour bookings. There are power sockets for recharging phones, too. There's also a booth on the Bourke St Mall (mostly for shopping and basic enquiries) and 'city ambassadors' (dressed in red) wandering around the city, who can help with info and directions.

WEBSITES

Lonely Planet's website (www.lonelyplanet.com) has useful links. Other online resources include:

Broadsheet Melbourne (www.broadsheet.com. au) Great source for reviews of the city's best eating, drinking and shopping spots.

That's Melbourne (www.thatsmelbourne.com. au) Downloadable maps, info and podcasts from the City of Melbourne.

Three Thousand (www.threethousand.com.au) A weekly round-up of (cool) local goings on.

Visit Victoria (www.visitvictoria.com.au) Highlights events in Melbourne and Victoria.

❶ Getting There & Away

AIR

Two airports serve Melbourne: **Melbourne** (MEL; ☑03-9297 1600; www.melbourneairport.com. au), also known as Tullamarine, and **Avalon** (AVV;

03-5227 9100, 1800 282 566; www.avalonairport.com.au), located en route to Geelong. From Melbourne, domestic and international flights are offered by Qantas (p345), Jetstar (p345), Virgin Australia (p345) and Tiger Air (p345). Presently only Jetstar serves Avalon.

QantasLink (☑13 13 13; www.qantas.com.au) and **Regional Express** (☑13 17 13; www.regionalexpress.com.au) fly from Melbourne to Mildura, while Sharp Airlines (p345) has services from Melbourne to Portland, Hamilton and Flinders Island from smaller **Essendon Airport** (MEB; ☑03-9948 9300; www.essendonairport.com.au).

There is a **left-luggage facility** (www.baggagestorage.com.au; Ground Fl, International Terminal 2; $15 per 24hr; ☉5.30am-12.30am) in Terminal 2 at Melbourne Airport.

BOAT

Spirit of Tasmania (☑1800 634 906; www.spiritoftasmania.com.au; adult/car one way from $174/89) crosses Bass Strait from Melbourne to Devonport, Tasmania, at least nightly; there are also day sailings during peak season. It takes 11 hours and departs from Station Pier, Port Melbourne.

BUS

The following long-distance buses depart from **Southern Cross Station** (www.southerncrossstation.net.au; cnr Collins & Spencer Sts, Melbourne) main terminal.

V/Line (☑1800 800 007; www.vline.com.au) Around Victoria.

Firefly (☑1300 730 740; www.fireflyexpress.com.au) To/from Adelaide, Canberra and Sydney.

Greyhound (☑1300 473 946; www.greyhound.com.au) Australia-wide.

There's a **left-luggage facility** (☑03-9619 2588; ☉during train service hours) at Southern Cross Station. It costs $12 to store a backpack or suitcase for 24 hours.

TRAIN

Interstate trains arrive and depart from **Southern Cross Station**.

ⓘ Getting Around

TO/FROM THE AIRPORT

Melbourne (Tullamarine) Airport

Inconveniently, there are no direct train or tram routes from Melbourne Airport to the city.

The most popular airport transport option is **SkyBus** (Map p50; ☑03-9335 2811; www.skybus.com.au; adult/child one way $18/7; ⊠ Southern Cross Station), a 24-hour express-bus service from Southern Cross Station to Melbourne Airport (20 to 30 minutes; departs every 10 minutes from 4.30am to midnight, every 20 to 30 minutes from midnight to 4.30am). It offers a free transfer service to several city hotels to/from Southern Cross Station (6am to 10.30pm Monday through Friday and 7.30am to 5.30pm on Saturday and Sunday; no service Christmas Day); otherwise you'll need to catch onward transport or a taxi to your destination.

Alternatively, budget travellers can chance their luck on **Bus 901**, departing Terminal 1 to Broadmeadows station (not the best place to hang out at night) from where you can catch the train to the city. It'll cost around $10 (including myki card; see p128) and take a minimum of 40 minutes; the last bus to/from the airport is around 11pm.

The fare for a **taxi** to Melbourne's city centre will start from $50, depending on traffic (expect around $65 to $75, including surcharges and tolls, from midnight to 5am).

Drivers need to be aware that part of the main route into the city from Melbourne (Tullamarine) Airport is a toll road run by CityLink (p128). You'll need to buy a **Tulla Pass** ($5.30) or, if you're travelling on toll roads (including CityLink and EastLink) for less than 30 days, a **Melbourne Pass** ($5.50 start-up fee, plus tolls and a vehicle-matching fee). If you have more time than money, take the exit ramp at Bell St, then turn right onto Nicholson St and follow it all the way south to the city centre.

Avalon Airport

Sita Coaches (☑03-9689 7999; www.sitacoaches.com.au; adult/child $22/10) meets all flights flying into and out of Avalon. It departs from Southern Cross Station and meets all flights. No pre-bookings are required. One way to/from Avalon Airport for an adult/child is $22/10, and takes 50 minutes.

BICYCLE

See the section on Cycling (p75) for the best way to pedal around town.

CAR & MOTORCYCLE

Car Hire

Avis (☑13 63 33; www.avis.com.au)
Budget (☑1300 362 848; www.budget.com.au)
Europcar (☑1300 131 390; www.europcar.com.au)
Hertz (☑13 30 39; www.hertz.com.au)
Thrifty (☑1300 367 227; www.thrifty.com.au)
Rent a Bomb (☑13 15 53; www.rentabomb.com.au)

Car Sharing

Car-sharing companies that operate in Melbourne include: **Flexi Car** (☑1300 363 780; www.flexicar.com.au), **Go Get** (☑1300 769 389; www.goget.com.au) and **Green Share Car** (☑1300 575 878; www.greensharecar.com.au). You rent

MELBOURNE GETTING AROUND

TRAM ROUTES

Brunswick/Parkville 1, 8, 19, 55, 96

Carlton 1, 3, 8, 96

Collingwood 86, 109

Docklands 30, 48, 70, 86, 109

Fitzroy 86, 96, 112

North Melbourne 55, 57, 68

Northcote 86

Prahran 6, 64, 72, 78, 79

Richmond 24, 45, 48, 70, 75, 78, 109

St Kilda 3, 3a, 16, 67, 78, 96, 112

South Melbourne 1, 55, 96, 109, 112

South Yarra 8, 72, 78

Toorak 8

the cars by the hour (from $14) or the day (from $80) and prices includes petrol. They vary on joining fees (free to $40) and how they charge (insurance fees, per hour and per kilometre). The cars are parked in and around the city centre and inner suburbs in designated 'car share' spots.

Parking

Parking inspectors are particularly vigilant in the city centre. Most of the street parking is metered and it's more likely than not that you'll be fined (between $72 and $144) if you overstay your metered time. Also keep an eye out for 'clearway' zones (prohibited kerb-side parking indicated by signs), which can result in sizeable fines. Central city parking is around $5.50 per hour, and $3.20 per hour in the outer central areas. There are plenty of parking garages in the city; rates vary. Motorcyclists are allowed to park on the footpath.

Toll Roads

Both drivers and motorcyclists will need to purchase a toll pass if they're planning on using one of the two toll roads: **CityLink** (☑13 26 29; www.citylink.com.au) from Melbourne (Tullamarine) Airport to the city and eastern suburbs or **EastLink** (☑13 54 65; www.eastlink.com.au), which runs from Ringwood to Frankston. Pay online or via phone – but pay within three days of using the toll road to avoid a fine.

PUBLIC TRANSPORT

Flinders Street Station is the main metro **train** station connecting the city and suburbs. The 'City Loop' runs under the city, linking the four corners of the CBD.

An extensive network of **trams** covers every corner of the city, running north–south and east–west along most major roads. Trams run roughly every 10 minutes Monday to Friday, every 15 minutes on Saturday and every 20 minutes on Sunday.

Check **Public Transport Victoria** (PTV; ☑1800 800 007; www.ptv.vic.gov.au; Southern Cross Station; ⓡ Southern Cross) for more information. Also worth considering is the free City Circle Tram (p81), which loops around town.

Bicycles cannot be taken on trams or buses, but can be taken on metropolitan trains.

Melbourne's buses, trams and trains use **myki** (www.myki.com.au), the controversial 'touch-on, touch-off' travel-pass system. It's not particularly convenient for short-term visitors, requiring you to purchase a $6 plastic myki card and then put credit on it before you travel. Cards can be purchased from machines at stations, 7-Eleven stores or newsagents, but some hostels collect myki cards from travellers who leave Melbourne. Travellers are best advised to buy a myki Visitor Pack ($14), which gets you one day's travel and discounts on various sights; available only from the airport, SkyBus terminal or the PTV Hub at Southern Cross Station.

The myki card can be topped up at 7-Eleven stores, myki machines at most train stations and at some tram stops in the city centre; frustratingly, online top-ups take at least 24 hours to process. For Zone 1, which is all that most travellers will need, costs $3.50 for two hours, or $7 for the day. Machines don't always issue change, so bring exact money. The fine for travelling without a valid myki card is $212 – ticket inspectors are vigilant and unforgiving.

TAXI

Melbourne's taxis are metered and require an estimated prepaid fare when hailed between 10pm and 5am. You may need to pay more or get a refund depending on the final fare. Toll charges are added to fares. Two of the largest taxi companies are **Silver Top** (☑131 008; www.silvertop.com.au) and **13 Cabs** (☑13 22 27; www.13cabs.com.au).

Around Melbourne

Includes ➡

The Dandenongs 131

Healesville & the
Lower Yarra Valley . . .134

Warburton & the
Upper Yarra Valley . . .138

Marysville 139

Lake Mountain 141

Daylesford &
Hepburn Springs 141

Macedon Ranges &
Around. 147

Best Places to Eat

➡ Lake House (p144)

➡ Sault (p144)

➡ Du Fermier (p148)

➡ Giant Steps & Innocent Bystander (p136)

➡ Reefton Hotel (p138)

Best Places to Stay

➡ Lake House (p143)

➡ Hepburn Springs Chalet (p144)

➡ Delderfield B&B (p141)

➡ Healesville Hotel (p136)

Why Go?

Getting out of the city for a day, a weekend or longer is easy – the question is not why, but where to first? Should you spend a day tripping from one winery to the next in the Yarra Valley? Disappear into the tall forest with a pair of walking boots and a keen eye for native wildlife? Indulge in some of Victoria's finest regional produce? Or pamper yourself with a massage and mineral spa? Just a short drive from Melbourne you can experience historic towns, mountains, rivers, waterfalls, bush, vine-covered hills, cycle paths and wildlife. And don't think you have to rough it – around Daylesford and the Yarra Valley you'll find some of the finest boutique accommodation, cafes and restaurants in regional Victoria, with fresh country air to match.

When to Go
Dandenong

Feb–May
The Yarra Valley is at its most colourful; grape harvest starts in February.

Jun–Sep
Cross-country skiing at Lake Mountain or a hot winter soak in Spa Country.

Oct–Nov
Festivals and spring weather make this a good time to hit the Dandenongs.

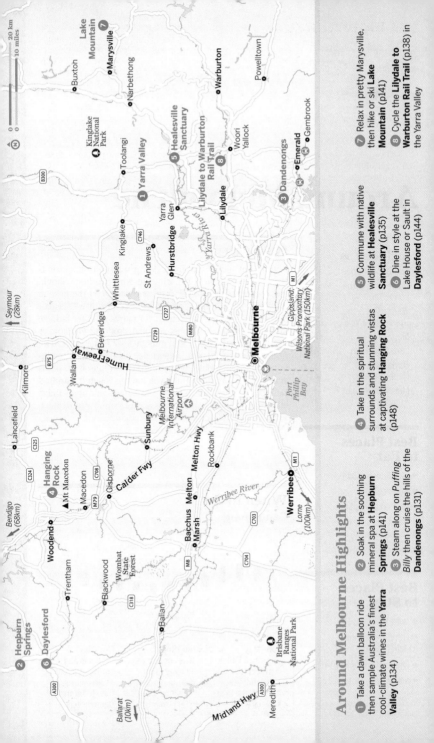

Around Melbourne Highlights

1 Take a dawn balloon ride then sample Australia's finest cool-climate wines in the **Yarra Valley** (p134)

2 Soak in the soothing mineral spa at **Hepburn Springs** (p141)

3 Steam along on *Puffing Billy* then cruise the hills of the **Dandenongs** (p131)

4 Take in the spiritual surrounds and stunning vistas at captivating **Hanging Rock** (p148)

5 Commune with native wildlife at **Healesville Sanctuary** (p135)

6 Dine in style at the Lake House or Sault in **Daylesford** (p144)

7 Relax in pretty Marysville, then hike or ski **Lake Mountain** (p141)

8 Cycle the **Lilydale to Warburton Rail Trail** (p138) in the Yarra Valley

THE DANDENONGS

The low ranges of the verdant Dandenongs, just 35km from Melbourne, feel a world away from the city and make a fantastic day trip. Mt Dandenong (633m) is the tallest peak and the landscape is a patchwork of exotic and native flora with a lush understorey of tree ferns. Take care driving on the winding roads – apart from other traffic, you might see a lyrebird wandering across.

The consumption of tea and scones is de rigueur in the many cafes in the hills, or you can stop for lunch at some quality restaurants in towns such as Olinda, Sassafras and Emerald.

On summer weekends, the hills are alive with day trippers – visit midweek for the best experience.

⦿ Sights & Activities

Puffing Billy   TRAIN
(☑ 03-9757 0700; www.puffingbilly.com.au; Old Monbulk Rd, Belgrave; return adult/child/family $59/30/119; 🚆 Belgrave) Holding fond childhood memories for many a Melburnian, popular Puffing Billy is an iconic restored steam train that toots its way through the ferny hills from Belgrave to Emerald Lake Park and Gembrook. Kids love to dangle their legs out the sides of the open-air compartments, and you can hop on and hop off en route to enjoy a picnic or walk. Puffing Billy train station is a short walk from Belgrave train station on Melbourne's suburban network.

Trees Adventure   ADVENTURE SPORTS
(☑ 0410 735 288; www.treesadventure.com.au; Old Monbulk Rd, Glen Harrow Gardens; 2hr session adult/child $39/25; ⊙ 11am-5pm Mon-Fri, 9am-5pm Sat & Sun; 🚆 Belgrave) Reminiscent of the Ewok village out of *Return of the Jedi*, Trees Adventure is a blast of tree-climbs, flying foxes and obstacle courses in a stunning patch of old-growth forest boasting sequoia, mountain ash and Japanese oak trees. The safety system for the course ensures you're always attached to a secure line and the beginner sections are suitable for kids as young as five.

Emerald Lake Park   SWIMMING, BOATING
(☑ 1300 131 683; www.emeraldlakepark.com.au; Emerald Lake Rd, Emerald) Featuring two man-made lakes, Nobelius and Treganowan, this garden has picnic areas, a water slide and swimming pool, paddle boats and **Emerald Lake Model Railway** (☑ 03-5968 3455; adult/

child $6/4; ⊙ 11.30am-4pm Thu-Sun), the largest HO scale model (1:87) railway in the southern hemisphere.

Dandenong Ranges National Park   PARK
(www.parkweb.vic.gov.au; 🚆 Upper Ferntree Gully, Belgrave) This national park contains the four largest areas of remaining forest in the Dandenongs. The Ferntree Gully area has several short walks, including the popular **1000 Steps** up to **One Tree Hill Picnic Ground** (two hours return), part of the **Kokoda Memorial Track**, which commemorates Australian WWII servicemen who served in New Guinea. Bring sturdy shoes as its steps get slippery.

Sherbrooke Forest, just north of Belgrave, has a towering cover of mountain ash trees and several walking trails. **Grants Picnic Ground**, at Kallista, attracts flocks of sulphur-crested cockatoos.

National Rhododendron Gardens   GARDENS
(☑ 03-9751 1980; www.parkweb.vic.gov.au; Georgian Rd, Olinda; ⊙ 10am-5pm) **FREE** Giant eucalypts tower over shady lawns and brilliant flowerbeds at these gardens with more than 15,000 rhododendrons and 12,000 azaleas. The best time to see the rhododendrons is September to November.

William Ricketts Sanctuary   SCULPTURE GARDEN
(☑ 13 19 63; www.parkweb.vic.gov.au; 1402 Mt Dandenong Tourist Rd, Mt Dandenong; ⊙ 10am-4.30pm) **FREE** This ferny garden features William Ricketts' sculptures of Aboriginal people, inspired by years spent living among them. You can also see his log cottage and gallery.

SkyHigh Mt Dandenong   VIEWPOINT
(☑ 03-9751 0443; www.skyhighmtdandenong.com.au; 26 Observatory Rd, Mt Dandenong; vehicle entry $5; ⊙ 9am-10pm Mon-Thu, 9am-10.30pm Fri, 8am-11pm Sat & Sun; 🚍 688) Drive up to SkyHigh for amazing views over Melbourne and Port Phillip Bay from the highest point in the Dandenongs. The view of the city lights at dusk is spectacular. There's a cafe-restaurant, a garden, picnic areas, and a maze (adult/child/family $6/4/16).

🛏 Sleeping

Loft in the Mill   GUESTHOUSE $$
(☑ 03-9751 1700; www.loftinthemill.com.au; 1602 Mt Dandenong Tourist Rd, Olinda; d $130-300; ❄ @) In the centre of Olinda, Loft in the

The Dandenongs

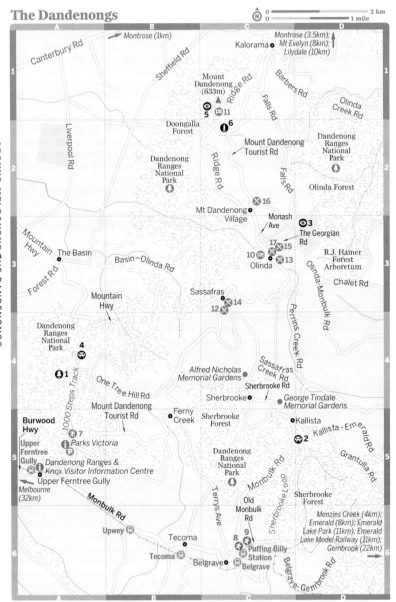

Mill is a welcoming place with nine cosy suites in two bluestone buildings modelled on an old flour mill and a 19th-century carriage house.

Observatory Cottages B&B $$$
(☏03-9751 2436; www.observatorycottages.com. au; 10 Observatory Rd, Mt Dandenong; r $285-330) Near the peak of Mt Dandenong, the four sumptuous self-contained cottages are

The Dandenongs

⊙ Sights
1 Dandenong Ranges National Park...................................... A4
2 Grants Picnic Ground............................ D5
3 National Rhododendron Gardens......... D3
4 One Tree Hill Picnic Ground.................. A4
5 SkyHigh Mt Dandenong......................... C1
6 William Ricketts Sanctuary C2

⊙ Activities, Courses & Tours
7 1000 Steps A5
8 Puffing Billy... C6
9 Trees Adventure C6

⊙ Sleeping
10 Loft in the Mill C3
11 Observatory Cottages C1

⊗ Eating
12 Cafe de Beaumarchais C3
13 Ivy C3
14 Miss Marple's Tearoom......................... C3
15 Pie in the Sky C3
16 Pig & Whistle Tavern.............................. C2
17 Ranges at Olinda C3

⊙ Shopping
Tea Leaves .... (see 14)

beautifully decorated in heritage style, furnished with antiques and surrounded by lovely grounds. All have a double spa and views.

✗ Eating & Drinking

Cafe de Beaumarchais　　　　　　CAFE $
(372 Mt Dandenong Tourist Rd, Sassafras; snacks $5-15; ⊗8.30am-5pm Mon-Sun; ☏) This dimly-lit Parisian-style cafe is a great spot for a breakfast pie, freshly baked croissant, baguettes or homemade sweet treats.

Pie in the Sky　　　　　　AUSTRALIAN $
(www.pieinthesky.net.au; 43 Olinda-Monbulk Rd, Olinda; pies from $5; ⊗10am-4.30pm Mon-Fri, 9.30am-5pm Sat & Sun) Try an Aussie *poi*, mate – go the award-winning classic Aussie or beef burgundy.

Miss Marple's Tearoom　　　　　TEAHOUSE $$
(www.missmarples.com.au; 382 Mt Dandenong Tourist Rd, Sassafras; dishes $13-17, Devonshire scones $9 for two; ⊗11am-4pm Mon-Fri, 11am-4.30pm Sat & Sun) This quaint English tearoom, inspired by an Agatha Christie character, comes with floral tablecloths, Devonshire scones and sticky toffee pudding, as well as lunch mains. It's wildly popular on weekends; two-hour waits are not unusual.

Ranges at Olinda　　　　　　CAFE $$
(☏03-9751 2133; 5 Olinda-Monbulk Rd, Olinda; lunch $12-25, dinner $22-42; ⊗8.30am-5pm daily & 5.30-9pm Tue-Sat; ☏) This popular spot on the main strip serves big breakfasts and lunch staples (fish and chips, steak sandwiches), while dinner might feature pasta dishes and crispy Atlantic salmon.

Pig & Whistle Tavern　　　　　　PUB $$
(☏03-9751 2366; www.pigandwhistletavern.com; 1429 Mt Dandenong Tourist Rd, Olinda; mains $17-33; ⊗11am-9pm) This English-style pub has a cosy dining room in which to enjoy the hearty meals, and has Guinness, Old Speckled Hen and Newcastle Brown beers on tap.

Ivy　　　　　　PIZZERIA $$
(☏03-9751 2388; www.theivyrestaurant.com.au; 540 Mt Dandenong Tourist Rd, Olinda; mains $21-35; ⊗noon-8.30pm Fri-Tue & 6-8.30pm Thu) Cracking thin-crust pizzas and a perfect people-watching terrace on Olinda's main strip. Also has live music.

⌂ Shopping

Tea Leaves　　　　　　DRINK
(www.tealeaves.com.au; 380 Mt Dandenong Tourist Rd, Sassafras; ⊗10am-5.30pm) Speciality tea store selling an impressive range, from organic Assam and caramel rooibos to the 'Melbourne cuppa'.

ⓘ Information

Dandenong Ranges & Knox Visitor Information Centre (☏03-9758 7522; www.dandenongrangestourism.com.au; 1211 Burwood Hwy, Upper Ferntree Gully; ⊗1-5pm Mon, 9am-5pm Tue-Sat, 10.30am-2.30pm Sun; ◨Upper Ferntree Gully) Outside the Upper Ferntree Gully train station. Good for walking maps.

ⓘ Getting There & Away

It's just under an hour's drive from Melbourne's city centre to Olinda, Sassafras or Belgrave. The quickest route is via the Eastern Fwy, exiting on Burwood Hwy or Boronia Rd. Suburban trains from Melbourne (Belgrave Line) head to Belgrave station.

YARRA VALLEY

The lush Yarra Valley is Victoria's premier wine region and weekend getaway – partly for its close proximity to Melbourne, but mainly for the 80-plus wineries, superb restaurants, national parks and wildlife. This is the place to rise at dawn in a hot-air balloon over patchwork fields and vineyards and kick back with a pinot noir at world-class wineries.

The Yarra River starts its journey in the upper reaches of the Yarra Ranges National Park, passing through Warburton and close to Healesville before winding into Greater Melbourne and emptying into Port Phillip Bay near Williamstown.

The valley covers a huge area from the ruggedly beautiful Yarra Ranges National Park in the east to Kinglake National Park in the west, a huge eucalypt forest on the slopes of the Great Dividing Range. In the centre of Kinglake National Park is Kinglake, a small township devastated by the 2009 bushfires

(see p140) but now rebuilding itself, with a great country pub, a few shops and cafes, and an inspiring community spirit. Toolangi, 18km east, was the home of CJ Dennis, who wrote 'The Sentimental Bloke'.

In between is the vine-covered valley itself. Coldstream is considered the gateway to the Yarra Valley winery region and most of the wineries are found within the triangle bound by Coldstream, Healesville and Yarra Glen. Further southeast, Warburton is the gateway to the Upper Yarra Valley region. There's another knot of wineries around Wandin and Seville along the Warburton Hwy (B380).

Healesville & the Lower Yarra Valley

Pretty little Healesville is the main town and base for exploring the triangular area of the Lower Yarra Valley. It's famous for its wildlife sanctuary, and perfectly located for easy

Yarra Valley

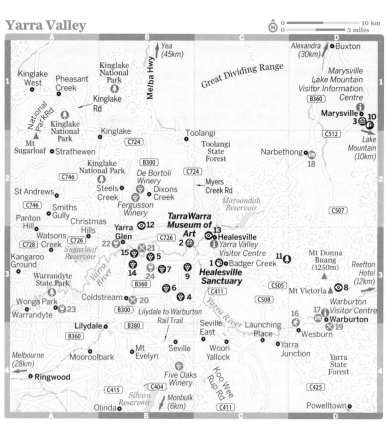

Yarra Valley

◉ Top Sights
1 Healesville Sanctuary C3
2 TarraWarra Museum of Art B3

◉ Sights
3 Black Saturday Exhibition D1
Bruno's Art & Sculptures Garden ..(see 3)
4 Coldstream Hills B3
5 Domain Chandon B3
6 Medhurst Wines B3
7 Oakridge B3
8 Rainforest Gallery D3
9 Rochford B3
10 Steavenson Falls D1
TarraWarra Estate .... (see 2)
11 Yarra Ranges National Park C3
12 Yarra Valley Chocolaterie & Ice
Creamery B2
13 Yarra Valley Railway C3
14 Yering Farm Wines B3
15 Yering Station B3

◉ Activities, Courses & Tours
Go Wild Ballooning .... (see 20)
16 Lilydale to Warburton Rail Trail D3
Marysville Ski Centre .... (see 3)

◉ Sleeping
17 Alpine Retreat Hotel D3
Badger Creek Holiday Park .... (see 1)
18 Black Spur Inn D2

Crossways Historic Country Inn ... (see 3)
Delderfield B&B .... (see 3)
Healesville Hotel .... (see 13)
Marysville Caravan Park .... (see 3)
The Tower .... (see 3)
Tuck Inn .... (see 13)

◉ Eating
19 Cog Bike Cafe... D4
20 Coldstream Brewery B3
Fraga's Café .... (see 3)
Giant Steps & Innocent
Bystander .... (see 13)
The Gilded Lily .... (see 13)
Healesville Harvest......................... (see 13)
Healesville Hotel .... (see 13)
Little Joe .... (see 19)
Yarra Valley Dairy .... (see 14)
21 Zonzo B3

◉ Drinking & Nightlife
Buckley's Beer .... (see 13)
Grind n' Groove .... (see 13)
22 Hargreaves Hill Brewing Co B3
23 Kelly Brothers Cider Co A3
24 Napoleone Cider B3
White Rabbit Brewery.................... (see 13)

◉ Shopping
Marysville Lolly Shop .... (see 3)

access to some of the region's finest wineries – from here it's a scenic drive or cycle circuit to Yarra Glen and Coldstream.

◉ Sights & Activities

★ **Healesville Sanctuary** WILDLIFE SANCTUARY
(☑03-5957 2800; www.zoo.org.au/healesville; Badger Creek Rd, Healesville; adult/child/family $30/13.20/68.50; ☺9am-5pm; 🚌685, 686) One of the best places in southern Australia to see native fauna, this wildlife park is full of kangaroos, dingoes, lyrebirds, Tasmanian devils, bats, koalas, eagles, snakes and lizards. The Platypus House displays the shy underwater creatures, and there's a daily interactive show at 11.30am (plus 2pm weekends). The exciting Birds of Prey presentation (noon and 2.30pm daily) features huge wedge-tailed eagles and owls soaring through the air. Admission for kids is free on weekends.

★ **TarraWarra Museum of Art** GALLERY
(☑03-5957 3100; www.twma.com.au; 311 Healesville-Yarra Glen Rd, Healesville; admission $5; ☺11am-5pm Tue-Sun) In a striking building at TarraWarra Estate, this excellent gallery showcases Australian art from the 1950s onwards and fea-

tures regularly changing, Australian and international contemporary art exhibitions. The rotating permanent collection includes work from heavyweights Arthur Boyd, Fred Williams, Sidney Nolan and Brett Whiteley.

Yarra Valley Railway HISTORIC RAILWAY
(☑03-5962 2490; www.yarravalleyrailway.org.au; Healesville Railway Station; adult/child/family $15/9/39; ☺10am-4pm Sun & holidays) This historical railway has reopened on a restored track with short train rides from Healesville station to Tunnel Hill and back. Future plans include extending the line to Yarra Glen.

Yarra Valley Chocolaterie & Ice Creamery CHOCOLATERIE
(☑03-9730 2777; www.yvci.com.au; 35 Old Healesville Rd, Yarra Glen; ☺9am-5pm) A bit of Willy Wonka has arrived in the Yarra Valley – this is the perfect winery break for the kids. Brightly uniformed staff carry trays piled high with free samples made with imported Belgian chocolate and you can watch the European chocolatiers at work through floor-to-ceiling glass windows. The Bushtucker range makes for great souvenirs.

☞ Tours

Ballooning over the Yarra Valley is a peaceful way to view the hills and vineyards. One-hour dawn flights with the following operators include a champagne breakfast and cost about $275 midweek and around $300 on weekends: **Global Ballooning** (☎1800 627 661; www.globalballooning.com.au) and **Go Wild Ballooning.** (☎03-9739 0772; www.gowildballooning.com.au; 621 Maroondah Hwy, Coldstream; ⊙9am-4pm Mon-Fri).

Eco Adventure Tours   CULTURAL TOUR
(☎03-5962 5115; www.ecoadventuretours. au; walks from $35) Offers nocturnal wildlife-spotting and daytime cultural walks in the Healesville, Toolangi and Dandenongs area.

Yarra Valley Winery Tours   WINE
(☎1300 496 105; www.yarravalleywinerytours. au; tours from Yarra Valley/Melbourne $105/140) Daily tours taking in four or five wineries, plus lunch.

🛌 Sleeping

A number of wineries offer luxury accommodation and there are lots of B&Bs, farmstays and guesthouses in the Yarra Valley – check out the accommodation booking service at www.visityarravalley.com.au.

Badger Creek Holiday Park   CAMPGROUND $
(☎03-5962 4328; www.badgercreekholidays. com.au; 419 Don Rd, Healesville; unpowered/powered sites $35/45, d cabins $145-225; ❊⊛❄) Among trees and birdlife, this riverside park is well kitted out with comfortable cabins and campsites, and has an adventure playground, pool and tennis courts.

Healesville Hotel   HOTEL $$
(☎03-5962 4002; www.yarravalleyharvest.com.au; 256 Maroondah Hwy, Healesville; d midweek/weekend from $110/130, Sat incl dinner $325; ❊⊛) An iconic Healesville landmark, this restored 1910 hotel offers boutique rooms upstairs with crisp white linen, pressed-metal ceilings and spotless shared bathrooms. Also has chic apartments behind the hotel in Furmston House (studio from $180).

Tuck Inn   B&B $$
(☎03-5962 3600; www.tuckinn.com.au; 2 Church St, Healesville; d midweek/weekend from $140/170; ❊) This former Masonic lodge has been refitted in a contemporary style – a beautiful and stylish five-room guesthouse with friendly hosts. Full breakfast included.

🍴 Eating & Drinking

Healesville Harvest   CAFE $
(☎03-5962 4002; www.yarravalleyharvest.com. au; 256 Maroondah Hwy, Healesville; snacks $7-20; ⊙8am-4pm; 🐾) Sidling up next to the Healesville Hotel, the Harvest is perfect for fresh Genovese coffee and light meals made with local produce – salads, sandwiches, cakes, breakfast eggs and soups. Head next door to **Kitchen & Butcher** to pick up gourmet picnic goodies and hampers.

★**Giant Steps &**
Innocent Bystander   TAPAS, PIZZA $$
(☎03-5962 6111; www.innocentbystander.com. au; 336 Maroondah Hwy, Healesville; mains $20-45; ⊙10am-10pm, from 8am Sat & Sun; 🐾) The industrial-sized Giants Steps & Innocent Bystander is a buzzing restaurant and cellar door – a great place for delicious pizzas, tapas and cheese platters or a lazy afternoon drink. Wine-tasting is free at the bar, or tour its barrel hall to sample the vintages for $10 (redeemable upon wine purchase).

Healesville Hotel   PUB $$
(☎03-5962 4002; www.yarravalleyharvest.com.au; 256 Maroondah Hwy, Healesville; ⊙mains $24-32) One of the area's culinary show-stoppers, historic Healesville Hotel is split into a formal dining room (Quince; two-courses from $55), and an inviting front bar with pub meals; the latter is a perfect spot for a pint or bottle of red by the fire.

Zonzo   ITALIAN $$
(☎03-9730 2500; www.zonzo.com.au; 957 Healesville-Yarra Glen Rd, Yarra Glen; pizza $24, share menu $45; ⊙noon-3pm Wed-Sun & 6pm-late Fri-Sun) At the Train Trak Winery, this stylish Italian and traditional pizza restaurant features a family-friendly shared dining experience and fine wines, with super views out over the valley. The thin-crust pizzas just fly off the plate. Bookings recommended.

The Gilded Lily   CAFE $$
(www.thegildedlily.com.au; 242 Maroondah Hwy, Healesville; dishes $8-18; ⊙8am-5pm; 🐾) At this cute, retro cafe/vintage store you can breakfast on bagels, spin vinyl and stock up on '50s dresses and leather bags.

Yarra Valley Dairy   CHEESE, WINE $$
(☎03-9739 1222; www.yvd.com.au; 70-80 McMeikans Rd, Yering; cheese plates from $27; ⊙10.30am-5pm) 🍴 This renowned cheesemaker sells cheese, produce and wine from

its picturesque farm gate. Take part in the cheese tasting, pick your favourites and order a platter to eat in the dairy's refurbished milking shed.

Grind n' Groove BAR, LIVE MUSIC
(☑03-5962 6840; www.grindngroove.com.au; 274 Maroondah Hwy, Healesville; ☉7pm-1am Wed-Sat) Cool music bar with band-poster-plastered walls and an outdoor covered beer garden. Wednesdays are open-mic night, and there's original live music on Friday and Saturday courtesy of local and Melbourne-based artists.

ⓘ Information

Yarra Valley Visitor Centre (☑03-5962 2600; www.visityarravalley.com.au; Harker St, Healesville; ☉9am-5pm) The main info centre for the Lower Yarra Valley with loads of brochures as well as maps for sale.

ⓘ Getting There & Away

Healesville is 65km north of Melbourne, an easy one-hour drive via the Eastern Fwy and Maroondah Hwy/B360.

McKenzie's Bus Lines (☑03-5962 5088; www.mckenzies.com.au) runs daily from Melbourne's Southern Cross Station to Healesville (1½ hours, $6) en route to Marysville and Eildon; check website for schedule.

From Melbourne, suburban trains run to Lilydale, where there are regular buses to Healesville.

YARRA VALLEY WINERIES

The Yarra Valley (www.wineyarravalley.com) has more than 80 wineries and 50 cellar doors scattered around its rolling, vine-cloaked hills, and is recognised as Victoria's oldest wine region – the first vines were planted at Yering Station in 1838. The region produces cool-climate, food-friendly drops such as chardonnay, pinot noir and pinot gris, as well as not-half-bad, full-bodied reds.

Of the many food and wine festivals in the region, our favourite is Grape Grazing (www.grapegrazing.com.au) in February, celebrating the beginning of the grape harvest. Rochford hosts a series of concerts throughout the year. Shedfest, in mid-October, is a showcase of the southern wineries near Warburton.

Some cellars charge a small fee for tasting, which is redeemable on purchase. Top Yarra Valley wineries with cellar-door sales and tastings include:

Coldstream Hills (☑03-5960 7000; www.coldstreamhills.com.au; 31 Maddens Lane, Coldstream; ☉10am-5pm) The chardonnay, pinot noir and merlot are the star picks here; good views of the vineyard and valley.

Domaine Chandon (☑03-9738 9200; www.chandon.com; 727 Maroondah Hwy, Coldstream; ☉10.30am-4.30pm) Established by the makers of Moët & Chandon, this slick operation with stunning views is worth a visit for the free guided tours at 11am, 1pm and 3pm, which include a peek at its atmospheric riddling hall.

Medhurst Wines (☑03-5964 9022; www.medhurstwines.com.au; 24/26 Medhurst Rd, Coldstream; ☉11am-5pm Thu-Mon) Polished concrete and glass work well together at this modern winery.

Oakridge (☑03-9738 9900; www.oakridgewines.com.au; 864 Maroondah Hwy, Coldstream; ☉10am-5pm) The cellar door affords stunning views at this award-winning winery. Contemporary fare is dished up in its chic restaurant.

Rochford (☑03-5962 2119; www.rochfordwines.com.au; 878-880 Maroondah Hwy, cnr Hill Rd, Coldstream; ☉9am-5pm) A huge complex with a restaurant, cafe and regular concerts.

TarraWarra Estate (☑03-5957 3510; www.tarrawarra.com.au; 311 Healesville–Yarra Glen Rd, Healesville; ☉11am-5pm) A convivial bistro and winery in a striking building. Sip away while lazing on the grassy knolls and visit the superb adjoining art gallery (p135).

Yering Farm Wines (☑03-9739 0461; www.yeringfarmwines.com; St Huberts Rd, Yering; ☉10am-5pm) A rustic, family-owned little cellar door in an old hayshed with lovely views.

Yering Station (☑03-9730 0100; www.yering.com; 38 Melba Hwy, Yering; ☉10am-5pm Mon-Fri, 10am-6pm Sat & Sun) Victoria's first vineyard, and home to the heady shiraz-viognier blend.

WORTH A TRIP

ST ANDREWS

Sleepily ensconced in the hills 35km north of Melbourne, this little town is best known for the weekly **St Andrews Community Market** (www.standrewsmarket.com.au; ⊗8am-2pm Sat). Every Saturday morning the scent of eucalypt competes with incense as an alternative crowd comes to mingle and buy handmade crafts, enjoy a shiatsu massage, sip chai, have their chakra aligned or just listen to the street musos. To get here, a shuttle bus departs from Hurstbridge train station.

Beyond, the winding road from St Andrews up to Kinglake is one of the region's great touring routes.

Warburton & the Upper Yarra Valley

The riverside town of Warburton has a very different feel from its Lower Valley neighbours – most visitors here are more interested in communing with nature than sipping chardonnay. The youthful Yarra River flows right through town and a lovely 6km walking and cycling trail follows both sides of the river.

The town of Warburton has an interesting history, first in gold mining, then as a timber town. From the early 20th century, much of the industry here was established by the Seventh-Day Adventist Church, which operated the Sanitarium Health Food factory (makers of Weet-Bix) here for many year. The architectural award-winning (now derelict) deco building still stands.

◉ Sights & Activities

Lilydale to Warburton Rail Trail   CYCLING
(Warby Trail; ☑1300 368 333; www.railtrails.org.au) Following a disused 1901 railway line, the 38km Lilydale to Warburton Rail Trail is a popular cycling route passing through farmland and wine country. The whole route takes about four hours one way, but it's relatively flat. Bike hire is available at **Yarra Valley Cycles** (☑03-9735 1483; www.yarravalleycycles.com; 108 Main St, Lilydale; per day $40) in Lilydale and Cog Bike Cafe in Warburton.

Yarra Ranges National Park   NATIONAL PARK
(☑13 19 63; www.parkweb.vic.gov.au) Towering above Warburton is the ruggedly beautiful Yarra Ranges National Park. **Mt Donna Buang** (1250m) is the highlight of the park, snow-topped in winter. Toboggans can be rented at the toboggan run. A few kilometres before the summit, the **Rainforest Gallery** (☑03-5966 5996; Acheron Way; admission free), also known as the Mt Donna Buang Skywalk, is a fantastic treetop walk along a 40m observation platform into the rainforest canopy, and a 350m boardwalk through the forest floor.

🛏 Sleeping & Eating

Alpine Retreat Hotel   HOTEL $
(☑03-5966 2411; www.alpineretreat.com.au; 12 Main St, Warburton; d from $50-110; 🕸) Once catering to Melbourne honeymooners, the sprawling 1920s faux-Tudor Alpine Retreat has cheap and cheerful rooms.

Reefton Hotel   PUB $
(☑03-5966 8555; 1600 Woods Point Rd, McMahons Creek; s/d $60/80, meals $12-26; ⊗noon-2.30pm & 5.30-8.30pm; 🕸) A bona fide slice of colonial Australiana, the Reefton is a real Aussie bush pub. Eat your homemade pie or Reefton burger out back near the old kiln or in the 'fancier' restaurant. To the side are four cosy cabins each with separate but private bathroom. It's 16km east of Warburton at McMahon's Creek.

Cog Bike Cafe   CAFE $
(☑03-5966 2213; www.cogbikecafe.com.au; 42 Station Rd, Warburton; mains $8-18; ⊗9am-4pm Thu-Sun; 🕸) Part of the Warby bike trail, this is the perfect pit stop for good coffee and lunch snacks, as well as offering all your bike-hire and service needs. It's behind the train station.

Little Joe   PIZZERIA $$
(☑03-5966 5635; 3416 Warburton Hwy, Warburton; pizzas $16-25; ⊗9am-late Thu-Sun) Owned by locals who met working at Healesville's renowned winery restaurant Innocent Bystander, this new wood-fired pizzeria is a stylish addition to Warburton's dining scene.

ℹ Information

Warburton Visitor Centre (☑03-5966 9600; www.warburtoninfocentre.com.au; 3400 Warburton Hwy, Warburton; ⊗10am-4pm) Plenty of brochures and info here, as well as a replica of the old Water Wheel. Also sells local handicrafts and arts by local artists.

Marysville

POP 520

Spread across a valley between Narbethong and Lake Mountain, Marysville was at the epicentre of the tragic 2009 bushfires (see p140), during which most of the town's buildings were destroyed and 34 people lost their lives. The town's tight-knit community is steadily and courageously rebuilding; a huge hotel conference complex is due for completion in 2014.

Marysville was a private mountain retreat as far back as 1863, and by the 1920s was known as Melbourne's honeymoon capital. Today it's still the main base for the cross-country ski fields at Lake Mountain and is reached via a beautiful drive over the Black Spur from Healesville; look out for lyrebirds on the way.

�) Sights & Activities

There are a number of great walking trails around town. Pick up maps and info from the visitor centre.

Steavenson Falls   WATERFALL
Spectacular Steavenson Falls, about 2km from town, is Victoria's highest waterfall

(84m). The infrastructure has been rebuilt since the fires, with a viewing platform spanning the river and floodlights illuminating the falls to 11pm.

Black Saturday Exhibition   MUSEUM
(5 Murchison St; entry $5; ⊙9am-5pm) Inside the visitor centre, this sobering exhibition of photos, video and salvaged items from the 2009 bushfires shows the devastating impact it had on the town.

Bruno's Art & Sculpture Garden   GALLERY, GARDENS
(☑03-5963 3513; www.brunosart.com; 51 Falls Rd; adult/child $10/5; ⊙ garden 10am-5pm daily, gallery Sat & Sun) This off-beat sculpture garden was badly damaged in the fires but more than 100 of the terracotta sculptures have been lovingly repaired – a fantasy land of figures representing the world's cultures and characters.

Beeches Rainforest Walk   WALKING
The Beeches Rainforest Walk is 4km (return) from the Beeches car park, which takes you through mountain ash and myrtle beech rainforest. It's a relatively easy walk with a few steep hills; look out for platypuses in the river, as well as lyrebirds, wallabies and echidnas.

AROUND MELBOURNE MARYSVILLE

YARRA VALLEY CIDER & ALE TRAIL

While it's wine that brings most visitors to the Yarra Valley, the **Cider & Ale Trail** (www.ciderandaletrail.com.au) will lead you on a fantastic route visiting local microbreweries and cider producers. Melbourne-based Aussie Brewery Tours (p108) offers popular tours.

Buckley's Beer (☑0408 354 909; www.buckleysbeer.com.au; 30 Hunter Rd, Healesville; ⊙11am-5pm Sat & Sun) On a mission to 'save the world one brew at a time', Buckley's has been hand-crafting its traditional lagers and ales for over a decade. Tours and tastings on weekends only.

Coldstream Brewery (☑03-9739 1794; www.coldstreambrewery.com.au; 694 Maroondah Hwy, Coldstream; mains $23-30; ⊙11am-11pm Wed-Fri, 8am-11pm Sat, 8am-10pm Sun) No longer brewing on-site, this great gastropub has all its selection on tap.

Hargreaves Hill Brewing Co (☑03-9730 1905; www.hargreaveshill.com.au; 25 Bell St, Yarra Glen; ⊙11.30am-8pm Mon-Sat, 11.30am-4.30pm Sun) Sample European-style beers within an 1890s building (a former bank) with quality restaurant.

Kelly Brothers Cider Co (☑03-9722 1304; www.kellybrothers.com.au; Fulford Rd, Wonga Park; ⊙10am-5pm Mon-Sat, from 11am Sun) In the business of making ciders since the 1960s; sample their goods made with local pears and apples.

Napoleone Cider (☑03-9739 0666; www.napoleonecider.com.au; 10 St Huberts Rd, Coldstream; ⊙10am-5pm) Produces a variety of pear and apple ciders crushed on-site using fruits picked from its orchard. Also does a pale ale beer. Free tastings.

White Rabbit Brewery (☑03-5962 6516; www.whiterabbitbeer.com.au; 316 Maroondah Hwy, Healesville; ⊙11am-5pm, to 9pm Fri) Enjoy a few cold ones at the Yarra Valley's most well-known brewery, and snack on a pizza on its retro couches surrounded by huge vats and bottling machines.

BLACK SATURDAY

Victoria is no stranger to bushfires. In 1939, 71 people died in the Black Friday fires; in 1983 Ash Wednesday claimed 75 lives in Victoria and South Australia. But no one was prepared for the utter devastation of the 2009 bushfires that became known as Black Saturday.

On 7 February 2009, Victoria recorded its hottest temperature on record, with Melbourne exceeding 46°C and some parts of the state topping 48°C. Strong winds and tinder-dry undergrowth from years of drought, combined with the record-high temperatures, created conditions in which the risk of bushfires was extreme. The first recorded fires began near Kilmore and strong winds from a southerly change fanned the flames towards the Yarra Ranges. Within a few devastating hours a ferocious firestorm engulfed the tiny bush towns of Marysville, Kinglake, Strathewen, Flowerdale and Narbethong, while separate fires started at Horsham, Bendigo and an area southeast of Beechworth. The fires virtually razed the towns of Marysville and Kinglake and moved so quickly that many residents had no chance to escape. Many victims of the fires died in their homes or trapped in their cars, some blocked by trees that had fallen across the road.

Fires raged across the state for more than a month, with high temperatures, winds and practically no rainfall making it impossible for fire crews to contain the worst blazes. New fires began at Wilson's Promontory National Park (burning more than 50% of the park area), the Dandenong Ranges and in the Daylesford area.

The statistics tell a tragic tale: 173 people died; more than 2000 homes were destroyed; an estimated 7500 people were left homeless; and more than 4500 sq km was burned. What followed from the shell-shocked state and nation was a huge outpouring of grief, humanitarian aid and charity. Strangers donated tonnes of clothing, toys, food, caravans and even houses to bushfire survivors, while an appeal set up by the Australian Red Cross raised more than $300 million.

Today the blackened forests around Kinglake and Marysville are regenerating, and the communities are rebuilding. Tourism remains a big part of the economy, and visiting the shops, cafes and hotels in the area continues to boost their recovery.

Keppel Lookout Trail WALKING

The Keppel Lookout Trail is a challenging walk with spectacular views from the lookout point and at the top of the picturesque Steavenson Falls.

🛏 Sleeping & Eating

Black Spur Inn INN $

(📞 03-5963 7121; www.blackspurinn.com.au; 436 Maroondah Hwy; s without bathroom $40, d from $85; ❊ 🐾) Just the kind of place every weary traveller hopes to stumble upon, this historic 1863 inn has farmhouse-style rooms in the main building and no-frills portable cabins out back (used as lodging for athletes during the Sydney 2000 Olympics before relocation). There's an atmospheric bar and restaurant with roaring fireplace. It's 14km out of town on the Black Spur, with a courtesy bus to/from Marysville.

Marysville Caravan Park CAMPGROUND $

(📞 03-5963 3247; www.marysvillecaravanpark. com.au; 1130 Buxton Rd; powered site from $33, cabins $95-160) Located at the edge of town,

Marysville Caravan Park has excellent self-contained riverside cabins, camping and a play area for kids.

The Tower MOTEL $$

(📞 03-5963 3225; www.towermotel.com.au; 33 Murchison St; s/d/f $125/135/165; ❊ 🐾) One of the few buildings on the main road to survive Black Saturday, the Tower embraces its 1970s motel facade, and recent renovations have jazzed it up to almost boutique levels. The owners are ultra-friendly and it has an attractive courtyard and wine bar, while rooms come with minibars, cable TV and free wi-fi. Rates increase $20 in ski season.

Crossways Historic Country Inn MOTEL $$

(📞 03-5963 3290; www.crosswaysmarysville.com. au; 4 Woods Point Rd; d $120, 2-bedroom cottages $195) Crossways has been around since the 1920s and, remarkably, survived the Black Saturday bushfires. Family-friendly accommodation includes individual log-cabin-style units and the River Cottage, a modern two-bedroom unit.

Delderfield B&B B&B **$$$**
(☑03-5963 4345; www.delderfield.com.au; 1 Darwin St; d $285-340) The two spacious boutique cottages overlooking a gorgeous garden make for a romantic retreat, just one street back from Marysville's centre. They come with spa bath, BBQ on the deck, and log fires.

Fraga's Café CAFE **$$**
(☑03-5963 3216; 19 Murchison St; meals $10-26; ⊙9am-4.30pm) A vibrant, arty cafe serving the town's best coffee, creative mains, pies and cakes, as well as local beers.

🛍 Shopping

Marysville Lolly Shop FOOD
(8 Murchison St; ⊙10am-4pm Mon-Fri, to 5pm Sat & Sun) Symbolic of Marysville's rise from the ashes, this old favorite has been rebuilt following the fires, and is a must visit for sweet-tooths. Also stocks local organic produce.

ℹ Information

Marysville Lake Mountain Visitor Information Centre (☑03-5963 4567; www.marysville tourism.com; 5 Murchison St; ⊙9am-5pm Mon-Fri, 10am-4pm Sat & Sun) The slick new tourist office provides helpful, friendly service.

ℹ Getting There & Away

Marysville is 100km from Melbourne, a 1½-hour drive via the Maroondah Hwy. It's 40 minutes from Healesville.

McKenzie's Bus Lines (p137) has a daily service to/from Melbourne ($10.40) via Healesville.

Lake Mountain

Part of the Yarra Ranges National Park, Lake Mountain (1433m) is the premier cross-country skiing resort in Australia, with 37km of trails and several toboggan runs. In summer there are marked hiking and mountain-biking trails. There's no on-mountain accommodation but Marysville is only 10km away.

During the ski season the daily gate fee is $35 per car on weekends and holidays, and $25 midweek; the trail fee costs from $11.90/5.90 per adult/child. Outside the season there's only a parking fee of $2.

Lake Mountain Alpine Resort (☑03-5957 7222; www.lakemountainresort.com.au; Snowy Rd; ⊙8am-4.30pm Mon-Fri Oct-May, until 6.30pm Jun-Sep) has ski hire, a ski school, a cafe and undercover barbecue areas. In town, **Marysville Ski Centre** (www.marysvilleski.com.au; 27 Murchison St; ⊙Jun-Sep) hire skis, toboggans, clothing and car chains.

The **Lake Mountain Snow Bus** (Country Touch Tours; ☑03-5963 3753; 24 Murchison St, Marysville) operates a return service including gate entry fee from Marysville (adult/child $40/35) and Healesville (adult/child $45/40). The bus returns from Lake Mountain at 3pm. Book online at www.visityarra valley.com.au.

THE SPA COUNTRY

Daylesford & Hepburn Springs

POP DAYLESFORD 3073, HEPBURN SPRINGS 601

Set among the scenic hills, lakes and forests of the Central Highlands, Daylesford and Hepburn Springs form the 'spa centre of Victoria', a fabulous year-round destination where you can soak away your troubles and sip wine by the fireside. The health-giving properties of the area's mineral springs were first claimed back in the 1870s, attracting droves of fashionable Melburnians. The well-preserved and restored buildings show the prosperity of these towns, as well as the lasting influence of the many Swiss-Italian miners who came to work the tunnel mines in the surrounding hills.

These days, the Daylesford region is one of Victoria's favourite boutique weekend getaways – even if you don't indulge in a spa treatment, there are plenty of great walks, a fabulous foodie scene and remnants of an arty, alternative vibe. The local population is a blend of hippies and old-timers, and there's also a thriving gay and lesbian scene here. During the week some businesses close so it's best to visit Thursday to Sunday.

⊙ Sights & Activities

Daylesford sits above pretty man-made Lake Daylesford, a popular fishing and picnicking area; boats and kayaks are available for hire. It's an easy walk or cycle around the lake, passing the Wombat Flat Mineral Spring (Map p145). Jubilee Lake, about 3km southeast of town, is another pretty picnic spot with canoe hire.

Good local walks incorporating various mineral-spring pumps include Sailors Falls, Tipperary Springs, Central Springs Reserve and the Hepburn Springs Reserve; take a water bottle with you to taste-test the pump water. The visitor centre has maps and walking guides.

Hepburn Springs

ⓝ 0 ——— 200 m
0 ——— 0.1 miles

Hepburn Springs

◉ **Top Sights**
1 Hepburn Bathhouse & Spa B1

◉ **Sights**
2 Hepburn Mineral Springs Reserve B2

🟢 **Activities, Courses & Tours**
3 Hepburn Springs Golf Club A2
Mineral Spa at Peppers .... (see 7)
Shizuka Ryokan .... (see 6)

🛏 **Sleeping**
4 Daylesford Cottage Directory B3
5 Hepburn Springs Chalet B2
Mooltan Guesthouse .... (see 1)
6 Shizuka Ryokan A2

❌ **Eating**
7 Argus at Peppers B1
8 Red Star Café B1

🍷 **Drinking & Nightlife**
9 Old Hepburn Hotel A1
10 Savoia Hotel B2

★ **Hepburn Bathhouse & Spa**   DAY SPA
(Map p142; ✆ 03-5321 6000; www.hepburnbath
house.com; Mineral Springs Reserve Rd, Hepburn Springs; 2 hr bathhouse entry $26; ⊙9am-
6.30pm) Within the Hepburn Mineral
Springs Reserve, the main bathhouse is a
sleek, ultramodern building where you can
gaze out on the bush setting while soaking
in the public pool or lazing on spa couches.
The spa offers various treatments or a soak
in a private mineral-spring pool in the original historic building. Around the bathhouse
are picnic areas, mineral-spring pumps and
the historic Pavilion cafe.

Convent Gallery   GALLERY
(Map p145; ✆ 03-5348 3211; www.theconvent.com.
au; 7 Daly St, Daylesford; admission $5; ⊙10am-
4pm) This beautiful 19th-century convent on
Wombat Hill has been brilliantly converted
into an art gallery with soaring ceilings,
grand archways and magnificent gardens.
Head up the path in the gardens behind
the convent for sweeping views over the
town. There's also an atrium cafe, bar and
penthouse apartment. They run night ghost
tours for the brave ($45; book ahead).

Wombat Hill Botanic Gardens   GARDENS
(Map p145; Central Springs Rd, Daylesford) Oak,
pine and cypress trees fill these beautiful
gardens, which have a picnic area and lookout tower with fine views of the countryside.

Daylesford Spa Country Railway   TRAIN
(Map p145; ✆ Sundays only 03-5348 3503; www.
dscr.com.au; 18 Raglan St, Daylesford train station;
adult/child/family $10/8/25; ⊙10am-2.30pm Sun)
This old rail-motor has popular half-hour
rides to Musk and back every Sunday. It's
a leisurely ride, but for extra sparkle go on
the first Saturday of the month (at 5.30pm)
when the Silver Streak Food & Wine Train
(✆ 0421 780 100; adult $35) indulges you with
drinks and finger food served on board. The
line to Bullarto was damaged in the 2009
bushfires but repair work is ongoing.

Hepburn Springs Golf Club   GOLF
(Map p142; ✆ 0458 560 592; www.hepburngolf.
com.au; 18 holes $25) An attractive course dou-
bling as a good place to spot kangaroos (ask
staff where they are). Golfers use an honour
system of putting your money in a bucket if
no one is around at reception.

Boomerang Holiday Ranch   HORSE RIDING
(Map p145; ✆ 03-5348 2525; www.boomerang
ranch.com.au; Ranch Rd, Daylesford; 1hr ride adult/
child $35/30) Offers leisurely trail rides in the
state forest.

⭐ Festivals & Events

ChillOut Festival   GAY, LESBIAN
(www.chilloutfestival.com.au) Held over the Labour Day weekend in March, this gay and

lesbian Pride festival is Daylesford's biggest annual event, attracting thousands of people for street parades, music and dance parties.

Swiss Italian Festa   CULTURAL
(www.swissitalianfesta.com) Held in late October, this festival draws on the region's European roots with literary events, music, food, wine and art.

🛏 Sleeping

Bookings for B&Bs can be made through agencies in Daylesford: try **Daylesford Cottage Directory** (Map p142; ☑ 03-5348 1255; www.cottagedirectory.com.au; 16 Hepburn Rd, Daylesford), **Daylesford Getaways** (Map p145; ☑ 03-5348 4422; www.dayget.com.au; 14 Vincent St, Daylesford) and **Escapes Daylesford** (Map p145; ☑ 03-5348 1448; www.dabs.com.au; 94 Vincent St, Daylesford).

Other than camping, genuine budget accommodation is basically nonexistent; however it's worth checking if the Continental Hotel has reopened.

Daylesford

2 Dukes   GUESTHOUSE $
(Map p145; ☑ 03-5348 4848; 2 Duke St, Daylesford; r from $99; 🐾) Flying the flag for affordable accommodation in Daylesford, this former doctor's surgery turned guesthouse is kitted out with vintage finds and original bright artworks. The five rooms each have their own personalities and share a bathroom (one room has en-suite). Light breakfast is included and there's free wi-fi rounding out the best offer in town.

Jubilee Lake Holiday Park   CAMPGROUND $
(Map p145; ☑ 1800 686 376, 03-5348 2186; www.jubileelake.com.au; 151 Jubilee Lake Rd, Daylesford; unpowered/powered sites $21/30, cabins $85-170; ❄🐾) Set in bushland on the edge of pretty Jubilee Lake, this friendly place is the best caravan park in the region. There is an open-air cinema in summer, paddle-boat and canoe hire is available, and lower rates apply out of the summer high season.

Central Springs Inn   MOTEL $$
(Map p145; ☑ 03-5348 3134; www.centralspringsinn.com.au; cnr Howe & Camp Sts, Daylesford; d from $115; 🐾) In a town full of pricey B&Bs, Central Springs offers more affordable motel-style lodging without skimping on character. Choose from large rooms in its 1875 heritage Provender building, or spa rooms in its newer section.

Lake House   BOUTIQUE HOTEL $$$
(Map p145; ☑ 03-5348 3329; www.lakehouse.com.au; King St, Daylesford; d incl half board from $550; ❄🐾) Overlooking Lake Daylesford, the famous Lake House is set in rambling gardens with bridges and waterfalls. Its 35 rooms are split into spacious waterfront rooms with balcony decks, and lodge rooms with

AROUND MELBOURNE DAYLESFORD & HEPBURN SPRINGS

PAMPERING

The Daylesford and Hepburn Springs region is famous for its rejuvenating mineral spa treatments. Aside from the well-known Hepburn Bathhouse & Spa, there are plenty of places to pamper yourself:

Daylesford Day Spa (Map p145; ☑ 03-5348 2331; www.daylesforddayspa.com.au; 25 Albert St, Daylesford; ☺10am-6pm Mon-Fri, 9am-7pm Sat, 10am-5pm Sun) Start with a vitamin-rich mud body mask followed by a hot-stone foot massage, then finish with a rose milk spa bath.

Massage Healing Centre (Map p145; ☑ 03-5348 1099; www.massagehealing.com.au; 5/11 Howe St, Daylesford) For a modest, down-to-earth alternative to the glitz-and-glam spa resorts, try this place.

Mineral Spa at Peppers (Map p142; ☑ 03-5348 2100; www.mineralspa.com.au; 124 Main Rd, Springs Retreat, Hepburn Springs) Have an exfoliation with Australian desert salts, an algae gel wrap, or relax in the lavender-infused steam room.

Salus (Map p145; ☑ 03-5348 3329; www.lakehouse.com.au; King St, Lake House, Daylesford) The pampering starts as you walk through a small rainforest to your exotic jasmine-flower bath in a cedar-lined tree house overlooking the lake.

Shizuka Ryokan (Map p142; ☑ 03-5348 2030; www.shizuka.com.au; 7 Lakeside Dr, Hepburn Springs) Shiatsu massage and spa treatments with natural sea salts and seaweed extracts feature at this Japanese-style country spa retreat.

private courtyards. Rates include breakfast and three-course dinner at its famed restaurant; two-night minimum on weekends.

Hepburn Springs

★ Hepburn Springs Chalet HOTEL $$

(Map p142; ✆ 03-5348 2344; www.hepburnsprings chalet.com.au; 78 Main Rd, Hepburn Springs; r midweek/weekends $120/180; ☜) If Don Draper was in town, this is where he'd drop his briefcase. It was originally a 1920s guesthouse, and the owners have retained the original features, complementing them with retro charm thanks to deco mirrors and velvet lounges in the sitting areas and bar. Rooms are basic, but comfortable, and come with en suite bathrooms.

Mooltan Guesthouse GUESTHOUSE $$

(Map p142; ✆ 03-5348 3555; www.mooltan.com. au; 129 Main Rd, Hepburn Springs; midweek s/d from $80/100, weekend from $100/130) Behind a well-clipped hedge, this inviting, quaint Edwardian country home has large lounge rooms, a billiard table and a tennis court. Some bedrooms open onto a broad verandah overlooking the Mineral Springs Reserve. The cheapest rooms have shared facilities.

Shizuka Ryokan GUESTHOUSE $$$

(Map p142; ✆ 03-5348 2030; www.shizuka.com.au; 7 Lakeside Dr, Hepburn Springs; d $280-380) Inspired by traditional places of renewal and rejuvenation in Japan, this traditional minimalist getaway has six rooms with private Japanese gardens, tatami matting and plenty of green tea. Not suitable for children.

✗ Eating

Daylesford and Hepburn Springs are walkin gourmet treats. Every second business on Vincent St in Daylesford is a cafe or foodstore and there's a buzzing atmosphere on weekends.

Daylesford

Cliffy's Emporium DELI, CAFE $

(Map p145; ✆ 03-5348 3279; www.cliffys.com.au; 30 Raglan St, Daylesford; mains $9-21; ⊙9am-5pm daily, till late Sat; ☜) ✎ Behind the vine-covered verandah of this local institution is an old-world shop crammed with organic vegetables, cheese and preserves. The busy cafe is perfect for breakfast, pies and baguettes.

Wombat Hill House CAFE $

(Map p145; www.wombathillhouse.com.au; Wombat Hill Botanic Gardens, Daylesford; mains $9-17; ⊙9am-4pm Thu-Mon) Recently taken over by the folks from the Lake House, this cutesy cafe in the Wombat Hill Botanic Gardens is a great spot to grab breakfast next to the fireplace or out in the patio garden. Also on offer are takeaway lunch boxes perfect for a picnic in the gardens.

Farmers Arms GASTROPUB $$

(Map p145; ✆ 03-5348 2091; www.farmersarms. com.au; 1 East St, Daylesford; mains $26-36; ⊙noon-3pm & 6pm-late) Modern and rustic – both the surroundings and the food – meld tastefully in this classic country red-brick gastropub. There's a welcoming front bar and a beer garden for summer days.

Koukla Café PIZZA $$

(Map p145; ✆ 03-5348 2363; www.frangosand frangos.com.au; 82 Vincent St, Daylesford; pizzas $21; ⊙7am-late; ☜) This moody European-style cafe is a great place to warm yourself by the fire with coffee on the couch. Has great sourdough wood-fired pizzas, including Vegemite and mozzarella pizzas for breakfast.

★ Lake House MODERN AUSTRALIAN $$$

(Map p145; ✆ 03-5348 3329; www.lakehouse.com. au; King St, Daylesford; 2-4 course lunch from $76, dinner from $80; ⊙noon-2.30pm & 6-9.30pm; ☜) You can't talk about Daylesford without waxing on about the Lake House, long regarded as Daylesford's top dining experience. It doesn't disappoint, with stylish purple high-back furniture, picture windows showing off Lake Daylesford, a superb seasonal menu, an award-winning wine list and impressive service. Book well ahead for weekends.

Sault MODERN AUSTRALIAN $$$

(✆ 03-5348 6555; www.sault.com.au; 2349 Ballan-Daylesford Rd, Daylesford; mains $34-40; ⊙6pm-late Wed & Thu, 11am-late Fri-Sun) Surrounded by lavender and a lake, and situated in a grand building about 7km south of Daylesford, stylish Sault has a reputation for serving innovative contemporary Australian dishes with a Spanish twist and a focus on local produce. Wednesday is 'locals' night' – a meal and a glass of wine cost $30.

Kazuki's JAPANESE $$$

(Map p145; ✆ 03-5348 1218; www.kazukis.com.au; cnr Raglan & Camp Sts, Daylesford; 2-/3-courses $65/80, tasting menu 5-/7-course $90/110; ⊙noon-2pm Fri-Mon, 6pm-late Thu-Tue) Kazuki's brings an unexpected twist to Daylesford's

Daylesford

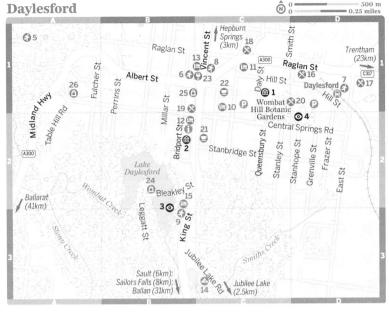

Daylesford

⊚ Sights
1 Convent Gallery	C1
2 Daylesford Museum	B2
Daylesford Sunday Market	(see 7)
3 Wombat Flat Mineral Spring	B2
4 Wombat Hill Botanic Gardens	D2

⊕ Activities, Courses & Tours
5 Boomerang Holiday Ranch	A1
6 Daylesford Day Spa	B1
7 Daylesford Spa Country Railway	D1
8 Massage Healing Centre	C1
9 Salus	B3

⊜ Sleeping
10 2 Dukes	C1
11 Central Springs Inn	C1
12 Daylesford Accommodation Escapes	B2
13 Daylesford Getaways	C1

14 Jubilee Lake Holiday Park	C3
15 Lake House	B2

⊗ Eating
16 Cliffy's Emporium	D1
17 Farmers Arms	D1
18 Kazuki's	C1
19 Koukla Café	B1
Lake House	(see 15)
20 Wombat Hill House	D1

⊝ Drinking & Nightlife
21 Breakfast & Beer	C2
22 Buffalo Girls	C1
23 Daylesford RSL	C1

⊜ Shopping
24 Book Barn	B2
25 Frances Pilley	B1
26 Mill Markets	A1

dining scene with its fusion of Japanese and French cuisine. The two-room restaurant, incorporating a wine and *sake* bar, is intimate, and there's an al fresco courtyard at the side.

✗ Hepburn Springs

Red Star Café   CAFE **$$**

(Map p142; ☑ 03-5348 2297; www.theredstar. com.au; 115 Main Rd, Hepburn Springs; mains $8-

24; ⊘ 8am-4pm) The weatherboard shopfront feels like someone's home, with loungy couches, bookshelves full of reading material, great music, a garden out the back and a funky local vibe. Great place for a morning coffee or lunch of foccacia, curry or steak sandwich.

WORTH A TRIP

MT FRANKLIN & AROUND

Just 10km north of Daylesford, **Mt Franklin** is an extinct volcanic crater that you can drive straight into. Known to the Dja Dja Wurrung people as Lalgambook, it's a beautiful place with forest-covered walking trails that take you through lush vegetation, a picnic area and a summit lookout. Free short-term camping is permitted in the crater (it's part of the Hepburn Regional Park).

Heading back towards Hepburn Springs, take the turn-off to **Shepherds Flat**, where there are two interesting spots. **Cricket Willow** (☑ 03-5476 4277; www.cricketwillow.com.au; 355 Hepburn-Newstead Rd; museum adult/child $3/1, tours $6; ◷ 10.30am-5.30pm Sat & Sun) has been making its Jabaroo cricket bats for over a century using the willow grown on-site since 1802. Check out the immaculate cricket oval, then tour the workshop, willow-tree nursery and sport memorabilia museum, or line up against the bowling machine ($25).

Further along, **Lavandula** (☑ 03-5476 4393; www.lavandula.com.au; 350 Hepburn-Newstead Rd; adult/child $4/1; ◷ 10.30am-5.30pm Sep–mid-Jul) is a lovely Swiss-Italian farm and stone cottage where you can meet the farm animals, check out the gardens and produce, wander between lavender bushes and enjoy lunch in the Ticinese grotto. There are free tours of the farm and cottage at noon, 2pm and 4pm.

Argus at Peppers MODERN AUSTRALIAN $$$
(Map p142; ☑ 03-5348 4199; www.peppers.com.au; 124 Main Rd, Hepburn Springs; mains $33-44; ◷ noon-3pm & 6pm-late) Within the Peppers Mineral Springs Retreat, the Argus dining room flickers with tealight candles amid art deco touches and dark wood. Local seasonal produce is the focus in the creative contemporary Australian dishes with fusion twists. Choose from the à la carte menu or sample the five-course degustation at $95 ($80 vegetarian).

 Drinking & Entertainment

For a budget option in Daylesford, try the **Daylesford RSL** (Map p145; 20 Vincent St, Daylesford), an unpretentious local hang-out with cheap drinks and live music. For more live music, try the **Savoia Hotel** (Map p142; ☑ 03-5348 2314; 69 Main Rd, Hepburn Springs) and Old Hepburn Hotel.

Buffalo Girls CAFE
(Map p145; ☑ 0423 250 713; 4c Duke St, Daylesford; espresso $3; ◷ 9am-1pm) The industrial warehouse space of Buffalo Girls is as cool as any cafe you'd find in Melbourne's hip inner north, as are its single-origin Ethiopian espressos and cold drips. It's well hidden within an unsigned red-brick facade in a car park off Duke St.

Breakfast & Beer CAFE, BAR
(Map p145; ☑ 03-5348 1778; www.breakfastandbeer.com.au; 117 Vincent St, Daylesford; ◷ 8am-4pm daily & 6-11pm Wed-Sun) Straight out of a Belgian backstreet, this European-style cafe stocks fine local and imported beer, and a boutique menu strong on local produce including innovative breakfast/brunch fare.

Old Hepburn Hotel PUB
(Map p142; ☑ 03-5348 2207; www.oldhepburnhotel.com.au; 236 Main Rd, Hepburn Springs; ◷ 4pm-midnight Mon & Tue, noon-midnight Wed & Thu, noon-1am Fri & Sat, noon-11pm Sun; 🛜) A country pub with taste, the Old Hepburn makes for a great night out with live music on weekends (usually free). The pub food hits the spot, plus the hotel has a ripper beer garden and friendly locals. Free bus pick-up and drop-off service from Hepburn.

🛍 **Shopping**

Daylesford is jam-packed with shops selling antiques, vintage and new-age paraphernalia. Check out the **Daylesford Sunday Market** (Map p145; ◷ 8am-3pm Sun) at the old train station.

Mill Markets MARKET
(Map p145; ☑ 03-5348 4332; www.millmarkets.com.au; 105 Central Springs Rd, Daylesford; ◷ 10am-6pm) You could just about fit a Boeing 747 in the enormous Mill Markets, housing a mind-boggling collection of furniture, collectables, antiques, books and retro fashions.

Frances Pilley HOMEWARES
(Map p145; www.francespilley.com.au; 78 Vincent St, Daylesford; ◷ 10am-5pm) Stocks beauti-

ful homewares imported from around the globe; think French striped deckchairs and homemade Syrian soaps.

Book Barn BOOKS
(Map p145; ☑03-5348 3048; 1 Leggatt St, Daylesford; ☺10am-5pm) This tiny bookshop by the lake manages to squeeze in a big range of quality secondhand books, and a cafe overlooking the lake.

ⓘ Information

Daylesford Visitors Centre (Map p145; ☑1800 454 891, 03-5321 6123; www.visit daylesford.com; 98 Vincent St, Daylesford; ☺9am-5pm) Within the old fire station, this excellent tourist centre has good information on the area and mineral springs. There's a history museum (Map p145; ☑03-5348 1453; www.daylesfordhistory.com.au; 100 Vincent St, Daylesford; adult/child $3/1; ☺1.30-4.30pm Sat & Sun) next door.

Daylesford Library (☑03-5348 2800; cnr Bridport & Albert Sts, Daylesford; ☺10am-6pm Mon-Fri, 10am-1pm Sat; 🛜) Free internet access.

ⓘ Getting There & Away

Daylesford is 115km from Melbourne, a 1½-hour drive via the Calder Hwy; take the Woodend turnoff from where it's a 35-minute drive.

Daily **V/Line** (☑1800 800 007; www.vline. com.au) train and coach services connect Melbourne by train to Woodend then bus to Daylesford ($11, two hours). The buses run from Bridport St opposite the fire station.

Local buses operate the 3km journey between Daylesford (from Bridport St) and Hepburn Springs; it's a 15-minute journey.

MACEDON RANGES & AROUND

A short distance off the Calder Fwy, less than an hour's drive north of Melbourne, the Macedon Ranges are a beautiful area of low mountains, native forest, excellent regional produce and wineries, often enveloped in cloud in winter, but great on a sunny day. The Macedon Ranges cover the towns of Gisborne, Woodend, Trentham, Lancefield, Romsey and Kyneton, and the legendary Hanging Rock.

The scenic drive up Mt Macedon, a 1010m-high extinct volcano, passes grand mansions and gardens, taking you to picnic areas, walking trails, sweeping lookouts and the huge memorial cross near the summit

car park. There's a cafe and barbecue area at Cameron's Picnic Area.

There are some great wineries (www. macedonrangeswineries.com.au) in the area. Wine Tours Victoria (☑1300 946 386; www.winetours.com.au) can arrange tours.

Trentham & Around

The small historic township of Trentham (population 630) sits at the top of the Great Dividing Range, midway between Woodend and Daylesford, 97km from Melbourne. At an elevation of 700m it's noticeably cooler than the surrounding areas, and is worth a visit to stroll its quaint streetscape with some excellent new eateries.

A 10-minute drive from Trentham is the tiny hamlet of Blackwood surrounded by state forest, which also has plenty of charm.

Two to four buses run daily to Trentham from Woodend station ($4, 22 minutes) en route to Daylesford.

◉ Sights & Activities

Trentham Falls WATERFALL
Situated in the Wombat State Forest and just a short drive from the Trentham township is one of Victoria's highest single-drop waterfalls – the Coliban River cascades 32m over a sheer face of basalt rock.

Domino Trail WALKING
This walking trail follows the old Trentham railway through the Wombat State Forest, the habitat of the endangered powerful owl. Trail maps are available from the tourist office (☑03-5424 1178; www.visittrentham.com.au; Victoria St, Trentham; ☺10am-4pm Sat & Sun) at the old train station.

Garden of St Erth GARDENS
(☑03-5368 6514; www.diggers.com.au/gardens-cafes/gardens/st-erth.aspx; Simmons Reef Rd, Blackwood; entry $10; ☺garden 9am-5pm, cafe 10am-4pm Thu-Mon) Located in Blackwood, this quaint, historic garden and nursery is centred around an 1860s sandstone cottage with a cafe serving produce grown on-site.

✕ Eating & Drinking

Colliban Foodstore CAFE $$
(☑03-5424 1774; www.collibanfoodstore.com; 18 Market St, Trentham; mains $10-30; ☺lunch Thu-Sun, 6-8pm Fri; 🛜) Fill up on tasty cafe fare surrounded by imported foodie goods at this cafe-providore in a converted weatherboard building. The wine list bulges at over 800

DON'T MISS

HANGING ROCK

Hanging Rock (www.visitmacedonranges.com; per vehicle $10; ⊙ 9am-5pm) is an ancient and captivating place, made famous by the spooky Joan Lindsay novel (and subsequent film by Peter Weir) *Picnic at Hanging Rock*, about the disappearance of a group of 19th-century schoolgirls.The volcanic rock formations are the sacred site of the traditional owners, the Wurundjeri people, but you're welcome to clamber up the rocks along the 20-minute path. It was once also a hideout for bushrangers – many mysteries and legends surround it and an eerie energy is said to be felt by many who climb among the boulders. From the summit there are views of Mt Macedon and the surrounding countryside.

The walk-through **Hanging Rock Discovery Centre** explains its history and geology, and there's a cafe next door. Guided night walks operate in summer months; call to book on ☑ 03-5421 1469.

Spreading out below the rock is a cricket ground, where you can see kangaroos, and its famous **racecourse** (www.hangingrockracingclub.com.au), which hosts two excellent picnic race meetings, on New Year's Day and Australia Day. It's also a venue for 'A Day on the Green' concerts, hosting big-name acts from the Rolling Stones to Leonard Cohen.

varietals, mainly European, and it has great ice cream too.

★ **Du Fermier**　　　　CAFE, FRENCH $$
(☑ 03-5424 1634; www.dufermier.com.au; 42 High St, Trentham; mains $12-35; ⊙ 10am-4pm Thu-Sun, & 6-9pm Fri & Sat) Celebrity chef Annie Smithers' Du Fermier, translated as 'from the farmhouse', focuses on rustic French provincial cooking, with 90% of the produce sourced from her own garden.

RedBeard Historic Bakery　　CAFE, BAKERY $$
(www.redbeardbakery.com.au; Old Bakery Lane, Trentham; mains $12-24; ⊙ 8am-5pm; 🛜) Tucked down a lane off the main strip, RedBeard is owned by brothers with more than 25 years' baking experience, and is famous for its sourdough breads baked in a huge 19th-century wood-fired Scotch oven. They also do good breakfasts. While RedBeard was for sale at the time of research, it's expected to continue as is.

Blackwood Merchant　　　　CAFE $$
(21 Martin St, Blackwood; mains $12-28; ⊙ 9am-5pm Sun-Thu, to 11pm Fri & Sat) In Blackwood, this rustic cafe/general store specialises in local produce and wines. Its back patio has lovely forest views.

The Cosmopolitan　　　　GASTROPUB
(☑ 03-5424 1516; www.thecosmopolitanhotel.com.au; cnr High St & Cosmo Rd, Trentham; mains from $25; ⊙ noon-late Fri-Sun) The historic Cosmo recently reopened (after it was destroyed by fire in 2005), pleasing many waiting locals. Cosy up by the open fire with a local beer or

cider under pressed-metal ceilings. In summer, the huge beer garden beckons.

Woodend

POP 5400

This pleasant town 13km from Mt Macedon is easily reached by train from Melbourne (70km away) and makes a popular base for road cyclists and mountain-bikers exploring the Macedon Ranges. It's also the gateway to Hanging Rock and the wineries in the region.

✗ Eating & Drinking

Village Larder　　　　CAFE $$
(☑ 03-5427 3399; www.thevillagelarder.com.au; 81 High St; mains $12-24; ⊙ 8am-4pm daily, & 6-10pm Sat) There's retro style at the Village Larder, where local organic produce is crafted into some interesting dishes with a hearty Modern British twist.

★ **Holgate Brewhouse**　　　　PUB
(☑ 03-5427 2510; www.holgatebrewhouse.com; 79 High St; d $135-185; mains $19-29; ⊙ noon-late) The excellent Holgate Brewhouse, at Keatings Hotel, is a cracking brewery pub producing a range of hand-pumped European-style ales and lagers on site. Serves hearty Mod Oz bistro food and has pub accommodation upstairs.

ⓘ Information

Woodend Visitor Centre (☑ 03-5427 2033; www.visitmacedonranges.com; High St; ⊙ 9am-5pm)

Great Ocean Road & Bellarine Peninsula

Includes ➡

Geelong 152
Bellarine Peninsula . . 157
Torquay 162
Lorne 166
Apollo Bay..........170
Cape Otway 173
Port Campbell
National Park 174
Warrnambool 177
Port Fairy...........181
Portland............184

Best Places to Eat

➡ Brae (p168)
➡ A La Grecque (p166)
➡ Merrijig Kitchen (p183)
➡ Wye General (p170)
➡ Chris's Beacon Point (p172)

Best Places to Stay

➡ Kennett River
Holiday Park (p170)
➡ Great Ocean
Ecolodge (p173)
➡ Beacon Point Ocean
View Villas (p172)
➡ Vue Grand (p159)
➡ Cimarron B&B (p166)

Why Go?

The Great Ocean Road (B100) is one of Australia's most famous road-touring routes. It takes travellers past world-class surfing breaks, through pockets of rainforest and calm seaside towns, and under koala-filled tree canopies. It shows off heathlands, dairy farms and sheer limestone cliffs, and gets you up close and personal with the crashing waves of the Southern Ocean.

Hunt out the isolated beaches and lighthouses in between the towns, and the thick eucalypt forests in the Otway hinterlands to really escape the crowds. Rather than heading straight to the Great Ocean Road, a fork in the road in Geelong allows you to take the long, leisurely way there via the Bellarine Peninsula, which allows you to visit charming coastal towns and wineries en route.

Day-tripping tourists from Melbourne rush into and out of the area in fewer than 12 hours, but, in a perfect world, you'd spend a couple of weeks here.

When to Go
Cape Otway

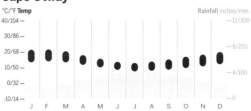

Mar Chill out to folk and roots tunes from around the globe at the popular Port Fairy Folk Festival.

Easter (Mar/Apr) Head to Bells Beach during the Rip Curl Pro to witness spectacular surfing action.

Jul Visit coastal towns mid-winter for bright seascapes, cosy cafes and whale watching.

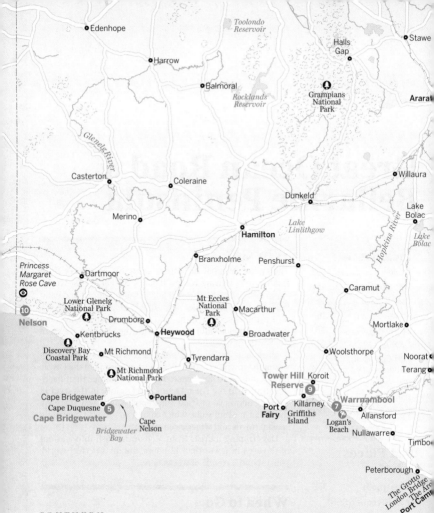

Great Ocean Road & Bellarine Peninsula Highlights

1 Count the upstanding **Twelve Apostles** (p174) near Port Campbell

2 Camp by beaches abutting **Cape Otway lighthouse** (p173)

3 Lap up the resort-style living in **Lorne** (p166)

4 Get tree-top high on the **Otway Fly** (p173)

5 Check out the seals at isolated and beautiful **Cape Bridgewater** (p185)

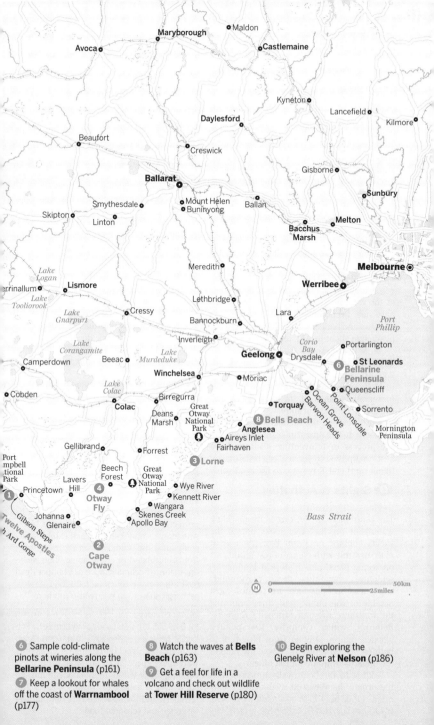

Maldon
Maryborough
Avoca
Castlemaine

Kyneton
Daylesford
Lancefield
Kilmore

Beaufort
Creswick
Gisborne

Ballarat
Mount Helen
Ballan
Sunbury

Smythesdale
Buninyong
Melton

Skipton
Linton
Bacchus
Marsh

Meredith
Melbourne

errinallum
Lismore
Werribee

Lake
Logan
Lethbridge

Lake
Tooliorook
Cressy
Lara

Lake
Gnarpurt
Bannockburn
Port
Phillip

Lake
Corangamite
Inverleigh
Corio
Bay
Portarlington

Camperdown
Lake
Murdeduke
Geelong
Drysdale

Beeac
St Leonards
6 Bellarine
Peninsula

Cobden
Winchelsea
Moriac
Queenscliff

Lake
Colac
Point Lonsdale
Sorrento

Birregurra
Ocean Grove

Colac
Great
Otway
National
Park
Torquay
Barwon
Heads

Deans
Marsh
8 Bells Beach
Mornington
Peninsula

Gellibrand
Anglesea

Port
mpbell
tional
Park
Forrest
Aireys Inlet
Fairhaven

Beech
Forest
Great
Otway
National
Park
3 Lorne

Princetown
Lavers
Hill
4
Otway
Fly
Wye River

Johanna
Wangara
Kennett River
Bass Strait

Glenaire
Skenes Creek
Apollo Bay

Twelve Apostles
h Ard Gorge
Gibson Steps
2
Cape
Otway

N
0   50km
0   25miles

6 Sample cold-climate
pinots at wineries along the
Bellarine Peninsula (p161)

7 Keep a lookout for whales
off the coast of **Warrnambool**
(p177)

8 Watch the waves at **Bells
Beach** (p163)

9 Get a feel for life in a
volcano and check out wildlife
at **Tower Hill Reserve** (p180)

10 Begin exploring the
Glenelg River at **Nelson** (p186)

GEELONG & BELLARINE PENINSULA

Geelong

POP 216,000

Geelong is Victoria's second-largest centre, a proud, industrial town with an interesting history and pockets of charm. While Melburnians love to deride its little cousin as a boring backwater, in reality few of the knockers have veered off its main thoroughfare to really get to know what makes the town tick. A new bypass means travellers can skip the city and head straight to the Great Ocean Road, however, there are lots of reasons to make a stop here.

The Wathaurung people – the original inhabitants of Geelong – called the area Jillong. Today the town is centred on sparkling Corio Bay waterfront and its city centre, where heritage buildings from the boom days of the wool industry and the gold-rush era have now been converted into swanky restaurants and bars. It's also a footy-mad town, passionate about its AFL team, the Cats.

As well as being a gateway to the Bellarine Peninsula and Great Ocean Road, it's also a laid-back alternative to staying in Melbourne, only an hour away. With the imminent closures of its oil refinery and the iconic Ford motor-industry hub, both of which have been the lifeblood of Geelong's economy, it is a town in transition and in the process of reinventing itself, perhaps best exemplified by its new celebrity mayor, flamboyant ex-UK paparazzo Darryn Lyons.

◎ Sights & Activities

Geelong Waterfront   WATERFRONT

The centrepiece of Geelong is its sparkling waterfront precinct that looks out to the yachts bobbing on Corio Bay. It's a great place to stroll, with plenty of restaurants set on scenic piers, plus historical landmarks, sculptures, swimming areas, playgrounds and grassy sections ideal for picnics. Most notable of the public sculptures adorning the foreshore are Jan Mitchell's *Baywalk Bollards,* which comprise 104 painted wooden figures ranging from lifesavers to bathing beauties; pick up a walking map of the bollards from the tourist office.

Adding to the boardwalk atmosphere is the ornate, hand-carved, 19th-century **carousel** ([✐]03-5224 1547; adult/child $4.40/3.90; ⊙10.30am-5pm Mon-Fri, to 8pm Sat, to 6pm Sun),

fully restored and housed within a glass pavilion.

In summer you can cool off at popular **Eastern Beach**, which features a sandy beach and **art deco bathing pavilion** with classic European-style enclosed bay swimming, complete with diving boards, sunbathing area and toddler pool.

Walking and jogging trails extend from **Rippleside Park** (Bell Pde) right up the hill to Limeburners Point.

Geelong Art Gallery   GALLERY
(www.geelonggallery.org.au; Little Malop St; ⊙10am-5pm) FREE With over 4000 works in its collection this excellent gallery has celebrated Australian paintings such as Eugene von Guérard's *View of Geelong* and Frederick McCubbin's 1890 *A Bush Burial.* Also exhibits contemporary works and has free tours on Saturday at 2pm.

National Wool Museum   MUSEUM
([✐]03-5272 4701; www.geelongaustralia.com.au/nwm; 26 Moorabool St; adult/child/family $7.50/4/25; ⊙9.30am-5pm Mon-Fri, from 10am Sat & Sun) More interesting than it may sound, this museum showcases the importance of the wool industry in shaping Geelong economically, socially and architecturally. Many of the grand buildings in the area are former wool-store buildings, including the museum's 1872 bluestone. There's a sock-making machine and a massive 1910 Axminster carpet loom that gets chugging on weekends.

Old Geelong Gaol   HISTORIC BUILDING
([✐]03-5221 8292; www.geelonggaol.org.au; cnr Myers & Swanston Sts; adult/child $10/5; ⊙1-4pm Sat & Sun, every day school holidays) Built in 1849, HSM Prison Geelong may have closed its doors in 1991, but this old bluestone jail remains as terrifying as ever. You'll see its grim cells set over three levels, shower block, watchtowers and gallows. Each exhibit is accompanied by audio, covering everything from contraband of crude homemade weapons to former cellmates such as Chopper Read (cell 39). **Ghost tours** ([✐]1300 856 668; www.geelongghosttours.com.au) are also run here.

Boom Gallery   GALLERY
([✐]0417 555 101; www.boomgallery.com.au; 11 Rutland St, Newtown; ⊙Wed-Sat 8.30am-4pm) Down an industrial street off Pakington St, Boom's warehouse space in an old wool mill shows contemporary works by Melbourne and local artists. It sells great design objects and jewellery, and the attached cafe does fantastic coffee and seasonal food.

Geelong

Geelong

◎ Sights
1 Botanic Gardens	D2
2 Geelong Art Gallery	B2
3 Geelong Play Space	D2
4 Geelong Waterfront	B1
5 National Wool Museum	B1
6 Old Geelong Gaol	C3

◈ Activities, Courses & Tours
7 Bathing Pavilion	D2
City Walking Tours	(see 5)
8 Freedom Bay Cruises	B1
9 Geelong Helicopters	B1
10 Geelong Waterfront Carousel	B1

◉ Sleeping
11 Four Points by Sheraton Geelong	B1
12 Gatehouse on Ryrie	B2
13 Irish Murphy's	A2

◈ Eating
14 Beach House	D2
15 Geelong Boat House	B1
16 Go!	C2
17 Jack & Jill	B3
18 Khan Curry Hut	B2
19 Mrs Hyde	B2

◉ Drinking & Nightlife
20 Beav's Bar	B2
21 CQ	B1
22 Little Creatures Brewery	B4

◈ Entertainment
23 Barwon Club	A4
24 Geelong Performing Arts Centre	B2
25 Kardinia Park	A3
26 Wool Exchange	B2

Botanic Gardens GARDENS

([✐]03-5272 4379; www.geelongaustralia.com.au/gbg; cnr Podbury & Eastern Park Drs; ⊙7.30am-5pm) FREE The 1851 Botanic Gardens are a peaceful place for a stroll or picnic. The '21st-century' garden at the entrance features indigenous plants from across Australia. It houses the great and ultra-kid-friendly **Geelong Play Space**.

Narana Creations CULTURAL CENTRE

(www.narana.com.au; 410 Torquay Rd, Grovedale; ⊙9am-5pm Mon-Fri, 10am-4pm Sat) On the road to Torquay in Grovedale, on Geelong's far outskirts, this Aboriginal cultural centre has didgeridoo performances (or play it yourself), a boomerang-throwing gallery and a native garden. Daily tours are at 11am and 2pm, and its gift shop sells indigenous books and music.

City Walking Tours TOUR

([✐]03-5222 2900; 26 Moorabool St; tours $12) Volunteer-led city tours show Geelong's historic architecture and landmarks. Prices include a ride on the carousel, tea and cake, and two-for-one admission to the National Wool Museum. Book one day in advance.

Freedom Bay Cruises BOAT CRUISE

([✐]0418 522 328; www.freedombaycruises.com.au; Geelong Waterfront; adult/child $25/10; ⊙11am, 1pm & 3pm) Join a one-hour scenic cruise around Corio Bay.

Geelong Helicopters SCENIC FLIGHTS

([✐]0422 515 151; www.geelonghelicopters.com.au; Geelong Waterfront; adult/child $45/35; ⊙10am-5pm) Check out Geelong and the coast from the air on a scenic chopper flight.

✪ Festivals & Events

Festival of Sails SAILING

([✐]03-5229 3705; www.festivalofsails.com.au; ⊙late Jan) This week-long sailing regatta began in 1854 and these days brings sailing to the public along Geelong's waterfront, where around 450 yachts compete. There's a heap of shore-based entertainment as well.

Pako Festa CULTURAL FESTIVAL

(www.pakofesta.com.au; Pakington St, Geelong West; ⊙last Sat in Feb) A celebration of cultural diversity that livens up Pakington St annually.

Avalon Airshow AIRCRAFT

(www.airshow.net.au; Avalon Airport) Held in Avalon, 20km north of Geelong's city centre, this display of sky-bound might and power is held every two years, usually in late summer/early autumn, and attracts thousands of viewers.

Geelong Cup HORSE RACING

(www.geelongcup.com.au; ⊙last Wed Oct) Melbourne's not only the town that gets the day off for a horse race, with this sporting event a big day on Geelong's social calendar.

Toast to the Coast FOOD, WINE

(www.toasttothecoast.com.au; tickets $40; ⊙early Nov) This wine festival, held on Melbourne Cup weekend, takes place at wineries from Geelong to the Bellarine. Shuttle service is an additional $25.

🛏 Sleeping

Irish Murphy's HOSTEL $

([✐]03-5221 4335; www.irishmurphysgeelong.com.au; 30 Aberdeen St, Geelong West; dm/s/d $35/45/70; [P][🛜]) Upstairs from an Irish pub, Geelong's only backpacker's hostel is a family-owned affair with clean dorms, most of which only have two beds – a good deal. Plus guests get 20% off pub meals downstairs. It's a short walk from the city, Pakington St and Geelong station.

Gatehouse on Ryrie GUESTHOUSE $$

([✐]0417 545 196; www.gatehouseonryrie.com.au; 83 Yarra St; d incl breakfast $95-130; [P][🛜]) Geelong's best midrange choice, this guesthouse was built in 1897 with gorgeous timber floorboards throughout, spacious rooms (most with shared facilities) and a communal kitchen and lounge area. Breakfast is held in the glorious front room.

Four Points by Sheraton Geelong HOTEL $$

([✐]03-5223 1377; www.fourpoints.com/geelong; 10-14 Eastern Beach Rd; r from $170; [✳][🛜][🏊]) Prime location on Geelong's waterfront, most rooms here have bay views (or glimpses). Rooms are a tad bland, but balconies and sitting areas are lovely additions, and staff are helpful.

🍴 Eating

Go! CAFE $

(www.cafego.com.au; 37 Bellarine St; mains from $10; ⊙7am-4pm Mon-Fri & 8am-4pm Sat; [🛜]) Go! is a local favourite for its fun, colourful atmosphere, good coffee and breakfasts. Head out to its lovely leafy courtyard.

Geelong Boat House FISH & CHIPS $

(Geelong Waterfront; mains from $8; ⊙10am-8pm) Jutting out to the water, this fish-and-chip joint is built on top of a barge once used to dredge the Yarra. Grab a chair on the deck or the rooftop, or laze on one of its picnic blankets on the grassy banks. There's also a seafood restaurant in its attached boat shed.

Khan Curry Hut
INDIAN $

(www.khancurryhut.com.au; 101-103 Ryrie St; mains from $10; ⊘noon-2.30pm Mon-Fri, 5.30-10pm daily) Head to Khan for a cheap and boozy (free BYO) meal featuring authentic Indian flavours. Fresh ingredients are used, and South Indian dishes are available.

Mrs Hyde
MODERN AUSTRALIAN $$

(☑03-5223 1228; www.mrshyde.com.au; 11 Malop St; tapas from $11; ⊘5pm-late Wed-Sun) Get snug in a high-backed Chesterfield booth and dine on tasty tapas share plates in this beautiful old bank building. Otherwise forgo dinner, prop up at the marble bar and get to work on the excellent cocktail list.

★ Jack & Jill
MODERN AUSTRALIAN $$$

(☑03-5229 9935; www.jackandjillrestaurant.com.au; 247 Moorabool St; tasting plates $32.50; ⊘6pm-late daily, noon-2.30pm Fri) Choose three small dishes from the menu of regional produce (perhaps parmesan-encrusted scallops, or a dish featuring ostrich) and they'll all be served to you on one plate. Upstairs has a rooftop beer garden with top craft beers. Roll the dice Fridays for free drinks between 5pm and 6.30pm. Also has regular live music.

Beach House
MODERN AUSTRALIAN $$$

(☑03-5221 8322; www.easternbeachhouse.com.au; Eastern Beach Reserve; mains $30-42; ⊘noon-2.30pm Fri-Sun; 6pm-late Wed-Sat; 🔊) In a town blessed with fantastic waterfront restaurants, this might just be the best. The modern international menu includes ravioli filled with rock flathead and fennel, and tempura catch of the day. It also has a casual cafe downstairs that serves breakfast and lunch daily.

🍷 Drinking & Entertainment

Pick up a free copy of *Forte* (www.fortemag.com.au) for upcoming gigs.

★ Little Creatures Brewery
BREWERY, BAR

(www.littlecreatures.com.au; cnr Fyans & Swanston Sts; ⊘11am-5pm Mon-Tue, to 9pm Wed-Fri, 8am-9pm Sat, 8am-5pm Sun; 🔊) Geelong is the newest addition to the growing Little Creatures beer empire. Within an old red-brick wool mill and kitted out in an industrial warehouse feel, this is a cracking place to sample its brews with a thin-crust pizza (from $17). Tours of the brewery operate a few times a day and include free tastings. Kids will love the sandboxes and room to run around.

Beav's Bar
BAR, LIVE MUSIC

(☑03-5222 3366; www.beavsbar.com.au; 77-79 Little Malop St; ⊘4pm-late Wed-Sat, 7-11pm Tue) A former auction house, this happening bar is decorated with eclectic art, retro couches and soft lighting. Regular live music as well as film screenings on Tuesdays ($7).

Cartel Roasters
CAFE

(www.coffeecartel.com.au; 6/21 Leather St, Breakwater; ⊘7am-4.30pm Mon-Sat; 🔊; 🚌61) An unexpected find in South Geelong's industrial backstreets, this hipster-haven coffeehouse roasts a range of African single-origins, to go with a menu of dude food. Tea lovers will be equally delighted with a refined tearoom serving leaves from around the world, set up by a certified 'tea master'.

CQ
COCKTAIL BAR

(City Quarter; www.thecityquarter.com.au; 10 Western Beach Foreshore Rd; ⊘noon-late Thu-Sun) Cunningham Pier's redevelopment (partly funded by ex-Cats captain Cameron Ling) has brought a restaurant, cafe and boutique bar to this stunning location. Climb the sweeping steps to CQ, and check out its smart fit-out and cocktail and tapas menus. Oh, and the view, which you can't miss.

Geelong Performing Arts Centre
THEATRE

(GPAC; ☑03-5225 1200; www.gpac.org.au; 50 Little Malop St) Geelong's major arts venue uses three theatres and a variety of outdoor venues to show local amateur productions, as well as touring professional dance, musicals and theatre shows.

Barwon Club
LIVE MUSIC

(☑03-5221 4584; www.barwonclub.com.au; 509 Moorabool St; ⊘11am-late) The Barwon has long been Geelong's premier live music venue, and has spawned the likes of Magic Dirt, Bored! and Warped, seminal bands in the 'Geetroit' rock scene. As well as catching local and international bands, it's a great pub for a beer.

Wool Exchange
LIVE MUSIC

(☑03-5222 2322; www.thewoolexchange.com.au; 44 Corio St) A former wool-industry building (c 1927) turned entertainment complex with a good roster of Aussie indie bands.

Kardinia Park
STADIUM

(Simonds Stadium; ☑03-5225 2300; www.ticketmaster.com.au; Moorabool St; tickets from $25) Recently renovated and fitted with light

GREAT OCEAN ROAD & BELLARINE PENINSULA GEELONG

towers; check to see if the mighty Geelong Cats are playing a home game here during winter. Book well ahead.

Shopping

Head to Pakington St in Geelong West for a few boutique shops. There's also a bunch of retro, bric-a-brac stores in town, such as the sprawling Geelong Vintage Market (www.geelongvintagemarket.com.au; 287-301 Melbourne Rd, North Geelong; ⊙10am-6pm) and How Bazaar (☑03-5278 5453; www.howbazaarantiques.com.au; 310 Melbourne Rd, North Geelong).

🛈 Information

Pick up a copy of *What's On* for the local happenings:

Geelong Library (www.grlc.vic.gov.au; 30-38 Little Malop St; ⊙8.30am-5pm Mon-Fri; 🛜 @) Free wi-fi and internet. Plans to relocate across the road in 2015.

National Wool Museum Visitors Centre (www.visitgreatoceanroad.org.au; 26 Moorabool St; ⊙9am-5pm; 🛜) Brochures on Geelong, Bellarine Peninsula and the Otways, plus free wi-fi. Also has a **visitor centre** (⊙9am-5pm) on the Geelong Rd stretch of Princes Hwy at the service station near Little River for those bypassing Geelong and heading directly to the Great Ocean Road.

🛈 Getting There & Away

AIR

Jetstar (p345) has services to/from Avalon Airport (p126).

BUS

Avalon Airport Shuttle (☑03-5278 8788; www.avalonairportshuttle.com.au) Meets all flights at Avalon Airport and goes to Geelong ($17, 35 minutes) and along the Great Ocean Road to Lorne ($70, 1¾ hours).

Gull Airport Service (☑03-5222 4966; www.gull.com.au; 45 McKillop St) Has 14 services a day between Geelong and Melbourne (Tullamarine) Airport ($30, 1¼ hours) from the city centre and Geelong station.

McHarry's Buslines (☑03-5223 2111; www.mcharrys.com.au) Frequent buses from Geelong station to Torquay ($3.70) and the Bellarine Peninsula ($3.50, 20 minutes).

V/Line (☑1800 800 007; www.vline.com.au) Runs buses from Geelong station to Apollo Bay ($16.40, 2½ hours, four daily) via Torquay ($3.60, 25 minutes), Anglesea ($5.40, 45 minutes), Lorne ($10, 1½ hours) and Wye River ($12.40, two hours). On Monday, Wednesday and Friday a bus continues to Port Campbell ($28.60, five hours) and Warrnambool ($32.20, 6½ hours), with bus transfer at Apollo Bay. The train is a much quicker and cheaper option for those heading direct to Warrnambool. V/Line also runs to Ballarat ($8.80, 1½ hours, three or four daily).

CAR

The 25km Geelong Ring Rd runs from Corio to Waurn Ponds, bypassing Geelong entirely. To get to Geelong city, be careful not to miss the Princes Hwy (M1) from the left lanes. For Geelong's waterfront, take Bell Pde and follow the Esplanade along the bay.

CYCLING

Pick up the *Great Ocean Trails* booklet from the tourist office for cycling routes around Geelong and beyond, or visit www.visitgeelongbellarine.com.au/cycling.

TAXI

For a taxi, contact **Geelong Taxi Network** (☑131 008)

GREAT OCEAN ROAD DISTANCES & TIMES

DESTINATION	DISTANCE	TIME
Melbourne to Geelong	75km	1hr
Geelong to Torquay	21km	15-20min
Torquay to Anglesea	16km	13min
Anglesea to Aireys Inlet	10km	10min
Aireys Inlet to Lorne	19km	22min
Lorne to Apollo Bay	45km	1hr
Apollo Bay to Port Campbell	96km	1½hr
Port Campbell to Warrnambool	66km	1hr
Warrnambool to Port Fairy	28km	20min
Port Fairy to Portland	72km	1hr
Portland to Melbourne	via Great Ocean Rd 440km/ via Hamilton Hwy 358km	6½hr/ 4hr 10min

V/Line (p156) runs from **Geelong train station** (☑ 03-5226 6525; Gordon Ave) to Melbourne's Southern Cross Station ($7.80, one hour, frequently). Trains also head from Geelong to Warrnambool ($22.20, 2½ hours, three daily).

Bellarine Peninsula

For centuries Melburnians have been coming to the Bellarine Peninsula for its seaside village ambience. It has a good mix of family and surf beaches, diving and snorkelling, historic towns and relaxed wineries.

This stretch of coast not only joins up with the Great Ocean Road, but is just a short ferry trip over to the Mornington Peninsula.

❶ Getting There & Away

BUS

McHarry's Buslines (☑ 03-5223 2111; www.mcharrys.com.au) Connects Geelong with Barwon Heads (30 minutes), Ocean Grove (45 minutes), Portarlington (45 minutes), Point Lonsdale (55 minutes) and Queenscliff (one hour). A two-hour ticket costs $3.70, full-day is $7.10. Myki cards accepted.

CAR

From Melbourne, the Bellarine Peninsula is easily accessible via the Princess Fwy (M1) to Geelong. Rather than taking the Geelong bypass, head through Geelong to the Bellarine Hwy (B110), which links up to Torquay and the Great Ocean Road.

FERRY

Queenscliff Sorrento Ferry (☑ 03-5258 3244; www.searoad.com.au) one-way foot passenger adult/child $10/8, 2 adults & car $69; ☺ hourly 7am-6pm) Runs between Queenscliff and Sorrento (40 minutes); till 7pm peak times.

Queenscliff

POP 3300

Historic Queenscliff is a lovely spot, popular with day-tripping and overnighting Melburnians who come to stroll its heritage streetscapes and soak up its nautical atmosphere. The views across the Port Phillip Heads and Bass Strait are glorious.

Queenscliff was established for the pilots who to this day steer all ships through the treacherous Port Phillip Heads. Known as 'the Rip', this is one of the most dangerous seaways in the world. In the 1850s Queenscliff was a favoured settlement for diggers who'd struck it rich on the goldfields, and wealthy Melburnians and the Western Dis-

trict's squattocracy flocked to the town. Extravagant hotels and guesthouses built then still operate today, giving Queenscliff a historic charm and grandness.

◉ Sights & Activities

The visitor centre runs the 45-minute guided **Queenscliff Heritage Walk** (☑ 03-5258 4843; incl afternoon tea $12) at 2pm each Saturday or by appointment, which takes in the town's historic buildings. Golfers can have a scenic hit at **Queenscliff Golf Club** (☑ 03-5258 1951; www.queenscliffgolfclub.com.au) on rugged Swan Island and cyclists can hire bicycles from **Big4 Beacon Resort** (☑ 03-5258 1133; www.beaconresort.com.au; 78 Bellarine Hwy; bike hire half-/full day $15/25).

Marine & Freshwater Discovery Centre　　　　AQUARIUM
(☑ 03-5258 3344; www.dpi.vic.gov.au/fisheries/education/mfdc; 2a Bellarine Hwy; adult/child $8/5; ☺ 11am-3pm Mon-Fri) While this education centre is primarily aimed at school children, it's still worth popping in to have a gawk at the local species that live under the sea, with tanks containing the deadly blue ring octopus, seahorses, fish and a touch pool where you can handle slimy creatures.

Observation Tower　　　　LANDMARK
(Larkin Pde, Queenscliff Harbour) **FREE** Check out the 360-degree views from this hard-to-miss tower.

Fort Queenscliff　　　　HISTORIC SITE
(☑ 03-5258 1488, for midweek tours 0403 193 311; www.fortqueenscliff.com.au; cnr Gellibrand & King Sts; adult/child/family $10/5/25; ☺ tours 1pm Mon-Fri, 1pm & 3pm Sat & Sun) Queensliff's fort was first used as a coastal defence in 1882 to protect Melbourne from a feared Russian invasion. It remained a base until 1946, before being used as Army Staff College until late 2012; today it functions as the defence archive centre. The 30-minute guided tours take in the military museum, magazine, cells and its twin lighthouses. Bring ID for entry.

Queenscliff Maritime Museum　　　　MUSEUM
(☑ 03-5258 3440; www.maritimequeenscliffe.org.au; 2 Wharf St; adult/child $7/5; ☺ 10.30am-4.30pm Mon-Fri, 1.30-4.30pm Sat & Sun) Home to the last lifeboat to serve the Rip, this museum has displays on the pilot boat process, shipwrecks, lighthouses and steamships. Don't miss the historic 1895 boatshed with its paintings that served as a record of passing ships in the bay.

Queenscliff

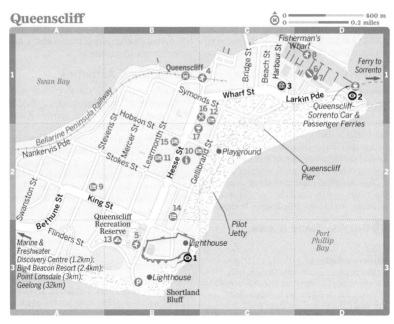

Queenscliff

◎ Sights
1 Fort Queenscliff B3
2 Observation Tower D1
3 Queenscliff Maritime Museum C1

⊕ Activities, Courses & Tours
4 Bellarine Peninsula Railway................. C1
5 Queenscliff Bowling Club.................... B3
6 Queenscliff Dive Centre D1
7 Sea-All Dolphin Swims D1
8 South Bay Eco Adventures................. D1

⊜ Sleeping
9 Albion.. A2
10 Athelstane House B2
11 Queenscliff Dive Centre B2
12 Queenscliff Hotel C1
13 Queenscliff Tourist Parks B3
14 Twomey's Cottage............................... B2
15 Vue Grand B2

⊗ Eating
16 Café Gusto C1
Vue Street Bar...............................(see 15)

⊜ Drinking & Nightlife
17 The Lounge @ Salt B2

Queenscliff Dive Centre   DIVING
(☎03-5258 1188; www.divequeenscliff.com.au; Queenscliff Harbour; per dive with/without gear $130/65) Victoria's premier dive operator of-fers trips to over 140 sites in the area, taking in rich marine life and shipwrecks from the past three centuries, including ex-HMAS *Canberra* (scuttled in 2009), and WWI submarines. Also does snorkel trips and dive lessons.

Bellarine Peninsula Railway   TRAIN TRIP
(☎03-5258 2069; www.bellarinerailway.com.au; Queenscliff train station; return adult/child/fam-ily $30/20/70; ⊙departs 11am & 2.45pm Sun, plus Tue & Thu during school holidays) Run by a group of cheerful volunteer steam-train enthusiasts, the railway has beautiful her-itage steam and diesel trains that ply the 1¾-hour return journey to Drysdale.

Sea-All Dolphin Swims   SNORKELLING
(☎03-5258 3889; www.dolphinswims.com.au; Queenscliff Harbour; sightseeing adult/child $70/60, 3½hr snorkel $135/115; ⊙8am & 1pm Oct-Apr) Offers sightseeing tours and swims with seals and dolphins in Port Phillip Bay; seal sightings are guaranteed, dolphins are not always seen but there's a good chance.

South Bay Eco Adventures   ADVENTURE TOUR
(☎03-5258 4019; www.southbayecoadventures.com; Wharf St East, Queenscliff Harbour; discovery tour adult/child $85/45) ⯑ Want to see a pilot in action guiding container ships through the Port Phillip Heads? Sign up here.

Bellarine Rail Trail
CYCLING

Popular with cyclists, joggers and walkers, the Bellarine Rail Trail runs 34km along the historic rail line between the Geelong Showgrounds and Queenscliff.

Queenscliff Bowling Club
LAWN BOWLS

(☑03-5258 1773; www.queenscliffbowling.com.au; 118 Hesse St; bowls $8; ◷10am-late; 🕿) Cheap beer, barefoot bowls and free wi-fi.

✪ Festivals & Events

Queenscliff Music Festival
MUSIC

(☑03-5258 4816; www.qmf.net.au; ◷late Nov) One of the coast's best festivals features big-name Australian musos with a folksy, bluesy bent.

Blues Train
MUSIC

(www.thebluestrain.com.au; tickets $95) Get your foot tapping with irregular train trips that feature rootsy music and meals; check the website for dates and artists.

🛏 Sleeping

Queenscliff Tourist Parks
CAMPGROUND $

(☑03-5258 1765; www.touristparks.queenscliffe. vic.gov.au; 134 Hesse St; non-powered/powered sites $26/32, cabins from $106; 🕿) A basic council-run campground around Queenscliff's footy field is five minutes' walk from town and almost on the beach. It has comfortable cabins, too.

Queenscliff Dive Centre
HOSTEL $

(☑03-5258 1188; www.divequeenscliff.com.au; 37 Learmonth St; dm/d incl breakfast $35/140; 🕿🖵) Run by the dive centre, this hostel-style accommodation was formerly used as historic Cobb & Co stables. The modern shared kitchen and lounge facilities are bright and airy, while the simple rooms are out the back.

Athelstane House
BOUTIQUE HOTEL $$

(☑03-5258 1024; www.athelstane.com.au; 4 Hobson St; r incl breakfast from $150; 🕿) Athelstane House has comfortable rooms with corner spa baths in a beautifully kept historical building. Its restaurant will keep you well fed and there's a lovely verandah for warmer nights. The owners also run the two-bedroom Murray's Cottage (from $200 per night) on the main street.

Twomey's Cottage
B&B $$

(☑0400 265 877; www.classiccottages.com.au; 13 St Andrews St; d from $105) Just the place to soak up Queenscliff's historic atmos-phere, this heritage fisherman's cottage is fantastic value. Its claim to fame is as the residence of Fred Williams when he painted his Queenscliff series, plus renowned recitalist Keith Humble composed music here, so creative vibes abound. The owners also have the similarly great-value **Albion** (43 Stevens St; d from $140) Victorian rental house nearby.

Queenscliff Hotel
HOTEL $$

(☑03-5258 1066; www.queenscliffhotel.com.au; 16 Gellibrand St; d from $170; 🗱@) Classified by the National Trust, this is a superb, authentically old-world luxury hotel. Small Victorian-style rooms have no telephones or TVs, and bathrooms are shared. You can relax in the comfortable guest lounges or dine and drink at the wonderful restaurant and bar.

Vue Grand
HOTEL $$$

(☑03-5258 1544; www.vuegrand.com.au; 46 Hesse St; std/turret r incl breakfast from $200/400) The Vue's standard pub rooms are nothing on its modern turret suite (boasting 360-degree views) and bay-view rooms (with freestanding baths in the lounge), but prices differ by hundreds. If you can't get the room, the turret-level deck is a fine spot for a beverage or two on a sunny day.

🍴 Eating & Drinking

Café Gusto
CAFE $$

(☑03-5258 3604; 25 Hesse St; mains $12-23; ◷8.30am-4pm) A favourite Queenscliff eatery, which is great for breakfast. It has a spacious garden courtyard out the back.

Vue Street Bar
PIZZERIA $$

(www.vuegrand.com.au; 46 Hesse St; pizzas $17; ◷11.30am-8pm Wed-Sat, noon-5pm Sun) Sit, a local beer in one hand and slice of pizza in the other, and watch the people of Queenscliff wander by. Terrific meals, great ambience.

The Lounge @ Salt
COCKTAIL BAR

(www.salt-art.com.au; 33-35 Hesse St; ◷4pm-late Fri-Sun) This glamorous bar has quality retro furniture, sea views from the balcony and art on its walls.

ℹ Information

Queenscliff Visitors Centre (☑03-5258 4843; www.queenscliffe.vic.gov.au; 55 Hesse St; ◷9am-5pm; @) Plenty of brochures, plus internet access for $6 per hour (though it's free next door at the library).

GREAT OCEAN ROAD & BELLARINE PENINSULA BELLARINE PENINSULA

Point Lonsdale

POP 2500

Point Lonsdale, 5km southwest of Queenscliff, is a laid-back community with cafes across from its family-friendly front beach. From the foreshore car park you can walk to the **Rip View lookout** to watch ships entering the Rip, to Point Lonsdale Pier and to the lighthouse. Along from here is the rugged 'back beach'; swimmers should stay between the flags.

◉ Sights

Point Lonsdale Lighthouse   LIGHTHOUSE
(☑ 0419 513 007; www.maritimequeenscliffe.org.au; adult/child $7/5; ◷ 9.30am-1pm Sun) Take a Sunday morning tour (they run every half hour) up this atmospheric and still-operational 1902 lighthouse.

🛏 Sleeping & Eating

Point Lonsdale Guest House   GUESTHOUSE $$
(☑ 03-5258 1142; www.pointlonsdaleguesthouse.com.au; 31 Point Lonsdale Rd; r $110-250; 🛜 ❄) The huge range of rooms in the former Terminus House (1884) range from basic motel rooms to lavish B&B affairs. Lighthouse views come at a premium. There's a communal kitchen, a tennis court, a games room and barbecue facilities.

Pasquinis   CAFE $
(89 Point Lonsdale Rd; mains from $10; ◷ 7am-4pm) Opposite the beach on the main strip, this is the locals' pick of cafes serving breakfasts and filling lunches. Cash only.

Cafe Amore   ITALIAN $$
(79-81 Point Lonsdale Rd; mains $15-18; ◷ 7am-5pm Mon & Tue, 7am-late Wed-Sun) A cosy Italian trattoria keeping things real with tasty homestyle cooking and good seafood.

Ocean Grove

POP 11,300

Ocean Grove, 3km northeast of Barwon Heads and 12km west of Queenscliff, is the big smoke of the Bellarine Peninsula, where folks come for their supermarket and department-store shopping. There are some good surf breaks around here and family-friendly beaches.

🛏 Sleeping & Eating

Ti-Tree Village   CABIN $$
(☑ 03-5255 4433; www.ti-treevillage.com.au; 34 Orton St; cottages $170-230; ❄) Log cabins are cosy and self-contained, and some have gardens and spas. It's a short walk to the beach and town.

**Piping Hot
Chicken Shop**   AMERICAN $
(☑ 03-5255 1566; www.pipinghotchickenshop.com.au; 63a the Terrace; mains $7-15; ◷ 8am-6pm, late when bands are on) Not your ordinary take-away barbecue-chook joint, the 'chicken shop' is straight outta Louisiana, with buffalo wings and pulled-pork rolls (and, yes, barbecue chicken) to go with a monthly roster of blues and rock gigs, all in its cool retro interior. It does great coffee, too.

Rolling Pin Pies and Cakes   BAKERY $
(www.rollingpin.com.au; 12 Park Lane; pies $5; ◷ 7.30am-5pm Mon-Fri, 7.30am-2.30pm Sat, 9am-2.30pm Sun) Duck in for one of the regular winners of Australia's best pie.

Dunes   CAFE $$
(☑ 03-5256 1944; www.dunescafe.com.au; Surf Beach Rd; breakfast from $9, mains from $18; ◷ 6.30am-10pm) Enjoy Mod Oz classics with a beer or wine while gazing out to crashing waves at this surf-side eatery.

Barwon Heads

POP 3000

At the mouth of the broad Barwon River, Barwon Heads is a haven of sheltered beaches, tidal river flats and holidaymakers. Barwon Heads was made famous as the setting for *SeaChange,* a popular TV series, and, over a decade on, still trades on the kudos. In a case of life imitating TV, the original bridge linking Barwon Heads with Ocean Grove was controversially recently replaced with two modern bridges.

Feisty **Thirteenth Beach**, 2km west, is popular with surfers. There are short walks around the headland and the **Bluff**, with panoramic sea vistas.

◉ Sights

**Jirrahlinga Koala & Wildlife
Sanctuary**   WILDLIFE RESERVE
(☑ 03-5254 2484; www.jirrahlinga.com.au; Taits Rd; adult/child $18/10; ◷ 9am-5pm) 🍃 This koala sanctuary also has roos and reptiles.

Lobster Pot Heritage Centre   CULTURAL CENTRE
(Jetty Rd; gold coin donation; ◷ summer holidays & weekends till Easter) Just before the bridge is this interpretive centre featuring info on the Indigenous Wathaurung people, marine life and local history.

🛏 Sleeping

Barwon Heads Caravan Park   CAMPGROUND **$**
(📞 03-5254 1115; www.barwoncoast.com.au; Ewing Blyth Dr; unpowered/powered sites $43/57, d/f cabins $100/155, beach house $280) Overlooking the sea, this park contains comfortable cabins – including Laura's house from *SeaChange* – as well as tea-tree-shaded sites.

There's a seven-night minimum between 19 December and 30 January.

Seahaven Village   APARTMENT **$$**
(📞 03-5254 1066; www.seahavenvillage.com.au; 3 Geelong Rd; d $145-295; ❄ 🌐) Across from a park, Seahaven's cluster of modern self-contained units are a bit sterile, but

THE BELLARINE TASTE TRAIL

The Bellarine/Geelong area has over 50 wineries (www.winegeelong.com.au), and is known for its cool-climate pinot, shiraz and chardonnay. Combine a winery hop with the **Bellarine Taste Trail** (www.thebellarinetastetrail.com.au), and you've got yourself a fantastic day out.

If you don't have your own wheels, **For the Love of Grape** (📞 0408 388 332; www.fortheloveofgrape.com.au/bellarine-wine-tours; half-/full-day tours from Geelong) and **Beacon Tours** (📞 03-5258 1672; www.beacontours.com.au; tours $137) offer winery tours, otherwise visit during Toast to the Coast (p154) festival in November.

Most listings here are open daily during summer and on weekends; other times call ahead.

Jack Rabbit (📞 03-5251 2223; www.jackrabbitvineyard.com.au; 85 McAdams Lane, Bellarine; ⊗ noon-3pm Sun-Thu, from 6pm Fri & Sat) Boutique winery with spectacular bay views and restaurant featuring local produce. Enjoy drinks on the outdoor decking or indoors by the fire.

PIKNIK (📞 03-5258 5155; www.piknik.com.au; 1195 Queenscliff Rd, Swan Bay; ⊗ 7.30am-3.30pm Wed-Sun) Fantastic breakfasts and lunches using local ingredients, plus great coffee and homemade ice cream.

Banks Road (📞 03-5258 3777; www.banksroad.com.au; 600 Banks Rd, Marcus Hill; ⊗ 11am-5pm Fri-Sun) Enjoy the wine while looking out to open-air sculptures in a pastoral setting shared with the outstanding Bistro at Banks French restaurant.

Scotchmans Hill (📞 03-5251 3176; www.scotchmans.com.au; 190 Scotchmans Rd, Drysdale; ⊗ 11am-4.30pm) Large-scale winery with a beautiful, lush setting; also has the Hill Winery outside Geelong, which hosts 'A Day on the Green' gigs, featuring artists such as Neil Young & Crazy Horse.

Oakdene (📞 03-5256 3886; www.oakdene.com.au; 255 Grubb Rd, Wallington; ⊗ cellar door 10am-4pm) Set in a quirky upside down barn and surrounded by eclectic arty objects, this is a vineyard with a difference. It also does fine dining and casual eating.

Elk Horn Roadhouse (📞 03-5250 6056; www.elkhornroadhouse.com.au; 420a Wallington Rd, Wallington; ⊗ 8am-5pm; 🌐) Just outside Ocean Grove, this rustic roadside cafe prides itself on gourmet homemade produce, best sampled in its tasting plates ($19). Also sells bottled relishes.

Terindah Estate (📞 03-5251 5536; www.terindahestate.com; 90 McAdams Lane, Bellarine; ⊗ 10am-4pm) Across from Jack Rabbit, Terindah winery boasts incredible views and fine dining in its glasshouse shed.

McGlashan's Wallington Estate (📞 03-5250 5760; www.mcglashans.com.au; 225 Swan Bay Rd, Wallington; ⊗ 11am-5pm Sat & Sun) Non-pretentious winery with tastings in a large barn covered in memorabilia, plus delicious seafood platters featuring abalone.

Tuckerberry Hill (📞 03-5251 3468; 35 Becks Rd; ⊗ 9am-5pm Sat & Sun) Pick your own blueberries, or sample its blueberry muffins, pancakes or shakes in the cafe.

Drysdale Cheeses (📞 0437 816 374; www.drysdalecheeses.com; 2140 Portarlington Rd, Bellarine; ⊗ 1-4pm first Sun of the month) Taste award-winning goats cheese and yoghurts.

Manzanillo Olive Grove (📞 03-5251 3621; Whitcombes Rd, Drysdale; ⊗ 11am-4.30pm Sat & Sun) Dunk bread into samples of cold-pressed extra-virgin and chilli-infused olive oils.

make for a comfortable choice. There's usually a two-night minimum stay.

✕ Eating & Drinking

Little Tuckles   CAFE $

(1 Flinders Pde; mains $8-12; ⊙ 6.30am-2pm Mon-Fri, from 7am Sat & Sun) At the end of the bridge, this cute hole-in-the-wall cafe does good coffee and yummy brekky tortillas. Its tiny space has a vintage farmhouse feel, while its courtyard is popular when the sun's shining.

At the Heads   MODERN AUSTRALIAN $$

(☑ 03-5254 1277; www.attheheads.com.au; Jetty Rd; meals $26-32; ⊙ 8am-9pm) Built on stilts over the river, this light, airy cafe-restaurant has huge breakfasts, local fare and the most amazing views. Its bustling ambience makes it a fun daytime locale. After dark try the seafood bouillabaisse.

Barwon Heads Hotel   PUB

(☑ 03-5254 2201; www.barwonheadshotel.com.au; 1 Bridge Rd) Raucous coastal pub with a bistro and live music featuring Aussie indie bands. There are no-frills rooms upstairs.

GREAT OCEAN ROAD

Torquay

POP 15,700

In the 1960s and '70s Torquay was just another sleepy seaside town. Back then surfing in Australia was a decidedly countercultural pursuit, its devotees crusty hippie drop-outs living in clapped-out Kombis, smoking pot and making off with your daughters. Since then it's become unabashedly mainstream and a huge transglobal business. Torquay's rise and rise directly parallels the boom of the surfing industry (and especially the surf-apparel industry). The town's proximity to world-famous Bells Beach and status as home of two iconic surf brands – Rip Curl and Quicksilver, both initially wetsuit makers – ensured Torquay's place as the undisputed capital of the Australian surf industry.

Other than the beach, Torquay's not a particularly attractive town, due to its suburban sprawl and housing estates.

◉ Sights & Activities

Torquay's beaches lure everyone from kids in floaties to backpacker surf-school pupils. **Fisherman's Beach**, protected from ocean swells, is the family favourite. Ringed by shady pines and sloping lawns, the **Front Beach** beckons lazy bums, while surf lifesavers patrol the frothing **Back Beach** during summer. Famous surf beaches include nearby Jan Juc, Winki Pop and, of course, Bells Beach.

Surf World Museum   MUSEUM

(www.surfworld.com.au; Surf City Plaza; adult/child/family $12/8/30; ⊙ 9am-5pm) The perfect starting point for those embarking on a surfing safari, this well-curated museum pays homage to Australian surfing: from Simon Anderson's ground-breaking 1981 thruster to Mark Richard's board collection and, most notably, Australia's Surfing Hall of Fame. It's full of great memorabilia (including Duke Kahanamoku's wooden longboard), videos and displays on surfing culture in the 1960s to '80s.

Surf Schools   SURFING

Several companies based in Torquay will help you learn how to surf, offering two-hour lessons from around $60. **Great Ocean Road Surf Tours** (☑ 1800 787 353; www.gorsurftours.com.au; 106 Surf Coast Hwy) has multiday surf trips down the coast from $295, including accommodation in Torquay and transport from Melbourne. Other reputable companies include **Go Ride A Wave** (☑ 1300 132 441; www.gorideawave.com.au; 1/15 Bell St; 2hr lesson incl hire $65), **Torquay Surfing Academy** (☑ 03-5261 2022; www.torquaysurf.com.au; 34a Bell St) and **Westcoast Surf School** (☑ 03-5261 2241; www.westcoastsurfschool.com; 2hr lesson $55).

Tiger Moth World Adventure Park   SCENIC FLIGHTS

(☑ 03-5261 5100; www.tigermothworld.com; 325 Blackgate Rd; 15min flights per person from $75, min 2 people; ⊙ 10am-5pm Wed-Mon) Strap on your goggles and hop into a Tiger Moth for a coastal joy flight. It also has a giant play park and skydiving for thrillseekers.

🛏 Sleeping

Bells Beach Backpackers   HOSTEL $

(☑ 03-5261 4029; www.bellsbeachbackpackers.com.au; 51-53 Surfcoast Hwy; dm/d $26/80; @ 🛜) On the main highway, this friendly backpackers does a great job of fitting into the fabric of this surf town with board hire, daily surf reports and a good collection of surf vids. Its basic rooms are clean and in good nick.

Torquay Foreshore Caravan Park   CAMPGROUND $

(☑ 03-52612496;www.torquaycaravanpark.com.au; 35 Bell St; powered sites $31-70, d cabins $99-280) Just behind Back Beach, this is the largest camping ground on the Surf Coast. It has good facilities and new premium-priced cabins with sea views.

Woolshed B&B   B&B $$$
(☑ 0408 333 433; www.thewoolshedtorquay.com.au; 75 Aquarius Ave; apt incl breakfast $250; ✹ ✺) Set on a gorgeous farm on Torquay's outskirts, this century-old woolshed has been converted into a great open and airy space with two bedrooms. It sleeps up to six, and guests can use the pool and tennis court.

✗ Eating & Drinking

Cafe Moby   CAFE $
(41 The Esplanade; mains $9-19; ⊘ 7am-4pm; 🛜) This old weatherboard house on the Esplanade harks back to a time when Torquay was simple, which is not to say its meals are not modern: fill up on linguini or a honey-roasted lamb souvlaki. There's a whopping great playground in the back for kids.

Bottle of Milk   BURGERS $
(☑ 0456 748 617; www.thebottleofmilk.com; 24 Bell St; burgers from $10; ⊘ 10.30am-late) Trading off the success of its Lorne branch (p169), the winning formula of burgers, beaches and beers makes Bottle of Milk rightfully popular. There's a beer garden, too, and great coffee.

Sticks and Stones   CAFE $$
(www.sticksandstonescafe.com.au; 61 Surfcoast Hwy; mains $7-19; ⊘ 8am-4pm) Part of the Surf World precinct, Sticks and Stones brings Melbourne cafe culture to the coast, with single-origin coffee (roasted by Axis in Melbourne) and breakfasts and lunches using fresh produce.

Bomboras Kiosk   CAFE $$
(www.bomboras.com.au/kiosk.html; The Esplanade, Fisherman's Beach; mains $18-36; ⊘ 7.30am-3pm) Run by local surfers, Bomboras is right on the sand and just the place for hungry beach-goers to recharge with sausage rolls, salads, milkshakes, coffee or a cold beer.

Ridestylz   CAFE, BAR
(www.ridestylz.com.au; 3/34a Bell St) An old-school '80s skateboard shop that doubles as a cafe, with longneck beers, coffees and milkshakes. It has another cafe on Baines Crescent.

Shopping

A smorgasbord of surf shops lines Torquay's main thoroughfare, from big brands to local board shapers. For bargains head down

ℹ️ ORGANISED TOURS

It's highly recommended you take your time along the Great Ocean Road (ideally a couple of nights to one week), but for those short on time the following tours depart from Melbourne and often cover it in one whirlwind day.

Go West Tours (☑ 1300 736 551; www.gowest.com.au; tours $120) Full-day tours visit Bells Beach, koalas in the Otways, Port Campbell and back to Melbourne. Free wi-fi on bus.

Otway Discovery Tour (☑ 03-9629 5844; www.greatoceanroadtour.com.au; tours $95) Very affordable one-day Great Ocean Road tours.

Ride Tours (☑ 1800 605 120; www.ridetours.com.au; tours $195) Two-day, one-night trips along the Great Ocean Road.

Baines Crescent alongside Surf City Plaza for discount surf seconds.

ℹ️ Information

Torquay Visitor Information Centre (www.greatoceanroad.org; Surf City Plaza, Beach Rd; ⊘ 9am-5pm) Well-resourced tourist office next to Surf World Museum. There's free wi-fi and internet available at the library next door.

ℹ️ Getting There & Away

Torquay is 15 minutes south of Geelong on the B100.

BUS

McHarry's Buslines (☑ 03-5223 2111; www.mcharrys.com.au) Hourly from 9am to 8pm (around 5pm weekends) from Geelong to Torquay ($3.70, 30 minutes), arriving and departing Torquay from the corner of Pearl and Boston Sts (behind the Gilbert St shopping centre).
V/Line (☑ 1800 800 007; www.vline.com.au) Four times daily Monday to Friday (two on weekends) from Geelong to Torquay ($3.60, 25 minutes).

Torquay to Anglesea

The Great Ocean Road officially begins on the stretch between Torquay and Anglesea. A slight detour takes you to famous **Bells Beach**, the powerful point break that is part of international surfing folklore (it's here, in name only, that Keanu Reeves and Patrick Swayze have their ultimate showdown in

GREAT OCEAN ROAD HISTORIC MARKERS

Work on the Great Ocean Road began in September 1919, and the road between Anglesea and Apollo Bay was completed in 1932. It was an effort that involved more than 3000 workers, mostly returned WWI soldiers, with initial construction done by hand, using picks, shovels and crowbars.

On the road from Torquay to Lavers Hill, keep an eye out for 13 bronze plaques that tell the story of its construction, most with spectacular views that are great photo ops. At Eastern View (just after Fairhaven en route to Lorne) you'll find the *Diggers* sculpture, which sits beneath the historic Memorial Arch and depicts an ex-WWI soldier labourer.

For further info on its construction visit the Great Ocean Road National Heritage Centre (p166) in Lorne.

the film *Point Break*). When the long right-hander is working it's one of the longest rides in the country. Since 1973, Bells has hosted the **Rip Curl Pro** (www.aspworldtour.com) every Easter. The world championship ASP tour event draws thousands to watch the world's best surfers carve up the big autumn swells, where waves have reached 5m during the contest! The Rip Curl Pro occasionally decamps to Johanna Beach, two hours west, when fickle Bells isn't working. Contact **Surfing Victoria** (☎03-5261 2907; www.surfingaustralia.com) for more details.

Nine kilometres southwest of Torquay is the turn-off to spectacular **Point Addis**, a vast sweep of pristine 'clothing optional' beach that attracts surfers, nudists, hang-gliders and swimmers. There's a signposted **Koorie Cultural Walk**, a 1km circuit trail to the beach through the **Ironbark Basin** nature reserve.

The **Surf Coast Walk** (www.visitgreatoceanroad.org.au/surfcoastwalk) follows the coastline for 30km from Jan Juc to Moggs Creek south of Aireys Inlet, and can be done in stages – the full route takes 11 hours. It's marked on the *Surf Coast Touring Map*, available from tourist offices.

There's a few nice wineries this way, too – **Bellbrae Estate** (☎03-5264 8480; www.bellbraeestate.com.au; 520 Great Ocean Rd, Bellbrae; ⊙11am-4pm Sat & Sun) and **Brown Magpie** (☎03-5266 2147; www.brownmagpiewines.com/; 125 Larcombes Rd, Modewarre; ⊙11am-4pm Sat-

Sun Nov-Mar) both offer tastings of award-winning cool-climate wines.

Anglesea

POP 2300

Mix orange cliffs falling into the ocean with hilly, tree-filled 'burbs and a population that booms in summer and you've got Anglesea.

Sharing fish and chips with seagulls by the Anglesea River is a family tradition for many, and caravan parks burst at their seams come school holidays. Life hits the fast lane during January when the wide riverbank is taken over by a Sunday market.

◉ Sights & Activities

Main Beach is the ideal spot to learn to surf, while sheltered **Point Roadknight Beach** is good for families. The Anglesea **heathlands** have a huge diversity of flora and fauna, particularly the wild orchids, with around 100 varieties found around September.

Bicycle hire is available from **Big4 Anglesea Holiday Camp** (bike hire half-/full day $10/20).

Anglesea Golf Club   GOLF
(☑03-5263 1582; www.angleseagolfclub.com.au; Noble St; 9 holes $25; ⊙clubhouse 8am-midnight) You can watch kangaroos graze on the fairways from the big glass windows at the clubhouse here, or, even better, pair your sightings with a round of golf.

Go Ride A Wave   SURFING
(☑1300 132 441; www.gorideawave.com.au; 143b Great Ocean Rd; 2hr lessons $65, board hire from $25; ⊙9am-5pm) Long-established surf school that runs lessons and hires out boards, SUPs and kayaks.

Anglesea Surf Centre   SURFING
(☑03-5263 1530; www.secondhandsurfboards.com.au; cnr Great Ocean Rd & McMillan St; surfboard hire from $25, wetsuit hire $15; ⊙9am-6pm) Sells second-hand surfboards, and hires out boards and wetsuits. Good local knowledge, too.

Anglesea Paddleboats   CANOEING
(☑0408 599 942; www.angleseapaddleandcanoe.com) Hires out canoes (per hour $25), paddleboats (per 15 minutes $16) and motorboats along Anglesea River.

★ Festivals & Events

Anglesea Music Festival   MUSIC
(AMF; www.angleseamusicfestival.com.au) The grassroots AMF features local and regional performers over three days in October.

🛏 Sleeping

Surfcoast Holiday Rentals (✎03-5263 3199; www.surfcoastrentals.com.au; 69 Great Ocean Rd) offers houses from $180 per night.

Anglesea Backpackers HOSTEL $
(✎03-5263 2664; www.angleseabackpackers.com; 40 Noble St; dm from $30, d $95-115, family $150; @) While most hostels like to cram 'em in, this simple, homely backpackers has just two dorm rooms and one double/triple, and is clean, bright and welcoming. In winter the fire glows warmly in the cosy living room.

**Anglesea Beachfront
Family Caravan Park** CAMPGROUND $
(✎03-5263 1583; www.angleseabeachfront.com.au; 35 Cameron Rd; powered sites $38-75, cabin d $107-310; @ 🛜 🐾) Beach- and river-fronting caravan park with a pool, wi-fi, two camp kitchens, a jumping pillow, an indoor spa and a games room. No, you probably won't get that book read.

Anglesea Rivergums B&B $$
(✎03-5263 3066; www.anglesearivergums.com.au; 10 Bingley Pde; d $125-160; ❄) Tucked by the river with tranquil views, these two spacious, tastefully furnished rooms (a self-contained bungalow and a room attached to the house) are excellent value.

🍴 Eating & Drinking

The **Anglesea Hotel** (✎03-5263 1210; www.angleseahotel.com.au; 1 Murch Cres) is the main spot for a drink.

Red Till CAFE $
(143a Great Ocean Rd; mains $10-20; ⊘7am-4pm; 🛜) Across from the main beach, Red Till is decked out in eclectic retro style, with fantastic all-day breakfasts and the best coffee in town.

McGain's Cafe CAFE $
(✎03-5263 3841; 1 Simmons Ct; dishes from $7; ⊘8.30am-4pm; 🛜) 🍃 Snack among the foliage at this lovely sunlit cafe in an atrium-like nursery setting. The menu is largely organic using produce from the attached foodstore. It's left off the Great Ocean Road before you hit the Anglesea shops.

Bakery Cafe BAKERY $
(Anglesea Shopping Centre; pies $5; ⊘6am-4.30pm) Delicious pies, including its signature prawn and scallop, and brekky ones.

Locanda Del Mare ITALIAN $$
(5 Diggers Pde; mains $19.50-25; ⊘from 6pm Thu-Mon summer, from 6pm Thu-Sun winter) Don't be deceived by its ugly exterior, this authentic Italian restaurant hidden behind Anglesea's petrol station gets rave reviews, especially for its wonderful desserts.

ℹ Information

Visitor Centre (16/87 Great Ocean Rd; ⊘9am-5pm) On the river, this small information centre is the first point of contact for many visitors along the Great Ocean Road, with useful info and maps.

ℹ Getting There & Away

The new Geelong bypass has reduced the time it takes to drive from Melbourne to Anglesea to around 75 minutes.

Aireys Inlet & Around
POP 1200

Aireys Inlet is midway between Anglesea and Lorne, and is home to glorious stretches of beach, including **Fairhaven** and **Moggs Creek**. It's hard to beat a stroll along Fairhaven beach, whether in winter or summer. In Aireys itself, the beaches are backed by tall, volcanic cliffs, with tidal rock pools along the foreshore just below the lighthouse. A Surf Life Saving Club patrols the beach at Fairhaven during summer.

◎ Sights & Activities

The lovely 3.5km **Aireys Inlet Cliff Walk** begins at Painkalac Creek, rounds Split Point and makes its way to Sunnymead Beach. The **Surf Coast Walk** continues along the coast here – pick up a copy of *Walks of Lorne & Aireys Inlet* from visitor centres.

⭐**Split Point Lighthouse** LIGHTHOUSE
(✎03-5263 1133; www.splitpointlighthouse.com.au; 45min tours adult/child/family $12/7/35; ⊘hourly 11am-2pm, summer holidays 10am-4pm) Scale the 136 steps to the top of the beautiful 'White Queen' lighthouse for sensational 360-degree views. Built in 1891, the 34m-high lighthouse is still operational (though now fully automated). It's only accessible by booking a tour. The historic **Willows Tea House** (⊘9.30am-4pm), formerly the lightkeeper's stables, does yummy scones.

Blazing Saddles HORSE RIDING
(✎03-5289 7322; www.blazingsaddlestrailrides.com; Lot 1 Bimbadeen Dr; 1/2½hr rides $45/100) People come from around the world to hop on a Blazing Saddles horse and head along the stunning beach or into the bush.

🛏 Sleeping

Cimarron B&B
B&B $$

(☑ 03-5289 7044; www.cimarron.com.au; 105 Gilbert St; d $150-175; 🐾) Built in 1979 from local timbers and using only wooden pegs and shiplap joins, Cimarron is an idyllic getaway with views over Point Roadknight. The large lounge area has book-lined walls and a cosy fireplace, while upstairs there are two unique, loft-style doubles with vaulted timber ceilings; otherwise there's a den-like apartment. Out back, it's all state park and wildlife. Gay friendly, but no kids.

Lightkeepers Inn
MOTEL $$

(☑ 03-5289 6666; www.lightkeepersinn.com.au; 64 Great Ocean Rd; d $130; 🐾⬜) Convenient for the shops, here you can expect clean motel rooms with extra-thick walls for peace and quiet.

Inlet Caravan Park
CABIN $$

(☑ 03-5289 6230; www.aicp.com.au; 19-25 Great Ocean Rd; unpowered/powered sites from $36/40, en suite cabin d $95-168; @🐾⬜) More cabin-oriented than a tent city, this neat park is close to the township's few stores.

Pole House Rental
RENTAL HOUSE $$$

(☑ 03-5220 0200; www.greatoceanroadholidays.com.au; 60 Banool Rd, Fairhaven; 2-night min mid-week from $435) The Pole House, in Fairhaven, is a Great Ocean Road landmark, sitting, as the name suggests, atop a pole, with extraordinary views.

🍴 Eating & Drinking

★ A La Grecque
GREEK $$

(☑ 03-5289 6922; www.alagrecque.com.au; 60 Great Ocean Rd; mains $28-38; ⊙ 9-11.30am, 12.30-2.30pm & 6-10pm daily Dec-Mar, Wed-Sun Apr-May & Sep-Nov) Be whisked away to the Mediterranean at this outstanding modern Greek taverna. Mezze including cured kingfish with apple, celery and a lime dressing, and mains such as grilled baby snapper are sensational. Kosta, the host, ran Kosta's in Lorne for 27 years before decamping to Aireys.

Freestone's Roadhaven
AMERICAN $$

(☑ 03-5289 6912; www.freestonesroadhaven.com.au; 85 Great Ocean Rd; milkshakes $6, burgers from $16; ⊙ cafe 11am-late daily, diner 11am-late Fri-Sun) Bringing '60s Americana to the coast, this roadhouse diner is decked out in retro furniture, motoring memorabilia and a classic-car display in its garage. The malt shop has hot dogs, milkshakes and booze (happy hour 5.30pm to 6.30pm), while the upstairs diner has uniformed waitresses serving burgers and wings, and views over Painkalak Creek.

Truffles Cafe Deli
CAFE $$

(☑ 03-5289 7402; 34 Great Ocean Rd; mains $15-20; ⊙ 8am-4pm Wed-Mon, from 6pm Thu-Sun; 🐾) Truffles does the lot – eat-in or takeaway, pizza, Thai curries, good vegetarian choices, regional wines, BYO, coffee, free wi-fi and a happy ambience.

Aireys Pub
PUB

(☑ 03-5289 6804; www.aireyspub.com.au; 45 Great Ocean Rd; ⊙ noon-late; 🐾) Established in 1904, this coastal pub is a survivor, twice burning to the ground, before closing its doors in 2011 only to be saved by a bunch of locals who chipped in to save it. Now it's better than ever, with a fantastic kitchen, roaring fire, sprawling beer garden, live music and its very own Aireys draught beer.

Fairhaven Surf Life Saving Club
BAR

(www.fairhavenslsc.org; ⊙ from 4pm daily Jan, Fri-Sun Feb-Easter) The newly rebuilt surf club runs a bar and bistro from its commanding dune location overlooking Fairhaven beach; a glorious spot for sunset.

Lorne
POP 1000

Lorne has an incredible natural beauty, something you see vividly as you drive into town from Aireys Inlet. Old, tall gumtrees line its hilly streets, and Loutit Bay gleams irresistibly. It's this beauty that has attracted visitors for centuries – Rudyard Kipling's 1891 visit led him to pen the poem 'Flowers': 'Gathered where the Erskine leaps/Down the road to Lorne...'

It gets busy; in summer you'll be competing with day-trippers for restaurant seats and lattes, but, thronged by tourists or not, Lorne is a lovely place to hang out.

◎ Sights & Activities

Kids will love the beachside swimming pool, trampolines and skate park.

There's more than 50km of bushwalking tracks around Lorne, taking in lush forests and waterfalls. There are also self-guided walks in Lorne, including historical and shipwreck trails; pick up the *Lorne Walks & Waterfalls* brochure from the visitors centre.

Great Ocean Road
National Heritage Centre
MUSEUM

(15 Mountjoy Pde; ⊙ 9am-5pm) Scheduled to open mid-2014, this museum will tell the story of the construction of the Great Ocean Road; see boxed text, p164.

Lorne

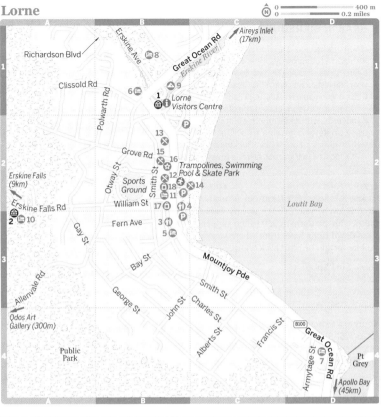

Lorne

⊚ Sights
1 Great Ocean Road National
   Heritage Centre.....................................B1
2 Qdos Art Gallery A3

⊙ Activities, Courses & Tours
3 Lorne Surf Shop.....................................B3
4 Southern Exposure...............................B2

⊜ Sleeping
5 Cumberland Lorne Resort.....................B3
6 Erskine River Backpackers....................B1
7 Grand Pacific Hotel...............................D4
8 Great Ocean Road Backpackers...........B1
9 Lorne Camping Grounds Booking
   Office...B1

10 Qdos...A3
11 Sandridge Motel....................................B2

⊗ Eating
12 Arab...B2
13 Bottle of Milk...B2
   Kafe Kaos ....(see 13)
14 Lorne Beach Pavilion C2
15 Mexican Republic B2

⊛ Entertainment
16 Lorne Theatre B2

⊜ Shopping
17 Fowlers Lorne Bookshop.......................B2
18 Lorne Beach Books...............................B2

Qdos Art Gallery   GALLERY
(☑ 03-5289 1989; www.qdosarts.com; 35 Allenvale
Rd; ⊙ 9am-6pm daily Dec & Jan, 9am-5.30pm Thu-
Mon Feb-Nov) **FREE** Amid the lush forest that
backs on to Lorne, Qdos always has something interesting showing at its gallery, to go
with its open-air sculpture garden. Refuel at
the on-site cafe and treat yourself to a night
in the accommodation (p169).

DON'T MISS

BRAE IN BIRREGURRA

Given the success chef Dan Hunter had at the Royal Mail Hotel in Dunkeld (p212), the Birregurra tourism guys must've been licking their lips for several reasons when they heard he was moving to their town to open his new restaurant, **Brae** (☑ 03-5236 2226; www.braerestaurant.com; 4285 Cape Otway Rd, Birregurra; 8-course tasting plates per person $180; ⊘ noon-3pm Fri-Mon, from 6pm Thu-Sun).

Opening its doors at the time of research, Brae takes over from the much-loved Sunnybrae, with its farmhouse getting a refit by renowned architects Six Degrees, and using whatever is growing in its 30 acres of organic gardens. Reservations are essential, well in advance. Future plans include boutique accommodation on-site.

It's located in the small historic town of Birregurra between Colac and Lorne.

Erskine Falls   WATERFALL
(Erskine Falls Access Rd) Head out of town to see this lovely waterfall. It's an easy walk to the viewing platform or 250 (often slippery) steps down to its base, from where you can explore further or head back on up.

Lorne Surf Shop   SURFING
(☑ 03-5289 1600; www.lornesurf.com.au; 130 Mountjoy Pde; ⊘ 9.30am-5.30pm) Rents surfboards, body boards and wetsuits.

Southern Exposure   SURFING, KAYAKING
(☑ 03-5261 9170; www.southernexposure.com.au) Offers surfing lessons (two hours $65), is big on kayaking, and, in Torquay, mountain biking.

⚑ Festivals & Events

Falls Festival   MUSIC
(www.fallsfestival.com; 2-/3-/4-day tickets $320/390/433; ⊘ 28 Dec-1 Jan) A four-day knees-up over New Year's on a farm just out of town, this stellar music festival attracts a top lineup of international rock and indie groups. Past headliners include Iggy Pop, Kings of Leon and the Black Keys. Sells out fast, and tickets include camping.

Pier to Pub Swim   SWIMMING
(www.lornesurfclub.com.au; ⊘ mid-Jan) This popular event in January inspires up to 4500 swimmers to splash their way 1.2km across Loutit Bay to the Lorne Hotel; it's a photo opportunity for local politicians and celebrities.

Lorne Film   FILM
(www.lornefilm.com.au; Lorne Theatre; ⊘ mid-Nov) This new three-day boutique film festival screens local and international docos and features, mostly with a coastal theme.

🛏 Sleeping

Erskine River Backpackers   HOSTEL $
(☑ 03-5289 1496; 6 Mountjoy Pde; dm/d $30/80; ⊘ Nov-Apr) Beautiful verandahs line this classic old building located by the river at the north end of town. It's a relaxed place with four-bunk dorms and great communal spaces. Call ahead to check it's open.

Great Ocean Road Backpackers   HOSTEL $
(☑ 03-5289 1070; 10 Erskine Ave; dm/d $35/90; ❄ ☎) Tucked away in the bush among the cockatoos, koalas and other wildlife, this two-storey timber lodge has dorms and good-value doubles. Unisex bathrooms take some getting used to. Also has pricier A-frame cottages that come with kitchens and en suites.

**Lorne Camping
Grounds Booking Office**   CAMPGROUND $
(☑ 03-5289 1382; www.lornecaravanpark.com.au; 2 Great Ocean Rd; unpowered/powered sites from $33/38, cabin d from $115; ☎) Book here for Lorne's five caravan parks. Of the five, Erskine River Caravan Park, where the booking office is located, is the prettiest. It's on the left-hand side as you enter Lorne, just before the bridge. Book well ahead for peak-season stays.

Grand Pacific Hotel   HOTEL $$
(☑ 03-5289 1609; www.grandpacific.com.au; 268 Mountjoy Pde; d/apt from $120/180; ☎) An iconic Lorne landmark, harking back to 1875, the Grand Pacific has been restored with a sleek modern decor that retains some classic period features. The best rooms have balconies and stunning sea views looking out to the pier. Plainer rooms are boxy, but still top value, and there are self-contained apartments, too.

Cumberland Lorne Resort   RESORT $$
(☑ 03-5289 2256; www.cumberland.com.au; 150 Mountjoy Pde; 1-bed apt $179-250; ❄ @ ☎ ⚊) A behemoth of a resort still may not suit Lorne,

however, once inside, it's hard to knock its self-contained apartments with unbeatable ocean views, including from within its spa baths. Other perks include free surfboard rental, indoor pool, day spa and tennis courts.

Sandridge Motel   MOTEL, APARTMENT **$$**
(📞 03-5289 2180; www.sandridgemotel.com.au; 128 Mountjoy Pde; r $150-350, apt $250-500; 🛜) Smack bang in the centre of Lorne's main strip, here everything's literally on your doorstep, including the ocean. There are self-serviced aparments or less flashy motel-style rooms. Aim for a sea-facing room with balcony, especially if you can snare a mid-week/low-season deal.

Qdos   RYOKAN **$$$**
(📞 03-5289 1989; www.qdosarts.com; 35 Allenvale Rd; r incl breakfast $250; 🛜) The perfect choice for those seeking a romantic getaway or forest retreat, Qdos' luxury zen treehouses are fitted with tatami mats, rice-paper screens and no TV. Two-night minimum; no kids.

✖ Eating

Mexican Republic   MEXICAN **$**
(📞 03-5289 1686; 1a Grove Rd; tacos from $7; ⏰ noon-9pm summer, noon-3pm & 6-9pm weekends winter) Bringing Melbourne's Mexican street-food craze to Lorne, this pop-up style eatery does authentic soft corn tortilla tacos, burritos with smoky chipotle mayo and imported Mexican beers.

Bottle of Milk   BURGERS **$**
(📞 03-5289 2005; www.thebottleofmilk.com; 52 Mountjoy Pde; burgers from $11.50; ⏰ 8am-3pm Mon-Fri, to 5pm Sat & Sun, 8am-9pm Nov-Feb) With a menu of 24 different, inventive burgers all stacked with fresh ingredients, it's hard to go wrong at this popular hangout on the main strip.

Kafe Kaos   CAFE **$**
(52 Mountjoy Pde; lunch $8-15; ⏰ 8am-4.30pm; 🛜) Bright and perky, Kafe Kaos typifies Lorne's relaxed foodie philosophy – barefoot patrons in boardies or bikinis tuck into first-class panini, bruschetta, burgers and chips, and all-day breakfasts. There's also a bar.

Lorne Beach Pavilion   MODERN AUSTRALIAN **$$**
(📞 03-5289 2882; www.lornebeachpavilion.com.au; 81 Mountjoy Pde; ⏰ 8am-9pm) With its unbeatable spot on the foreshore, here life's literally a beach, especially with a cold beer in hand. Come at happy hour for 1kg of mussels for $10 and two-for-one cocktails. Cafe-

style breakfasts and lunches are tasty, while a more upmarket Modern Australian menu is on for dinner.

Arab   CAFE **$$**
(📞 03-5289 1435; 94 Mountjoy Pde; mains $20-24; ⏰ 7am-8pm Mon-Fri, to 9.30pm Sat & Sun) Arab started as a beatnik coffee lounge in 1956, and single-handedly transformed Lorne from a daggy family-holiday destination into a place for groovers and shakers. It's been trading ever since, and still hits the spot for coffee and all-day breakfasts.

★ Entertainment

Lorne Theatre   CINEMA
(📞 03-5289 1272; www.greatoceanroadcinemas.com.au; 78 Mountjoy Pde; adult/child $16.50/11.50) This grand old theatre shows new-release films daily in peak season.

🛍 Shopping

The main street has boutique clothing and beachware stores. **Lorne Beach Books** (www.lornebeachbooks.com.au; 108a Mountjoy Pde; ⏰ 9am-5pm Mon-Sat, 9am-4pm Sun) stocks interesting new releases, while **Fowlers** (📞 03-5289 1173; 1/1 William St; ⏰ 10am-5pm Mon-Wed & Sat, noon-4pm Sun) has second-hand paperbacks.

ℹ Information

Lorne Visitors Centre (📞 1300 891 152; www.visitgreatoceanroad.org.au/lorne; 15 Mountjoy Pde; ⏰ 9am-5pm; @ 🛜) Stacks of information (including walking maps), helpful staff, fishing licences, bus tickets and accommodation booking service. Has internet access and free wi-fi.

ℹ Getting Around

V/Line buses pass through daily from Geelong ($10,1½ hours) en route to Apollo Bay ($5.40, one hour). For taxis, try **Lorne Taxi Service** (📞 0409 892 304).

Cumberland River

Just 7km southwest of Lorne is Cumberland River, starting point for a lovely 6km return walk to Erskine Falls. There's also the wonderful **Cumberland River Holiday Park** (📞 03-5289 1790; www.cumberlandriver.com.au; Great Ocean Rd; unpowered sites $37, en suite cabins from $105), a splendidly located bushy camping ground next to the river and unique backdrop of craggy cliffs that rise on the far side. The ocean beach offers surfing and swimming, but watch out for rips.

Wye River

POP 140

The Great Ocean Road snakes spectacularly around the cliff-side from Cumberland River before reaching this little town with big ideas. Nestled discreetly in the pretty (steep) hillsides are some modest holiday houses and a few grander steel-and-glass pole-frame structures built on the 'challenging' housing sites.

🛏 Sleeping & Eating

Wye River Foreshore Camping Reserve (☑ 03-5289 0412; sites $40; ⊙ Nov-Apr) offers camping in summer, while **Big4 Wye River Holiday** (www.big4wyeriver.com.au; 25 Great Ocean Rd; unpowered/powered sites from $36/40, cabins from $100; @) has sites and cabins year-round. **Holiday Great Ocean Road** (☑ 03-5237 1098; www.holidaygor.com.au; studios from $190, 2BR cottage from $250) can arrange holiday 2-bed house rentals.

★**Wye General**　　　CAFE $$
(www.thewyegeneral.com; 35 Great Ocean Rd; mains $15-26; ⊙ 8am-5pm Mon-Sat, to 4pm Sun) This cafe has marched into town and there's nothing general about it. From fantastic burgers, homemade sourdough to perfect coffee, this smart indoor-outdoor joint has polished concrete floors, timber features and a sophisticated retro ambience that will impress.

Wye Beach Hotel　　　PUB $$
(☑ 03-5289 0240; www.wyebeachhotel.com.au; 19 Great Ocean Rd; mains $18-30 ⊙ 11am-11pm Mon-Fri, to late Sat; 🐾) People come here for pub food on a verandah with some of the most stunning views of the coast. The hotel also has comfortable motel-style double rooms ($120 to $260) with great views. Rooms are well priced midweek.

Deck House　　　RENTAL HOUSE $$$
(☑ 03-5289 0222; www.thedeckhouse.com.au; weekdays/weekends from $285/325, min 2-night stay; ❋ 🐾) Opening right up to the ocean and isolated from the world, this private studio apartment is perfect for couples looking for a romantic trip down the coast. There are wonderful views from its decking or glassed-in lounge with crackling fire.

Kennett River

Located 5km along from Wye River is Kennett River, which has some great **koala spotting** just behind the caravan park.

There are also **glow-worms** that shine at night up the same stretch of Grey River Rd (take a torch).

The friendly bush **Kennett River Holiday Park** (☑ 03-5289 0272; www.kennettriver.com; 1-13 Great Ocean Rd; unpowered/powered sites $29/35, d cabins from $115; @ 🐾) is one of the best sites along the coast, and equally popular with surfers, families, travellers and young couples. The beach-view cabins have amazing vistas.

Apollo Bay

POP 1800

One of the larger towns along the Great Ocean Road, Apollo Bay has a tight-knit community of fisherfolk, artists, musicians and sea-changers.

Majestic rolling hills provide a postcard backdrop to the town, while broad, white-sand beaches dominate the foreground. It's also an ideal base for exploring magical Cape Otway and Otway National Park. It has some of the best restaurants along the coast and two lively pubs.

◎ Sights & Activities

Signposted **Marriners Lookout** is 1.5km from town towards Cape Patton – from the car park the lookout is a rewarding 20-minute return walk. A **community market** (www.apollobay.com/market_place; ⊙ 9am-1pm Sat) is held Saturdays along the main strip.

Mark's Walking Tours　　　WALKING TOUR
(☑ 0417 983 985; www.greatoceanwalk.asn.au/markstours; 2-3hr tours adult/child $50/15) Take a walk around the area with local Mark Brack, son of the Cape Otway lighthouse keeper. He knows this stretch of coast, its history and its ghosts better than anyone around. Daily tours include shipwreck tours, historical tours, glow-worm tours and Great Ocean Walk tours. Minimum two people.

Apollo Bay Surf & Kayak　　KAYAKING, SURFING
(☑ 0405 495 909; www.apollobaysurfkayak.com.au; 157 Great Ocean Rd; 2hr kayak tours $65, 1½hr surf lessons $60) Head out to an Australian fur seal colony on a two-seated kayak. Tours (with full instructions for beginners) depart from Marengo beach (to the south of the town centre). Also offers surf lessons, plus boards, stand-up paddle boards and mountain bikes for hire. It also operates Walk 91 for the Great Ocean Walk (p172).

FORREST

Tucked away in the hinterland of the Otways, a 30-minute drive from Apollo Bay, the former logging town of Forrest has emerged as one of the new tourist hot spots in the Otways.

Since the decline of the logging industry, it's reinvented itself as one of the best **mountain-biking** destinations in the state. Parks Victoria and the Department of Environment and Primary Industries (DEPI) have opened 16 trails (adding up to more than 50km) – ranging from beginner to highly advanced. Grab a trail map (www.rideforrest. com.au/trails) from the **Corner Store** (www.thecornerstoreforrest.com.au; cnr Blundy & Station Sts, Forrest; ⊙10am-5pm), which also does the best coffee and pies in town, and rents out bikes and arranges tours through **MTB Skills** (www.mtbskills.com.au; bike hire half-/full day $65/85;). It hosts the **Otway Odyssey Mountain Bike Marathon** (www. rapidascent.com.au) in late February, and **Forrest Festival** (www.forrestfestival.com.au) stage race held in the first weekend of December.

Located 7km from Forrest is scenic **Lake Elizabeth**, famous for its population of platypus, and surreal scenery of dead trees jutting from its glassy water. **Otway Eco Tours** (☑0419 670 985; www.platypustours.net.au; adult/child $85/50) runs guided canoe trips at dusk and dawn to spot platypus. There's also free camping here; BYO drinking water.

The town is also known for the **Forrest Brewing Company** (☑03-5236 6170; www. forrestbrewing.com.au; Apollo Bay Rd, Forrest; 6-beer tasting pallet $10; ⊙Thu 10am-late, Fri-Sun 9am-late, daily Dec-Jan) microbrewery where you can sample eight different beers brewed on-site and dig into quality pub meals.

Accommodation options include the wonderful **Forrest Guesthouse** (☑03-5236 6446; www.forrestaccommodation.com.au; 16 Grant St; s/d $100/150; 🖝), with rustic rooms and a charming cafe, which has homemade pies and local beers on tap. It also rents out bikes. Otherwise, **Forrest Caravan Park** (☑0447 588 348; sites per person $10.50, cabins from $60) has campsites and cabins.

Otway Expeditions ADVENTURE SPORTS
(☑03-5237 6341; http://otwayexpeditions.tripod. com; 1hr argo rides $45, 3hr mountain-bike tours $65) Take a dual-suspension bike through the Otways (minimum six people), or go nuts in an amphibious all-terrain 8x8 argo buggy.

Surf'n'Fish DIVING
(☑03-5237 6426; www.surf-n-fish.com.au; 157 Great Ocean Rd) Authorised PADI dive centre that can arrange trips to Marengo reef and nearby wrecks, including SS *Casino*, which sank offshore in 1932. Rents out surfboards and fishing tackle, too.

★ Festivals & Events

Apollo Bay Music Festival MUSIC
(☑03-5237 6761; www.apollobaymusicfestival.com; weekend pass $125, under 15yr free; ⊙late Feb) Three-day music festival spanning most genres, showcasing Aussie talent and international acts. Book accommodation well ahead.

⨁ Sleeping

YHA Eco Beach HOSTEL $
(☑03-5237 7899; www.yha.com.au; 5 Pascoe St; dm from $35, d/f $95/119; @🖝) ⬦ This $3 million, architect-designed hostel is an out-

standing place to stay, with ecocredentials, great lounge areas, kitchens, boules pit and rooftop terraces. Rooms are generic but spotless. It's a block behind the beach.

Surfside Backpacker HOSTEL $
(☑03-5237 7263; www.surfsidebackpacker.com; cnr Great Ocean Rd & Gambier St; dm $25-30, d $65; 🖝) Right across from the beach, this fantastic sprawling, old-school 1940s beach house will appeal to those looking for budget accommodation with character (though possibly not to those seeking a sleek, modern hostel). It's run by a lovely lady, with a homely lounge full of couches, board games and huge windows looking out onto the ocean. It's a 15-minute walk from the bus stop.

Skenes Creek
Beachfront Park CAMPGROUND $
(☑03-5237 6132; www.skenescreek.com; 2 Great Ocean Rd, Skenes Creek; sites from $22, caravans $70; 🖝) Notable for being right on the beach, this simple campground is just outside Apollo Bay in Skenes Creek.

Pisces Big4 Apollo Bay CAMPGROUND $
(☑03-5237 6749; www.piscespark.com.au; 311 Great Ocean Rd; sites from $28, cabins from $80;

🛜🖥️) It's the unbeatable views from the ocean-front villas (from $170) that set this family-oriented park apart from the others.

★ **Beacon Point Ocean View Villas** VILLA **$$**
(☑03-5237 6196; www.beaconpoint.com.au; 270 Skenes Creek Rd; r from $160; ❄️) A commanding hill location among the trees, this wonderful collection of comfortable one- and two-bedroom villas is a luxurious yet affordable bush retreat. Most have great coast views, balconies and wood-fired heaters. Handy location for Chris's restaurant, too.

Sandpiper Motel MOTEL **$$**
(☑03-5237 6732; www.sandpiper.net.au; 3 Murray St; d low/high season from $130/165; 🛜) Simple beach-house-style rooms in sea blues and sandy tones make for a relaxing stay at this friendly modern motel.

🍴 Eating & Drinking

Bay Leaf Café CAFE **$**
(☑03-5237 6470; 131 Great Ocean Rd; mains $10-16; ⊙8.30am-2.30pm) A local favourite for its innovative menu, good coffee, friendly atmosphere and boutique beer selection.

Apollo Bay Bakery BAKERY **$**
(www.apollobaybakery.com.au; 125 Great Ocean Rd; pies $5; ⊙6am-4pm) Tasty selection of homemade pies and freshly baked sourdough sandwiches.

★ **Chris's Beacon**
Point Restaurant GREEK **$$$**
(☑03-5237 6411; www.chriss.com.au; 280 Skenes Creek Rd; mains from $38; ⊙8.30-10am & 6pm-late daily, plus noon-2pm Sat & Sun; 🛜) Feast on memorable ocean views, deliciously fresh seafood and Greek-influenced dishes at Chris's hilltop fine-dining sanctuary among the treetops. Reservations recommended. You can also stay in its wonderful stilted villas (including breakfast $265). It's accessed via Skenes Creek.

La Bimba MODERN AUSTRALIAN **$$$**
(☑03-5237 7411; 125 Great Ocean Rd; mains $36-42; ⊙8am-3pm & 5.30-10pm Wed-Mon) This upstairs Mod Oz restaurant is worth the splurge. Warm with a relaxed smart-casual vibe, it has ocean views and a good wine list. Try the local goodies: chilli Portarlington-mussel hotpot or a kangaroo main.

Apollo Bay Hotel PUB
(☑03-5237 6250; 95 Great Ocean Rd; ⊙11am-11pm) This pub's enticing street-front beer garden is the place to be in summer. The bistro has good seafood options, and there are live bands on weekends.

☆ Entertainment

Apollo Bay Cinema CINEMA
(☑03-5289 1272; www.greatoceanroadcinemas.com.au; cnr Great Ocean Rd & Nelson St; adult/child $16.50/11.50) Operates from the local hall during school holidays.

ℹ️ Information

Great Ocean Road Visitors Centre (☑1300 689 297; 100 Great Ocean Rd; ⊙9am-5pm; 🛜) Modern tourist office with heaps of info and an 'ecocentre' with displays. Free wi-fi and bookings for bus tickets.

DON'T MISS

WALKING THE GREAT OCEAN ROAD

The superb multiday **Great Ocean Walk** (www.greatoceanwalk.com.au) starts at Apollo Bay and runs all the way to the Twelve Apostles. It takes you through changing landscapes along spectacular clifftops, deserted beaches and forested Otway National Park.

It's possible to start at one point and arrange a pick-up at another (public transport options are few and far between). You can do shorter walks or the whole 104km trek over eight days. Designated camp sites are spread along the Great Ocean Walk catering for registered walkers only; bring cooking equipment and tents (no fires allowed). Otherwise there are plenty of comfortable accommodation options, from luxury lodges to caravan parks. Check out the helpful FAQ page on the website for all info.

Walk 91 (☑03-5237 1189; www.walk91.com.au; 157-159 Great Ocean Rd, Apollo Bay) can arrange your itinerary, transport, and equipment hire, and can take your backpack to your destination so you don't have to. **GOR Shuttle** (☑0428 379 278, 03-5237 9278) is a recommended shuttle service for luggage and walkers; it will pick you up when your walking's done (costing anywhere from $35 to $85, depending on the distance).

OTWAY FLY, FALLS & BREWERY DETOUR

Twenty kilometres inland from the logging town of **Lavers Hill** on the Colac Rd (C155) is the popular **Otway Fly** (☑03-5235 9200; www.otwayfly.com; 360 Phillips Track; adult/child $22.50/9; ⊙9am-5pm, last entry 4pm). It's an elevated steel walkway suspended among the forest canopy, and includes a swaying lookout tower, 50m above the forest floor. Kids will enjoy the 'prehistoric path' loaded with dinosaurs, and everyone can test their bravery on the guided **zipline** tour – including a 120m run. You can also abseil down one of the giant trees.

Along the same road as the Fly is **Triplet Falls**, which passes an historic timber site and is worth the 900m hike. The **Beauchamp** and **Hopetoun Falls** are just past Beech Forest, down the Aire Valley Rd, and are also worth the trip.

On the corner just before the Fly, pop into **Otway NouriShed** (☑03-5235 9226; www.otwaynourished.com; 3810 Colac-Lavers Hill Rd; mains $8-20; ⊙10am-6pm), an old potato shed converted into a rustic cafe serving meals and fair-trade coffee. Further afield towards Colac past Gellibrand is the **Otway Estate** (☑03-5233 8400; www.otwayestate.com.au; 10-30 Hoveys Rd) brewery, which produces Prickly Moses beer plus cider and wine; call ahead to check it's open. It has accommodation in self-contained cottages from $200.

Seven kilometres southwest of Lavers Hill is **Melba Gully**, with a rainforest nature walk under a canopy of blackwoods and myrtle beeches, ferns and 300-year-old 'Big Tree' – a messmate eucalypt. After dark, glow-worms glimmer in the park.

Cape Otway

Cape Otway is the second most southerly point of mainland Australia (after Wilsons Promontory) and one of the wettest parts of the state. This coastline is particularly beautiful, rugged and historically treacherous for passing ships. The turn-off for Lighthouse Rd, which leads 12km down to the lighthouse, is 21km from Apollo Bay.

◉ Sights & Activities

Cape Otway Lightstation   LIGHTHOUSE
(☑03-5237 9240; www.lightstation.com; Lighthouse Rd; adult/child/family $18.50/7.50/46.50; ⊙9am-5pm) Cape Otway lighthouse is the oldest surviving lighthouse on mainland Australia and was built in 1848 by more than 40 stonemasons without mortar or cement. The **Telegraph Station** has fascinating displays on the 250km undersea telegraph cable link with Tasmania laid in 1859. It's a sprawling complex with plenty to see, from Aboriginal cultural sites to WWII bunkers.

⨀ Sleeping

Blanket Bay   CAMPGROUND $
(☑13 19 63; www.parkweb.vic.gov.au; sites from $20) Blanket Bay is one of those 'secret' camping grounds that Melburnians love to lay claim to discovering. It's serene (depending on your neighbours) and the nearby beach is beautiful. It's not really a secret; in

fact it's so popular during summer and Easter holidays that sites must be won by ballot (held August to October).

Bimbi Park   CAMPGROUND $
(☑03-5237 9246; www.bimbipark.com.au; 90 Manna Gum Dr; unpowered/powered sites $20/30, dm $45, d cabins $50-185; ☎) ⬤ Down a dirt road 3km from the lighthouse is this character-filled caravan park with bush sites, cabins, dorms and old-school caravans. It's good for families, with plenty of wildlife, including koalas, horse rides ($45 per hour) and a rock-climbing wall. Good use of water-saving initiatives.

Cape Otway Lightstation   B&B $$$
(Cape Otway lighthouse; ☑03-5237 9240; www.lightstation.com; Lighthouse Rd; d from $250) There is a range of options at this wind-swept spot; you can book out the whole Head Lightkeeper's House (sleeps 16), or the smaller Manager's House (sleeps two); prices are halved if you stay a second night. Vans are also permitted to stay for $25, but you'll need to pay the admission fee.

★Great Ocean Ecolodge   LODGE $$$
(☑03-5237 9297; www.greatoceanecolodge.com; 635 Lighthouse Rd; r incl breakfast & activities from $370) ⬤ Reminiscent of a luxury African safari lodge, this mudbrick homestead stands among pastoral surrounds filled with wildlife. It's solar-powered, and rates go to the on-site **Centre for Conservation**

Ecology (www.conservationecologycentre.
org). It also serves as an animal hospital
for local fauna, and has a captive tiger quoll
breeding program, which you'll visit with an
ecologist on the dusk wildlife walk.

Cape Otway to Port Campbell National Park

After Cape Otway, the Great Ocean Road
levels out and enters the fertile Horden Vale
flats, returning briefly to the coast at tiny
Glenaire. Six kilometres north of Glenaire, a
5km detour goes to the wild, thrashing and
often massive surf of Johanna Beach (forget swimming). The world-famous Rip Curl
Pro surfing competition relocates here when
Bells Beach isn't working.

Johanna has a free campground (☑13
19 63; www.parkweb.vic.gov.au) here on a protected grassy area between the dunes and
the rolling hills; book ahead. Pebble Point
(☑03-5243 3579; www.pebblepoint.com.au) is an
upmarket alternative with luxury tents overlooking a valley, and a short drive from the
Twelve Apostles.

Port Campbell National Park

The road levels out after leaving the Otways
and enters narrow, flat, scrubby escarpment
lands that fall away to sheer, 70m cliffs along
the coast between Princetown and Peterborough – a distinct change of scene. This
is Port Campbell National Park, home to
the Twelve Apostles, and the most famous
and most photographed stretch of the Great
Ocean Road. For aeons, waves and tides have
crashed against the soft limestone rock, erod-
ing, undercutting and carving out a fascinating series of rock stacks, gorges, arches and
blowholes.

None of the beaches along this stretch
are suitable for swimming because of strong
currents and undertows.

◉ Sights & Activities

★ Twelve Apostles   NATURAL FORMATION
(Great Ocean Rd; ☉visitor centre 9am-5pm) The
most iconic sight and enduring image for
most visitors to the Great Ocean Road, the
Twelve Apostles provide a fitting climax to
the journey. Jutting out from the ocean in
spectacular fashion, these rocky stacks stand
like they've been abandoned to the ocean by
the retreating headland. Today only seven
Apostles can be seen from a network of viewing platforms connected via timber boardwalks around the clifftops.

There's pedestrian access to the viewing
platforms from the car park at the Twelve
Apostles Visitor Centre (more a kiosk and
toilets than info centre) via a tunnel beneath
the Great Ocean Road.

The best time to visit is sunset, not only
for optimum photography opportunities
and to beat the tour buses, but to see little
penguins returning from ashore. Sightings
vary, but generally they arrive 20 to 40 minutes after sunset. You'll need binoculars,
which can be borrowed from the Port Campbell Visitor Centre (p177).

HOW MANY APOSTLES?

The Twelve Apostles are not 12 in number, and, from all records, never have been. From
the viewing platform you can clearly count seven Apostles, but maybe some obscure
others? We consulted widely with Parks Victoria officers, tourist office staff and even the
cleaner at the lookout, but it's still not clear. Locals tend to say 'It depends where you
look from', which really is true.

The Apostles are called 'stacks' in geologic lingo, and the rock formations were originally called the 'Sow and Piglets'. Someone in the '60s (nobody can recall who) thought
they might attract some tourists with a more venerable name, so they were renamed 'the
Apostles'. Since apostles tend to come by the dozen, the number 12 was added sometime
later. The two stacks on the eastern (Otway) side of the viewing platform are not technically Apostles – they're Gog and Magog (picking up on the religious nomenclature yet?).

The soft limestone cliffs are dynamic and changeable, constantly eroded by the un-
ceasing waves – one 70m-high stack collapsed into the sea in July 2005 and the Island
Archway lost its archway in June 2009. If you look carefully at how the waves lick around
the pointy part of the cliff base, you can see a new Apostle being born. The labour lasts
many thousands of years.

THE SHIPWRECK COAST

In the era of sailing ships, Victoria's beautiful and rugged southwest coastline was one of the most treacherous on earth. Between the 1830s and 1930s, more than 200 ships were torn asunder along the so-called **Shipwreck Coast** between Cape Otway and Port Fairy. From the early 1850s to late 1880s, Victoria's gold rush and subsequent economic boom brought countless ships of prospectors and hopefuls from Europe, North America and China. After spending months at sea, many vessels (and lives) were lost on the final 'home straight'. The lighthouses along this coast – at Aireys Inlet, Cape Otway, Port Fairy and Warrnambool – are still operating.

You'll find shipwreck museums, memorial plaques and anchors that tell the story of wrecks along this coast. The most famous is that of the iron-hulled clipper **Loch Ard**, which foundered off Mutton Bird Island (near Port Campbell) at 4am on the final night of its long voyage from England in 1878. Of 37 crew and 19 passengers on board, only two survived. Eva Carmichael, a nonswimmer, clung to wreckage and was washed into a gorge (since renamed Loch Ard Gorge), where apprentice officer Tom Pearce rescued her. Eva and Tom were both 19 years old, leading to speculation in the press about a romance, but nothing actually happened – they never saw each other again and Eva soon returned to Ireland (this time, perhaps not surprisingly, via steamship).

Gibsons Steps   BEACH, VIEWPOINT

These 86 steps hacked by hand into the cliffs by 19th-century landowner Hugh Gibson (and more recently replaced by concrete steps), lead down to wild Gibson Beach. You can walk along the beach, but be careful not to be stranded by high tides.

Loch Ard Gorge   HISTORIC SITE

Close to the Twelve Apostles, Loch Ard Gorge is where the Shipwreck Coast's most famous and haunting tale unfolded when two young survivors of the wrecked iron clipper *Loch Ard* made it to shore. There are several walks in the area taking you down to the cave where they took shelter, plus a cemetery and rugged beach.

London Bridge   VIEWPOINT

Just outside Port Campbell en route to Peterborough, London Bridge indeed has fallen down. It was once a double-arched rock platform linked to the mainland, yet it remains a spectacular sight nevertheless. In January 1990, the bridge collapsed leaving two terrified tourists marooned on the world's newest island – they were eventually rescued by helicopter.

This is a great spot for seeing little penguins – if you hang around after sunset.

Just before London Bridge, the intact **Arch** formation is worth a stop, with the Twelve Apostles providing a memorable backdrop.

The Grotto   VIEWPOINT

A short drive on from London Bridge, another recommended stop is the Grotto, with

steep stairs leading down to its hollowed out cave-like formation where waves crash through.

Bay of Islands Coastal Park   VIEWPOINT

Past Peterborough (12km west of Port Campbell), the lesser-visited **Bay of Martyrs** and **Bay of Islands** both have spectacular lookout points of rock stacks and sweeping views comparable to the Twelve Apostles. Both have fantastic coastal walks, and there's a great beach at **Crofts Bay**.

The Great Ocean Road officially ends just beyond here onwards to Warrnambool, where it meets the Princess Hwy (A1).

12 Apostles Helicopters   SCENIC FLIGHTS

(☑ 03-5598 8283; www.12apostleshelicopters.com. au; 15min flights $145) For the undisputed best views head up into the skies for a chopper tour of the Twelve Apostles and surrounding sights. It's based at Twelve Apostles Visitor Centre.

Port Campbell Boat Charters   FISHING

(☑ 0428 986 366; per person from $50) Get up close and personal with the Twelve Apostles on a boat tour. There are also dive and fishing charters for groups.

Port Campbell

POP 400

This small, laid-back coastal town was named after Scottish Captain Alexander Campbell, a whaler who took refuge here on trading voyages between Tasmania and Port Fairy. It's a friendly spot with some great

12 APOSTLES GOURMET TRAIL

Head inland to the Corangamite hinterland on the **12 Apostles Gourmet Trail** (www. visit12apostles.com.au) to taste cheeses, chocolate, wine, whiskeys and ice cream among other gourmet regional produce.

Start at Timboon, an ex-logging town 15km from Point Campbell, home to **Timboon Railway Shed Distillery** (☑ 03-5598 3555; www.timboondistillery.com; Bailey St; meals $13-20; ⊙ 10am-5pm, from 6pm Fri), an historic railway shed converted into a vibrant cafe. Inspired by Timboon's illegal 19th-century whiskey trade, it produces single-malts and spirits on-site. Watch the distillery process, sample a few whiskeys and vodkas, and nab some keepsakes. The restaurant is big on local produce, and it makes its own ice cream and pizzas.

Still in Timboon, **Whiskey Creek Tours** (☑ 0434 509 693; www.newflutes.com/whiskeytales/tours/tours.html), run by the granddaughter of a notorious moonshiner, offers a fascinating backstory to Timboon's illegal whiskey industry.

Up the road you can pick your own strawberries and blackberries at **Berry World** (☑ 03-5598 3240; www.berryworld.com.au; Egan St, Timboon; ⊙ 10am-4pm Tue-Sun Nov-Apr) . Further along, French cheesemakers **L'Artisan Cheese** (☑ 03-5598 3244; www. lartisancheese.com.au; 23 Ford & Fells Rd, Timboon; ⊙ 11am-5pm daily Oct-Apr, 11am-4pm Thu-Sun May-Jul) does free tastings or platters of wonderful, pungent rind cheeses. **Apostle Whey Cheese** (☑ 03-5598 7367; www.apostlewheycheese.com.au; 9 Gallum Rd, Cooriemungle; ⊙ 10am-5pm) offers tastings of delicious award-winning blue cheeses, bries and gumtree-smoked cheddar on its dairy farm. Midweek you can watch cheesemaking in action.

The day wouldn't be complete without wine and chocolate. **Newtons Ridge Estate** (☑ 0407 878 213, 03-5598 7394; www.newtonsridgeestate.com.au; 1170 Cooriemungle Rd, Timboon; ⊙ 11am-4pm Thu-Mon Oct-May, daily Jan) offers tastings of its reds and chardonnays at its cellar door, while **GORGE Chocolates** (www.gorgechocolates.com.au; 1432 Princetown Rd, Cooriemungle; ⊙ 10am-5pm) is an essential stop for its handmade Belgian chocolates, with plenty of goodies and samples.

No doubt after this you'll feel a little bloated, so luckily the **Camperdown–Timboon Rail Trail** offers a 34km track for cyclists and walkers, following the historic railway line. You can hire mountain bikes from **Crater to Coast** (☑ 0438 407 777; www. timboonbikehireandtaxis.com; bike hire half-/full day $25/40, car tour per hour $50), which also offers gourmet-trail tours in the owner's '80s Jaguar.

budget accommodation options, which make for an ideal spot to debrief after the Twelve Apostles. Its tiny bay has a lovely sandy beach, the only safe place for swimming along this tempestuous stretch of coast.

⊙ Sights & Activities

A 4.7km **Discovery Walk**, with signage, gives an introduction to the area's natural and historical features. It's just out of town on the way to Warrnambool.

There is some good **snorkelling** off the beach, as well as excellent **diving** in the kelp forests, canyons and tunnels of the **Arches Marine Sanctuary** and the *Loch Ard* wreck.

Port Campbell Touring Company TOUR
(☑ 03-5598 6424; www.portcampbelltouring. com.au; half-day tours from $100) Runs Apostle Coast tours and walking tours, including a Loch Ard evening walk.

🛌 Sleeping

Port Campbell Guesthouse GUESTHOUSE **$**
(☑ 0407 696 559; www.portcampbellguesthouse. com; 54 Lord St; s/d incl breakfast from $40/70; ❄ @) It's great to find a home away from home, and this historic cottage close to town has four cosy rooms and relaxed lounge and country kitchen. For added privacy there's a separate motel-style section up front with en suite rooms. Its ultra-relaxed owner, Mark, is knowledgeable on the area.

Port Campbell Hostel HOSTEL **$**
(☑ 03-5598 6305; www.portcampbellhostel. au; 18 Tregea St; dm/d from $28/70; @ 🛜) 🌿 A modern, purpose-built, double-storey backpackers has rooms with western views, a huge shared kitchen and an even bigger lounge and bar area. It's big on recycling and the toilets are ecofriendly, too. Offers bike hire and tours in the area.

Port Campbell Holiday Park   CAMPGROUND **$**
(☑03-5598 6492; www.pchp.com.au; Morris St;
powered sites/cabins from $30/105; @ 🛜) Com-
fortable cabins are all neat with en suites;
a two-minute walk to the beach and town.

Port Bayou   B&B **$$**
(☑03-5598 6009; www.portbayou.portcampbell.
nu; 52 Lord St; d B&B $130, cottage $155; ❄)
Choose from the cosy B&B or a rustic self-
contained cottage fitted with exposed ceiling
beams and corrugated-tin walls (we'd go for
the cottage).

🍴 Eating & Drinking

12 Rocks Cafe Bar   CAFE **$$**
(19 Lord St; mains $20-36; ⊘9.30am-11pm)
Watch flotsam wash up on the beach from
this busy eatery, which has perfect beachfront views. Try a local Otways beer with a
pasta or seafood main, or just duck in for
a coffee.

Port Campbell Hotel   PUB
(40 Lord St; ⊘11am-1am Mon-Sat, noon-11pm Sun)
Head in for a beer and a feed with the locals.
Kitchen closes at 8.30pm.

🛈 Information

Port Campbell Visitor Centre (☑1300 137
255; www.visit12apostles.com.au; 26 Morris
St; ⊘9am-5pm) Stacks of regional information
and interesting shipwreck displays – the anchor
from the Loch Ard is out the front. Provides free
use of binoculars and GPS equipment.

🛈 Getting There & Away

V/Line buses leave Geelong on Monday,
Wednesday and Friday and travel through Port
Campbell ($28.60, five hours) and on to Warr-
nambool ($6.80, 1 hour 20 minutes).

Warrnambool
POP 28,100

Warrnambool was originally a whaling and
sealing station – now it's booming as a major regional commercial and whale-watching
centre. Its historic buildings, waterways and
tree-lined streets are attractive, and there's
a large population of students who attend
the local campus of Deakin University. The
major housing and commercial development
around the fringes of the city looks much like
city suburbs anywhere in Australia, but the
regions around the waterfront have largely
retained their considerable historic charm.

👁 Sights & Activities

Sheltered Lady Bay, with fortifications at the
breakwater at its western end, is the main
swimming beach. Logan's Beach has the best
surf, and there are breaks at Levy's Beach
and Second Bay.

⭐**Flagstaff Hill
Maritime Village**   HISTORIC SITE
(☑03-5559 4600; www.flagstaffhill.com;
89 Merri St; adult/child/concession/fam-
ily $16/6.50/12.50/39; ⊘9am-5pm) The world-
class Flagstaff Hill precinct is of equal
interest for its shipwreck museum, heritage-
listed lighthouses and garrison as it is for its
reproduction of a historical Victorian port
town. It also has the nightly Shipwrecked
(adult/child/family $26/14/67), an engaging
70-minute sound-and-laser show telling the
story of the *Loch Ard's* plunge.

The shipwreck museum is a definitive
stop for anyone interested in the story of
the 200 vessels that succumbed along this
stretch of coast, today known as the Shipwreck Coast. Also here are two historical
(and still operational) lighthouses and the
original flagstaff stand. The cannons and

GREAT OCEAN ROAD & BELLARINE PENINSULA WARRNAMBOOL

HAVE A WHALE OF A TIME IN WARRNAMBOOL

In the 19th century Warrnambool's whale industry involved hunting them with harpoons,
however, these days they're a major tourist attraction, with crowds gathering to see
them frolic offshore during their migration between May and September. Southern right
whales (named due to being the 'right' whales to hunt) are the most common visitors,
heading from Antarctica to these more temperate waters.

Although whales can be seen between Portland and Anglesea, undoubtedly the best
place to see them is at Warrnambool's Logan's Beach Whale-Watching Platform,
the beach they use as a nursery. Sightings aren't guaranteed but you've got a very good
chance of spotting them breaching and slapping their tails about as they nurse their
bubs in the waters. Call ahead to the visitors centre (p180) to check if the whales are
about, or visit www.visitwarrnambool.com.au for latest sightings.

Warrnambool

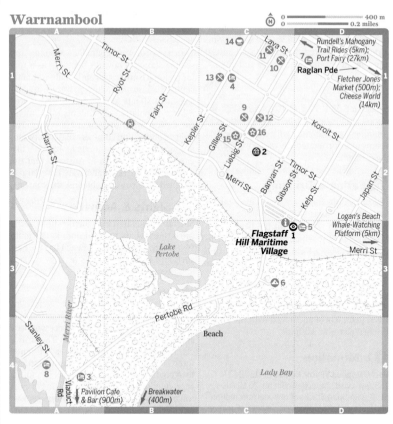

Warrnambool

◎ Top Sights
1 Flagstaff Hill Maritime Village C3

◎ Sights
2 Warrnambool Art Gallery C2

🛏 Sleeping
3 Bayside Lodge A4
4 Hotel Warrnambool C1
5 Lighthouse Lodge D3
6 Surfside Holiday Park C3
7 Victoria Hotel D1
8 Warrnambool Beach Backpackers A4

✪ Eating
9 Bojangles C1
10 Brightbird Espresso C1
   Fishtales Café .... (see 9)
   Hotel Warrnambool .... (see 4)
11 Kermond's Hamburgers C1
12 Pickled Pig C1
13 Wyton Events & Catering C1

◉ Drinking & Nightlife
14 Club Warrnambool C1

✪ Entertainment
15 Lighthouse Theatre C2
16 Loft C2

fortifications were built in 1887 to withstand the perceived threat of Russian invasion.

The village is modelled on a pioneer-era Australian coastal port, with ye olde shops such as blacksmiths, candlemakers and shipbuilders. **Stella Maris Tearooms** (Devonshire tea $8.50; ⏱ 11.30am-3pm) offers Devonshire tea, and you can also stay overnight in comfortable or budget lodging.

Cheese World
FACTORY

(www.cheeseworld.com.au; Great Ocean Rd, Allansford; ⊙9.30am-5pm Mon-Fri, 9am-4pm Sat & Sun) FREE On the outskirts of town in the dairy township of Allansford, Cheese World is run by the Warrnambool Cheese & Butter factory, whose processing plant across the road has been in business since 1888. Here you can sample cheeses, visit its dairy farm museum (surprisingly worthwhile) and get one of its famous creamy milkshakes from the cafe.

Warrnambool Art Gallery
GALLERY

(☑03-5559 4949; www.warrnambool.vic.gov.au; 165 Timor St; ⊙10am-5pm Mon-Fri, noon-5pm Sat & Sun) FREE Small but worthwhile collection of rotating permanent artworks by prominent Australian painters, as well as temporary exhibits.

Coastal Walks
WALKING

Walking trails in and around Warrnambool include the 5.7km Warrnambool Foreshore Promenade (from the breakwater to Logan's Beach) and the 3km Heritage Trail. The short Thunder Point stroll also shows off the best coastal scenery in the area; it's also the starting point for the 22km coastal Mahogany Walking Trail.

Rail Trail
CYCLING

(www.portfairytowarrnamboolrailtrail.com) Divided into three stages, the newly opened 38km-long cycling track follows the old railway line that links Warrnambool's breakwater to Port Fairy (via Koroit and Tower Hill). Map downloadable from website.

Rundell's Mahogany Trail Rides
HORSE RIDING

(☑0408 589 546; www.rundellshorseriding.com.au; 1½hr beach rides $60) Get to know Warrnambool's quiet beach spots by horseback.

Absolute Outdoors
SURFING, KAYAKING

(☑03-5521 7646; www.absoluteoutdoors.com.au; surfing lessons from $40) Runs surfing, kayaking and rock-climbing adventures.

Southern Coast Charters
WHALE WATCHING

(☑03-5598 3112; www.southerncoastcharters.com.au) Go fishing or whale watching on one of these charters.

🛏 Sleeping

Warrnambool Beach Backpackers
HOSTEL $

(☑03-5562 4874; www.beachbackpackers.com.au; 17 Stanley St; dm/d from $26/80; @奈) A short stroll to the beach, this hostel has all backpackers' needs, with huge living area, kitschy Aussie-themed bar, internet access,

kitchen and free pick-up service. Its rooms are clean and good value, and it hires surfboards and bikes. Vanpackers pay $12 per person to stay here.

Victoria Hotel
PUB $

(☑03-5562 2073; warvichotel@bigpond.com; 90 Lava St; r without bathroom per person $30) A good choice for those on a budget wanting their own space within no-frill pub rooms. The downstairs bar has friendly staff and decent food.

Hotel Warrnambool
PUB $$

(☑03-5562 2377; www.hotelwarrnambool.com.au; cnr Koroit & Kepler Sts; d incl breakfast without/with bathroom from $110/140; P❋奈) Renovations to this historic 1894 hotel have seen rooms upgraded to the more boutique end of the scale, while keeping a classic pub-accommodation feel.

Lighthouse Lodge
GUESTHOUSE $$

(www.lighthouselodge.com.au; Flagstaff Hill; d/house from $155/375; ❋奈) Once the former harbour master's residence, this charming weatherboard cottage can be rented as the entire house or separate rooms. It has a grassy area overlooking the Maritime Village and coastline. In the village there's also lodging in the Garrison Camp ($25 per person), a unique option for budget travellers within small wooden A-frame bunk cabins. BYO linen.

Bayside Lodge
MOTEL $$

(☑03-5562 7323; www.baysidelodge.com.au; 30 Pertobe Rd; d/q from $100/130; ❋奈) These large, self-contained, two-bedroom apartments are great value for a group. Stuck in a '70s time warp, but literally within spittin' distance from the beach.

Surfside Holiday Park
CAMPGROUND $$

(☑03-5559 4700; www.surfsidepark.com.au; Pertobe Rd; unpowered/powered sites from $30/32, cabins from $115) One of several Warrnambool caravan parks, this one offers good self-contained cabins, beach chalets, camping and caravan sites. It's perfectly situated between the town and the beach.

✕ Eating & Drinking

Brightbird Espresso
CAFE $

(www.brightbird.com.au; 157 Liebig St; mains $8-17; ⊙7.30am-4pm Mon-Fri, 8.30am-2pm Sat) Polished concrete floors, dangling light bulbs and single-origin coffees brewed by tattooed baristas bring a slice of inner-city Melbourne to the 'bool. All-day breakfasts include creative dishes and egg-and-bacon rolls.

GREAT OCEAN ROAD & BELLARINE PENINSULA TOWER HILL RESERVE

Wyton Events & Catering CAFE $
(www.wytonevents.com; 91 Kepler St; mains $12; ☉ 9am-6pm Mon-Thu, to 6.30pm Fri, 9am-1pm Sat) A classy cafe in a heritage building with minimalist decor and tables lined with butcher paper. Expect sophisticated breakfasts, homemade sausage rolls, cakes and coffee.

Kermond's Hamburgers BURGERS $
(📞 03-5562 4854; 151 Lava St; burgers $8; ☉ 9am-9.30pm) Likely not much has changed at this burger joint since it opened in 1949, with Laminex tables, wood-panelled walls and classic milkshakes served in stainless steel tumblers. Its burgers make this a local institution.

Fishtales Café CAFE $
(📞 03-5561 2957; 63 Liebig St; mains $7-16; ☉ 6am-8.30pm; 📶) Upbeat, earthy and friendly, with a massive menu covering the globe.

Bojangles PIZZERIA $$
(📞 03-5562 8751; www.bojanglespizza.com.au; 61 Liebig St; mains $16-31; ☉ 5-10pm; 📶) A step above your usual country pizza places with seriously delicious thin-crust pizzas.

Hotel Warrnambool PUB $$
(cnr Koroit & Kepler Sts; mains $18-24; ☉ noon-late; 📶) One of Victoria's best coastal pubs, Hotel Warrnambool mixes pub charm with bohemian character and serves wood-fired pizzas among other gastro-pub fare.

Pavilion Cafe & Bar CAFE $$
(www.pavilion.net.au; 50 Viaduct Rd; mains $8-25; ☉ 8am-5pm; 📶) Sun streams into this industrial-feel cafe right on the breakwater. Gaze out to the ocean over breakfast through big glass windows or out on the decking. Lunch is Mod Oz, the likes of salt-and-pepper calamari washed down with a couple of pots.

Pickled Pig MODERN EUROPEAN $$
(📞 03-5561 3188; 78 Liebig St; mains $12-28) Warrnambool's place to dress up, the Pickled Pig is smart dining, with linen-clad tables and chandeliers. Plenty of Spanish influences feature on the menu and bookings are advised.

Club Warrnambool AFTERNOON TEA
(📞 03-5562 2020; www.clubwarrnambool.com.au; 86 Kepler St; ☉ 9.30am-late Tue-Sat, 10am-4pm Sun; 📶) A former gentlemen's club, this grand 1873 Victorian building now hosts afternoon tea ($60) with silver service and fine china. Twice monthy; bookings essential.

☆ Entertainment

Loft LIVE MUSIC
(📞 03-5561 0995; www.theloftbar.com.au; 58 Liebig St; ☉ 5.30pm-1am Wed, Fri & Sat Mar-Nov, daily Dec-Feb) Warrnambool's premier live music venue, hosting Aussie indie bands like You Am I.

Lighthouse Theatre THEATRE
(📞 03-5559 4999; www.lighthousetheatre.com.au; cnr Liebig & Timor Sts) This is a major venue for live theatre, ballet and music.

🛍 Shopping

Fletcher Jones Market VINTAGE
(📞 03-5562 9936; Princes Hwy; ☉ 10am-6pm) The iconic Fletcher Jones clothes factory now houses an eclectic mix of collectables and vintage clothing.

ⓘ Information

Warrnambool Library (25 Liebig St; ☉ 9.30am-5pm Mon & Tue, to 6pm Wed-Fri, 10am-noon Sat; @ 📶) Free internet and wi-fi access.
Warrnambool Visitors Centre (📞 1800 637 725; www.visitwarrnambool.com.au; Merri St; ☉ 9am-5pm) Has the latest on whale sightings, as well as bike maps, several walking maps, and bicycle hire ($30 per day).

ⓘ Getting There & Away

Warrnambool is an hour's drive west of Port Campbell on the B100.

BUS

Three buses a week (Monday, Wednesday and Friday) travel from Geelong along the Great Ocean Road to Warrnambool ($32.20, 6½ hours).

V/Line and **Warrnambool Bus Lines** (📞 03-5562 1866; www.transitsw.com.au) run buses to Port Fairy ($4.20, 35 minutes), with V/Line continuing on to Portland ($11, 1½ hours).

Christians Bus Co (📞 03-5562 9432; www.christiansbus.com.au) also runs services on Tuesday, Friday and Sunday to Port Fairy ($4, departing 7.45am), continuing to Halls Gap ($25, 3¼ hours) and Ararat ($29.20, four hours).

TRAIN

V/Line (📞 1800 800 007; www.vline.com.au; Merri St) trains run to Melbourne ($31, 3¼ hours, three or four daily) via Geelong ($22.20, 2½ hours).

Tower Hill Reserve

Tower Hill, 15km west of Warrnambool, is a vast caldera born in a volcanic eruption 35,000 years ago. Aboriginal artefacts un-

THE MAHOGANY SHIP

The Mahogany Ship is said to be a Portuguese vessel that ran aground off Warrnambool in the 1500s – there have been alleged sightings of the elusive wreck sitting high in the dunes dating back to 1846. Portuguese naval charts from the 16th century, known as the Dieppe Maps, are said to depict parts of Australia's southern coastline, including Armstrong Bay 6km west of Warrnambool, and this has further fuelled the Mahogany Ship legend. Alternative theories claim that the Mahogany Ship was an even earlier Chinese junk. For 150 years people have been trying to find the remains of the Mahogany Ship – some say it's buried deep in the dunes or was swallowed by the sea. There's no direct evidence that the ship ever existed, but every decade or so it all rises to the surface again at the locally held Mahogany Ship Symposium.

earthed in the volcanic ash show that Indigenous people lived in the area at the time and, today, the Worn Gundidj Aboriginal Cooperative operates the Tower Hill Natural History Centre ([☎]03-5565 9202; www.worngundidj.org.au; walks adult/child $18.95/8.80; ⊙9am-5pm Mon-Fri, 10am-5pm Sat, Sun & public holidays). The centre is housed within the UFO-like building designed by renowned Australian architect Robin Boyd in 1962. Bush walks led by indigenous guides depart daily at 11am and include boomerang-throwing and bush-tucker demonstrations. The centre also sells handicrafts, artwork and accessories designed by the local Worn Gundidj community.

Parks Victoria manages the park and it's one of the few places where you'll spot wild emus, kangaroos and koalas hanging out together. It's also home to over 200 species of bird, with its wetland habitat attracting both resident and migratory birds.

There are excellent day walks, including the steep 30-minute Peak Climb with spectacular 360-degree views. After a century of deforestation and environmental degradation, a detailed 1855 painting of Tower Hill by Eugene von Guérard (now exhibited in the Warrnambool Art Gallery) was used to identify species in a replanting program; over 300,000 trees have been replanted since 1961.

Port Fairy

POP 2600

Settled in 1833 as a whaling and sealing station, Port Fairy retains its historic 19th-century charm with a relaxed, salty feel, heritage bluestone and sandstone buildings, whitewashed cottages, colourful fishing boats and wide tree-lined streets. It has a rich and sometimes gloomy heritage that enraptures local history buffs. In 2012

it was voted the world's most liveable community, and for most visitors it's not hard to see why.

⦿ Sights & Activities

A new Rail Trail (p179) runs between Port Fairy and Warrnambool.

Battery Hill HISTORIC SITE
Located across the bridge from the picturesque harbour, Battery Hill is worthy of exploration, with cannon fortifications positioned here in 1887 to protect the town from foreign warships. You'll also encounter resident black wallabies. It was originally used as a flagstaff, so the views are good.

Wharf Area PORT
Back in the 1850s Port Fairy's port was one of the busiest in Australia, serving as the main departure point for ships heading to England loaded up with wool, gold and wheat. Today there's still plenty going on at this charming marina, from the luxury yachts to the weather-worn fishing boats moored here.

Griffiths Island ISLAND
Where the Moyne River meets the ocean, Griffiths Island makes for a lovely one-hour walk with some good swimming spots. It's home to a protected mutton-bird colony; they descend on the town each October and stay until April (dusk is the best time to visit).

Port Fairy History Centre MUSEUM
([☎]03-5568 2682; www.historicalsociety.port-fairy.com; 30 Gipps St; admission adult/child $4/1; ⊙2-5pm Wed & Sat, 10.30am-12.30pm Sun) Housed in the old bluestone courthouse (complete with mannequins acting out a courtroom scene), this museum has shipping relics and old photos.

Port Fairy

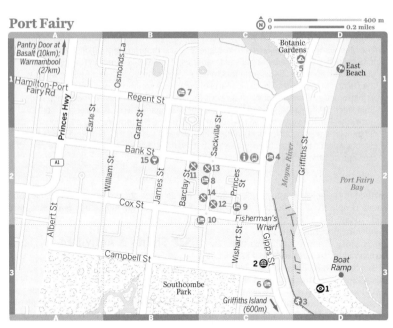

Port Fairy

⊙ **Sights**
1 Battery Hill D3
2 Port Fairy History Centre C3

⊕ **Activities, Courses & Tours**
3 Mulloka Cruises Boat D3

🛏 **Sleeping**
4 Douglas on River C2
5 Gardens Caravan Park D1
6 Merrijig Inn C3
7 Pelican Waters B1
8 Port Fairy Accommodation Centre C2
   Port Fairy Holiday Rentals ....(see 8)

9 Port Fairy YHA C2
10 Seacombe House C2

🍴 **Eating**
11 Cobb's Bakery B2
12 Coffin Sally C2
   Merrijig Kitchen .... (see 6)
13 Rebecca's Cafe C2
14 Rocksalt C2
   The Stag .... (see 10)

🍷 **Drinking & Nightlife**
15 Stump Hotel B2

Self-Guided Walking Tours   WALKING
Pick up a range of maps and brochures at the visitor centre that will guide you through various aspects of the town's heritage. The visitor centre also has maps of the popular Maritime & Shipwreck Heritage Walk, while architecture buffs will want to buy a copy of *Historic Buildings of Port Fairy*.

Mulloka Cruises Boat   CRUISE
(☏ 0408 514 382; cruises adult/child $10/free) Runs half-hour cruises of the port, bay and Griffiths Island.

Go Surf   SURFING
(☏ 0408 310 001; www.gosurf.com.au; 2hr lesson $40, board hire 2hr/1 day $25/50) Surf school and stand-up paddle board tours.

★☆ Festivals & Events

★ **Port Fairy Folk Festival**   MUSIC
(www.portfairyfolkfestival.com; tickets $75-210; ⊙ Mar) Australia's premier folk-music festival is held on the Labour Day long weekend in March. It includes an excellent mix of international and national acts, while the streets are abuzz with buskers. Accommodation can book out a year in advance.

🛏 Sleeping

Much of Port Fairy's holiday accommodation is managed by agents, including **Port Fairy Accommodation Centre** (📞03-5568 3150; www.portfairyaccom.com.au; 2/54 Sackville St) and **Port Fairy Holiday Rentals** (📞03-5568 1066; www.lockettrealestate.com.au; 62 Sackville St). The visitor centre (p184) offers a free booking service.

Port Fairy YHA   HOSTEL **$**
(📞03-5568 2468; www.portfairyhostel.com.au; 8 Cox St; dm $26-30, s/tw/d from $37/65/70; @) In the rambling 1844 home of merchant William Rutledge, this friendly, well-run hostel has a large kitchen, a pool table, free cable TV and peaceful gardens.

Gardens Caravan Park   CAMPGROUND **$**
(📞03-5568 1060; www.portfairycaravanparks.com; 111 Griffiths St; unpowered/powered sites $35/38, cabins from $112; 🐾) One of several local caravan parks, this place is next to the botanical gardens, 200m from the beach and a short walk to the town centre.

Seacombe House   GUESTHOUSE **$$**
(📞03-5568 1082; www.seacombehouse.com.au; 22 Sackville St; r without/with bathroom $93/155; ❄🐾) Built in 1847, historic Seacombe House has cosy (OK, tiny) rooms, but it offers all the atmosphere and romance you'd hope from this seafaring town. Modern motel rooms are available in its rear wing. It's above the acclaimed Stag restaurant.

Pelican Waters   CABIN **$$**
(📞03-5568 1002; www.pelicanwatersportfairy.com.au; 34 Regent St; cabins from $100; ❄) Why stay in a hotel when you can sleep in a train? This beautifully presented farm property has cabins as well as rooms in converted old-school Melbourne suburban trains. Has alpacas and llamas here too.

Merrijig Inn   HOTEL **$$**
(📞03-5568 2324; www.merrijiginn.com; 1 Campbell St; d from $110; 🐾) One of Victoria's oldest inns, at the heritage-listed Merrijig you can take your choice between the quaint dollhouse 'attic' rooms upstairs, and spacious and more comfortable rooms downstairs. There's a wonderful back lawn with fluffy chickens and comfy lounges throughout.

Douglas on River   B&B **$$**
(www.douglasonriver.com.au; 85 Gipps St; r incl breakfast from $120; 🐾) On the waterfront along the wharf, this 1852 heritage guest-house lays claims to being the oldest in Port Fairy, and a great choice for those seeking boutique accommodation. The lovely front lawn and common area are both perfect for relaxing, and there are wonderful breakfasts using local produce.

🍴 Eating

Coffin Sally   PIZZERIA **$**
(33 Sackville St; pizzas $9-19; ⊙4-10pm) Located within a former undertakers (relax, it was 100 years ago), traditional thin-crust pizzas are cooked in an open kitchen and wolfed down on streetside stools or in the dimly lit dining nooks out back next to an open fire.

Cobb's Bakery   BAKERY **$**
(📞03-5568 1713; 25 Bank St; pies $6; ⊙7am-5.30pm Mon-Fri, to 4.30pm Sat & Sun) Great selection of homemade pies, including curried scallop and bolognese.

Rebecca's Cafe   CAFE **$**
(http://rebeccasatportfairy.com; 70-72 Sackville St; mains $10-20; ⊙7am-6pm) Excellent for breakfast and light lunches, Rebecca's has interesting items on the menu, including rich wild-rice porridge topped with rhubarb.

Rocksalt   CAFE **$$**
(📞03-5568 3452; 42 Sackville St; mains $12-34; ⊙7.30am-4pm year-round & 6-8.30pm summer; 🐾) Homely, nonpretentious cafe with baked eggs, beans and chorizo for breakfast, steak sandwiches for lunch and pork belly for dinner.

Stag   MODERN AUSTRALIAN **$$**
(22 Sackville St; mains from $29; ⊙6-10pm Tue-Sat) Fine dining within a heritage atmosphere; the soft lighting from this candlebra-lit restaurant makes it a special-occasion kind of place. Go the tasting menu ($80) to sample everything from confit duck to grain-fed beef cheek to grilled local fish.

Pantry Door at Basalt   CAFE **$$**
(📞03-5568 7442; 1131 Princes Hwy, Killarney; $12-25; ⊙9am-4pm Thu-Mon; 🐾) Just outside Port Fairy in the township of Killarney, the bluestone homestead cafe focuses on seasonal local produce and has an outdoor decking among fruit trees. Next door is **Basalt Wines** (www.basaltwines.com), a family-run biodynamic winery that does tastings in its shed.

★ Merrijig Kitchen   MODERN AUSTRALIAN **$$$**
(📞03-5568 2324; www.merrijiginn.com; 1 Campbell St; mains $30-38; ⊙6-9pm Thu-Mon; 🐾) One of coastal Victoria's most atmospheric

restaurants, warm yourself by the open fire and enjoy superb dining with a menu that changes according to what's seasonal. Delectable food with great service.

Stump Hotel PUB
(☑ 03-5568 1044; www.caledonianinnportfairy.com.au; 41 Bank St; ⊙ lunch & dinner) Victoria's oldest continuously licensed pub (1844), the Stump, aka Caledonian Inn, has a beer garden and pub grub. Also has no-frills motel rooms from $100.

ⓘ Information

Port Fairy Library (www.corangamitelibrary.vic.gov.au; cnr Sackville & Bank Sts; ⊙ 10am-1pm & 1.30-4.30pm Mon, Wed & Fri, to noon Sat; @ 🛜) Free wi-fi and internet.

Port Fairy Visitors Centre (☑ 03-5568 2682; www.visitportfairy-moyneshire.com.au; Bank St; ⊙ 9am-5pm) Spot-on tourist information, walking-tour brochures, V/Line tickets and bike hire (half-/full day $15/25).

ⓘ Getting There & Away

Port Fairy is 20 minutes west of Warrnambool on the A1.

BUS

V/Line (☑ 1800 800 007; www.vline.com.au) buses run three times daily on weekdays (and twice on Saturday and once on Sunday) to Portland ($7.80, 55 minutes) and Warrnambool ($4.20, 35 minutes). Christian's Bus Co (p180) connects Port Fairy with Halls Gap ($21.60, 2½ hours) and Ararat ($27.20, 3¼ hours) on Tuesday, Friday and Sunday at around 8am.

Portland

POP 9800

Portland's claim to fame is as Victoria's first permanent European settlement, founded as a whaling and sealing base in the early 1800s. Despite its colonial history and architecture, for a town its size, blue-collared Portland lacks a real drawcard, which sees it fall short of its potential. There are some good beaches and surf breaks outside town.

⊙ Sights & Activities

Portland is the start and end of the Great South West Walk.

Whales often visit during winter; see www.whalemail.com.au for latest sightings.

Historic Waterfront HISTORIC BUILDINGS
(Cliff St) The grassy precinct overlooking the harbour has several heritage bluestone buildings. The **History House** (☑ 03-5522 2266; adult/child $3/2; ⊙ 10am-noon & 1-4pm), located in the former town hall (1863), has an interesting museum detailing Portland's colonial past. **Customs House** (1850) has a fascinating display of confiscated booty, including a stuffed black bear.

Also here is the 1845 **courthouse**, the 1886 **Rocket Shed** with a display of ship rescue equipment, and the 1889 **battery** built as defence against feared Russian invasion.

Portland Cable Tram TRAM
(☑ 03-5523 2831; www.portlandcabletrams.com.au; adult/child/family $15/6/35; ⊙ departures 10am, 11.15am, 12.30pm & 1.45pm) This restored 1886 cable tram (now diesel-powered) does four trips a day, plying a 7.4km circular route on a track laid in 2002. It links the **vintage-car museum** (☑ 03-5523 5795; cnr Glenelg & Percy Sts; adult/child $6/1; ⊙ 10am-4pm), botanic gardens, Maritime Discovery Centre and WWII memorial water tower. Hop on and off as you please.

Portland Maritime Discovery Centre MUSEUM
(☑ 1800 035 567; Lee Breakwater Rd; adult/child $7/free; ⊙ 9am-5pm) Excellent displays on shipwrecks, Portland's whaling history, a sperm whale skeleton that washed ashore, and an original 1858 wooden lifeboat.

Historic Walking Tours WALKING TOUR
The tourist office offers several self-guided walking tours, including a heritage building tour and one that traces the steps of **St Mary MacKillop's** time in Portland.

🛏 Sleeping

Portland Holiday Village CAMPGROUND $
(☑ 03-5521 7567; www.holidayvillage.com.au; 37 Percy St; unpowered/powered sites from $25/30, cabins from $89; ❄🛜) Centrally located caravan park with decent facilities.

Annesley House BOUTIQUE HOTEL $$
(☑ 0429 852 235; www.annesleyhouse.com.au; 60 Julia St; d from $145; ❄🛜) This recently restored former doctor's mansion (c 1878) has six very different self-contained rooms, some featuring clawfoot baths and lovely views. All have a unique sense of style.

Clifftop Accommodation GUESTHOUSE $$
(☑ 03-5523 1126; www.portlandaccommodation.com.au; 13 Clifton Ct; d from $160; ❄🛜) The panoramic ocean views from the balconies

GREAT SOUTH WEST WALK

This 250km signposted loop begins and ends at Portland Visitors Centre, and takes in some of the southwest's most stunning natural scenery: from the remote, blustery coast, through the river system of the Lower Glenelg National Park, and back through the hinterland to Portland. The whole loop takes at least 10 days, but it can be done in sections, and parts can be done as day walks. Maps are available from visitors centres in Portland and Nelson (p186).

Visit www.greatsouthwestwalk.com for all information, FAQs and registration details.

here are incredible. Three self-contained rooms are huge, with big brass beds, telescopes and a modern maritime feel.

✗ Eating

Deegan Seafoods   FISH & CHIPS $
(106 Percy St; mains $10; ⊙ 9am-6pm Mon-Fri)
This fish-and-chip shop famously serves up the freshest fish in Victoria.

Cafe Bahloo   CAFE $$
(85 Cliff St; mains $12-28; ⊙ 7.30am-3.30pm Tue-Sat) Housed in the original bluestone watchkeeper's house across from the harbour, Bahloo serves good breakfasts and coffee.

ⓘ Information

Portland Visitors Centre (☑ 1800 035 567; www.glenelg.vic.gov.au; Lee Breakwater Rd; ⊙ 9am-5pm) Modern building on the waterfront, with a stack of suggestions of things to do and see.

ⓘ Getting There & Away

Portland is one hour west of Port Fairy on the A1.

BUS

V/Line (☑ 1800 800 007; www.vline.com.au) buses connect Portland with Port Fairy ($7.80, 55 minutes) and Warrnambool ($11, 1½ hours) three times daily on weekdays, twice on Saturdays and once on Sundays. Buses depart from Henty St.

Portland to South Australia

From Portland you can go north to Heywood and rejoin the Princes Hwy to South Australia, or head northwest along the slower, beautiful coastal route known as the Portland–Nelson Rd. This road runs inland from the coast, but along the way there are turn-offs leading to beaches and national parks.

Cape Bridgewater

Cape Bridgewater is an essential 21km detour off the Portland–Nelson Rd. The stunning 4km arc of **Bridgewater Bay** is perhaps one of Australia's finest stretches of white-sand surf beach. The road continues on to **Cape Duquesne** where walking tracks lead to a spectacular **blowhole** and the eerie **petrified forest** on the clifftop (the wind farm is a blight, but adds to its surreal feel). A longer two-hour return walk takes you to a **seal colony** where you can see dozens of fur seals sunning themselves on the rocks.

There's plenty of accommodation available at Cape Bridgewater (enquire at Portland Visitors Centre), but the following standouts have perfect ocean views: **Sea View Lodge B&B** (☑ 03-5526 7276; www.hotkey.net.au/~seaviewlodge; 1636 Bridgewater Rd; s/d incl breakfast $110/140; ♠), **Abalone Beach House** (☑ 0408 808 346; www.abalonehouse.com.au; Bridgewater Rd; 2 people from $250) and **Cape Bridgewater Bay House** (☑ 03-9439 2966; www.capebridgewater.com.au; Bridgewater Rd; up to 4 people $170, extra person $15). Sprawling **Cape Bridgewater Coastal Camp** (☑ 03-5526 7247; www.capebridgewatercoastalcamp.com.au; Blowhole Rd; unpowered/powered sites $20/30, dm/d/house $25/50/150; ❋) has budget options with large dorms, self-contained rooms, camping, a huge kitchen, and a cinema in an old church (c 1870) on its grassy property; check it's not booked out by school groups first. It also runs the exhilarating **Seals by Sea Tour** (☑ 03-5526 7247; www.sealsbyseatours.com.au; adult/child $35/20; ⊙ Aug-Apr), a 45-minute zodiac cruise to see Australian fur seals.

Right on the beach, **Bridgewater Bay Beach Cafe** (☑ 03-5526 7155; www.bridgewaterbay.com.au; 1611 Bridgewater Rd; mains $10-16; ⊙ 9am-5pm Sun-Thu, from 6pm Fri & Sat; ♠) serves meals all day, and has a bar and free wi-fi.

GREAT OCEAN ROAD & BELLARINE PENINSULA PORTLAND TO SOUTH AUSTRALIA

CAPE NELSON LIGHTHOUSE

Built in 1884, the still-operational **Cape Nelson Lighthouse** (13km southwest of Portland, but which is not on the road to Nelson) is accessed via **lighthouse tours** (www.cape nelsonlighthouse.com.au; adult/child $15/10; ⊙ 11am & 2pm), and has stunning views atop.

Isabella's Cafe (✍ 03-5523 5119; ⊙ 11am-4pm) takes pride of place at its blustering base and offers excellent deli-style food within its thick bluestone walls. Those wanting to stay can book into the self-contained **assistant lighthouse keeper's cottage** (✍ 03-5523 5119; www.capenelsonlighthouse.com.au; d from $180).

Nelson

POP 230

Tiny Nelson is the last vestige of civilisation before the South Australian border – just a general store, a pub and a handful of accommodation places. It's a popular holiday and fishing spot at the mouth of the **Glenelg River**, which flows through **Lower Glenelg National Park**. Note that Nelson uses South Australia's ✍ 08 telephone area code.

🏃 Activities

There's a rugged stretch of coast, but swimming is best suited to its Estuary Beach.

⭐ **Nelson Boat & Canoe Hire**　　BOATING
(✍ 08-8738 4048; www.nelsonboatandcanoehire. com.au) Exploring the 65km stretch of scenic river along Lower Glenelg National Park on a multiday canoe trip or a houseboat is one of Victoria's best hidden secrets. This outfit can rig you up for serious river-camping expeditions – canoe hire costs from $60 a day, or $45 for three days including waterproof barrels. Self-contained houseboats cost $410 for two nights. Also rents motorboats and paddles.

Nelson River Cruises　　CRUISE
(✍ 0448 887 1225, 08-8738 4191; www.glenelgriver-cruises.com.au; cruises adult/child $30/10; ⊙ Sep-Jun) These leisurely 3½-hour cruises head along the Glenelg River, departing Nelson at 1pm several times a week; check website for schedule. The tours include the impressive **Princess Margaret Rose Cave** (✍ 08-8738 4171; www.princessmargaretrosecave.com; adult/child/family $17.50/11.50/40; ⊙ hourly tours 11am to 4.30pm, reduced hours winter), with its gleaming underground formations; tickets for the cave cost extra.

🛏 Sleeping & Eating

There are nine camp sites between Nelson and Dartmoor along the Glenelg River, which are popular with canoeists but are also accessible by road, with ablutions and fireplaces (BYO firewood). Forest Camp South on the river is the nicest of these. Pre-arrange camping permits online.

Nelson Cottage　　COTTAGE $
(✍ 08-8738 4161; www.nelsoncottage.com.au; cnr Kellett & Sturt Sts; d from $90; ☎) This 1848 cottage, once used as a police station, has old-fashioned rooms with clean shared amenities.

Kywong Caravan Park　　CAMPGROUND $
(✍ 08-8738 4174; www.kywongcp.com; North Nelson Rd; unpowered/powered sites $22/27, cabin d from $65) Set 1km north of town, this 25-acre park is next to the national park and Glenelg River, with plenty of wildlife and great birdwatching.

⭐ **Nelson Hotel**　　PUB $$
(✍ 08-8738 4011; www.nelsonhotel.com.au; Kellett St; d/apt incl breakfast from $65/120, mains $17-35; ☎) As real as outback pubs come, the Nelson Hotel (established in 1855) is an essential stop for a beer and friendly yarn with locals. It's got a character-filled front bar and bistro serving hearty meals, and rooms are basic, but comfortable. For more privacy, go the fantastic attached studio.

❶ Information

Nelson Visitors Centre (✍ 08-8738 4051; http://parkweb.vic.gov.au; internet per 30min $2.50; ⊙ 9am-5pm daily summer, Mon, Wed & Thu winter; @) Good info for both sides of the border; has internet access.

❶ Getting There & Away

Nelson is 65km from Portland, and 4km from the South Australian border.

There's no public transport here, so you'll need your own wheels, or you can walk here on the Great South West Walk.

Goldfields & the Grampians

Includes ➡

Ballarat 190
Bendigo 196
Castlemaine 202
Grampians National
Park (Gariwerd) 207
Halls Gap 210
Dunkeld & the
Southern Grampians . . 212
Mt Arapiles
State Park 213
Little Desert
National Park 213

Best Places to Eat

➡ Royal Mail Hotel (p212)

➡ GPO Bar & Grill (p200)

➡ Dispensary
Enoteca (p200)

➡ Empyre Hotel (p204)

➡ Flouch's (p201)

Best Places to Stay

➡ Shamrock Hotel (p199)

➡ Theatre Royal
Back Stage (p203)

➡ D'Altons Resort (p211)

➡ Little Desert
Nature Lodge (p214)

➡ Comfort Inn
Sovereign Hill (p193)

Why Go?

History, nature and culture combine spectacularly in Victoria's regional heart. For a brief time in the mid-19th century, more than a third of the world's gold came out of Victoria and, today, the spoils of all that precious metal can be seen in the grand regional cities of Bendigo and Ballarat, and the charming towns of Castlemaine, Kyneton and Maldon. This is a fantastic region for touring, with a range of contrasting landscapes, from pretty countryside and green forests, red earth and granite country, to farmland, orchards and wineries.

Further west, there's a different type of history to experience at the Grampians National Park, one of Victoria's great natural wonders. Some 80% of Victoria's Aboriginal rock-art sites are found here, and the majestic ranges are an adventurer's paradise, lording it over the idyllic Wartook Valley and the towns of Halls Gap and Dunkeld.

When to Go

Ballarat

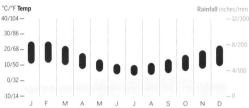

Easter Join the dragon procession at the Bendigo Easter Festival.

Mar–May Autumn colours, hiking and wine touring without the crowds.

Sep–Nov When the wildflowers bloom in Grampians National Park.

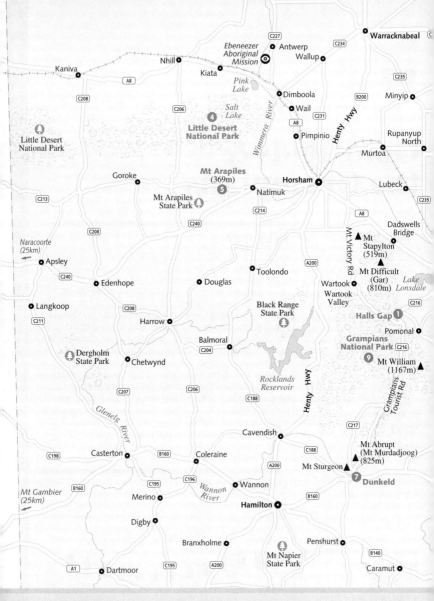

Goldfields & the Grampians Highlights

1 Discover the traditional stories of Gariwerd at **Brambuk Cultural Centre** (p210) in Halls Gap

2 Descend deep into a gold mine then ride the talking tram in **Bendigo** (p196)

3 Ride the restored **steam train** (p202) from Maldon to Castlemaine

4 Camp under the stars in **Little Desert National Park** (p213)

5 Scale the granite heights at **Mt Arapiles** (p213), Victoria's best rock-climbing destination

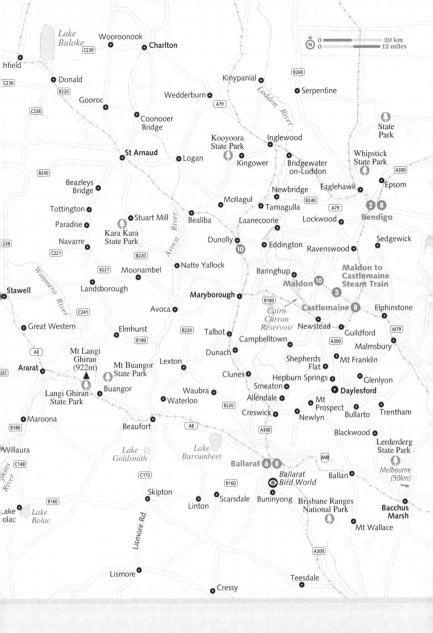

6 Experience the closest thing to a real gold-rush town at Ballarat's **Sovereign Hill** (p190)

7 Climb Mt Sturgeon then dine in style at the Royal Mail Hotel in **Dunkeld** (p212)

8 Admire the artworks at regional **galleries** in Bendigo (p196), Ballarat (p190) and Castlemaine (p202)

9 Set up camp and walk to waterfalls and stunning

lookouts at **Grampians National Park** (p207)

10 Revisit the past along the postcard-pretty main street of **Maldon** (p205)

BALLARAT

POP 85,935

Ballarat was built on gold and it's easy to see the proceeds of those days in the grand Victorian-era architecture around the city centre. The single biggest attraction here is the fabulous, re-created gold-mining village at Sovereign Hill, but there's plenty more in this busy provincial town to keep you occupied: a day spent admiring the architecture, wandering through the superb art gallery or hanging around Lake Wendouree and the botanical gardens is a day well spent. Rug up if you visit in the winter months – Ballarat is renowned for being chilly.

History

The area around here was known to the local indigenous population as 'Ballaarat', meaning 'resting place'. When gold was discovered here in August 1851 – giving irresistible momentum to the central Victorian gold rush that had begun two months earlier in Clunes – thousands of diggers flooded in, forming a shanty town of tents and huts. Ballarat's alluvial goldfields were the tip of the golden iceberg, and when deep shaft mines were sunk they struck incredibly rich quartz reefs. In 1854 the Eureka Rebellion pitted miners against the government and put Ballarat at the forefront of miners' rights. For more on the Eureka Rebellion, see p313.

◉ Sights & Activities

Take the time to walk along **Lydiard St**, one of Australia's finest streetscapes for Victorian-era architecture. Impressive buildings include **Her Majesty's Theatre** (1875), **Craig's Royal Hotel** (1853), **George Hotel** (1854) and the art gallery (1890). The main drag, impressive **Sturt St**, had to be three chains wide (60m) to allow for the turning circle of bullock wagons. The **Gold Monument** (cnr Sturt & Albert Sts) features a replica of the Welcome Nugget.

★ **Sovereign Hill**   HISTORIC VILLAGE
(☑03-5337 1100; www.sovereignhill.com.au; Bradshaw St; adult/student/child/family $47/37.60/21.40/117.50; ⊙10am-5pm) You'll need to set aside at least half a day to visit this fascinating re-creation of an 1860s gold-mining township. The site was mined in the gold-rush era and much of the equipment is original, as is the mine shaft. Kids love panning for gold in the stream, watching the hourly gold pour, and exploring the old-style lolly shop.

The main street here is a living history museum with people performing their chores dressed in costumes of the time. Several places offer food, from pies at the Hope Bakery to a three-course lunch at the United States Hotel. Sovereign Hill opens again at night for the impressive sound-and-light show **Blood on the Southern Cross** (☑03-5337 1199; adult/student/child/family $57/45.60/30.50/154.50, combined with Sovereign Hill ticket $104/83.20/51.90/272.50), a dramatic simulation of the Eureka Stockade battle. There are two shows nightly but times vary so check in advance; bookings are essential.

Your ticket also gets you into the nearby **Gold Museum** (Bradshaw St; adult/child $11.20/5.90; ⊙9.30am-5.30pm), which sits on a mullock heap from an old mine. There are imaginative displays and samples from all the old mining areas, as well as gold nuggets, coins and a display on the Eureka Rebellion.

★ **Art Gallery of Ballarat**   GALLERY
(☑03-5320 5858; www.balgal.com; 40 Lydiard St Nth; ⊙10am-5pm) **FREE** Established in 1884 and moved to its current location in 1890, the Art Gallery of Ballarat is the oldest provincial gallery in Australia. The architectural gem houses a wonderful collection of early colonial paintings, works from noted Australian artists (including Tom Roberts, Sir Sidney Nolan, Russell Drysdale and Fred Williams) and contemporary works. Free iPod tours are available and there are free guided tours at 2pm Wednesday to Sunday.

Lake Wendouree   LAKE
Lake Wendouree, a large artificial lake used for the 1956 Olympics rowing events, is a natural focal point for the town. Old timber boatsheds spread along the shore, and a popular walking and cycling track encircles the lake.

On the western side of the lake, Ballarat's beautiful and serene **botanical gardens** (Wendouree Pde; ⊙sunrise-sunset) **FREE** were first planted in 1858. Stroll through the 40 hectares of immaculately maintained rose gardens, wide lawns and the colourful conservatory. Visit the cottage of poet Adam Lindsay Gordon or walk along Prime Ministers Avenue, a collection of bronze busts of Australia's prime ministers. There's a visitor centre in the glass Robert Clark Conservatory.

A **tourist tramway** (☑03-5334 1580; www.btm.org.au; rides adult/child $4/2; ⊙12.30-5pm Sat & Sun, daily during holidays) operates on a short section of tramline around the lake, departing from the tram museum. Horse-drawn trams started running in the city in 1887, but were later replaced by electric trams, which ran until 1971.

★ Museum of Australian Democracy at Eureka   MUSEUM

(MADE; ☑ 1800 287 113; www.made.org; cnr Eureka & Rodier Sts; adult/child/family $12/8/35; ⊙ 10am-5pm) Standing on the site of the Eureka Rebellion, this fine museum opened in May 2013 and has already established itself as one of Ballarat's top attractions. Taking the Eureka Rebellion as its starting point – pride of place goes to the preserved remnants of the original Eureka flag, and multimedia displays re-create the events of 1854 – the museum then broadens out to discuss democracy in Australia and beyond through a series of interactive exhibits.

If you haven't visited Ballarat for a few years, this could be a good place to start. Either way, a visit here nicely complements the old-world charm of Sovereign Hill.

Ballarat Wildlife Park   ZOO

(☑ 03-5333 5933; www.wildlifepark.com.au; cnr York & Fussell Sts; adult/child/family $25/15/70; ⊙ 9am-5.30pm, tour 11am) Ballarat's tranquil wildlife park is strong on native fauna, from the sweet little King Island wallabies to Tasmanian devils, emus, quokkas, snakes, eagles and crocs. There's a daily guided tour, and weekend programs include a koala show, a wombat show, a snake show and crocodile-feeding.

Ballarat Bird World   WILDLIFE RESERVE

(☑ 03-5341 3843; www.ballaratbirdworld.com.au; 408 Eddy Ave, Mt Helen; adult/child/family $10/6/30; ⊙ 10am-5pm) Forty different types of bird hang out here in peaceful gardens with ponds and waterfalls. Located 10km south of Ballarat.

Kryal Castle   CASTLE

(☑ 03-5334 7388; www.kryalcastle.com.au; 121 Forbes Road, Leigh Creek; adult/child/family $31/19/89; ⊙ 10am-4pm) It may be kitsch but the kids will love a day out at this mock medieval castle and self-styled medieval adventure park. Knights and damsels in distress wander the grounds and there's everything from a Dragon's Labyrinth and Wizard's Workshop to jousting re-enactments and a torture dungeon. You can also sleep overnight in one of the semi-luxurious Castle Suites (rooms $179 to 260).

ⓘ BALLARAT PASS

If you plan on visiting a number of attractions while in Ballarat, the **Ballarat Pass** (☑ 1800 446 633; www.visitballarat.com.au/things-to-do/ballarat-pass; adult 3-/4-day pass $85/93, child $45/51, family $225/252) covers entry to Sovereign Hill, the Museum of Australian Democracy at Eureka, Kryal Castle and Ballarat Wildlife Park. The three-day pass alone will save you around $30 on an adult ticket if you visit all four attractions. The pass can be bought over the phone or at the Ballarat Visitors Centre.

Gold Rush Mini Golf   MINI GOLF

(☑ 03-5334 8150; www.goldrushgolf.com.au; Western Hwy, Warrenheip; 1/2 rounds adult $13/17, child $8/12, family $34/50; ⊙ 10am-7pm Sun-Thu, to 8pm Fri & Sat) If Sovereign Hill doesn't wear the kids out, take them to Gold Rush Mini Golf, with two themed 18-hole courses – naturally the main theme is gold-mining.

Gold Shop   EQUIPMENT HIRE

(☑ 03-5333 4242; www.thegoldshop.com.au; 8a Lydiard St Nth; ⊙ 10am-5pm Mon-Sat) Hopeful prospectors can pick up miners' rights and rent metal detectors at the Gold Shop in the historic Mining Exchange.

☞ Tours

Eerie Tours   TOUR

(☑ 1300 856 668; www.eerietours.com.au; adult/child/family $27.50/17.50/65; ⊙ 8pm or 9pm Wed-Sun) Relive the ghoulish parts of Ballarat's past with a night-time ghost tour or cemetery tour.

★★ Festivals & Events

Organs of the Ballarat Goldfields   MUSIC

(www.ballarat.com/organs; ⊙ mid-Jan) A week of recitals and musical celebrations, held outdoors, in grand cathedrals and churches, in mid-January.

Summer Sundays   MUSIC

(www.ballarat.vic.gov.au; ⊙ Jan) Free music on the foreshore of Lake Wendouree every Sunday in January.

Begonia Festival   STREET FESTIVAL

(www.ballaratbegoniafestival.com; ⊙ Mar) This 100-year-old festival, held over the Labour Day weekend in early March, includes sensational floral displays, a street parade, fireworks, art shows and music.

GOLDFIELDS & THE GRAMPIANS BALLARAT

Ballarat

GOLDFIELDS & THE GRAMPIANS BALLARAT

N

0   0.5 miles
0   1 km

Lake
Wendouree
Wendouree Pde

Tourist Tramway (400m);
Tram Museum (400m);
Botanic Gardens (500m);
Pipers by the Lake (2km)

The Ballarat
Market (700m);
Daylesford (44km)

Gold Rush
Mini Golf (2km);
Kryal Castle (9km);
Melbourne (115km)

Museum of
Australian
Democracy
at Eureka 2

Stawell St Sth

York St

Rodier St

Queen St

Joseph St

Victoria St

Eureka St

Otway St

York St

Humffray St Nth

Mair St

Peel St Nth

BAKERY
HILL

Main Rd

Main Rd 16

Scott Pde

Bridge St
Mall

Ballarat

Sturt St

See Enlargement

Humffray St

Grant St

Clayton St

Main Rd

Wainwright
St

22 6

Bradshaw St

3 Sovereign
Hill

Magpie St

11 12

Ballarat–Buninyong Rd

Buninyong (8km);
Ballarat Bird
World (10km)

Lookout

P

10

Yarrowee River

Humffray St Sth

Dawson St

Raglan St

Errard St

Drummond St

Webster St

Mair St

Mair St

Sturt St

Sturt St

20

Pleasant St

Ripon St

Urquhart St

Eyre St

South St

9

Scott Pde

Enlargement

Art Gallery
of Ballarat

Ballarat

Mair St

Camp St 25

Field St

Grenville St

21 23

Curtis St

Bridge St Mall

Little Bridge St

0   0.1 miles
0   200 m

Lydiard St Nth

1 7

18

13

Sturt St

17

24

8

5

Lydiard St Sth

Armstrong
St Sth

Doveton St Nth

Doveton St Sth

Lydiard St Sth

19

14

15

Dawson St Nth

Doveton St Nth

Ballarat

◉ **Top Sights**
1 Art Gallery of Ballarat B3
2 Museum of Australian
  Democracy at Eureka......................G2
3 Sovereign Hill D4

◉ **Sights**
4 Ballarat Wildlife Park G3
5 Gold Monument B4
6 Gold Museum E4

◔ **Activities, Courses & Tours**
7 Gold Shop B4

◒ **Sleeping**
8 Ansonia on Lydiard B4
9 Ballarat Backpackers Hostel E1
10 Ballarat Goldfields Holiday
   Park...E3
11 Ballarat Sovereign Hill YHA D4
12 Comfort Inn Sovereign Hill D4
13 George Hotel B3
14 Oscar's A4
15 Quest Ballarat A3

◉ **Eating**
16 Catfish D2
17 Craig's Royal Hotel B4
18 The Lane B3
19 L'Espresso A4
20 Olive Grove B1
21 Phoenix Brewery B4
22 Restaurante Da Uday E3

◉ **Drinking & Nightlife**
Haida .... (see 21)
23 Irish Murphy's......................................B4

◉ **Entertainment**
24 Her Majesty's Theatre B4
25 Karova Lounge B3

Ballarat Antique Fair ANTIQUES
(www.ballaratantiquefair.com.au; ☺mid-Mar) Three days in mid-March, with exhibitors and antiques, buyers and sellers from all over Australia. There's a smaller version in October.

Royal South Street Eisteddfod MUSIC
(www.royalsouthstreet.com.au; ☺Sep or Oct) If you lived in Victoria and learnt music as a child, you were probably dragged off to Australia's oldest eisteddfod.

🛏 Sleeping

Ballarat's grand old pubs, B&Bs and cottages all offer gracious accommodation, and there are many motels and holiday resorts.

Ballarat Goldfields Holiday Park CAMPGROUND $
(☏03-5332 7888; www.ballaratgoldfields.com.au; 108 Clayton St; powered sites from $38, cabins $79-150; ❄@☎❄) Close to Sovereign Hill, with a good holiday atmosphere. The cabins are like miners' cottages, and some have three bedrooms.

Ballarat Backpackers Hostel HOSTEL $
(☏0427 440 661; www.ballarat.com/eastern-station/index.htm; 81 Humffray St Nth; s/d/f $40/70/100) In the old Eastern Station Hotel (1862), this refurbished guesthouse is also a decent corner pub with occasional live music. Rooms are simple but fresh and good value.

Ballarat Sovereign Hill YHA HOSTEL $
(☏03-5337 1159; www3.yha.com.au/hostels/vic/regional-victoria/ballarat-sovereign-hill; Magpie St; s/d $43/63) This cute but simple and compact YHA cottage has just four rooms around a central kitchen/dining area, as well as dormitory-style bunkhouse accommodation for groups or families.

★**Oscar's** BOUTIQUE HOTEL $$
(☏03-5331 1451; www.oscarshotel.com.au; 18 Doveton St; d $150-200, spa $225; ❄☎) The 13 rooms of this attractive art deco hotel have been tastefully refurbished to include double showers and spas (watch TV from your spa).

★**Comfort Inn Sovereign Hill** HISTORIC HOTEL $$
(☏03-5337 1159; www.sovereignhill.com.au/comfort-inn-sovereign-hill; 39-41 Magpie St; r $170-190; ❄☎) Formerly known as Sovereign Hill Lodge, this excellent place has bright, modern rooms that are located a stone's throw from Sovereign Hill itself. Ask about the accommodation-and-entertainment packages. The 'Night in the Museum' package (singles/doubles $410/670) lets you stay in the Steinfeld's building at the top of Main St within Sovereign Hill, where you'll be served by staff in period dress.

Ansonia on Lydiard B&B $$
(☏03-5332 4678; www.theansoniaonlydiard.com.au; 32 Lydiard St Sth; r $125-204; ❄☎) One of Lydiard St's great hotels, the Ansonia exudes calm with its minimalist design, polished floors, dark-wood furnishings and light-filled atrium. Stylish rooms have large-screen TVs and range from studio apartments for two to family suites.

George Hotel
HOTEL **$$**

(☑ 03-5333 4866; www.georgehotelballarat.com. au; 27 Lydiard St Nth; d/f/ste from $150/195/220; ✳ ☎) This grand old pub has seen bags of history since it was first built in 1852. It's right in the thick of things and the recently refurbished rooms are tasteful and comfortable, and there is a good bar and restaurant. If you're thinking of staying here on a weekend, though, remember that the nightclub below is open till 5am.

Quest Ballarat
APARTMENT **$$**

(www.questapartments.com.au; 7-11 Dawson St Nth; studio from $159, 1-/2-bed apt from $175/275; ✳ ☎) A world (and walking distance) away from Ballarat's gold-mining heritage, these ultra-modern, large apartments feature exemplary service, as you'd expect from a place that attracts a lot of midweek business traffic. Highly recommended.

✗ Eating

L'Espresso
ITALIAN **$**

(☑ 03-5333 1789; 417 Sturt St; mains $11-20; ☺ 7.30am-6pm Sun-Thu, to 11pm Fri & Sat) A mainstay on Ballarat's cafe scene, this trendy Italian-style place doubles as a record shop – choose from the whopping jazz, blues and world-music selection while you wait for your espresso or Tuscan bean soup. Fabulous risotto.

★ The Lane
CAFE, PIZZERIA **$$**

(☑ 03-5333 4866; 27 Lydiard St Nth; pizza $16-22, mains $23-39; ☺ 7am-late) The laneway running beside the George Hotel buzzes with all-day diners. At the front is a bright cafe with breakfast, light meals and a bar; at the back is a great little pizzeria which doubles as an à la carte restaurant in the evenings.

Olive Grove
DELI, CAFE **$$**

(☑ 03-5331 4455; 1303 Sturt St; mains $12-24; ☺ 8am-4pm; ☎) The Olive Grove buzzes with locals lingering over coffee, gourmet baguettes or bagels, or browsing the deli delights of cakes, cold meats and cheeses.

Restaurante Da Uday
INTERNATIONAL **$$**

(☑ 03-5331 6655; www.dauday.com; 7 Wainwright St; mains $18-28, pizza $10-18; ☺ noon-2pm & 5.30pm-late Tue-Sun; ☎) This pretty converted cottage near Sovereign Hill has a lovely atmosphere and the intoxicating aromas of authentic Indian, Thai and (oddly enough) Italian. It's curry meets pizza, with plenty of vegetarian choices and takeaway available.

Pipers by the Lake
CAFE **$$**

(☑ 03-5334 1811; www.pipersbythelake.com.au; 403 Wendouree Pde; lunch mains $18-32, dinner mains $27-32; ☺ 9am-4pm Sat-Thu, 9am-4pm & 6-10pm Fri) The 1890 Lakeside Lodge was designed by WH Piper and today it's a lovely light-filled cafe with huge windows looking out over the lake and an alfresco courtyard. Dishes range from lentil burgers or beetroot risotto to pork chops with mango and coriander sauce.

Catfish
THAI **$$**

(☑ 03-5327 2787; www.catfishthai.com.au; 42-44 Main Rd; ☺ Tue-Sat 6pm-late) Catfish is the brand-new kitchen of chef Damien Jones, who made the Lydiard Wine Bar such a treasured local secret. Thai cooking classes only add to what is an increasingly popular package.

VICTORIA'S GOLD RUSH

When gold was discovered in New South Wales in May 1851, a reward was offered to anyone who could find gold within 300km of Melbourne, amid fears that Victoria would be left behind. They needn't have worried. By June, a significant discovery was made at Clunes, 32km north of Ballarat, and prospectors flooded into central Victoria.

Over the next few months, fresh gold finds were made almost weekly around Victoria. Then in September 1851 the greatest gold discovery ever known was made at Moliagul, followed by others at Ballarat, Bendigo, Mt Alexander and many more places. By the end of 1851 hopeful miners were coming from England, Ireland, Europe, China and the failing goldfields of California across the Pacific.

While the gold rush had its tragic side (including epidemics that swept through the camps), plus its share of rogues (including bushrangers who attacked the gold shipments), it ushered in a fantastic era of growth and prosperity for Victoria. Within 12 years, the population had increased from 77,000 to 540,000. Mining companies invested heavily in the region, the development of roads and railways accelerated, and huge shanty towns were replaced by Victoria's modern provincial cities, most notably Ballarat, Bendigo and Castlemaine, which reached the height of their splendour in the 1880s.

Craig's Royal Hotel   MODERN AUSTRALIAN $$$

(☏ 03-5331 1377; www.craigsroyal.com.au; 10 Lydiard St Sth; mains $20-42; ☺ 7am-10pm) Even if you can't afford to stay here, you can experience some royal treatment with a cocktail in historic Craig's Bar, or a coffee in Craig's Cafe & Larder. For fine dining, the Gallery Bistro is a sumptuous atrium dining room serving European-inspired cuisine.

Phoenix Brewery   MODERN AUSTRALIAN $$$

(☏ 03-5333 2686; 10 Camp St; 2-/3-course set menu $68/88; ☺ 5-10pm Mon, 11am-10pm Tue-Sat) Although this isn't really a brewery, it might as well be with 19 beers to choose from. But it's the food that really wins plaudits, with dishes such as cheese soufflé and crispy-skinned snapper fillet in a lavender-infused broth.

🍷 Drinking & Entertainment

With its large student population, Ballarat has a lively nightlife. There are some fine old pubs around town but most of the entertainment is centred on Lydiard St and the nearby Camp St precinct.

Irish Murphy's   PUB

(☏ 03-5331 4091; www.murphysballarat.com.au; 36 Sturt St; mains $18-30; ☺ 11am-11pm Mon-Tue, to 3am Wed-Sun) The Guinness flows freely at this atmospheric Irish pub. It's a welcoming place and the live music draws people of all ages. There's nothing too sophisticated about it all, but it's a formula that works.

Haida   LOUNGE

(☏ 03-5331 5346; www.haidabar.com; 12 Camp St; ☺ 5pm-late Wed-Sun) Haida is a loungy two-level bar where you can relax with a cocktail by the open fire or chill out to DJs and live music downstairs.

Karova Lounge   LIVE MUSIC

(☏ 03-5332 9122; www.karovalounge.com; cnr Field & Camp Sts; ☺ 9pm-late Wed-Sat) Ballarat's best original live-music venue showcases local and touring bands in a grungy, industrial style.

Her Majesty's Theatre   THEATRE

(☏ 03-5333 5888; www.hermaj.com; 17 Lydiard St Sth) Ballarat's main venue for the performing arts since 1875, 'Her Maj' is in a wonderful Victorian-era building and features theatre, live music, comedy and local productions. Check the website for a calendar of shows.

🛍 Shopping

Ballarat's shopping strip is Sturt St and the streets running off it. At the Ballarat Show-

WORTH A TRIP

CLUNES

It was in Clunes, roughly halfway between Maryborough and Ballarat, that a find in June 1851 sparked the gold rush that would transform Victoria's fortunes. These days, the small town (population 1373) is a quintessential gold-mining relic, with gorgeous 19th-century porticoed buildings whose grandeur seems way out of proportion to the town's current size.

But Clunes has another, more modern claim to fame. The town hosts the annual **Booktown Book Fair** in early May and is home to no fewer than (at last count) seven bookstores, most of which are a bibliophile's delight, with a focus on the second-hand trade.

For more information on the town, visit the **Clunes Visitor Centre** (☏ 03-5345 3896; www.visitclunes.com.au; Bailey St; ☺ 10am-4pm Sat & Sun), or check out its website.

grounds there's a fine Sunday **market** (Creswick Rd; ☺ 8am-1pm Sun).

Mill Markets   MARKET

(☏ 03-5334 7877; www.millmarkets.com.au; 9367 Western Hwy; ☺ 10am-6pm) A little sister of the popular Mill Market at Daylesford, this huge collection of antiques, retro furnishings and knick-knacks is in the old woolsheds.

① Information

Ballarat Visitors Centre (☏ 03-5320 5741, 1800 446 633; www.visitballarat.com.au; 43 Lydiard St; ☺ 9am-5pm) Opposite the art gallery.

① Getting There & Away

Greyhound Australia (☏ 1300 473 946; www.greyhound.com.au) buses between Adelaide and Melbourne stop in Ballarat (to Melbourne $28, two hours) if you ask the driver (departs Adelaide 8.15pm, $84, 8¾ hours). **Airport Shuttle Bus** (☏ 03-5333 4181; www.airportshuttlebus.com.au) goes direct from Melbourne Airport to Ballarat train station (adult/child $32/17, 1½ hours, nine daily, seven on weekends).

V/Line (☏ 1800 800 007; www.vline.com.au) has frequent direct trains between Melbourne (Southern Cross Station) and Ballarat (from $12.80, 1½ hours, 18 daily) and at least three services via Geelong.

GOLDFIELDS & THE GRAMPIANS BALLARAT

BENDIGO

POP 82,800

You don't have to look far to find evidence of Bendigo's heritage, whether in the magnificent Shamrock Hotel, the Central Deborah Goldmine or the Chinese dragons that awaken for the Easter Festival. At the same time, modern-day Bendigo is a prosperous, upbeat and thoroughly enjoyable regional city with one of the best regional art galleries in Australia, plenty of family attractions and some great wineries in the surrounding district. It's also a place with star potential where things seem to be moving – watch this space.

History

The fantastically rich Bendigo Diggings covered more than 360 sq km after gold was discovered in nearby Ravenswood in 1851, and later Bendigo Creek. It is said the maids at the Shamrock Hotel mopped the floor every night to collect the gold dust brought in on the drinkers' boots. The arrival of thousands of Chinese miners in 1854 had a lasting effect on the town, despite the racial tensions that surfaced.

In the 1860s the scene changed again as independent miners were outclassed by the powerful mining companies with their heavy machinery. The companies poured money into the town and some 35 quartz reefs were found. The ground underneath Bendigo is still honeycombed with mine shafts, and the gold is still around – Bendigo Mining successfully resumed operations at the Kangaroo Flat mine in 2008.

◉ Sights

The city's impressive buildings are first seen in Pall Mall as a splendid trio: the Shamrock Hotel (p199), **Law Courts** and **former Post Office**, which is now the visitor centre. Take a look inside all three – the interiors are just as elaborate as the exteriors. **View St** is a historic streetscape with some fine buildings, including the **Capital**, which houses the Bendigo Art Gallery, and **Dudley House**, classified by the National Trust.

If you plan on seeing the main sights, the **Bendigo Experience Pass** (adult/child/family $50/26.50/128) is good value. Ask at the visitor centre.

★ **Central Deborah Goldmine**   HISTORIC SITE
(☑03-5443   8322;   www.central-deborah.com; 76 Violet St; adult/child/family mine experience $28.50/15/78.50; ◎9.30am-5pm) For a very

deep experience, descend into this 500m-deep mine with a geologist. The mine has been worked on 17 levels, and about 1000kg of gold has been removed. After donning hard hats and lights, you're taken down the shaft to inspect the operations, complete with drilling demonstrations. There are five tours on weekdays and six on weekends and they last about 75 minutes. Other tours include the 2½-hour Underground Adventure ($75/45/190), or, for the claustrophobes, a self-guided surface tour ($14/7/35).

★ **Bendigo Talking Tram**   TRAM
(☑03-5442   2821;   www.bendigotramways.com; adult/child/family $16/10/47, valid 2 days; ◎10am-5pm) For an interesting tour of the city, hop aboard one of the restored vintage 'talking' trams. The hop-on hop-off trip runs from the Central Deborah Goldmine to the **Tramways Museum** (1 Tramways Rd; admission free with tram ticket; ◎10am-5pm) every half-hour, making half-a-dozen stops, including at the Golden Dragon Museum and Lake Weeroona.

★ **Golden Dragon
Museum & Gardens**   MUSEUM
(☑03-5441   5044;   www.goldendragonmuseum. org; 1-11 Bridge St; adult/child/family $11/6/28; ◎9.30am-5pm) Bendigo's obvious Chinese heritage sets it apart from other goldfields towns, and this fantastic museum and garden is the place to experience it. Walk through a huge wooden door into an awesome chamber filled with dragons, including the imperial dragons Old Loong (the oldest in the world) and Sun Loong (the longest in the world at over 100m).

Old Loong arrived in 1892 to feature in the Easter procession. Sun Loong took over in 1970 when Old Loong retired, and it comes out each year to lead the Easter parade. The museum also displays amazing Chinese heritage items and costumes. Outside, the Yin Yuan (Garden of Joy) classical Chinese gardens are a tranquil little haven with bridges, water features and ornamental shrubs. The tearoom serves simple, Chinese-style dishes. The area outside the museum has been redeveloped as the Dai Gum San Chinese precinct, complete with a large lotus flower.

Joss House Temple   TEMPLE
(☑03-5443   8255;   www.bendigojosshouse.com; Finn St; adult/child/family $5.50/3.50/11; ◎11am-4pm) Painted red, the traditional colour for strength, this is the only remaining practising joss house in central Victoria. It's 2km northwest of the centre.

Bendigo

Bendigo

◎ Top Sights
1 Bendigo Art Gallery B2
2 Bendigo Talking Tram A4
3 Central Deborah Goldmine A4
4 Golden Dragon Museum &
   Gardens C1

◎ Sights
5 Discovery Science & Technology
   Centre.. C4
6 Dudley House B2
7 Former Post Office C2
8 Law Courts C2
9 Rosalind Park B2
10 Sacred Heart Cathedral A3
11 Tramways Museum D1

◉ Sleeping
12 Allawah Bendigo B2
13 Bendigo Backpackers B3

14 Bendigo Holiday Accommodation B3
15 City Centre Motel B2
16 Quest Bendigo D1
17 Shamrock Hotel.. C2

✸ Eating
18 Dispensary Enoteca C2
19 Gillies Bendigo Original Pie Shop C2
20 GPO Bar & Grill C2
21 Mason's of Bendigo................................. C3
22 Piyawat Thai C3
23 Toi Shan C3
24 Whirrakee Restaurant & Wine Bar B2
   Wine Bank.......................................(see 12)

◉ Drinking & Nightlife
25 Metro & Puggs Irish Bar C2

◉ Entertainment
26 Capital.. B2

★ Bendigo Art Gallery GALLERY

(☑ 03-5434 6088; www.bendigoartgallery.com.au; 42 View St; admission by donation; ☺ 10am-5pm, tours 2pm) One of Victoria's finest regional galleries, the permanent collection here includes outstanding colonial and contemporary Australian art, such as work by Charles Blackman, Fred Williams, Rupert Bunny and Lloyd Rees; the annual temporary exhibitions are cutting edge. The Gallery Café overlooks Rosalind Park and is a good spot for coffee or a light lunch.

Sacred Heart Cathedral CHURCH

(cnr Wattle & High Sts) You can't miss the soaring steeple of this magnificent cathedral. Construction began in the 19th century and was only completed in 2001 with the installation of bells from Italy in the belfry. Inside, beneath the high vaulted ceiling, there's a magnificently carved bishop's chair, some beautiful stained-glass windows, and wooden angels jutting out of the ceiling arches.

Lake Weeroona LAKE

(cnr Nolan & Napier Sts) Bendigo's little lake is a favourite spot for boating, kayaking or just walking around the path that encircles it. There are barbecue and picnic areas, toilets, a children's adventure playground on the eastern side and the Boardwalk Restaurant at the southern end.

Parks & Gardens GARDENS

Right in the city centre, **Rosalind Park** is a lovely green space, with lawns, big old trees, fernery and the fabulous **Cascades Fountain**, which was excavated after being buried for 120 years. Climb to the top of the lookout tower for sensational 360-degree views or, if you love roses, wander through the **Conservatory Gardens**.

The **White Hills Botanic Gardens**, 2km north of town, features many exotic and rare plant species, a small fauna park, aviary and barbecue facilities.

Bendigo Pottery POTTERY

(☑ 03-5448 4404; www.bendigopottery.com.au; 146 Midland Hwy; ☺ 9am-5pm) FREE Australia's oldest pottery works, the Bendigo Pottery was founded in 1857 and is classified by the National Trust. The historic kilns are still used; watch potters at work, admire the gorgeous ceramic pieces or throw a pot yourself (half-/full day $15/30). The attached museum (adult/child $8/4) tells the story of pottery through the ages. It's just over 4km north of the town centre.

O'Keefe Rail Trail HIKING, CYCLING

(www.railtrails.org.au) This hike-or-bike trail, along a disused railway line, starts at Lake Weeroona and meanders for 23km to Axedale.

BENDIGO FOR KIDS

Bendigo has lots of parks, gardens and activities to keep kids happy.

About 4km north of the town centre is the **Ironbark Complex** (Watson St), with three major activities: **Ironbark Riding Centre** (☑ 03-5436 1565; www.bwc.com.au/ironbark; 1hr/2hr rides $40/70; ☺ 8.30am-5pm Mon-Sat) offers trail rides, riding lessons and the Great Australian Pub Ride to Allies Hotel in Myers Flat (with lunch $100); **Bendigo Gold World** (☑ 03-5448 4140; www.bendigogold.com.au; half-/full-day tours $280/380; ☺ 8.30am-5pm Mon-Sat) has fossicking and detecting tours in the bush with metal detectors, plus gold panning – with guaranteed gold! – at the mobile gold-panning centre ($12 per hour); and **Bendigo Water World** (☑ 03-5448 4140; www.bendigowaterworld.com.au; admission $3, with unlimited rides $21; ☺ 4-7pm Mon-Wed, noon-8pm Thu & Fri, 10.30am-8pm Sat, 10.30am-6pm Sun), where the 'Big Bendi' waterslide zaps you into a pool.

Discovery Science & Technology Centre (☑ 03-5444 4400; www.discovery.asn.au; 7 Railway Pl; adult/child/family $12.50/9.50/39.50; ☺ 10am-4pm), in an old railway goods shed, has a wide range of interesting and educational exhibits, including a planetarium, science lab and kaleidoscope.

A complete kids' entertainment complex, the **Zone** (www.thezone.net.au; 1 Gildea Lane; admission from $20; ☺ 3.30-8pm Mon-Thu, noon-10pm Fri, 10am-10pm Sat, 10am-8pm Sun), has a playground, mini golf, go-karting and paintball.

Confectionery Capers (☑ 0458 650 003, 03-5449 3111; www.confectionerycapers.com; 1028 McIvor Hwy, Junortoun; adult/child/family $8/5/20; ☺ 10am-5pm Mon-Sat, 1-5pm Sun), 8km southeast of town, is an amazing display of whirls, whizzes, word plays and oddball machines: Barbie dolls in a line? A tree in a toilet? You have to go there for it all to make sense...

✷ Festivals & Events

Easter Festival
CARNIVAL

Bendigo's major festival (⊙Mar or Apr) attracts thousands with its carnival atmosphere and colourful and noisy procession of Chinese dragons, led by Sun Loong, the world's longest imperial dragon.

Bendigo Cup
HORSE RACING

(⊙Oct-Nov) Part of the Spring Racing Carnival.

Swap Meet
VINTAGE CARS

(www.bendigoswap.com.au; ⊙Nov) For enthusiasts in search of that elusive vintage-car spare part. It's so popular that accommodation is at a premium.

🛏 Sleeping

Several accommodation services offer lovely maisonettes, townhouses, suites and apartments in the heart of the city, including **Abode Bendigo** (☎03-5442 5855; www.abode-bendigo.com.au), **Allawah Bendigo** (☎03-5441 7003; www.allawahbendigo.com; 45 View St) and **Bendigo Holiday Accommodation** (☎03-5443 7870; www.bendigoholidayaccommodation.com; 20 High St).

Bendigo Backpackers
HOSTEL $

(☎03-5443 7680; www.bendigobackpackers.com.au; 33 Creek St Sth; dm/d/f $30/70/100; ❄) This small, homey hostel is in a weatherboard cottage in a great central location. It has bright cheery rooms with all the usual amenities, as well as bike hire.

Central City Caravan Park
CAMPGROUND $

(☎03-5443 6937, 1800 500 475; www.centralcitycaravanpark.com.au; 362 High St, Golden Sq; unpowered/powered sites from $30/36, cabins $79-185; ❄⛱) The closest caravan park to the city centre has shady sites, a camp kitchen and en suite cabins.

★ Shamrock Hotel
HOTEL $$

(☎03-5443 0333; www.hotelshamrock.com.au; cnr Pall Mall & Williamson St; d $140-195, ste $245) One of Bendigo's historic icons, the Shamrock is a stunning Victorian building with stained glass, original paintings, fancy columns and a *Gone with the Wind*–style staircase. The refurbished upstairs rooms range from small standard rooms to spacious deluxe and spa suites.

City Centre Motel
MOTEL $$

(☎03-5443 2077; www.citycentremotel.com.au; 26 Forest St; s/d from $80/115, weekends d $130; ☎) One of Bendigo's most central motels –

a block from the art gallery. The cheaper rooms here are a little dated but very good value.

Quest Bendigo
APARTMENT $$

(☎03-5410 1300; www.questapartments.com.au; 228 McCrae St; studio $140, 1-/2-bed apt $158/240; ❄☎) The Bendigo outpost of this excellent chain offers stylish, spacious and modern serviced apartments close to the city centre.

Lakeview Resort
MOTEL $$

(☎03-5445 5300; www.lakeviewresort.com.au; 286 Napier St; d/f incl breakfast $150/200; ❄☎⛱) You've got Lake Weeroona across the road, spacious units around the central courtyard, shaded pool, piazza, and Quills, a fine-dining restaurant with a great reputation.

✗ Eating

Gillies Bendigo Original Pie Shop
BAKERY $

(Hargreaves St Mall; pies from $4.50; ⊙9am-5.30pm Sat-Thu, to 7pm Fri) The pie window on the corner of the mall here is a Bendigo institution, and the pies are as good as you'll find.

Piyawat Thai
THAI $

(☎03-5444 4450; 136 Mollison St; mains $12-18; ⊙6-11pm Tue-Sun; ✗) Tucked away in a cosy house a couple of blocks south of the centre, this authentic Thai restaurant serves fabulously fragrant curries, noodles and Thai stir-fries at affordable prices.

Toi Shan
CHINESE $

(☎03-5443 5811; 67 Mitchell St; mains $12-19, buffet $13-17; ⊙noon-2.30pm & 5-10pm) Cheap and cheerful Chinese: Toi Shan has been around since the gold rush and you can fill up on the lunchtime smorgasbord.

★ **Dispensary Enoteca**   MODERN AUSTRALIAN **$$**
(☑ 03-5444 5885; www.thedispensaryenoteca.com;
9 Chancery Lane; mains $18-35; ☺11.30am-late
Tue-Sat, 11.30am-3pm Sun & Mon) Local produce,
a hip eating space and a talented chef make
this one of regional Victoria's more creative
restaurants. The chestnut croquettes are a
fine prelude to the cinnamon-cured duck
breast. The abundance of beer bottles and
the laneway location add to the sense of a
designer eating (and, later, drinking) den for
people in the know.

★ **GPO Bar & Grill**   MEDITERRANEAN **$$**
(☑ 03-5443 4343; www.gpobendigo.com.au; 60-64
Pall Mall; tapas $3.50-14, lunch mains $14-25, dinner
mains $22-32; ☺11am-late; 🛜) The food and at-
mosphere here is superb and rated highly by
locals. Confit pork belly and roasted kingfish
grace the Mediterranean menu, or go for
the innovative pizza, pasta or tapas plates.
The bar is a chilled place for a drink from
the impressive wine and cocktail list.

Mason's of Bendigo   MODERN AUSTRALIAN **$$**
(☑ 03-5443 3877; www.masonsofbendigo.com.au;
25 Queen St; mains $14-34; ☺8.30am-9.30pm
Tue-Sat) Casual yet sophisticated, dominated
by local produce yet influenced by cooking
techniques from around the world, Mason's
is an agreeable mix of fine food and a great
atmosphere at any time of the day. Dishes
might include beetroot gnocchi, roasted
goat shoulder or quail and pistachio-nut
terrine. Great beer list, too.

Wine Bank   TAPAS **$$**
(☑ 03-5444 4655; www.winebankonview.com; 45
View St; mains $14-38; ☺7.30am-11pm Mon-Thu,
7.30am-1am Fri, 8.30am-1am Sat, 8.30am-4pm Sun)
Wine bottles line the walls in this former
bank building, which serves as a wine shop
and bar specialising in central Victorian
wines, and an atmospheric Italian-style cafe
serving tapas and platters.

Boardwalk   CAFE **$$**
(☑ 03-5443 9855; www.theboardwalkbendigo.com.
au; Nolan St; mains $16-30; ☺7.30am-4.30pm
Mon-Fri, 8am-4.30pm Sat & Sun) The location
on the edge of Lake Weeroona is the big tick
here – full-length windows and an alfresco
deck offer prime views of waterbirds and
rowers. Good for coffee or a lazy lunch.

Whirrakee
Restaurant & Wine Bar   FRENCH **$$$**
(☑ 03-5441 5557; www.whirrakeerestaurant.com.
au; 17 View St; lunch 2-/3-courses $30/45, dinner

mains $32; ☺ 6.30-9.30pm Mon, noon-3pm & 6.30-
9.30pm Tue-Sun Tue-Sun) In another of Bendigo's historic buildings (the 1908 Royal Bank),
Whirrakee has a French-influenced menu
featuring dishes such as gorgonzola souffle,
with some surprises such as spiced kangaroo
salad. Downstairs there's a small wine bar
with cosy sofas, and there's live music in the
gold-weighing room on Friday night.

Bendigo Ninesevensix   TRAM RESTAURANT **$$$**
(☑ 03-5444 4655; www.bendigoninesevensix.com.
au; set menu $98; ☺7pm-late Sat) Every Satur-
day night a 1952 Melbourne W-class tram be-
comes a rolling restaurant, with a set menu
including four courses and free drinks –
a great way to see the city.

🍷 **Drinking & Entertainment**

Bendigo has a lively nightlife – uni nights
are Tuesday and Thursday. Although some
clubs remain open as late as 5am, all have a
2am lockout. The main nightlife zone is Bull
St and along Pall Mall. Many restaurants, in-
cluding Wine Bank, the Dispensary Enoteca
and Whirrakee, segue easily into classy wine
bars after the kitchen closes.

Metro & Puggs Irish Bar   PUB
(☑ 03-5443 4916; 224 Hargreaves St; ☺10.30am-
late Mon-Sat) With Guinness (and many other
beers) on tap, Puggs has a thickly welcoming
atmosphere, not unreasonable door staff, a
beer garden and live music every Thursday,
Friday and Saturday night till 3am.

Capital   THEATRE
(☑ 03-5434 6100; www.bendigo.vic.gov.au; 50 View
St) The beautifully restored Capital theatre
is the main venue for the performing arts,
with hundreds of performances and exhibi-
tions each year.

ℹ️ **Information**

Bendigo Visitors Centre (☑ 03-5434 6060,
1800 813 153; www.bendigotourism.com; 51-67
Pall Mall; ☺9am-5pm) In the historic former
post office; offers an accommodation booking
service and the Post Office Gallery.

ℹ️ **Getting There & Away**

Bendigo Airport Service (☑ 03-5444 3939;
www.bendigoairportservice.com.au) runs direct
between Melbourne Airport and Bendigo train
station (one-way/return adult $42/78, child
$20/40, two hours, four daily). Bookings
essential.

V/Line ([phone]13 61 96; www.vline.com.au) has frequent trains between Melbourne (Southern Cross Station) and Bendigo (from $19.40, two hours, 12 to 18 daily) via Kyneton and Castlemaine.

GOLDFIELDS TOWNS

As splendid as Ballarat and Bendigo are, to really appreciate this part of the world you need to get out and explore the country towns and former gold-mining relics that make up central Victoria. Touring the likes of Castlemaine, Kyneton, Maldon and Maryborough – and the tiny communities in between – will give you a good understanding of the incredible growth and inevitable decline of the gold towns, but you'll also pass through gorgeous countryside and an increasingly flourishing (and trendy) wine and food region. Head north of Melbourne along the Calder Hwy (M79 and A79) to start the journey.

Kyneton

POP 4460

Kyneton, established a year before gold was discovered, was the main coach stop between Melbourne and Bendigo, and the centre for the farmers who supplied the diggings with fresh produce. Today Piper St is a historic precinct lined with bluestone buildings that have been transformed into cafes, antique shops, museums and restaurants.

Sights & Activities

Kyneton Historical Museum   MUSEUM
([phone]03-5422 1228; 67 Piper St; adult/child $3/1; [clock]11am-4pm Fri-Sun) The old bank building (1855) is now Kyneton Historical Museum, housing a display of local history items – the upper floor is furnished in period style.

Botanic Gardens   GARDENS
(Clowes St) It's worth a walk to the Botanic Gardens, established by Baron Ferdinand von Mueller in the 1860s, beside the Campaspe River.

Festivals & Events

Kyneton Daffodil & Arts Festival   FLOWERS
(www.kynetondaffodilarts.org.au; [clock]Sep) Kyneton is renowned for its daffodils. The annual Kyneton Daffodil & Arts Festival is held each September, with 10 days of gala evenings, markets, concerts, fairs, and art and flower shows.

Budburst   FOOD, WINE
([phone]1800 244 711; www.macedonrangeswine.com.au/budburst-festival/; [clock]mid-Nov) Budburst is a wine and food festival hosted over several days at wineries throughout the Macedon Ranges region.

Eating

Kyneton's eat street is historic Piper St, with a fabulous cafe and restaurant scene.

Dhaba at the Mill   INDIAN $
([phone]03-5422 6225; www.dhaba.com.au; 18 Piper St; mains $10-14; [clock]6-9pm Thu-Sat, noon-2.30pm & 5-9pm Sun; [icon]) Behind the heavy wooden doors at the old bluestone steam mill you can tuck into authentic, affordable curries – classics such as butter chicken, palak paneer and lamb vindaloo.

★ Flouch's   AUSTRALIAN $$
([phone]03-5422 3683; www.flouchs.com.au; 12-14 Piper St; mains $17-36; [clock]11am-3pm Wed-Fri, 6pm-late Sat, 10am-3pm Sun) Celebrated chef Michael Flouch presides over perfectly prepared contemporary dishes; the focus is on updated classic tastes without too many frilly elaborations. Try the French-style potato gnocchi with blue-cheese sauce and roasted pear, or the more traditional chargrilled eye fillet steak.

Mr Carsisi   MIDDLE EASTERN $$
([phone]03-5422 3769; www.mrcarsisi.com; 37c Piper St; mains $14-35; [clock]11.30am-late Fri-Tue) Turkish tastes and Middle Eastern mezze dominate this well-regarded place, which does a faultless job of combining foreign flavours with local produce – the honey-and-cardamom Milawa duck breast is typical of the genre.

Royal George   MODERN AUSTRALIAN $$
([phone]03-5422 1390; www.royalgeorge.com.au; 24 Piper St; mains $27-38; [clock]6pm-late Wed, noon-3pm & 6pm-late Thu-Sat, noon-3pm Sun) The historic Royal George hotel has been transformed into a glamorous one-hat restaurant and makes for a sublime fine-dining experience.

Information

Kyneton Visitor Centre ([phone]1800 244 711, 03-5422 6110; www.visitmacedonranges.com; 127 High St; [clock]9am-5pm) On the southeastern entry to town. Ask for the brochures *Town Walks*, *Self Drive Tour* and *Campaspe River Walk*.

Getting There & Away

Kyneton is just off the Calder Hwy about 90km northwest of Melbourne. Regular V/Line trains

GOLDFIELDS & THE GRAMPIANS KYNETON

on the Bendigo line run here from Melbourne (from $10.40, 1¼ hours). The train station is 1km south of the town centre.

Castlemaine

POP 9130

At the heart of the central Victorian goldfields, Castlemaine is a rewarding working-class town where a growing community of artists and tree-changers live amid some inspiring architecture and gardens.

History

After gold was discovered at Specimen Gully in 1851, the Mt Alexander Diggings attracted some 30,000 diggers and Castlemaine became the thriving marketplace for the goldfields. The town's importance waned as the surface gold was exhausted by the 1860s but, fortunately, the centre of town was well established by then and remains relatively intact.

Even after the gold rush subsided, Castlemaine has always had a reputation for industry and innovation – this was the birthplace of the Castlemaine XXXX beer-brewing company (now based in Queensland) and Castlemaine Rock, a hard-boiled sweet lovingly produced by the Barnes family since 1853. It's also the 'Street Rod Centre of Australia', where hot rods have been built and shown off since 1962.

◉ Sights & Activities

Castlemaine has a number of interesting historic buildings, including the Roman basilica facade of the old **Castlemaine Market** (1862) on Mostyn St; the Theatre Royal (1856; p204) on Hargreaves St; the **post office** (1894); and the original **courthouse building** (1851) on Goldsmith Cres. For a good view over town, head up to the **Burke & Wills Monument** on Wills St (follow Lyttleton St east of the centre). Robert O'Hara Burke was a police superintendent in Castlemaine before his fateful trek.

★ **Castlemaine Art Gallery & Historical Museum**   GALLERY, MUSEUM
(☑ 03-5472 2292; www.castlemainegallery.com; 14 Lyttleton St; adult/student/child $4/2/free; ◎ 10am-5pm Mon-Fri, noon-5pm Sat & Sun) A superb art deco building houses this gallery, which features colonial and contemporary Australian art, including work by well-known Australian artists such as Frederick McCubbin and Russell Drysdale. The museum, in the basement, provides an insight into local history, with costumes, china and gold-mining relics.

Buda   MUSEUM
(☑ 03-5472 1032; www.budacastlemaine.org; 42 Hunter St; adult/child/family $11/5/26; ◎ noon-5pm Wed-Sat, 10am-5pm Sun) Home to a Hungarian silversmith and his family for 120 years, Buda has permanent displays of the family's extensive art and craft collections, furnishings and personal belongings. There's an interesting mix of architectural styles: the original Indian-villa influence, and later Edwardian-style extensions dating from 1861.

Castlemaine Botanic Gardens   GARDENS
These majestic gardens, some of the oldest in Victoria (established 1860), strike a perfect balance between sculpture and wild bush among beautiful National Trust–registered trees and the artificial Lake Joanna.

Hadfield's Rod Museum   MUSEUM
(☑ 0428 122 206, 03-5472 3868; www.rodshop.com.au; Pyrenees Hwy; adult/child $5/free) If you're into hot rods and custom cars, take a trip out to the shop about 7km east of town in Chewton. The big green shed contains around 20 custom-built vehicles and drag racers. Call ahead to check it's open.

Victorian Goldfields Railway   SCENIC TRAIN
(☑ 03-5470 6658; www.vgr.com.au; adult/child return $35/15) This historic steam train heads through the box-ironbark forests of Victoria's gold country, running between Castlemaine and Maldon up to three times a week.

★ Festivals & Events

Castlemaine State Festival   ARTS
(www.castlemainefestival.com.au) One of Victoria's leading arts events, featuring theatre, music, art and dance; held in March or April in odd-numbered years.

Festival of Gardens   GARDENS
(www.festivalofgardens.org) Over 50 locals open their properties to the public; held in November in even-numbered years.

⌴ Sleeping

Bookings are essential during festival times so make use of the free **accommodation booking service** (☑ 1800 171 888; www.maldoncastlemaine.com).

Castlemaine Gardens Caravan Park   CAMPGROUND $
(☑ 03-5472 1125; www.castlemaine-gardens-caravanpark.vic.big4.com.au; Doran Ave; unpowered/powered sites $31/36, cabins $85-135) Beautifully situated next to the Botanic Gardens and

Castlemaine

Castlemaine

⊙ Top Sights
1 Castlemaine Art Gallery &
Historical Museum B2

⊙ Sights
2 Buda C1
3 Burke & Wills Monument....................D3
4 Castlemaine Market B2
5 Old Courthouse....................................A3

🛏 Sleeping
6 Colonial Motel B2
7 Midland Private Hotel B2
Theatre Royal Back Stage .... (see 14)

⊗ Eating
8 Apple Annie's.......................................B2
9 Empyre Hotel.......................................C3
10 Good Table B2
11 Naam Pla Thai Kitchen.......................B2
12 Public Inn B2
13 Saffs Cafe...C2

⊕ Entertainment
14 Theatre Royal C3

public swimming pool, this leafy park has a camp kitchen, barbecues and recreation hut.

Colonial Motel   MOTEL **$$**
(☑03-5472 4000; www.castlemainemotel.com.au; 252 Barker St; s/d $115/125, spa unit $155, apt $195; ❇🐾) Conveniently central and the best of Castlemaine's motels, the Colonial has modern rooms, some with spa, and high-ceilinged apartments in a beautifully converted school building.

Midland Private Hotel   GUESTHOUSE **$$**
(☑0487 198 931; www.themidland.com.au; 2 Templeton St; d $150) Opposite the train station, this lace-decked 1879 hotel is mostly original so the rooms are old-fashioned, but it has plenty of charm, from the art deco entrance to the magnificent guest lounge and attached Maurocco Bar. No children.

**★Theatre Royal
Back Stage**   BOUTIQUE HOTEL **$$$**
(☑03-5472 1196; www.theatreroyal.info; 30 Hargreaves St; B&B d $220; ❇🐾) It's a unique experience staying backstage at this 1854 theatre. The two suites are compact but beautifully decorated with period furniture and cinema memorabilia, and are literally right behind the velvet curtain – you can clearly hear any performances. The rate includes admission to all movies screened during your stay. The suites can be rented together for $240 (sleeping four) plus you get the 'Harry Potter' single (under the stairs) free.

GOLDEN TRIANGLE TOURING

The so-called central Victorian 'Golden Triangle' has yielded plenty of gold over the years and is still popular with prospectors and fossickers using metal detectors.

The world's largest alluvial nugget, the 72kg Welcome Stranger, was found in Moliagul in 1869, while the 27kg Hand of Faith (the largest nugget found with a metal detector) was found near Kingower in 1980. A good touring route starts in Castlemaine or Maryborough and heads up to the historic town of Maldon. From there take the back road through the farmland and canola fields of the Loddon Valley to Dunolly. It was here that miners John Deason and Richard Oates first brought the Welcome Stranger nugget, where it was cut into pieces because it was too big to fit on the scales! See a replica of the nugget and the anvil it was cut up on at the **Goldfields Historical Museum** (☑ 03-5468 1405; Broadway, Dunolly; adult/child $4/0.20; ⊙ 10am-3pm Tue & Wed; 1.30-4pm Sat & Sun) Dunolly's main street is lined with historic buildings and you can hire metal detectors in town for $45 a day. From here it's a pleasant drive to Moliagul, where signs point to the Moliagul Historic Reserve and the **Welcome Stranger Memorial**, erected in 1897 roughly where the nugget was unearthed. Moliagul is also known as the birthplace of Reverend John Flynn, the founder of the Royal Flying Doctor Service, the world's first air-ambulance service that still brings medical care to remote corners of rural Australia. It's a further 15km east to Tarnagulla, another interesting old mining town, and from there it's an easy drive back to Maldon or across to Bendigo.

✖ Eating

Apple Annie's   BAKERY, CAFE $
(☑ 03-5472 5311; www.appleannies.com.au; 31 Templeton St; mains $5-17; ⊙ 8am-5pm Wed-Sat, 8am-3pm Sun) For freshly baked bread and mouth-watering cakes and pastries it's hard to beat this country-style cafe and bakery.

Saffs Cafe   CAFE $
(☑ 03-5470 6722; 64 Mostyn St; mains $8-22; ⊙ 8am-5pm Mon & Tue, till late Wed-Sun) A local favourite, Saffs is a bright, friendly place with good coffee, cake, brilliant breakfasts, local artwork on the walls and a rear courtyard.

Naam Pla Thai Kitchen   THAI $$
(217 Barker St; mains $13-19; ⊙ noon-2.30pm & 4-9pm Wed-Sun) Occupying a tiny old pharmacy, this fragrant little den of excellent Thai cooking doesn't mess with unnecessary things like phones or a website – instead the staff put all their energy into the cooking and it shows.

Good Table   EUROPEAN $$
(☑ 03-5472 4400; www.thegoodtable.com.au; 233 Barker St; mains $14-37; ⊙ noon-2pm Thu-Sun, from 6pm daily) There have been numerous incarnations of this lovely corner hotel, but the Good Table does it well with a thoughtful European-influenced menu, featuring smoked eel terrine and pickled garfish.

Empyre Hotel   MODERN AUSTRALIAN $$$
(☑ 03-5472 5166; www.empyre.com.au; 68 Mostyn St; lunch $17-25, dinner $34-36; ⊙ noon-3pm & 6-9pm Wed-Sat, 6-9pm Sun) In a beautifully restored 19th-century hotel, dinner at the Empyre is a sumptuous fine-dining experience – the focus is on classic dishes, local produce and a refined setting. There's more relaxed lunchtime dining in the cafe.

Public Inn   MODERN AUSTRALIAN $$$
(☑ 03-5472 3568; www.publicinn.com.au; 165 Barker St; mains $31-38; ⊙ 4pm-late Mon-Thu, noon-late Fri-Sun) The former Criterion Hotel has been transformed into a slick bar and restaurant that, with its plush tones and leather couches, wouldn't look out of place in Manhattan. Food is high-end 'gastropub', and there's a two-course lunch menu for $39. Check out the 'barrel wall', where local wines are dispensed.

☆ Entertainment

Bridge Hotel   LIVE MUSIC
(☑ 03-5472 1161; 21 Walker St; ⊙ 4-11pm Mon-Wed, 4pm-1am Thu, noon-1am Fri, noon-midnight Sat, noon-11pm Sun) It's always worth checking out what's on here at one of regional Victoria's best live-music venues. It's an unassuming venue with a regular calendar of live acts, including indie gems and star performers plus karaoke and trivia nights.

Theatre Royal   CINEMA
(☑ 03-5472 1196; www.theatreroyal.info; 28 Hargreaves St; adult/child $15/12) A continually operating theatre since the 1850s, this is a fabulous entertainment venue – classic cinema (dine while watching a movie), touring live performers, a bar and a cafe. Check the program on the website.

Shopping

Castlemaine is a good place to go hunting for collectables.

Book Heaven BOOKS
(☑03-5472 4555; 47 Main Rd, Campbells Creek) An awesome second-hand bookshop crammed with 90,000 titles!

XXXX Antiques ANTIQUES
(☑03-5470 5989; www.xxxxantiques.com.au; 1-5 Elizabeth St; ☉9.30am-5pm) Houses a museum collection of antiques and collectables, partly in the original XXXX brewery (Bond Store).

Information

Castlemaine Visitors Centre (☑03-5471 1795; www.maldoncastlemaine.com; 44 Mostyn St; ☉9am-5pm) In the magnificent old Castlemaine Market, a building fronted with a classical Roman-basilica facade complete with a statue of Ceres, the Roman goddess of the harvest, on top.

Getting There & Away

V/Line (☑13 61 96) trains run hourly between Melbourne and Castlemaine (from $14.20, 1½ hours) and continue on to Bendigo ($4.20).

Around Castlemaine

About 10km northwest of Castlemaine, the **Harcourt** region (bypassed by the new Calder Fwy) is known as Victoria's 'apple centre', but in recent years it has also developed as an excellent mini-wine centre, an extension of the Bendigo wine region (for which the Castlemaine Visitors Centre can provide a map and a list of cellar doors). Check out **Bress** (☑03-5474 2262; www.bress.com.au; 3894 Calder Hwy; ☉11am-5pm Sat & Sun), a combined winery, restaurant and cidery, and **Blackjack Wines** (☑03-5474 2355; www.blackjack-wines.net.au; Calder Hwy).

Maldon

POP 1240

Like a pop-up folk museum, the whole of tiny Maldon is a well-preserved relic of the gold-rush era, with many fine buildings constructed from local stone. The population is significantly lower than the 20,000 who used to work the local goldfields, but this is still a living, working town – packed with tourists on weekends but reverting to its sleepy self during the week.

The town centre consists of High St and Main St, lined with antique stores, cafes, old toy shops, bookshops and the local pubs – the Maldon, Grand and Kangaroo hotels.

Sights & Activities

Evidence of the mining days can be seen around town – you can't miss the 24m-high **Beehive Chimney**, just east of Main St. A short trip south along High St reveals remains of the **North British Mine**, where interpretive boards tell the story of what was once one of the world's richest mines.

Maldon & District Museum MUSEUM
(☑03-5474 1633; adult/child $5/1; ☉1.30-4pm Fri-Wed) Situated behind the visitor centre, the old marketplace is now the Maldon & District Museum, with historical photos and a research room.

Old Post Office HISTORIC BUILDING
(95 High St) The Old Post Office, built in 1870, was the childhood home of local author Henry Handel Richardson. She (yes, she!) writes about it in her autobiography, *Myself When Young* (1948).

Carman's Tunnel HISTORIC SITE
(☑03-5475 2656; off Parkin's Reef Rd; adult/child $7.50/2.50; ☉tours 1.30pm, 2.30pm & 3.30pm Sat & Sun, daily school holidays) For a hands-on experience, Carman's Tunnel is a 570m-long mine tunnel that was excavated in the 1880s and took two years to dig, yet produced only $300 worth of gold. Now you can descend with a guide for a 45-minute candlelit tour.

Mt Tarrengower LOOKOUT
Don't miss the 3km drive up to Mt Tarrengower for panoramic views from the poppethead lookout.

Victorian Goldfields Railway SCENIC TRAIN
(☑03-5470 6658; www.vgr.com.au; adult/child/family single $25/15/55, return $35/15/75) This beautifully restored steam train runs along the original line through the Muckleford forest to Castlemaine (and back) up to three times a week. For a little extra, go first class (adult/child/family $45/25/100, Sunday only) in an oak-lined viewing carriage. Magic! The Maldon train station dates from 1884.

Festivals & Events

Twilight Food & Wine Festival WINE, FOOD
(www.tasteofgold.com; ☉Jan) Fine food, lanterns, live music and wine tasting in early January. Arrive by steam train.

Maldon Easter Fair FAIR
(www.facebook.com/maldoneasterfair; ☉Mar or Apr) Held March or April.

Maldon Folk Festival · MUSIC

(www.maldonfolkfestival.com; tickets 1-/2-days $60/110; ⊙ Oct-Nov) Maldon's main event, this four-day festival in late October and early November attracts dozens of performers, who provide a wide variety of world music at venues around town and at the main stage at Mt Tarrengower Reserve.

🛏 Sleeping & Eating

There are plenty of self-contained cottages and charming B&Bs in restored buildings that are located around town. **Heritage Cottages of Maldon** (🖉 0413 541 941; www. heritagecottages.com.au; 41 High St) manages numerous properties, and there's also the accommodation booking service (p202).

Butts Reserve Camp Site · CAMPGROUND

(Mt Tarrengower Rd) **FREE** Has toilets and picnic tables. From High St, head west along Franklin St and follow the signs to Mt Tarrengower.

Calder House · B&B $$

(🖉 03-5475 2912; www.calderhouse.com.au; 44 High St; d $130-160) If you're in the mood for grand, you'll step back in time at this formal, yet very inviting, place.

Gold Exchange Cafe · CAFE $

(44 Main St; meals $7-14; ⊙ 9am-5pm Wed-Sun) This tiny licensed cafe is worth a visit for the yabby pies, made from locally farmed yabbies.

ℹ Information

Maldon Visitors Centre (🖉 03-5475 2569; www.maldoncastlemaine.com; 95 High St; ⊙ 9am-5pm) Has internet access. Pick up the *Information Guide* and *Historic Town Walk* brochure, which guides you past historic buildings.

Maryborough

POP 7180

Maryborough is part of central Victoria's 'Golden Triangle', where prospectors still turn up a nugget or two. The town's pride and joy is the magnificent railway station, and now that passenger trains are running here again from Melbourne it's worth a day trip.

◎ Sights & Activities

Maryborough Railway Station · HISTORIC BUILDING

(🖉 03-5461 4683; www.stationantiques.com.au; 38 Victoria St; ⊙ 10am-5pm) **FREE** The town boasts plenty of impressive Victorian-era buildings, but Maryborough Railway Station leaves them all for dead. Built in 1892, the inordinately large station, complete with clock tower, was described by Mark Twain as 'a train station with a town attached'. Today it houses a mammoth antique emporium, a regional wine centre and an excellent cafe. An antique fair is held here three times a year.

Worsley Cottage · MUSEUM

(🖉 03-5461 2518; www.vicnet.net.au/~mbhs; 3 Palmerston St; adult/child $5/1; ⊙ 10am-noon Tue & Thu, 2-4pm Sun) Built in 1894, Worsley Cottage is the local historical society museum. Every room is furnished with pieces from the times, often donated by local people, and there's a large photographic collection. Records held here are used in family history research.

Coiltek Gold Centre · PROSPECTING

(🖉 03-5460 4700; www.coiltek.com.au; 6 Drive-in Ct; ⊙ 9am-5pm) If you're interested in finding your own gold nuggets, Coiltek Gold Centre offers full-day prospecting courses (one/two people $120/200) with state-of-the-art metal detectors. It also sells and hires out prospecting gear.

✯ Festivals & Events

Highland Gathering · SCOTTISH

(www.maryboroughhighlandsociety.com; ⊙ 1 Jan) Have a fling at Maryborough's Scottish festival, with races, stalls, tossing the caber and highland music; held every New Year's Day since 1857 (except during World War II).

Energy Breakthrough Festivals · CARS

(www.racvenergybreakthrough.net; ⊙ Nov) Focusing on alternative energy sources, school groups bring their inventive vehicles for the 24-hour and 16-hour (for juniors) RACV Energy Breakthrough Grand Prix; held late November.

🛏 Sleeping & Eating

There's plenty of accommodation in the region. Contact Central Goldfields visitor centre or browse its website. The historic **Bull & Mouth** (🖉 03-5461 3636; cnr High & Nolan Sts) had been renovated in a boutique style and was up for sale at the time of research – check to see if it has reopened.

High St is the foodie area, with cafes, restaurants, bakeries, takeaways, pubs and clubs.

Maryborough Caravan Park · CAMPGROUND $

(🖉 03-5460 4848; www.maryboroughcaravanpark. com.au; 7-9 Holyrood St; unpowered/powered sites $22/27, bunkhouse dm $25, cabins $75-95; ⊛ ⊠) Close to the town centre and nicely located beside Lake Victoria, the caravan park is well set up, with Maryborough's cheapest accommodation.

Station Cafe
CAFE **$$**

(☑ 03-5461 4683; www.stationantiques.com.au; 38c Victoria St; mains $14-31; ☺ 10am-4pm Mon & Wed-Fri, 9.30am-4.30pm Sat & Sun) This excellent cafe is in a lovely light-filled room in the grand Maryborough train station. Stop in for a coffee or speciality crêpe. The dining menu features pasta and Black Angus steaks.

ℹ️ Information

Central Goldfields Visitor Centre (☑ 03-5460 4511, 1800 356 511; www.visitmaryborough. com.au; cnr Alma & Nolan Sts; ☺ 9am-5pm; @) Loads of helpful maps and friendly staff. There's also a replica of the famous Welcome Stranger gold nugget here, and internet access and a library in the same complex.

ℹ️ Getting There & Away

The passenger train to Maryborough finally resumed in 2010. Currently there's only one direct train a day from Melbourne. You can also go via Geelong, Ballarat or Castlemaine by bus.

THE GRAMPIANS

Rising up from the western Victorian plains, acting as a haven for bushwalkers, rock-climbers and nature lovers, the Grampians are one of the state's most outstanding natural and cultural features. The rich diversity of wildlife and flora, unique rock formations, Aboriginal rock art, spectacular viewpoints and an extensive network of trails and bush camp sites offer something for everyone. The local indigenous Jardwadjali people called the mountains Gariwerd – in the local language *'gari'* means 'pointed mountain', while *'werd'* means 'shoulder'. Explorer Major Thomas Mitchell named the ranges the Grampians after the mountains in Scotland. In 1836 he eloquently described them as: '...a noble range of mountains, rising in the south to a stupendous height, and presenting as bold and picturesque an outline as a painter ever imagined.'

It's really something to be surrounded by these spectacular shapes, whether you're abseiling down in a harness or peering over a cascading waterfall. Over 900 species of native trees, shrubs and wildflowers have been recorded here, with everything from fern gullies to redgum forests. It's worth visiting at any time of year, but it's at its colourful best in spring when the wildflowers (including 20 species that don't exist anywhere else in the world) are at their peak. Water supplies can be erratic so take your own supplies to picnic areas and camping grounds.

Grampians National Park (Gariwerd)

The four greatest mountain ranges of the Grampians are the **Mt Difficult Range** in the north, **Mt William Range** in the east, **Serra Range** in the southeast and **Victoria Range** in the southwest. They spread from Ararat to the Wartook Valley and from Dunkeld almost to Horsham. **Halls Gap**, the main accommodation base and service town, lies in the Fyans Valley. The smaller **Wonderland Range**, close to Halls Gap, has some of the most splendid and accessible outlooks, scenic drives, picnic grounds and gum-scented walks, such as those that go to the Pinnacles or to Silverband Falls.

There are more than 150km of well-marked **walking tracks**, ranging from half-hour strolls to overnight treks through difficult terrain, all starting from car parks, picnic grounds and camping areas. For longer walks, let someone know where you're going (preferably the Parks Victoria rangers).

One of the most popular sights is spectacular **MacKenzie Falls**. From the car park the steep 600m path leads to the base of the falls and a large plunge pool (no swimming). Other popular places include **Boroka Lookout**, with views over Halls Gap and Lake Bellfield, and **Reed Lookout** with the short walk to the **Balconies** and views over Lake Wartook.

Zumstein Reserve in the western Grampians is named after Walter Zumstein, a bee-keeper and naturalist who settled in the area in 1910 and developed it into a wildlife reserve. There are picnic facilities, free electric barbecues and short walks. **Mt Stapylton** and **Hollow Mountain** in the north are renowned as abseiling and rock-climbing spots.

During a ferocious heatwave across Victoria in mid-January 2014, a series of bushfires swept through the Grampians region. Embers rained down on Halls Gap but an earlier-than-expected wind change spared the town. The northern Grampians region was particularly hardest hit with homes lost around Wartook and Brimpaen, while large swaths of forest turned to ash in the areas around Mt Difficult. In spite of the fires, the Grampians remains very much open for business – check with the various visitors centres and Parks Victoria to see which, if any, trails are closed.

👉 Tours

Absolute Outdoors
ADVENTURE
(☑ 03-5356 4556; www.absoluteoutdoors.com. au; 105 Main Rd, Halls Gap) Rock climbing,

abseiling, mountain biking, canoeing and guided nature walks. Also offers equipment hire.

Brambuk Cultural Centre   HIKING, INDIGENOUS
(☑ 03-5361 4000; www.brambuk.com.au; Grampians Tourist Rd; 3-/5hr tours $70/140) Rangers lead cultural and rock-art tours with numerous fascinating insights into local indigenous culture. Bookings essential.

**Grampians
Horseriding Adventures**   HORSE RIDING
(☑ 03-5383 9255; www.grampianshorseriding.com.au; 430 Schmidts Rd, Wartook Valley; 2½hr rides $100; ⊙ 10am & 2pm) Horse-riding adventures around a grand property with sweeping views, lakes and wandering bush tracks. Beginners are well looked after and there are pony rides ($30) for the kids.

**Grampians Mountain
Adventure Company**   ADVENTURE
(GMAC; ☑ 0427 747 047; www.grampiansadventure.com.au; half-/full day from $95/145) Specialises in rock climbing and abseiling adventures and instruction from beginner to advanced.

**Grampians Personalised
Tours & Adventures**   ADVENTURE
(☑ 0429 954 686, 03-5356 4654; www.grampianstours.com; half-/full-day 4WD tours from $79/149) Offers a range of 4WD tours (with off-road options), rock climbing and abseiling, discovery walks (from half a day to four days), photography, and scenic flights over the ranges ($170/280 for three/five people). Tours include stop-offs at picturesque locations.

**Grampians Quad
Bike Adventures**   QUAD BIKING
(☑ 03-5383 9215; www.grampiansquadbikes.com.au; 130 Schmidts Rd, Brimpaen; 2hr/half-day tour $130/198) Tool around the bush on a quad bike (on private property, not in the park). No experience required; minimum age is 12.

Hangin' Out   ROCK CLIMBING
(☑ 03-5356 4535, 0407 684 831; www.hanginout.com.au; 4hr/full-day rock climbing $75/130) Rock-climbing specialists who will get you started with a four-hour introductory session ($75) and private guiding from $175. Experienced guide Earl will get you onto the cliff faces, giving you a lively interpretation of the surrounding country as you go. His adventure walk (full-day $135) includes rock climbs and abseils – an exhilarating Grampians experience.

🛏 Sleeping

Parks Victoria maintains **campsites** (03-5361 4000; sites per vehicle or 6 people $14) throughout the park, with toilets, picnic tables and fireplaces (BYO water). Be warned that camping fees are slated for a significant increase in the not-too-distant future. Permits are required; you can register and pay at the office at the Brambuk Cultural Centre. Bush camping is permitted (no camp fires), except in the Wonderland Range area, around Lake Wartook and in parts of the Serra, Mt William and Victoria Ranges.

Pay close attention to fire restrictions – apart from the damage you could do to yourself and the bush, you can be jailed for lighting *any* fire, including a fuel stove, on days of total fire ban. Check www.cfa.vic.gov.au for details of fire restrictions before heading out.

ⓘ Information

Parks Victoria (☑ 13 19 63, 03-5361 4000; www.parkweb.vic.gov.au) In the Brambuk Cultural Centre, the parks office is the place for park maps and the rangers can advise you about where to go, where to camp and what you might see. They also issue camping permits and fishing permits required for fishing in local streams.

ROCK ART

Traditional Aboriginal owners have been occupying Gariwerd for more than 20,000 years and this is the most accessible place in Victoria to see indigenous rock art. Sites include **Bunjil's Shelter**, near Stawell, one of Victoria's most sacred indigenous sites, best seen on a guided tour from the Brambuk Cultural Centre. Other rock art sites in the west of the park are the **Manja Shelter**, reached from the Harrop Track car park; the **Billimina Shelter**, near the Buandik camping ground; and in the north is the **Ngamadjidj Shelter**, reached from the Stapylton camping ground.

These paintings, in protected rock overhangs, are mostly hand prints, animal tracks and stick figures. They indicate the esteem in which these mountains are held by local Indigenous communities and should be treated with respect.

The Grampians (Gariwerd)

0 —————— 10 km
0 —————— 5 miles

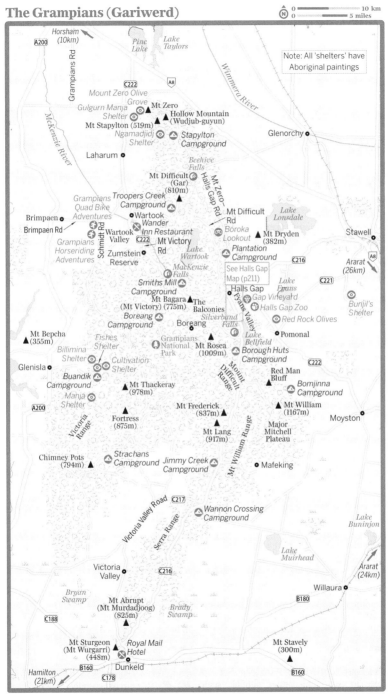

Note: All 'shelters' have Aboriginal paintings

Horsham (10km)
A200
Grampians Rd
Pine Lake
Lake Taylors
Wimmera River
C222
A8
Mount Zero Olive Grove
Gulgurn Manja Shelter
Mt Zero
Hollow Mountain (Wudjub-guyun)
Mt Stapylton (519m)
Ngamadjidj Shelter
Stapylton Campground
Glenorchy
McKenzie River
Laharum
Beehive Falls
Mt Difficult (Gar) (810m)
Mt Zero–Halls Gap Rd
Troopers Creek Campground
Brimpaen
Brimpaen Rd
Grampians Quad Bike Adventures
Wartook
Wander Inn Restaurant
Mt Difficult Rd
Boroka Lookout
Mt Dryden (382m)
Lake Lonsdale
Stawell
Grampians Horseriding Adventures
Schmidt Rd
Wartook Valley
C222
Mt Victory Rd
Plantation Campground
C216
Ararat (26km)
A8
Zumstein Reserve
Lake Wartook
MacKenzie Falls
Smiths Mill Campground
Halls Gap
See Halls Gap Map (p211)
Lake Fyans
Gap Vineyard
Halls Gap Zoo
C221
Bunjil's Shelter
Mt Bepcha (355m)
Mt Bagara (Mt Victory) (775m)
The Balconies
Boreang Campground
Boreang
Silverband Falls
Red Rock Olives
Pomonal
Fishes Shelter
Grampians National Park
Mt Rosea (1009m)
Lake Bellfield
Borough Huts Campground
Billimina Shelter
Cultivation Shelter
Glenisla
Evans Valley
C222
Buandik Campground
Red Man Bluff
Bornjinna Campground
Manja Shelter
A200
Victoria Range
Mt Thackeray (978m)
Mount Difficult Range
Mt Frederick (837m)
Mt William (1167m)
Moyston
Fortress (875m)
Mt Lang (917m)
Major Mitchell Plateau
Mt William Range
Chimney Pots (794m)
Strachans Campground
Jimmy Creek Campground
Mafeking
Victoria Valley Road
C217
Wannon Crossing Campground
Serra Range
Lake Buninjon
Victoria Valley
C216
Lake Muirhead
Ararat (24km)
Bryan Swamp
Mt Abrupt (Mt Murdadjoog) (825m)
Brady Swamp
Willaura
C188
B180
Mt Sturgeon (Mt Wurgarri) (448m)
Royal Mail Hotel
Dunkeld
Mt Stavely (300m)
Hamilton (21km)
B160
C178
B160

Halls Gap

POP 620

Nudging up against the craggy Wonderland Range, Halls Gap is a pretty little town – some might even say sleepy if you visit midweek in winter, but boy does it get busy during holidays. This is the main accommodation base and easiest access for the best of the Grampians. The single street through town has a neat little knot of shops, a supermarket, adventure-activity offices, restaurants and cafes. The Halls Gap general store and post office has an ATM and Eftpos.

◎ Sights & Activities

★ Brambuk
Cultural Centre   CULTURAL BUILDING
(☑ 03-5361 4000; www.brambuk.com.au; Grampians Tourist Rd; ⊙ 9am-5pm, cafe 9am-4pm) ✦ FREE Your first stop should be the superb cultural centre at Brambuk, 2.5km south of Halls Gap. Run by five Koorie communities in conjunction with Parks Victoria, the centre offers insights into local culture and history through Koorie stories, art, music, dance, weapons, tools and photographs.

The building itself is a striking design that combines timeless Aboriginal motifs with contemporary design and building materials. Its flowing orange roof represents the open wings of the cockatoo, as well as referencing the peaks of the Grampians.

The Gariwerd Dreaming Theatre (adult/child/family $6/4/15) shows hourly films explaining Dreaming stories of Gariwerd and the creation story of Bunjil. The ceiling here represents the southern right whale (totem of the Gunditjmara people). There's an art room where kids can try their hand at indigenous painting, classes on boomerang throwing and didgeridoo playing, and holiday programs are organised. Outside are native plants used for food and medicine.

In a separate building – where you first enter the complex – is the Parks Victoria office where rangers can advise on walks and sell camping permits. Also here are interesting educational displays covering the natural features and the history of the Grampians, a souvenir shop and Brambuk Bush Tucker Café (meals $11-26; ⊙ 9am-4pm) with a lovely deck overlooking the gardens.

Halls Gap Zoo   ZOO
(☑ 03-5356 4668; www.hallsgapzoo.com.au; adult/child/family $24/12/60; ⊙ 10am-5pm) Get up close to Australian native animals such as wallabies, grey kangaroos, quolls and wombats, but also exotic critters such as meerkats, spider monkeys, bison and tamarin. This is a top-notch wildlife park with breeding and conservation programs and a natural bush setting. Call ahead to find out about feeding times or check the website for details of close encounters.

Grampians Adventure Golf   MINI GOLF
(☑ 03-5356 4664; www.grampiansadventuregolf.com.au; 475-481 Grampians Tourist Rd; adult/child/family $12.50/9/38; ⊙ 10am-5pm Wed-Sun, daily in school holidays) There's minigolf, and then there's this 18-hole extravaganza squeezed into a bush setting just south of Halls Gap. Great for kids. There's a licensed cafe and the MOCO gallery attached.

Gap Vineyard   WINERY
(☑ 03-5356 4252; Ararat-Halls Gap Rd; ⊙ 10am-5pm Wed-Sun) The road out to Pomonal, 11km southeast of Halls Gap, has a neat little cluster of attractions. Just before the turn-off to the Halls Gap Zoo, you pass Gap Vineyard, with cellar door sales and tastings.

Next door, Red Rock Olives (☑ 03-5356 6168; www.redrockolives.com.au; cnr Ararat-Halls Gap & Tunnel Rds; ⊙ 10am-5pm Fri-Sun) has olive products to sample and buy, or you can just wander around the olive groves.

★ Festivals & Events

Grampians Jazz Festival   MUSIC
(www.visithallsgap.com.au; ⊙ mid-Feb) Three days of jazz music around town and a street parade.

Grampians Grape Escape   WINE, FOOD
(www.grampiansgrapeescape.com.au; ⊙ May) Two-day wine and food extravaganza at various venues and wineries, including live music and kids' entertainment. First weekend in May.

🛏 Sleeping

Halls Gap and the surrounding region has a huge range of accommodation – with more than 6000 beds, this is regional Victoria's most visited area after the Great Ocean Road, and tourists far outnumber locals. Whether you're camping, backpacking or looking for a motel or log cabin, there's plenty to choose from, but it still gets very busy in holiday periods – book ahead.

★ Grampians Eco YHA   HOSTEL $
(☑ 03-5356 4544; www3.yha.com.au; cnr Grampians Tourist Rd & Buckler St; dm/d from $30.50/85; @) ✦ This architecturally designed and

ecofriendly hostel utilises solar power and rainwater tanks and makes the most of light and space. It's beautifully equipped with a spacious lounge, a *MasterChef*-quality kitchen and spotless rooms.

Brambuk Backpackers
HOSTEL **$**

(☑03-5356 4250; www.brambuk.com.au; Grampians Tourist Rd; dm/d $30/75; @ 🛜) 🍃 Across from the cultural centre, this friendly Aboriginal-owned and -run hostel gives you a calming sense of place with a relaxed feel and craggy views out of the lounge windows. All rooms, including dorms, have en suites and the lounge, dining room, kitchen and barbecue deck are all top-notch.

Tim's Place
HOSTEL **$**

(☑03-5356 4288; www.timsplace.com.au; 44 Grampians Rd; dm/s/d $27/55/70, apt from $90; @ 🛜) Friendly, spotless backpackers with eco-feel; free mountain-bike hire and herb garden.

Halls Gap Caravan Park
CAMPGROUND **$**

(☑03-5356 4251; www.hallsgapcaravanpark.com. au; Grampians Rd; unpowered/powered sites from $29/36, cabins $70-185; ✳) Camping and cabins right in the town centre. Gets crowded at peak times.

★D'Altons Resort
COTTAGES **$$**

(☑03-5356 4666; www.daltonsresort.com.au; 48 Glen St; studio/deluxe/family cottages from $110/125/160; ✳ 🛜 ♨) These delightful timber cottages, with lounge chairs, verandahs and log fires, spread up the hill between the gums and kangaroos, back from the main road. It's immaculately kept and the friendly owners are a mine of local information. There's even a tennis court and a saltwater pool.

Pinnacle Holiday Lodge
MOTEL **$$**

(☑03-5356 4249; www.pinnacleholiday.com.au; 21-45 Heath St; 1-/2-bedroom unit from $97/157, d with spa from $145; ✳ 🛜 ♨) Right in the centre of Halls Gap, this gorgeous property behind the Stony Creek shops is a cut above most of Halls Gap's motels. The spacious grounds have a bucolic feel, with barbecue areas, an indoor pool and tennis courts. Modern self-contained units, two-bedroom family apartments and a swanky spa suite feature gas log fires.

Mountain Grand Guesthouse
GUESTHOUSE **$$**

(☑03-5356 4232; www.mountaingrand.com.au; Grampians Tourist Rd; s/d incl breakfast $146/166; ✳ 🛜) This gracious, old-fashioned timber guesthouse prides itself on being a traditional old-fashioned lodge where you can take a pre-dinner port in one of the lounge areas

Halls Gap

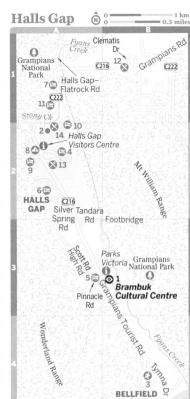

Halls Gap

◎ Top Sights
1 Brambuk Cultural Centre B3

❸ Activities, Courses & Tours
2 Absolute Outdoors A2
Brambuk Cultural Centre ....(see 1)
3 Grampians Adventure Golf.................B4

⛤ Sleeping
4 Aspect Villas...A2
5 Brambuk Backpackers A3
6 D'Altons Resort....................................A2
7 Grampians YHA Eco-Hostel A1
8 Halls Gap Caravan Park A2
9 Mountain Grand Guesthouse..............A2
10 Pinnacle Holiday Lodge A2
11 Tim's Place A1

⊗ Eating
12 Halls Gap Hotel.....................................B1
13 Kookaburra Restaurant A2
14 Livefast Lifestyle Cafe.........................A2

GOLDFIELDS & THE GRAMPIANS HALLS GAP

and mingle with other guests. The rooms are still quaint but with a bright, fresh feel. The Balconies Restaurant here is well regarded.

Aspect Villas BOUTIQUE VILLA **$$$**
(✆03-5356 4457; www.aspectvillas.com.au; off Mackey's Peak Rd; d $475; ❋) These two luxury villas are situated close to town but seem a world away when you're reclining on your bed or by the log fire, taking in views of the Wonderland Ranges through floor-to-ceiling windows. The villas make the most of local building materials, such as Grampians stone, and sit on a secluded property complete with its own lagoon. With a spa and king-size bed, it's a real couples getaway. There's a minimum two-night stay ($750) on weekends.

✖ Eating

Livefast Lifestyle Cafe CAFE **$**
(www.livefast.com.au; Shop 5 Stony Creek Stores; light meals $8-16, mains $24-28; ⊙7am-5pm Mon & Tue, 7am-late Wed-Sun) Good coffee, sunny atmosphere and energetic staff are the hallmarks of here, where you can get an early breakfast, a focaccia for lunch or call in for a glass of Grampians wine with live music in the evening.

Kookaburra Restaurant MODERN AUSTRALIAN **$$**
(✆03-5356 4222; www.kookaburrabarbistro.com. au; 125-127 Grampians Rd; mains $19-35; ⊙6-9pm Tue-Sat, noon-3pm & 6-9pm Sun) This Halls Gap institution is famed for its excellent pub food such as the sublime crispy-skin duck and Aussie dishes such as barramundi and kangaroo fillet. The wine list features mostly Grampians-area wines, and there's beer on tap at the convivial bar.

Halls Gap Hotel PUB **$$**
(✆03-5356 4566; www.hallsgaphotel.com.au; 2262 Grampians Rd; mains $19-32; ⊙noon-2pm Wed-Sun, from 6pm daily) For generous, no-nonsense bistro food or a family dinner, you can't beat the local pub, about 2km north of town, with views of the Grampians. Dishes include the seafood risotto and the warm Moroccan chicken salad. There are indoor and outdoor play areas for kids, and it's a social place for a beer after a day's bushwalking.

❶ Information

Halls Gap Visitors Centre (✆1800 065 599; www.grampianstravel.com.au; Grampians Rd; ⊙9am-5pm) The staff here are helpful, and can book tours, accommodation and activities.

Dunkeld & the Southern Grampians

The southern point of access for the Grampians, Dunkeld is a sleepy little town with a very big-name restaurant. The setting is superb, with Mt Abrupt and Mt Sturgeon rising up to the north, while the Grampians Tourist Rd to Halls Gap gives you a glorious passage into the park, with the cliffs and sky opening up as you pass between the Serra and Mt William Ranges. Fit hikers can walk to the summit of **Mt Abrupt** (6.5km, three hours return) and **Mt Sturgeon** (7km, three hours return) for panoramic views of the ranges. Both walks leave from signposted car parks off the Grampians Tourist Rd.

The town was established in the 1860s, but much of it was destroyed by bushfires in 1944. The **Historical Society Museum** (✆03-5577 2386; cnr Wills & Templeton Sts, Dunkeld; admission $2; ⊙1-5pm Sun), in an old bluestone church, has a local history collection, including Aboriginal artefacts and old photographs.

Dunkeld has a couple of cafes in the main street and a number of holiday cottages dotted around the region, but the main attraction is the restaurant at the **Royal Mail Hotel** (✆03-5577 2241; www.royalmail.com.au; Parker St; bar meals $31-44, restaurant set menu $120-140; ⊙bar & bistro noon-2.30pm & 6-9pm, restaurant from 6pm Wed-Sun). The hotel has been continuously licensed since 1855 but today it's a stylish modern hotel with a fine bar, bistro and one of Victoria's top restaurants. Chef Robin Wickens oversees the kitchens for the upmarket showpiece restaurant but also for the more affordable bistro. If you only splurge once while travelling around the state, do it here. And if you can't, at the very least spoil yourself in the bistro. You need to book months ahead to dine in the main restaurant. The attached motel-style rooms and apartments, with mountain or garden views, are elegant with all mod-cons, while the cottages across the road make up for the lack of views with their spaciousness.

Dunkeld visitor centre (✆03-5577 2558; www.visitsoutherngrampians.com.au; Parker St) has useful information.

Wartook Valley & the Northern Grampians

Lush Wartook Valley runs along the Grampians' western foothills, giving a completely different perspective of the mountains. Heading to or from Horsham, this is the scenic alternative to the Western Hwy (A8). From Wartook, the sealed Roses Gap Rd and Mount Victoria Rd pass through the park, and there are lots of unsealed roads and tracks passing little creeks, waterfalls and idyllic picnic spots. The northern Grampians region suffered one of its worst bushfires in recent times in mid-January 2014. Most of the tourist infrastructure was spared, but much of the land has turned from green to black and will take some time to recover.

You can buy olives and other farm produce at the **Mt Zero Olive Grove** (☑ 03-5383 8280; www.mountzeroolives.com; Mt Zero Rd; ☺10am-4pm). Although it was affected by the January 2014 bushfires, fire damage at the olive grove was minimal and it remains in business. Walk to the top of **Mt Zero** from the nearby picnic area. Further south off Roses Gap Rd, it's a short walk to the base of **Beehive Falls**.

Wander Inn Restaurant (☑ 03-5383 6377; 2637 Northern Grampians Rd; mains $14-29; ☺noon-2.30pm Tue-Sun, 6-8.30pm Thu-Sun) has a certain rustic old-world charm in the licensed restaurant and a tranquil tearoom and artists' studio attached.

NORTHWEST OF THE GRAMPIANS

Horsham

The major town to the northwest of the Grampians and the capital of the Wimmera region, Horsham makes a convenient base for exploring the surrounding national parks and Mt Arapiles. The main shopping strip has postal and banking facilities, supermarkets and plenty of other shops and eateries. **Grampians & Horsham Visitors Centre** (☑ 03-5382 1832; www.visithorsham.com.au; 20 O'Callaghan's Pde; ☺9am-5pm) has information on the surrounding areas.

Horsham Regional Art Gallery (☑ 03-5362 2888; www.horshamartgallery.com.au; 21 Roberts Ave; gold coin donation; ☺10am-5pm Tue-Fri, 1-4.30pm Sat & Sun) houses the Mack Jost Collection of significant Australian artists, including works by Rupert Bunny, Sir Sidney Nolan, John Olsen and Charles Blackman.

Horsham's **Botanic Gardens** (Firebrace St) were established in the 1870s and designed by the curator of Melbourne's Royal Botanic Gardens, William Guilfoyle.

Mt Arapiles State Park

Mt Arapiles, 37km west of Horsham and 12km west of Natimuk, is Australia's premier rock-climbing destination. At 369m it's not the world's highest mountain but with more than 2000 routes to scale, it attracts salivating climbers from around the world. Popular climbs include the Bard Buttress, Tiger Wall and the Pharos. In the tiny nearby town of Natimuk a community of avid climbers has set up to service the visitors, and the town has also developed into something of a centre for artists – the biennial **Nati Frinj Festival**, held in November in odd years, includes performances and a colourful street parade.

Even if you're not into climbing, there are two short and steep walking tracks from Centenary Park to the summit, or you can drive up along the sealed Lookout Rd.

Arapiles Mountain Shop (☑ 03-5387 1529; 67 Main St, Natimuk) sells and hires climbing equipment. If you want to learn to climb or hire a guide, the **Natimuk Climbing Company** (☑ 03-5387 1329; www.climbco.com.au; 6 Jory St, Natimuk) and **Arapiles Climbing Guides** (☑ 03-5384 0376; www.arapiles.com.au; Natimuk) are two professional outfits offering instruction and group courses. Most climbers head for the popular **Pines Camping Ground** (Centenary Park; camp sites $5) at the base of the mountain.

Duffholme Cabins (☑ 03-5387 4246; Natimuk-Goroke Rd; d $48, extra adult $15) comprises a self-contained cottage sleeping seven. Call to make a booking (it's not staffed). **National Hotel** (☑ 03-5387 1300; 65 Main St, Natimuk; d $70-80) has tidy motel-style units at the back and pub rooms upstairs, plus good counter meals.

Little Desert National Park

Don't expect rolling sand dunes, but this arid park is rich in flora and fauna that thrive in the dry environment. There are over 670 indigenous plant species here, and in spring and early summer the landscape is transformed into a colourful wonderland of wildflowers. The best-known resident is the mallee fowl, an industrious bird that can be seen in an aviary at the Little Desert Nature Lodge.

The park covers a huge 132,000 hectares, and the vegetation varies substantially due to the different soil types, climate and rainfall in each of its three blocks (central, eastern and western). The rainfall often reaches 600mm per year, but summers are dry and very hot.

The Nhill–Harrow Rd through the park is sealed and the road from Dimboola is gravel, but in the park the tracks are mostly sand and only suitable for 4WD vehicles or walking. Some are closed to 4WDs in the wet season (July to October).

If you want a brief introduction to the park there are several well-signposted walks: south of Dimboola is the **Pomponderoo Hill Nature Walk**, south of Nhill is the **Stringybark Nature Walk** and south of Kiata is the **Sanctuary Nature Walk**. Other longer walks leave from the camping ground south of Kiata, including a 12km trek south to the Salt Lake.

🛏 Sleeping

There are national park **camping grounds** (www.parkweb.vic.gov.au; sites $21) in the eastern block at Horseshoe Bend and Ackle Bend, both on the Wimmera River south of Dimboola; and south of Kiata. They have toilets, picnic tables and fireplaces. Or you can bush camp in the more remote central and western blocks; see the rangers first.

★ Little Desert Nature Lodge   CAMPGROUND, RESORT $
(☎03-5391 5232; www.littledesertlodge.com.au; camp sites $25, bunkhouse d $44, B&B r $125; ❄) 🏊 On the northern edge of the desert, 16km south of Nhill, this well-equipped bush retreat is a superb base for exploring the park. With a spacious camping ground, bunkhouse, comfortable en suite motel-style rooms and a restaurant, there's something for everyone. A key attraction here is the tour of the mallee-fowl aviary ($15), where you can see these rare birds in a breeding program; otherwise, take the mallee-fowl sanctuary tour ($130) and a night spotlighting walk ($15).

ℹ Information

Little Desert Park Office (☎13 19 63; www.parkweb.vic.gov.au; Nursery Rd) Off the Western Hwy south of Dimboola.

Dimboola

Located on the eastern edge of the Little Desert, beside the Wimmera River, Dimboola is a classic country town made famous by Jack Hibberd's play *Dimboola,* and the subsequent 1979 John Duigan film of the same name about a country wedding. The historic Dimboola Hotel was gutted by fire in 2003 and has since lain dormant. The park entrance is about 4km south of town on a sealed road, but from then on it's gravel. There are numerous easily accessed walks around the flats area along the river.

Beside the Western Hwy, 19km northwest of Dimboola, the **Pink Lake** is a colourful salt lake with a bright pink-purple hue.

Ebeneezer Aboriginal Mission, near Antwerp, 18km north of Dimboola, was established by German missionaries in 1859 and ceased operation in 1904. You can wander around the well-preserved mission buildings and cemetery.

There's tourist information and internet access at **Dim-e-Shop** (☎03-5389 1588; 109 Lloyd St) on the main street.

Dimboola celebrates with a **German Fest** in April, and the **Dimboola Rowing Regatta** in November.

🛏 Sleeping

Riverside Host Farm   CABINS $
(☎03-5389 1550; 150 Riverside Rd; sites $28, cabins d $95; ❄) This friendly working farm on a bend in the Wimmera River is a lovely place to stay, with cosy self-contained cabins, camp sites and a rustic open-sided camp kitchen lounge area with pot-belly stove. Hire canoes, take a boat tour from here into the Little Desert or help out with farm activities.

Dimboola Riverside Caravan Park   CAMPGROUND $
(☎03-5389 1416; dimboolacaravanpark@bigpond.com; 2 Wimmera St; unpowered/powered sites $23/30, cabins from $55) Set among eucalypts and pine trees beside the Wimmera River.

Nhill

Nhill is the main base for the northern entrance to the Little Desert National Park and Kiata campground. It's a big town for this part of the world – the main industries here are wheat farming and producing ducks for Victorian restaurant tables. Nhill is an Aboriginal word meaning 'mist over the water' – check out the artificial **Lake Nhill** and surrounding wetlands to see if there's any water.

Nhill has some grand old pubs, cafes, motels and a caravan park, but your best bet for accommodation is to head down to Little Desert Nature Lodge near the park entrance.

Hindmarsh visitor centre (☎03-5391 3086; www.wimmeramalleetourism.com.au; Victoria St; ⏱9am-5pm), in Goldsworthy Park in the town centre, has plenty of information on the park, local sights and accommodation.

Mornington Peninsula & Phillip Island

Includes ➡

Mornington
Peninsula...................216

Sorrento 220

Portsea 222

Point Nepean
National Park 222

Mornington Peninsula
National Park 223

Flinders 223

Red Hill & Around .. 224

French Island 224

Phillip Island....... 225

Best Places to Eat

➡ Montalto (p224)

➡ Red Hill Estate (p224)

➡ Terminus (p224)

➡ Portsea Hotel (p222)

➡ The Baths (p222)

Best Places to Stay

➡ Carmel of Sorrento (p221)

➡ Hotel Sorrento (p221)

➡ Glen Isla House (p229)

➡ Clifftop (p229)

➡ Tortoise Head
Lodge (p225)

Why Go?

More a playground for locals than a lure for foreign travellers, Mornington Peninsula is a string of holiday communities that curls around Port Phillip Bay's eastern half. At the tip of the peninsula, a world of rugged ocean surf beaches, sublime links golf courses and coastal bushwalks opens up. Away from the coast, the peninsula's interior is a wine- and food-lover's paradise, with more than 50 cellar doors and some of Victoria's finest winery restaurants. Away to the east, it's a short ferry ride to wild and isolated French Island and to Phillip Island, one of Victoria's premier attractions. Apart from the famous nightly parade of little penguins, Phillip Island is blessed with wonderful surf beaches, accessible wildlife and enough activities to keep you (and the kids) busy for a week.

When to Go
Phillip Island

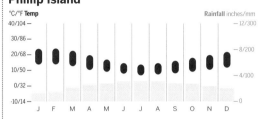

Jan–Feb Phillip Island is one of the closest summer playgrounds to Melbourne.

Mar–May, Sep–Oct Hit the beaches and wineries, after the holiday crowds have departed.

Nov–Dec The best time to view seals and penguins at Phillip Island.

MORNINGTON PENINSULA

The Mornington Peninsula – the boot-shaped area of land between Port Phillip Bay and Western Port Bay – has been Melbourne's summer playground since the 1870s, when paddle steamers ran down to Portsea. Today, much of the interior farming land has been replaced by vineyards and orchards – foodies love the peninsula, where a winery lunch is a real highlight – but it still retains lovely stands of native bushland.

The calm 'front beaches' are on the Port Phillip Bay side, where families holiday at bayside towns from Mornington to Sorrento. The rugged ocean 'back beaches' face Bass Strait and are easily reached from Portsea, Sorrento and Rye; there are stunning walks along this coastal strip, part of the Mornington Peninsula National Park.

The bay heads are so close that it's just a short hop by ferry across from Sorrento to Queenscliff on the Bellarine Peninsula.

ℹ️ Information

Peninsula Visitor Information Centre (☎03-5987 3078, 1800 804 009; www.visitmorningtonpeninsula.org; 359b Nepean Hwy, Dromana; ⏰9am-5pm) The main visitor information centre for the peninsula can book accommodation and tours. There are also visitor centres in Mornington (p218) and **Sorrento** (☎03-5984 1478; cnr George St & Ocean Beach Rd).

ℹ️ Getting There & Away

Moorooduc Hwy (11) and Point Nepean Rd (B110) both feed into the Mornington Peninsula Fwy (M11), the main peninsula access. Alternatively, exit the Moorooduc Hwy to Mornington and take the coast road around Port Phillip Bay.

Frequent Metlink trains run from Melbourne to Frankston, Hastings and Stony Point.

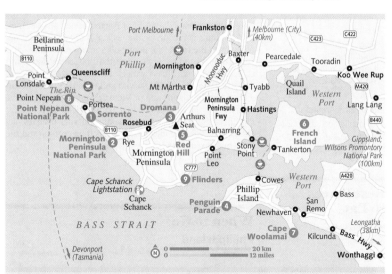

Mornington Peninsula & Phillip Island Highlights

1 Swim with dolphins and soak up the history at **Sorrento** (p220)

2 Walk the cliff tops and surf the back beaches of **Mornington Peninsula National Park** (p223)

3 Catch a film at the **Dromana Drive-In** (p218), one of the few left in Australia

4 Settle in at dusk for the famous **Penguin Parade** (p226) at Phillip Island

5 Kick off with a long, liquid lunch then an afternoon of wine tasting at the **wineries** around Red Hill (p224)

6 Take the ferry to **French Island** and hike or cycle in blissful isolation (p224)

7 Catch a wave at beautiful **Cape Woolamai** (p226)

8 Cycle out to the peninsula's tip at **Point Nepean National Park** (p222)

9 Challenge yourself to a round of golf at the **Flinders Golf Club** (p223)

THE MAZE TRAIL

When did hedge mazes become so popular? The Mornington Peninsula has a few of these English-garden curiosities to get lost in.

Ashcombe Maze & Lavender Gardens (☑ 03-5989 8387; www.ashcombemaze.com.au; 15 Shoreham Rd, Shoreham; adult/child/family $18.50/10/52; ☺ 10am-5pm) Brilliant mazes, including a circular rose maze, fields of lavender and blooming gardens.

Boneo Maze & Wetlands (☑ 03-5988 6385; www.boneomaze.com.au; 695 Limestone Rd, Fingal; adult/child/family $15/10/45; ☺ 10am-4pm Mon-Thu, 10am-5pm Fri-Sun) Several mazes, boardwalks through wetlands and a giant chess set.

Enchanted Maze Garden (☑ 03-5981 8449; www.enchantedmaze.com.au; 55 Purves Rd, Arthurs Seat; adult/child $29/19; ☺ 10am-6pm) This remarkably well-clipped hedge maze, ornamental garden, sculpture park and lolly shop will make the kids squeal with delight.

BOAT

Inter Island Ferries (p230) runs between Stony Point and Cowes via French Island (p224).

Queenscliff–Sorrento Car & Passenger Ferries (Map p158; ☑ 03-5258 3244; www.searoad.com.au; one-way foot passenger adult/child $10/8, 2 adults & car standard one-way/return $69/132; ☺ hourly 7am-6pm, to 7pm Jan & long weekends) sails between Sorrento and Queenscliff, enabling you to cross Port Phillip Bay by car or bicycle.

BUS

Portsea Passenger Service (☑ 03-5986 5666; www.ptv.vic.gov.au) runs the following services:

➡ 788 from Frankston to Portsea via Mornington, Dromana and Sorrento

➡ 786 from Rye to St Andrews Beach

➡ 787 from Safety Beach to Sorrento

Peninsula Bus Lines (☑ 03-9786 7088; www.grenda.com.au) runs bus 782 from Frankston train station to Flinders via Hastings and Balnarring.

Mornington

POP 22,421

Pretty Mornington, with its cute bathing boxes and swimming beaches, is the gateway to the peninsula's holiday coastal strip – just beyond the reaches of Melbourne's urban sprawl. Originally part of the lands of the Boonwurrung people, it was founded as a European township in 1854. The town thrived and by 1890 there were steamers and a daily train service from Melbourne – now sadly defunct.

◉ Sights & Activities

For views over the harbour, take a walk along the 1850s **pier** and around the Schnapper Point foreshore boardwalk past the **Matthew**

Flinders **monument** that commemorates his 1802 landing. **Mothers Beach** is the main swimming beach, while at **Fossil Beach**, where limestone was mined in the 1860s, there are remains of a lime-burning kiln. Fossils found here date back 25 million years! At Mills Beach you can see colourful and photogenic **bathing boxes**.

Historic Buildings   NOTABLE BUILDINGS
There are several grand old buildings around Main St, including the 1892 **Grand Hotel**. The **Old Court House**, on the corner of Main St and the Esplanade (C783), was built in 1860, and the **Police Lock-Up** behind it was built in 1862. On the opposite corner is the **Old Post Office Museum** (☑ 03-5976 3203; cnr Main St & The Esplanade; admission by donation; ☺ 1.30-4.30pm Sun & public holidays, 11am-3pm Wed in summer) in the 1863 post office building. Nearby is a **monument** to the 15 members of Mornington's football team who lost their lives when their boat, *Process*, sank while returning from a game against Mordialloc in 1892.

Mornington Botanical Rose Gardens   GARDENS
(cnr Mornington-Tyabb Rd & Dunns Rd) FREE Away from the beach, the Mornington Botanical Rose Gardens is a beautifully landscaped garden with over 4000 flowers.

Mornington Peninsula Regional Gallery   GALLERY
(☑ 03-5975 4395; www.mprg.mornpen.vic.gov.au; Dunns Rd; adult/child $4/free; ☺ 10am-5pm Tue-Sun) In the Civic Reserve alongside the Botanical Rose Gardens, the outstanding Mornington Peninsula Regional Gallery has changing exhibitions and a permanent collection of Australian prints and paintings.

Mornington Street Market MARKET
(Main St; ⊙9am-3pm Wed) Every Wednesday, the Mornington Street Market takes over Main St with stalls and crafts.

Mornington Railway HISTORIC RAILWAY
(☑1300 767 274; www.morningtonrailway.org.au; Mornington train station; return adult/child $16/5) On the first three Sundays of each month the popular Mornington Railway runs steam locomotives between Mornington and Moorooduc.

Schnapper Point Boat Hire BOATING
(☑03-5975 5479; www.fishingmornington.com; Boatshed 7, Scout Beach) Rents out kayaks (first hour $30) and small motor boats (from $85 for two hours), and sells fishing tackle and bait.

🍴 Sleeping & Eating

Main St is lined with cafes and restaurants, particularly at the bay end.

Royal Hotel HOTEL $$
(☑03-5975 9115; www.theroyal.com.au; 770 The Esplanade; ❋) Classified by the National Trust, the Royal is tastefully renovated, offering authentic old-world accommodation in a range of rooms and bay views. The latest round of renovations was underway when we last visited but we expect the best rooms to still be the balcony suites with bathrooms and sea views.

The Rocks SEAFOOD $$
(☑03-5973 5599; www.therocksmornington.com. au; 1 Schnapper Point Dr; mains $18-36; ⊙8am-10pm) At the Mornington Yacht Club, this restaurant, with an open-sided deck overlooking the marina, is the perfect place for a drink or light meal. The restaurant is strong on fresh seafood, with oysters done every which way.

Afghan Marco Polo MIDDLE EASTERN $$
(☑03-5975 5154; www.afghanmarcopolo.com.au; 9-11 Main St; mains $23-37; ⊙6pm-late) Marco Polo is an atmospheric place with Persian rugs and brass hookahs, that serves traditional Afghan cuisine. Kebabs, kormas, *boranis* and *kulfi* ice cream – a Central Asian mash up!

ℹ️ Information

Mornington Library (☑03-5950 1820; Vancouver St; ⊙9am-2pm Mon & Sat, 9am-8pm Tue & Thu, 9am-6pm Wed & Fri; 🛜) Free internet access.

Mornington Visitors Centre (☑03-5975 1644; www.visitmorningtonpeninsula.org; 320 Main St; ⊙9am-5pm) Has useful regional information and a Mornington walking-tour map.

Mornington to Blairgowrie

From Mornington, the Esplanade heads south for the gorgeous scenic drive towards Sorrento, skirting the rocky Port Phillip Bay foreshore. Inland, the Nepean Hwy (B110) takes a less-scenic route and again becomes the Mornington Peninsula Fwy.

From **Dromana** take the steep hairpin-bend Arthurs Seat Rd inland up to the lookout at **Arthurs Seat** (called Wonga by the Boonwurrung people), which, at 305m, is the highest point on the Port Phillip Bay coast, with fine views across the bay. The famous chairlift here was closed after a series of accidents but there are plans to revive it, if safety demands can be met. Back at Dromana there's a relic of the 1960s, a time when there were more than 330 drive-in cinemas across Australia. The National Trust–listed **Dromana Drive-In** (☑03-5987 2492; www.drivein.net.au; 113 Nepean Hwy; adult/child $16/10; ⊙7.30pm & 10pm Thu-Sun) is one of just a handful that remain.

◎ Sights & Activities

The Briars HISTORIC BUILDING
(☑03-5974 3686; 450 Nepean Hwy, Mt Martha; adult/child $5/4, park only free; ⊙10am-4pm, park 9am-5pm) The Briars is the 1840 homestead of one of the peninsula's first pastoral runs. Sitting on 96 hectares, it includes original farm buildings, parklands and a wildlife reserve. The homestead houses the Dame Mabel Brookes collection of Napoleon relics, which includes locks of the emperor's hair and his death mask.

Jillian Fishing Trips FISHING
(☑0418 148 426; www.thejillian.com.au; adult/child from $50/40) For a relaxed afternoon of fishing on the bay, Jillian Fishing Trips has family-friendly morning, afternoon and twilight fishing charters, picking up from Rosebud Pier.

Peninsula Hot Springs SPA
(☑03-5950 8777; www.peninsulahotsprings.com; Springs Lane, Rye; bathhouse adult/child Tue-Thu $30/15, Fri-Mon $35/20) There are lots of spas and massage centres popping up along the peninsula, but none better than Peninsula Hot Springs, a large and luxurious complex that utilises hot, mineral-rich waters pumped from deep underground. There's a huge menu of spa, private bathing and massage treatments available, or you can just relax in the bathhouse. It's about 7km inland from Rye, off Browns Rd.

Mornington Peninsula

10 km
5 miles

N

Phillip Island (70km); Gippsland
Watson Inlet
Western Port
Sandstone Island
Crib Point
Stony Point
Ferry to French Island & Cowes
Cowes

Yabb-Tooradin Rd
A780
Somerville
Tyabb

Jones Rd
C777
Hastings
Stony Point Rd
Crib Point
Stony Point
Flinders Naval Depot
Sandy Point
Phillip Island
C473
B420
C478

Coolart Rd
Hendersons Rd
C782
C785
Bittern
Morradoo
Flinders
C473

Frankston (12km); Melbourne (53km)
Mornington–Tyabb Rd
Mooranduc
Mooroduc
M11
Stumpy Gully Rd
Bittern Reservoir
Devilbend Reservoir
Tubbarubba Rd
C784
Salix at Willow Creek Vineyard
Stanleys Rd
Merricks North
Port Phillip Estate
Balnarring
C777
Merricks
Somers
Western Port

Mornington
The Briars
Mt Martha
B110
Marina Cove
Martha Point
Balcombe Point
C783
Red Hill
C788
C787
Red Hill South
Red Hill Estate
Montalto
Point Leo
Point Leo Surf Beach
Shoreham
Flinders Golf Club
West Head

Port Phillip
South Channel Fort
Safety Beach
Dromana
Arthurs Seat (305m)
McCrae
Arthurs Seat State Park
Ten Minutes By Tractor
T'Gallant
Sunny Ridge
Strawberry Farm
Main Ridge
Mornington Peninsula National Park
Flinders
C787
C777
The Arch
Picnic Point

Mud Islands
West Rosebud
Rosebud
B110
M11
Browns Rd
Tootgarook
Fingal
Moonah
Links
Boneo
Boneo Maze & Wetlands
C777
Cape Schanck
Bushrangers Bay
Cape Schanck Lighthouse
Cape Schanck
Fingal Beach

Swan Bay
Queenscliff
Collins Settlement Historic Site
Sorrento
Portsea
Point Nepean National Park
Pope's Eye
Blairgowrie
B110
Rye
Dundas St
The Dunes
Peninsula Hot Springs
St Andrews
St Andrews Ocean Beach
Gunnamatta Beach
Rye Ocean Beach

The Rip
Point Nepean
Fort Nepean
Cheviot Beach
Portsea (Golf Course)
London Bridge
Portsea Surf Beach
Sorrento Ocean Beach
Koonya Beach
Blairgowrie Ocean Beach
Melbourne Rd

Bass Strait
Ferries to Tasmania

🛏 Sleeping & Eating

There's holiday accommodation all along the coast, and council-managed **foreshore camping** (☏03-5986 8286; www.mornpen.vic. gov.au; unpowered/powered sites $26/31, peak season $41/46) at Rosebud, Rye and Sorrento. These camping areas are close to the beach and are open from September to April – it's next to impossible to get a site during the Christmas and Easter holidays.

Bayplay Lodge HOSTEL $
(☏03-5984 0888; www.bayplay.com.au; 46 Canterbury Jetty Rd, Blairgowrie; per person from $50; ❋ ⚛ ☷) Tucked away off the Esplanade in Blairgowrie, this rustic house has backpacker-style accommodation, with a big communal lounge and kitchen area, and a pool.

Two Buoys TAPAS $
(☏03-5981 8488; www.twobuoys.com.au; 209 Point Nepean Rd, Dromana; tapas $4-9, mains $13-20; ⊙11.30am-9pm Mon-Fri, 8am-9pm Sat & Sun) This funky Dromana tapas restaurant with a view of the bay is a real shared-dining experience. You can choose from small or medium plates such as twice-cooked pork belly and Dromana mussels, as well as flat-bread pizzas.

Fed-Up Fish Café SEAFOOD $$
(☏03-5986 4716; 1571 Point Nepean Rd, Rosebud; mains $18-35; ⊙5.30-9.30pm Wed & Thu, noon-2pm & 5.30-9.30pm Fri-Sun) It doesn't look like much from the outside, but this fading retro bayside restaurant consistently serves up good, fresh seafood. Try the chowder.

Sorrento

POP 1448

Historic Sorrento is the standout town on the Mornington Peninsula for its beautiful limestone buildings, ocean and bay beaches, and buzzing seaside summer atmosphere. This was the site of Victoria's first official European settlement, established by an expedition of convicts, marines, civil officers and free settlers who arrived from England in 1803.

Sorrento boasts some of the best cafes and restaurants on the peninsula, and the main street is lined with galleries, boutiques, and craft and antique shops – naturally, it gets ridiculously busy in summer. Dolphin swims and cruises are popular, and the trip to Queenscliff on the ferry is a fun outing. The small **Sorrento visitor centre** (☏03-5984 5678; 2 St Aubins Way; ⊙10am-4pm) is on the main street.

◉ Sights & Activities

The calm bay beach is good for families and you can hire **paddle boards** on the foreshore. At low tide, the **rock pool** at the back beach is a safe spot for adults and children to swim and snorkel, and the surf beach is patrolled in summer. The 10-minute climb up to **Coppins Lookout** offers good views.

Historic Buildings NOTABLE BUILDINGS
The grand 19th-century buildings constructed from locally quarried limestone, including the Hotel Sorrento (1871), **Continental Hotel** (1875) and **Koonya Hotel** (1878), look fabulous in the late-afternoon sun.

Collins Settlement
Historic Site HISTORIC SITE
(Leggett Way; ⊙1.30-4pm Sat & Sun) Apart from four graves that are believed to hold the remains of 30 original settlers, there's little evidence of Sorrento's original abandoned settlement. The Collins Settlement Historic Site, midway between Sorrento and Blairgowrie, marks the 1803 settlement site at Sullivan Bay, and a display centre tells its story.

Sorrento Museum MUSEUM
(☏03-5984 0255; 827 Melbourne Rd; adult/child $5/free; ⊙1.30-4.30pm Sat, Sun & public holidays) Sorrento Museum has interesting displays on the early history of Sorrento and Portsea, and a pioneer garden.

☞ Tours

★**Moonraker Charters** SWIMMING
(☏03-5984 4211; www.moonrakercharters.com.au; 7 George St; adult/child sightseeing $65/55, dolphin & seal swimming $125/115) Operates three-hour dolphin- and seal-swimming tours from Sorrento Pier.

★**Polperro Dolphin Swims** SWIMMING
(☏03-5988 8437; www.polperro.com.au; adult/child sightseeing $55/35, dolphin & seal swimming $130) Popular morning and afternoon dolphin-and seal-swimming tours from the pier.

Sorrento Tours BOAT TOUR
(☏0418 374 912; www.adventuresails.com.au; adult/child $38/25; ⊙12.30pm & 2.30pm) Sightseeing tours aboard a catamaran. Also sunset sails ($80 per person).

🛏 Sleeping

Sorrento Foreshore
Camping Ground CAMPGROUND $
(☏03-5950 1011; Nepean Hwy; unpowered/powered sites $26/31, peak season $41/46; ⊙Nov-May)

Hilly, bush-clad sites between the bay beach and the main road into Sorrento.

Sorrento Beach House YHA
HOSTEL $

(✓03-5984 4323; www.sorrento-beachhouse.com; 3 Miranda St; dm/d from $30/90) This purpose-built hostel situated in a quiet but central location maintains a relaxed atmosphere – the back deck and garden are great places to catch up with other travellers. Staff can also organise horse riding, snorkelling and diving trips.

Carmel of Sorrento
GUESTHOUSE $$

(✓03-5984 3512; www.carmelofsorrento.com.au; 142 Ocean Beach Rd; d $130-220, apt from $210) This lovely old limestone house, right in the centre of Sorrento, has been tastefully restored in period style and neatly marries the town's history with contemporary comfort. There are three Edwardian-style suites with bathrooms and continental breakfast, and two modern self-contained units.

Whitehall Guesthouse & Oceanic Apartments
B&B, APARTMENTS $$

(✓03-5984 4166; www.oceanicgroup.com.au; 231 Ocean Beach Rd; d $130-290, apt $200-290; ❄☀) This gracious limestone, two-storey guesthouse on the road to the back beach has dreamy views from its timber verandah, though most rooms are small and old-style with shared bathrooms down the hall – the rooms with bathrooms are more spacious. Across the road, Oceanic Apartments ditch the period charm with spruce self-contained, split-level apartments.

Hotel Sorrento
HOTEL $$$

(✓03-5984 8000; www.hotelsorrento.com.au; 5-15 Hotham Rd; motel r $220-280, apt $220-320; ❄@) The legendary Hotel Sorrento is well known as a pub and restaurant but it also has some slick accommodation. The motel-style Heritage and Garden suites are modern and well appointed, but the On the Hill apartments are the ones to go for, with airy living spaces, spacious bathrooms, private balconies, spas and bay views. The hotel has its own spa centre.

✗ Eating & Drinking

Sorrento's main street, Ocean Beach Rd, has most of the town's cafes and restaurants, with tables and chairs spilling out along the footpaths in summer. The town's three pubs, the historic Hotel Sorrento, Continental Hotel and Koonya Hotel are all good places for a meal or drink, and all have live music in summer.

Stringer's
CAFE, DELI $

(✓03-5984 2010; 2 Ocean Beach Rd; light meals $4-9; ☉8am-2.30pm) Stringer's is a Sorrento institution with thoughtfully prepared sandwiches, snacks and light meals. If it has the egg, bacon and chive tart for breakfast, you've hit the jackpot.

Sisters
CAFE $

(✓03-5984 4646; 151 Ocean Beach Rd; mains $12-20; ☉8am-4pm Mon, Tue, Thu & Fri, 8am-5pm Sat & Sun) The dishes at this gorgeous courtyard cafe burst with goodness, whether it's the eggplant parmigiana, chickpea salad or the frangipani tart.

BUCKLEY'S CHANCE

In October 1803 William Buckley (1780–1856), a strapping 6ft 7in bricklayer, was transported to Victoria's first settlement (now Sorrento) as a convict for receiving stolen goods.

Buckley and three others escaped in December, though one was shot dead during the escape. The remaining three set off around the bay, thinking they were heading to Sydney, but two turned back and died from lack of food and water.

Buckley wandered for weeks, surviving on shellfish and berries. He was on his last legs when two Wathaurong women found him, and Buckley spent the next 32 years living with the nomadic clan on the Bellarine Peninsula, learning their customs and language.

In 1835 Buckley surrendered to a party from a survey ship. He was almost unable to speak English, and the startled settlers dubbed him the 'Wild White Man'. Buckley was subsequently pardoned and acted as an interpreter and mediator between white settlers and the Wathaurong people. John Morgan's 1852 book *The Life & Adventures of William Buckley* provides an insight into Aboriginal life before white settlement.

The Australian colloquialism 'Buckley's chance' (a very slim or no chance) is said to be based on William Buckley's story, but there's dispute about this. Some claim the expression gained currency in the late 1800s and derived from the name of the Melbourne department store Buckley's & Nunn ('You've got two chances – Buckley's and none').

WORTH A TRIP

MERRICKS & BALNARRING

On the Western Port Bay side of the peninsula, tiny Merricks is worth a stop for its **Merricks General Store** (✍03-5989 8088; www.merricksgeneralstore.com.au; 3460 Frankston-Flinders Rd/C777; meals $16-34; ⊙9am-5pm). The bistro is renowned for its hearty breakfasts and quality meals using fresh, local produce. The cellar door showcases wines from the Elgee Park, Baillieu Vineyard and Quealy wineries.

Further east, Balnarring has an excellent foreshore camping ground in a bush setting, and the **Balnarring Picnic Races** (✍03-5986 3755; www.balnarringraces.com; adult/child $10/free), a great country race meeting held at various times throughout the year.

The Baths
FISH & CHIPS $

(✍03-5984 1500; www.thebaths.com.au; 3278 Point Nepean Rd; fish & chips $10, restaurant mains $25-33; ⊙noon-8pm) The waterfront deck of the former sea baths is the perfect spot for lunch or a romantic sunset dinner overlooking the jetty and the Queenscliff ferry. The menu has some good seafood choices.

Smokehouse
ITALIAN $$

(✍03-5984 1246; 182 Ocean Beach Rd; mains $20-34; ⊙6-9pm) Gourmet pizzas and pastas are the speciality at this local family favourite. Innovative toppings and the aromas wafting from the wood-fired oven hint at the key to its success.

Acquolina Ristorante
ITALIAN $$

(✍03-5984 0811; 26 Ocean Beach Rd; mains $26-36; ⊙6-10pm Thu-Mon, daily in summer, closed Jun-Sep) Acquolina set the bar when it opened in Sorrento with its authentic northern-Italian fare. This is hearty, simple food – handmade pasta and ravioli dishes matched with imported Italian wines and homemade (utterly irresistible) tiramisu.

Loquat
MODERN AUSTRALIAN $$

(✍03-5984 4444; www.loquat.com.au; 3183 Point Nepean Rd; 2-course meal from $30, mains $30-38) An in-crowd frequents this trendily converted cottage, but its staying power is due to excellent food – everything from fish and chips to chargrilled quail.

Portsea

POP 446

The last village on the peninsula, wee Portsea is where many of Melbourne's wealthiest families have built seaside mansions. You can walk the Farnsworth Track (1.5km, 30 minutes) out to scenic **London Bridge**, a natural rock formation, and spot middens of the Boonwurrung people who once called this area home.

Bayplay (✍03-5984 0888; www.bayplay.com.au; 3755 Point Nepean Rd) offers aquatic activities and tours (PADI courses, snorkelling and sea kayaking) and hires equipment (kayaks four/eight hours $50/80).

Dive Victoria (✍03-5984 3155; www.divevictoria.com.au; 3752 Point Nepean Rd; snorkelling $85, s/d dive with gear $130/210) runs diving and snorkelling trips.

Portsea's pulse is the iconic, sprawling, half-timber **Portsea Hotel** (✍03-5984 2213; www.portseahotel.com.au; Point Nepean Rd; s/d from $85/105, s/d with bathroom from $135/175), an enormous pub with a great lawn and terrace area looking out over the bay. There's an excellent bistro (mains $20 to $28) and old-style accommodation (most rooms have shared bathrooms) that increases in price based on bay views and season.

Point Nepean National Park

The peninsula's tip is marked by the scenic **Point Nepean National Park** (http://parkweb.vic.gov.au; Point Nepean Rd), originally a quarantine station and army base. A large section of the park is a former range area and is still out of bounds due to unexploded weapons, but there's plenty to see here and long stretches of traffic-free road that make for excellent cycling. There are also plenty of **walking trails** throughout the park and at the tip is **Fort Nepean**, which played an important role in Australian defence from the 1880s to 1945. On the parade ground are two historic **gun barrels** that fired the first Allied shots in WWI and WWII. **Quarantine** is a legendary surf break at the Rip, and is still only accessible by boat.

Point Nepean visitor information centre (✍03-5984 6014; Point Nepean Rd; ⊙9am-6pm Jan, 9am-5pm Feb-Apr & Oct-Dec, 10am-5pm May-Sep) will give you the lowdown on the park and hires bikes for $25 per day. You can walk or cycle to the point (12km return), or take the shuttle bus (adult/child return $10/7.50), a hop-on, hop-off bus service that departs the visitor centre six times daily.

Mornington Peninsula National Park

Stretching from Portsea on the sliver of coastline to Cape Schanck and inland to the Greens Bush area, this national park showcases the peninsula's most beautiful and rugged ocean beaches. Along here are the cliffs, bluffs and crashing surf beaches of Portsea, Sorrento, Blairgowrie, Rye, St Andrews, Gunnamatta and Cape Schanck. This is spectacular coastal scenery – well known to the surfers, hikers and fisherfolk who have their secret spots – and it's possible to walk all the way from Portsea to Cape Schanck (26km, eight hours). Swimming and surfing is dangerous at these beaches: the undertow and rips can be severe, and drownings continue to occur. Swim only between the flags at Gunnamatta and Portsea during summer.

If you want to learn to surf, contact East Coast Surf School (☑ 0417 526 465, 03-5989 2198; www.eastcoastsurfschool.net.au; 226 Balnarring Rd, Merricks North; lessons per person $55) or Mornington Peninsula Surf School (☑ 0417 338 079; www.greenroomsurf.com.au; 6 Chetwyn Ct, Frankston South; group/private lessons $55/150).

You can ride a horse along Gunnamatta Beach with Gunnamatta Trail Rides (☑ 03-5988 6755; www.gunnamatta.com.au; 150 Sandy Rd, Fingal; rides per person $70-120) on excursions ranging from half an hour to a full day.

Built in 1859, Cape Schanck Lightstation (☑ 03-5988 6184; www.capeschancklighthouse.com.au; 420 Cape Schanck Rd; museum only adult/child/family $13.50/9.50/37, museum & lighthouse $16.50/10.50/44; ☉ 10.30am-4pm) is a photogenic working lighthouse with a kiosk, a museum, information centre and regular guided tours. You can stay at Cape Schanck B&B (☑ 1300 885 259; www.capeschancklighthouse.com.au; 420 Cape Schanck Rd; d from $130) in the limestone Keeper's Cottage.

From the light station, descend the steps of the boardwalk that leads to the craggy cape for outstanding views. Longer walks include tracks to Bushrangers Bay, which can be approached from Cape Schanck or the Bushrangers Bay car park on Boneo Rd (C777) – 5km return. Wild Fingal Beach is a 6km return walk.

Flinders

POP 622

Flinders, where the thrashing ocean beaches give way to Western Port Bay, has so far been largely spared the development of the Port Phillip Bay towns. It's a delightful community and home to a busy fishing fleet. Surfers have been coming to Flinders for decades, drawn by ocean-side breaks such as Gunnery, Big Left and Cyril's, and golfers know the cliff-top Flinders Golf Club course as the most scenic and wind blown in Victoria.

The historic Flinders Hotel (☑ 03-5989 0201; www.flindershotel.com.au; cnr Cook & Wood Sts; d $225-500; ❋) has been a beacon on this sleepy street corner longer than anyone can remember. Modern motel units are well equipped. For meals there's the indoor-outdoor Deck Bar Bistro (mains $18-36; ☉ noon-3pm & 5.30-9pm) where pub grub goes gastronomic – nothing too fussy, just staple dishes such as steak and parma done really well – or the celebrated fine-dining

TOP FIVE FOR GOLFERS

The Mornington Peninsula has some of Victoria's most picturesque and challenging links golf courses, all with ocean views:

The Dunes (☑ 03-5985 1334; www.thedunes.com.au; Browns Rd, Rye; 18 holes midweek/weekend $52/79)

Flinders Golf Club (☑ 03-5989 0312; www.flindersgolfclub.com.au; Bass St, Flinders; 18 holes midweek/weekend $35/49)

Cape Schanck (☑ 03-5950 8000; Boneo Rd/C777, Cape Schanck; 18 holes midweek/weekend $50/56)

Moonah Links (☑ 03-5988 2000; www.moonahlinks.com.au; 55 Peter Thomson Dr, Fingal; 18 holes $75-95)

Portsea Golf Club (☑ 03-5984 3521; www.portseagolf.com.au; Relph Ave, Portsea; 18 holes $60-70)

experience of **Terminus** (2-/3-course meal $69/89; ⊘ 6-10pm Fri, noon-2.30pm & 6-10pm Sat, noon-2.30pm Sun).

Red Hill & Around

POP 731

The undulating hills of the peninsula's interior around Red Hill and Main Ridge are the centre of the region's viticulture and winemaking industries, and a favourite destination for foodies. It's a lovely region of trees and tumbling hills where you can visit the popular **Red Hill Market** (www.craftmarkets.com.au; ⊘ 8am-1pm 1st Sat of month Sep-May) or spend a sublime afternoon hopping around the winery cellar doors and restaurants.

Red Hill Brewery (⊘ 03-5989 2959; www.redhillbrewery.com.au; 88 Shoreham Rd; ⊘ 11am-6pm long weekends & by appointment) is a great spot to sample some of the 10 handcrafted European-style beers with a plate of mussels or a ploughman's lunch.

If all this booziness is too much, pick your own strawberries at **Sunny Ridge Strawberry Farm** (⊘ 03-5989 4500; www.sunnyridge.com.au; cnr Shands & Mornington-Flinders Rds; adult/child $8/4; ⊘ 9am-5pm Nov-Apr, 11am-4pm Sat & Sun May-Oct). Admission includes 500g of strawberries and there's a cafe serving all things strawberry.

FRENCH ISLAND

POP 116

Exposed, windswept and wonderfully isolated, French Island is two-thirds national park and it retains a real sense of tranquillity – you can only get here by passenger ferry, so it's virtually traffic-free, and there's no mains water or electricity! The main attractions are bushwalking and cycling, taking in wetlands, checking out one of Australia's largest

---

LIQUID LUNCH

Most of the peninsula's wineries are in the hills between Red Hill and Merricks, and most have excellent cafes or restaurants attached. Several companies offer winery tours – ask at the visitor centre (p216). Wineries to consider include the following:

Montalto (⊘ 03-5989 8412; www.montalto.com.au; 33 Shoreham Rd, Red Hill South; cafe mains $14-18, restaurant mains $35-39; ⊘ cellar door 11am-5pm, cafe noon-4pm Sat & Sun, restaurant noon-3pm daily, 6.30-11pm Fri & Sat) Montalto is one of the Mornington Peninsula's best winery restaurants, and the pinot noir and chardonnay here are terrific. There's also the piazza and garden cafe for casual dining, as well as an olive grove and shop.

Port Phillip Estate (⊘ 03-5989 4444; www.portphillipestate.com.au; 263 Red Hill Rd, Red Hill South; 2-/3-course meal from $68/85, cellar door mains $15-22; ⊘ cellar door 11am-5pm, restaurant noon-3pm Wed-Sun, 6.30-9pm Fri & Sat) Home of Port Phillip Estate and Kooyong wines, this award-winning winery has an excellent, breezy restaurant and some lighter cellar-door meals.

Red Hill Estate (⊘ 03-5931 0177; www.redhillestate.com.au; 53 Shoreham Rd, Red Hill South; ⊘ cellar door 11am-5pm, restaurant noon-5pm daily, 6.30-11pm Fri & Sat) Red Hill Estate's signature pinot noir and sparkling wines are outstanding, while Max's Restaurant is one of the best on the peninsula.

Ten Minutes by Tractor (⊘ 03-5989 6080; www.tenminutesbytractor.com.au; 1333 Mornington-Flinders Rd, Main Ridge; 5-/8-course tasting menu $109/139, 2-/3-course meal $69/89; ⊘ cellar door 11am-5pm, restaurant noon-3pm Wed-Sun, 6.30-9pm Thu-Sat) This is one of regional Victoria's best restaurants and you won't find a better wine list on the peninsula. The name comes from the three vineyards, which are each 10 minutes apart by tractor.

T'Gallant (⊘ 03-5989 6565; www.tgallant.com.au; 1385 Mornington-Flinders Rd, Main Ridge; mains $16-32; ⊘ noon-3pm) This winery pioneered luscious pinot gris in Australia and produces the country's best. There's fine dining at La Baracca Trattoria and sometimes live music on weekends.

Willow Creek Vineyard (⊘ 03-5989 7640; www.willow-creek.com.au; 166 Balnarring Rd/C784, Merricks North; mains $36-38; ⊘ noon-3pm daily, 6-10pm Fri & Sat) Renowned for its sparkling wines, chardonnay and pinot noir. Chef Bernard McCarthy's Salix Restaurant is a serene place for a sophisticated lunch on the deck or an intimate dinner.

koala colonies and observing a huge variety of birds.

Pick up the Parks Victoria brochure at the Tankerton Jetty for a list of walks and cycling routes. All roads on the island are unsealed and some are quite sandy.

The island served as a penal settlement for prisoners serving out their final years from 1916 and you can still visit the original prison farm.

The ferry docks at Tankerton; from there it's around 2km to the licensed French Island General Store ([🖉]03-5980 1209; Tankerton Rd, Lot 1; bike hire $25; ⊘8am-6pm, from 9am Sun), which also serves as post office, and tourist-information and bike-hire centre, and has accommodation ($120 per person). Bikes can also be hired at Tankerton Jetty.

Located 10km from Tankerton is the Bayview Chicory Kilns (Bayview Rd; ⊘daily), where fourth-generation local Lois will give you a tour of the historic kilns (by donation), show you a few resident koalas and whip up chicory coffee and Devonshire teas in her rustic cafe. Chicory (a coffee substitute) was the island's biggest industry from 1897 to 1963. You can camp here for $8/5 per adult/child.

Tours

If you want to see the best of the island, especially if your time is limited, a tour is the best way to go. Book ahead and arrange a pick up from Tankerton Jetty.

French Island Biosphere Bus Tours   BUS TOUR
([🖉]0412 671 241, 03-5980 1241; www.frenchislandtours.com.au; half-day adult/child $25/12, full day $49/22; ⊘Tue, Thu, Sun, plus Sat during school holidays) Lois from the Bayview Chicory Kilns runs half-day tours with morning or afternoon tea. The full-day tour includes lunch. The ferry to the island costs extra.

Sleeping

Fairhaven   CAMPGROUND
([🖉]03-5986 9100; www.parkweb.vic.gov.au) `FREE`
On the western shore where the wetlands meet the ocean, this camping ground provides a real getaway experience, with sites offering little more than a compost toilet. Bookings essential.

Tortoise Head Lodge   B&B $
([🖉]03-5980 1234; www.tortoisehead.net; 10 Tankerton Rd, Tankerton; budget s/d/f $60/90/120, cabins s/d $90/130) A short stroll from the ferry, this has knock-out water views and is great value.

McLeod Eco Farm   GUESTHOUSE $
([🖉]03-5980 1224; www.mcleodecofarm.com; McLeod Rd; per person with breakfast & dinner $98)
🍃 Formerly the island's prison, this organic farm offers cosy guesthouse rooms (former officers' quarters) and makes abundant use of recycled furniture. All rooms have shared bathrooms. The meals here are outstanding.

❶ Getting There & Around

Inter Island Ferries ([🖉]03-9585 5730; www.interislandferries.com.au) runs a service between Stony Point and Tankerton (10 minutes, at least two daily, four on Tue, Thu, Sat & Sun, adult/child return $24/12). You can reach Stony Point directly from Frankston on a Metlink train.

You can hire bikes ($25 per day) from the kiosk at the jetty in summer and from the general store.

PHILLIP ISLAND
POP 9406

Famous for the Penguin Parade and Motorcycle Grand Prix circuit, Phillip Island attracts a curious mix of surfers, petrolheads and international tourists making a beeline for those little penguins.

At its heart, Phillip Island is still a farming community, but nature has conspired to turn it into one of Victoria's hottest tourist destinations. Apart from the nightly waddling of the penguins, there's a large seal colony, abundant bird life around the Rhyll wetlands and a koala colony. The rugged south coast has some fabulous surf beaches and the swell of tourists – the holiday population jumps to around 40,000 over summer – means there's a swag of family attractions, plenty of accommodation, and a buzzing if unexciting cafe and restaurant scene in the island capital, Cowes. Visit in winter, though, and you'll find a very quiet place where the local population of farmers, surfers and hippies go about their business.

'The Island', as it's locally known, is only about 100 sq km, so it's easy and quick to get around by car or bike – it's just a 15-minute drive from Cowes to the Penguin Parade or Grand Prix circuit. It's linked to the mainland by a bridge across the Narrows from San Remo to Newhaven. If you're on foot or bicycle, you can get here by ferry from Stony Point to Cowes. Cowes runs along the island's north coast, while Rhyll, 7km to the east, occupies a promontory that juts out from the island's northeast corner. Cape Woolamai, 14km southeast of Cowes, is a

ℹ️ PHILLIP ISLAND NATURE PARK

The Phillip Island Nature Park incorporates four of the island's biggest attractions: the Penguin Parade, the Nobbies, Koala Conservation Centre and Churchill Island. A Three Parks Pass (the Nobbies Centre is free) costs $40.40/20.20/101 per adult/child/family, or you can buy tickets for each attraction individually. Passes are available from the information centre (p230) and online at www.penguins.org.au.

long finger of land that extends out into the ocean from the island's far southeast, south of Newhaven.

The Boonwurrung people are the traditional inhabitants of the island, though what they'd have made of coachloads of Penguin Parade tourists and biker gangs making their way over the San Remo bridge is anyone's guess.

⊙ Sights & Activities

★ **Penguin Parade**   WILDLIFE RESERVE
(Map p227; ☑03-5951 2800; www.penguins.org.au; Summerland Beach; adult/child/family $23.80/11.90/59.50; ☉10am-dusk, penguins arrive at sunset) The Penguin Parade attracts more than half-a-million visitors annually to see the little penguins (Eudyptula minor), the world's smallest, and probably cutest, of their kind. The penguin complex includes concrete amphitheatres that hold up to 3800 spectators who come to see the little fellas just after sunset as they waddle from the sea to their land-based nests.

Penguin numbers swell in summer, after breeding, but they're in residence year-round. After the parade, hang around the boardwalks for a closer view as the stragglers search for their burrows and mates. Bring warm clothing. There are a variety of specialised **tours** (adult $44-80) where you can be accompanied by rangers to explain the behaviour of penguins, or see the penguins from the vantage of a Skybox (an elevated platform). There's also a cafe and an interpretive centre at the complex.

Koala Conservation Centre   ZOO
(Map p227; ☑03-5951 2800; www.penguins.org.au; 1810 Phillip Island Rd, Cowes; adult/child/family $11.30/5.65/28.25; ☉10am-5pm, extended hours

in summer) From the boardwalks at the Koala Conservation Centre you're certain to see koalas chewing on eucalyptus leaves or dozing away – they sleep about 20 hours a day!

Churchill Island   FARM
(Map p227; ☑03-5956 7214; www.penguins.org.au; Phillip Island Rd, Newhaven; adult/child/family $11.30/5.65/28.25; ☉10am-5pm) Churchill Island, connected to Phillip Island by a bridge near Newhaven, is a working farm where Victoria's first crops were planted. There's a historic homestead and garden, and pleasant walking tracks looping around the island.

★ **Seal Rocks & the Nobbies**   WILDLIFE WATCHING
(Map p227) The Nobbies are a couple of large, craggy, offshore rocks at the island's southwestern tip. Beyond them are Seal Rocks, which are inhabited by Australia's largest fur-seal colony. The **Nobbies Centre** (Map p227; ☑03-5951 2852; www.penguins.org.au; ☉11am-1hr before sunset) FREE offers great views over the Nobbies and the 6000 distant Australian fur seals that sun themselves there. You can view the seals from boardwalk binoculars or use the centre's underwater cameras ($5). The centre also has some fascinating interactive exhibits, a kids games room and a cafe.

★ **Grand Prix Circuit**   RACE TRACK
(Map p227; Back Beach Rd) Even when the motorbikes aren't racing, petrol-heads love the Motorcycle Grand Prix circuit, which was souped up for the Australian Motorcycle Grand Prix in 1989. The **visitor centre** (☑03-5952 9400; www.phillipislandcircuit.com.au; Back Beach Rd; ☉9.30am-5pm) FREE runs **guided circuit tours** (adult/child/family $19/10/44; ☉tours 2pm), or check out the **History of Motorsport Museum** (adult/child/family $13.50/6.50/30). The more adventurous can cut laps of the track with a racing driver in hotted-up V8s ($295; bookings essential). Drive yourself in a go-kart around a scale replica of the track with **Champ Karts** (per 10/20/30min $30/53/68).

Swimming & Surf Beaches   BEACH
Cowes Main Beach is calm and safe for swimming – head over to the long Cowes East Beach for a quieter time. The best surf beaches are along the southern coast.

Spectacular Cape Woolamai is the most popular surf beach but rips and currents make it suitable only for experienced surfers. Beginners and families head to Smiths

Phillip Island

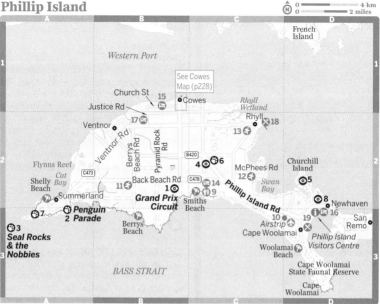

Phillip Island

◎ Top Sights
1 Grand Prix Circuit B2
2 Penguin Parade..................................... A3
3 Seal Rocks & the Nobbies A3

◎ Sights
4 Amaze'n Things C2
5 Churchill Island D2
6 Koala Conservation Centre C2
7 Nobbies Centre A3
8 Phillip Island Chocolate Factory D2

◎ Activities, Courses & Tours
9 Island Surfboards (Smiths Beach)....... C2
10 Phillip Island Helicopters D3

11 Phillip Island Winery.............................. B2
12 Purple Hen Winery C2
13 Rhyll Trout & Bush Tucker Farm C2

◎ Sleeping
14 Clifftop C2
15 Glen Isla House B1
16 The Island Accommodation YHA D3
17 Surf & Circuit Accommodation B2

◎ Eating
18 Big Fat Greek Bar & Grill........................ C2
19 Curry Leaf D3
    Foreshore Bar & Restaurant.........(see 18)
    White Salt ....(see 19)

Beach, which is often teeming with surf-school groups. Both are patrolled in summer. Berrys Beach is another beautiful spot and usually quieter than Woolamai or Smiths. Around the Nobbies, Cat Bay and Flynns Reef will often be calm when the wind is blowing onshore at the Woolamai and Smiths areas.

Island Surfboards (Map p228; ☑ 03-5952 3443; www.islandsurfboards.com.au; lessons $60, surfboard hire per hr/day $12.50/40) offers surfing lessons and hires gear.

Phillip Island Winery WINERY
(Map p227; ☑ 03-5956 8465; www.phillipisland-wines.com.au; Berrys Beach Rd; ⊙11am-5.30pm Thu-Sun, daily in school holidays) Sample excellent estate wines and share platters platters ($14-30) of cheese, terrine, smoked salmon, trout fillets and pâté.

Purple Hen Winery WINERY
(Map p227; ☑ 03-5956 9244; www.purplehenwines. com.au; 96 McPhees Rd, Rhyll; ⊙10am-5.30pm Fri-Mon) Try the signature pinot noir and chardonnay at the cellar door of this pretty

Cowes

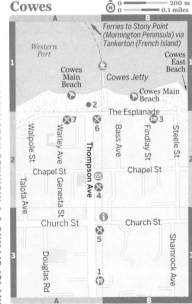

Ferries to Stony Point (Mornington Peninsula) via Tankerton (French Island)

Cowes

☺ Activities, Courses & Tours
1 Island Surfboards A3
2 Wildlife Coast Cruises A1

🛏 Sleeping
3 Waves Apartments B2

⊗ Eating
4 Café Lugano A2
5 Fig & Olive at Cowes A3
6 Hotel A2
7 Madcowes A2

winery off the main tourist route, with views over Western Port Bay.

Amaze'n Things　　　　　AMUSEMENT PARK
(Map p227; ☑03-5952 2283; www.amazenthings. com.au; 1805 Phillip Island Rd; adult/child/family $33/23/99.50; ☺10am-5pm, last admission 4pm) With a maze, crazy illusion rooms, minigolf, a puzzle island and lots of activities, this wacky fun park is great for kids, but gets the adults in too.

Rhyll Trout & Bush Tucker Farm　　FARM
(Map p227; ☑03-5956 9255; www.rhylltroutand-bushtucker.com.au; 36 Rhyll-Newhaven Rd; adult/child/family $9/7/34, rod hire $4; ☺10am-5pm) A

fun day out for kids, here you can fish for trout in a lake or indoor pond or follow the bushtucker-trail.

Phillip Island Chocolate Factory　　CHOCOLATE FACTORY
(Map p227; ☑03-5956 6600; www.phillipisland-chocolatefactory.com.au; 930 Phillip Island Rd; tours adult/child/family $15/10/45; ☺9am-6pm) Like Willy Wonka's, Panny's place has a few surprises. As well as free samples of handmade Belgian-style chocolate, there's a walk-through tour of the chocolate-making process, including a remarkable gallery of chocolate sculptures, from Michelangelo's *David* to an entire model village! Naturally, you can buy chocolate penguins, but most of the chocolate is prepackaged.

⌖ Tours

Go West　　　　　　　　　　　TOUR
(☑03-9485 5290, 1300 736 551; www.gowest.com. au; 1-day tour $130) One-day tour from Melbourne that includes lunch and iPod commentary in several languages. Includes entry to the Penguin Parade.

Phillip Island Helicopters　　SCENIC FLIGHTS
(Map p227; ☑03-5956 7316; www.pih.com.au; Phillip Island Tourist Rd, Newhaven; flights per person $80-225) Scenic flights over the island.

Wildlife Coast Cruises　　　BOAT TOUR
(Map p228; ☑03-5952 3501; www.wildlifecoastcruises.com.au; Rotunda Bldg, Cowes Jetty; seal-watching adult/child $72/49; ☺departures 2pm Fri-Wed May-Sep, 2pm & 4.30pm daily Oct-Apr) Runs a variety of cruises including seal-watching, twilight and cape cruises; also runs a two-hour cruise to French Island (adult/child $30/20) and a full-day cruise to Wilsons Promontory ($190/140).

✪ Festivals & Events

Pyramid Rock Festival　　　　MUSIC
(☺New Year) This huge event which coincided with New Year's festivities and featured some of the best Aussie bands was cancelled in 2013 and it's unclear what the future holds for this fine event.

Australian Motorcycle Grand Prix　　MOTORCYCLE RACING
(www.motogp.com.au; ☺Oct) The island's biggest event – three days of bike action in October.

V8 Supercars　　　　　MOTOR RACING
(www.v8supercars.com.au) Racing events throughout the year.

🛌 Sleeping

Most of the accommodation is in and around Cowes, although there are a few places in Rhyll and Newhaven, and B&Bs and caravan parks are scattered around the island. During big motor-racing events, Christmas, Easter and school holidays, rates are sky high and you'll need to book way in advance.

The Island Accommodation YHA   HOSTEL $$
(Map p227; ☑ 03-5956 6123; www.theislandaccommodation.com.au; 10-12 Phillip Island Rd, Newhaven; dm/d from $30/155; @🛜) 🏊 This purpose-built backpackers has huge identical living areas on each floor, complete with table-tennis tables and cosy fireplaces for winter. Its rooftop deck has terrific views and its eco-credentials are excellent. Cheapest dorms sleep 12 and doubles are motel-standard.

Surf & Circuit Accommodation   APARTMENT $$
(Map p227; ☑ 03-5952 1300; www.surfandcircuit. com; 113 Justice Rd, Cowes; apt $115-230; ❄🖥) Ideal for families or groups, these eight spacious, modern and comfortable two- and three-bedroom units accommodate up to six and 10 people, respectively. All have kitchens, lounges with plasma TVs, and patios, and some have spas. Outside there are barbecue areas, a tennis court and a playground.

Waves Apartments   APARTMENT $$
(Map p228; ☑ 03-5952 1351; www.thewaves.com. au; 1 Esplanade, Cowes; d/tr/q from $180/195/210; ❄🛜) These slick apartments overlook Cowes Main Beach so you can't beat the balcony views if you go for a beachfront unit. The modern, self-contained apartments come with spa, and balcony or patio.

Clifftop   BOUTIQUE HOTEL $$$
(Map p227; ☑ 03-5952 1033; www.clifftop.com.au; 1 Marlin St, Smiths Beach; d $235-290; ❄) It's hard to imagine a better location for your island stay than perched above Smiths Beach. Of the seven luxurious suites here, the top four have ocean views and private balconies, while the downstairs rooms open onto gardens – all have fluffy beds and slick contemporary decor.

Glen Isla House   BOUTIQUE HOTEL $$$
(Map p227; ☑ 03-5952 1882; www.glenisla.com; 230 Church St, Cowes; d incl breakfast $299-439, self-contained cottage $325-395; ❄🛜) This brilliant boutique hotel is one of the best addresses on the island. Ensconced in a renovated 1870 homestead and outbuildings, Glen Isla is all about understated, old-world luxury with modern touches such as huge plasma TVs.

🍴 Eating & Drinking

Regional Victoria's gastronomic revolution has yet to sweep Phillip Island and the places to eat here are surprisingly unexciting. Most of the eateries are in Cowes – the Esplanade and Thompson Ave are crowded with fish-and-chip shops, cafes and takeaways – but there are a few gems scattered around the island.

Cowes

Café Lugano   CAFE $
(Map p228; ☑ 03-5952 5636; 71 Thompson Ave; mains $7-17; ⏱8am-3pm) Cool hole-in-the-wall joint for good coffee or a healthy lunch of focaccia, rice burger or falafel salad.

Madcowes   CAFE, DELI $
(Map p228; ☑ 03-5952 2560; www.madcowescafe. com.au; 17 The Esplanade; mains $9-19; ⏱7am-4pm) This stylish cafe-foodstore looks out to the main beach and cooks up some of the heartiest breakfasts and light lunches on the island. Staples include chicken parma and fish and chips, while the tempura prawns are memorable for all the right reasons.

Hotel   AUSTRALIAN $$
(Map p228; ☑ 03-5952 2060; www.hotelphillipisland.com; 11-13 The Esplanade; mains $10-32; ⏱noon-late) So cool that it only goes by its first name (like Cher...), this breezy corner pub is all leather, sleek lines and big windows. The menu is honest and good value, with all-day tapas plates, pizza and the standard steak and chicken parma. Has live music on weekends.

Fig & Olive at Cowes   MODERN AUSTRALIAN $$
(Map p228; ☑ 03-5952 2655; www.figandoliveatcowes.com.au; 115 Thompson Ave, Cowes; mains $24-38; ⏱9am-late Wed-Mon) A groovy mix of timber, stone and lime-green decor makes this a relaxing place to enjoy a beautifully presented meal, or a late-night cocktail. The eclectic menu is strong on seafood and moves from paella or pork belly to wood-fired Tasmanian salmon.

Rhyll

Rhyll has a neat little strip of eateries by the waterfront, including a Greek restaurant and fish and chippery.

Big Fat Greek Bar & Grill GREEK **$$**
(Map p227; ☑ 03-5956 9511; 9 Beach Rd; mains $26-34; ⊙ 6-9pm Thu-Mon, longer hours in summer) Across the road from the beach, this family-run Greek restaurant serves large helpings of perfectly prepared Greek staples – the grilled seafood and cheeses taste even better when a sea breeze wafts in the door.

Foreshore Bar & Restaurant PUB **$$**
(Map p227; ☑ 03-5956 9520; www.theforeshore.com.au; 11 Beach Rd; mains $17-36; ⊙ 11am-late) The water views and nautical theme from the timber deck of the classy pub-turned-restaurant complement your lunchtime steak sandwich or bowl of mussels. The evening has a relaxed, fine-dining feel with a gastro-pub menu from bangers and mash to Indonesian pork curry.

Cape Woolamai

White Salt FISH & CHIPS **$**
(Map p227; ☑ 03-5956 6336; 7 Vista Pl; fish from $6, meal packs from $15; ⊙ noon-8pm Thu-Tue, from 4.30pm Wed) White Salt serves the best fish and chips on the island – select from fish fillets and hand-cut chips, tempura prawns and marinated barbecue octopus salad with corn, pesto and lemon.

Curry Leaf INDIAN **$**
(Map p227; ☑ 03-5956 6772; 9 Vista Pl; mains $12-25; ⊙ noon-8pm Wed-Mon; ☑) This cheery Indian restaurant and takeaway is popular for its piquant meat, seafood and vegetarian curries, samosas and aromatic biryani dishes.

❶ Information

Phillip Island Visitors Centre (☑ 1300 366 422; www.visitphillipisland.com; ⊙ 9am-5pm, till 6pm school holidays) Newhaven (Map p227; 895 Phillip Island Tourist Rd, Newhaven); Cowes (Map p228; cnr Thompson & Church Sts, Cowes) The main visitor centre for the island is on the main road at Newhaven, and there's a smaller centre at Cowes. Both sell the Three Parks Pass (adult/child/family $40.40/20.20/101), and the main centre has a free accommodation- and tour-booking service.

❶ Getting There & Away

BUS
V/Line (☑ 1800 800 007; www.vline.com.au) has train-bus services from Melbourne's Southern Cross Station via Dandenong station or Koo Wee Rup ($12.40, 2½ to 3½ hours). There are no direct services.

CAR
About 140km from Melbourne, Phillip Island can only be accessed by car across the bridge between San Remo and Newhaven. From Melbourne take the Monash Fwy (M1) and exit at Pakenham, joining the South Gippsland Hwy at Koo Wee Rup.

FERRY
Inter Island Ferries (☑ 03-9585 5730; www.interislandferries.com.au; adult/child/bike return $24/12/8) runs between Stony Point on the Mornington Peninsula and Cowes to French Island (45 minutes). There are two sailings Monday and Wednesday, and three on Tuesday, Thursday, Friday, Saturday and Sunday.

❶ Getting Around

Ride On Bikes (☑ 03-5952 2533; www.rideon-bikes.com.au; 43 Thompson Ave, Cowes; day/week from $50/200; ⊙ 9am-6pm Mon-Fri, 9am-5pm Sat, 10am-4pm Sun) There's no public transport around Phillip Island but you can hire mountain bikes here.

Gippsland & Wilsons Promontory

Includes ➡

Walhalla 234

Wilsons Promontory
National Park 238

Sale 242

Ninety Mile Beach . . 243

Paynesville
& Raymond Island . . 244

Lakes Entrance 246

Snowy River
National Park 249

Orbost 251

Croajingolong
National Park 254

Best Places to Eat

➡ Koonwarra Store (p237)

➡ Metung Galley (p245)

➡ Ferryman's Seafood
Cafe (p248)

➡ Wildfish (p242)

➡ The Boathouse (p248)

Best Places to Stay

➡ Walhalla Star Hotel (p235)

➡ Lighthouse Keepers'
Cottage (p239)

➡ Wilderness Retreat (p239)

➡ Moilong Express (p236)

➡ Adobe Mudbrick Flats
(p253)

Why Go?

The Great Ocean Road may get the crowds, but Gippsland hides all the secrets. Gippsland is one region where it pays to avoid the cities – the towns along the Princes Hwy are barely worth a traveller's glance. Elsewhere are some of the most absorbing, unspoilt and beautiful wilderness areas and beaches in the state.

Along the coast there's Wilsons Promontory National Park, a fabulous destination for hikers and the less energetic alike. This is only the start when it comes to stirring beaches. Epic Ninety Mile Beach yields to the Cape Conran Coastal Park and Croajingolong National Park. Put them together and it's one of the wildest, most beautiful coastlines on earth.

Inland, Walhalla is an utterly beguiling village, while the national parks at Snowy River and Errinundra are as deeply forested, remote and pristine as any in the country.

When to Go
Point Hicks

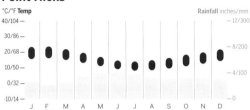

Feb–Mar For toe-tapping jazz festivals at Inverloch and Paynesville.

Sep–Nov Spring is the time for wildflowers and wildlife, as well as bushwalking.

Dec–Jan It gets busy, but there's no better time to hit the oceans and lakes than summer!

Gippsland & Wilsons Promontory Highlights

① Hike from Tidal River to Sealers Cove at spectacular **Wilsons Promontory** (p238)

② Saddle up for the **East Gippsland Rail Trail** (p251), Gippsland's longest cycle path

③ Camp in the dunes and fish from the beach at legendary **Ninety Mile Beach** (p243)

④ Hike deep into the forest or drive along the remote tracks of **Snowy River National Park** (p249)

⑤ Step back in time at **Walhalla** (p234), an authentic gold-mining village

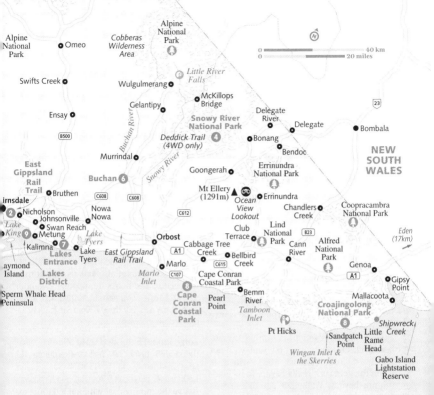

Alpine National Park

Omeo

Cobberas Wilderness Area

Alpine National Park

Swifts Creek

Little River Falls

Wulgulmerang

Gelantipy

McKillops Bridge

Delegate River

Delegate

Bombala

Ensay

B500

Snowy River National Park

Deddick Trail (4WD only)

Bonang

Bendoc

NEW SOUTH WALES

Murrindal

Buchan River

Snowy River

Goongerah

Errinundra National Park

23

East Gippsland Rail Trail

Buchan

C608

C608

Mt Ellery (1291m)

Ocean View Lookout

Errinundra

Chandlers Creek

Cooracambra National Park

irnsdale

Bruthen

Nicholson

Johnsonville

Swan Reach

C612

Nowa Nowa

Lind National Park

Cann River

B23

Eden (17km)

Lake King

Metung

Kalimna

Lakes Entrance

Lake Tyers

Orbost

Cabbage Tree Creek

A1

Club Terrace

Alfred National Park

Genoa

A1

aymond Island

Lakes District

Lake Tyers

East Gippsland Rail Trail

Marlo

C107

Bellbird Creek

C615

Gipsy Point

Sperm Whale Head Peninsula

Marlo Inlet

Cape Conran Coastal Park

Cape Conran Coastal Park

Pearl Point

Bemm River

Tamboon Inlet

Pt Hicks

Croajingolong National Park

Sandpatch Point

Mallacoota

Shipwreck Creek

Little Rame Head

Wingan Inlet & the Skerries

Gabo Island Lightstation Reserve

BASS STRAIT

0 — 40 km
0 — 20 miles

6 Descend into ancient limestone caves and camp outside at **Buchan** (p249)

7 Take an afternoon winery cruise and then feast on a

seafood dinner at **Lakes Entrance** (p246)

8 Find your quiet corner of the world in humbling **Croajingolong National Park**

(p254) and **Cape Conran Coastal Park** (p252)

9 Cruise the waters of the **Lakes District** (p242) from the tranquil marina villages of Metung and Paynesville

WEST GIPPSLAND

The Princes Hwy heads east from Melbourne to the Latrobe Valley, an area known for its dairy farming and coal-fired power stations. Avoid the main towns of Moe, Morwell and Traralgon and head instead for the coast, or north into the foothills of the Great Dividing Range, where you'll find Baw Baw National Park, the Thomson Dam and the historic gold-mining town of Walhalla.

Walhalla

POP 16

As you travel along the Latrobe Valley, there's little to suggest that a mere 35km north of the main road is Victoria's best-preserved and most charming historic town. Tiny Walhalla lies hidden high in the green hills and forests of west Gippsland, a postcard-pretty collection of sepia-toned period cottages and other timber buildings (some original, most reconstructed). The setting, too, is gorgeous, strung out along a deep, forested valley with Stringers Creek running through the centre of the township.

Gold was discovered here on 26 December 1862, although the first find was not registered until January 1863, which is when the gold rush really began. In its gold-mining heyday, Walhalla's population was 5000. It fell to just 10 people in 1998 (when mains electricity arrived in the town). Like all great ghost towns, the dead that are buried in the stunningly sited cemetery vastly outnumber the living.

AUSTRALIAN ALPS WALKING TRACK

One of Australia's best and most challenging walks, the Australian Alps Walking Track begins in Walhalla and ends close to Canberra. This 655km epic traverses the valleys and ridgelines of Victoria's High Country, and en route to Tharwa in the ACT it climbs to the summit of Mt Bogong, Mt Kosciuszko and Bimberi Peak, the highest points in Victoria, New South Wales and the ACT respectively. Making the full trek is a serious undertaking that requires good navigational skills and high levels of fitness and self-sufficiency. If you're planning on making the trek, which takes up to eight weeks to complete, track down a copy of *Australian Alps Walking Track* by John and Monica Chapman.

◉ Sights & Activities

The best way to see the town is on foot – take the **tramline walk** (45 minutes) that begins from opposite the general store soon after you enter town. Other good (and well-signposted) walks lead up from the valley floor. Among them, a trail leads to the **Walhalla Cricket Ground** (2km, 45 minutes return). Another trail climbs to the extraordinary **Walhalla Cemetery** (20 minutes return), where the gravestones cling to the steep valley wall and through their inscriptions tell a sombre yet fascinating story of the town's history.

During August the town lights up for the **Walhalla Vinter Ijusfest** (Winter Lights Festival).

Walhalla Historical Museum MUSEUM
(☑ 03-5165 6250; admission $2; ⊙10am-4pm) Located in the old post office in the group of restored shops along the main street, Walhalla Historical Museum also acts as an information centre and books the popular two-hour **ghost tours** (www.walhallaghosttour.info; adult/child/family $25/20/75; ⊙ 7.30pm Sat, 8.30pm Sat during daylight saving).

Long Tunnel Extended Gold Mine MINE
(☑03-5165 6259; off Walhalla-Beardmore Rd; adult/child/family $19.50/13.50/49.50; ⊙tours 1.30pm daily, plus noon & 3pm Sat, Sun & holidays) Relive the mining past with guided tours exploring Cohens Reef, once one of Australia's top reef-gold producers. Almost 14 tonnes of gold came out of this mine.

Walhalla Goldfields Railway HISTORIC RAILWAY
(☑03-5165 6280; www.walhallarail.com; return adult/child/family $20/15/50; ⊙from Walhalla Station 11am, 1pm & 3pm, from Thomson Station 11.40am, 1.40pm & 3.40pm Wed, Sat, Sun & public holidays) A star attraction is the scenic Walhalla Goldfields Railway, which offers a 20-minute ride between Walhalla and Thomson Stations (on the main road, 3.5km before Walhalla). The train snakes along Stringers Creek Gorge, passing lovely, forested gorge country and crossing a number of trestle bridges.

☞ Tours

Mountain Top Experience ADVENTURE TOUR
(☑03-5134 6876; www.mountaintopexperience.com) Mountain Top Experience operates nature-based 4WD tours that head north along remote trails from Walhalla and nearby Rawson into the Victorian High Country. Departure dates depend on demand.

🛏 Sleeping & Eating

You can camp for free at North Gardens, a camp site with toilets and barbecues (but no showers), at the north end of the village. Walhalla has a handful of cottages and B&Bs, and there are a couple of old-style cafes among the group of shops in the village centre.

Chinese Garden   CAMPGROUND $
(www.walhallaboard.org.au; off Main St; per person $25) At the northern end of town, this recently opened camping ground has full toilet and shower facilities, a laundrette and a barbecue area.

Rawson Caravan Park   CARAVAN PARK $
(☑ 03-5165 3439; www.rawsoncaravanpark.com.au; Depot Rd, Rawson; powered sites/dm/cabins $30/45/95) Located about 12km from Walhalla, Rawson Caravan Park has a native-bush setting, en suite sites and the popular Stockyard Bar & Bistro, which opens on weekends and features live music and boisterous crowds up from the Latrobe Valley.

★ Walhalla Star Hotel   HISTORIC HOTEL $$
(☑ 03-5165 6262; www.starhotel.com.au; Main St; d incl breakfast from $175; 🌐 @ 🛜) The rebuilt historic Star offers stylish boutique accommodation with king-sized beds and simple but sophisticated designer decor, making good use of local materials such as corrugated-iron water tanks. Guests can dine at the flash **Parker's Restaurant** (☑ 03-5165 6262; mains from $30, 2-/3-course set meals from $30/40; ⏰ 6.30-9.30pm); others need to reserve in advance. Or you can get good breakfasts, pies, coffee and cake at the attached **Greyhorse Café** (mains from $5; ⏰ 10am-2pm).

Windsor House   B&B $$
(☑ 03-5165 6237; www.windsorhouse.com.au; off Walhalla Rd; d $160, ste $175-200) The five rooms and suites in this beautifully restored two-storey 1878 home are fittingly old fashioned and ghost-free. No children under 12.

Wild Cherry B&B   B&B $$
(☑ 03-5165 6245; www.wildcherrywalhalla.com.au; Church Hill Rd; d $180; 🌐 🛜) The Wild Cherry is a sweet little B&B perched on the hill above Walhalla and has comfy motel-style rooms.

Walhalla Lodge Hotel   PUB $$
(☑ 03-5165 6226; Main St; mains $16-25; ⏰ noon-2pm & 6-9pm Wed-Mon) The cosy, one-room Wally Pub is decked out with prints of old Walhalla and serves good-value counter meals – think burgers, pasta, schnitzels and T-bone steaks.

❶ Getting There & Away

Walhalla lies approximately 180km east of Melbourne. There's no public transport. By road, Walhalla can be reached via a lovely, winding forest drive from Moe or Traralgon.

SOUTH GIPPSLAND

South Gippsland has plenty of gems along the coast between Inverloch and Wilsons Promontory – Venus Bay, Cape Liptrap Coastal Park and Waratah Bay are all worth exploring. Inland among the farming communities are some great drives through the Strzelecki Ranges, the Great Southern Rail Trail cycle path and trendy villages such as Koonwarra and Fish Creek.

Inverloch
POP 4460

Fabulous surf, calm inlet beaches and outstanding diving and snorkelling make the coast along the road between Cape Paterson and Inverloch a popular destination. You'll wonder what all of the fuss is about if you pass through in winter, but stay for a few days in summer and you'll come to appreciate Inverloch's charms, not least among which is its unpretentious vibe.

🎉 Festivals & Events

Inverloch Jazz Festival   MUSIC
(www.inverlochjazzfest.org.au; ⏰ Mar) Inverloch draws the crowds when it hosts the popular Inverloch Jazz Festival on the Labour Day long weekend each March.

🎓 Courses

Offshore Surf School   SURFING
(☑ 0407 374 743; www.offshoresurfschool.com.au; 32 Park St; 2hr lesson $60) If you want to learn to catch a wave, the Offshore Surf School offers lessons at the main town surf beach.

🛏 Sleeping

There's plenty of holiday accommodation around Inverloch – the visitor centre can help with bookings.

Inverloch Foreshore Camping Reserve   CAMPGROUND $
(☑ 03-5674 1447; www.inverlochholidaypark.com.au; cnr Esplanade & Ramsey Blvd; unpowered/powered sites from $26/30) Camping is a pleasure at this camp site set just back from the inlet beach and offering shade and privacy.

LOCAL MARKETS

Food is an increasingly important part of the traveller experience in Gippsland, and it's always worth checking the dates of the farmers and other markets in the small towns across the region.

➡ Koonwarra – 1st Saturday of the month

➡ Korumburra – 2nd Saturday of the month

➡ Foster – 3rd Saturday of the month

➡ Mirboo North – last Saturday of the month

➡ Inverloch – last Sunday of the month

★ **Moilong Express** BOUTIQUE HOTEL **$$**
(☑ 0439 842 334; www.coastalstays.com/moilongexpress; 405 Inverloch-Venus Bay Rd; d $120) This quirky former railway train carriage, on a hillside property about 3km from Inverloch, has been converted into very comfortable accommodation. There's a kitchen, queen-sized bed, traditional wood panelling and an old railway station clock.

Lofts APARTMENT **$$$**
(☑ 03-5674 2255; www.theloftapartments.com.au; Scarborough St; apt from $200; ❋) Spread yourself out in these sleek, architect-designed apartments with high ceilings and lofts. They're handily adjacent to the park, beach and shops. Some have water views and most have a spa. Prices drop the longer you stay.

✖ Eating

Cafes and restaurants are clustered around Williams and A'Beckett Sts.

Red Elk Café CAFE **$**
(☑ 03-5674 3264; 27 A'Beckett St; mains $10-16.50; ◷ 8.30am-3.30pm Mon-Fri, to 4pm Sat & Sun) In a weatherboard corner cottage, this new cafe and bar is a buzzing place for coffee and a hearty breakfast. Try the quinoa salad or the chicken-and-brie toasted roll.

Tomo's JAPANESE **$$**
(☑ 03-5674 3444; www.tomos-japanese.com; 23 A'Beckett St; sushi from $4, mains $21-39; ◷ noon-2pm & 6-9pm Wed-Sun, daily Dec-Feb) Modern Japanese cuisine prepared to perfection. Start with tender sushi or sashimi, but don't miss the *gyoza* (dumplings) or tempura tiger prawns.

Vela 9 MEDITERRANEAN **$$$**
(☑ 03-5674 1188; www.velanine.com.au; 9 A'Beckett St; mains $30-38; ◷ 6-9.30pm Thu-Mon) Spanish flavours dominate at this wine-and-tapas bar that opens out onto a more upmarket restaurant at night. Get started with a cured meats board and follow it up with some local seafood.

ⓘ Information

Inverloch Visitor Centre (☑ 1300 762 433; www.visitbasscoast.com; 39 A'Beckett St; ◷ 9am-5pm) Helpful staff can make accommodation bookings for free.

Bunurong Environment Centre & Shop (☑ 03-5674 3738; www.sgcs.org.au; cnr Esplanade & Ramsey Blvd; ◷ 10am-4pm Fri-Mon, daily in school holidays) An abundance of books and brochures on environmental and sustainable-living topics. Also here is the Shell Museum (admission $2) with more than 6000 shells.

ⓘ Getting There & Away

V/Line (☑ 13 61 96; www.vline.com.au) trains depart daily from Melbourne's Flinders St and Southern Cross Stations for Dandenong, connecting with buses to Inverloch ($16.40, 3½ hours). A quicker option (2½ hours) is the V/Line coach with a change at gloriously named Koo Wee Rup.

If you're driving to Inverloch from Melbourne (148km), follow the signs to Phillip Island and Wonthaggi. The route via Leongatha, 27km northeast of Inverloch, is less scenic but slightly quicker.

Bunurong Marine & Coastal Park

This surprising little marine and coastal park offers some of Australia's best snorkelling and diving, and a stunning, cliff-hugging drive between Inverloch and Cape Paterson. It certainly surprised the archaeological world in the early 1990s when dinosaur remains dating back 120 million years were discovered here. Eagles Nest, Shack Bay, the Caves and Twin Reefs are great for snorkelling. The Oaks is the locals' favourite surf beach. The Caves is where the dinosaur dig action is.

SEAL Diving Services (☑ 03-5174 3434; www.sealdivingservices.com.au; 7/27 Princes Hwy, Traralgon) has shore dives at Cape Paterson and boat dives in Bunurong Marine & Coastal Park.

Korumburra

POP 3350

The first sizeable town along the South Gippsland Hwy, Korumburra is scenically situated on the edge of the Strzelecki Ranges.

Coal Creek Village (☑ 03-5655 1811; www.coalcreekvillage.com.au; 12 Silkstone Rd; ◷ 10am-4.30pm Thu-Mon, daily during school holidays)

FREE is an interesting re-creation of a 19th-century mining town, with a museum, activities for kids and a regional visitor centre (☎1800 630 704, 03-5655 2233; www.visitpromcountry.com.au; ☻9am-5pm). V/Line coaches from Melbourne's Southern Cross Station stop outside en route to Leongatha and Yarram.

Volunteers at the South Gippsland Railway (☎03-5658 1111, 1800 442 211; www.sgr.org.au; adult/child/family return $30/20/100) operate heritage diesel trains along scenic tracks from Korumburra to Leongatha and Nyora on Sundays and public holidays (four services).

Koonwarra

POP 380

This tiny township on the South Gippsland Hwy has built itself a reputation around its general store and cafe. There's also an organic fruit-and-vegetable shop and a popular organic farmers market (☎0408 619 182; www.kfm.org.au; Memorial Park, Koala Dr; ☻8am-1pm 1st Sat of month).

🏃 Activities

Milly & Romeo's Artisan Bakery & Cooking School　COOKING COURSE
(☎03-5664 2211; www.millyandromeos.com.au; Koala Dr; adult/child from $90/50; ☻9.30am-4.30pm Thu & Fri, 8.30am-4.30pm Sat & Sun, longer hours in summer) Victoria's first organic-certified cooking school offers short courses in making cakes, bread, traditional pastries, French classics and pasta, as well as running cooking classes for kids.

Koonwarra Day Spa　SPA
(☎03-5664 2332; www.koonwarraspa.com.au; 9 Koala Dr; spa from $45, massage from $55; ☻10am-5pm Tue-Sat, plus Mon Dec & Jan) Indulge yourself with spas, saunas and body treatments ranging from a 30-minute mineral spa to a six-hour pamper package.

🛏 Sleeping & Eating

Lyre Bird Hill Winery & Guest House　B&B $$
(☎03-5664 3204; www.lyrebirdhill.com.au; 370 Inverloch Rd; guesthouse s/d $125/175, cottage $150; ☻cellar door 10am-5pm Wed-Mon Oct-Nov & Feb-Apr, daily Dec & Jan, by appointment May-Sep; ✲) Stay among the vines 4km southwest of Koonwarra. The quaint, old-fashioned B&B has light-filled rooms overlooking the garden, while the self-contained country-style cottage is perfect for a family. The vineyard is right next door.

★**Koonwarra Store**　CAFE $$
(☎03-5664 2285; www.koonwarrastore.com; cnr South Gippsland Hwy & Koala Dr; mains $12.50-24; ☻8.30am-5.30pm) Local produce and wines are on sale in this renovated timber building. Inside is a renowned cafe that serves simple food with flair, priding itself on using organic, low-impact suppliers and products. The arrival of a Spanish chef has added tapas to the mix. Soak up the ambience in the wooded interior, or relax at a table in the shaded cottage gardens, home to the Outside Bit, a quirky little nursery.

❶ Getting There & Away

Koonwarra is served by buses running between Korumburra and Foster three times a day on weekdays and up to six times daily on weekends. By road the town is 32km southeast of Korumburra and 21km northeast of Inverloch.

Fish Creek

POP 790

For years travellers in the know have been stopping for a bite to eat at Fish Creek on their way to the coast or the Prom. These days it has developed into a little bohemian artists community with craft shops, galleries, studios, bookshops and some great cafes. The Great Southern Rail Trail passes through.

Celia Rosser Gallery (☎03-5683 2628; www.celiarossergallery.com.au; Promontory Rd; ☻10am-4pm Fri-Sun) FREE is a bright art space featuring the works of renowned botanical

GREAT SOUTHERN RAIL TRAIL

This 58km cycling and walking path (www.railtrails.org.au) follows the old rail line from Leongatha to Foster, passing through the villages of Koonwarra, Meeniyan, Buffalo and Fish Creek, where you can stop and refuel. The trail meanders through farmland with a few gentle hills, trestle bridges and occasional views of the coast and Wilsons Prom. The first section from Leongatha to Koonwarra is through the rolling open country of the region's dairy farms. The middle section from Koonwarra to Meeniyan and on to Foster is the most scenic section of the route, with plenty of bridges, eucalypt forests and fine views.

GRAND RIDGE ROAD

The spectacular 132km Grand Ridge Road winds along the top of the Strzelecki Ranges, running from midway between Warragul and Korumburra to midway between Traralgon and Yarram. The (mostly) gravel road provides a fabulous excursion through fertile farmland once covered with forests of giant mountain ash and valleys of giant tree ferns.

The drive is a great alternative to the Princes Hwy, but if you're going to travel the length of it, allow the best part of a day. Pick the road up (signposted from the highway) south of Warragul. Just 3km along is the excellent **Wild Dog Winery** (☑ 03-5623 2211; www.wild-dogwinery.com; Warragul-Korumburra Rd; restaurant mains around $35; ⊙ cellar door 10am-5pm, restaurant 11.30am-2.30pm Wed & Thu, to 2.30pm & 6-9pm Fri, 10am-3pm Sat & Sun), one of Gippsland's first wineries. It produces a range of cool-climate wines, all grown and bottled on its 30 acres, and has an excellent restaurant with views across the Strzelecki Ranges.

The only community of any size along the Grand Ridge Road is the pretty township of **Mirboo North**. It's home to Gippsland's only brewery, the award-winning **Grand Ridge Brewery & Restaurant** (☑ 03-5668 2222; www.grand-ridge.com.au; Main St; mains $20-28; ⊙ brewery daily, restaurant noon-3pm & 6-9pm Wed-Sun), producing a range of chemical- and preservative-free beer. The restaurant food is fresh, prepared from local produce, and includes steaks from the local beef producer, tapas plates and roo fillet.

Continuing, you'll pass through the rainforest gully of **Tarra-Bulga National Park**, one of the last remnants of the magnificent forests that once covered all of south Gippsland. There are some good short walks here, including the Tarra Valley Rainforest Walk to **Cyathea Falls** (1.5km, 35 minutes return) and the easy **Fern Gully Nature Walk** (750m, 15 minutes return). Camping is not permitted in the park but you can stay at the nearby **Tarra Valley Tourist Park** (☑ 03-5186 1283; www.tarra-valley.com; 1906 Tarra Valley Rd; unpowered/powered sites $26/36, cabins $120-175) nestled in rainforest, with camping in a pretty riverside setting and cabin accommodation.

For sheer indulgence, stop at the **Tarra Valley Rainforest Retreat** (☑ 03-5186 1313; www.tarravalleyrainforestretreat.com; 1788 Tarra Valley Rd; d $180; ❋), elegant Swiss chalet–style accommodation that doubles as a chocolate-making school. Chocolate appreciation courses with the resident chocolate maker cost $50/55 for guests/nonguests.

---

artist Celia Rosser and various visiting artists. The attached Banksia Café has a sunny deck.

The art deco **Fish Creek Hotel** (☑ 03-5683 2416; www.fishcreekhotel.com.au; Old Waratah Rd; mains $16-30; ⊙ noon-2pm & 6-9pm), universally known as the Fishy Pub (but also called the Promontory Gate Hotel), is an essential stop for a beer or bistro meal, and there's motel accommodation at the back.

Fish Creek lies along the Korumburra–Foster bus line with at least three departures daily. By road, follow the signs off the South Gippsland Hwy at Foster (13km) or Meeniyan (28km).

WILSONS PROMONTORY NATIONAL PARK

If you like wilderness bushwalking, stunning coastal scenery and secluded white-sand beaches, you'll absolutely love this place. 'The Prom', as it's affectionately known, is one of the most popular national parks in Australia. Hardly surprising, given its accessibility from Melbourne, its network of more than 80km of walking tracks, its swimming and surf beaches, and the abundant wildlife.

Wilsons Promontory was an important area for the Kurnai and Boonwurrung indigenous peoples, and middens have been found in many places, including Cotters and Darby Beaches, and Oberon Bay. The southernmost part of mainland Australia, the Prom once formed a land bridge that allowed people to walk to Tasmania.

Tidal River, 30km from the park entrance, is the hub: it's home to the Parks Victoria office, a general store, cafe and accommodation. The wildlife around Tidal River is incredibly tame: kookaburras and rosellas lurk expectantly (resist the urge to feed them) and wombats nonchalantly waddle out of the undergrowth.

Although there's a staffed **entrance booth** (⊙ 9am-sunset), where you receive a ticket, entry is free. There's no fuel available in Tidal River.

🏃 Activities

There's an extensive choice of marked **walking trails** (see p241), taking you through forests, marshes, valleys of tree ferns, low granite mountains and along beaches lined with sand dunes. The Parks Victoria office at Tidal River has brochures with details of walks, from 15-minute strolls to overnight and longer hikes. Even nonwalkers can enjoy some of the park's beauty, with car park access off the Tidal River road leading to gorgeous beaches and lookouts. The northern area of the park is much less visited – most walks in this wilderness area are overnight or longer, and mainly for experienced bushwalkers; permits are required.

Swimming is safe from the gorgeous beaches at Norman Bay (Tidal River) and around the headland at Squeaky Beach – the ultrafine quartz sand here really does squeak beneath your feet!

You can hire camping equipment, including tents, stoves, sleeping bags and backpacks, from **Wilsons Prom Hiking Hire** (☑ 0400 377 993; www.wilsonspromhikinghire.com.au; 3670 Prom Rd, Yanakie).

👉 Tours

Bunyip Tours BUS TOUR
(☑ 1300 286 947; www.bunyiptours.com; tours from $120; ⊙ Wed & Sun, plus Fri in summer) Proudly carbon-neutral, Bunyip Tours offers a one-day guided tour to the Prom from Melbourne, with the option of staying on another two days to explore by yourself.

First Track Adventures ADVENTURE TOUR
(☑ 03-5634 2761; www.firsttrack.com.au) This Yarragon-based company organises customised bushwalking, canoeing and abseiling trips to the Prom for individuals and groups. Prices vary according to group size and activity.

🛏 Sleeping

The main accommodation base is at Tidal River, but there are 11 bush-camping (outstation) areas around the Prom, all with pit or compost toilets, but no other facilities; you need to carry in your own drinking water. Overnight hikers need camping permits (adult/child per night $11.30/5.70), which must be booked ahead through Parks Victoria (p241).

For bookings in the Prom's hinterland, try the **Wilsons Prom & Surrounds Accommodation Service** (www.promcountry.com.au).

Tidal River

Situated on Norman Bay and a short walk to a stunning beach, Tidal River is incredibly popular. Book accommodation well in advance through Parks Victoria (p241), especially for weekends and holidays.

★ **Lighthouse Keepers' Cottages** COTTAGE $
(☑ Parks Victoria 13 19 63; www.parkweb.vic.gov.au; 8-bed cottage $90-100, 20-bed cottage $120-134) These isolated, heritage-listed 1850s cottages with thick granite walls are a real getaway, attached to a working lightstation on a pimple of land that juts out into the wild ocean. Kick back after the 19km hike from Tidal River and watch ships or whales passing by. The cottages have shared facilities, including a fully equipped kitchen.

Camp Sites CAMPGROUND $
(unpowered sites per vehicle & 3 people $29.60-32.80, powered sites per vehicle & up to 8 people $49.30-54.70) Tidal River has 484 camp sites, but only 20 powered sites. For the Christmas school-holiday period there's a ballot for sites (apply online by 30 June at www.parkweb.vic.gov.au).

Park Huts CABINS $
(4-/6-bed huts from $72/109) If you're travelling tent-free, these cosy wooden huts are a decent budget option, with bunks and kitchenettes, but no bathrooms.

Park Cabins CABINS $$
(d $186-207, additional adult/child $27/18) The spacious and private self-contained cabins sleep up to six people and have large, sliding-glass doors and a deck, and overlook the bush or river. The Lorikeet Units are equally comfortable, sleeping up to four people, but they're closer to the visitor centre and parking area.

★ **Wilderness Retreat** SAFARI TENT $$$
(www.wildernessretreats.com.au; d $302.50, extra person $24.50) Nestled in bushland at Tidal River, these are the most expensive tents on the Prom. The luxury safari tents, each with their own deck, sleep up to four people and are pretty cool, with a bathroom, queen-sized beds, heating and a communal tent kitchen. It's like being on an African safari with a kookaburra soundtrack.

Yanakie & Foster

The tiny, dispersed settlement of Yanakie offers the closest accommodation outside the

Wilsons Promontory National Park

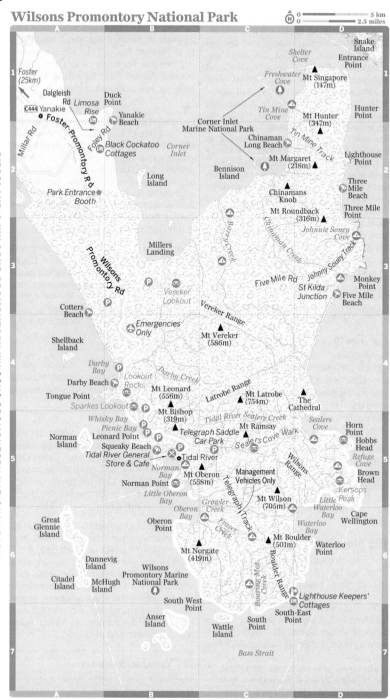

0 ————— 5 km
0 ————— 2.5 miles

Foster
(25km)

Dalgleish
Rd
C444 Yanakie
Foster-Promontory Rd
Millar Rd
Limosa
Rise
Duck
Point
Yanakie
Beach
Foley Rd
Black Cockatoo
Cottages
Corner
Inlet
Park Entrance
Booth
Wilsons
Promontory Rd
Long
Island
Millers
Landing
Barry Creek
Snake
Island
Entrance
Point
Shelter
Cove
Freshwater
Cove
Mt Singapore
(147m)
Tin Mine
Cove
Mt Hunter
(347m)
Hunter
Point
Corner Inlet
Marine National Park
Chinaman
Long Beach
Bennison
Island
Mt Margaret
(218m)
Lighthouse
Point
Chinamans
Knob
Mt Roundback
(316m)
Three
Mile
Beach
Three Mile
Point
Johnnie Souey
Cove
Johnny Souey Track
Chinaman Creek
Tin Mine Track

Cotters
Beach
Shellback
Island
Vereker
Lookout
Vereker Range
Emergencies
Only
Mt Vereker
(586m)
Five Mile Rd
St Kilda
Junction
Monkey
Point
Five Mile
Beach

Darby
Bay
Darby Beach
Tongue Point
Lookout
Rocks
Sparkes Lookout
Darby Creek
Mt Leonard
(556m)
Mt Bishop
(319m)
Latrobe Range
Mt Latrobe
(754m)
The
Cathedral
Whisky Bay
Picnic Bay
Norman
Island
Leonard Point
Squeaky Beach
Tidal River General
Store & Cafe
Tidal River
Norman
Bay
Norman Point
Mt Oberon
(558m)
Telegraph Saddle
Car Park
Tidal River
Sealers Creek
Mt Ramsay
Sealers Cove Walk
Sealers
Cove
Horn
Point
Hobbs
Head
Refuge
Cove
Brown
Head
Wilsons
Range
Kersops
Peak
Management
Vehicles Only
Mt Wilson
(705m)
Little
Waterloo
Bay
Cape
Wellington
Great
Glennie
Island
Oberon
Point
Little Oberon
Bay
Oberon
Bay
Growler
Creek
Fraser
Creek
Telegraph Track
Waterloo
Bay
Mt Boulder
(501m)
Waterloo
Point
Dannevig
Island
Citadel
Island
McHugh
Island
Wilsons
Promontory Marine
National Park
Mt Norgate
(419m)
South West
Point
Anser
Island
Wattle
Island
South
Point
Roaring Meg Creek
Boulder Range
South-East
Point
Lighthouse Keepers'
Cottages

Bass Strait

park boundaries – from cabins and camping to luxury cottages. Foster, the nearest main town, has a backpackers and several motels.

Prom Coast Backpackers HOSTEL **$**
(☑ 0427 875 735; www.promcoastyha.com.au; 40 Station Rd, Foster; dm/d from $30/70; @) The closest backpacker hostel to the park is this friendly YHA in Foster. The cosy renovated cottage sleeps only 10 so it's always intimate.

Black Cockatoo Cottages COTTAGES **$$**
(☑ 03-5687 1306; 60 Foley Rd, Yanakie; d $140-160, 6-person house $180) You can take in glorious views of the national park without leaving your very comfortable bed – or breaking the bank – in these private, stylish, black-timber cottages. There are three modern cottages and a three-bedroom house.

Warrawee Holiday Apartments APARTMENTS **$$**
(☑ 03-5682 2171; www.warraweeapartments.com.au; 38 Station Rd, Foster; d $100-130; ❀) Next to Prom Coast Backpackers in Foster and under the same management, these simple but comfortable two-bedroom apartments are good value.

Limosa Rise COTTAGES **$$$**
(☑ 03-5687 1135; www.limosarise.com.au; 40 Dalgleish Rd, Yanakie; d $250-440; ❀) The views are stupendous from these luxury, self-contained

cottages near the Prom entrance. The three tastefully appointed cottages (a studio, one-bedroom and two-bedroom) are fitted with full-length glass windows taking complete advantage of sweeping views across Corner Inlet and the Prom's mountains.

✖ Eating

Tidal River General Store & Cafe CAFE **$**
(mains $5-22; ⊙ 9am-5pm Sun-Fri, to 6pm Sat) The Tidal River general store stocks grocery items and some camping equipment, but if you're hiking or staying a while it's cheaper to stock up in Foster. The attached cafe serves takeaway food such as pies and sandwiches, as well as breakfast, light lunches and bistro-style meals on weekends and holidays.

ℹ Information

Parks Victoria (☑ 03-5680 9555, 13 19 63; www.parkweb.vic.gov.au; ⊙ 8.30am-4.30pm) The helpful visitor centre at Tidal River books all park accommodation, including permits for camping away from Tidal River.

ℹ Getting There & Away

Tidal River lies approximately 224km southeast of Melbourne. There's no direct public transport between Melbourne and the Prom, but the **Wilsons Promontory Bus Service** (Moon's Bus Lines; ☑ 03-5687 1249) operates from Foster to

---

TOP PROM WALKS

The Prom's delights are best discovered on foot. From Christmas to the end of January a free shuttle bus operates between the Tidal River visitors car park and the Telegraph Saddle car park (a nice way to start the Prom Circuit Walk). Here are six of the best:

Great Prom Walk This is the most popular long-distance hike, a moderate 45km circuit across to Sealers Cove from Tidal River, down to Refuge Cove, Waterloo Bay, the lighthouse and the return loop back to Tidal River via Oberon Bay. Allow three days, and coordinate your walks with tide times, as creek crossings can be hazardous. It's possible to visit or stay at the lighthouse by prior arrangement with the parks office.

Sealers Cove Walk The best overnight hike, this two-day walk starts at Telegraph Saddle and heads down Telegraph Track to stay overnight at beautiful Little Waterloo Bay (12km, 4½ hours). The next day walk on to Sealers Cove via Refuge Cove and return to Telegraph Saddle (24km, 7½ hours).

Lilly Pilly Gully Nature Walk An easy 5km (two-hour) walk through heathland and eucalypt forests, with lots of wildlife.

Mt Oberon Summit Starting from the Mt Oberon car park, this moderate-to-hard 7km (2½-hour) walk is an ideal intro to the Prom, with panoramic views from the summit. The free Mt Oberon shuttle bus can take you to the Telegraph Saddle car park and back.

Little Oberon Bay An easy-to-moderate 8km (three-hour) walk over sand dunes covered in coastal tea trees with beautiful views over Little Oberon Bay.

Squeaky Beach Nature Walk An easy 5km return stroll through coastal tea trees and banksias to a sensational white-sand beach.

Tidal River (via Fish Creek) on Friday at 4.30pm, returning on Sunday at 4.30pm. This service connects with the V/Line bus from Melbourne at Fish Creek.

V/Line (☑ 13 61 96; www.vline.com.au) buses from Melbourne's Southern Cross Station travel to Foster ($19.80, three hours, four daily) via Dandenong and Koo Wee Rup.

EAST OF THE PROM

Port Albert

POP 250

This little old fishing village, 111km by road northeast of Tidal River, is developing a reputation as a trendy stopover for boating, fishing and sampling the local seafood. The town proudly pronounces itself Gippsland's first established port, and the many historic timber buildings in the main street dating from the 1850s bear a brass plaque, detailing their age and previous use.

◉ Sights & Activities

Gippsland Regional Maritime Museum   MUSEUM
(☑ 03-5183 2520; Tarraville Rd; adult/child $5/1; ☉ 10.30am-4pm daily Sep-May, Sat & Sun Jun-Aug) The Gippsland Regional Maritime Museum, in the old Bank of Victoria (1861), will give you an insight into the highlights of Port Albert's maritime history, with stories of shipwrecks, the town's whaling and sealing days, and local Aboriginal legends.

Nooramunga Marine & Coastal Park   CANOEING, BOATING
You can hire boats and canoes from the Slip Jetty for cruising around the sheltered waters of the Nooramunga Marine & Coastal Park.

🛏 Sleeping & Eating

There's a caravan park at Seabank, about 6km northwest of Port Albert, and there are a few B&Bs in town.

Port Albert Hotel   HOTEL
Sadly this historic timber hotel – which could formerly lay claim to being Victoria's oldest continually licensed pub (since 1842) – burned to the ground in February 2014. No plans to rebuild were in place at time of publication, but watch this space.

Port Albert Wharf   FISH & CHIPS $
(☑ 03-5183 2002; 40 Wharf St; mains from $7; ☉ 11am-7.30pm) The fish and chips here are renowned, perfectly presented and as fresh as you'd expect from a town built on fishing.

★ **Wildfish**   SEAFOOD $$
(☑ 03-5183 2002; www.wildfish-restaurant.com.au; 40 Wharf St; lunch mains $8-17, dinner mains $26-36; ☉ noon-3pm & 6-8pm Thu-Sun) With a sublime harbour-side location and the freshest local seafood, Wildfish is earning a well-deserved reputation for serving good food. By day it's a cafe offering coffee and sandwiches; by night the menu turns to thoughtful seafood dishes such as flake-and-scallop pie or tempura garfish fillets.

❶ Getting There & Away

The closest public transport from Melbourne is the V/Line bus service to Yarram, 12km to the north of Port Albert. By road, take the South Gippsland Hwy and follow the signs to Port Albert along the Yarram–Port Albert Rd.

LAKES DISTRICT

The Gippsland Lakes form the largest inland waterway system in Australia, with the three main interconnecting lakes – Wellington, King and Victoria – stretching from Sale to beyond Lakes Entrance. The lakes are actually saltwater lagoons, separated from the ocean by the Gippsland Lakes Coastal Park and the narrow coastal strip of sand dunes known as Ninety Mile Beach. You really need a boat to explore the lakes in depth, but it's hard to beat camping and fishing along the beach or hanging out at the pretty seaside communities.

Sale

POP 12,800

Gateway to the Lakes District, Sale has plenty of accommodation, shops, restaurants and pubs, making it a good town-sized base for exploring Ninety Mile Beach.

◉ Sights & Activities

Port of Sale   PORT
The Port of Sale is a redeveloped marina area in the town centre with boardwalks, cafes and a canal leading out to the Gippsland Lakes.

Sale Wetlands Walk   WALKING
The Sale Wetlands Walk (4km, 1½ hours) is a pleasant wander around Lake Gutheridge

(immediately east of where the Princes Hwy does a dogleg in the centre of Sale) and its adjoining wetlands, and incorporates an Indigenous Art Trail commemorating the importance of the wetlands to the local Kurnai community.

Sale Common BIRDWATCHING

Sale Common, a 300-hectare wildlife refuge with bird hides, an observatory, a waterhole, boardwalks and other walking tracks is part of an internationally recognised wetlands system. The best time to visit is early morning or late evening (wear some mosquito repellent), when you'll see lots of bird life. The visitor centre has a list of recorded species.

🛏 Sleeping & Eating

Cambrai Hostel HOSTEL $

(☑ 03-5147 1600; www.maffra.net.au/hostel; 117 Johnson St; dm per night/week $28/160; @) In Maffra, 16km north of Sale, this relaxed hostel is a budget haven and one of the few true backpacker hostels in Gippsland. In a 120-year-old building that was once a doctor's residence, it has a licensed bar, an open fire and a pool table in the cosy lounge, a tiny self-catering kitchen and clean, cheerful rooms. The owners can sometimes arrange work in the region.

Quest Serviced Apartments APARTMENT $$

(☑ 03-5142 0900; www.questapartments.com.au; 180-184 York St; studio/1-bedroom/2-bedroom apt $120/199/285; ❄ 🛜 🖥) This reliable chain offers up modern, self-contained apartments that feel more luxurious than you'd expect for these prices. As such, it's streets ahead of most other motels around town.

Bis Cucina CAFE $$

(☑ 03-5144 3388; 100 Foster St; breakfast & lunch $12-23, dinner $23-36; ☺ 8am-2pm daily, 6-8pm Fri, Sat & show nights) At the Wellington Entertainment Centre, Bis Cucina offers relaxed and attentive service combined with carefully chosen modern Australian cuisine with Mediterranean influences. This is a good choice for serious foodies, theatre-goers wanting a preshow meal, or those after just a coffee or lazy breakfast.

ℹ Information

Wellington Visitor Information Centre (☑ 03-5144 1108; www.tourismwellington.com.au; 8 Foster St; ☺ 9am-5pm) Internet facilities and a free accommodation-booking service.

ℹ Getting There & Away

Sale lies along the Princes Hwy, 214km from Melbourne.

V/Line (☑ 1800 800 007; www.vline.com. au) has train and train-bus services between Melbourne and Sale ($24.60, three hours, four daily), sometimes with a change in Traralgon.

Ninety Mile Beach

To paraphrase the immortal words of Crocodile Dundee: that's not a beach...*this* is a beach. Isolated Ninety Mile Beach is a narrow strip of sand backed by dunes, featuring lagoons and stretching unbroken for more or less 90 miles (150km) from near McLoughlins Beach to the channel at Lakes Entrance. It's arguably Australia's longest single beach. The area is great for surf fishing, camping and long beach walks, though the crashing surf can be dangerous for swimming, except where patrolled at Seaspray, Woodside Beach and Lakes Entrance.

Between Seaspray and Lakes Entrance, the Gippsland Lakes Coastal Park is a protected area of low-lying coastal shrubs, banksias and tea trees, bursting with native wildflowers in spring. Permits for remote camping can be obtained from Parks Victoria (☑ 13 19 63; www.parkweb.vic.gov.au).

The main access road to Ninety Mile Beach is the South Gippsland Hwy from Sale or Foster, turning off to Seaspray, Golden Beach and Loch Sport.

Seaspray

You'll think you've travelled back to the 1950s at this low-key, low-rise seaside village of prefab houses. It gets busy during the summer holidays but otherwise it's a quiet place with just a few shops, a cafe, holiday accommodation and a near-deserted beach.

Northeast of Seaspray are a string of superb free Parks Victoria camping grounds, just back from the dunes and with beach access. Camp sites include the Honeysuckles, Flamingo Beach, Golden Beach and Paradise Beach. They're hugely popular in summer and during holiday weekends, but at other times you can just drive straight in. Some sites have barbecues and pit toilets, but you need to bring your own water and firewood. Hot showers are available at Golden Beach ($2).

BAIRNSDALE BYPASS?

Bustling Bairnsdale (population 11,820) is East Gippsland's commercial hub and the turn-off north for the Great Alpine Rd (B500) to Omeo or south to Paynesville and Raymond Island. There's better accommodation in Sale, Metung or Lakes Entrance. Otherwise, the only reason we can think to stop in the town itself is the **Krowathunkoolong Keeping Place** (☑ 03-5152 1891; 37-53 Dalmahoy St; adult/child $3.50/2.50; ⊙ 9am-5pm Mon-Fri), a stirring and insightful Koorie cultural exhibition space that explores Kurnai life from the Dreaming until after European settlement. The exhibition traces the Kurnai people from their Dreaming ancestors, Borun the pelican and his wife Tuk the musk duck, and covers life at Lake Tyers Mission, east of Lakes Entrance, now a trust privately owned by Aboriginal shareholders. The massacres of the Kurnai from 1839 to 1849 are also detailed. For more information, try the **Bairnsdale Visitor Centre** (☑ 03-5152 3444, 1800 637 060; www.discovereastgippsland.com.au; 240 Main St; ⊙ 9am-5pm). Bairnsdale lies 67km from Sale and 280km from Melbourne.

Loch Sport & Lakes National Park

◉ Sights & Activities

The small, bushy holiday town of Loch Sport – where wallabies graze serenely on residents' front lawns – sprawls between the ocean and Lake Victoria. The main road comes to an abrupt halt at Lakes National Park, a narrow strip of coastal bushland surrounded by water. Banksia and eucalypt woodland abound, along with areas of low-lying heathland and some swampy salt-marsh scrub. In spring the park is carpeted with native wildflowers and has one of Australia's best displays of native orchids. A loop road through the park provides good vehicle access, and there are well-marked walking trails. Point Wilson, at the eastern tip of the mainland section of the park, is the best picnic spot and a popular gathering place for kangaroos. Industrial-strength mosquito repellent is a must here.

⊨ Sleeping & Eating

Emu Bight Camp Site　　CAMPGROUND $
(☑ 13 19 63; unpowered sites per 6 people $15) The only camping area in the park itself, this place has pit toilets and fireplaces but you must BYO water.

90 Mile Beach Holiday Retreat　　CAMPGROUND $
(☑ 03-5146 0320; www.90milebeachholidayretreat.com; Track 10, off Golden Beach-Loch Sport Rd; unpowered/powered sites from $36/38, lodge & cottage d from $95) ⬝ On a huge chunk of land a few kilometres from Loch Sport, this retreat has 2.4km of pristine beach frontage, lots

of camp sites and spacious, airy lodges. It's separated from the rest of the world by 6km of dirt track. The whole place is run on solar- and wind-powered generators.

Marina Hotel　　SEAFOOD $$
(☑ 03-5146 0666; Basin Blvd, Loch Sport; mains $16-28; ⊙ noon-2pm & 6-9pm) Perched by the lake and marina, the local pub has a friendly vibe, superb sunset views and decent seafood dishes on the bistro menu.

ⓘ Getting There & Away

To get to Loch Sport, turn off the South Gippsland Hwy at Longford. From the turn-off, it's a 61km drive along the C485.

Paynesville & Raymond Island

◉ Sights & Activities

Paynesville is a relaxed little lake town where life is all about the water, and some residents have their luxury boats moored right outside their house on purpose-built canals. A good reason to detour here is to take the ferry on the five-minute hop across to Raymond Island for some koala spotting. There's a large colony of koalas here, mostly relocated from Phillip Island in the 1950s. The flat-bottom car and passenger ferry operates every half-hour from 7am to 11pm and is free for pedestrians and cyclists; cars and motorcycles cost $10. Several operators hire out boats.

Aquamania　　WATER SPORTS
(☑ 0417 163 365; www.aquamania.com.au) Organises boat tours, waterski and wakeboard instruction, and operates a water taxi.

✦ Festivals & Events

Paynesville Jazz Festival MUSIC
(⊙Feb) The popular Paynesville Jazz Festival happens on the last weekend in February.

🛏 Sleeping & Eating

Mariners Cove MOTEL **$$**
(☑03-5156 7444; www.marinerscoveresort.com; d $100-165, f $165, apt $160-225; ❄) These bright, sunny, waterside motel-style units are well located near the Raymond Island ferry. Boat hire is available.

Fisherman's Wharf Pavilion CAFE, SEAFOOD **$$**
(☑03-5156 0366; 70 The Esplanade; lunch $8-24, dinner $22-43; ⊙8am-3pm & 6-8pm Tue-Sun) Perched over the water and with an alfresco deck, this airy cafe is a sublime place for a pancake breakfast or quiche for lunch on a sunny day. By night it's a fine-dining steak-and-seafood restaurant, using fresh, local produce.

❶ Getting There & Away

Paynesville is 16km south of Bairnsdale along the C604 – watch for signs to the turn-off along the Princes Hwy in the centre of Bairnsdale.

V/Line coaches travel twice daily between Bairnsdale and Paynesville (30 to 40 minutes), connecting with onward, Melbourne-bound trains.

Metung

POP 1010

Curling around Bancroft Bay, little Metung is one of the prettiest towns in the Lakes District. Besotted locals call it the Gippsland Riviera, and with its absolute waterfront location and unhurried charm it's hard to argue.

At high noon pelicans fly in like dive bombers for fish dispensed outside the Metung Hotel. Pelicans can tell time – or at least when it's time for a free feed.

🏃 Activities

Riviera Nautic BOATING
(☑03-5156 2243; www.rivieranautic.com.au; 185 Metung Rd; yachts & cruisers for 3 days from $1089) Getting out on the water is easy enough: Riviera Nautic hires out boats and yachts for cruising, fishing and sailing on the Gippsland Lakes.

Slipway Boat Hire BOATING
(☑03-5156 2469) At the Metung Visitors Centre, Slipway Boat Hire has small motor boats for hire from $60 per hour to $175 per day, including fuel.

Director BOAT TOUR
(☑03-5156 2628; www.thedirector.com.au; 2½hr cruise adult/child/family $45/10/105; ⊙3pm Tue, Thu & Sat) If you'd like to take it easy, take a cruise on board the *Director* to Ninety Mile Beach and back.

🛏 Sleeping

The only budget accommodation is at the Metung Hotel (p246). The nearest camping ground is up the road at Swan Reach.

Metung Holiday Villas CABINS **$$**
(☑03-5156 2306; www.metungholidayvillas.com; cnr Mairburn & Stirling Rds; cabins $150-250; ❄ ❄) Metung's former caravan park has reinvented itself as a minivillage of semiluxury cabins, and is one of the best deals in Metung.

Moorings at Metung APARTMENT **$$$**
(☑03-5156 2750; www.themoorings.com.au; 44 Metung Rd; apt $150-390; ❄ ❄ ❄) At the end of the road in Metung village and with water views to either Lake King or Bancroft Bay, this contemporary apartment complex has a range of apartments, from spacious studios to two-bedroom, split-level townhouses. Outside the peak season it's good value, with a tennis court, indoor and outdoor pools, spa and marina.

McMillans of Metung RESORT **$$$**
(☑03-5156 2283; www.mcmillansofmetung.com.au; 155 Metung Rd; cottages $82-440, villas $88-367; ❄ ❄ ❄) This swish lakeside resort has won stacks of tourism awards for its complex of English country–style cottages set in 3 hectares of manicured gardens. It has modern villas, a private marina and a spa centre.

🍴 Eating

★Metung Galley CAFE **$$**
(☑03-5156 2330; www.themetunggalley.com.au; 50 Metung Rd; lunch $9-15, dinner $19.50-34; ⊙8am-4pm Tue, to late Wed-Fri, 7.30am-late Sat, to 4pm Sun) Felicity and Richard's city hospitality experience shines through in this friendly, innovative cafe. It serves up beautifully presented, quality food using local ingredients such as fresh seafood and Gippsland lamb (try the lamb 'cigars' with tzatziki).

Lakes Entrance

Lakes Entrance

◉ Sights
1 Jemmy's Point Lookout B2
2 Kalimna Lookout B1

⊙ Activities, Courses & Tours
3 Boat Hire C1
4 Illuka Day Spa C2
5 Lonsdale Cruises D2
6 Mulloway Fishing Charters C1
7 Peels Lake Cruises D2
  Sea Safari .... (see 7)
8 Surf Shack E1

⊚ Sleeping
9 Bellevue on the Lakes D2
10 Kalimna Woods A1

⊗ Eating
  The Boathouse .... (see 9)
11 Ferryman's Seafood Cafe D2
12 Floating Dragon D2
13 Miriam's Restaurant E1
14 Omega 3 .... D1
15 Six Sisters & A Pigeon E1

Bancroft Bites CAFE $$
(☑ 03-5156 2854; www.bancroftbites.com.au; 2/57 Metung Rd; lunch $8-22, dinner $20-34; ⊙ 8am-3pm & 6-8pm Thu-Tue) This is a seriously good cafe-by-day, fine-dining-by-night place. Seafood chowder and glazed roast duck grace the contemporary menu.

Metung Hotel PUB $$
(☑ 03-5156 2206; www.metunghotel.com.au; 1 Kurnai Ave; mains $25-33; ⊙ noon-2pm & 6-8pm) You can't beat the location overlooking Metung Wharf, and the big windows and outdoor timber decking make the most of the water views. The bistro serves top-notch pub food. The hotel also has the cheapest rooms in town ($85).

ⓘ Information

Metung Visitors Centre (☑ 03-5156 2969; www.metungtourism.com.au; 3/50 Metung Rd; ⊙ 9am-5pm) Accommodation-booking and boat-hire services.

ⓘ Getting There & Away

Metung lies south of Princes Hwy along the C606; the turn-off is signposted at Swan Reach. The nearest major towns are Bairnsdale (28km) and Lakes Entrance (24km). The nearest intercity rail services are at Bairnsdale.

Lakes Entrance

POP 5970

With the shallow Cunninghame Arm waterway separating town from the crashing ocean beaches, Lakes Entrance basks in an undeniably pretty location, but in holiday season it's a packed-out tourist town with a graceless strip of motels, caravan parks, minigolf courses and souvenir shops lining the Esplanade. Still, the bobbing fishing boats, fresh seafood, endless beaches and cruises out to Metung and Wyanga Park Winery should win you over. There's plenty here for families and kids, and out of season there's an unhurried pace and accommodation bargains.

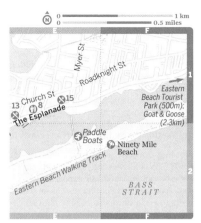

The town is named for the channel, artificially created in 1889 to provide ocean access from the lakes system and create a harbour for fishing boats.

◉ Sights & Activities

Lakes Entrance is all about the beach and boating. A long footbridge crosses the Cunninghame Arm inlet from the east of town to the ocean and Ninety Mile Beach. From December to Easter, paddle boats, canoes and sailboats can be hired by the footbridge on the ocean side. This is also where the **Eastern Beach Walking Track** (2.3km, 45 minutes) starts, taking you through coastal scrub to the entrance itself.

To explore the lakes, three companies along Marine Pde (on the back-side of the town centre) offer **boat hire** (hire per 1/4/8hr $50/90/150).

On the Princes Hwy on the western side of town is **Kalimna Lookout**, a popular viewing spot with coin-operated binoculars. For an even better view of the ocean and inlet (and a quieter location), take the road directly opposite to **Jemmy's Point Lookout**.

Surf Shack   SURFING
(☑03-5155 4933; www.surfshack.com.au; 507 The Esplanade; 2hr lesson $50) Surfing lessons (gear provided) are run by the Surf Shack at nearby Lake Tyers Beach, around 10km from Lakes Entrance.

Illuka Day Spa   SPA
(☑03-5155 3533; www.illukadayspa.com.au; 1 The Esplanade; ⊙9am-5pm Sat-Mon, Wed & Thu, to 8pm Tue, to 7pm Fri) For a bit of indulgence, Illuka Day Spa, at the Esplanade Resort, has a

range of massage therapies, facials and seaweed scrubs from $70.

☞ Tours

Several companies offer cruises on the lakes.

Lonsdale Cruises   CRUISE
(☑03-9013 8363; Post Office Jetty; 3hr cruise adult/child/family $50/25/120; ⊙1pm) ✐ Scenic eco-cruises out to Metung and Lake King on a former Queenscliff–Sorrento passenger ferry.

Mulloway Fishing Charters   FISHING
(☑03-5155 3304, 0427 943 154; 3hr cruise adult/child $50/25) Fishing cruises departing the jetty opposite 66 Marine Pde. Rods, tackle, bait and morning or afternoon tea provided.

Peels Lake Cruises   CRUISE
(☑0409 946 292; www.peelscruises.com.au; Post Office Jetty; 4hr Metung lunch cruise adult/child $55/16, 2½hr cruise $41; ⊙11am Tue-Sun, 2pm Tue-Thu & Sat) This long-running operator has daily lunch cruises aboard the *Stormbird* to Metung and two-and-a-half-hour cruises on the *Thunderbird*.

Sea Safari   CRUISE
(☑0458 511 438; www.lakes-explorer.com.au; Post Office Jetty; 1/2hr cruise $15/25) ✐ These safaris aboard the *Lakes Explorer* have a focus on research and ecology, identifying and counting seabirds, testing water for salinity levels and learning about marine life.

★ Festivals & Events

Seafarers Multicultural Festival   CULTURAL
(www.seafarersfestival.com.au; ⊙Dec) The Seafarers Multicultural Festival, in early December, celebrates the region's culture and fishing industry with a multicultural parade, a Koorie art festival, music and boat races.

⎵ Sleeping

Lakes Entrance has stacks of accommodation, much of it your typical motels, holiday apartments and caravan parks squeezed cheek by jowl along the Esplanade. Prices more than double during holiday periods (book ahead), but there are good discounts out of season.

Eastern Beach Tourist Park   CAMPGROUND **$**
(☑03-5155 1581; www.easternbeach.com.au; 42 Eastern Beach Rd; unpowered/powered sites from $26/31, cabins $105-185; @ 🛜 ⊠ 🐾) Most caravan parks in Lakes pack 'em in, but this one has space, grassy sites and a great

GIPPSLAND & WILSONS PROMONTORY LAKES ENTRANCE

location away from the hubbub of town in a bush setting back from Eastern Beach. A walking track takes you into town (30 minutes). New facilities are excellent, including a camp kitchen, barbecues and a kids' playground.

Kalimna Woods COTTAGE **$$**
(☑03-5155 1957; www.kalimnawoods.com.au; Kalimna Jetty Rd; d $99-130, with spa $129-170; ❋) Retreat 2km from the town centre to Kalimna Woods, set in a large rainforest-and-bush garden, complete with friendly resident possums and birds. These self-contained country-style cottages with either spa or wood-burning fireplace are spacious, private and cosy.

Bellevue on the Lakes HOTEL **$$**
(☑03-5155 3055; www.bellevuelakes.com; 201 The Esplanade; d from $159, 2-bedroom apt from $244; ❋ ☎ ❋) Right in the heart of the Esplanade, Bellevue brings a bit of style to the strip with neatly furnished rooms in earthy tones, most with water views. For extra luxury, go for the spacious spa suites or two-bedroom self-contained apartments.

Goat & Goose B&B **$$**
(☑03-5155 3079; www.goatandgoose.com; 16 Gay St; d $160) Bass Strait views are maximised at this wonderfully unusual, multistorey, timber pole–framed house. The friendly owners are long-time locals, and all the gorgeously quaint rooms have spas.

✕ Eating & Drinking

With the largest fishing fleet in the state, Lakes Entrance is a great place to indulge in fresh seafood. You can sometimes buy shellfish (prawns, bugs) straight from local boats (look for signs) or try Ferryman's. Omega 3 (Shop 5, Safeway Arcade, Church St; ☉9am-5pm) is the shop front for the local Fishermen's Co-op, so the seafood is always fresh.

The best cafe strip is on the Esplanade and around the corner on Myer St, right opposite the Cunninghame Arm footbridge.

Six Sisters & A Pigeon CAFE **$**
(☑03-5155 1144; 567 The Esplanade; mains $9-18; ☉7am-3pm Tue-Sun; ✐) The name alone should guide you to this quirky, licensed cafe on the Esplanade opposite the footbridge. Good coffee; all-day breakfasts – Mexican eggs, French toast or Spanish omelettes; lunches of focaccias and baguettes; and light mains with an Asian-Italian influence.

★**Ferryman's Seafood Cafe** SEAFOOD **$$**
(☑03-5155 3000; www.ferrymans.com.au; Middle Harbour, The Esplanade; lunch mains $19-23, dinner $22.50-43.50; ☉10am-late, seafood sales 8.30am-5pm) It's hard to beat the ambience of dining on the deck of this floating cafe-restaurant, which will fill you to the gills with fish and seafood dishes, including good ol' fish and chips. The seafood platter is a great order. It's child-friendly, and downstairs you can buy fresh seafood, including prawns and crayfish.

Floating Dragon CHINESE **$$**
(☑03-5155 1400; www.floatingdragon.com.au; 160 The Esplanade; mains $23-49; ☉6pm-late Tue-Sat, noon-2pm Sun) This floating restaurant dishes up high-end Cantonese cuisine with soothing views through the floor-to-ceiling windows. The best deal is yum cha for Sunday lunch, but the pork belly has its admirers.

Miriam's Restaurant STEAKHOUSE, SEAFOOD **$$**
(☑03-5155 3999; www.miriamsrestaurant.com.au; cnr The Esplanade & Bulmer St; mains $25-39; ☉6pm-late) The upstairs dining room at Miriam's overlooks the Esplanade, and the Gippsland steaks, local seafood dishes and casual cocktail-bar atmosphere are excellent. Try the epic 'Greek fisherman's plate' – half a kilo of local seafood for $55.

★**The Boathouse** MODERN AUSTRALIAN **$$$**
(☑03-5155 3055; www.bellevuelakes.com; 201 The Esplanade; mains $38; ☉6-9pm Tue-Sat) This much-awarded restaurant is Lakes Entrance's most celebrated kitchen. The atmosphere is refined and the emphasis is on creatively conceived seafood. Start with the Atlantic scallops with pea purée, pancetta and ocean foam.

❶ Information

Lakes Entrance Visitors Centre (☑03-5155 1966, 1800 637 060; www.discovereastgippsland.com.au; cnr Princes Hwy & Marine Pde; ☉9am-5pm) Free accommodation- and tour-booking services. Also check out www.lakesentrance.com.

Lakes Entrance Library (☑03-5153 9500; 18 Mechanics St; ☉8.30am-5pm Mon-Fri) Free internet access.

❶ Getting There & Away

Lakes Entrance lies 314km from Melbourne along the Princes Hwy.

V/Line (☑1800 800 007; www.vline.com.au) runs a train-bus service from Melbourne to Lakes Entrance via Bairnsdale ($34.20, 4½ hours, three daily).

EAST GIPPSLAND & THE WILDERNESS COAST

Beyond Lakes Entrance stretches a wilderness area of spectacular coastal national parks and old-growth forest. Much of this region has never been cleared for agriculture and contains some of the most remote and pristine national parks in the state, making logging in these ancient forests a hot issue.

Inland you'll find the glorious Snowy River and Errinundra National Parks, while the stunning coast is home to Cape Conran, Croajingolong and Mallacoota – all uncrowded, unspoilt and undeveloped. Even on the highway, the winding forest drive to the state's most easterly point is magnificent.

Buchan

POP 380

The sleepy town of Buchan, in the foothills of the Snowy Mountains, is famous for the spectacular and intricate limestone cave system at the Buchan Caves Reserve, open to visitors for almost a century. Underground rivers cutting through ancient limestone rock formed the caves and caverns, and they provided shelter for Aboriginal people as far back as 18,000 years ago. Parks Victoria (☑13 19 63; www.parks.vic.gov.au; tours adult/child/family $20.30/11.90/56.10, two caves $30.40/17.60/83.70; ⊙10am, 11.15am, 1pm, 2.15pm & 3.30pm, hours vary seasonally) runs guided cave tours daily, alternating between Royal and Fairy Caves. They're both impressive: Royal has more colour, a higher chamber and extinct kangaroo remains; Fairy has more delicate decorations and potential fairy sightings. The rangers also offer hard-hat guided tours to the less-developed Federal Cave during the high season. The reserve itself is a pretty spot with shaded picnic areas, walking tracks and grazing kangaroos. Invigoration is guaranteed when taking a dip in the icy rock pool.

🛏 Sleeping & Eating

Buchan Caves Reserve   CAMPGROUND $
(☑13 19 63; www.parks.vic.gov.au; unpowered/powered sites $23.40/30.20, d cabins $86.10, wilderness retreats d $181.50; ☎) You can stay right by the caves at this serene Parks Victoria camping ground edged by state forest. There are a couple of standard cabins, plus safari-style tents providing a 'luxury' wilderness experience (think comfortable queen-sized bed) without having to pitch your own tent.

Buchan Lodge   HOSTEL $
(☑03-5155 9421; www.buchanlodge.com.au; 9 Saleyard Rd; dm $25; ☎) A short walk from the caves and the town centre, and just by the river, this welcoming pine-log backpackers is great for lounging about and taking in the country views. It boasts a big country-style kitchen, convivial lounge and has campfires out the back.

Caves Hotel   PUB $$
(☑03-5155 9203; 49 Main St; mains $16-26; ⊙11.30am-2.30pm & 6-9pm) This century-old timber pub is a good place for a drink and serves decent bistro meals.

ⓘ Getting There & Away

Buchan is an easy drive 56km north of Lakes Entrance. Buchan Bus 'n' Freight (☑03-5155 0356) operates a service on Wednesday and Friday from Bairnsdale to Buchan ($18, 1¾ hours). It meets the train at Bairnsdale. At other times you'll need your own transport.

Snowy River National Park

Northeast of Buchan, this is one of Victoria's most isolated and striking national parks, dominated by deep gorges carved through limestone and sandstone by the Snowy River on its route from the Snowy Mountains in NSW to its mouth at Marlo. The entire park is a smorgasbord of unspoilt, superb bush and mountain scenery. It covers more than 950 sq km and includes a huge diversity of vegetation, ranging from alpine woodlands and eucalypt forests to rainforests.

The road north of Buchan continues across the border to Jindabyne – the gravel track to Suggan Buggan, just short of the state border, is spectacular, but not for those with a fear of heights.

Equally dramatic is the 85km gravel road that crosses the park from north of Gelantipy in the west to Bonang in the east. It's suitable for 2WD vehicles but not after rain. Coming from the west, the views from the well-signposted cliff-top lookouts over Little River Falls and Little River Gorge, Victoria's deepest gorge, are awesome; watch for the rare brush-tailed rock wallaby around the lookout at the latter. From there it's about 20km along a steep, narrow track to McKillops Bridge. En route expect utterly splendid views of the high alpine country and some glimpses of the

GIPPSLAND OFF-ROAD TOURS

Most of the Snowy River and Errinundra National Parks are inaccessible with a 2WD, and sections of Croajingolong are only open to a limited number of walkers. An easier way to see these beautiful wilderness areas is with an organised tour.

An ecotourism award winner, **Gippsland High Country Tours** (☑ 03-5157 5556; www. gippslandhighcountrytours.com.au) 🖉 is an East Gippsland–based company running easy, moderate and challenging five- to seven-day hikes in Errinundra, Snowy River and Croajingolong National Parks. The Croajingolong trips include three nights' accommodation in the Point Hicks Lighthouse. There's also a five-day bird-watching tour in Snowy River country.

Snowy River Expeditions (☑ 03-5155 0220; www.karoondapark.com/sre; Karoonda Park; tours per day $150-275) is an established company running adventure tours, including one-, two- or four-day rafting trips on the Snowy. Half- or full-day abseiling or caving trips are also available. Costs include transport, meals and camping gear.

charming Snowy River, not to mention some alarming drops if you're nervous about heights... The bridge itself spans the Snowy River, making it possible to drive across the park to Errinundra National Park – the road from here to Bonang is mostly gravel, but less precipitous, and follows the pretty Deddick River.

The hilly and difficult **Silver Mine Walking Track** (15km, six hours) starts at the eastern end of McKillops Bridge. Walking and canoeing are the most popular activities, but you need to be well prepared for both – conditions can be harsh and subject to sudden change. The classic canoe or raft trip down the Snowy River from McKillops Bridge to a pull-out point near Buchan takes at least four days and offers superb scenery: rugged gorges, raging rapids, tranquil sections and excellent camping spots on broad sandbars.

🛏 Sleeping

There is free camping at a number of basic sites around the park, but the main site is McKillops Bridge. It's a beautiful spot, and has toilets and fireplaces.

Karoonda Park FARM $
(☑ 03-5155 0220; www.karoondapark.com; 3558 Gelantipy Rd; s/d/tr $50/70/90, cabins per 6 people $115; ✸ @ ✸) At Gelantipy, 40km north of Buchan on the road to Snowy River National Park, this cattle-and-sheep property has comfortable backpacker and cabin digs. Rates include breakfast; other meals are available. Activities available include abseiling, horse riding, wild caving, whitewater rafting, mountain-bike hire and farm activities.

❶ Getting There & Away

The two main access roads to the park are the Buchan-Jindabyne Rd from Buchan, and the Bonang Rd north from Orbost. These roads are joined by McKillops Rd (also known as Deddick Valley Rd), which runs across the northern border of the park. Various minor access roads and scenic routes run into and alongside the park from these three main roads. The 43km Deddick Trail, which runs through the middle of the park, is only suitable for 4WDs.

Buchan Bus 'n' Freight (☑ 03 5155 0356) operates a bus service from Bairnsdale to Karoonda Park (via Buchan) on Wednesday and Friday ($24.50, 2¾ hours).

Errinundra National Park

Errinundra National Park contains Victoria's largest cool-temperate rainforest and is one of East Gippsland's most outstanding natural areas. The gorgeous forests surrounding the park are a constant battleground between loggers and environmentalists.

The national park covers an area of 256 sq km and has three granite outcrops that extend into the cloud, resulting in high rainfall, deep, fertile soils and a network of creeks and rivers that flow north, south and east. The park has several climatic zones – some areas of the park are quite dry, while its peaks regularly receive snow. This is a rich habitat for native birds and animals, which include many rare and endangered species, such as the potoroo.

◉ Sights & Activities

You can explore the park by a combination of scenic drives, and short- and medium-length walks. **Mt Ellery** has spectacular views; **Erri-**

nundra Saddle has a rainforest boardwalk; and from **Ocean View Lookout** there are stunning views down the Goolengook River as far as the town of Bemm River. The park also has **mountain plum pines**, some of which are more than 400 years old, and are easily accessible from Goonmirk Rocks Rd.

Nestled by the edge of the national park is tiny **Goongerah** (population 50), where there's a thriving community with two active community environmental organisations, **Goongerah Environment Centre** (☑ 03-5154 0156; www.geco.org.au) 🖋 and **Environment East Gippsland** (☑ 03-5154 0145; www.eastgippsland.net.au) 🖋.

🛏 Sleeping

There are free camping areas on the park's edges – at Ellery Creek in Goongerah and at Delegate River.

Frosty Hollow Camp Site   CAMPGROUND $
(sites free) This is the only camping area within the national park, on the eastern side. The only way to reach the camp site is along unsealed tracks into the park off the Bonang Rd north of Goongerah.

ℹ Getting There & Around

Errinundra National Park lies approximately 490km east of Melbourne. The main access roads to the park are Bonang Rd from Orbost and Errinundra Rd from Club Terrace. Bonang Rd passes along the western side of the park, while Errinundra Rd passes through the centre. Roads within the park are all unsealed, but are 2WD accessible. Road conditions are variable. Expect seasonal closures between June and November, though roads can deteriorate quickly at any time of year after rain and are often closed or impassable after floods (check Parks Victoria in Orbost or Bendoc first). Also watch out for logging trucks when driving.

Orbost

POP 2140

Orbost services the surrounding farming and forest areas. Most travellers fly through as the Princes Hwy passes just south of the town, while the Bonang Rd heads north towards the Snowy River and Errinundra National Parks, and Marlo Rd follows the Snowy River south to Marlo and continues along the coast to Cape Conran Coastal Park.

Orbost Visitor Information Centre (☑ 03-5154 2424; 39 Nicholson St; ◷ 9am-5pm) is in the historic 1872 Slab Hut.

The impressive **Orbost Exhibition Centre** (☑ 03-5154 2634; www.orbostexhibitioncentre.org; Clarke St; adult/child $4/free; ◷ 10am-4pm Mon-Sat, 1-4pm Sun), next to the visitor centre, showcases stunning works by local timber artists.

Marlo

POP 438

Rather than barrel down the highway from Orbost to Mallacoota, turn off to Marlo, a sleepy beach town at the mouth of the Snowy River just 15km south of Orbost. It's a lovely spot, popular with anglers. The road continues on to Cape Conran Coastal Park before rejoining the highway.

Aside from the coast, the main attraction here is the **PS Curlip** (☑ 03-5154 1699; www.paddlesteamercurlip.com.au; adult/child/family $25/15/60; ◷ cruises 10.30am Sat & Sun, extra cruises Dec & Jan), a re-creation of an 1890 paddle steamer that once chugged up the Snowy River to Orbost. The vessel was rebuilt as a community project. You can buy tickets at the general store in town.

EAST GIPPSLAND RAIL TRAIL

The **East Gippsland Rail Trail** (www.eastgippslandrailtrail.com) is a 94km walking/cycling path along the former railway line between Bairnsdale and Orbost, passing through Bruthen and Nowa Nowa and close to a number of other small communities. The trail passes through undulating farmland, temperate rainforest, the Colquhoun Forest and some impressive timber bridges. On a bike the trail can comfortably be done in two days, but allow longer to explore the countryside and perhaps detour on the Gippsland Lakes Discovery Trail to Lakes Entrance. Arty Nowa Nowa is a real biking community, with a new mountain-bike park and trails leading off the main rail trail. There are plans to extend the trail from Orbost down to Marlo along the Snowy River.

If you don't have your own bike, **Snowy River Cycling** (☑ 0428 556 088; www.snowyrivercycling.com.au) offers self-guided tours with a bike (from $35), map and transfers ($35) plus luggage transport ($15). It also runs guided cycle adventures.

You can't beat an afternoon beer on the expansive wooden verandah of the **Marlo Hotel** (☑03-5154 8201; www.marlohotel.com.au; 17 Argyle Pde; mains $14-30), which offers a sublime view of the Snowy River emptying into the sea. The boutique rooms (double $140) are above average for a pub – some come with spa ($130-160) – and the restaurant serves local seafood such as gummy shark and king prawns (mains from $14 to $30).

Cape Conran Coastal Park

This blissfully undeveloped part of the coast is one of Gippsland's most beautiful corners, with long stretches of remote white-sand beaches. The 19km coastal route from Marlo to Cape Conran is particularly pretty, bordered by banksia trees, grass plains, sand dunes and the ocean.

🏃 Activities

Cape Conran is a fabulous spot for **walking**. One favourite is the nature trail that meets up with the East Cape Boardwalk, whose signage gives you a glimpse into how indigenous peoples lived in this area. Following an indigenous theme, take the West Cape Rd off Cape Conran Rd to **Salmon Rocks**, where there's an Aboriginal **shell midden** dated at more than 10,000 years old.

For some relaxed swimming, canoeing and fishing, head to the Yerrung River, which shadows the coast east of the cape and can be reached along Yerrung River Rd. There's good surfing at West Cape Beach, extending northwest from the cape and accessible from West Cape Rd. For qualified divers, Lakes Entrance–based **Cross Diving Services** (☑03-5155 1397, 0407 362 960; www.crossdiving.com.au) offers dives on most weekends (equipment hire available).

If you're staying in the park, keep an eye out for bandicoots and potoroos, whose numbers have increased in recent years following the introduction of the park's fox management program. Check out the **cabbage tree palms**, which can be accessed from a number of points and are a short detour off the road between Cape Conran and the Princes Hwy. This is Victoria's only stand of native palms – a tiny rainforest oasis.

🛏 Sleeping

Banksia Bluff Camping Area   CAMPGROUND $
(☑03-5154 8438; www.conran.net.au; per person $30.20) Run by Parks Victoria, this excellent camping ground is right by the foreshore, with generous sites surrounded by banksia woodlands offering shade and privacy. The camping ground has toilets, cold showers and a few fireplaces, but you'll need to bring drinking water. A ballot is held for using sites over the Christmas period.

Cape Conran Cabins   CABIN $
(☑03-5154 8438; www.conran.net.au; 4 people from $161.90) These self-contained cabins, which can sleep up to eight people, are surrounded by bush and are just 200m from the beach. Built from local timbers, the cabins are like oversized cubby houses with lofty mezzanines for sleeping. BYO linen. An excellent option run by Parks Victoria.

Cape Conran Wilderness Retreat   SAFARI TENT $$
(☑03-5154 8438; www.conran.net.au; d $181.50) Nestled in the bush by the sand dunes, these stylish safari tents are a great option for accommodation, run by Parks Victoria. All the simplicity of camping, but with comfortable beds and a deck outside your fly-wire door. Two-night minimum stay.

West Cape Cabins   CABIN $$
(☑03-5154 8296; www.westcapecabins.com; 1547 Cape Conran Rd; d $175-215) Crafted from locally grown or recycled timbers, these self-contained cabins a few kilometres from the park are works of art. The timbers are all labelled with their species, and even queen-sized bed bases are made from tree trunks. The outdoor spa baths add to the joy. The larger cottage sleeps eight. It's a 15-minute walk through coastal bush to an isolated beach.

❶ Getting There & Away

Cape Conran Coastal Park lies south of the Princes Hwy, 405km from Melbourne. The well-signposted turn-off from the highway lies just east of the small settlement of Cabbage Tree. The park is around 15km south of the turn-off along Cabbage Tree–Conran Rd.

Mallacoota

POP 1031

One of Gippsland's, and indeed Victoria's, little gems, Mallacoota is the state's most easterly town, snuggled on the vast Mallacoota Inlet and surrounded by the tumbling hills and beachside dunes of beautiful Croajingolong National Park. Those prepared to come this far are treated to long, empty, ocean-surf beaches, tidal river mouths and swimming, fishing and boating on the inlet.

On the road in from Genoa you pass turn-offs to **Gipsy Point** and **Karbeethong**, beautiful little communities on the inlet offering a few places to stay. At Christmas and Easter Mallacoota is a crowded family holiday spot – it's certainly no secret these days – but most of the year it's pretty quiet and very relaxed.

⊙ Sights & Activities

One of the best ways to experience the beauty of Mallacoota is by boat. The calm estuarine waters of Mallacoota Inlet have more than 300km of shoreline. There are many public jetties where you can tie up your boat and come ashore for picnic tables and toilets, or take a dip. **Mallacoota Hire Boats** (☑ 0438 447 558; Main Wharf, cnr Allan & Buckland Drs; motor boats per 2/4/6hr $60/100/140) is centrally located and hires out canoes and boats. No licence required; cash only.

On Gabo Island, 14km offshore from Mallacoota, the windswept 154-hectare **Gabo Island Lightstation Reserve** is home to seabirds and one of the world's largest colonies of little penguins – far outnumbering those at Phillip Island. Whales, dolphins and fur seals are regularly sighted offshore. The island has an operating **lighthouse**, built in 1862 and the tallest in the southern hemisphere, and you can stay in the old keepers' cottages here. **Mallacoota Air Services** (☑ 0408 580 806; return per 3 adults or 2 adults & 2 children $300) offers fast access to the island on demand, or you can get there by boat with Wilderness Coast Ocean Charters.

There are plenty of great short walks around the town, inlet and in the bush. It's an easy 4km walk or cycle around the inlet to Karbeethong. From there the **Bucklands Jetty to Captain Creek Jetty Walk** (one-way 5km, 1½ hours) follows the shoreline of the inlet past the Narrows. The **Mallacoota Town Walk** (7km, five hours) loops round Bastion Point, and combines five different walks. Walking notes with maps are available from the visitor centre.

For good **surf**, head to Bastion Point or Tip Beach. There's swimmable surf and some sheltered waters at Betka Beach, which is patrolled during Christmas school holidays. There are also good **swimming spots** along the beaches of the foreshore reserve, at Bastion Point and Quarry Beach.

☞ Tours

MV Loch-Ard CRUISE
(☑ 03-5158 0764; Main Wharf; 2hr cruise adult/child $30/12) Runs several inlet cruises, including wildlife spotting and a twilight cruise.

Porkie Bess CRUISE, FISHING
(☑ 0408 408 094; 2hr cruise $30, fishing trip $60) A 1940s wooden boat offering fishing trips and cruises around the lakes of Mallacoota Inlet, and ferry services for hikers ($20 per person, minimum four people).

Wilderness Coast Ocean Charters BOATING
(☑ 0417 398 068, 03-5158 0701) Runs day trips to Gabo Island ($70, minimum eight people; $70 each way if you stay overnight) and may run trips down the coast to view the seal colony off Wingan Inlet if there's enough demand.

⏢ Sleeping

There are quite a few options in Mallacoota, but during Easter and Christmas school holidays you'll need to book well ahead and expect prices to be significantly higher.

Mallacoota Foreshore Holiday Park CAMPGROUND $
(☑ 03-5158 0300; cnr Allan Dr & Maurice Ave; unpowered sites $20-29, powered sites $26-38; 🛜) Curling around the waterfront, the grassy sites here morph into one of Victoria's most sociable and scenic caravan parks, with sublime views of the inlet and its resident population of black swans and pelicans. No cabins, but the best of Mallacoota's many parks for campers.

★ **Adobe Mudbrick Flats** APARTMENT $
(☑ 0409 580 329, 03-5158 0329; www.adobeholidayflats.com.au; 17 Karbeethong Ave; d $75, q $90-170) 🐾 A labour of love for Margaret and Peter Kurz, these unique mudbrick flats in Karbeethong are something special. With an emphasis on recycling and ecofriendliness, the flats have solar hot water and guests are encouraged to compost their kitchen scraps. Birds, lizards and possums can be hand-fed outside your door. The whimsical apartments are comfortable, well equipped and cheap. A real find.

★ **Gabo Island Lighthouse** COTTAGE $$
(☑ 03-5161 9500, Parks Victoria 13 19 63; www.parkweb.vic.gov.au; up to 8 people $148-190) For a truly wild experience head out to stay at this remote lighthouse. Accommodation

GIPPSLAND & WILSONS PROMONTORY MALLACOOTA

is available in the three-bedroom assistant lighthouse keeper's residence. Watch for migrating whales in autumn and late spring. Pods of dolphins, and seals basking on the rocks are also regular sightings. There's a two-night minimum stay, and a ballot for use during the Christmas and Easter holidays.

Karbeethong Lodge   GUESTHOUSE $$
(☑ 03-5158 0411; www.karbeethonglodge.com.au; 16 Schnapper Point Dr; d $110-220) It's hard not to be overcome by a sense of serenity as you rest on the broad verandahs of this early 1900s timber guesthouse, which gives uninterrupted views over Mallacoota Inlet. The large guest lounge and dining room have an open fire and period furnishings, and there's a mammoth kitchen if you want to prepare meals. The pastel-toned bedrooms are small but neat and tastefully decorated.

Mallacoota Wilderness Houseboats   HOUSEBOAT $$$
(☑ 0409 924 016; www.mallacootawildernesshouseboats.com.au; Karbeethong Jetty; 4 nights midweek from $750, weekly from $1200) These six-berth houseboats are not as luxurious as the ones you'll find on the Murray, but they are the perfect way to explore Mallacoota's waterways, and they are economical for a group or family.

✗ Eating & Drinking

Most visitors consider the best eating to be the fish you catch yourself; otherwise there are a few good places along Maurice Ave.

★ Lucy's   ASIAN $
(☑ 03-5158 0666; 64 Maurice Ave; mains $10-22; ☺ 8am-8pm) Lucy's is popular for delicious and great-value homemade rice noodles with chicken, prawn or abalone, as well as dumplings stuffed with ingredients from the garden. It's also good for breakfast.

Croajingolong Cafe   CAFE $
(☑ 03-5158 0098; Shop 3, 14 Allan Dr; mains $6-14; ☺ 8.30am-4pm Tue-Sun; ☏) Overlooking the inlet, this is the place to spread out the newspaper over coffee, baguettes or a pancake breakfast.

Mallacoota Hotel   PUB $$
(☑ 03-5158 0455; www.mallacootahotel.com.au; 51-55 Maurice Ave; mains $17-32; ☺ noon-2pm & 6-8pm) The local pub bistro serves hearty meals from its varied menu, with reliable favourites such as chicken parmigiana and Gippsland steak. Bands play regularly in the summer.

❶ Information

Mallacoota Visitors Centre (☑ 03-5158 0800; www.visitmallacoota.com.au; Main Wharf, cnr Allan Dr & Buckland Dr; ☺ 10am-4pm) Operated by friendly volunteers.

❶ Getting There & Away

Mallacoota is 23km southeast of Genoa (on the Princes Hwy), which is 492km from Melbourne. Take the train to Bairnsdale (3¾ hours), then the V/Line bus to Genoa ($44.20, 3½ hours, one daily). **Mallacoota–Genoa Bus Service** (☑ 1800 800 007) meets the V/Line coach on Monday, Thursday and Friday, plus Sunday during school holidays, and runs to Mallacoota ($4.50, 30 minutes).

Croajingolong National Park

Croajingolong is one of Australia's finest coastal wilderness national parks, recognised by its listing as a World Biosphere Reserve by Unesco (one of 12 in Australia). The park covers 875 sq km, stretching for about 100km from the town of Bemm River to the NSW border. Magnificent, unspoilt beaches, inlets, estuaries and forests make it an ideal park for camping, walking, swimming and surfing. The five inlets, **Sydenham**, **Tamboon**, **Mueller**, **Wingan** and **Mallacoota** (the largest and most accessible), are popular canoeing and fishing spots.

Two sections of the park have been declared wilderness areas (which means no vehicles, access to a limited number of walkers only and permits required): the **Cape Howe Wilderness Area**, between Mallacoota Inlet and the NSW border, and the **Sandpatch Wilderness Area**, between Wingan Inlet and Shipwreck Creek. The **Wilderness Coast Walk** runs for 100km between the eastern shores of Sydenham Inlet to Wonboyn in the Nadgee Nature Reserve, across the border in New South Wales. You can walk shorter sections of the walk; Thurra River is a good starting point, making the walk an easy-to-medium hike (59km, five days) to Mallacoota.

Croajingolong is a birdwatcher's paradise, with more than 300 recorded species (including glossy black cockatoos and the rare ground parrot), while the inland waterways are home to myriad water birds, such as the delicate azure kingfisher and the magnificent sea eagle. There are also many small mammals here, including possums, bandicoots and gliders, and some huge goannas.

Park vegetation ranges from typical coastal landscapes to thick eucalypt forests, with areas of warm-temperate rainforest. The heathland areas are filled with impressive displays of orchids and wildflowers in the spring.

Point Hicks was the first part of Australia to be spotted by Captain Cook and the *Endeavour* crew in 1770, and was named after Lieutenant Zachary Hicks. There's a lighthouse here and accommodation in the old cottages. You can still see remains of the SS *Saros*, which ran ashore in 1937, on a short walk from the lighthouse.

Access roads of varying quality lead into the park from the Princes Hwy. Apart from Mallacoota Rd, all roads are unsealed and can be very rough in winter, so check road conditions with Parks Victoria before venturing on, especially during or after rain.

🛏 Sleeping

Given their amazing beauty, the park's main camping grounds are surprisingly quiet, and bookings only need to be made for the Christmas and Easter holiday periods, when sites are issued on a ballot system.

Wingan Inlet   CAMPGROUND **$**
(☑13 19 63; www.parkweb.vic.gov.au; unpowered sites $25.20) This serene and secluded site has superb sandy beaches and great walks. The Wingan River Walk (5km, 2½ hours return) through rainforest has great waterholes for swimming. Bookings though Parks Victoria.

Shipwreck Creek   CAMPGROUND **$**
(☑13 19 63; www.parkweb.vic.gov.au; unpowered sites $25.20) Only 15km from Mallacoota, this is a beautiful camping ground set in forest above a sandy beach. It's a small area with just five sites, and there are lots of short walks to do here. Bookings through Parks Victoria.

Mueller Inlet   CAMPGROUND **$**
(☑03-5158 4268, 03-5156 0432; www.pointhicks. com.au; unpowered sites $20) The calm waters

here are fantastic for kayaking and swimming, and the camp sites are only a few metres from the water. It has eight sites, three of them walk-in, but has no fireplaces. There's no vegetation to provide privacy, but outside Christmas and Easter holidays it's usually quiet. Bookings are made through Point Hicks Lighthouse.

Thurra River   CAMPGROUND **$**
(☑03-5158 4268, 03-5156 0432; www.pointhicks. com.au; unpowered sites $20) This is the largest of the park's camping grounds, with 46 well-designed sites stretched along the foreshore from the river towards the lighthouse. Most of the sites are separated by bush, and there are communal fireplaces and pit toilets. Bookings are made through Point Hicks Lighthouse.

Point Hicks Lighthouse   COTTAGE **$$**
(☑03-5158 4268, 03-5156 0432; www.pointhicks. com.au; bungalow $100-120, cottage $330) This remote lighthouse has two comfortable, heritage-listed cottages and one double bungalow, which originally housed the assistant lighthouse keepers. The cottages sleep six people, and have sensational ocean views and wood-burning fireplaces.

ℹ Information

Parks Victoria (☑13 19 63, Cann River 03-5158 6351, Mallacoota 03-5161 9500; www. parkweb.vic.gov.au) Contact offices in Cann River or Mallacoota for information on road conditions, overnight hiking, camping permits and track notes.

ℹ Getting There & Away

Croajingolong National Park lies 492km east of Melbourne. Unsealed access roads lead south off Princes Hwy and into the park from various points between Cann River and the New South Wales border. Among these are tracks leading to campgrounds at Wingan Inlet, Mueller Inlet, Thurra River and Shipwreck Creek.

GIPPSLAND & WILSONS PROMONTORY CROAJINGOLONG NATIONAL PARK

The High Country

Includes ➡

Baw Baw National Park	257
Eildon	260
Mt Buller	263
Beechworth	266
Mt Buffalo	270
Bright	271
Mt Beauty	274
Falls Creek	275
Mt Hotham	278

Best Places to Eat

➡ Mansfield Regional Produce Store (p263)

➡ Provenance (p268)

➡ Pepperleaf Bushtucker Restaurant (p273)

➡ Myrtleford Butter Factory (p270)

➡ Simone's Restaurant (p273)

Best Places to Stay

➡ Freeman on Ford (p268)

➡ Odd Frog (p273)

➡ Dreamers (p275)

➡ Houseboat on Lake Eildon (p260)

➡ Shady Brook Cottages (p277)

Why Go?

With its enticing mix of history, adventure and culinary temptations, Victoria's High Country is a wonderful place to spend some time. The Great Dividing Range – Australia's eastern mountain spine – curls around eastern Victoria from the Snowy Mountains to the Grampians, peaking in the spectacular High Country. These are Victoria's Alps – a mountain playground attracting skiers and snowboarders in winter and bushwalkers and mountain bikers in summer. Here, the mountain air is clear and invigorating, winter snowfalls at the resorts of Mt Buller, Mt Hotham and Falls Creek are fairly reliable, and the scenery is stunning.

Away from the mountain tops, there are activities aplenty and Bright is one of the loveliest gateway towns in the state. Throw in historic towns such as Beechworth, the wineries of King Valley and the gourmet food offerings of Milawa and you'll find plenty of reasons to linger.

When to Go
Mt Hotham

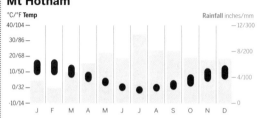

Apr–May Best time for glorious autumn colours around Bright and Omeo.

Winter Hit the snowy mountain slopes; July/August is peak season.

Dec–Feb The green season for mountain biking, horse riding and wine touring.

Baw Baw National Park

Baw Baw National Park, an offshoot of the Great Dividing Range, is the southernmost region of Victoria's High Country. The Baw Baw Plateau and the forested valleys of the Thomson and Aberfeldy Rivers are wonderful places for bushwalking, with marked tracks through subalpine vegetation, ranging from open eucalypt stands to wet gullies and tall forests on the plateau.

The 3km **Mushroom Rocks Walk** from Mt Erica car park leads to huge granite tors (blocks of granite broken off from the massif). The highest points are **Mt St Phillack** (1566m) and **Mt Baw Baw** (1564m). The higher sections of the park are snow-covered in winter, when everyone heads for Baw Baw Village ski resort and the **Mt St Gwinear** cross-country skiing area. A section of the **Australian Alps Walking Track**, which starts its 655km journey in the historic township of Walhalla in Gippsland, passes by a few kilometres from Baw Baw Village. Quiet back roads connect this region with Walhalla.

There is a camping area in the northeastern section of the park, with picnic tables, fireplaces and pit toilets. Dispersed free bush camping is also allowed on the Baw Baw Plateau (fuel stove only).

Baw Baw Village

POP 25

Baw Baw is Victoria's smallest (and also cheapest) downhill-skiing resort and is a relaxed option for both beginners and families. The downhill-skiing area is set over 35 hectares with a vertical drop of 140m and seven ski lifts. Baw Baw is also a base for cross-country skiing, with plenty of trails, including one that connects to the Mt St Gwinear trails on the southern edge of the plateau. In winter the day car park costs $35/40 (weekday/weekend) per car; during green season it's $8 per day. Lifts per adult/child cost from $65/45 per day midweek and $72/50 on weekends; cross-country passes cost $12/7 and toboggan passes are $8 per person. **Mt Baw Baw Ski Hire** (☑03-5165 1120; www.bawbawskihire.com.au) rents out equipment. For freestyle riders, **Cactus Rail Park** has rails and kick boxes, and there's the **Big Air Bag**, where you can practise your snowboarding stunts with a guaranteed soft landing!

🛏 Sleeping & Eating

Most lodges and eateries are open year-round. For full listings, check out www.mountbawbaw.com.au.

Alpine Hotel   HOTEL $
(☑03-5165 1136; Currawong Rd; dm from $30, d/tr from $70/85) Superb value, year-round backpacker and motel-style accommodation. In winter the sports bar-cafe and attached lounge is *the* place to hang while local bands belt out rock covers until 2am.

Kelly's Lodge   B&B $$
(☑03-5165 1129; www.kellyslodge.com.au; 11 Frosti Lane; 4-bed r summer/winter from $120/370, budget r per person $45-70) This long-running, superfriendly place, with comfortable rooms and a cosy lounge, is in the centre of everything on the mountain. The ski-in cafe (mains $15 to $32) is a Baw Baw favourite, with pizzas and lamb shanks.

Village Central   MODERN AUSTRALIAN $$
(☑03-5165 1123; Alpine Resort, Currawong Rd; mains $8-28; ⊙10.30am-late daily winter, 11am-late Mon-Fri, 10.30am-late Sat & Sun summer) This cafe-restaurant at Village Central specialises in local produce and has good valley views.

ℹ Information

Mt Baw Baw Alpine Resort Management Board (☑03-5165 1136; www.mountbawbaw.com.au; ⊙8.30am-8.30pm ski season, 9am-5pm rest of year) In the centre of the village, this office provides general tourist information and an accommodation service.

ℹ Getting There & Away

Located about 120km east of Melbourne, the main access road to Baw Baw Village is the windy Baw Baw Tourist Rd via Noojee, reached off the Princes Hwy at Drouin. An alternative back route from the Latrobe Valley is the unsealed, but all-season, South Face Rd from Rawson, north of Moe. Either way, the last 5km up to Baw Baw Village is probably the steepest road in the country – low gear all the way.

Lake Eildon National Park & Around

ℹ Getting There & Away

Lake Eildon, 215km northeast of Melbourne, can be reached via the Hume Fwy (take the turn-off at Seymour) or via the far prettier route through Healesville.

High Country Highlights

1 Cycle the **Murray to Mountains Rail Trail** (p268), Victoria's longest bike path

2 Visit Ned Kelly's haunts in historic **Beechworth** (p266), then sample the brews at Bridge Road Brewers

3 Hit the gourmet trail in **Milawa and the King Valley** (p265), tasting wine, cheese, mustard and olives

4 Mountain-bike the green-season trails down **Mt Buller** (p264)

5 Hit the piste at one of the big three ski resorts: **Mt Buller** (p263), **Mt Hotham** (p278) or **Falls Creek** (p275)

6 Enjoy the vibrant colours of the autumn and spring festivals in **Bright** (p271)

7 Holiday on a houseboat or camp by the shores on the beautiful lake at **Eildon** (p260)

8 Make like *The Man from Snowy River* and go horse riding on the high plains around **Mansfield** (p261)

9 Drive along the **Great Alpine Road** to the isolated gold-mining town of **Omeo** (p280)

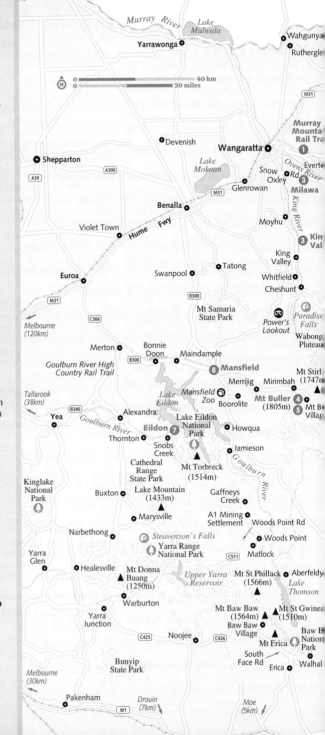

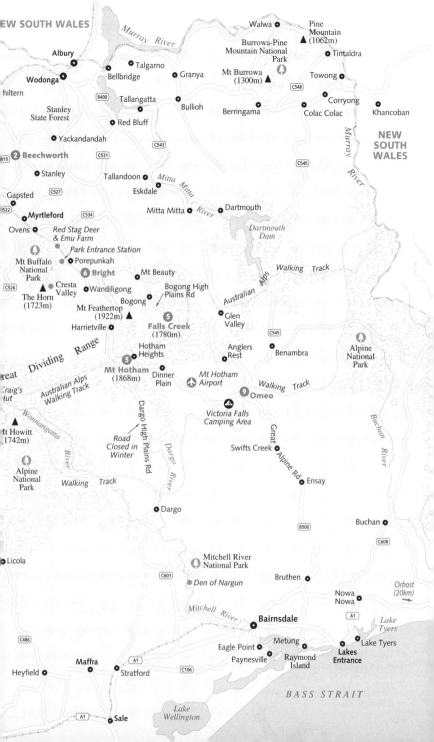

Lake Eildon National Park

Surrounding most of its namesake lake, Lake Eildon National Park is the low-lying southern gateway to the High Country, covering over 270 sq km and providing superb opportunities for walking and camping. From the 1850s, the areas around Lake Eildon were logged and mined for gold, so much of the vegetation is regrowth eucalypt forest.

Originally called Sugarloaf Reserve, **Lake Eildon** was created as a massive reservoir for irrigation and hydroelectric schemes. It was constructed between 1915 and 1929 and flooded the town of Darlingford and surrounding farm homesteads. After years of drought, recent rains have brought the lake back to near capacity. Behind the dam wall, the 'pondage' (outflow from the dam) spreads below Eildon township.

On the northern arm of the lake is **Bonnie Doon**, a popular weekend base, which reached icon status as the nondescript spot where the Kerrigan family enjoyed 'serenity' in the satirical 1997 Australian film *The Castle*.

🛏 Sleeping

Lake Eildon is a beautiful place for bush camping, with several lakeside national-park sites. All sites ($25.20) must be booked online at www.parkweb.vic.gov.au. Fraser Camping Area, on Coller Bay 14km northwest of Eildon along Skyline Dr, comprises three separate camp sites, while the Jerusalem Creek Camping Area is about 8km southwest of Eildon. If you have your own boat or are prepared to hike in, there are (free) remote camp sites at Taylor's Creek, Mountaineer Creek and Cooper Point.

If the Murray River is too far – or you want more room to manoeuvre – Lake Eildon is the next best place in Victoria to stay on a houseboat. Here, you can hire a luxurious 10- or 12-berth houseboat (minimum hire per weekend from $1500). Book well ahead for holiday periods.

Eildon Houseboat Hire HOUSEBOAT $$$
(☑ 0408 005 535; www.eildonhouseboathire.com.au; per week winter/summer $2400/3500)

**Lake Eildon Marina
& Houseboat Hire** HOUSEBOAT $$$
(☑ 03-5774 2107; www.houseboatholidays.com.au; 190 Sugarloaf Rd; high season per week $2500-3800)

Eildon

POP 730

The little one-pub town of Eildon, which sits on the edge of the pondage, is a popular holiday recreation base, built in the 1950s to house Eildon Dam project workers.

◎ Sights & Activities

Lake Eildon and the rivers that feed into it are popular for fishing, but you don't have to be a dedicated angler to have fun here. You can drive up to and across the dam's massive retaining wall to a **lookout point**, with sensational views over the lake, town and houseboat-building yards. There are quiet walking and cycling trails along the shores that give easy access to the best fishing spots.

Eildon Trout Farm FISHING
(☑ 03-5773 2377; www.eildontroutfarm.com.au; 460 Back Eildon Rd; entry/fishing $2/2; ⊙ 9am-5pm) Catching a trout or salmon is guaranteed at this farm located on the back road between Thornton and Eildon.

**Goulburn Valley
Fly-Fishing Centre** FISHING
(☑ 03-5773 2513; www.goulburnvlyflyfishing.com.au; 1270 Goulburn Valley Way; introductory/4hr trip $65/250) If you're looking for specialist tuition and guided fishing trips, either on private waterways or local rivers, this is the place to go.

Rubicon Valley Horse-Riding HORSE RIDING
(☑ 03-5773 2292; www.rubiconhorseriding.com.au; Rubicon Rd; introductory/2hr/half-day/full-day rides $50/75/110/195) This company caters for all levels, including children, and runs overnight safaris ($475).

Stockman's Reward HORSE RIDING
(☑ 03-5774 2322; Goulburn Valley Hwy; 1-/2hr rides $40/70) There are horse-riding adventures available for everyone here, with ponies for young riders and trail rides in the hills.

🛏 Sleeping & Eating

There are a few places to stay in Eildon and on the back road to Thornton, but the best accommodation is on board a houseboat on Lake Eildon – they build 'em in Eildon. Eating options in town are limited to a few cafes in the small shopping strip and the local pub.

Blue Gums Caravan Park
CAMPGROUND **$**

(☑ 03-5774 2576; www.bluegums.com.au; 746 Back Eildon Rd; dm $25, unpowered/powered site from $27/30, cabins $100-135; ✳ 🐾 🏊) On the banks of the Goulburn River about 5km southwest of Eildon, this is a fabulous family caravan park with two swimming pools, a playground, manicured lawns for camping and slick self-contained cabins.

Golden Trout Hotel Motel
MOTEL **$**

(☑ 03-5774 2508; www.goldentrout.com.au; 1 Riverside Dr; d $95) The local pub has standard, slightly tired motel rooms attached, but the location makes up for it – ask for a 'pondage view' room (they're all the same price). The bistro does good pub food ($14 to $28) and is the best bet for an evening meal in town.

❶ Information

Eildon Visitor Information Centre (☑ 03-5774 2909; www.lakeeildon.com; Main St; ⊙ 10am-2pm) Friendly staff run this small office opposite the shopping centre.

Jamieson

POP 250

From Eildon, the sealed and scenic back road skirts the southern edge of the national park to Jamieson, a charming little town where the Goulburn and Jamieson Rivers join Lake Eildon. Jamieson was established as a supply town for gold-miners in the 1850s and a number of interesting historical buildings remain.

🛏 Sleeping & Eating

There's good bush camping along the Jamieson and Goulburn Rivers but you must be self-sufficient and camp at least 20m from the water – take the Jamieson-Licola Rd east or the Woods Point Rd to the south. In town, accommodation includes a caravan park and motel.

Twin River Cabins
CABIN **$**

(☑ 03-5777 0582; www.twinrivercabins.com.au; 3 Chenery St; s/d $50/90) These rustic little cabins make a great budget retreat close to town. They sleep four to six people and have basic kitchen facilities and shared amenities. The owners rent mountain bikes for $20 a day.

Jamieson Brewery
PUB **$$**

(☑ 03-5777 0515; www.jamiesonbrewery.com.au; Eildon-Jamieson Rd; mains $16-30; ⊙ from 11am)

An essential stop 3km from town, the Jamieson Brewery produces flavoursome beers on-site, including a raspberry ale and the knockout 'Beast'. Try a tasting plate of four beers and homemade pesto ($12) and take the free, daily brewery tour at 12.30pm. There's even free tastings of homemade fudge. The bistro serves up good pub food for lunch and dinner daily – enjoy it on the deck overlooking a large garden.

Mansfield

POP 3067

Mansfield is the gateway to Victoria's largest snowfields at Mt Buller, but also an exciting all-seasons destination in its own right. There's plenty to do here in *The Man from Snowy River* country, with horse riding and mountain biking popular in summer, and a buzzing atmosphere in winter when the snow bunnies hit town.

◉ Sights

On the fourth Saturday of each month, the **Mansfield Farmers Market** (www.mansfieldfarmersmarket.com.au; Highett St; ⊙ 8.30am-1pm) brings farmers' produce to town at the Mansfield Primary School.

Mansfield Cemetery
CEMETERY

The three Mansfield police officers killed at Stringybark Creek by Ned Kelly and his gang in 1878 (see p303) rest in Mansfield Cemetery.

Mansfield Zoo
ZOO

(☑ 03-5777 3576; www.mansfieldzoo.com.au; 1064 Mansfield Woods Point Rd; adult/child/family $15/8/44; ⊙ 10am-5.30pm, to 6.30pm or sunset in

CRAIG'S HUT

Cattlemen built huts throughout the High Country from the 1850s onwards, but the most iconic is Craig's Hut, built in 1981 for the film *The Man from Snowy River*. It was converted from a film set into a visitors centre 10 years later, then rebuilt in 2003. In 2006 it burned down in bushfires, before being rebuilt (again) in 2007. It's on Mt Stirling in the Alpine National Park about 53km east of Mansfield. The last 1.2km is accessible only by walking or 4WD, but it's worth it for the breathtaking views.

summer) Mansfield Zoo is a surprisingly good wildlife park with lots of native fauna and some exotics, such as a pair of lions. If you're older than eight, you can sleep in the paddocks in a swag (adult/child $65/45, including zoo entry for two days) and wake to the dawn wildlife chorus.

🏃 Activities & Tours

Mansfield is an action town. In winter, plenty of places hire chains and ski and snowboarding gear. At other times, this is one of the best places in the state for horse riding and mountain biking. Horse-riding season in the High Country is generally from late October to May.

Mansfield marks the start or end of the **Goulburn River High Country Rail Trail**, a walking/cycling path that runs from Tallarook to Mansfield via Yea, Alexandra and Bonnie Doon.

All Terrain Cycles MOUNTAIN BIKING
(📞 03-5775 2724; www.allterraincycles.com.au; 58 High St) Hires out top-quality mountain bikes and safety equipment. Also runs guided tours and mountain-biking clinics.

Alpine Helicopter Charter SCENIC FLIGHTS
(📞 0428 376 619; www.alpineheli.com.au; 325 Mt Buller Rd; flights from $185) Themed helicopter flights, such as 'Bushranger Tour', 'Kinlock Winery Experience' and 'Mount Buller Express'. The one-hour adventure flight costs $185 per person.

High Country Horses HORSE RIDING
(📞 03-5777 5590; www.highcountryhorses.com.au; Mt Buller Rd, Merrijig; 2hr/half-day rides $90/120, overnight from $550; ☉ Oct-May) Based at Merrijig on the way to Mt Buller, High Country Horses offers anything from a short trot to overnight treks to Craig's Hut, Howqua River and Mt Stirling.

McCormack's Mountain Valley Trail Rides HORSE RIDING
(📞 03-5777 5542; www.mountainvalleytrailrides. com.au; 43 McCormack's Rd, Merrijig; day ride from $260; ☉ Oct-May) Experienced locals take you into the King Valley and High Country; options include a four-day adventure for $1200.

Watson's Mountain Country Trail Rides HORSE RIDING
(📞 03-5777 3552; www.watsonstrailrides.com.au; Three Chains Rd; 1-/2hr $40/80, 1-/2-day rides from $200/555) A peaceful property where

children can learn with pony rides or short trail rides, or take off on overnight catered rides. One of the highlights is the view from Kate Cameron's Peak, looking down the steep run featured in *The Man from Snowy River*.

🎊 Festivals & Events

High Country Autumn Festival CULTURAL
(www.mansfieldmtbuller.com.au) Held over the March Labour Day weekend; there are markets, picnics, and a rodeo at nearby Merrijig.

Upper Goulburn Wine Region Vintage Celebration WINE
(www.uppergoulburnwine.org.au) Local wines, musicians and chefs make for three fun days in April.

High Country Festival & Spring Arts ARTS
(www.highcountryfestival.com.au) A week of arts, bush markets and activities from late October, culminating in the Melbourne Cup day picnic races.

🛏 Sleeping

Mansfield has a good range of accommodation. Prices are slightly higher during ski season.

Mansfield Holiday Park CAMPGROUND $
(📞 03-5775 1383; www.mansfieldholidaypark.com. au; Mt Buller Rd; unpowered/powered sites from $28/32, d cabins $70-120; ☀) On the edge of town, this is a spacious caravan park with a pool, minigolf, camp kitchen and comfortable cabins.

Mansfield Travellers Lodge HOSTEL, MOTEL $$
(📞 03-5775 1800; www.mansfieldtravellers lodge.com.au; 116 High St; dm $35, s/d/f from $100/120/170; ☀) Located close to the centre of town, this is a long-time favourite for backpackers and families. The spacious dorms are in a restored heritage building, while the motel section features spotless one- and two-bedroom units. Facilities include a kitchen, games rooms, laundry and drying room.

Banjo's Accommodation CABIN $$
(📞 03-5775 2335; www.banjosmansfield.com.au; cnr Mt Buller Rd & Greenvale Lane; d/q $120/180; ☀) These family-friendly, self-contained units on the edge of town can sleep up to five people in the studios and six in the two-bedroom units. They're modern and spacious and the expansive grounds are perfect for the kids to run around.

Highton Manor BOUTIQUE HOTEL **$$**
(☑ 03-5775 2700; www.hightonmanor.com.au; 140 Highton Lane; d stable/tower incl breakfast $130/365; ❄) Built in 1896 for Francis Highett, who sang with Dame Nellie Melba, this stately two-storey manor has style and romance but doesn't take itself too seriously. There is group accommodation in the shared room, modern rooms in the converted stables and lavish period rooms in the main house. If you want the royal treatment, choose the tower room.

Wappan Station FARMHOUSE **$$**
(☑ 03-5778 7786; www.wappanstation.com.au; Royal Town Rd; cottages d from $200, shearers quarters for 20 people $450; ❄) Watch farm activities from your deck at this sheep-and-cattle property on the banks of Lake Eildon.

✖ Eating & Drinking

★ **Mansfield Regional**
Produce Store CAFE **$**
(☑ 03-5779 1404; www.theproducestore.com.au; 68 High St; mains $12-18; ⊙ 9am-5pm Tue-Thu & Sat-Sun, to 9pm Fri; ⊿) The best spot in town for coffee or a light lunch, this rustic store stocks an array of local produce, wine and freshly baked artisan breads. The ever-changing blackboard menu offers full breakfasts, baguettes and salads.

Forty One CAFE **$**
(☑ 03-5775 2951; 39-41 High St; mains $8-17; ⊙ 8am-2.30pm) It's famous for its creamy vanilla slice, but you can enjoy a range of gourmet surprises in the sunny courtyard here.

Mansfield Hotel PUB **$$**
(☑ 03-5775 2101; www.mansfieldhotel.com.au; 86 High St; mains $18-32; ⊙ noon-2pm & 6-9pm) Newly renovated after a 2010 fire, the Mansfield has a huge dining room and extensive bistro menu to go with it. Pull up a couch by the fireplace in winter or eat out on the sunny beer terrace in summer.

Deck on High MODERN AUSTRALIAN **$$**
(☑ 03-5775 1144; www.thedeckonhigh.com.au; 13-15 High St; mains $26-37; ⊙ 11am-late Mon & Wed-Fri, 10am-late Sat & Sun) A sophisticated but relaxed bar-restaurant serving up genuinely good contemporary Aussie cuisine such as tiger-prawn fettucini or chargrilled swordfish. The upper deck is brilliant for a drink on a summer's afternoon and the downstairs bar, with soft couches and sleek lines, is a cosy place to explore the extensive local wine list in winter.

ℹ Information

Mansfield & Mt Buller High Country Visitors Centre (☑ 1800 039 049; www.mansfieldmt-buller.com.au; 175 High St; ⊙ 9am-5pm) In a modern building next to the town's original railway station, the visitors centre books accommodation for the region, and sells lift tickets.

ℹ Getting There & Away

Mansfield is 209km northeast of Melbourne, but allow at least 2½ hours if you're driving; take the Tallarook or Euroa exits from the Hume Fwy.

V-Line (www.vline.com.au) coaches run between Melbourne's Southern Cross Station and Mansfield (three hours, $25) at least once daily, with more frequent departures during the ski season.

Mt Buller

ELEV 1805M
Victoria's largest and busiest ski resort is also the closest major resort to Melbourne, so it buzzes all winter long. It's also developing into a popular summer destination for mountain bikers and hikers, with a range of cross-country and downhill trails. The extensive lift network includes the Horse Hill chairlift that begins in the day car park and drops you off in the middle of the ski runs. The downhill-skiing area is 180 hectares with a vertical drop of 400m. Cross-country trails link Mt Buller with Mt Stirling.

⊙ Sights & Activities

Buller is a well-developed resort with a vibrant village atmosphere in the white season and on summer weekends. In winter there's **night skiing** on Wednesday and Saturday, and for nonskiers there's tobogganing, snowtubing and excellent snowshoeing. The entrance fee to the Horse Hill day car park in winter is $35 per car (free in summer).

At least eight outlets spread across Mansfield and Mt Buller rent ski and other equipment – check out www.mtbuller.com.au for a full list of options.

Mt Buller holds an array of event weekends throughout the year. Check the calendar on www.mtbuller.com.au.

National Alpine
Museum of Australia MUSEUM
(NAMA; ☑ 03-5777 6077; www.nama.org.au; Level 1, Community Centre, Summit Rd; admission by

THE HIGH COUNTRY MT BULLER

BIKING MT BULLER

Mt Buller has developed into one of the great summer mountain-biking destinations in Victoria, with a network of trails around the summit, and exhilarating downhill tracks. From 26 December to the end of January, the Horse Hill chairlift operates on weekends, lifting you and your bike up to the plateau (all-day lift and trails access $55). If you're not biking you can still ride the chairlift all day (adult/child $18/13).

From 26 December till the Easter weekend a bus shuttle runs every weekend from the **Mirimbah Store** (☑03-5777 5529; www.mirimbah.com.au; per ride $15, daily $35; ⊙8am-4pm Thu-Sun Sep-May, daily in winter) at the base of the mountain, to the summit car park, from where you can ride all the way back down on a number of trails. The most popular trail is the **River Spur** (60 to 90 minutes), partly following the Delatite River with 13 river crossings. More challenging is the new one-to-1½-hour **Klingsbourne Trail**. The owners of the Mirimbah Store (which, incidentally, is also a fabulous cafe) are experienced riders and a mine of information on the trails.

You can hire quality mountains bikes from All Terrain Cycles (p262) in Mansfield. During the biking season it also has a hire service at Buller village.

donation; ⊙1-4pm winter, by appointment summer) ⊘ The only alpine museum in Australia, this institution highlights the fascinating history of this area.

Ducks & Drakes SNOW SPORTS (www.ducksanddrakes.net; tours $45-55) Ducks & Drakes runs one- to two-hour guided snowshoeing tours, including equipment and hot chocolate, starting at the clock tower.

Breathtaker on High Spa Retreat SPA (☑1800 088 222; www.breathtaker.com.au; massage per hr from $130) This retreat offers the chance to soak and revive with a range of luxurious treatments, a 20m lap pool and a hydrotherapy 'geisha tub'. It's open by appointment only and for long weekends outside the winter season.

🛏 Sleeping

There are over 7000 beds on the mountain. Rates vary throughout the ski season, with cheaper rates midweek. A handful of places are open year-round. **Mt Buller Alpine Reservations** (☑03-5777 6633; www.mtbuller-reservations.com.au) books accommodation; there's generally a two-night minimum stay on weekends.

YHA Mt Buller HOSTEL $ (☑03-5777 6181; www3.yha.com.au/hostels/vic/ski-region/mount-buller; The Ave; dm $60-70) In winter this well-known and cosy little YHA has good facilities and friendly staff.

Mt Buller Chalet CHALET $$$ (☑03-5777 6566; www.mtbullerchalet.com.au; Summit Rd; d incl breakfast summer/winter from

$215/604; ☞🔲) With a central location, the chalet offers a sweet range of suites, a library with billiard table, well-regarded eateries, an impressive sports centre and a heated pool. It also operates nearby **Buller Backpackers** (www.bullerbackpackers.com.au; dm $55).

Hotel Enzian CHALET $$$ (☑03-5777 6996; www.enzian.com.au; 69 Chamois Rd; r $230-390) Year-round Enzian has a good range of lodge rooms and apartments (sleeping up to eight) with all the facilities, alpine charm and an in-house restaurant.

🍴 Eating & Drinking

You'll find plenty of great dining experiences here in winter, and a few places open year-round. There's a licensed and reasonably well-stocked supermarket in the village centre.

There's no shortage of entertainment and après-ski fun here in winter, but most places close up for the summer.

Cattleman's Café CAFE $ (☑03-5777 7970; Village Centre; mains $8-18; ⊙8am-2pm Oct-May, 8am-9pm Jun-Sep) At the base of the Blue Bullet chairlift and open year-round, this is the place for breakfast, coffee or a bistro meal of steak, burgers or fish and chips.

Black Cockatoo MODERN AUSTRALIAN $$ (☑03-5777 6566; Summit Rd; lunch from $8.50, mains $31-42, 2-/3-course menu $55/65; ⊙7-11am & 6-9pm) At the Mt Buller Chalet, this is year-round fine dining – the best on the mountain. In winter, the Après Bar & Cafe has more casual dining.

Pension Grimus   AUSTRIAN **$$**
(☑ 03-5777 6396; www.pensiongrimus.com.au;
Breathtaker Rd; mains $25-39; ⊗ 6-9pm Mon-Fri,
noon-2pm & 6-9pm Sat & Sun) One of Buller's
originals, there's Austrian-style food at the
Kaptan's Restaurant, impromptu music and
a pumping bar that will give you a warm,
fuzzy feeling after a day on the slopes.

Kooroora Hotel   PUB
(☑ 03-5777 6050; Village Sq; ⊗ to 3am in winter)
Rocks hard and late during the ski season.
There's live music on Wednesday night and
most weekends, and the popular Hoohah
Kitchen serves good bistro meals.

❶ Information

Mt Buller Resort Management Board (☑ 03-
5777 6077; www.mtbuller.com.au; Community
Centre, Summit Rd; ⊗ 8.30am-5pm) Also runs
an information office in the village-square clock
tower during winter.

❶ Getting There & Around

Mansfield–Mt Buller Buslines (☑ 03-5775
2606; www.mmbl.com.au) runs a winter service
from Mansfield (adult/child return $58/40,
48km), while **V/Line** (www.vline.com.au) oper-
ates at least one daily bus between Melbourne
and Mt Buller (adult/child return from $130/81).

Ski-season car parking is below the village;
a 4WD taxi service transports people to their
village accommodation.

Day-trippers park in the Horse Hill day car park
and take the quad chairlift into the skiing area,
or there's a free day-tripper shuttle-bus service
between the day car park and the village. Ski
hire and lift tickets are available at the base of
the chairlift.

King Valley
& the Snow Road

King Valley

From Melbourne, turning east off the Hume
Fwy near Wangaratta and onto the Snow Rd
brings you to the King Valley, a prosperous
cool-climate wine region and an important
gourmet food region. The valley extends
south along the King River, through the
tiny towns of Mohyu, Whitfield and Ches-
hunt, with a sprinkling of 20 or so wineries
noted for Italian varietals and cool-climate
wines such as sangiovese, barbera, sparkling
prosecco and pinot grigio. Check out www.
winesofthekingvalley.com.au.

Among the best are **Dal Zotto Estate**
(☑ 03-5729 8321; www.dalzotto.com.au; Main Rd,
Whitfield; ⊗ 10am-5pm), which also has an
Italian-style trattoria open on weekends,
and **Pizzini** (☑ 03-5729 8278; www.pizzini.com.
au; 175 King Valley Rd, Whitfield; ⊗ 10am-5pm).

There's good camping along the King Riv-
er and a few places to stay around Whitfield.

Milawa Gourmet Region

On the Snow Rd, between Wangaratta and
Myrtleford, the Milawa/Oxley gourmet re-
gion (www.milawagourmet.com) is the place
to indulge your tastebuds. As well as wine
tasting, you can sample cheese, olives, mus-
tards and marinades, or dine in some of the
region's best restaurants.

At Oxley, wineries include **John Gehrig
Wines** (☑ 03-5727 3395; www.johngehrigwines.
com.au; 80 Gehrigs Lane; ⊗ 10am-5pm), which

WORTH A TRIP

POWER'S LOOKOUT

The back road from Mansfield to Whitfield in the King Valley is a seriously scenic drive –
sure beats the Hume Hwy. About 20km from Whitfield and 3km down a signposted
gravel road is Power's Lookout, with the greatest view over the King Valley and the
Victorian Alps you could hope to see. The lookout was named after Harry Power, a 19th-
century bushranger who teamed up with a young Ned Kelly and taught him a thing or
two. Although he committed more than 30 armed crimes, Power was considered some-
thing of a gentleman, never killing anyone and occasionally offering not to rob those he
thought couldn't afford it. He even apologised as he departed with his loot and horses.
Power knew the mountains intimately and used this lookout as his hideout, from where
he could survey the land for approaching trouble. But in 1870 he was betrayed for a
£500 reward, captured here as he slept, and sent to jail for 15 years.

Today, you can survey the valley and ranges just as Power did. There's a lookout at the
picnic area, but don't miss the short walk to the rocky No 2 lookout – superb!

has rare varieties such as verjuice, and the unmistakeable **Sam Miranda** ([☑] 03-5727 3888; www.sammiranda.com.au; 1019 Snow Rd ⊙ 10am-5pm) with its architecturally-designed cellar door and wide range of Italian-style wines.

About 5km further on, the main street of Milawa boasts **Milawa Mustards** ([☑] 03-5727 3202; www.milawamustards.com.au; The Cross Roads; ⊙ 10am-5pm), which offers tastings of its handmade seeded mustards, herbed vinegars and preserves; the **Olive Shop** ([☑] 03-5727 3887; www.theoliveshop.com.au; 1605 Snow Rd; ⊙ 10am-5pm), an olive 'gallery' with oils and tapenades for sampling; and **Walkabout Honey** ([☑] 03-5727 3468; Snow Rd; ⊙ 10am-5pm), where you can sample a range of honeys.

Next stop is the region's best-known winery, **Brown Brothers Vineyard** ([☑] 03-5720 5500; www.brownbrothers.com.au; Bobbinawarrah Rd, Milawa; ⊙ 9am-5pm). The winery's first vintage was in 1889, and it has remained in the hands of the same family ever since. As well as the tasting room, there's the superb Epicurean Centre restaurant, a gorgeous garden, kids' play equipment and picnic and barbecue facilities.

About 2km north of Milawa, **Milawa Cheese Company** ([☑] 03-5727 3589; www.milawacheese.com.au; Factory Rd, Milawa; ⊙ 9am-5pm, meals 9.30am-3pm) is our favourite produce store. From humble origins, it now produces a mouth-watering array of cheeses to sample or buy. It excels at soft farmhouse brie (from goat or cow) and pungent washed-rind cheeses. There's a bakery here and an excellent restaurant where the speciality is a variety of pizzas using Milawa cheese. Also here is the cellar door for **Wood Park Wines** ([☑] 03-5727 3500; www.woodparkwines.com.au; ⊙ 11am-4pm Fri-Wed), so you can complement your cheese tasting with some quality wine tasting, or pop around the back to the **Muse Gallery of Milawa** ([☑] 03-5727 3599; www. musegallery.com.au; ⊙ 10am-5pm Thu-Mon).

Further northeast on the road to Everton is **EV Olives** ([☑] 03-5727 0209; www.evolives. com; 203 Everton Rd, Markwood; ⊙ 10am-5pm), offering the fruity taste of oils, olives and tapenades.

Back in Milawa, the **Milawa Gourmet Hotel** ([☑] 03-5727 3208; cnr Snow & Factory Rds; mains $15-33; ⊙ noon-2.30pm & 6-8.30pm) is a traditional country pub, but it lives up to the region's reputation, serving good bistro food and local produce with gourmet flair. Try the Milawa chicken stuffed with local Camembert, wrapped in bacon and served with Milawa mustard.

Just north of Snow Rd on the Ovens River flood plain is the little farming community of Whorouly, home to the **2 Cooks Cafe** ([☑] 03-5783 6110; www.the2cookscafe.com.au; 577 Whorouly Rd; mains $12.50-17.50; ⊙ 9am-5pm Fri-Mon, 6-9pm Fri), a sweet deli, food store and cafe. Nearby is the **Whorouly Hotel** ([☑] 03-5727 1424; www.whoroulyhotel.com; 542 Whorouly Rd; mains $6-24; ⊙ 6-9pm Fri & Sat), a friendly country pub where you can get a hearty bistro meal (it's known for its beef parma).

Where the Snow Rd meets the Great Alpine Rd (B500), **Gapsted Wines** ([☑] 03-5751 1383; www.gapstedwines.com.au; Great Alpine Rd; ⊙ 10am-5pm, lunch daily) is another outstanding winery where you can eat from the seasonal lunch menu in beautiful surroundings.

TOP 10 HIGH COUNTRY FOOD EXPERIENCES

➡ Milawa Cheese Company (p266)

➡ Brown Brothers Vineyard (p266), Milawa

➡ Myrtleford Butter Factory (p270)

➡ Patrizia Simone Country Cooking School (p272), Bright

➡ King Valley wine region (p265)

➡ Rutherglen wine region (p300)

➡ Bridge Road Brewers (p268), Beechworth

➡ Provenance (p268), Beechworth

➡ Mt Buffalo Olives (p271)

➡ Å Skafferi (p275), Mt Beauty

Beechworth

POP 2789

Beechworth's historic honey-coloured granite buildings and wonderful gourmet offerings make this one of northeast Victoria's most enjoyable towns. It's also listed by the National Trust as one of Victoria's two 'notable' towns (the other is Maldon), and you'll soon see why: this living legacy of the gold-rush era will take you back to the days of miners and bushrangers – Ned Kelly was tried here for the murder of three Mansfield policemen.

Most of the town spreads along two intersecting streets – Ford and Camp Sts – where you'll find old-fashioned shops and some of the best food stores, cafes and restaurants in the region.

◎ Sights & Activities

Historic Precinct
NEIGHBOURHOOD

Beechworth's main attraction is the group of well-preserved, honey-tinged buildings that make up the **Historic & Cultural Precinct** (☑1300 366 321; ticket for all sites plus 2 guided tours adult/child/family $25/15/50; ⊙9am-5pm) – if you're going to visit more than a couple of the museums, it's worth buying the combined ticket. First is the **Town Hall**, where you'll find the visitors centre and the free *Echoes of History* audiovisual tour. Across the road is the **Beechworth Courthouse** (adult/child/family $8/5/16; ⊙9.30am-5pm), where the trials of many key historical figures took place, including those of Ned Kelly and his mother; their cells can still be seen. Behind the courthouse is the **Old Police Station Museum** (admission $2; ⊙10am-2pm Fri-Sun). You can send a telegram to anywhere in the world from the **Telegraph Station** on Ford St, the original Morse-code office. Walk through to Loch St to the **Burke Museum** (adult/child/family $8/5/16; ⊙10am-5pm), which is named after the hapless explorer Robert O'Hara Burke, who was Beechworth's superintendent of police before he set off on his historic trek north with William Wills.

Beechworth Sweet Co
FOOD

(www.beechworthsweetco.com.au; 7 Camp St; ⊙9.30am-5.30pm Tue-Sat, to 5pm Sun & Mon) You'll get all nostalgic over the eye-popping range of old-time sweets and lollies at the Beechworth Sweet Co. So popular it's one-way traffic only!

Murray Breweries Historic Cellars
MUSEUM

(☑03-5728 1304; 29 Last St; admission $1; ⊙10am-4pm) Old brewery paraphernalia is on display at MB Historic Cellars, a former brewery that now produces traditional cordials such as ginger beer. In the same premises is the **Carriage Museum**, displaying gorgeous old horse-drawn carriages.

Golden Horseshoes Monument
MONUMENT

(cnr Sydney Rd & Gorge Scenic Dr) The Golden Horseshoes Monument is where, in 1855, a horse was shod with golden shoes and ridden into town by candidate Donald Cameron on the nomination day of Victoria's first parliamentary elections. The Victorian-era PR stunt seemed to work – Cameron was duly elected to parliament.

Chinese Gardens
GARDENS

Down near pretty Lake Sambell you'll find the Chinese Gardens, a tribute to the Chinese gold miners.

★ Sticks & Stones Adventures
OUTDOORS

(☑02-6027 1483; www.sticksandstonesadventures. com.au) This company offers some of Victoria's more intriguing excursions, with a mix of bush survival skills (learning how to start fires without a match or to find medicinal plants) to interesting bush experiences (panning for gold or cooking damper). Wildlife and local foods also feature high on the itineraries.

Beechworth Honey Experience
FOOD

(☑03-5728 1432; www.beechworthhoney.com.au; cnr Ford & Church Sts; ⊙9am-5pm) **FREE** Beechworth Honey Experience takes you into the world of honey and bees with a self-guided audiovisual tour, live hive and honey tastings. The shop sells locally made honey, beeswax candles, nougat and soaps.

☞ Tours

Daily guided **walking tours** (adult/child/family $10/7.50/25) leave from the visitors centre and feature lots of gossip and interesting details. The Gold Rush tour starts at 10.15am; the Ned Kelly–themed tour at 1.15pm.

Beechworth Ghost Tours
GUIDED TOUR

(☑0447 432 816; www.beechworthghosttours.com; asylum tour adult/child/family $30/15/85, murder tour $25/15/75; ⊙from 8pm) Beechworth's most popular after-dark outing is Beechworth Ghost Tours, which explore the town's former lunatic asylum by lamplight, with plenty of eerie tales of murder and mayhem. There are four tours on weekends, including a midnight walk.

★ Festivals & Events

Golden Horseshoes Festival
CULTURAL

(⊙Easter) Donald Cameron's ride on a gold-shod horse is re-enacted in a grand parade at this Easter event. Food stalls, Easter-egg hunt, music and fun.

Harvest Celebration
FOOD

(www.harvestcelebration.com.au; ⊙May) Food and wine stalls and workshops take to the streets in May.

Beechworth Oktoberfest
DRINK

(⊙Oct) Beer-drinking and oompah in early October, hosted by Bridge Road Brewers.

MURRAY TO MOUNTAINS RAIL TRAIL

The **Murray to Mountains Rail Trail** (www.murraytomountains.com.au) is Victoria's second-longest bike path and one of the High Country's best walking/cycling trails for families or casual riders. It's sealed and relatively flat for much of the way, and passes through spectacular rural scenery of farms, forest and vineyards, with views of the alpine ranges. The 94km trail runs from Wangaratta to Bright via Beechworth, Myrtleford and Porepunkah. A newly completed section heads northwest from Wangaratta to Wahgunyah via Rutherglen, completing the true Murray to Mountains experience.

Break up the journey and explore the area: stop off for a cold beer in a country pub such as the Ovens Hotel, sample local produce in the gourmet region, jump off for tastings and lunch at a winery (such as Pennyweight, Michelton or Boynton's), or spend a day or two in one of the many comfortable local B&Bs.

Aficionados say the 16km between Everton and Beechworth, which detours off the main trail, is the best part of the ride (despite a challenging uphill section), as you're cycling through the bush. Bikes can be hired in Wangaratta and Bright, as well as towns in between. **Bus-a-Bike** (☑ 03-5752 2974) carries up to 11 people and their bikes to wherever, from wherever, along the trail. Call to arrange your pick-up.

Celtic Festival   CULTURAL
(www.beechworthcelticfestival.com.au; ⊗ Nov) Art, entertainment, food, music and mayhem in mid-November.

🛏 Sleeping

Beechworth is well-endowed with cottages and heritage B&Bs; check out www.beechworthonline.com.au. Provenance has some stunning rooms that start at $285 a double.

Old Priory   GUESTHOUSE $
(☑ 03-5728 1024; www.oldpriory.com.au; 8 Priory Lane; dm/s/d $45/65/95, cottages $140) This historic convent is a spooky but charming old place. It's often used by school groups, but it's the best budget choice in Beechworth, with lovely gardens and a range of rooms, including beautifully renovated miners' cottages.

Lake Sambell Caravan Park   CAMPGROUND $
(☑ 03-5728 1421; www.caravanparkbeechworth.com.au; Peach Dr; unpowered/powered sites from $28/34, cabins $95-170; ❄ 🛜) This shady park next to beautiful Lake Sambell has great facilities including a camp kitchen, a playground and bike hire. The sunsets reflected in the lake are spectacular.

★ Freeman on Ford   B&B $$$
(☑ 03-5728 2371; www.freemanonford.com.au; 97 Ford St; s/d incl breakfast from $255/275; ❄) In the 1876 Oriental Bank, this sumptuous but homely place offers Victorian luxury in six beautifully renovated rooms, right in the heart of town. The owner, Heidi, will make you feel very special.

🍴 Eating & Drinking

For a town of its size, Beechworth has some fantastic feasting, from provedores and pantries stocking fresh local produce to serious fine-dining restaurants in historic buildings.

Beechworth Bakery   BAKERY $
(☑ 1300 233 784; 27 Camp St; light meals $4-10; ⊗ 6am-7pm) This popular place is the original in a well-known, statewide bakery chain; great for pies and pastries, cakes and sandwiches.

Beechworth Provender   CAFE, DELI $
(☑ 03-5728 2650; 18 Camp St; ⊗ 8am-5.30pm) Crammed with delectable local produce (and wines) for filling a gourmet hamper, the Provender is also an excellent cafe. Courtyard seating outside.

★ Bridge Road Brewers   BREWERY, PIZZERIA $$
(☑ 03-5728 2703; www.bridgeroadbrewers.com.au; Old Coach House Brewers Lane, 50 Ford St; pizza $12-21; ⊗ 11am-5pm Mon-Sat, 11am-11pm Sun) Hiding behind the imposing Tanswells Commercial Hotel, Beechworth's gem of a microbrewery produces some excellent beers (taste 10 for $15), with nine of them on tap, and serves freshly baked pretzels and super housemade pizzas.

★ Provenance   MODERN AUSTRALIAN $$$
(☑ 03-5728 1786; www.theprovenance.com.au; 86 Ford St; 2-/3-course meals $63/80, degustation menu without/with matching wines $100/155; ⊗ 6.30pm-late Wed-Sat, noon-3pm & 6.30pm-late Sun) In an 1856 bank building, Provenance has elegant but contemporary fine dining.

Under the guidance of acclaimed local chef Michael Ryan, the innovative menu features dishes such as Berkshire pork belly, tea-smoked duck breast and some inspiring vegetarian choices. If you can't decide, go for the degustation menu. Bookings essential.

ⓘ Information

Beechworth Visitors Centre (☎1300 366 321; www.beechworthonline.com.au; 103 Ford St; ☉9am-5pm) An accommodation and activity booking service located in the Town Hall. Ask about the Golden Ticket, which includes admission to the historic precinct and two guided walking tours (valid for two days).

ⓘ Getting There & Away

Beechworth is just off the Great Alpine Rd, 36km east of Wangaratta, and 280km northeast of Melbourne.

V/Line (☎1800 800 007; www.vline.com.au) runs a train/bus service between Melbourne and Beechworth with a change at Seymour or Wangaratta ($31, 3½ hours, three daily). There are direct buses from Wangaratta ($4.50, 35 minutes, six daily) and Bright ($4.60, 50 minutes, two daily).

Yackandandah

POP 950

An old gold-mining town nestled in beautiful hills and valleys east of Beechworth, 'Yack', as it's universally known, is original enough to be classified by the National Trust. You might even recognise it as the setting for the 2004 film *Strange Bedfellows*, starring Paul Hogan and Michael Caton.

In mid- to late March, Yack celebrates the **Yackandandah Folk Festival** (www.folkfestival.yackandandah.com; ☉Mar) – three days of music, parades, workshops and fun.

⊙ Sights & Activities

A stroll along the historic main street is the town's highlight. Before setting out, pick up the free *A Walk in High Street* brochure from the visitor centre (p270).

Karr's Reef Goldmine   MINE TOUR
(☎0408 975 991; adult/child $25/20; ☉10am, 1pm & 4pm Sat & Sun) Karr's Reef Goldmine dates from 1857. On the 1½-hour guided tour you don a hard hat and descend into the original tunnels to learn a bit about the mine's history. Bookings can be made through the visitors centre.

Schmidt's Strawberry Winery   WINERY
(☎02-6027 1454; 932 Osborne's Flat Rd, Allans Flat; ☉9am-5pm Mon-Sat, 10am-4pm Sun) Fresh strawberries are on sale here from mid-October to mid-January, but what makes this place stand out are its strawberry wines. They won't be to everyone's taste, but they're unlike anything you'll try elsewhere. It's around 5km northeast of Yackandandah along the road to Baranduda.

🛍 Shopping

Many of the historic shops in the main street contain galleries, antiques and curios.

Kirby's Flat Pottery   CERAMICS
(☎02-6027 1416; www.johndermer.com.au; 225 Kirby's Flat Rd; ☉10.15am-5.30pm Sat & Sun) The studio-cum-gallery-cum-shop at Kirby's Flat Pottery is 4km south of Yackandandah. Even if you're not interested in buying, the gallery contains a stunning collection.

A Bear's Old Wares   CRAFT
(☎02-6027 1114; www.abearsoldwares.com; 12 High St; ☉9am-5.30pm) A Bear's Old Wares is a fascinating shop crammed with Buddhist and Hindu idols, prayer flags, Tibetan jewellery and wall hangings.

🛏 Sleeping & Eating

Yackandandah Holiday Park   CAMPGROUND $
(☎02-6027 1380; www.yhp.com.au; Taymac Dr; powered sites $32-43, cabins $105-170) Beside pretty Yackandandah Creek but close to the town, this well-equipped park is a little oasis of greenery and autumn colours.

Sticky Tarts Cafe   CAFE $
(☎02-6027 1853; 26 High St; breakfast $5-13.50, lunch mains $5-16.50; ☉8am-2.30pm) With fabulous cafe food on the main street, Sticky Tarts Cafe makes a great breakfast or lunch stop. For the former, try the pumpkin bread with maple butter or you can build your own breakfast, while lunch is more about sandwiches and risotto.

Star Hotel   PUB $$
(☎02-6027 1493; 30 High St; mains $18-20; ☉3pm-late Mon-Thu, noon-late Fri-Sun) This 1863 hotel, known locally as the 'top pub', has good bistro meals that range from a mixed grill or steak sandwich to vegetarian lasagne or red chicken curry.

ⓘ Information

Yackandandah Visitors Centre (☑ 02-6027 1988; www.uniqueyackandandah.com.au; 27 High St; ☺ 9am-5pm) In the grand 1878 Athenaeum building.

ⓘ Getting There & Away

Yackandandah is 307km northeast of Melbourne – take the Hume Fwy to the Great Alpine Rd exit north of Wangaratta, and then follow the signs to Beechworth, from where it's a further 22km into Yackandandah.

Myrtleford

POP 2707

Along the Great Alpine Hwy near the foothills of Mt Buffalo, Myrtleford is a 'Gateway to the Alps', and a worthwhile stop if you're heading to the snowfields or exploring the gourmet region.

Myrtleford Cycle Centre (☑ 03-5752 1511; www.myrtlefordcycle.com; 59 Clyde St; per day/weekend $25/45; ☺ 9am-5.30pm Tue-Sat, 10am-2pm Sun) rents out bikes and helmets.

🛏 Sleeping

Myrtleford Caravan Park　　CAMPGROUND $
(☑ 03-5752 1598; www.myrtlefordholidaypark.com.au; Lewis Ave; unpowered/powered sites from $25/27, dm $29, cabins $83-134; ❄) Grassy sites, well-maintained cabins, kids' playground and a 40-bed bunkhouse for groups or backpackers.

Motel on Alpine　　MOTEL $$
(☑ 03-5752 1438; www.motelonalpine.com; 258 Great Alpine Rd; d/f from $129/190; ❄ 🛜 ⛲) Quality motel close to the town centre with a pool and spa, manicured garden and a highly regarded restaurant. Breakfast included.

Carawah Ridge　　B&B $$$
(☑ 03-5752 2147; www.carawahridge.com.au; 514 Buffalo Creek Rd; d $215, minimum 2-night stay; ❄ ⛲) These two secluded apartments, 7km from Myrtleford in the Buffalo Creek Valley, make a delightful getaway. Gorgeous gardens, cosy bedrooms and modern amenities, including kitchenette, with a full breakfast delivered to your door.

🍴 Eating

★ **Myrtleford Butter Factory**　　CAFE $
(☑ 03-5752 2300; www.thebutterfactory.com.au; Great Alpine Rd; mains $6.50-18.50; ☺ 9am-5pm; 🛜 🚗) This cafe, produce store and restaurant is in an old butter factory, and you can still see butter being churned here. It offers 45-minute guided tours ($8) of the factory at 11am on Thursdays. The produce store stocks a wide range of local products, while the cafe is a special place for an organic breakfast or lunch of local trout or innovative tasting plates.

ⓘ Information

Myrtleford Visitors Centre (☑ 03-5755 0514; www.visitmyrtleford.com; 38 Myrtle St; ☺ 9am-5pm) Information and a booking service for the alpine valley area ski fields. Ask for the *Myrtleford Discovery Trail Guide*, which outlines historical sites around town.

ⓘ Getting There & Away

Myrtleford lies 296km northeast of Melbourne. The easiest access road is the Great Alpine Rd (B500) between Wangaratta (46km) and Bright (30km).

Mt Buffalo National Park

Beautiful **Mt Buffalo** is an easily accessible year-round destination – in winter it's a tiny family-friendly ski resort with gentle runs, and in summer it's a great spot for bushwalking, mountain biking and rock climbing.

It was named in 1824 by the explorers Hume and Hovell on their trek from Sydney to Port Phillip – they thought its bulky shape resembled a buffalo – and declared a national park in 1898. The main access road is out of Porepunkah, between Myrtleford and Bright.

You'll find granite outcrops, alpine lookouts, streams and waterfalls, wildflowers and wildlife here. The **Big Walk**, an 11km, five-hour ascent of the mountain starts from Eurobin Creek Picnic Area, north of Porepunkah, and finishes at the Gorge Day Visitor Area. A road leads to just below the summit of the Horn (1723m), the highest point on the massif. Nearby **Lake Catani** is good for swimming, canoeing and camping. There are 14km of groomed **cross-country ski trails** starting out from the Cresta Valley car park, as well as a **tobogganing area**. In summer Mt Buffalo is a **hang-gliding** paradise, and the near-vertical walls of the Gorge provide some of Australia's most challenging **rock climbing**.

THE HIGH COUNTRY MYRTLEFORD

✦ Activities

Adventure Guides Australia
OUTDOORS
(☑0419 280 614; www.visitmountbuffalo.com.au)
This established operator offers abseiling
(from $88), rock climbing (from $88) and
caving with glow worms through an underground river system (from $120). It also runs
a cross-country ski school in winter.

Mt Buffalo Olives
FARM
(☑03-5756 2143; www.mtbuffaloolives.com.au;
307 Mount Buffalo Rd, Porepunkah) On the road
up to Mt Buffalo from Porepunkah, this
working olive grove has tastings and sales
of olives, olive oils and other locally farmed
products. It also has a lovely place to stay.

🛏 Sleeping

Remote camping is possible at Rocky Creek,
which has pit toilets only.

Lake Catani Campground
CAMPGROUND $
(per person $31.40; ☺Nov-Apr) A summer
campground with toilets and showers. Book
through **Parks Victoria** (☑13 19 63; www.park
web.vic.gov.au).

Bright
POP 2165

Famous for its glorious autumn colours,
Bright is a popular year-round destination
in the foothills of the alps and a gateway to
Mt Hotham and Falls Creek. Skiers make a
beeline through Bright in winter, but it's a
lovely base for exploring the Alpine National
Park, paragliding, fishing and kayaking on
local rivers, bushwalking, and exploring the
region's wineries. Plentiful accommodation
and some sophisticated restaurants and
cafes complete the picture.

⊙ Sights & Activities

Walking trails around Bright include the
3km loop **Canyon Walk**, 4km **Cherry Walk**
and a 6km track to **Wandiligong** that follows Morses Creek. Bright is also a base for
all sorts of adventure activities, including
paragliding – enthusiasts catch the thermals
from nearby Mystic Mountain.

Bright Markets
MARKET
(☺9am-1pm) The Bright Markets are held in
Howitt Park on the third Saturday of each
month.

Great Alpine Liqueurs
DISTILLERY
(☑03-5755 1002; www.greatalpineliqueurs.com.
au; 36 Churchill Ave; ☺10am-4.30pm Fri-Mon,
daily during holidays) There are plenty of wineries in the region, but for something different you can sample a range of liqueurs,
schnapps and brandy distilled at Great
Alpine Liqueurs.

Wandiligong Maze
MAZE
(☑03-5750 1311; www.wandimaze.com.au; White
Star Rd; adult/child $12/10; ☺10am-5pm Wed-Sun,
daily school holidays, closed Aug) Wandiligong
Maze is a fun hedge maze, minigolf course
and cafe about 8km from Bright.

Murray to Mountains Rail Trail
CYCLING
The Murray to Mountains Rail Trail between
Bright and Wangaratta starts (or ends) behind the old train station. Bikes, tandems
and baby trailers can be rented from **Cyclepath** (☑03-5750 1442; www.cyclepath.com.
au; 74 Gavan St; per hr from $20, half-/full-day from
$24/32, per day mountain/road bikes $44/60;
☺9am-5.30pm Mon-Fri, 9.30am-4pm Sat & Sun).
See p268 for more information on the rail
trail.

Active Flight
ADVENTURE SPORTS
(☑0428 854 455; www.activeflight.com.au) Intro-
ductory paragliding course (from $265) or
tandem flights (from $150).

Alpine Paragliding
ADVENTURE SPORTS
(☑0428 352 048; www.alpineparagliding.com;
☺Oct-Jun) Tandem flights from Mystic
($130) and two-day courses ($500).

Bright Microflights
MICROLIGHTING
(☑03-5750 1555; brightmicroflights@swiftdsl.
com.au; Buckland Valley Rd, Porepunkah; flights
per person $70-155) Powered hang-glider
flights over Porepunkah ($70) or Mt
Buffalo ($155).

Eagle School of Microlighting
SCENIC FLIGHTS
(☑0428 570 168; www.eagleschool.com.au; flights
$80-350) Exhilarating tandem flights over
the Mt Buffalo region, as well as flying lessons. Flights include an unpowered glide
back to base.

Alpine Gravity
MOUNTAIN BIKING
(☑03-5758 3393; www.alpinegravity.net; 100
Gavan St; half-/full-day tours $60/75) This expe-
rienced operator runs a mountain-biking
festival in mid-November and spends the
rest of the year taking people out onto the
trails on half-, full- and multiday tours.

Bright

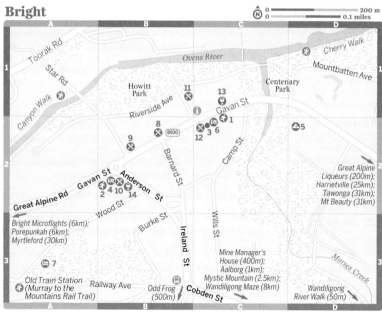

Bright

Activities, Courses & Tours
1 Alpine Gravity C2
2 Cyclepath B2
3 Patrizia Simone Country Cooking
   School C2

Sleeping
4 Bright Escapes B2
5 Bright Holiday Park D2
6 Coach House Inn C2
7 Elm Lodge Motel A3

Eating
8 Beanz of Bright B2
9 Blackbird Café & Food Store B2
10 Pepperleaf Bushtucker
    Restaurant B2
11 Riverdeck Cafe B1
12 Simone's Restaurant C2

Drinking & Nightlife
13 Bright Brewery C1
14 Grape & Grain B2

🎓 Courses

★ Patrizia Simone
Country Cooking School COOKING COURSE
(☑ 03-5755 2266; www.simonesbright.com.au; 98
Gavan St; per person $180) One of northeastern
Victoria's most celebrated chefs, Patrizia
Simone runs fabulous four-hour cooking
classes centred on Italian (especially Um-
brian) cooking techniques using local in-
gredients. Her signature class is 'Umbrian
Experience'.

✹ Festivals & Events

Bright Autumn Festival STREET FESTIVAL
(www.brightautumnfestival.org.au; ⊙ April or May)
Open gardens, scenic convoy tours and a
popular gala day.

Bright Spring Festival STREET FESTIVAL
(www.brightspringfestival.com.au; ⊙ Oct-Nov)
Celebrate all things Bright and beautiful
over the Melbourne Cup weekend and beyond in late October/early November.

🛏 Sleeping

There's an abundance of accommodation here, but rooms are scarce during the
holiday seasons. If you're stuck, check out
Bright Escapes (☑ 1300 551 117; www.bright
escapes.com.au; 76a Gavan St) or **Bright Holiday
Accommodation** (www.brightholidays.com.au).

Bright Holiday Park CAMPGROUND $
(☑ 03-5755 1141; www.brightholidaypark.com.au;
Cherry Ave; unpowered/powered sites from $31/36,

cabins $110-230; ☎) Straddling pretty Morses Creek, this lovely park is five minutes' walk to the shops. The riverside spa cabins are very nice.

Coach House Inn   MOTEL $$
(☑1800 813 992; www.coachhousebright.com.au; 100 Gavan St; s/d from $85/105, apt $125-205; ❄ ☒) This central place has simple but super-value rooms and self-contained units sleeping two to six people. In winter there's a ski-hire shop with discounts for guests, and the popular Lawlers Hut Restaurant is next door. High-season surcharge is a flat $22 per unit.

Elm Lodge Motel   MOTEL $$
(☑03-5755 1144; www.elmlodge.com.au; 2 Wood St; d $110-150, spa cottage $160; ☒) This slightly quirky set of burgundy and pine units has rooms for all budgets, from a shoebox cheapie to spacious two-bedroom self-contained apartments with polished floorboards, and spa rooms. The owners run limousine winery tours (from $75).

Odd Frog   BOUTIQUE HOTEL $$
(☑0418 362 791; www.theoddfrog.com; 3 Mc-Fadyens Lane; d $150-195, q $250) 🖉 Designed and built by the young architect/interior-designer owners, these contemporary, eco-friendly studios feature light, breezy spaces and fabulous outdoor decks with a telescope for star gazing. The design features clever use of the hilly site with sculptural steel-frame foundations and flying balconies.

Mine Manager's House   B&B $$
(☑03-5755 1702; www.brightbedandbreakfast.com. au; 30 Coronation Ave; d $155-195; ❄ ☎) Dating from 1892 and now sumptuously restored to the finest detail, this traditional B&B offers couples a complete experience. Enjoy warm hospitality, beautiful rooms and a delightful English garden. The claw-foot bath in the self-contained cottage offers an extra treat.

Aalborg   APARTMENTS $$$
(☑0401 357 329; www.aalborgbright.com.au; 6 Orchard Ct; r $200-240; ☎) Clean-lined Scandinavian design and pine-and-white furnishings dominate this gorgeous place. Every fitting is perfectly chosen and abundant glass opens out onto sweeping bush views.

✕ Eating & Drinking

Riverdeck Cafe   CAFE $
(☑03-5755 2199; 119 Gavan St; mains $13-16; ☺8am-2.30pm) Behind the visitor centre, the

deck here overlooks the Ovens River and park. It's a great place for coffee, a pancake breakfast or sandwich.

Beanz of Bright   CAFE $$
(103 Gavan St; mains $15-16; ☺8am-2.30pm Tue-Sun) This local favourite is a loungey hole-in-the-wall cafe and bar serving good coffee and decent food. All-day breakfasts, local cheeses and Asian inflections such as Thai fish cakes round out an eclectic mix.

★**Pepperleaf Bushtucker Restaurant**   MODERN AUSTRALIAN $$
(☑03-5755 1537; 2a Anderson St; 1/10 tapas dishes $8/70, mains $19-30; ☺noon-2pm & 6pm-late Fri-Tue, breakfast Sat & Sun) This place doesn't look fancy but the philosophy and flavours – using 'native' ingredients such as wattle-seed, quandong, wild limes and lemon myrtle – are something of a taste revelation. Tapas-style plates give you an opportunity to sample the goods. Mains range from emu or kangaroo fillet to Harrietville rainbow trout, while the indigenous tapas include crocodile skewers or wallaby.

Blackbird Café & Food Store   CAFE $$
(☑03-5750 1838; www.blackbirdfood.com.au; 95 Gavan St; mains $8-23; ☺8am-late) Newspapers spread across couches and coffee tables, while locals mingle with tourists in this light-filled corner cafe that captures the essence of laid-back, food-loving Bright.

★**Simone's Restaurant**   ITALIAN $$$
(☑03-5755 2266; www.simonesbright.com.au; 98 Gavan St; mains $37-40, vegetarian/non-vegetarian tasting menu $85/95; ☺from 6.30pm Tue-Sat) For 20 years owner-chef Patrizia Simone has been serving outstanding Italian food, with a focus on local ingredients and seasonal produce, in the rustic dining room of this heritage-listed house. This is one of regional Victoria's great restaurants and well worth the splurge. Bookings are essential.

★**Bright Brewery**   BREWERY
(☑03-5755 1301; www.brightbrewery.com.au; 121 Gavan St; ☺noon-10pm; ☎) This small boutique brewery produces a quality range of beers (sample five for $10) and beer-friendly food such as pizza, kranskys and nachos. There's a guided tour and tasting on Friday at 3pm ($18), live blues on Sunday, or you can learn to be a brewer for a day ($360) – see the website for course dates.

Grape & Grain WINE BAR
(☎03-5750 1112; www.grapeandgrainbar.com.au; 2c Anderson St; ⊙4-10pm Tue-Thu, 4-11pm Fri & Sat) Swanky bar serving hard-to-find wines, local beers and plenty of the good stuff, such as Milawa cheeses and antipasto.

❶ Information

Alpine Visitor Information Centre (☎03-5755 0584, 1800 111 885; www.brightvictoria.com.au; 119 Gavan St; ⊙9am-5pm) Has a busy accommodation booking service, Parks Victoria information and the attached Riverdeck Cafe (p273).

❶ Getting There & Away

Bright is 310km northeast of Melbourne.
V/Line (☎1800 800 007; www.vline.com.au) runs train/coach services from Melbourne with a change at Wangaratta ($32.20, 4½ hours, two daily). During the ski season the **Snowball Express** (☎1300 656 546; www.snowballexpress.com.au) operates from Bright to Mt Hotham (adult/child return $50/30, 1½ hours).

Mt Beauty & the Kiewa Valley

POP 1654

Huddled at the foot of Victoria's highest mountain, Mt Bogong (1986m), on the Kiewa River, Mt Beauty and its twin villages of Tawonga and Tawonga South are the gateways to Falls Creek ski resort. It's reached by a steep and winding road from Bright with some lovely alpine views, particularly from **Tawonga Gap Lookout**. A scenic loop drive is via the **Happy Valley Tourist Road** from Ovens to Mt Beauty.

The **Mt Beauty Music Festival** (www.musicmuster.org.au) brings together folk, blues and country musicians in April.

◉ Sights & Activities

The 2km **Tree Fern Walk** and the longer **Peppermint Walk** both start from **Mountain Creek Picnic and Camping Ground**, on Mountain Creek Rd, off the Kiewa Valley Hwy (C531). Located about 1km south of Bogong Village (towards Falls Creek), the 1.5km return **Fainter Falls Walk** takes you to a pretty cascade. For information on longer walks in the area, visit the Mt Beauty Visitors Centre.

Bogong Power Station NOTABLE BUILDING
(☎03-5754 3318; Bogong High Plains Rd; ⊙11am-3pm Sun & Mon) FREE There's a fascinating visitor information centre at the Bogong Power Station, a working hydroelectric plant about 20km from Mt Beauty. The centre explains the history of the hydro scheme and has a water wall and a viewing window into the plant.

Rocky Valley Bikes BICYCLE RENTAL
(☎03-5754 1118; www.rockyvalley.com.au; Kiewa Valley Hwy) Rocky Valley Bikes hires mountain and cross-country bikes from $35/50 per half-/full day, and snow-sports equipment in the white season.

THE MAN FROM SNOWY RIVER

You've seen the film and probably read Banjo Paterson's famous poem, but out at Corryong, close to the source of the Murray River, they live the legend. It looked like so much fun in the film that the locals just had to try it – mountain horse-racing where 'the hills are twice as steep and twice as rough'. Yes, it's the **Country Wide Challenge**, Australia's ultimate test of horse-riding prowess! The race is a feature of the **Man From Snowy River Bush Festival** (☎02-6076 1992; www.manfromsnowyriverbushfestival.com.au; ⊙Mar-Apr) – four days of whip-cracking and yarn-spinning fun.

Corryong is a pretty township ringed by mountains – a natural playground for trout fishing, canoeing, cycling and bushwalking. The **Man From Snowy River Museum** (☎03-6076 2600; www.manfromsnowyrivermuseum.com; 103 Hanson St; adult/child $5/1; ⊙10am-4pm Sep-May, 11am-3pm Jun-Aug) tells the story of Jack Riley, a stockman who lived and worked near Corryong and might have been Paterson's inspiration. It's also a local history museum, featuring a set of snow skis from 1870 and the Jarvis Homestead, a 19th-century slab-timber hut.

Corryong visitors centre (☎03-6076 2277; 50 Hanson St; ⊙9am-5pm) has info on the region, including **Jack Riley's Grave** (Corryong Cemetery) which is inscribed with the words, 'In memory of the Man from Snowy River, Jack Riley, buried here 16th July 1914.'

Annapurna Estate WINERY
(☑03-5754 4517; www.annapurnaestate.com.au;
217 Simmonds Creek Rd, Tawonga South; ☺11am-
4pm Fri-Sun) Annapurna Estate, about 3km
from Mt Beauty, is a stunning vineyard with
cellar door sales and a restaurant where you
can dine on the lovely deck looking over the
vines.

Angling Expeditions FISHING
(☑03-5754 1466; 82 Kiewa Valley Hwy, Tawonga;
per person from $100) This is world-renowned
trout-fishing territory. Angling Expeditions
specialises in fly-fishing trips to a private
creek as well as river expeditions.

**Bogong
Horseback Adventures** HORSE RIDING
(☑03-5754 4849; www.bogonghorse.com.au;
Mountain Creek Rd; 2-/3hr $90/110, full-day with
lunch $220) Horse riders can experience this
beautiful area on horseback with Bogong
Horseback Adventures. It's 12km northwest
of Tawonga.

🛏 Sleeping

Mount Beauty Holiday Centre CAMPGROUND $
(☑03-5754 4396; www.holidaycentre.com.au;
Kiewa Valley Hwy; unpowered/powered sites
$28/33, cabins & yurts $75-150; ❄🛜) This family caravan park close to Mt Beauty town
centre has river frontage, games and an interesting range of cabins, including hexago-
nal 'yurts'.

★Dreamers APARTMENT $$$
(☑03-5754 1222; www.dreamersmtbeauty.com.
au; Kiewa Valley Hwy, Mt Beauty; d $200-490;
🛜🐾) 🍴 Each of Dreamers' stunning self-
contained eco apartments offers something
special and architecturally unique. Sunken
lounges, open fireplaces, loft bedrooms and
balcony spas are just some of the highlights.
Great views and a pretty lagoon complete a
dreamily romantic five-star experience.

✕ Eating

★Å Skafferi SWEDISH $
(☑03-5754 4544; 84 Bogong High Plains Rd, Mt
Beauty; mains $8-18; ☺8am-4pm Thu-Mon) This
cool Swedish pantry and food store is a fabu-
lous place to stop. Try the grilled Milawa
cheese sandwiches for breakfast and the
Swedish meatballs or the sampler of herring
and *knäckebröd* for lunch. It sells a range of
local and Scandinavian produce.

Roi's Diner Restaurant ITALIAN $$
(☑03-5754 4495; 177 Kiewa Valley Hwy; mains
$27-35; ☺6.30-9.30pm Thu-Sun) It's hard to
believe this unassuming timber shack on
the highway 5km from Mt Beauty is an
award-winning restaurant, specialising in
exceptional modern-Italian cuisine. Great
risotto.

ℹ Information

Mt Beauty Visitors Centre (☑03-5755 0596,
1800 111 885; www.greatalpinevalleys.com.au;
31 Bogong High Plains Rd, Mt Beauty; ☺9am-
5pm) Has an accommodation-booking service,
a working hydroelectric model and displays on
the history and nature of the region.

ℹ Getting There & Away

V/Line (☑1800 800 007) operates a train/
bus/taxi service from Melbourne to Mt Beauty,
via Seymour and Bright ($36, 5½ hours). In
winter **Falls Creek Coach Service** (☑03-5754
4024; www.fallscreekcoachservice.com.au)
operates direct buses to Mt Beauty from Melbourne on Wednesday, Friday, Saturday and
Sunday (one-way/return $85/134), and from
Albury from Thursday to Sunday ($34/53), both
continuing on to Falls Creek ($37/58).

Falls Creek
ELEV 1780M
Falls Creek, Victoria's glitzy, fashion-
conscious resort, combines a picturesque
alpine setting with impressive skiing and
infamous après-ski entertainment.

◎ Sights & Activities

Skiing at Falls Creek is spread over two areas – the **Village Bowl** and **Sun Valley** –
with 19 lifts, a vertical drop of 267m and
Australia's longest beginner's run at **Wombat's Ramble**. Falls is also the free-ride
snowboard capital, with four parks. Night
skiing in the Village Bowl operates several
times a week.

Other popular winter activities include a
bungee trampoline ($12), snow bikes ($45),
snowtubing and tobogganing, snowmobile
tours (from $130), kiteboarding (from $70)
and snowshoe tours ($28). For more infor-
mation, call the **Activities Hotline** (☑1800
204 424).

It's not all snow sports though, and Falls
has a great **summer program**, which includes an outdoor cinema (free) on an in-
flatable screen, hiking, horse riding and a

Alpine National Park – Bogong Region

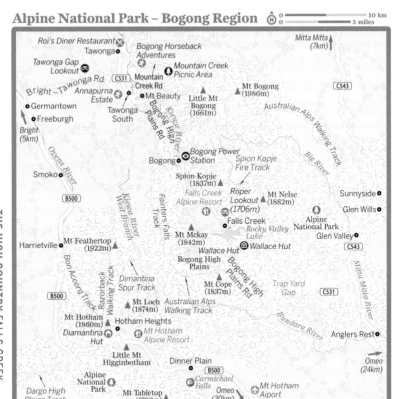

rock-climbing wall. The **Summit chairlift** operates during the summer school holidays (per ride/day $15/25). Mountain biking is popular here in the green season, with downhill trails, three lift-accessed trails, spur fire trails, aqueduct trails, road circuits and bike rental (from $55 per day).

The best local hiking trails include the walk to **Wallace Hut**, built in 1889 and said to be the oldest cattleman's hut in the High Country; and **Rocky Valley Lake**.

Packers High Country Horse Riding
HORSE RIDING

(☎03-5159 7241; www.horsetreks.com; Anglers Rest; 1½hr $80, half-/full day $150/240) Packers High Country Horse Riding, based at Anglers Rest on the road to Omeo, offers true High Country riding through river valleys and snowgum forests.

✯✯ Festivals & Events

Mile High Dragon Boat Festival   CULTURAL
(www.fallscreek.com.au/dragonboats) Gorgeous, glorious dragon boats race on Rocky Valley Lake. Held from 26 to 27 January.

Easter Festival   EASTER
(www.fallscreek.com.au/easterfestival) A giant Easter-egg hunt.

🛏 Sleeping

Accommodation can be booked via several agencies, such as **Falls Creek Central Reservations** (☎1800 033 079; www.fallscreek.com.au/centralreservations) or **Falls Creek Reservation Centre** (☎1800 453 525; www.fallscreek.com.au/rescentre). Most lodges stipulate a minimum two-night stay, particularly on weekends.

Alpha Lodge LODGE $
(☑ 03-5758 3488; www.alphaskilodge.com.au; dm summer/winter from $61/122) A spacious, affordable lodge with a sauna, a large lounge with panoramic views, and a communal kitchen.

Viking Alpine Lodge LODGE $$
(☑ 03-5758 3247; 13 Parallel St; d/q summer from $110/200, ski season from $320/500) Viking offers good-value accommodation all year with excellent communal facilities, including lounge, kitchen and great views. Ski in, ski out.

Frueauf Village APARTMENT $$$
(☑ 1300 300 709; www.fvfalls.com.au; 4 Schuss St; d 2-nights from $561; ☎) These luxurious, architect-designed apartments have everything, including private outdoor hot tubs, and the funky Milch Cafe Wine Bar.

✕ Eating & Drinking

Three Blue Ducks CAFE $$
(☑ 03-5758 3863; www.huski.com.au; 3 Sitzmark St; mains $12-28; ☉ 7.30am-11pm Jun-Sep) Chic store and cafe with great casual dining, coffee and High Country produce.

Mo's Restaurant at Feathertop MODERN AUSTRALIAN $$
(☑ 03-5758 3232; www.feathertoplodge.com.au/mo; 14 Parallel St; mains $18-34; ☉ 4pm-late) This inviting winter-only restaurant at the Feathertop Lodge features leather chesterfield couches, private alcoves and mood lighting. The food ranges from tapas to contemporary Australian cooking.

Man Hotel PUB
(☑ 03-5758 3362; www.themanfallscreek.com; 20 Slalom St; ☉ 4pm-late) 'The Man' has been around forever, is open all year and is the heart of Falls' nightlife. In winter it fires up as a club, cocktail bar and live-music venue featuring popular Aussie bands. Good pub dinners and pizzas are available.

❶ Information

Ski-season daily resort entry is $32 per car. One-day lift tickets per adult/child cost $110/55. Combined adult lift-and-lesson packages cost $169. Lift tickets also cover Mt Hotham. An over-snow taxi service ($38 return) operates between the car parks and the lodges from 7am to midnight Monday to Thursday (to 2am Friday night, to 1am Saturday & Sunday). Car parking for day visitors is at the base of the village, next to the ski lifts.

Falls Creek Resort Management (☑ 03-5758 1202; www.fallscreek.com.au; 1 Slalom St; ☉ 8.30am-5pm daily winter, 9am-5pm Mon-Fri, 10am-3pm Sat & Sun summer) Has informative pamphlets, including *Crosscountry* (about ski trails that are also good for summer walking).

❶ Getting There & Around

Falls Creek is 375km, and a 4½ hour drive, from Melbourne. During winter **Falls Creek Coach Service** (☑ 03-5754 4024; www.fallscreekcoachservice.com.au) operates four times a week between Falls Creek and Melbourne (one-way/return $97/170) and also runs services to and from Albury ($60/95) and Mt Beauty ($37/58). There's a reduced service in summer.

If you want to ski Mt Hotham for the day, jump on the **Heli-Link** (☑ 03-5759 4444) for $150 return (if you have a valid lift ticket).

Harrietville
POP 234

Harrietville, a pretty little town nestled on the Ovens River below Mt Feathertop, is the last stop before the start of the winding road up to Mt Hotham. During ski season a bus shuttles between the town and Mt Hotham, making it a good choice for slightly cheaper off-mountain accommodation.

Harrietville is the starting/finishing point for various alpine walking tracks, including the popular **Mt Feathertop walk**, **Razorback Ridge** and **Dargo High Plains walks**. The town is also developing as a mountain-biking centre – you can hire bikes (half-/full day $30/40) from Snowline Hotel, which also runs mountain-bike tours and mountain transfers.

🛏 Sleeping & Eating

Snowline Hotel MOTEL $$
(☑ 03-5759 2524; www.snowlinehotel.com.au; Great Alpine Rd; d from $120) The Snowline has been operating for over 100 years, and offers inexpensive off-mountain accommodation in comfortable motel rooms. The pub bistro (mains $20 to $29) has a loyal following, especially for its chicken parma, Harrietville trout and Tasmanian Angus steak.

★ Shady Brook Cottages COTTAGE $$
(☑ 03-5759 2741; www.shadybrook.com.au; Mountain View Walk; d from $140; ❀ @) A magnificent garden envelopes this lovely, peaceful group

of self-contained country-style cottages. Two come with a spa and all have balconies and mod cons.

Bella's
CAFE $

(☑ 03-5759 2750; 231 Great Alpine Rd; mains $7-17; ⊙ 8am-3pm Thu-Tue) For an all-day breakfast, or lunch of antipasto, damper rolls and pizza with a glass of local wine or hot coffee, this welcoming cafe is Harrietville's best.

Big Shed Café
CAFE $

(☑ 03-5759 2672; Great Alpine Rd, Smoko; meals $6-18; ⊙ 8am-2.30pm Wed-Mon) You can't miss this giant roadside restaurant in the beautifully named hamlet of Smoko, 7km north of Harrietville. The former tobacco shed is now a popular gourmet cafe dishing up focaccias, Camembert wedges, and fish and chips.

Mt Hotham & Dinner Plain

ELEV 1868M

Serious hikers, skiers and snowboarders make tracks for Mt Hotham, with some of the best and most challenging downhill runs in the country.

🏃 Activities

Mt Hotham is home to 320 hectares of downhill runs, with a vertical drop of 428m. About 80% of the ski trails are intermediate or advanced black diamond runs. Beginners hit the Big D, which is open for night skiing every Wednesday and Saturday in winter.

MT HOTHAM BOOKING AGENCIES

Ski-season accommodation generally requires a minimum two-night stay. Booking agencies include the following:

Mt Hotham Accommodation Service (☑ 1800 032 061; www.mthothamaccommodation.com.au) Books mountain accommodation throughout the year.

Dinner Plain Accommodation (☑ 03-5159 6696, 1800 444 066; www.accommdinnerplain.com.au; Big Muster Dr)

Dinner Plain Central Reservations (☑ 1800 670 019; www.dinnerplain.com; Big Muster Dr)

Over at Dinner Plain, 10km from Hotham village and linked by a free shuttle, there are excellent **cross-country trails** around the village, including the Hotham-Dinner Plain Ski Trail.

At least six operators offer ski and other equipment hire; the visitors centres have full lists of outlets, or visit www.mthotham. com.au.

From November to May, Hotham and Dinner Plain boast some stunning alpine trails for hiking and mountain biking; the most popular is to **Mt Feathertop** (1922m). This crosses the Razorback Ridge starting at the **Diamantina Hut** (2.5km from Mt Hotham village). It's 22km return and requires sound walking shoes.

Dinner Plain is particularly well set up for summer activities.

Mountain-Bike Park
MOUNTAIN BIKING

(per day $45; ⊙ weekends) This mountain-bike park in Dinner Plain has downhill and cross-country trails and jumps.

Onsen Retreat and Spa
SPA

(☑ 03-5150 8880; www.onsen.com.au; Big Muster Dr, Dinner Plain; massage/treatment from $70/145; ⊙ daily winter) In need of pampering? Head to Onsen Retreat and Spa, a divine Japanese-influenced, indoor-outdoor experience where the body gets to feel beautiful. It's open only during the ski season.

✦ Festivals

Cool Summer Festival
MUSIC

(www.coolsummerfestival.com) Three days of music in the middle of nowhere; held in January or February.

🛏 Sleeping

Leeton Lodge
LODGE $

(☑ 03-5759 3283; www.leetonlodge.com; Dargo Ct, Mt Hotham; dm summer $45, winter $65-85) Classic family ski-club lodge with 30 beds, cooking facilities and good views. Open year-round.

General Lodge
LODGE $$

(☑ 03-5759 3523; www.thegeneral.com.au; Great Alpine Rd, Mt Hotham; 1-/2-bedroom apt $190/285) Behind the General pub are these brand new, fully self-contained apartments with lounge and kitchen, and views from the balcony.

Currawong Lodge LODGE **$$**
(☑1800 635 589, 03-5159 6452; www.currawong-lodge.com.au; Big Muster Dr, Dinner Plain; summer s/d $80/130, ski season 2-night minimum d $220) Currawong Lodge welcomes you with a huge communal lounge-and-kitchen area with a monster open fireplace, TV, DVD and stereo. At this price you can ski without breaking the bank.

Rundell's Alpine Lodge LODGE **$$$**
(☑03-5159 6422; www.rundells.com.au; Big Muster Dr, Dinner Plain; summer d from $225, ski season 2-night minimum d $450; ☎) Originally an Australian Army retreat, this sprawling complex is a well-run hotel with all the comforts – spa, sauna and restaurant/bar – but a definite lack of pretension. The restaurant-cafe (mains $15 to $36) is open year-round.

Arlberg Resort APARTMENT **$$$**
(☑03-5986 8200; www.arlberghotham.com.au; Mt Hotham; 2 nights d $430-830; ☎☎) The largest resort on the mountain, the Arlberg has a large range of apartments and motel-style rooms, plus restaurants, bars, ski hire and a heated pool. Ski season only.

✕ Eating

In winter, there are plenty of great eating choices at Mt Hotham. In summer a couple of places serve meals and the small supermarket at the General is open.

Zirky's CAFE **$**
(☑03-5759 3518; Great Alpine Rd, Mt Hotham; mains $10-14; ⏲8am-2.30pm Wed-Sun) The Z cafe at the base of the summit run is open year-round. Andrew Blake's fine-dining restaurant (open for dinner in winter) is highly regarded.

General PUB **$$**
(☑03-5759 3523; Great Alpine Rd, Mt Hotham; meals $10-30; ⏲noon-2pm & 6-8.30pm; @) The ever-reliable 'Gen' is open all year and is a popular watering hole, with a menu of pizzas and good bistro meals, as well as internet access.

Dinner Plain Hotel PUB **$$**
(☑03-5159 6462; www.dinnerplainhotel.com.au; Dinner Plain; mains $10-28; ⏲noon-2pm & 6-9pm) The barn-sized local pub is the social hub of Dinner Plain and is a friendly place to hang out year-round, with roaring

DOG-SLED TOURS

For a real Arctic-style adventure, try a dog-sledding tour, where you're pulled along on a traditional sled behind a team of huskies.

Australian Sleddog Tours (☑0418 230 982; www.sleddogtours.com.au; Dinner Plain; adult/child/family $130/80/400) Day tours from Dinner Plain.

Howling Husky Sled Dog Tours (☑0409 517 633; www.howlinghuskys.com.au; tandem rides $120/490) Short rides from its base at Omeo Caravan Park (p280), and weekend tours at Mt Baw Baw.

open fires and a bistro serving good pub grub and pizzas.

ℹ Information

The ski-season admission fee is $40 per car per day, and $15 for bus passengers (this may be included in your fare). Lift tickets (peak) per adult/student/child cost $115/95/55. Passes are cheaper in September and there are packages that include gear hire and lessons. Lift tickets also cover Falls Creek.

Dinner Plain Visitor Centre (☑1300 734 365; www.visitdinnerplain.com) In the village centre.

Hotham Central Guest Services (☑03-5759 4470; Hotham Central) Open during winter.

Mt Hotham Alpine Resort Management Board (☑03-5759 3550; www.mthotham.com.au) At the village administration centre. Collect a range of brochures with maps for short, eco, heritage and village walks.

ℹ Getting There & Around

Mt Hotham is 360km northeast of Melbourne. By car, take the Hume Hwy to Wangaratta, then follow the Great Alpine Rd to Mt Hotham.

During the ski season, **Snowball Express** (☑1800 659 009, 03-9370 9055; www.snowballexpress.com.au) has daily buses from Melbourne to Mt Hotham ($160 return, six hours), via Wangaratta, Myrtleford, Bright and Harrietville.

O'Connell's Bus Lines (☑0428 591 377; www.omeobus.com.au) operates an 'Alps Link' service between Omeo and Bright ($11) via Mt Hotham ($5.40) and Dinner Plain ($4.40) daily in summer.

A free shuttle runs frequently around the Mt Hotham resort from 7am to 3am; a separate shuttle service also operates to Dinner Plain. The free 'zoo cart' takes skiers from their lodges to the lifts between 8am and 6pm.

Mt Hotham Airport (☑ 03-5159 6777) services Mt Hotham and Dinner Plain, but it's currently only served in winter by **QantasLink** (www.qantas.com) from Sydney, and by charter flights.

Heli-Link (p277) takes six minutes to fly to Falls Creek (on clear days) so you can spend a day skiing there.

Omeo

POP 487

High in the hills, historic Omeo is a pretty town reached after the winding drive up from the coast or down from the mountains. This is the southern access route to Mt Hotham and Falls Creek and the main town on the eastern section of the Great Alpine Rd. The road is sometimes snowbound in winter; always check conditions before heading this way and carry chains.

In the gold-rush days of the 1850s, Omeo was the wildest and most remote gold field in the state. It attracted many Chinese diggers whose legacy you can see today on the **Oriental Claims Walk**. Stay a while to wander the steep main street and breathe in the crisp mountain air.

🛏 Sleeping & Eating

The scenic Victoria Falls Camping Area, off the Great Alpine Rd, 18km west of Omeo, has pit toilets and a picnic area. In town, there's a bakery, a couple of cafes and takeaways.

Omeo Caravan Park　　CAMPGROUND $
(☑ 03-5159 1351; www.omeocaravanpark.com.au; Old Omeo Hwy; unpowered/powered sites $28/32, d cabins from $100) In a pretty valley alongside the Livingstone Creek about 2km from town, this park has spacious, grassy sites. Bike hire is available. This is also the base for Howling Husky Sled Dog Tours (p279),

who offer short local rides and longer weekend packages at Mt Baw Baw.

Golden Age Hotel　　HOTEL $
(☑ 03-5159　1344; www.goldenageomeo.com.au; Day Ave; s/d from $50/80, d with spa $157) This beautiful art-deco corner pub dominates Omeo's main street. Upstairs are simple but elegant pub rooms, some with en suite and spa – the best rooms open onto the balcony. The welcoming restaurant (mains $15 to $25) serves plates piled high with reliable fare of steaks, salads and gourmet pizzas.

Snug as a Bug Motel　　MOTEL $$
(☑ 03-5159　1311; www.motelomeo.com.au; 188 Great Alpine Rd; d/f from $100/180; 🖥) There's a range of accommodation here in lovely country-style historic buildings, including family motel rooms, the main guesthouse, a cute self-contained cottage and the two-room Omeo Backpackers (doubles $70).

Twinkles Café　　CAFE $
(☑ 03-5159 1484; 174 Day Ave; mains $5-14; ⊙ 8am-2.30pm) The place for a coffee or toasted sandwich.

❶ Information

Omeo Service Station (☑ 03-5159 1312; www.omeoskihire.com.au; Day Ave) Ski and chain hire.

Omeo Visitor Information Centre (☑ 03-5159 1455; www.omeoregion.com.au; 179 Day Ave; ⊙ 8.30am-5pm Mon-Fri, 10am-2pm Sat & Sun) Friendly visitor centre in the library.

❶ Getting There & Away

Omeo is 400km from Melbourne. **Omeo Bus Lines** (☑ 0427 017 732) runs one bus on weekdays between Omeo and Bairnsdale ($21, two hours). **O'Connell's Bus Lines** (☑ 0428 591 377; www.omeobus.com.au) operates a daily summer 'Alps Link' service between Omeo and Bright ($11) via Mt Hotham ($5.40) and Dinner Plain ($4.40). A winter service to Dinner Plain and Mt Hotham operates on Sunday, Wednesday and Friday.

The Murray River & Around

Includes ➡

Mildura 284
The Mallee 288
Swan Hill 289
Echuca 292
Yarrawonga 298
Rutherglen 299
Benalla 302
Woodonga 304

Best Places to Eat

➡ Stefano's Restaurant (p287)

➡ Oscar W's Wharfside (p297)

➡ Spoons Riverside Café (p291)

➡ Pickled Sisters Café (p301)

➡ Parkers Pies (p300)

Best Places to Stay

➡ Houseboat in Mildura (p286) or Echuca (p296)

➡ Quality Hotel Mildura Grand (p286)

➡ Adelphi Boutique Apartments (p297)

➡ Linesman's Cottage (p301)

➡ Tuileries (p300)

Why Go?

The mighty Murray is Australia's longest and most important inland waterway and arrayed along its shores are some of Victoria's most captivating towns. It's a stirring place of wineries and orchards, bush camping, balmy weather and river-red-gum forests.

The Murray changes character constantly along its 2400km route. Here, history looms large in towns such as Echuca and Glenrowan, food and wine dominate proceedings around Rutherglen and Mildura, and national parks enclose soulful desert expanse in the far west. It's a world of picturesque river beaches, of paddle steamers that were once the lifeblood of Victoria's inland settlements, and of unending horizons that serve as a precursor to the true outback not far away. It's an intriguing, if relatively far-flung mix, one that enables you to follow in the footsteps of some of Australia's earliest explorers who travelled along the river.

When to Go

Mildura

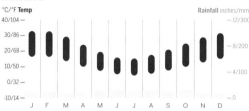

All year The Murray region enjoys year-round sunshine, especially in Mildura.

Feb–Mar A good time for camping on the river after the holiday crowds have left.

Sep–Nov Springtime sees some of the best local festivals, without the heat.

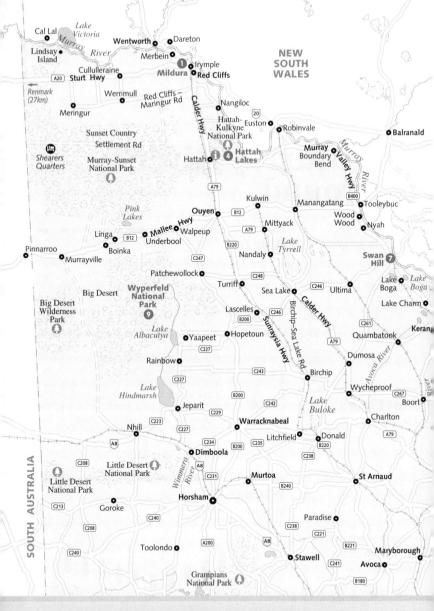

The Murray River & Around Highlights

1 Relax on a houseboat and dine out on 'Feast Street' in sunny **Mildura** (p284)

2 Ride an original paddle steamer from the **historic Port of Echuca** (p292)

3 Time your visit to **Rutherglen** (p299) for one of the great winery festivals

4 Spot the many species of waterbirds at beautiful **Hattah Lakes** (p289)

5 Set up a bush camp and a fishing rod on the banks of the Murray at **Gunbower National Park** (p292)

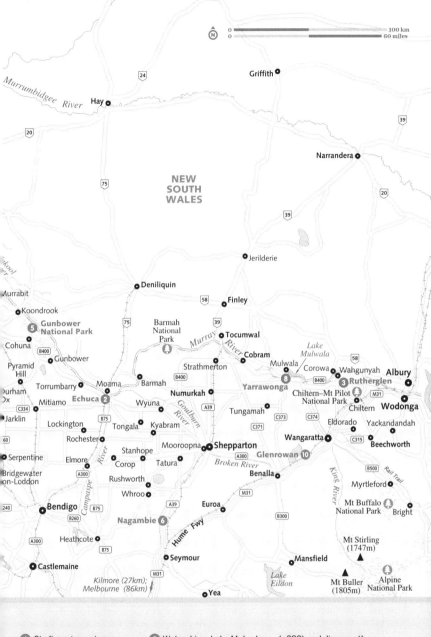

6 Sip fine wine or jump out of a plane at lakeside **Nagambie** (p302)

7 Take the kids on a trip back in time at the Pioneer Settlement in **Swan Hill** (p289)

8 Waterski on Lake Mulwala or play a round of golf at **Yarrawonga** (p298)

9 Disappear in remote **Wyperfeld National Park**

(p288) and discover the vastness of the Mallee

10 Relive Ned Kelly's last stand at tiny **Glenrowan** (p302)

MILDURA

POP 31,400

After crossing windswept deserts and pale-golden wheat fields, it comes as something of a shock to see the miles of fertile vineyards and orchards that thrive in the far northwestern corner of the state. Mildura (meaning 'red soil') is a true oasis, a modern town with its roots firmly in the grand old pastoralist era.

Considering its remote location, Mildura is a remarkably prosperous and progressive city with fun nightlife, decent shopping, art deco buildings (such as Mildura Brewery, Sandbar and T&G Tower) and some of the best dining in provincial Victoria. Thanks to irrigation, this is also one of Australia's richest agricultural areas – it was once a major citrus-growing region and is now the second-largest producer of wine in the country. If you're looking for casual work, this is a popular destination for fruit-picking and agricultural labour.

Of course, the region makes full use of the Murray so it's very easy to get out fishing, swimming, canoeing, waterskiing, house-boating, taking a paddle-steamer cruise or playing on riverside golf courses. The weather up here is very much blue sky – you can expect warm, sunny days even in midwinter.

Most places of interest are around the riverside wharf and the main boulevard, Deakin Ave, but Mildura sprawls through the suburbs of Red Cliffs and Irymple. Across the river in New South Wales are the towns of Buronga and Wentworth.

◉ Sights

Historic **Mildura Wharf** is now a mooring for paddle boats. The lock is operated at 11am, 12.30pm, 2pm and 3.30pm daily.

★ Rio Vista & Mildura Arts Centre
HISTORIC BUILDING

(☑03-5018 8330; www.milduraartscentre.com.au; 199 Cureton Ave; ☺10am-5pm) **FREE** William B Chaffey's grand homestead, the historic Queen Anne–style Rio Vista, has been beautifully preserved and restored. Each room is set up as a series of historical displays depicting colonial life in the 19th century, with period furnishings, costumes, photos and a collection of letters and memorabilia.

The Mildura Arts Centre, in the same complex, combines a modern-art gallery with changing exhibitions and a theatre.

★ Old Mildura Homestead
HISTORIC SITE

(Cureton Ave; admission by donation; ☺9am-6pm) Along the river near Rio Vista, this cottage was the first home of William B Chaffey. The heritage park here contains a few other historic log buildings and has picnic and barbecue facilities.

Old Psyche Bend Pump Station
HISTORIC SITE

(☑03-5024 5637; Kings Billabong; adult/family $3/8; ☺1-4pm Tue & Thu, 10.30am-12.30pm Sun) This station is where Chaffey set up his system to supply irrigation and drainage over 115 years ago. (The modern pumps are electric now and have been placed a bit further up the river.) You can walk around the old centrifugal pumps and Chaffey's triple-expansion steam-engine pump. The station is within **Kings Billabong**, a pretty nature reserve on the Murray floodplain about 8km southeast of the town centre.

Chateau Mildura
WINERY, MUSEUM

(☑03-5024 5901; www.chateaumildura.com.au; 191 Belar Ave; adult/child $10/free; ☺10am-4pm) Established in 1888 and still producing table wines, Chateau Mildura is part vineyard, part museum, with wine tastings and historical displays.

Apex Beach
BEACH

About 3km northwest of the centre, with a sandy river beach on the Murray, is this popular swimming and picnic spot. There's a good walking and cycling track from here to the Old Mildura Homestead.

🏃 Activities

Golfers are spoilt for choice in Mildura – check out www.visitmildura.com.au/golf for a full list of courses.

Paddle-steamer cruises depart from the Mildura Wharf, and most go through a lock: you'll be able to see the gates opening and the water levels changing. For bookings on all of the boats listed here, call ☑03-5023 2200, or go to www.paddlesteamers.com.au.

PS Melbourne
CRUISE

(2hr cruise adult/child $29/13; ☺10.50am & 1.50pm) One of the original paddle steamers, and the only one still driven by steam power: watch the operator stoke the original boiler with wood. On Friday and Saturday this cruise is aboard the PV *Rothbury*.

PV Mundoo
CRUISE

(dinner cruise adult/child $65/32; ☺7pm Thu) The newest riverboat has a dinner cruise every Thursday from 7pm. This cruise is sometimes aboard the PV *Rothbury*.

Mildura

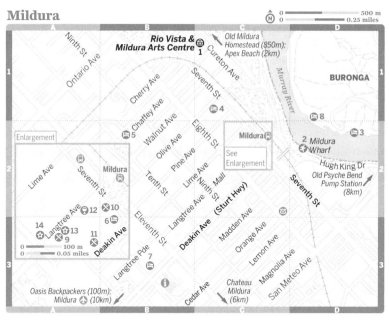

Mildura

⊙ Top Sights
1 Rio Vista & Mildura Arts Centre C1

⊙ Activities, Courses & Tours
2 PS Melbourne... D2
PV Mundoo ....(see 2)
PV Rothbury ....(see 2)

🛏 Sleeping
3 Acacia Houseboats................................ D2
4 Misty's Manor & Ditto Daddy's C1
5 Pied-à-Terre B2
6 Quality Hotel Mildura Grand..................B3
7 Sandors Motor Inn.................................B3
8 Willandra Houseboats............................D1

✗ Eating
Pizza Café at the Grand ....(see 10)
9 Restaurant Rendezvous..........................A3
10 Spanish Bar & Grill.................................B2
11 Stefano's Café Bakery A3
Stefano's Restaurant.....................(see 6)

🍷 Drinking & Nightlife
12 Mildura Brewery A2

🎭 Entertainment
13 Dom's Nightclub.....................................A3
14 Sandbar A3

PV Rothbury　　　　CRUISE
(winery cruise adult/child $65/32, lunch cruise $32/15; ☺10.30am Thu) The fastest of the riverboats, it offers a winery cruise from 10.30am on Thursday, with a visit to Trentham Estate Winery and a barbecue lunch at Kings Billabong. On Tuesday there's a lunch cruise to Gol Gol Hotel, where you buy your own meal.

🚩 Tours

The best tours out of Mildura focus on the region's history, adventure opportunities and

cultural heritage. A standout is the extraordinary and ancient natural formations of Mungo National Park (in NSW). Several operators run tours out there, focusing on its culture, its 45,000 years of history and its wildlife.

★ Harry Nanya Tours　　CULTURAL TOUR
(☎03-5027 2076; www.harrynanyatours.com.au; tours adult/child $180/110, tag along in your own car $90/45) 🖉 Indigenous guide Graham Clarke keeps you enchanted with Dreaming stories and his deep knowledge and understanding

of the Mungo region. Between November and March, there's a spectacular sunset tour.

Moontongue Eco-Adventures　　KAYAKING
(🗹 0427 898 317; www.moontongue.com.au; kayak tours $25-50) 🏊 A sunset kayaking trip is a great way to see the river and its wildlife. Local guide Ian will tell you about the landscape and bird life as you work those muscles in the magnificent, peaceful surroundings of Gol Gol Creek and the Murray.

Wild Side Outdoors　　ADVENTURE TOUR
(🗹 0428 242 852, 03-5024 3721; www.wildsideoutdoors.com.au) 🏊 Wild Side is an ecofriendly outfit offering a range of activities, including a sunset kayaking tour at Kings Billabong (adult/child $35/15) and a six-hour 4WD tour into the Hattah-Kulkyne National Park (adult/child $85/30). It also has canoe/kayak/mountain-bike hire for $30/20/20 per hour.

Mildura Ballooning　　SCENIC FLIGHTS
(🗹 03-5024 6848; www.miluraballooning.com.au; adult/child $320/220; ⊙ dawn) Enjoy the sunrise from the air with a one-hour balloon flight, at dawn, over the wonderful patchwork of vineyards, orchards and the Murray. Includes champagne breakfast.

Discover Mildura Tours　　GUIDED TOUR
(🗹 03-5024 7448; www.discovermildura.com.au; tours per person $140-155) The guided tours here cover wine tasting, Mungo National Park or farm visits.

MILDURA HOUSEBOATS

Staying on a houseboat is bliss. The Mildura region has over a dozen companies that hire houseboats ranging from two- to 12-berth boats and from modest to luxurious. Most have a minimum hire of three days; prices increase dramatically in summer and during school holidays. The following operators are located just across from Mildura Wharf in Buronga:

Acacia Houseboats (🗹 03-5022 1510, 1800 085 500; www.murrayriver.com.au/acacia-houseboats-949/fleet; 3 nights $600-1800) Has seven houseboats, ranging from four to 12 berths, with everything supplied except food and drink.

Willandra Houseboats (🗹 03-5024 7770; www.willandrahouseboats.com.au; 3 nights $700-3600) Willandra has six houseboats sleeping two to 12 people. Offers gourmet and golf packages.

🎊 Festivals & Events

Mildura Wentworth Arts Festival　　ARTS
(www.artsmildura.com.au/mwaf;　　⊙ Feb-Mar) Magical concerts by the river, in the sandhills, and all around.

Mildura Country Music Festival　　MUSIC
(www.milduracountrymusic.com.au; ⊙ Sep-Oct) Ten days of free concerts in late September and/or early October.

Mildura Show　　AGRICULTURAL
(www.mildurashow.org.au; ⊙ Oct) One of the largest shows in rural Victoria; held mid-October.

Mildura Jazz, Food & Wine Festival　　MUSIC
(www.artsmildura.com.au/jazz; ⊙ Oct or Nov) Traditional bands, great food, good wine; held in October or November.

🛏 Sleeping

Mildura is a real holiday destination, with houseboats, dozens of family motels, apartments and caravan parks, and a few big hotels and boutique B&Bs close to the river.

Apex RiverBeach Holiday Park　CAMPGROUND $
(🗹 03-5023 6879; www.apexriverbeach.com.au; Cureton Ave; unpowered/powered sites $34/39, cabins $69-125; ❄ 🛜) Thanks to a fantastic location on sandy Apex Beach just outside town, this bush park is always popular – prices are 25% higher during school holidays. There are campfires, a bush kitchen, barbecue area, boat ramp, good swimming and a cafe.

Oasis Backpackers　　HOSTEL $
(🗹 0401 344 251, 03-5022 8200; www.mildura oasisbackpackers.com.au; 230-232 Deakin Ave; dm/d per week $155/330; ❄ @ 🛜) Mildura is a big destination for travellers looking for fruit-picking work, so most of the city's half-dozen hostels are set up with them in mind. Oasis is Mildura's best-equipped backpacker hostel, with a great pool and patio bar area, ultramodern kitchen and free internet. The owners can organise plenty of seasonal work. Minimum one-week stay.

⭐ **Quality Hotel Mildura Grand**　HOTEL $$
(🗹 1800 034 228, 03-5023 0511; www.qualityhotel-milduragrand.com.au; Seventh St; s/d incl breakfast from $75/120; ❄ 🛜 🏊) The standard rooms at the Grand aren't the most luxurious in town but staying at this landmark hotel – Mildura's top address – gives you the feeling of being part of something special. Although cheaper rooms in the original wing are com-

fortable, go instead for one of the stylish suites with private spa. Many rooms open onto a delightful courtyard garden, and there's a gym, pool and spa.

**Misty's Manor
& Ditto Daddy's**   APARTMENT **$$**
(☑0419 840 451; www.couplesretreatsmildura. com.au; 16 Olive Ave; d $130-200; ✳☎) These two apartments are spectacular in their design and decoration – a beautifully designed but unlikely mix of corrugated iron, stone and recycled timber, with a lilac, mauve and canary-yellow colour scheme in Ditto Daddy's and a tartan theme in Misty's Manor. There are king-sized beds, plasma TVs, modern kitchens, double spas and showers.

Pied-à-Terre   B&B **$$**
(☑03-5022 9883; www.piedaterre.com.au; 97 Chaffey Ave; d $175, per night extra adult/child $25/15; ✳☎) It's French for 'a home away from home', but we doubt home ever looked this good! Five stylish and luxurious bedrooms sleep up to 10 people, with amenities including free wi-fi, boat storage, car parking and a barbecue area.

Sandors Motor Inn   MOTEL **$$**
(☑03-5023 0047, 1800 032 463; www.sandorsmotorinn.com; 179 Deakin Ave; d $95-135; ✳☒) Mildura has plenty of motels, but Sandors, virtually opposite the visitor centre, is well located, with spacious, tidy rooms and an inviting pool set in a tropical garden. Breakfast is included.

 Eating

Mildura's cafe and restaurant precinct runs along Langtree Ave (otherwise known as 'Feast Street') and around the block dominated by the Quality Hotel Mildura Grand. Italian raconteur Stefano de Pieri perhaps single-handedly stamped the town on the foodie map, but others are jumping on board.

Stefano's Café Bakery   CAFE **$**
(☑03-5021 3627; www.stefano.com.au; 27 Deakin Ave; meals $10-23; ☉7.30am-4pm Mon-Thu, 7.30am-4pm & 6-9pm Fri, 7.30am-3pm Sat, 8am-noon Sun) Fresh bread baked daily, Calabrese eggs, pastries and, of course, good coffee – Stefano's casual daytime cafe and bakery (now run by his talented in-laws) keeps things fresh and simple. It's also a gourmet grocery store selling foodstuffs and wines.

Pizza Café at the Grand   PIZZERIA **$**
(☑03-5022 2223; www.pizzacafe.com.au; 18 Langtree Ave; pizza & pasta $15-22; ☉11am-11pm Mon-

Sat, 11.30am-11pm Sun) For simple and inexpensive (but stylish) family dining – with all the atmosphere of the Grand Hotel dining strip – Pizza Café is perfect. The wood-fired pizzas hit the spot and there's a supporting cast of salads, pastas and chicken dishes.

Spanish Bar & Grill   STEAKHOUSE **$$**
(☑03-5021 2377; www.seasonsmildura.com.au; cnr Langtree Ave & Seventh St; lunch mains $18-38, dinner $22-39; ☉6-10pm Mon-Thu & Sat, noon-3pm & 6-10pm Fri) In the Grand Hotel, this place keeps it simple with top-quality steaks and barbecue food, including kangaroo and Mallee rump. No tapas, but it is a carnivore's heaven.

Restaurant Rendezvous   FRENCH **$$**
(☑03-5023 1571; www.rendezvousmildura.com. au; 34 Langtree Ave; mains $18-48; ☉noon-4pm & 6pm-late Mon-Fri, 6pm-late Sat) The warm, casual atmosphere of this long-running place that's almost swallowed up by the Grand Hotel complements the perfectly prepared Mediterranean-style seafood, grills, pastas, crepes and unusual specials.

★**Stefano's Restaurant**   ITALIAN **$$$**
(☑03-5023 0511; www.stefano.com.au; Seventh St; 2-/3-course lunch set menu $45/52, dinner set menu $110-150; ☉7-11pm Tue-Thu, noon-3pm & 7-11pm Fri & Sat) Descend into the former underground wine cellar at the Grand Hotel to see Stefano work his magic with the ever-changing six- to eight-course Italian dinner. The food is exquisite, combining local produce with Italian recipes. It's an intimate, candlelit experience and very popular – book well in advance.

🍷 **Drinking & Entertainment**

Mildura has a compact but lively nightlife scene, buoyed by an ever-changing crew of backpackers and itinerant fruit-pickers.

★**Mildura Brewery**   BREWERY
(☑03-5022 2988; www.mildurabrewery.com.au; 20 Langtree Ave; ☉noon-late) Set in the former Astor cinema, in the same block as the Grand Hotel, this is Mildura's trendiest drinking hole. Shiny stainless-steel brewing equipment makes a great backdrop to the stylish lounge, and the beers brewed here – Honey Wheat and Mallee Bull among them – are superb. Good food, too. The interior retains many of the sleek art deco features from the original theatre.

Sandbar   LIVE MUSIC
(☑03-5021 2181; www.thesandbar.com.au; cnr Langtree Ave & Eighth St; ☉noon-late Tue-Sun)

THE MURRAY RIVER & AROUND MILDURA

On a balmy evening locals flock to the fabulous beer garden at the back of this lounge bar in a classic art deco building. Local, national, original and mainstream bands play in the front bar nightly from Thursday to Sunday.

Dom's Nightclub   CLUB
(☑03-5021 3822; www.doms.com.au; 28 Langtree Ave; ⊙9pm-late Sat) The upstairs club at Dom's, in the heart of Feast Street, attracts the after-pub crowd on a Saturday night for music and dancing.

❶ Information

Mildura Visitors Centre (☑03-5018 8380, 1800 039 043; www.visitmildura.com.au; cnr Deakin Ave & 12th St; ⊙9am-5.30pm Mon-Fri, to 5pm Sat & Sun) In the Alfred Deakin Centre. There's a free service for booking accommodation, interesting displays, local produce, a cafe and helpful staff who book tours and activities.

❶ Getting There & Away

Mildura is 542km northwest of Melbourne along the Calder Hwy (A79).

AIR

Regional Express Airlines (Rex; ☑13 17 13; www.rex.com.au), **Qantas** (☑13 13 13; www.qantas.com.au) and **Virgin** (☑13 67 89; www.virginaustralia.com) all fly between Mildura and Melbourne daily. Virgin has the cheapest fares – as low as $60 one way for advance online fares.

Victoria's busiest regional airport, **Mildura Airport** (MQL; ☑03-5055 0500; www.milduraairport.com.au) is about 10km west of the town centre off the Sturt Hwy.

BUS & TRAIN

Long-distance buses operate from a depot at the train station on Seventh St, but there are currently no direct passenger trains to or from Mildura.

V/Line (☑1800 800 007; www.vline.com.au) has a train-bus service to/from Melbourne via Bendigo or Swan Hill ($44.20, 7½ hours, four daily). V/Line's Murraylink is a daily bus service connecting Mildura with towns along the Murray: Swan Hill ($26.20, three hours, three daily), Echuca ($36.40, six hours, one daily) and Albury-Wodonga ($45.50, 11 hours, one daily).

THE MALLEE

Occupying the relatively vast northwestern corner of Victoria, the Mallee appears as a flat horizon and endless, undulating, twisted mallee scrub and desert. The attractions – other than the sheer solitude – are the semi-arid wilderness areas, such as Wyperfeld National Park, Big Desert Wilderness Park

and Murray-Sunset National Park. Collectively these parks cover over 7500 sq km, and are particularly notable for their abundance of native plants, spring wildflowers and birds. This is 'Sunset Country', the one genuinely empty part of the state. Nature-lovers might delight in it, but much of it is inaccessible to all but experienced 4WD enthusiasts. Like most outback areas, visiting here is best avoided in the hot summer months.

The main route through the Mallee is the Sunraysia Hwy (B220), via the towns of Birchip and Ouyen, but if you want to explore the region's national parks, turn off to the historic farming towns of **Jeparit** (birthplace of Sir Robert Menzies, and the jumping-off point for Lake Hindmarsh), **Rainbow**, **Yaapeet** and **Hopetoun**.

Wyperfeld National Park

Wyperfeld is a vast but accessible park of river red gum, mallee scrub, dry lake beds, sand plains and, in the spring, a carpet of native wildflowers. It's a naturalist's paradise, with over 200 species of birds and a network of walking and cycling tracks. A sealed road from the southern park entrance near Yaapeet leads to the visitor centre at **Wonga Campground** (camp sites $25.20) with pit toilets, picnic tables and fireplaces. **Casuarina Campground** (sites free), in the north, is reached via a gravel road off the Patchewollock-Baring Rd.

To the west, along the South Australian border, is the **Big Desert Wilderness Park**, which has no roads, facilities or water. Walking and camping are permitted but only for the experienced and totally self-sufficient.

Murray-Sunset National Park

If you've packed your hat and filled your water bottle, you're ready to enjoy the stunning 6330 sq km of mallee woodland in the Murray-Sunset National Park, reaching from the river red gums of Lindsay Island down to Underbool. Most of the park is remote 4WD-only territory.

The **Pink Lakes**, near Underbool, get their colour from the millions of microscopic organisms in the lake, which concentrate an orange pigment in their bodies. From **Linga**, on the Mallee Hwy, there's a signed, unsealed road that was built when salt was harvested

MALLEE SCRUB

A mallee is a hardy eucalypt with multiple slender trunks. Its roots are twisted, gnarled, dense chunks of wood, famous for their slow-burning qualities and much sought after by woodturners. Mallee gums are canny desert survivors – root systems of over a thousand years old are not uncommon – and are part of a diverse and rich biosystem with waterbirds, fish in the huge (but unreliable) lakes, kangaroos and other marsupials, emus, and the many edible plants that thrive in this environment.

When the railway line from Melbourne to Mildura was completed in 1902, much of the region was divided into small blocks for farming. The first Europeans had terrible problems trying to clear the land. They used a method called mullenising (crushing the scrub with heavy red-gum rollers pulled by teams of bullocks, then burning and ploughing the land), but after rain the tough old mallee roots regenerated and flourished. Farmers also had to deal with rabbit and mouse plagues, sand drifts and long droughts. Today the Mallee is a productive sheep-grazing and grain-growing district, with more exotic crops, such as lentils, also appearing.

from the lakes. Nearby is a basic camping ground, but beyond that you need a 4WD.

It you go for walks along the tracks, leave before dawn and be out of the sun before noon. As the wide sky turns pink at dusk, venture out again to watch the bird life and the magic of the night sky.

On the western side of the park, the **Shearer's Quarters** (☑ 03-5028 1218; dm $61) has hostel-type accommodation. It's pretty basic (hot and cold water and a fridge are supplied) and is accessible only by 4WD.

For more information, and to let someone know your whereabouts, contact the rangers of **Parks Victoria** (☑ 13 19 63, Underbool 03-5094 6267, Werrimull 03-5028 1218; www.parkweb.vic.gov.au) in Underbool on the Mallee Hwy (B12), or north at Werrimull.

Hattah-Kulkyne National Park

The vegetation of the beautiful and diverse Hattah-Kulkyne National Park ranges from dry, sandy mallee-scrub country to the fertile riverside areas closer to the Murray, which are lined with red gum, black box, wattle and bottlebrush.

The **Hattah Lakes** system fills when the Murray floods, which is great for waterbirds. The many hollow trees here are perfect for nesting, and more than 200 species of birds have been recorded in the area. There are many native animals, mostly nocturnal desert types and wetland species, such as the burrowing frog, which digs itself into the ground and waits until there's enough water to start breeding. Reptiles here include the mountain devil, the inspiration for the Aus-

tralian saying, 'flat out like a lizard drinking', because it draws surface water into its mouth by lying flat on the ground.

The main access road is from **Hattah**, 70km south of Mildura on the Calder Hwy. There are two **nature drives**, the Hattah and the Kulkyne, and a network of old camel tracks that are great for **cycling**, although you'll need thorn-proof tubes. Tell the rangers where you're going, and carry plenty of water, a compass and a map.

You can **camp** (unpowered sites $16.50) at Lake Hattah and Lake Mournpall, but there's limited water and the lake water is undrinkable. Free camping is possible anywhere along the Murray River frontage.

Hattah-Kulkyne National Park visitor centre (☑ 03-5029 3253), 5km into the park, is a cool building with posters, tables and chairs. Ring the ranger to find out if the tracks are passable.

SWAN HILL

POP 9900

Swan Hill is a sleepy river town without the tourist hype of Mildura and Echuca, but with undeniable appeal. The riverside Pioneer Settlement is one of the best open-air museums in Victoria and the town has some good places to eat. While you wouldn't cross the state just to come here, it makes an ideal stopover as you meander along the Murray or head for the Outback.

Back in 1836, Major Mitchell, explorer and surveyor, was kept awake all night by swans on the nearby lagoon, thus giving the town its name. The area was settled by sheep graziers soon after, and the original

THE MURRAY RIVER & AROUND SWAN HILL

homesteads of the two major properties in the area, Murray Downs and Tyntyndyer, are still looking magnificent.

◎ Sights & Activities

Here there are plenty of opportunities for walking, fishing or swimming along the Murray. If you just want a place to picnic, head to **Riverside Park** (Monash Dr), which has barbecue facilities and a playground. From here, a riverside walk explores the banks of the Murray and Marraboor (Little Murray) rivers. If you share Australia's passion for 'big things', check out the **Giant Murray Cod** outside the train station. The **Burke & Wills Tree**, an enormous Moreton Bay fig tree planted to commemorate the explorers as they passed through Swan Hill on their ill-fated journey, is located on Curlewis St.

Pioneer Settlement   HISTORIC VILLAGE, MUSEUM
(☑ 03-5036 2410; www.pioneersettlement.com. au; Monash Dr, Horseshoe Bend; adult/child/family $27/20.50/74; ⊙ 9.30am-4pm) Swan Hill's main tourist attraction is a fun re-creation of a riverside port town of the paddle steamer–era. The settlement's displays include the restored PS *Gem,* one of Australia's largest riverboats, a great collection of old carriages and buggies, an old-time photographic parlour, an Aboriginal keeping place, a lolly shop, a school classroom and the fascinating Kaiser Stereoscope. The paddle steamer PS *Pyap* makes short **cruises** (adult/child/family $21/14.50/55; ⊙ cruises 2.30pm daily, also 10.30am on weekends & school holidays) along the Murray.

TWIN TOWNS

There's almost always a 'twin' town across the Murray River in New South Wales (technically the river itself is in NSW) but generally the most interesting towns are on the Victorian side – the main exception being Albury-Wodonga (sorry, Wodonga). Before Federation in 1901, all major river crossings had customs houses on each bank, from which the two states levied tariffs on goods carried across their borders. Before poker machines were introduced into Victoria in 1990, many of the twin towns on the NSW side made a fortune from punters travelling across by the busload to play the 'pokies'. Now they're on both sides and gambling has spread throughout Victoria.

Other attractions include vintage-car and wagon rides. Every night at dusk the 45-minute **sound-and-light show** (adult/child/family $21/14.50/55) entails a dramatic journey through the settlement in an open-air transporter. A combined package for cruise and show works out to reduce the cost.

Swan Hill Regional Art Gallery   GALLERY
(☑ 03-5036 2430; www.swanhillart.com; Monash Dr, Horseshoe Bend; admission by donation; ⊙ 10am-5pm Tue-Sun) Opposite the Pioneer Settlement, this gallery has a permanent collection of more than 300 pieces, focusing on the works of contemporary and local artists.

Murray Downs Resort   GOLF
(☑ 03-5033 1427, 1800 807 574; www.murraydowns resort.com.au; Murray Downs Dr; 9/18 holes $25/40, club hire $25) Itching for a round? One of the Murray's superb public-resort golf courses, Murray Downs is 5km east of Swan Hill in NSW, but is regarded as a Swan Hill club.

✦ Festivals & Events

Swan Hill has a racecourse, and the three-day **racing carnival** over the Queen's Birthday weekend in June is the main event of the year. It culminates with the Swan Hill Cup on the Sunday. Book accommodation well in advance.

Australian Inland Wine Show   WINE
(www.inlandwine.com; ⊙ Mar 3rd weekend Oct) Usually held in October, in 2014 this festival shifted to March to coincide with the Swan Hill Food & Wine Festival. Whether that continues remains to be seen – check at the Swan Hill Region Information Centre. Whenever it's held, the region's motto is the same: 'Life is too short to drink bad wine.'

⌂ Sleeping

Riverside Caravan Park   CAMPGROUND $
(☑ 1800 101 012, 03-5032 1494; www.riverside-swanhill-holiday-park.vic.big4.com.au; 1 Monash Dr; unpowered/powered sites from $31/35, cabins $105-160) On the banks of the Murray, close to the Pioneer Settlement, this park enjoys a fabulous central location. There's a good range of cabins but prices soar by more than 50% in holiday periods.

Travellers Rest Motor Inn   MOTEL $$
(☑ 03-5032 9644; www.bestwestern.com.au/travellersrest; 110 Curlewis St; d $145; ❀ ≋ ⊠) Sitting in the shade of the Burke & Wills Tree, rooms here are spacious and comfort-

MURRAY COD

The Murray River is great for fishing, from the upper reaches where anglers cast flies in search of trout and salmon to the slow-moving, deep-water sections hiding perch (yellow belly), redfin, bream and the dreaded European carp. The introduced carp has long been a problem in the Murray-Darling system, breeding intensively, muddying the waters and generally upsetting the riverine ecology. They are a declared pest, so it's illegal to release them back into the water once caught. And don't bother eating them – they taste like mud.

The big prize, though, is the elusive Murray cod, Australia's largest freshwater fish and native to these waters. The Murray cod is a long-lived fish – the biggest and oldest can weigh upwards of 100kg and there are plenty of tales of the ones that got away. The cod is carnivorous and can be caught using yabbies, grubs, river shrimp, small fish or trolling with a lure. Anything under 60cm must be released back into the water; the bag limit is two. To fish in Victorian waters you need a recreational fishing licence ($12/24.50 per month/year), available from many shops along the Murray or from the **Department of Primary Industries** (www.depi.vic.gov.au).

able with the usual motel accompaniments. There's a heated spa and outdoor pool.

Murray Downs Houseboats　HOUSEBOAT **$$$**
(☑ 03-5032 2160, 0428 500 066; www.murraydownsmarina.com.au; Murray Downs Marina; 12-berth 3 nights from $1950; ❋) Nothing beats a luxury houseboat for relaxing on the Murray. The 12-berth comes with four bedrooms, two bathrooms and a deck spa. High-season rates are significantly higher ($2650 over the Christmas period). The marina is 2km from town, on the NSW side.

✖ Eating

The main cafe and dining scene is on Campbell St. Otherwise, head down to the riverside park for a barbecue or picnic.

Jilarty Gelato Bar　ICE CREAM **$**
(☑ 03-5033 0042; 233 Campbell St; ☉ 8am-5.30pm Mon-Sat, 10am-4pm Sun) Gelati on a hot summer's day? Unbeatable. This little cafe specialises in Italian-style gelati with local fruit flavours, along with great coffee and Spanish *churros* (fried dough dusted in sugar).

Yutaka Sawa　JAPANESE **$$**
(☑ 03-5032 3515; www.yutakasawa.com.au; 107 Campbell St; mains $14-27; ☉ 11am-8pm Mon & Wed-Sat, 5-8pm Sun) A Japanese restaurant in a small country town may sound a bit dodgy but this one has the goods, with expertly prepared sushi and sashimi, and a fine choice of noodle dishes, teriyaki and tempura.

Java Spice　THAI **$$**
(☑ 03-5033 0511; www.javaspice.com.au; 17 Beveridge St; mains $19-32; ☉ noon-2pm & 6pm-late Fri & Sat, 6pm-late Tue-Thu & Sun; ☑) Dining

under open-sided thatched and teak-wood huts in a tropical garden, you'll think you've been transported to Southeast Asia. The authentic cuisine is predominantly Thai, with some Malaysian and Indonesian influences mixed in.

★ Spoons
Riverside Café　MODERN AUSTRALIAN **$$**
(☑ 03-5032 2601; www.spoonsriverside.com.au; 125 Monash Dr, Horseshoe Bend; lunch mains $9.50-20, dinner $28-35; ☉ 8am-5pm Sun-Wed, to 11pm Thu-Sat) The riverside location alone is enough to lure you to this licensed cafe, which offers a big timber deck overlooking the Marraboor River and Pioneer Settlement. As well as light lunches and innovative dinners (in which fresh, local ingredients take centre stage), there's a provedore deli selling fresh produce and gourmet hampers.

❶ Information

Swan Hill Region Information Centre (☑ 03-5032 3033, 1800 625 373; www.swanhillonline.com; cnr McCrae & Curlewis Sts; ☉ 9am-5pm) Helpful maps and brochures on the region.

❶ Getting There & Away

Swan Hill is 338km northwest of Melbourne, travelling via Bendigo and Kerang; it sits on the Murray Valley Hwy (B400), 218km from Mildura and 156km from Echuca.

V/Line (☑ 1800 800 007; www.vline.com.au) runs trains between Melbourne and Swan Hill ($35.80, four hours, three to four daily), and some train and coach services with a change at Bendigo. There are daily V/Line coaches to Mildura ($25, three hours) and Echuca ($15.30, two hours).

THE MURRAY RIVER & AROUND SWAN HILL

WORTH A TRIP

GUNBOWER NATIONAL PARK

One of the great spots for free camping along the Murray River, superb **Gunbower Island** is formed the Murray River and Gunbower Creek and is said to be the largest inland island in the world. In 2010 Parks Victoria created the 88 sq km Gunbower National Park (previously a state forest) to protect its beautiful river-red-gum forests. As well as the majestic red gums, which have been extensively logged for timber since the 1870s, the park is home to abundant animals and bird life. You might see kangaroos, possums, goannas, turtles and snakes, and more than 200 species of birds have been recorded here. A network of 'river tracks' criss-cross the island and lead to more than 100 numbered bush-camping spots by the riverbank (only on the Victorian side). The roads are dirt and a bit rough, but are passable to conventional vehicles when it's dry – after heavy rain, though, it's 4WD-only.

The main access points to the island are from Cohuna in the north and tiny Gunbower in the south.

AROUND SWAN HILL

The Swan Hill region doesn't compare with Mildura in grape production but there are a few wineries you can visit with cellar-door sales and tastings, including **Brumby Wines** (☑ 03-5030 5366; www.brumbywines.com.au; cnr Murray Valley Hwy & Cannon Lane, Wood Wood).

Historic **Tyntyndyer Homestead** (☑ 03-5030 2416; Murray Valley Hwy, Beverford; admission $8.50; ☺ by appointment only), located 16km north of town, has a small museum and many reminders of the hardships of colonial life. Guided group tours require an appointment.

Just 16km southeast of Swan Hill, **Lake Boga** is an interesting little town – especially now that its namesake lake is full of water again. The famous Catalina flying boat *A24-30* is on display at the **Lake Boga Flying Boat Museum** (☑ 03-5037 2850; www.flyingboat.org.au; Catalina Park; adult/child/family $10/3/20; ☺ 9.30am-4pm). Flying boats were repaired and tested at Lake Boga during WWII. Inside are lots of displays and photographs.

Further down the highway is a patchwork of lakes, including **Kangaroo Lake** and **Lake Charm**, which are popular watersports destinations. Just before you reach Kerang is the **Middle Lake Ibis Rookery**, where birdwatchers can spy the huge flocks of ibis from a bird hide.

Overlooking the water at Lake Boga, the luxurious **Burrabliss B&B** (☑ 03-5037 2527; www.burrabliss.com.au; 169 Lakeside Dr; d/ste/villas $150/180/300) is a fine choice. Go with the friendly owners to see their ultra-fine-wool sheep, go birdwatching in the wetlands, or walk by the lake and enjoy the gardens.

ECHUCA

POP 12,620

One of the loveliest towns in rural Victoria, Echuca is the paddle-steamer capital of Victoria and a classic Murray River town, bursting with history, nostalgia and, of course, riverboats. The Aboriginal name translates as 'meeting of the waters', as it's here that three great rivers meet – the Goulburn, Campaspe and the Murray. The highlight here is unquestionably the historic port area and the rivers themselves, best enjoyed on a riverboat cruise or a sunset stroll along the river as cockatoos and corellas screech overhead. While it might feel a bit touristy, the town glows with an upbeat atmosphere and some fabulous restaurants and bars that will bring a smile to the face of riverside campers and travelling gastronomes alike.

History

Echuca was founded in 1853 by ex-convict Henry Hopwood. He settled on the banks of the Murray, converted some rough sheds into an inn and a store, then established punt and ferry crossings over the Murray and Campaspe Rivers; with his monopoly on transport and the gold rush in full swing, he profited handsomely. At the peak of the riverboat era there were more than 100 paddle steamers carting wool, timber and other goods between Echuca and the outback sheep stations.

It was too good to last, though: the Melbourne–Echuca railway line opened in 1864, and within a decade the boom years of the riverboat trade had ended.

◉ Sights

Ask at Echuca Visitors Centre for the *Heritage Walk Echuca* brochure, which outlines a self-guided walking itinerary taking in the town centre's historic buildings.

★ Historic Port of Echuca   HISTORIC SITE
(☑ 03-5481 0500, 1300 942 737; www.portofechuca.org.au; 74 Murray Esplanade; adult/concession/child/family $14/11/8/37; ☉ 9am-5pm, guided tours 11.30am & 1.30pm) Echuca's star attraction is the historic Port of Echuca. Everything is original – you're exploring living history as you walk along the pedestrian-only **Murray Esplanade**, which you can wander for free.

At the northern end of Murray Esplanade, the **Port of Echuca Discovery Centre** is your gateway to the **Echuca Wharf** area (admission ticket required), with excellent displays (some of them interactive) on the port's history, the paddle steamers and the riverboat trade. Guided tours set out from the discovery centre twice daily.

In the wharf's cargo shed, there's an interesting audiovisual presentation and dioramas depicting life on the riverboats. Walk along the various levels of the massive wharf and onto the restored historic paddle steamers PS *Pevensey* (built in 1911) and PS *Adelaide* (1866), the oldest operating paddle steamer in the world. The wharf was built with three tiers because of the changing river levels; there are gauges marking the highest points.

Back on the Esplanade, stop in at the Star Hotel (1867) and escape through the underground tunnel, which helped drinkers avoid the police during the years when the pub was a 'sly grog shop'.

On Hopwood Pl at the far end is the **Bridge Hotel**, where your ticket admits you to a historic upstairs gallery. The pub now operates as a restaurant and bistro.

Sharp's Magic Movie House & Penny Arcade (☑ 03-5482 2361; 43 Murray Esplanade; adult/child/family $15/10/45; ☉ 9am-5pm) has authentic and fully restored penny-arcade machines – you're given a fist-full of pennies. Free fudge tasting is another blast from the past. The movie house shows old films such as Buster Keaton or Laurel and Hardy classics.

Other port-area sights include **Red Gum Works** (Murray Esplanade; ☉ 9am-4pm) **FREE**, a historic sawmill that recreates old timber-milling days. Watch wood-turners and blacksmiths work with traditional equipment, and purchase red-gum products.

There are free tastings of local wines at **St Anne's** (☑ 03-5480 6955; www.stanneswinery.com.au; 53 Murray Esplanade; ☉ 10am-6pm), where the giant port barrels will inspire you to taste the range of ports, aged in bourbon and rum barrels.

★ National Holden Museum   MUSEUM
(☑ 03-5480 2033; www.holdenmuseum.com.au; 7 Warren St; adult/child/family $7/3/16; ☉ 9am-5pm) Car buffs should check out this museum dedicated to Australia's four-wheeled icon, with more than 40 beautifully restored Holdens, from FJ to Monaro, as well as racing footage and memorabilia.

Echuca Historical Museum   MUSEUM
(☑ 03-5480 1325; www.echucahistoricalsociety.org.au; 1 Dickson St; adult/child $5/1; ☉ 11am-3pm) This historical museum is located in the old police station, classified by the National Trust. It has a collection of local history items, charts and photos from the riverboat era and early records.

Great Aussie Beer Shed   MUSEUM
(☑ 03-5480 6904; www.greataussiebeershed.com.au; 377 Mary Ann Rd; adult/child/family $9.50/3.50/19; ☉ 9am-5pm Sat, Sun & holidays) This is a wall-to-wall shrine of beer cans in a huge shed. It's the result of 30 years of collecting. Guided tours will take you through the history of beer. Very Aussie.

---

① PORT OF ECHUCA COMBINATION TICKETS

Echuca's old port recently got an overhaul with a new discovery centre. It sells a series of combination tickets, including the following:

Discovery Centre & One-Hour Cruise Package (adult/concession/child/family $34/28/16/70) Includes all-day access to the historic port area (guided tours offered at 11.30am and 1.30pm) and a one-hour paddle steamer cruise.

Heritage Package (adult/concession/child/family $52/45.25/24.30/137.25) All of the above, but also includes admission to the National Holden Museum, Echuca Historical Museum and admission to and guided tour of the Great Aussie Beer Shed.

Wharf to Winery Package (per person $69) Paddle-steamer cruise to Morrisons Winery, two-course lunch and wine tasting.

THE MURRAY RIVER & AROUND ECHUCA

Echuca

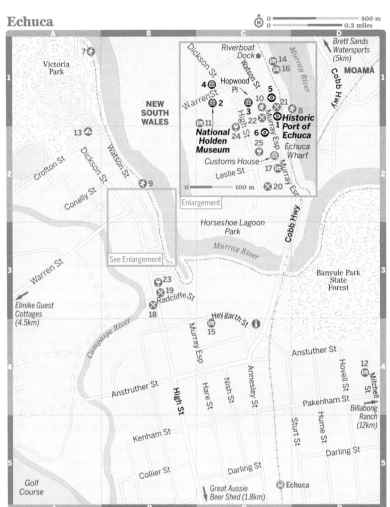

N 0 —— 400 m
0 —— 0.2 miles

Activities

Paddle-Steamer Cruises

A paddle-steamer cruise here is almost obligatory – there are at least six operating at one time or another, wood-fired, steam-driven and with interesting commentary. Buy tickets from the Port of Echuca Discovery Centre (p293), Echuca Visitors Centre (p297) or at the sales points along Murray Esplanade. Check out the timetable for lunch and dinner, twilight and sunset cruises.

Most of the following offer cruise and either lunch or dinner packages. One is the 'Wharf to Winery' package, which costs $69 and includes a cruise aboard the PS *Alexander Arbuthnot* or PS *Pevensey* to a local winery, two-course lunch, glass of wine and wine-tasting.

PS Alexander Arbuthnot   CRUISE
(☏03-5482 4248; www.echucapaddlesteamers. net.au; adult/child/family $23.50/9.80/61.50) One-hour cruises four times daily.

PS Canberra   CRUISE
(☏03-5482 5244; www.emmylou.com.au; adult/ child/family $23.50/10/62.50) One-hour cruises three times daily.

Echuca

⊙ Top Sights
1 Historic Port of Echuca C1
2 National Holden Museum C1

⊙ Sights
3 Bridge Hotel...C1
4 Echuca Historical Museum....................C1
5 Red Gum Works C1
6 Sharp's Magic Movie House &
    Penny Arcade C2

⊙ Activities, Courses & Tours
7 Echuca Boat & Canoe Hire A1
  MV Mary Ann.......................................(see 8)
8 PS Alexander Arbuthnot D1
  PS Canberra...(see 8)
9 PS Emmylou B2
  PS Pevensey...(see 8)
  PS Pride of the Murray ....(see 8)
10 St Anne's...C1

⊙ Sleeping
11 Adelphi Boutique Apartments C1
12 Echuca Gardens D4
13 Echuca Holiday Park A2
14 Murray River Houseboats C1
15 Quest Echuca..C4
16 Rich River Houseboats C1
17 Steampacket B&B....................................C2

⊗ Eating
18 Beechworth Bakery B3
19 Ceres..B3
20 Fish in a Flash..C2
21 Oscar W's Wharfside............................... C1
22 Star Hotel & Wine Bar C1

⊙ Drinking & Nightlife
23 Bordello Wine Bar....................................B3
24 Shamrock Hotel..C2
25 Speakeasy C2

PS Emmylou
CRUISE

(☎03-5482 5244; www.emmylou.com.au; 1hr cruise adult/child $27/12.50, 2hr cruise $34/15.50) One of the most impressive boats in Echuca, fully restored and driven by an original engine. Offers two one-hour cruises and one two-hour cruise daily, plus lunch cruises and overnight cruises.

PS Pevensey
CRUISE

(☎03-5482 4248; www.echucapaddlesteamers.net.au; adult/child/family $23.50/9.80/61.50) Star of the TV miniseries *All the Rivers Run;* offers one-hour cruises four times daily, and winery cruises ($30).

PS Pride of the Murray
CRUISE

(☎03-5482 5244; www.emmylou.com.au; adult/child/family $23.50/10/62.50) One-hour cruises three times daily.

MV Mary Ann
CRUISE

(☎03-5480 2200; www.maryann.com.au) Not a traditional paddle steamer, but this restaurant boat combines a river cruise with lunch or dinner. Prices include a two-course meal and entertainment. Call ahead for times.

Horse Riding

Billabong Ranch
HORSE RIDING

(☎03-5483 5122; www.billabongranch.com.au; 1hr/2hr/half-day ride $45/80/110) This ranch offers rides through the bush and along the Murray and Goulburn Rivers from its base, 12km east of Echuca. It also has minigolf, pedal boats, an animal nursery, tenpin bowling, a playground, pony rides, off-road buggies ($30 per 15 minutes), a cafe and a bar, among other things.

Water Sports

Echuca Boat & Canoe Hire
BOAT HIRE

(☎03-5480 6208; www.echucaboatcanoehire.com; Victoria Park Boat Ramp) Hires out motor boats (one/two hours $40/60), 'barbie boats' with onboard BBQs (10 people $120/170), kayaks ($16/26) and canoes ($20/30). Multiday, self-guided 'campanoeing' trips are also available, where you can arrange to be dropped upstream and canoe back.

River Country Adventours
KAYAKING

(☎0428 585 227; www.adventours.com.au; half-/full-/2-day safaris $55/88/185) For organised canoe safaris on the Goulburn River, this Kyabram-based team are the experts in this part of the world, with canoe and camping safaris around the Barmah and Goulburn regions, as well as on the Murray.

Brett Sands Watersports
WATERSPORTS

(☎03-5482 1851; www.brettsands.com; Merool Lane, Moama; half-/full day $140/220) Several operators offer waterskiing trips and classes, but this outfit will teach you skills behind a boat on skis, wakeboard, kneeboard or barefoot. It also hires out gear.

☞ Tours

The Echuca region is home to a few wineries, and local operators can take you there.

Echuca Moama Wine Tours
WINE

(☎1300 798 822; www.echucamoamawinetours.com.au; tours from $85; ⊙Tue-Sun) Tours include the historic port, a cruise along the Murray and local wineries.

✦✦ Festivals & Events

Check the online event calendar at www.echucamoama.com.

Club Marine Southern 80   WATER SPORTS
(www.southern80.com.au) The world's largest waterskiing race; held in February.

Riverboats Music Festival   MUSIC
(www.riverboatsmusic.com.au) Music, food and wine by the Murray; held in late February. Recent past performers include Tim Finn, Archie Roach and Colin Hay.

Steam, Horse & Vintage Rally   VINTAGE TRANSPORT
(www.echucasteamrally.com.au) On the Queen's Birthday weekend in June; classic and historic vehicles and steam engines powered by all imaginable methods.

Echuca-Moama Winter Blues Festival   MUSIC
(www.winterblues.com.au) Blues and folk musos play in the streets and at venues around town at this weekend music festival in late July.

🛏 Sleeping

Echuca has plenty of accommodation, from quaint B&Bs and backpacker hostels to caravan parks, huge brick motels and old lace-trimmed hotels, much of it conveniently close to the port area.

About 5km east of town, Christies Beach is a free camping area on the banks of the Murray. There are pit toilets, but bring water and firewood.

Echuca Holiday Park   CAMPGROUND $
(☑03-5482 2157; www.echucacaravanpark.com.au; 51 Crofton St; unpowered/powered sites from $25/30, d cabins $82-188; ❉ 🙴 ❉) Beside the river just a short walk from town, this park is pretty cramped but the facilities are good, with modern timber camp kitchens and shady river red gums.

Echuca Gardens   HOSTEL, GUESTHOUSE $
(☑03-5480 6522; www.echucagardens.com; 103 Mitchell St; dm $30, wagon d $80-150, guesthouse d $110-180; @) Run by inveterate traveller Kym, this enjoyable place is part YHA hostel and part guesthouse, all set in beautiful gardens with ponds, statues, chickens and fruit trees. The 140-year-old workers cottage has bunk beds, smart bathrooms, a country kitchen and a TV room. The cute 'gypsy wagons' in the garden offer unique accommodation, complete with en suite and kitchenette, and there are two guesthouse rooms in the main house. Something for everyone and a warm atmosphere.

Steampacket B&B   B&B $$
(☑03-5482 3411; www.steampacketinn.com.au; cnr Murray Esplanade & Leslie St; d $135-205; ❉) Staying in the old port area is all part of the Echuca experience. This 19th-century National Trust–classified B&B offers genteel rooms with all the old-fashioned charm, linen and lace, and brass bedsteads you could want (but with air-con and flat-screen TVs, too). Ask for the large corner rooms for a view of the wharf. The lounge room is cosy and breakfast is served on fine china.

Quest Echuca   APARTMENT $$
(☑03-5481 3900; www.questechuca.com.au; 25-29 Heygarth St; studio/1-/2-bed apt from $135/165/275; ❉ 🙴) Stylish modern apartments a block back from the Murray River and main street make this a fine choice if the usual doily-and-lace Echuca aesthetic is not your thing.

Elinike Guest Cottages   COTTAGE $$
(☑03-5480 6311; www.elinike.com.au; 209 Latham Rd; d incl breakfast $160-195) These romantic little self-contained cottages are set in rambling gardens on the Murray River around 5km out of town, blending old-world style with modern conveniences such as double spas. The lilac cottage ($195) has a glass-roofed garden room.

ECHUCA HOUSEBOATS

Echuca is a great place to hire a houseboat. They range from six-berth to luxurious 12-berth crafts with spa baths. Four nights midweek in the low season will cost from $900 to $2500, depending on the boat. The following outfits are based at the Riverboat Dock, while the Echuca Visitors Centre has brochures from and information about other operators.

Murray River Houseboats (☑03-5480 2343; www.murrayriverhouseboats.com.au; Riverboat Dock; 2- to 7-bed houseboat per week $1290-2460) Five houseboats in the fleet, including the stunning four-bedroom *Indulgence*.

Rich River Houseboats (☑03-5480 2444; www.richriverhouseboats.com.au; Riverboat Dock; 8-bed houseboat per week $3850-6800) The six beautiful boats here include a budget six-berth and a couple of floating palaces.

Adelphi

Boutique Apartments APARTMENT $$

(☏ 03-5482 5575; www.adelphiapartments.com.au; 25 Campaspe St; 1-/2-bedroom apt from $170/295; ❋) The semiluxurious riverside accommodation here, a block back from the main street, is a good choice, especially if you're willing to pay a little more for the ones with a terrace overlooking the Campaspe River.

Eating

Conveniently, some of the best places to eat in Echuca are around the port area and the top end of High St.

Beechworth Bakery BAKERY $

(☏ 1300 233 784; www.beechworthbakery.com.au; 513 High St; meals $5-12; ⊙ 6am-6pm) In a magnificent old building with wrap-around balcony and deck overlooking the Campaspe River, this cheerful bakery prepares a high standard of breads, pies, cakes and sandwiches.

Fish in a Flash FISH & CHIPS $

(☏ 03-5480 0824; 602 High St; fish & chips from $8.90; ⊙ 11am-8pm) Consistently ranked among the best fish-and-chip places in Victoria, Fish in a Flash does fine river fish as well as the usual suspects, all dipped in the owner's secret batter. Great for a riverside picnic.

Ceres EUROPEAN $$

(☏ 03-5482 5599; www.ceresechuca.com.au; 554 High St; lunch $19-25, dinner $25-35; ⊙ 10am-late Mon-Fri, 9am-late Sat & Sun) Located in the old town-hall hotel building, Ceres oozes style with its high-back leather chairs, starched tablecloths and occasional couches. It's a relaxed place for lunch with all-day coffee and tapas, but there's an atmospheric fine-dining evening restaurant with an innovative menu of Italian-influenced pastas, steaks and roast duckling. Among the tapas and antipasto choices, the slow-cooked, sticky fried pork belly, seared scallops, black pudding and cauliflower purée caught our eye.

★ Oscar W's Wharfside MODERN AUSTRALIAN $$

(☏ 03-5482 5133; www.oscarws.com.au; 101 Murray Esplanade; lunch $22-27, mains $37.50-58; ⊙ 11am-late) The glorious location in the old port area, with a terrace overlooking the Murray, is unbeatable, but Oscar's really delivers with its food and service – this is easily Echuca's best place to eat. Start with the smaller shared plates or go straight to thoughtful Mod Oz mains of pan-fried Murray cod, kangaroo and local steak. Big wine list, great atmosphere.

Star Hotel & Wine Bar BAR, BISTRO $$

(☏ 03-5480 1181; www.starhotelechuca.com.au; 45 Murray Esplanade; mains $13-24; ⊙ 8am-2pm & 6pm-late Wed-Sun) The historic 'Star Bar' is still one of the liveliest places in town for a meal or drink, especially on weekends when there's live music. Full cooked breakfasts and a reasonably priced lunch of calamari or chicken parma can be enjoyed right beside the port.

🍷 Drinking

The Bridge Hotel (p293) and Star Hotel & Wine Bar in the port area are atmospheric places for a drink.

Bordello Wine Bar WINE BAR

(www.rivergalleryinn.com.au; 578 High St; ⊙ 5-11pm Thu-Sun) Ideal for fine local wines, a fabulous range of world beers, comfy armchairs and occasional live music, Bordello, along the main street, is Echuca's most intimate venue.

Shamrock Hotel IRISH PUB

(☏ 03-5482 1058; www.shamrockhotel.com.au; 583 High St) Close to the port area, the Shamrock is full of Irish-themed fun and frivolity, with live music, good food and Guinness on tap.

Speakeasy WINE BAR

(☏ 0408 551 017; 620 High St; ⊙ from 3pm Thu-Sun, closed Aug) Tucked away behind the port area, Speakeasy is a relaxed bar with a focus on good wines and boutique beers. There's live music at the Sunday sessions from 5pm.

ℹ️ Information

Echuca Library (☏ 03-5482 1997; 524-528 High St; ⊙ 10am-5.30pm Mon, Tue, Thu & Fri, noon-8pm Wed, 10am-1pm Sat, 2-4.30pm Sun; @) Free internet access.

Echuca Visitors Centre (☏ 1800 804 446; www.echucamoama.com; 2 Heygarth St; ⊙ 9am-5pm) In the old pump station, the visitor centre has helpful staff and an accommodation booking service.

ℹ️ Getting Around

Echuca offers an enlightened free bicycle service, called the 'Port Picnic Bike'. Bikes can be picked up at St Anne's (p293); ask there or at the Echuca Visitors Centre for more information.

ℹ️ Getting There & Away

Echuca lies 222km north of Melbourne. Take the Hume Fwy (M31) and then the well-signposted turn-off to the B75, which then passes through Heathcote and Rochester en route to Echuca.

V/Line (☑ 13 61 96; www.vline.com.au) has two direct Melbourne–Echuca trains on weekends and train and bus services (return $24.60, 2¾ hours) on weekdays, with changes at Bendigo, Murchison, Heathcote or Shepparton.

AROUND ECHUCA

Barmah National Park

About 40km northeast of Echuca via the Cobb Hwy in NSW, Barmah is a significant wetlands area of the Murray River floodplain. It's the largest remaining red-gum forest in Australia, and the swampy understorey usually floods, creating a wonderful breeding area for many species of fish and birds; it's one of few places in Victoria to see the Superb Parrot.

The park entry is about 6km north of the tiny town of Barmah (turn at the pub). From the day-use area, **Kingfisher Cruises** (☑ 03-5855 2855; www.kingfishercruises.com.au; adult/child/family $35/21/100; ⊙ 10.30am Mon, Wed, Thu, Sat & Sun) takes you out in a flat-bottom boat for an informative two-hour cruise. Your captain points out bird and mammal species along the way. Call ahead for departure times and bookings.

You can camp for free in the park, or at the Barmah Lakes camping area, which has tables, barbecue areas and pit toilets.

YARRAWONGA

POP 6800

Arrayed along the southern shores of Lake Mulwala, which was created when the Murray River was dammed for irrigation back in 1939, Yarrawonga is beloved by boaters, waterskiers, golfers and retirees. It also enjoys more sunshine hours than anywhere else in Victoria. Such positives make up for a lack of old-world character, it being a fairly run-of-the-mill provincial Victorian town.

◎ Sights & Activities

Byramine Homestead   HISTORIC BUILDING
(☑ 03-5748 4321; www.byraminehomestead.com.au; 1436 Murray Valley Hwy; adult/child/family $5/2.50/15; ⊙ 10am-4pm Sun, Mon, Wed, Thu & Sat) When Elizabeth Hume's husband was killed by bushrangers, she moved here and built in 1842 a safe haven that saw her become the first permanent European settler in the area. The homestead is shaped like a fortress and is set in magnificent grounds 14km west of town.

Paradise Queen   CRUISE
(☑ 0418 508 616; www.paradisequeen.com; cruises $15-26) Paradise Queen can take you cruising along the lake and the Murray River, pointing out historic spots and bird life. There are 1½-hour sunrise breakfast cruises ($24), barbecue cruises ($26) at noon and scenic cruises ($15) at 2pm, as well as dinner cruises during summer.

Action Bike & Ski   KAYAKING, CYCLING
(☑ 03-5744 3522; www.actionbikeski.com.au; 81 Belmore St; ⊙ 9am-5pm Mon-Fri, to 1pm Sat, open some Sun) Hires out kayaks ($55) and bikes ($20). To really discover the lake and river, take one of the half-day guided kayak tours ($100).

Yarrawonga & Border Golf Club   GOLF
(☑ 03-5744 1911; www.yarragolf.com.au; Gulai Rd, Mulwala; 9/18 holes $28/45) Across the water, in Mulwala, NSW, is Australia's largest public golf course, with 45 beautifully manicured holes, resort accommodation and a bar and bistro.

🛏 Sleeping

Murray Valley Resort   RESORT $$
(☑ 03-5744 1844; www.murrayvalleyresort.com.au; Murray Valley Hwy; s/d from $140/174, condos from $275; ❄ ☲) This place is a good reflection of the town itself – the modern, motel-style rooms don't have much character but the facilities (a gym, indoor and outdoor pools, tennis courts, billiard tables and spas) are excellent.

Coghill Cottages   COTTAGE $$
(☑ 03-5744 2271; www.coghill.com.au; 6 Coghill St; 1-/2-/3-bedroom cottages from $110/160/220; ❄ ☲) These smart, modern, self-contained cottages have a range of sizes and are close to the lake. There's a minimum two-night stay and pets are welcome.

✕ Eating & Drinking

There's a reasonable cafe and pub scene on Belmore St, between the Murray Valley Hwy and the lake.

Nosh Deli   CAFE $
(☑ 03-5744 1756; 42 Belmore St; mains $9-20; ⊙ 8am-4pm Sun-Thu, to 7pm Fri) Top spot for breakfast, coffee, spot-on smoothies or tasty lunches of enchiladas and frittata.

Deck One Pub   PUB $$
(☑ 03-5744 3839; www.criterionyarrawonga.com.au; 1 Belmore St; mains $13-25; ⊙ 11am-9pm) The beer deck here takes up as much real estate

as the Criterion Hotel, to which it's attached. Shady umbrellas, good views of the lake and a kids' playground. Good pub food is complemented with pizzas and pasta.

ⓘ Information

Yarrawonga Visitor Centre (☑03-5744 1989, 1800 062 260; www.yarrawongamulwala.com. au; 1 Irvine Pde; ☺9am-5pm) Right beside the Mulwala Bridge and with a cafe overlooking the lake; book accommodation and tours here.

ⓘ Getting There & Away

Yarrawonga is 283km northeast of Melbourne. By car, take the Hume Fwy (M31) and then head north from Benalla or Wangaratta.

V/Line (☑13 61 96; www.vline.com.au) train and coach services run between Melbourne and Yarrawonga ($28.60, four hours, three daily), with a change at Benalla or Seymour.

NORTHEAST VICTORIA

Rutherglen

POP 2500

Rutherglen combines some marvellous gold rush–era buildings (gold was discovered here in 1860) with northern Victoria's most celebrated winemaking tradition. The town itself has all the essential ingredients that merit a stopover, among them a great pie shop, antique dealers and a labyrinthine second-hand bookshop. It all adds up to an engaging destination in its own right and a good base for exploring the Murray's Victorian hinterland.

◉ Sights & Activities

First up should be the Rutherglen Wine Experience (p300), with a wine-tasting room where you can sample local fortifieds, book tours and hire bikes ($25/35 per half-/full day).

The visitor centre at the Wine Experience provides maps and touring information for cycling tours around the region, including the Rutherglen–Wahguynah extension to the Murray to Mountains Rail Trail (see p268).

ⓒ Tours

There are lots of ways to get out to the wineries without driving or cycling yourself, including chauffeured limousine tours. The visitor centre has a full list.

Behind the Scenes WINERY
(www.rutherglenvic.com/behind-the-scenes-tours; ☺2pm Mon, Wed & Thu, 11am Fri-Sun) **FREE** Five local wineries offer fantastic 'Behind the Scenes' winery tours that take you into the world of the winemaking process, but advance bookings are essential. Check the website to match your day with a winery.

Walkabout Limousines WINERY
(☑02-6032 9572; www.walkaboutmotel.com.au; Murray Valley Hwy) Winery tours in an impeccably restored Lincoln limousine.

★ Festivals & Events

There are special events on almost every weekend here, all featuring a wide range of activities, especially focused on eating and drinking. See www.rutherglenvic.com.

Tastes of Rutherglen WINE, FOOD
(☺Mar) Two weekends of total indulgence, with food-and-wine packages at dozens of vineyards and restaurants.

Winery Walkabout Weekend WINE, MUSIC
(☺Jun) Australia's original wine festival – there's music, barrel racing and probably some wine.

Rutherglen Wine Show WINE
(www.rutherglenwineshow.com.au; ☺Sep) Don't miss this late-September show with gourmet dinners and public tastings.

⊨ Sleeping

Accommodation is tight (and rates are higher) during major festivals and on weekends and public holidays – book ahead.

Rutherglen Caravan & Tourist Park CAMPGROUND $
(☑02-6032 8577; www.rutherglentouristpark. com; 72 Murray St; unpowered/powered sites from $25/32, d cabins $88-140; ✿) This friendly park with good facilities sits on the banks of Lake King, close to the golf course and swimming pool.

Victoria Hotel HOTEL $$
(☑02-6032 8610; www.victoriahotelrutherglen. com.au; 90 Main St; s/d without bathroom from $45/75, d with bathroom $90-160; ✿) This beautiful National Trust–classified pub has history, great bistro food and some very inviting accommodation – the spruced-up front rooms have en suites and views over Main St, with access to the wide, lace-trimmed balcony. At the back is a three-room suite that can sleep up to 11.

Carlyle House   B&B **$$**

(☑02-6032 8444; www.carlylehouse.com.au; 147 High St; r incl breakfast $150-240; ❋) The four traditional suites and modern garden apartments are beautifully presented in this lovingly restored home. The Tokay suite boasts a private lounge. Although a change of owner is in the offing, we don't expect too much to change here.

★**Tuileries**   BOUTIQUE HOTEL **$$$**

(☑02-6032 9033; www.tuileriesrutherglen.com.au; 13-35 Drummond St; d incl breakfast $199, with dinner $299; ❋ 🛜 ☲) All rooms are individually decorated in bright, contemporary tones at this luxurious place next to Jolimont Cellars. There's a guest lounge, a tennis court, a pool and an outstanding restaurant and cafe.

✖ Eating

In addition to the following, a number of wineries also have quality restaurants, including All Saints and Vintara.

★**Parkers Pies**   BAKERY **$**

(☑02-6032 9605; www.parkerspies.com.au; 86-88 Main St; pies $5-7.50; ⊙8am-5pm Mon-Sat, 9am-4.30pm Sun) If you think a pie is a pie, this award-winning local institution might change your mind. Try the gourmet pastries – emu, venison, crocodile or buffalo, or the lovely Jolly Jumbuck (lamb pastry with rosemary and mint).

Forks & Corks   INDIAN **$$**

(☑02-6032 7662; 82 Main St; mains $18-21; ⊙noon-2.30pm & 5.30-9pm Fri & Sat, noon-2.30pm Sun-Thu) This bright, airy place dishes out North Indian tandoori specialities, as well as curries and seafoods.

**Tuileries
Restaurant & Cafe**   MEDITERRANEAN **$$**

(☑02-6032 9033; www.tuileriesrutherglen.com.au; 13-35 Drummond St; lunch mains $12.90, dinner $31.50-36; ⊙noon-2pm & 6.30-9pm) The courtyard cafe is a fine place for lunch, and in the evening the fine-dining restaurant produces superb Mediterranean-influenced dishes, with local produce such as gum-smoked kangaroo fillet or Murray Valley pork belly.

❶ Information

Rutherglen Wine Experience (☑02-6033 6306, 1800 622 871; www.rutherglenvic.com; 57 Main St; ⊙9am-5pm) combines the visitor information centre with a cafe and wine-tasting room. It also provides information about Rutherglen's busy calendar of wine and food events, including Tastes of Rutherglen in March and Winery Walkabout Weekend in June.

❶ Getting There & Away

Rutherglen is 295km northeast of Melbourne. To get there by car, take the Hume Fwy (M31) and turn off at Chiltern.

   V/Line (☑1800 800 007; www.vline.com. au) has a train and coach service between

---

RUTHERGLEN REDS

Rutherglen's wineries produce superb fortifieds (port, muscat and tokay) and some potent durifs and shirazes – among the biggest, baddest and strongest reds. See www. winemakers.com.au for more information. Some of the best are:

All Saints (☑02-6035 2222; www.allsaintswine.com.au; All Saints Rd, Wahgunyah; ⊙9am-5.30pm Mon-Sat, 10am-5.30pm Sun) Fairy-tale castle, restaurant and cheese tasting.

Buller Wines (☑03-9936 0200; www.buller.com.au; Three Chain Rd; ⊙9am-5pm Mon-Sat, 10am-5pm Sun) Fine shiraz, plus a bird park.

Morris (☑02-6026 7303; www.morriswines.com.au; Mia Mia Rd; ⊙9am-5pm Mon-Sat, 10am-5pm Sun)

Pfeiffer (☑02-6033 2805; www.pfeifferwinesrutherglen.com.au; 167 Distillery Rd, Wahgunyah; ⊙9am-5pm Mon-Sat, 10am-5pm Sun)

Rutherglen Estates (☑02-6032 7999; www.rutherglenestates.com.au; 13-35 Drummond St, Tuileries Complex; ⊙10am-5.30pm) Closest winery to town.

Stanton & Killeen Wines (☑02-6032 9457; www.stantonandkilleenwines.com.au; Jacks Rd; ⊙9am-5pm Mon-Sat, 10am-5pm Sun)

Vintara (☑0447 327 517; www.vintara.com.au; Fraser Rd; ⊙10am-4pm) Includes Bintara Brewery.

Warrabilla Wines (☑02-6035 7242; www.warrabillawines.com.au; Murray Valley Hwy; ⊙10am-5pm) Small winery but quality reds.

Melbourne and Rutherglen with a change at Seymour ($31, 3½ hours, eight weekly). During festivals, bus transport to wineries can be organised through the visitor centre.

Wahgunyah

POP 890

A short drive northeast of Rutherglen on the Murray River is the quiet township of Wahgunyah. At the height of the riverboat era, Wahgunyah was a thriving port town and trade depot. Now, wineries surround it, and historic Corowa is just across the bridge in NSW.

Visit Cofield Wines for tastings and a meal in the excellent **Pickled Sisters Café** (☑ 02-6033 2377; www.pickledsisters. com.au; Cofield Wines, Distillery Rd; mains $32; ☺ 10am-4pm Wed-Mon, 6-9pm Fri & Sat). For another fine dining experience, try the **Terrace Restaurant** (☑ 02-6035 2209; www.all-saintswine.com.au; All Saints Estate, All Saints Rd; 2-/3-course meal $60/75; ☺ noon-3pm Wed-Fri & Sun, noon-3pm & 6-11pm Sat).

Over in Corowa, in a revamped flour mill, is **Corowa Whisky & Chocolate** (☑ 0406 059 283; www.corowawhisky.com; Steele St; ☺ 9am-4pm), where sampling handmade chocolates and international whiskies is the perfect complement to all that wine tasting!

Chiltern

POP 1150

Like an old-time movie set, tiny Chiltern is one of Victoria's most historic colonial townships. Its two main streets are lined with 19th-century buildings, antique shops and a couple of pubs – authentic enough that the town has been used as a film set for period films, including the early Walt Disney classic *Ride a Wild Pony*. Originally called Black Dog Creek, it was established in 1851 and prospered when gold was discovered here in 1859.

◎ Sights & Activities

Old Town   NEIGHBOURHOOD
Pick up a copy of the *Chiltern Touring Guide* from the Chiltern Visitor Centre (p302) – it guides you around 20 historic sites scattered throughout the town.

Among the National Trust–classified sites are the **Athenaeum Library & Museum** (☑ 03-5726 1467; www.chilternathenaeum.com.au; Conness St; adult/child $2/free; ☺ 10am-4pm), in the former Town Hall (1866), with a collection of memorabilia, photos and equipment from the gold-rush days; **Dow's Pharmacy**

(☑ 03-5726 1597; www.nationaltrust.org.au/vic/dows-pharmacy; Conness St; adult/child $3/1; ☺ 11am-3pm Mon-Fri), a chemist's from 1859 to 1968, with lotions and potions from the early days; and **Lake View Homestead** (☑ 03-5726 1317; 18-22 Victoria St; adult/child $2/1; ☺ 10am-4pm Sun or by appointment), built in 1870 and overlooking Lake Anderson. It was the home of Henry Handel (Ethel Florence) Richardson, who wrote about life here in the book *Ultima Thule* (1929), the third part of her trilogy *The Fortunes of Richard Mahony* (1930).

Star Hotel Museum & Theatre (☑ 03-5726 1395; cnr Main & Conness Sts), once used for plays and dances, was the centrepiece of Chiltern's social and cultural life. Unfortunately the museum here is rarely open these days (call ahead for an appointment or ask at the visitor centre). The grapevine in the courtyard is the largest in Australia – you can just see it down the alleyway off Conness St.

Chiltern-Mt Pilot National Park   OUTDOORS
(Chiltern Box-Ironbark National Park; ☑ 13 19 63; www.parks.vic.gov.au) This important national park protects some of Victoria's last stands of Box-Ironbark forest in a patchwork of protected areas around the town. This is also one of the last Victorian refuges for the endangered regent honeyeater, along with more than 200 other bird species. The Chiltern Visitor Centre has maps, a park information sheet, a brochure entitled *Bird Trails of Chiltern*, and information on the best places to see the regent honeyeater. To immerse yourself in the Ironbarks, consider the 8.5km **Whitebox Walking Track**, which completes a circuit in the area of the park south of Chiltern; ask at the visitor centre for directions.

🛏 Sleeping & Eating

There are a couple of classic country pubs in town serving bistro food.

★**Linesman's Cottage**   GUESTHOUSE $$
(☑ 03-5726 1300; www.linesmanscottage.com.au; 56 Main St; 1-/2-/3-night stay $120/200/280; ❋) At the rear of Chiltern's historic post office, this 1950s cottage retains its historic facade but has been beautifully renovated within. With a kitchen, courtyard garden, a queen-sized bed and sofa bed, it's ideal for a family.

Mulberry Tree B&B & Tearooms   B&B $$
(☑ 03-5726 1277; www.mulberrytreechiltern.com. au; 28 Conness St; d incl breakfast $135-190) Mulberry Tree is a charming B&B in an old bank building with two cute rooms; one is self-contained with lounge and open fire. Even if

NAGAMBIE

In the Goulburn Valley just west of the Hume Fwy, Nagambie inhabits the shores of pretty Lake Nagambie – it's a popular centre for water sports and sky-diving. For the latter try **Skydive Nagambie** (☑1800 266 500, 03-5794 2626; www.skydivenagambie.com; 52 Kettles Rd; tandem dives $299-399). The surrounding area is known for its horse studs – superstar horse Black Caviar was born here – and wineries.

Two of Victoria's best wineries are just south of town: **Mitchelton Wines** (☑03-5736 2222; www.mitchelton.com.au; 470 Mitchellstown Rd; ☺10am-5pm), with an art gallery and award-winning shiraz; and **Tahbilk Winery** (☑03-5794 2555; www.tahbilk.com.au; 254 O'Neils Rd; ☺9am-5pm Mon-Fri, 10am-5pm Sat & Sun), which began in 1860 and claims to be the oldest winery and vineyard in Victoria. Tahbilk opens onto the **Wetlands & Wildlife Reserve** (admission by donation, wetlands cruise $5; ☺11am-4pm Thu-Mon), with boardwalks and boat tours through a natural area rich in bird life. Entry is via the excellent **Wetlands Café** (mains $18-36; ☺11am-4pm Thu-Mon).

Staff at **Nagambie Visitor Centre** (☑03-5794 1471, 1800 444 647; www.nagambielakes andstrathbogieranges.com.au; 317a High St; ☺9am-5pm) are passionate about their region.

you don't stay, the garden cafe is a great place for coffee, sandwiches or Devonshire tea.

ⓘ Information

Chiltern Visitor Centre (☑03-5726 1611; www.chilternvic.com; 30 Main St; ☺10am-4pm) Chiltern's helpful tourist office has information on the town and surrounding area, with useful tips on everything from birdwatching to gold prospecting.

ⓘ Getting There & Away

Chiltern is 290km northeast of Melbourne and lies just off the Hume Fwy (M31).

Up to three bus or train **V/Line** (☑1800 800 007; www.vline.com.au) services run from Melbourne's Southern Cross Station to Chiltern ($31, 3¼ hours).

Benalla

POP 9350

Just off the Hume Fwy, 212km north of Melbourne, Benalla is an important regional centre, although you won't need much more than an hour to take in its sights.

Benalla Visitor Centre (☑03-5762 1749; www.benalla.vic.gov.au; Mair St; ☺9am-5pm), by the lake, shares a home with the **Costume & Pioneer Museum** (adult/child $4/0.50), which has interesting exhibits, a delightful miniature house and a display on local war hero Sir Edward 'Weary' Dunlop. **Benalla Art Gallery** (☑03-5760 2619; www.benallaartgallery.com; Bridge St; ☺10am-5pm) **FREE** has a collection of Australian art, including paintings from the Heidelberg School, and a cafe that spreads onto a deck overlooking the lake. Outside is the moving Weary Dunlop Memorial.

Glenrowan

POP 300

Tiny Glenrowan is the epicentre of the legends surrounding Ned Kelly – it was here that the bushranger's exploits came to their bloody end in 1880. The main sites of the capture are signposted, so pick up a walking map and follow the trail.

Ned Kelly's Last Stand (☑03-5766-2367; 41 Gladstone St; tickets $25; ☺10am-4pm) is an animated theatre where Ned's story is told by a cast of surprisingly lifelike animatronic characters, and culminates in a smoky shootout and Ned's hanging (it may be too scary for young children). Original props include a Kelly-era handgun, Sgt Kennedy's hitching post and a rare copy of the findings of the Royal Commission into the Kelly manhunt. A few doors up, a **museum** holds Kelly memorabilia and artefacts gathered from all over the district, and a replica of the Kelly home.

The town has several country-style cafes and motels, as well as the local pub.

Glenrowan lies 235km northeast of Melbourne along the Hume Fwy (M31).

Wangaratta

POP 17,400

Wangaratta (or just plain old 'Wang' to the locals) is a busy commercial centre situated along the Hume Fwy. It's the turn-off for the ski fields along the Great Alpine Rd, and for the Rutherglen wine region. The name means 'resting place of the cormorants'.

The town sits neatly at the junction of the Ovens and King Rivers – the first buildings, in the 1840s, were based around a punt service that operated until 1855. Even so, what you see today is a modern provincial town with only faint echoes of that past.

◉ Sights & Activities

Free, one-hour guided walking tours of the town leave from the visitors centre (p304) at 10am every Saturday.

Wangaratta Cemetery   CEMETERY

At the Wangaratta Cemetery, south of town, is the grave of Dan 'Mad Dog' Morgan, a notorious bushranger. It contains most of Morgan's remains – after he was fatally shot at nearby Peechelba Station in April 1865, his head was taken to Melbourne for a study of the criminal mind (his scrotum was supposedly fashioned into a tobacco pouch). Pick up the brochure entitled *Wangaratta Cemetery – Self-Guided Tour* from the visitor centre.

Murray to Mountains Rail Trail   CYCLING, HIKING

(www.murraytomountains.com.au) Wangaratta is the start of the Murray to Mountains Rail Trail, which runs east via Beechworth to Bright and now links Wangaratta with Rutherglen and Wahgunyah. Ask at the Wangaratta Visitor Centre for information on local bike hire, although most who tackle the trail bring their own. For more info, see p268.

✯ Festivals & Events

Wangaratta Sports Carnival   SPORT

An athletics meeting featuring the Wangaratta Gift, one of Victoria's more prestigious regional foot races; held in late January.

Wangaratta Jazz & Blues Festival   MUSIC

(✆ 03-5722 8199; wangarattajazz.com) The main claim to fame here is the famous Wangaratta Jazz & Blues Festival, which attracts jazz players and buffs from around Australia and the world in early November.

🛏 Sleeping

Wangaratta has a decent range of typical motels, which can be booked online at www.visitwangaratta.com.au.

THE KELLY GANG

Bushranger and outlaw he may have been, but Ned Kelly is probably Australia's greatest folk hero. His life and death have been embraced as part of the national culture – from Sidney Nolan's famous paintings to Peter Carey's Man Booker Prize–winning novel *True History of the Kelly Gang*. Ned himself has become a symbol of the Australian rebel character.

Born in 1854, not far from Melbourne, to Irish parents, Ned was first arrested when he was 14 and had numerous brushes with the law over the next 10 years.

In 1878 a warrant was issued for his arrest for stealing horses. A trooper was trying to arrest Ned's brother Dan on a similar charge when he was wounded at the Kelly homestead. Ned and Dan went into hiding. Their mother and two friends were arrested, sentenced and imprisoned for aiding and abetting in the attempted murder of a policeman. The Kelly family had long felt persecuted by the authorities, and the jailing of Mrs Kelly, who was still breastfeeding a baby, was the last straw.

Ned and Dan were joined in their hideout in the Wombat Ranges, near Mansfield, by Steve Hart and Joe Byrne. Four policemen (Kennedy, Lonigan, Scanlon and McIntyre) came looking for them, and, in a shootout at Stringybark Creek, Kennedy, Lonigan and Scanlon were killed. McIntyre escaped to Mansfield and raised the alarm.

The government put up a £500 reward for any of the gang members, dead or alive, and declared them outlaws. In December 1878 the gang held up the National Bank at Euroa, and got away with £2000. Then, in February 1879, they took over the police station at Jerilderie, locked the two policemen in their log lock-up and robbed the Bank of New South Wales, with Ned wearing a police uniform. This robbery boosted the reward to £2000 a head.

After 20 months on the run, on 27 June 1880 the gang held 60 people captive in a hotel at Glenrowan, planning to destroy a trainload of police and trackers they had decoyed from Melbourne. Ned's plan was foiled when a schoolteacher warned the police. Surrounded, the gang holed up in the hotel and returned fire for hours, wearing heavy armour made from plough steel. Suffering 28 shot wounds, Ned was eventually captured while trying to rescue his men from the hotel. Dan Kelly, Joe Byrne and Steve Hart, along with two of the hostages, were killed.

Ned Kelly was brought to Melbourne to be tried, and was hanged on 11 November 1880. He met his end bravely; his last words are famously quoted as, 'Such is life.' His death mask, Gang armour and the gallows on which he died are on display in the Old Melbourne Gaol (p54). His 7500-word 'Jerilderie Letter' is considered a major historical document and is a 'treasure' of the State Library of Victoria (p54).

Painters Island Caravan Park CAMPGROUND $
(☑03-5721 3380; www.paintersislandcaravanpark.
com.au; Pinkerton Cres; unpowered/powered sites
from $30/32, cabins with bathrooms $85-160;
❄️🛜🏊) Set on 10 hectares along the banks
of the Ovens River, but close to the town centre, this impressive park has a playground, a
camp kitchen and a good range of cabins.

Hermitage Motor Inn MOTEL $$
(☑03-5721 7444; www.hermitagemotorinn.com.au;
cnr Cusack & Mackay Sts; d $115-160, f from $150;
❄️🛜🏊) Close to the town centre, the Hermi-
tage is one of Wang's better motels, with spa-
cious rooms, contemporary decor and a pool.

Quality Hotel Gateway Wangaratta HOTEL $$
(☑03-5721 8399; www.wangarattagateway.com.au;
29-37 Ryley St; d/f from $170/199; ❄️🛜🏊) On
the main road into town, this upmarket hotel has a clean-lined look, excellent facilities
(including a gym and heated outdoor pool)
and an attention to detail that elevates it
above other options scattered around town.

🍴 Eating & Drinking

There's a cafe scene along Murphy St and Reid
St, and a couple of good restaurants in town.

Rinaldo's Casa Cucina ITALIAN $$
(☑03-5721 8800; www.rinaldos.com.au; 8-10 Tone
Rd; mains $19-33; ☺ 6-10pm Tue-Thu, noon-2pm
& 6-10pm Fri & Sat) Formerly at the Dal Zotto
winery in Whitfield, Rinaldo's has moved
its hearty Northern Italian kitchen to this
industrial-sized venue in Wang, and is get-
ting plenty of attention. The seasonal menu
features fresh pasta dishes and modern
Mediterranean versions of steak and sea-
food; try the figs wrapped in prosciutto and
served with blue cheese. Ask about cooking
classes.

Vine Hotel PUB $$
(☑03-5721 2605; www.thevinehotel.net.au; 27 De-
tour Rd; mains $13-24; ☺noon-2pm daily, 6-8pm
Mon-Sat) Ned Kelly and his gang used to
hang out here; these days the food is better
and you're less likely to get shot. Go underground to the small museum and cellars.
The Vine is about 3km north of town, on the
road to Eldorado.

Buffalo Brewery PUB, BREWERY
(☑03-5726 9215; www.buffalobrewery.com.au;
1519 Boorhaman Rd, Boorhaman; ☺11am-8pm
Sun-Thu, to midnight Fri & Sat) At the Boorhaman Hotel, about 15km northwest of Wangaratta, this country pub-brewery produces
five award-winning beers, including a wheat
beer and a dark ale.

ℹ️ Information

Wangaratta Visitors Centre (☑03-5721 5711,
1800 801 065; www.visitwangaratta.com.au;
104 Murphy St; ☺9am-5pm; @) In the old
library, featuring displays, internet access, bike
hire and videos depicting local rail trails and
snippets from the annual Wangaratta Jazz &
Blues Festival.

ℹ️ Getting There & Away

Wangaratta lies 252km northeast of Melbourne
along the Hume Fwy (M31).

V/Line (☑1800 800 007; www.vline.com.au)
train and coach services operate at least five
times daily between Wangaratta and Melbourne's
Southern Cross Station ($26.60, 1½ to 3 hours).

Wodonga

POP 31,600

The border town of Wodonga is separated
from its NSW twin, Albury, by the Murray
River. Although a busy little town with a
lake formed off Wodonga Creek, most of the
attractions and the best of the accommodation are on the NSW side.

There are signed trails for the many walking and bike trails around Gateway Island,
along the Murray River and to the beautiful wetlands of **Sumsion Gardens**. This is
also the start of the **High Country Rail Trail**
(www.highcountryrailtrail.org.au), a cycling and
walking path that skirts around the southern end of Lake Hume to Old Tallangatta.

The **Army Museum Bandiana** (☑02-6055
2525; Anderson Rd; adult/child/family $5/2/10;
☺9.30am-5.30pm) displays a variety of war
weaponry, items from missions, and docu-
ments. There are also magnificent vintage
cars, including a Buick, Holden staff cars,
Chevy trucks, carriages and motorbikes.

For 24 years from the end of WWII,
Bonegilla, 10km east of Wodonga, was
Australia's first migrant-reception centre,
providing accommodation and training for
some 320,000 migrants. At the **Bonegilla
Migrant Experience** (☑02-6020 6912; www.
bonegilla.org.au; Bonegilla Rd; admission free,
group tours by appointment $5; ☺10am-4pm)
FREE you can visit some of the preserved
buildings and see photos and historical
memorabilia.

Gateway visitor information centre
(☑1300 796 222; www.alburywodongaaustralia.
com.au; Hume Hwy, Gateway Village; ☺9am-5pm)
has 24-hour touch-screen information and
an accommodation-booking service.

Wodonga is 323km northeast of Melbourne along the Hume Fwy (M31).

Understand Melbourne & Victoria

MELBOURNE & VICTORIA TODAY **306**
Melbourne's on a high and the regions have joined the party.
But will the good times continue?

HISTORY **308**
Victoria's rich and rollicking history doesn't require a textbook –
it's all around.

FOOD & DRINK **318**
It starts at breakfast and ends when you call time; welcome to a
culinary wonderland.

FASHION & SHOPPING **324**
Melbourne knows how to put on its best, from hipster cheek to
couture chic.

THE ARTS **326**
Pack your black skivvy: experimentation rules in the thriving
art scene.

SPORT **334**
Come watch the big men fly, or get out into the state's beautiful
outdoors.

Melbourne & Victoria Today

Melbourne may be a great place to live (and to visit), but maintaining its place at the top of the world and national liveability scale involves confronting the major issues of rising costs, urban planning and environmental sustainability. But of course Victoria is about more than just Melbourne, and regional Victorians have a different take on how those important questions are to be answered.

Top Films

The Castle (1997) Cult-comedy classic set in a working-class Melbourne suburb.
On the Beach (1957) Apocalypse Now-ish.
Picnic at Hanging Rock (1975) Elliptical, sensual classic.
Dogs in Space (1986) Chaotic chronicle of the city's punk past.
Animal Kingdom (2010) Menacing, moody crime-family thriller.
Red Hill (2010) 'Revisionist' Western/cop-thriller genre mash-up, set in breathtaking East Gippsland.

Top Playlist

'Carlton (Lygon Street Limbo)', Skyhooks
'Shivers', Boys Next Door
'Beautiful People', Australian Crawl
'Leaps and Bounds', Paul Kelly
'Under the Sun', Hunters & Collectors

Famous Victorians

St Mary MacKillop
Dame Nellie Melba
Barry Humphries
Nick Cave
Kylie Minogue
Cate Blanchett
Julian Assange

Melbourne's Liveability

Melbourne consistently ranks as one of the most liveable cities on earth. In 2013, and not for the first time, Melbourne basked in the title of the World's Most Liveable City according to the prestigious *Economist* Intelligence Unit. In the same year, *Monocle* magazine's quality of life index put Melbourne in a still-rather-enviable second (behind Copenhagen). So what makes Melbourne so good?

Melbourne always ranks highly when it comes to infrastructure and safety, while *Monocle*'s criteria takes in public transport, urban design and tolerance. And although the state (and Australia in general) hasn't been immune to the global financial crisis, Victoria has consistently recorded growth rates that are the envy of the industrialised world.

But the city does have some chinks in its armour. Perhaps Melbourne just couldn't win *Monocle*'s #1 ranking because climate and sunshine are among their criteria – Melbourne weather can be glorious, but it can also be wet, windy and changeable at a moment's notice. And then there's the spiralling cost of living. Salaries have largely kept pace, but everything from restaurant meals to hotel rooms have soared in recent years. To see what we mean, stop by a real-estate auction and watch the prices climb ever higher.

City Limits

Urban planning stands at the centre of public debate in Melbourne, not least because Melbourne's population is expected to almost double to eight million by 2050. All around its outer limits, new suburbs appear, often before transport infrastructure and other essential services are in place. And with inner Melbourne already out of reach for low-income home buyers and renters, these questions grow in importance with every passing year.

In the heart of the city, it's no less complicated. A decade ago, the shift to higher-density living saw the rise of the Docklands precinct and inner-city apartment complexes. Success, however, has been partial at best. A lack of after-hours life and a failure to develop the necessary services for those who remain in the centre after the sun sets continue to plague area development.

Connecting the two extremes of Melbourne's human geography could be one of its most controversial projects in a generation. The Liberal–National Party coalition of Premier Denis Napthine is pushing ahead with construction of the East West Link, an 18km-long, mostly underground freeway that will connect Melbourne's eastern suburbs with the west. With the loss of parkland in Royal Park, projected increases in traffic elsewhere and with no concomitant rise in public transport spending, many wonder whether the project (the first stage of which is due to be completed by 2019) will create more problems than it solves.

City–Rural Divide?

Country Victoria is so much more than a venue for a food lover's passions or a tree-changer's escape. It's also a pillar of the state's economy and the place where many of the state's most pressing environmental issues are being confronted.

The brown-coal power plants of Gippsland's Latrobe Valley may be a blight on the environment – the Hazelwood Power Station is the most polluting in the country – but they also supply 85% of the state's electricity. Victoria is Australia's most deforested state, with the highest number of threatened species. There's also an ongoing debate over whether grazing or logging should be allowed in national parks: the conservative government is generally in favour, predominantly city-based environmentalists less so. And then there are the water shortages in the state's north and wider Murray–Darling River Basin.

In country Victoria, these issues are very often seen primarily in terms of farmers' rights and important sources of employment for vulnerable communities. In the cities, they're environmental issues of wider global significance. And this city–rural divide is reflected, in part, in the state's political landscape: rural electorates are dominated by conservative independents or the National Party (which has its roots in rural farming communities), while the inner-city seat of Melbourne is the only lower-house seat in the country to be held by the Greens, whose federal MP Adam Bandt increased his majority at the 2013 election.

POPULATION: **5.74 MILLION**

AVERAGE WEEKLY EARNINGS: **$1338**

UNEMPLOYMENT RATE: **5.8%**

AREA OF VICTORIA: **227,415 SQ KM**

AREA OF GREATER MELBOURNE: **8806 SQ KM**

if Australia were 100 people

79 would speak English at home
3 would speak Chinese at home
2 would speak Italian at home
1 would speak Vietnamese at home
15 would speak another language at home

belief systems
(% of population)

64 Christian
19 Agnostic
2 Muslim
1 Hindu
12 Other

population per sq km

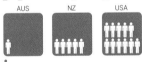

AUS   NZ   USA

≈ 3 people

History

Victoria's history is one of Australia's more picaresque tales. It begins with geological upheaval and flourishing Indigenous cultures, but the unravelling of the latter, which followed the European discovery of Australia in 1770, is a story of profound tragedy. The fraught and stop-start settlement of the state finally took hold with the discovery of gold in the mid-19th century – a find that thrust Victoria into the modern era, laying the foundation stones for the state's democracy, prosperity and multicultural make-up.

Creation Stories

A mere 120 million years ago, Australia broke away from the vast super-continent known as Gondwana, followed 40 million years later by another epic geological event – the separation of Australia from Antarctica. In prehistoric times, far lower sea levels exposed a land bridge between what is now Tasmania and Victoria. It was not until 10,000 years ago, with the rising sea levels that accompanied the end of the last Ice Age, that Victoria took on its current form as the southernmost extent of the Australian mainland.

Estimates suggest that before the Europeans arrived, Victoria's Aboriginal population was between 60,000 and 100,000; by the late 1840s it had dropped to 15,000. By 1860 scarcely 2000 Aboriginal people survived.

Victoria's human history begins somewhat later: the earliest records of Australia's Indigenous people inhabiting the land date back around 52,000 years. At the time, they hunted the giant marsupials that once roamed Australia, among them a species of wombat the size of a rhinoceros and possibly even a giant platypus as long as a metre.

The oral history of Indigenous Australians has its own version of Victoria's prehistory. For the Wurundjeri people, who lived in the catchment of the Yarra River where Melbourne is today, the land and the people were created in the Dreaming by the spirit Bunjil – 'the great one, old head-man, eagle hawk' – who continues to watch over all from Tharangalk-bek, the home of the spirits in the sky.

Indigenous Victoria

Victoria's Indigenous peoples lived in some 38 different dialect groups that spoke 10 separate languages. These groups, some matrilineal, others

TIMELINE	80 million years ago	50,000 BC	1770
	The Australian continent breaks away from Antarctica to form its own land mass.	The first humans colonise southeastern Australia. The people of the Kulin Nation live in the catchment of the Yarra River; various other tribes, speaking 38 dialects among them, are spread throughout Victoria.	Lieutenant Zachary Hicks becomes the first European to lay eyes on the Eastern Australian shoreline. Captain Cook will later name the spot in far-east Gippsland, 'Point Hicks'.

patrilineal, were further divided into clans and sub-clans, each with its own complex system of customs and laws, and each claiming custodianship of a distinct area of land. Despite this, the British considered the continent to be *terra nullius* – 'a land belonging to no one'.

The Wurundjeri were a tribe of the Woiwurrung, one of five distinct language groups belonging to southern Victoria's Kulin Nation. They often traded and celebrated with their coastal counterparts, the Boonwurrung, among the towering red gums, tea trees and ferns of the river's edge, as well as with other Kulin clans from the north and west.

As the flood-prone rivers and creeks broke their banks in winter, bark shelters were built north in the ranges. Possums were hunted for their meat and skinned to make calf-length cloaks. During the summer, camps were made along the Yarra and Maribyrnong Rivers and Merri Creek. Food – game, grubs, seafood, native greens and roots – was plentiful. Wurundjeri men and women were compelled to marry out of the tribe, requiring complex forms of diplomacy. Ceremonies and bouts of ritual combat were frequent.

Colonial Arrivals

Close to sunrise on 19 April 1770, Lieutenant Zachary Hicks, on watch duty on board the *Endeavour*, spied a series of low sand hills. He immediately called his commander, Captain Cook. Although they didn't know at the time whether it was an island or part of the mainland, it would later prove to be the first European sighting of Australia's east coast (although Dutch seamen had been intermittently exploring the west coast for more than a century). Point Hicks is now part of Croajingolong National Park, between Cape Conran Coastal Park and Mallacoota. In 1788, the first colony was established at Sydney Cove in New South Wales (NSW).

The first European settlement in Victoria in 1803 didn't have an auspicious start. With a missed mail-ship communiqué and a notoriously supercilious British government calling the shots, Surveyor-General Charles Grimes' recommendation – that the best place to found a southern settlement would be by the banks of the 'Freshwater River' (aka the Yarra) – went unheeded. The alternative, Sorrento, on what is now the Mornington Peninsula, was an unmitigated disaster from the beginning; as Lieutenant David Collins pointed out to his superiors, you can't survive long without drinkable water. The colony moved to Van Diemen's Land (Tasmania), but one extremely tenacious convict escapee, William Buckley, was left behind; he was still on the lam when John Batman turned up a few decades later.

After the failed Sorrento colony it was 20-odd years before explorers made their way overland to Port Phillip and another decade before a settlement was founded on the southwest coast at Portland. Around the same time, in the early 1830s, the Surveyor-General of NSW, Major

Indigenous Victoria

Koorie Heritage Trust, Melbourne

Bunjilaka Aboriginal Cultural Centre, Melbourne Museum

Brambuk Cultural Centre, Halls Gap

Harry Nanya Tours, Mildura

Tower Hill Natural History Centre, Warrnambool

Krowathunkoolong Keeping Place, Bairnsdale

Cape Conran Coastal Park

1803	1834	1835	1837
Victoria's first European settlement is at Sorrento. It is an unmitigated disaster, with no fresh water to be found; the settlers abandon the site after six months and relocate to Van Diemen's Land (Tasmania).	Portland pioneer Edward Henty, his family and a flock of sheep arrive from Van Diemen's Land, marking the first permanent European settlement in the region that will become Victoria.	John Batman meets with a group of local Aboriginal people and trades a casket of blankets, mirrors, scissors, handkerchiefs and other assorted curios for around 2400 sq km of land.	The military surveyor Robert Hoddle draws up plans for the city of Melbourne, laying out a geometric grid of broad streets in a rectangular pattern on the northern side of the Yarra River.

Thomas Mitchell, crossed the Murray River (then called the Hume) near Swan Hill and travelled southwest. He was delighted to find the rich volcanic plains of the Western District. His glowing reports of such fertile country included him dubbing the area 'Australia Felix' (Fortunate Australia) and encouraged pastoralists to venture into the area with large flocks of sheep and herds of cattle.

It was not until 1835, when Australian-born entrepreneur John Batman sailed from Van Diemen's Land to arrive in what we now know as Victoria, that the process of settling the area began in earnest. He would later write of travelling through 'beautiful land...rather sandy, but the sand black and rich, covered with kangaroo grass about ten inches high and as green as a field of wheat'. He noted stone dams for catching fish built across creeks, trees that bore the deep scars of bark harvesting, and women bearing wooden water containers and woven bags holding stone tools. However, the Indigenous people's profound spiritual relationship with the land and intimate knowledge of story, ceremony and season would be irrevocably damaged within a few short years.

As European settlement fanned out through Victoria, and the city of Melbourne transformed from pastoral outpost to a heaving, gold-flushed metropolis in scarcely 30 years, the cumulative effects of dispossession, alcohol and increasing acts of organised violence resulted in a shocking decline in Victoria's Indigenous population. From the earliest days, the colonial authorities evicted Aboriginal people from their traditional homes. By the early 1860s the Board for the Protection of Aborigines had begun to gather together surviving Aboriginal people in reserves run by Christian missionaries at Ebenezer, Framlingham, Lake Condah, Lake Tyers, Ramahyuck and Coranderrk. These reserves developed into self-sufficient farming communities and gave their residents a measure of 'independence' (along with twice-daily prayers and new boots at Christmas), but at the same time inflicted irreversible damage.

Around 25,000 people in Victoria have Aboriginal heritage, including about 15,000 in Melbourne and 5000 in the Shepparton region.

The Birth of Melbourne

'Modern' Melbourne's story begins in the 1830s. John Batman, an ambitious grazier from Van Diemen's Land, sailed into Port Phillip Bay in mid-1835 with an illegal contract of sale. (Britain's colonial claims of terra nullius relied on the fiction that the original inhabitants did not own the land on which they lived and hence could not sell it.) He sought out some tribal elders and on a tributary of the Yarra – it's been speculated that it was the Merri Creek, in today's Northcote – found some 'fine-looking' men, with whom he exchanged blankets, scissors, mirrors and handkerchiefs for over half a million acres (2400 sq km) of land surrounding Port Phillip.

Despite the fact that the Aboriginal people from Sydney who were accompanying Batman couldn't speak a word of the local language and

1838	1851	1854	1854
The *Melbourne Advertiser*, Melbourne's first newspaper, is first published, with 10 weekly handwritten editions; in 1839 it rolls off the presses daily as the *Port Phillip Patriot & Melbourne Advertiser*.	Victoria separates from the colony of New South Wales. Gold is discovered in central Victoria and the world's richest gold rush is on.	Gold miners rebel over unfair licences and conditions, raising the Southern Cross flag at the Eureka Stockade. Brutally suppressed by soldiers and police, their actions enter into Australia's nation-building mythology.	Australia's first significant rail line, from Melbourne Terminus on Flinders St, across the Yarra, to Station Pier in Port Melbourne, opens.

vice versa, Batman brokered the deal and signatures were gathered from the 'local chiefs' (three suspiciously called Jaga-jaga and all with remarkably similar penmanship). He noted a low, rocky falls several miles up the Yarra, where the Queens Bridge is today. Upstream fresh water made it a perfect place for, as Batman described it, 'a village'. Batman then returned to Van Diemen's Land to ramp up the Port Phillip Association.

It's at this point that the historical narrative becomes as turbid as the Yarra itself. Before Batman could get back to his new settlement of Bearbrass (along with 'Yarra', another cocksure misappropriation of the local dialect), John Pascoe Fawkner, a Launceston publican and childhood veteran of the failed Sorrento colony, got wind of the spectacular opportunity at hand. He promptly sent off a small contingent of settlers aboard the schooner *Enterprize*, who, upon arrival, started building huts and establishing a garden. On Batman's return there were words, and later furious bidding wars over allotments of land. Historians regard the two in various ways, but Fawkner's foremost place in Victoria's story was sealed by the fact he outlived the syphilitic Batman by several decades. Despite the bickering, hubris and greed of the founders, the settlement grew quickly; around a year later, almost 200 brave souls (and some tens of thousands of sheep) had thrown their lot in with the new colony.

New South Wales wasn't happy. Governor Bourke dispatched Captain William Lonsdale south in 1836, quashing any notion of ownership by the Port Phillip Association. Surveyors were sent for and the task of drawing up plans for a city began. Robert Hoddle, the surveyor in charge, arrived with the governor in March 1837, and was horrified by the lack of order, both that of his unruly staff – who had absconded upriver to get drunk or shoot kangaroos one too many times – and the antipodean topography itself. For Hoddle, it was all about straight lines; his grid, demarcated by the Yarra and what was once a 'hillock' where Southern Cross Station now lies, is Melbourne's defining feature. Land sales commenced almost immediately, and so the surveying continued, but with little Romantic notion of exploration or discovery. It was, by all accounts, a real-estate feeding frenzy. The British were well served by their *terra nullius* concept, as returns on investment were fabulous. The rouseabout 'Bearbrass' was upgraded to the rather more distinguished 'Melbourne', after the serving British prime minister.

During these years, the earliest provincial towns were also established along Victoria's coast, around the original settlement of Portland to the southwest and Port Albert to the southeast. Early inland towns rose up around self-sufficient communities of sheep stations, which at this stage were still the main source of Victoria's fast-increasing fortunes. This, however, was soon to change.

Various kings, queens and assorted contemporary bigwigs (including Governor Bourke himself) got the nod in the naming of Melbourne's streets.

1856–60	1858	1859	1880
Stonemasons building the University of Melbourne strike and the struggle for a shorter working day begins; the subsequent 'eight-hour day' campaign transforms Victorian working conditions.	The Melbourne Football Club is formed. Australian Rules football's first recorded match takes place between Scotch College and Melbourne Grammar School.	Thomas Austin releases rabbits onto his property at Winchelsea, west of Melbourne, beginning a rabbit infestation that will spread across the southern part of Australia and continue to this day.	The International Exhibition is held at the Royal Exhibition Building in Melbourne's Carlton Gardens. More than a million visitors come to see the fruits of the Empire.

Golden Years

In 1840 a local landowner described the fledgling city of Melbourne as 'a goldfield without the gold'. Indeed, with a steady stream of immigrants and confidence-building prosperity, there had been growing calls for separation from convict-ridden, rowdy New South Wales. By the end of 1850, the newly minted colony of Victoria had got its wish to go it alone. This quickly seemed like a cruel stroke of fate: gold was discovered near Bathurst in New South Wales in early 1851, sparking a mass exodus. Pastoral riches or not, there was every chance that without a viable labour force (many had already succumbed to the siren call of California) the colony would wither and die.

Melbourne jewellers had for some time been doing a clandestine trade with shepherds who came to town with small gold nuggets secreted in their kerchiefs. Wary of the consequences of a gold rush on civic order, but with few other options, the city's leading men declared that gold must indeed be found. As was the Victorian way, a committee was formed and a reward was offered. Slim pickings were discovered in the Pyrenees and Warrandyte, before a cluey Californian veteran looked north to Clunes. Just over a ridge, in what was to become Ballarat, was the proverbial pot at the end of the rainbow. It wasn't long before miners were hauling 27kg of the magic mineral into Geelong at a time, and the rush was well and truly on.

The news spread around the world and brought hopefuls from Britain, Ireland, China, Germany, Italy, the US and the Caribbean. By August 1852, 15,000 new arrivals were disembarking in Melbourne each month. Crews jumped ship and hotfooted it to the diggings, stranding ships at anchor. Chaos reigned. Everyone needed a place to stay, even if only for a night or two, and when there was no room at the inn, stables were let for exorbitant amounts. Wives and children were often dumped in town while husbands continued on to the diggings. Governor La Trobe despaired of his grand civic vision, as shanties and eventually a complete tent village sprung up. Canvas Town, on the south side of the Yarra, housed more than 8000 people.

Catherine Spence, a journalist and social reformer, visited Melbourne at the height of the hysteria and primly observed 'this convulsion has unfixed everything. Religion is neglected, education despised...everyone is engrossed with the simple object of making money in a very short time.' The 567,000kg of gold found between 1851 and 1860 represented a third of the world's total. That said, relatively few diggers struck it lucky. The licensing system favoured large holdings, policing was harsh and scratching out a living proved so difficult for many that dissent became as common as hope had been a few years before.

For some, 1852 was indeed a golden year, but by 1854, simmering tensions exploded in Ballarat.

Chinese migrants founded Melbourne's Chinatown in Little Bourke St in 1851, making it the longest continuous Chinese settlement in any Western country.

1883–85	1883	1884	1901
The railway line linking Sydney and Melbourne opens in 1883, followed two years later by Melbourne's first cable-tram service, running from the city centre to Richmond.	Yarra Falls, a rock bridge spanning the Yarra at Customs House that divided fresh water from salt and was used as a crossing, is removed by explosives.	HV McKay's invention of the Sunshine stripper harvester in Ballarat makes leaps and bounds in the efficient harvest of cereal crops, putting Australia on the map as a leading exporter of grain.	Australia's collection of colonies become a nation. The Federation's first parliament is held at the Royal Exhibition Building; parliament will sit in Melbourne for the next 27 years.

Growing Inequalities

As the easily won gold began to run out, Victorian diggers despaired of ever striking it rich, and the inequality between themselves and the privileged few who held the land that they worked stoked a fire of dissent.

Men joined together in teams and worked cold, wet, deep shafts. Every miner, whether or not gold was found, had to pay a licence fee of 30 shillings a month. This was collected by policemen who had the power to chain those who couldn't pay to a tree, often leaving them there until their case was heard.

In September 1854, Governor Hotham ordered that the hated licence hunts be carried out twice a week. A month later a miner was murdered near the Ballarat Hotel after an argument with the owner, James Bentley. When Bentley was found not guilty by a magistrate (who happened to be his business associate), miners rioted and burned the hotel down. Though Bentley was retried and found guilty, the rioting miners were also jailed, which enraged the miners.

The Ballarat Reform League was born. They called for the abolition of licence fees and for democratic reform, including the miners' rights to vote (universal suffrage was yet to exist) and greater opportunity to purchase land.

Gold Rush Sights

Sovereign Hill, Ballarat

Central Deborah Goldmine, Bendigo

Castlemaine Market building

Walhalla

Maldon

Beechworth

The Eureka Stockade: Victoria's Rebellion

On 29 November 1854, about 800 miners tossed their licences into a bonfire during a mass meeting, then, led by Irishman Peter Lalor, built a stockade at Eureka, where they prepared to fight for their rights. A veteran of Italy's independence struggle named Raffaello Carboni called on the crowd, 'irrespective of nationality, religion and colour', to salute the Southern Cross as the 'refuge of all the oppressed from all the countries on earth'.

On 3 December the government ordered troopers (the mounted colonial police) to attack the stockade. There were only 150 miners within the makeshift barricades and the fight lasted a short but devastating 20 minutes, leaving 25 miners and four troopers dead.

Though the rebellion was short-lived, the miners won the sympathy and support of many Victorians. The government deemed it wise to acquit the leaders of the charge of high treason. It's interesting to note that only four of the miners were Australian-born: the others hailed from Ireland, Britain, Italy, Greece, Germany, Russia, Holland, France, Switzerland, Spain, Portugal, Sweden, the US, Canada and the West Indies.

The licence fee was abolished and replaced by a Miners' Right, which cost one pound a year. This gave miners the right to search for gold; to fence in, cultivate and build a dwelling on a piece of land; and to vote

By 1840, when the young Queen Victoria took the throne, Melbourne had 10,000 (occasionally upstanding) citizens and was looking decidedly like a city.

1923	1925	1928	1930
Vegemite, a savoury sandwich spread and Australia's most enduring culinary quirk, is invented in Melbourne, using autolysis to break down yeast cells from waste provided by Carlton & United Breweries.	The first Australian-built Ford Model Ts roll off an improvised production line in a disused wool store in Geelong.	Australia's first set of traffic lights begins operation at the junction of Collins and Swanston Sts in Melbourne.	A plucky young chestnut gelding called Phar Lap wins the Melbourne Cup. His winning streak endears him to the nation and he remains one of the most popular exhibits in the Melbourne Museum.

GOLD

for members of the Legislative Assembly. The rebel miner Peter Lalor became a member of parliament some years later. Eureka remains a powerful symbol in Australian culture, standing as it does for the treasured notions of workers' rights, democracy and 'a fair go for all'.

Sadly, goldfield brotherhood in 1854 had its limits. The 40,000 miners who arrived from southern China to try their luck on 'the new gold mountain' were often a target of individual violence and systemic prejudice. Still, the Chinese community persevered, and it has to this day been a strong and enduring presence in the city of Melbourne and throughout regional Victoria.

More than 90% of Australia's $100 million gold haul in the 1850s was found in Victoria.

Boom & Crash

Gold brought undreamt-of riches and a seemingly endless supply of labour to Victoria. Melbourne became 'Marvellous Melbourne', one of the world's most beautiful Victorian-era cities, known for its elegance – as well as its extravagance. Grand expressions of its confidence include the University of Melbourne, Parliament House, the State Library and the Victorian Mint. Magnificent public parks and gardens were planted both in the city and in towns across the state. By the 1880s, Melbourne had become Australia's financial, industrial and cultural hub. The 'Paris of the Antipodes' claim was invoked: the city was flush with stylish arcades, and grand homes were decorated with ornate iron balconies. The city

---

OUR NED

Victorian bushranger Ned Kelly (1854–80) became a national legend when he and his gang donned homemade armour in an attempt to deflect the bullets of several dozen members of the constabulary. Kelly's story, set among the hills, valleys and plains of northeastern Victoria, has a Robin Hood–like quality, as well as the whiff of an Irish rebel song.

Kelly's passionate, articulate letters, handed to hostages while he was robbing banks, paint a vivid picture of the harsh injustice of his time, as well as his lyrical intelligence. These, as well as his ability to evade capture for so long, led to public outrage when he was sentenced to death and finally hanged at the Old Melbourne Gaol in 1880.

The enduring popularity of the Kelly legend is evident in the mass of historical and fictional accounts that continue to be written to this day. His life has also inspired a long string of films, from the world's first feature film, *The Story of the Kelly Gang* (1906), to two more recent versions, both simply called *Ned Kelly,* with the first starring Mick Jagger (1970) and the second, the late Heath Ledger (2003). A series of paintings by Sidney Nolan featuring Kelly in his armour are among Australia's most recognisable artworks. In 2001, Australian novelist Peter Carey won the Man Booker Prize for his *True History of the Kelly Gang*.

1953	1956	1964	1967
The first Italian Gaggia espresso machine is imported to Melbourne. Soon University Cafe in Carlton, Pellegrini's in the city and Don Camillo in North Melbourne are serving the city's first cappuccinos.	Melbourne hosts the summer Olympic Games. Despite this mark of sporting bonhomie, the event is marked with political unrest due to the Suez crisis and the Soviet invasion of Hungary.	The Beatles visit Melbourne, staying in the since-demolished Southern Cross Hotel on Bourke St and creating city-wide 'youthquake' hysteria.	Prime Minister Harold Holt disappears while swimming at Cheviot Beach near Portsea on the Mornington Peninsula; his body is never recovered.

spread eastwards and northwards over the surrounding flat grasslands and southwards along Port Phillip Bay. A public transport system of cable trams and railways spread into the growing suburbs.

Regional cities, especially those servicing the goldfields, such as Ballarat, Bendigo and Beechworth, also reaped the rewards of sudden prosperity, leaving a legacy of magnificent Victorian architecture throughout the state. 'Selection Acts' enabled many settlers and frustrated miners to take up small farm lots (selections). Although a seemingly reformist, democratic move, these farms were often too small to forge a real living from, and life in the bush proved tough. Grinding poverty and the heavy hand of the law led to some settlers turning to bushranging (rural armed robberies of money or livestock), variously considered a life of crime and/ or an act of subversion against British rule, depending on which side of the economic and religious divide you were on.

In 1880 (and again in 1888) Melbourne hosted an International Exhibition, pulling well over a million visitors. The Royal Exhibition Building was constructed for this event; Melbourne's soaring paean to Empire and the industrial revolution is one of the few 19th-century exhibition spaces of its kind still standing.

This flamboyant boast to the world was, however, to be Marvellous Melbourne's swansong. In 1889, after years of unsustainable speculation, the property market collapsed and the decades that followed were marked by severe economic depression.

A Difficult Half-Century

Despite the symbolic honour of becoming the new nation's temporary capital in 1901, Melbourne's fortunes didn't really rally until after WWI, and by then its 'first city' status had been lost to Sydney. When WWI broke out, large numbers of young men from throughout Victoria fought in the trenches of Europe and the Middle East, with enormous losses.

There was a renewed spirit of expansion and construction in Victoria in the 1920s, but this came to a grinding halt with another economic disaster, the Great Depression (in 1931 almost a third of breadwinners were unemployed). When war broke out once again in 1939, Melbourne became the heart of the nation's wartime efforts, and later the centre for US operations in the Pacific. It was boom time again, though no time for celebration.

The state's Victorian heritage did not fare well during the postwar construction boom – when Melbourne hosted the Olympic Games in 1956, hectares of historic buildings were bulldozed with abandon; this continued apace during the new boom days of the 1980s as well. However, significant parts of the city and many goldfield towns still echo with Victorian ambition and aspiration.

Kelly Gang Haunts

Glenrowan

Warby Range State Park

Beechworth

Old Melbourne Gaol

The Welcome Stranger, discovered in 1869 a few centimetres under the ground in the central Victorian town of Moliagul, was, at 72kg, the largest alluvial gold nugget ever found. At the time of its unearthing there were no scales capable of weighing a nugget of its size.

HISTORY A DIFFICULT HALF-CENTURY

1970	1977	1982–84	1988
Melbourne's West Gate Bridge collapses during construction, killing 35 workers; the impact and explosion that follows is heard more than 20km away. Melbourne's Tullamarine Airport opens in the same year.	The Centenary Test, commemorating the first cricket test match between Australia and England, is played at the MCG. Amazingly, Australia triumphs by the same margin as the original: 45 runs.	The Victorian Arts Centre, built to the design of Roy Grounds, opens in stages at the site now known as Southbank after a construction period of some 11 years.	The Australian Tennis Open moves from Kooyong to the hard-court venues of Melbourne Park. Attendance jumps by 90%, to well over 250,000 spectators.

Melbourne's Multicultural Midcentury

In 1901, one of the first things the newly created Australian government did was to pass legislation with the express wish to protect its security and assert its sense of identity as a member of the British Empire. The so-called White Australia policy restricted the entry of non-Europeans, and was followed a couple of years later by the Commonwealth Naturalisation Act, which excluded all non-Europeans from attaining citizenship, and limited both citizens' and non-citizens' ability to bring even immediate family to Australia. This subsequent piece of legislation was particularly devastating to Victoria's Chinese community, which maintained strong family and business ties with China. Victoria's early history of diversity came to an abrupt end.

Although the state's loyalties and most of its legal and cultural ties to Britain remained firm, the 1920s did herald change, as small Italian and Greek communities settled in both the city and the state's agricultural heartland, part of a renewed spirit of expansion and construction at the time. They set about establishing food production companies, cafes, restaurants, fish-and-chip shops, delis and grocers; the efforts of these small-business pioneers were to prove an inspiration for a new generation of migrants in the 1940s and '50s.

Close to a million non-British immigrants arrived in Australia during the 20 years after WWII; at first Jewish refugees from eastern and central Europe, then larger numbers from Italy, Greece, the Netherlands, Yugoslavia, Turkey and Lebanon. With the demise of the blatantly racist White Australia policy in early 1973, many migrants from Southeast Asia also settled in Victoria. These postwar migrants also embraced the opportunity to set up small businesses, adding a vibrancy and character to their new neighbourhoods, such as Carlton, Collingwood, Richmond, Brunswick and Footscray. Melbourne's cultural life was transformed by these communities, and diversity gradually became an accepted, and treasured, way of life.

During Melbourne's years as the capital, the city's population of just over half a million people was the largest in Australia, and in the British Empire it was second in size only to London.

Political & Social Machinations

Victoria's historical reputation as something of a conservative counterpoint to the more radical politics of racy Sydney was born as far back as the 19th century, when the money that flooded the state during the gold-rush years established Victoria as one of the wealthiest places in Australia. Family dynasties grew up and the powerful families that controlled the business and political levers of the state made Melbourne one of the most powerful cities in the country – hence its choice as the nation's temporary capital from 1901. By the middle of the 20th century, Melbourne was a conservative city, the seat of the state's old-money

1992	2002	2006	2006
Southgate shopping centre, built on a former industrial site, opens, connecting the Arts Centre with the city and marking the start of massive redevelopment of Melbourne's waterfront spaces.	Federation Square opens – a year late for the centenary of Federation – amid controversy about its final design and cost ($440 million), but to public praise.	With the failure of late-winter and spring rainfalls and the second-driest conditions since 1900, water restrictions are introduced across Victoria.	Melbourne hosts the Commonwealth Games, the largest sporting event ever to be held in the city: in numbers of teams, athletes and events it eclipses the 1956 Olympics.

A MULTICULTURAL STATE

Victoria's multicultural make-up continues to diversify. Around one out of every four Victorians was born overseas and Melbourne is home to people from, at last count, 180 countries. Together they speak 233 languages and dialects, and adhere to 116 religions. The largest group of foreign-born residents comes from the UK, more than double that of any other country. The other main source countries are Italy, Vietnam, China, New Zealand, Greece and India.

families and still Australia's economic capital. This history is reflected in the fact that conservative political forces – the Liberal Party, usually in coalition with the predominantly rural National Party – held power in Victoria from 1955 to 1982.

But things were changing. During the early 1970s, a burgeoning counterculture's experiments with radical theatre, drugs and rock 'n' roll rang out through the Melbourne suburb of Carlton. By the later years of that decade, Melbourne's reputation as a prim 'establishment' city was further challenged by the emergence of a frantically subversive art, music, film and fashion scene that launched bands like the Birthday Party onto the world stage. During the real-estate boom of the 1980s, a wave of glamorous shops, nightclubs and restaurants made way for Melbourne's emergence as Australia's capital of cool. Changes to the licensing laws in the 1990s saw a huge growth of small bars, cafes and venues – and the birth of the laneway phenomenon.

These changes were reflected in the political arena. A left-centre Labor Party government held power for 10 years from 1982, and it was during this period that Victoria's reputation as a seat for progessive politics and as a centre for the arts was born. In 1992, the Liberal Party, led by Jeff Kennett, won a landslide victory in statewide elections. Although from the conservative side of politics, Kennett pursued a quite radical agenda, modernising many government institutions but alienating large sections of the community (particularly when it came to school reforms) in the process. An unexpected victory for the Labor Party in 1999 ushered in a decade of left-of-centre rule – a significant part of their success was their surprisingly good electoral results in regional Victoria. The latest twist came in December 2010, when a Liberal–National Party coalition came to government. They remained in power at the time of writing, with the next elections due in late 2014.

2009	2010	2010	2011
Victoria records its hottest temperatures on record. The Black Saturday bushfires that follow leave 173 people dead, more than 2000 homes destroyed and 4500 sq km burned out.	Adam Bandt becomes the first member of the Greens Party to be elected to the federal House of Representatives in a general election. He retains the inner-city seat of Melbourne in the 2013 federal election.	The conservative Liberal–National Party coalition returns to power in the Victorian state parliament, after 11 years in the political wilderness.	Victoria is devastated by the worst 'flood events' in its recorded history, with the central and northern parts of the state worst hit, including the towns of Horsham, Shepparton and Swan Hill.

Food & Drink

Victoria's food and drink scene is one of almost limitless choice, with a constant flow of new ideas and new tastes. While Melbourne doesn't have the deeply ingrained traditions and profound self-confidence of, say, Paris or Tokyo, it has an exuberant culinary culture and a talent for innovation and adaptation – and a constantly evolving scene where new cafes, bars and restaurants open on a weekly basis.

From Fine Dining to Small Plates

At the top of the city's food chain, fine dining thrives. While many Melbourne chefs experiment widely, mixing and matching techniques and ingredients, you'll rarely find chefs doing fusion for fusion's sake. There's too much respect for providence and context. You'll instead find menus that rove across regions and riff on influences. Modern Australian cuisine is a search to find a nation's own unique food and is hard to define. Some chefss incorporate native ingredients, such as Shannon Bennett at Vue de Monde, Ben Shewry at Attica and Fitzroy's Charcoal Lane, while other chefs incorporate both modern Mediterranean and Asian ideas and flavours to greater or lesser degrees: Andrew McConnell at Fitzroy's Cutler & Co, St Kilda's Golden Fields and the city centre's Cumulus Inc manages to create a particularly thoughtful version of this style.

There's a long tradition of posh Italian dining in the city and it's often exemplary, with chefs such as Guy Grossi at Grossi Florentino. Mediterranean is also done with high-end flair and a modern sensibility by chefs such as Frank Camorra at MoVida and George Calombaris at Press Club and Gazi.

More recently, the city has been taken over by a growing fleet of Mexican restaurants ranging from upmarket chic to cheap and cheerful, many of them great-tasting and authentic. Mamasita is one of the long-standing originals to kick it all off and is still the best. The other dining trend popping up around town is the advent of food from the USA, ranging from Southern-style cooking to diner and deli fare, as well as 'dude food' where pulled pork features heavily.

Regional Victoria also has several 'destination' restaurants. Some fit the stereotype of hearty country fare, such as the 'agriturismo'-styled Sardinian cuisine at the Tea Rooms at Yarck. Others, such as acclaimed chef Dan Hunter's Brae at Birregurra (in the Otways), surprise with sophistication and creativity.

Gourmet Towns

Kyneton

Milawa

Beechworth

Red Hill

Mildura

NO RESERVATIONS

A recent trend in Melbourne's fine-dining scene has many of the city's hottest restaurants (MoVida, Mamasita, Longrain and Chin Chin, to name a few) taking the approach of a 'no bookings' policy. The move has received its share of love and criticism but is mostly aimed at delivering more flexibility and spontaneity. Most places will take your mobile number and call once a spot has opened so you're not awkwardly hanging around waiting – or else people make a drink at the bar or a pre-dinner stroll part of their night out.

THE GHOSTS OF DINNERS PAST

The site of Melbourne was known for its edible delights long before John Batman set eyes on the natural falls of the Yarra. The Wurundjeri thrived because of the area's incredible bounty: the wetlands that spread south of the Yarra were teeming with life, and the river itself brimmed with fish, eels and shellfish. Depending on the season, Indigenous 'Melburnians' would have eaten roast kangaroo, waterfowl, fish and eel, as well as greens, grubs, yam daisies and a sweet cordial concocted from banksia blossoms.

The first Europeans didn't stop to notice the veritable native feast they had stumbled upon, but instead quickly went about planting European crops and tending large flocks of sheep. Although many new arrivals were astounded by the ready supply of fresh food – especially the Irish, who were escaping the famine of the 1840s – the early settlers dined mainly on mutton, bread and butter, tea, beer and rum. (Though it's hard to imagine that those familiar with the gentle art of poaching didn't help themselves to ducks and geese.)

Given that there's always so much to try, city dwellers love to eat out often, rather than saving up restaurants for celebratory big nights out. Melbourne really comes into its own when it comes to a casual, grazing style of dining. Small and large plates override the rigid three-course chronology, but an informal menu and more modest price tag don't mean that high-quality produce or attention to detail are sacrificed.

In a similar manner, bar food is no longer seen as a mere consort to booze, but something that makes for an equal marriage of tastes and experiences. This kind of 'smart casual' eating out is an easy way to join the locals, and also a great way to sample widely without the price shock of fine dining. Pub grub is also a big part of Melbourne's eating-out repertoire, and ranges from a number of upmarket gastropub restaurants to basic counter-meal service, with nostalgic dishes such as bangers and mash (sausages and mashed potatoes), steaks, parmas (chicken parmigiana), roasts and curries.

There's no shortage of informal food that's cooked with love and is great value for money. Cafes often serve heartier dishes at lunchtime, and casual venues with wine licences are not uncommon. Look for authentic dishes from a smattering of cuisines from across the globe. A steaming bowl of *pho* (Vietnamese soup), a square of spanakopita (spinach and feta pie), a teriyaki salmon *maki* (hand roll) or a provolone-and-prosciutto *piadina* (Italian flatbread) will probably leave you change from $10 – and without any doubt about Melbourne's status as a great food city.

Dishing Up Diversity

Take 140 cultures, mix and let simmer for a few decades. While the recipe might not be quite that simple, Victoria's culinary habits are truly multicultural. Many Melburnians have grown up with at least one other culinary heritage besides the rather grim Anglo-Australian fare of the mid-20th century – plus they're generally also inveterate travellers, which makes for a city of adventurous, if often highly critical, palates.

'Mod Oz' cooking is a loose term that describes a mix of British, European, Asian and Middle Eastern techniques and ingredients, with a seasonal, fresh-produce-driven philosophy similar to Californian cuisine. There's a base of borrowed traditions, yes, but its style and attitude is unique. The Melbourne manifestation (and the state's culinary offerings in general) tends more towards European and Mediterranean tastes, rather than Sydney's firmly Pacific Rim take on the cuisine. This is both a product of the city's very untropical climate – with four distinct seasons and strongly demarked seasonal crops – and also due to the strong impact that Melbourne's Italian, Greek, Eastern European and Middle Eastern communities

The Wine Map of Victoria by Max Allen is a great visual guide to the topography, climate and most widely planted grape varieties of the state; it also details 900-plus cellar doors, wineries and vineyards.

VEG OUT

Vegetarians and vegans (and even raw-food enthusiasts) will have no trouble finding restaurants that cater specifically to them in Melbourne, particularly in neighbourhoods such as Fitzroy and St Kilda.

There will also be at least a couple of dishes on most restaurant menus that will please, and few restaurateurs will look askance at special requests. Many fine-dining restaurants (Vue de Monde, Attica, Moon Under Water, etc) offer vegetarian degustation tasting menus, and with advance warning these can usually be made dairy-free.

Most Asian and Indian restaurants will have large meatless menus, but with Chinese, Vietnamese and Thai cooking you'll need to be clear that you don't want the common additives of oyster or fish sauce. Casual Japanese places also have many vegetarian options, though similarly you'll need to ask if they can prepare your dish with *dashi* (stock) that hasn't been made with bonito fish (ask if they have mushroom or seaweed *dashi* instead).

had on the city from the 1950s onwards. But that's not to say that you won't find wonderful Asian cooking and a host of varied Asian influences as the city continues to absorb and reinvent these traditions, too.

Melbourne has long been a diverse city, but apart from the long-standing influence of the Chinese community via numerous restaurants and importing business, tastes didn't really begin to shift from the Anglo-Celtic basics until the postwar period. As well as importing the goods they couldn't do without (such as olive oil), the city's southern and eastern European migrants set to producing coffee, bread, cheeses and smallgoods, which gradually found their way from specialist delis into mainstream supermarkets. These communities also helped shape the agricultural traditions of the state, bringing new crops and production methods to a land that often resembled the parts of the Mediterranean they had left behind. The Vietnamese, Lebanese and Turkish migrants that followed in the 1970s also had a lasting impact on the way Victorians eat. Many of the state's culinary leading lights and rising stars are the children or grandchildren of these first-generation migrants (or are migrants themselves): Guy Grossi, Greg Malouf, Karen Martini, Con Christopoulos, George Calombaris, Rita Macali, Joseph Abboud, Shane Delia, Rosa Mitchell and Pietro Porcu, to name just a few.

While Victoria's eating habits have absorbed and incorporated a range of cuisines, creating something new in the process, many of the original inspirations are represented in kitchens across the city, and are constantly joined by those catering to its newest arrivals. Melbourne's ethnic restaurants, once clustered in tight community hubs, now flourish all over the city, though there are still loosely dedicated zones. Richmond's Victoria St is packed with Vietnamese restaurants and provedores while the western suburb of Footscray draws those looking for the most authentic Vietnamese, Laotian and Cambodian food, as well as great East African and Indian restaurants. Lygon St, Carlton, has long been home to simple red-sauce Italian cooking – with notable innovators such as D.O.C – and its coffee and Italian delis are excellent. Chinatown, in the city centre, is home to Flower Drum, one of Australia's most renowned restaurants of any culinary persuasion, and there are places doing regional cuisines such as Sichuan- and Beijing-style dumplings up every other laneway. You'll find Japanese *izakayas* (pubs) and Korean restaurants here, too. Just to the north, Lonsdale St has a handful of Greek taverns and bars. The northern suburb of Brunswick has a number of wonderful Middle Eastern bakers and grocers as well as cafes and restaurants. A large international student population has seen many Indian, Malaysian and Indonesian places spring up in the city and around the various university campuses, serving inexpensive and fabulously authentic dishes.

Cafes & Coffee Culture

Cafes are an integral part of daily Victorian life. Many city-dwellers are up early so they can catch up with colleagues or just the newspaper over a latte and a slice of sourdough before the workday begins, and weekends see cafes across the state fill (queues are not uncommon) with those looking for a long, leisurely, blow-out breakfast. Cafes also fill mid-morning with those out for a 'morning tea' coffee run, or freelancers conducting meetings or working quietly in a corner. This will then be repeated mid-afternoon, with a roaring lunch trade in between.

While socialising is a big part of this ritual, the coffee itself is definitely not an afterthought. Melbourne's coffee is far superior to what you'll get in London or Los Angeles, and often tops what you'll find in Italy. Bigger towns throughout the state are also not far behind. Neighbourhood cafes have begun to attract the kind of tribal devotion reserved for AFL teams. Soy milk is polarising; some purist cafes refuse to offer it, along with 'skinny' (skim) milk, while it forms a large part of many others' trade. Flavoured coffee? Forget about it. Yes, big chains such as Starbucks have sprung up, but an attempt to settle in the cafe heartland of Lygon St didn't last long – why would you need a cookie-cutter multinational to tell you how it's done when Melbourne's been getting the *crema* correct for well over 20 years?

The cafe tradition goes back to the early years of last century, with the arrival of Victoria's first wave of Italian and Greek migrants, but really took off post-WWII when large numbers of Italians settled in the inner city and the first Gaggia and La Cimbali espresso machines were imported under licence in 1953. Bourke Street's Pellegrini's is an ever-enchanting survivor of this generation. The brew in their signature Duralex glasses may be unremarkable by today's standards, but the Italian brio, urban bonhomie and original decor are as authentic as it gets. Melbourne *torrefazione* (Italian coffee roasters) such as Genovese and Grinders also date back to this era, and their bean blends now fuel cafes all over the country. Other local roasters include Atomic, Jasper and Gravity, and Castlemaine's Coffee Basics.

While these original family-run roasters have prospered and become household names, Melbourne is now firmly in the grip of coffee's third wave. Coffee talk now runs to terroir, and single-origin beans, premium small-batch roasts and alternative brewing methods such as siphon, pour-over, filter and cold-drip have taken coffee appreciation to a new level. Part of a global network that includes Chicago's Intelligentsia and Oslo's Tim Wendelboe, Melbourne is in an era of extreme coffee excellence.

Third-wave pioneer Mark Dundon owns Seven Seeds – part cafe, part retail outlet and part instructional facility, set in a warehouse conversion that wins in both the sustainability and style stakes. He also runs city cafes Brother Baba Budan and Traveller. Salvatore Malatesta took over South Melbourne's legendary St Ali from Dundon, and now also runs a stable of other cafes. Other third-wavers doing great things include Market Lane at Prahran Market, Lygon St's Brunswick East Project, Dukes in Windsor, Monk Bodhi Dharma in East St Kilda, Auction Rooms in North Melbourne and Proud Mary in Collingwood.

HOLD THE COFFEE

Tea and hot chocolate, although still lurking in coffee's deep shadow, are having something of a renaissance. Many Asian restaurants now offer artisanal teas and tisanes, and city hotels like the Windsor and the Langham book out for their traditional high teas. Hot chocolate is also a focus; the city's bourgeoning epicurean chocolate scene has a number of chocolatiers serving up ambrosial chocolate made in the Belgian, French or Italian style.

MELBOURNE CHEFS TO TAKE AWAY

Take home the recipes of some of Melbourne's most loved and respected chefs via their cookbooks:

➡ *MoVida: Spanish Culinary Adventures* (Frank Camorra & Richard Cornish of MoVida)

➡ *The Press Club: Modern Greek Cookery* (George Calombaris of the Press Club, Gazi, Hellenic Republic and more)

➡ *Origin* (Ben Shewry of Attica)

➡ *My French Vue: Bistro Cooking at Home* (Shannon Bennett of Vue de Monde)

➡ *The Cook's Companion* (Stephanie Alexander) – Although Stephanie no longer graces the city's stoves on a regular basis, her classic kitchen reference is one of Australia's most well-thumbed cookbooks.

➡ *Chin Chin* (Benjamin Cooper of Chin Chin)

Eating Local

Over the last decade, the organic and local food movement has gone from strength to strength in Victoria. Shopping at weekly markets and small grocers is a lifestyle choice that's embraced by many, and the Slow Food movement has a strong presence state-wide – news and events can be found at www.slowfoodaustralia.com.au/tag/victoria – as well as a monthly market at the Abbotsford Convent on the fourth Saturday of each month.

Queen Victoria Market in the city centre, and its suburban counterparts in South Melbourne and Prahran, are beloved by locals for their fresh fruit, vegetables, meat and fish, and their groaning deli counters, not to mention a catch-up with friends. There's also a weekly rota of inner-city farmers markets (see www.mfm.com.au) at Collingwood Children's Farm, Veg Out in St Kilda, and South Melbourne's Gasworks, which bring local artisan producers and fresh, often organic, produce to town. They make for a pleasant Saturday-morning coffee spot and food-related stroll.

A huge number of outer suburbs and regional towns also hold community markets, selling local produce as well as crafts and secondhand goods; a comprehensive list can be found at the Australian Farmers Market Association (www.farmersmarkets.org.au). The monthly markets at Red Hill, on the Mornington Peninsula, and St Andrews (www.standrewsmarket.com.au), around 40 minutes' drive north of Melbourne, are veterans of the scene and incredibly popular. Both are held in atmospheric, bush-ringed settings – the bellbird soundtrack is complimentary, no purchase required.

Food tourism is big news right throughout Victoria, with much of the action centred on wine-growing districts such as the Mornington and Bellarine Peninsulas and the Yarra Valley. The Goldfields-area spa towns of Kyneton, Trentham, Daylesford and Castlemaine, and alpine Mansfield, are home to ever-increasing numbers of provedores and cafes offering local produce. The Milawa Gourmet Region – the first to be given such a title in Australia – is unsurprisingly one of the state's richest; the foodie trail here also takes in the surrounding towns of Oxley and Beechworth. Out along the Murray, Mildura is also a destination for its produce and restaurants.

Cellar-Door Dining

Max's at Red Hill Estate, Mornington Peninsula

Salix at Willow Creek Vineyard, Mornington Peninsula

Oakridge, Yarra Valley

Port Phillip Estate, Mornington Peninsula

La Baracca at T'Gallant, Mornington Peninsula

Merricks General Wine Store, Mornington Peninsula

Jack Rabbit Winery, Bellarine Peninsula

Victorian Vino

Bacchus appears to have smiled upon the state of Victoria. Its small size belies the variety of its climates, which makes for a splendidly diverse wine scene, with around 900 vineyards spread over 21 growing regions. Melbourne itself is surrounded by five of these – the Yarra Valley,

Mornington Peninsula, Macedon Ranges, Geelong and Sunbury – all with distinct climates and soils. Wine-region weekends away and grape-grazing festivals are popular with Victorians, and with many of the regions close to favourite beach resorts or ski fields, they also provide a gourmet backdrop to seasonal holidays. Whether it's for confidently working your way through a Melbourne wine list or for creating a cellar-door itinerary, understanding what's what only makes the tasting sweeter.

Beginning at Melbourne's suburban fringe, the Yarra Valley is a patchwork of vines, and it's here that you'll find the glamorous big boys of the industry, Chateau Yering and Domain Chandon. These glistening temples to the grape absorb the tour-bus bustle surprisingly well, with a rota of produce markets and entertainment, as well as striking architecture, making up for the high traffic. The area still has its share of rustic tin sheds where it's just you and the winemaker if that's more your style. Fruity, unwooded pinot noirs, peachy chardonnay and crisp sparklings are the darlings here, but there's plenty of experimentation with other grapes, too.

A little further afield in Melbourne's southeast is the rarefied rusticity of the Mornington Peninsula. The hills and valleys of this favourite beach destination hide an embarrassment of riches in terms of small-scale viticulture – there's literally a winemaker around every bend (not to mention symbiotic cellar door, restaurant, gourmet provedore and shop selling French plimsolls). Mornington vignerons are a tenacious, innovative lot, who coax the most out of the volcanic soil and capricious, often chilly, maritime climate to produce beautiful, early ripening pinot noirs; subtle, honeyed chardonnay; and pinot gris, as well as fragrant Italian varietals such as arneis and pinot grigio, possibly Australia's best. The vineyards of the Bellarine Peninsula, on the opposite coast, have gained a following of their own, and their delicate maritime-climate aromatic whites are getting a lot of attention.

In Victoria's northeast, wine has been continuously produced since the thirsty days of the gold rush, with Brown Brothers making both fortified and table wines right through the 20th century. Northern Italian farmers also made a big contribution to this region's development. They noted similarities in the landscape and introduced grapes from their home regions that took to the local terroir. Today, the gloriously diverse geography, climate and soil, from the flats around Milawa to the high country of Beechworth and the cool, wet King Valley, see a huge variety of wines produced. Rieslings, sauvignon blancs and sparklings (including an Italian-styled prosecco) shine in the King Valley, along with the complex, tightly structured chardonnay and spicy shiraz of Beechworth, and Milawa's fortifieds, cabernet merlots, sangiovese, nebbiolos and pinot grigios. To the west of here, Rutherglen is also a pioneer, well known for its fortifieds and unctuous stickies. Big – well, absolutely huge – reds do well here too, but it's the long-cellared muscats and tokays (aka liquid Christmas-pud) that keep the faithful coming back.

Other less-visited regions include the Pyrenees, known for its French-influenced sparklings and, somewhat surprisingly, its absolutely Aussie big, ripe reds; Macedon, which produces crisp, cold-climate sparklings and minerally European-style chardonnay, riesling and sauvignon blancs; the Goulburn Valley's Nagambie and Shepparton, for marsanne, viognier and Rhône Valley reds, some of which are grown from original vines imported from France in the 1850s; and the Grampians for reds, such as cabernet and dolcetto, as well as an unforgettable sparkling shiraz.

Best Victorian Varietals

Pinot gris

Chardonnay

Viognier

Arneis

Savagnin

Marsanne

Pinot noir

Shiraz

Gamay

Durif

Tokay

Fashion & Shopping

Melbourne's reputation as a shopping mecca is, we are pleased to announce, utterly justifiable. Passionate retailers roam widely in search of the world's best as well as showcasing abundant local design talent. Fashion plays a huge part in Melbourne's self-image. Whether strictly suited or ultraglam, casual, creative or subversive, Melburnians of both sexes love to look good.

City Style

Ask any fashionista in Melbourne their favourite time of year and they'll invariably say it's winter – and usually for the fashion opportunities that crisp, cold days deliver. While Melbourne designers do produce swimwear (Gorman, Zoe Elizabeth and We Are Handsome's retro offerings are local favourites), it's during the autumn–winter season of the fashion cycle that the city comes into its own. Temperatures only have to drop a few degrees for boots and jackets to emerge, and unpredictable summers see many a cardigan or lightweight scarf thrown in the mix.

There is no shortage of places to shop in Melbourne. City laneways and Victorian shopping streets have long provided reasonably priced rental spaces that encourage creativity rather than conformity in shop owners; their vision contributes much to the city's eclectic identity and character. Yes, the chains and big global designers are all well represented, and there are suburban malls aplenty (including Chadstone, known as Chaddy, the largest in the southern hemisphere and Victoria's oldest; www.chadstone shopping.com.au), but the city and surrounds offer a host of alternatives.

Buoyed by a culture of small shops and an adventurous-minded public, young designers flourish. Rather than adhering to the established studios' hierarchies, many start their own labels straight out of design school, giving the scene an amazing energy and vitality.

Melbourne Black

One constant in Melbourne fashion is colour, or lack of it. You'll not go long without hearing mention of 'Melbourne black', and it's true that inky shades are worn not just during the cold months but right through the hottest days of summer. Perhaps it's because black somehow suits the soft light and often grey days, or maybe it's the subliminal influence of the city's moody bluestone. Some muse that it's the long-lingering fallout of the explosive 1980s postpunk scene or southern European immigration. The fact remains that black clothes sell far better here than in any other city in the country. In Melbourne, black is always the new black.

Local Talent

Melbourne's designers are known for their tailoring, luxury fabrics, innovation and blending of global elements, all underscored with a fuss-free Australian sensibility. Those to watch out for include the evergreen Scanlan & Theodore for smart, lyrical elegance; Tony Maticevski and Martin Grant for demi-couture and dark reworkings of the classics; Ess Hoshika, Dhini and Munk for conceptual, deconstructed pieces; Anna Thomas

DISCOUNTS

Discount factory outlets can be found aplenty in Bridge Rd, Richmond; the lower end of Smith St, Collingwood; or at South Wharf, but savvy Melbourne fashionistas prefer designer-specific sample sales, discovered via word-or-mouth or mailing lists – check out Missy Confidential (www.missyconfidential.com.au).

WHERE TO SHOP?

The city has national and international chains spread out over Bourke, Swanston and Collins Sts, as well as the city malls of Melbourne Central, QV, GPO, Australia on Collins St, Spencer St and South Wharf. Smaller retailers and design workshops inhabit the laneways as well as the vertical villages of Curtin House and the Nicholas Building. Flinders Lane and the arcades and laneways that feed into it are particularly blessed. A strip of Little Collins heading north from Swanston is dedicated to sartorially savvy gentlemen, while the length of leafy Collins St is lined with luxury retailers.

Chapel St, South Yarra, has all the chains and classic Australian names, as well as some edgier designers once you hit Prahran. Up the hill, head to Hawksburn Village or High St, Armadale, for fashion-forward labels, super-stylish children's clothes and homewares. You'll find streetwear in Greville St, Prahran, and in Windsor; the latter is also good for vintage shopping.

In the north, Lygon St, Carlton, has some great small shops specialising in European tailoring and local talent. Brunswick St, Fitzroy, has streetwear and vintage shops, and pulses with the energy of young designers, particularly in stores such as the legendary Fat. Gertrude St, Fitzroy, mixes vintage with many of the city's most sought-after innovators, as well as some up-and-coming menswear names, art-supply shops and vintage furniture.

and Vixen for the luxuriously grown-up; Gorman, Arabella Ramsay, Búl and Obüs for hipster cheek with a delightfully feminine twist; Alpha 60, Kloke, Schwipe and Claude Maus for clever, urban pieces; and finally, scene stalwarts Bettina Liano for straight-ahead glamour and Alannah Hill for the original girly-girl layers. For flattering and form-fitting jeans, you can't go past Fitzroy's Nobody Denim. Millinery is also a local speciality, due to the fondness for racing carnivals, with names such as Richard Nylon, Melissa Jackson and Louise Macdonald.

Crafts

Melbourne's penchant for small-scale design goes one further with a bubbling subculture that sells through markets and online. Craft Victoria is the grand old (if eternally cool) dame of the scene, with a commitment to showing and selling work that, as board member Pene Durston says, demonstrates 'the importance of the "hand" in the production of work, and the high level of skill invested by makers in their craft'. Thread Den, in North Melbourne, combines a craft, DIY and vintage ethos with classes augmenting their retail offerings. The Nicholas Building (thenicholasbuilding.blog spot.com), at the corner of Swanston St and Flinders Lane, is the city's most concentrated artisan hub, with both small shops (such as Buttonmania and L'uccello) as well as much-coveted studios and workshops.

Top Local Designers

Third Drawer Down

Craft Victoria

Obüs

Crumpler

Gorman

To Market, To Market

Melbourne's unpredictable weather hasn't deterred its entrepreneurial spirit, with many markets being held in all-weather venues. The twice-yearly Melbourne Design Market (www.melbournedesignmarket.com. au) is huge, attracting around 10,000 visitors. It showcases 'design-led' stallholders and has a rigorous selection process that keeps quality high. Fitzroy's Rose Street Artists' Market (www.rosestmarket.com.au) and the Skirts & Shirts Market (www.skirtandshirtmarkets.com.au) at the Abbotsford Convent are as much about the social buzz as the highly individual vendors. Monthly markets are also held in pubs (a clever use of drinking downtime in a post-sticky-carpet age). These include the Hello Sailor Vintage Fair (www.hellosailorvintagefair.com.au) at Collingwood's Grace Darling Hotel, held on the last weekend of the month, and the Lonely Hunter (www.lonelyhunter.com.au) at Fitzroy's Cape Lounge, held on the second Saturday of the month.

The Arts

Long regarded as the culture capital of Australia, Melbourne has always been a city for artists and art lovers. Its thriving live-music scene, strong community of street artists, and passion for literature, theatre and visual arts all provide a vibrant, creative backdrop fundamental to the fabric of the city. Art in Melbourne is highly accessible, both for the number of its art spaces as well as its appeal to a broad audience.

Visual Arts

Melbourne's visual-arts scene thrives and grows in myriad places: tucked away in basement galleries, exhibited in edgy spaces, stencilled on unmarked laneway walls, flaunted in world-class museums and sneaking up on you in parks and gardens.

Painting

Melbourne and Victoria's visual-arts culture began in the traditions of the Kulin Nation tribes, and ancestral design inspires contemporary Victorian Indigenous artists to this day. The late-19th-century artwork of Wurundjeri elder William Barak depicts ceremonial gatherings, several of which are displayed in the Ian Potter Centre: NGV Australia. Prominent contemporary Koorie artists in Victoria include Vicki Couzens, Esther Kirby, Mandy Nicholson and Trevor 'Turbo' Brown, who paint upon a mix of traditional artefacts, possum-skin cloaks and emu eggs, as well as canvas (note: there are no dots in Indigenous Victorian art). In Melbourne, the Koorie Heritage Trust and Melbourne Museum's Bunjilaka Aboriginal Centre all provide an intimate picture of Victorian Aboriginal culture.

Early Europeans who visited the fledgling colony of Melbourne presented a very different experience of Australia. The Vienna-born Eugene von Guérard is one of Australia's best-known colonial artists from the 1850s; his vast works include panoramic landscapes of early Geelong, the Otways, Gippsland and the Western District region, all depicted as colonial jewels with bucolic pastures and abundant forests.

In the late 19th century a new generation of Australian-born artists emerged, forming the Heidelberg School (aka the Australian Impressionists). Artists Tom Roberts, Arthur Streeton and Frederick McCubbin are fondly remembered for defining a more 'Australian' vision of the landscape and depicting the harshness in the beauty of the Victorian bush. They also created a heroic national iconography, ranging from the shearing of sheep to visions of a wide brown land.

The early- to mid-20th century saw the rise to prominence of a number of modernist painters, including internationally acclaimed Melbourne artists Sidney Nolan, John Brack, Charles Blackman, Fred Williams and Russell Drysdale. Heide, the Melbourne home of arts patrons John and Sunday Reed, played a pivotal role in the development of Australian modernism; Nolan's famous *Ned Kelly* series is said to have been painted at the Reeds' dining-room table. The Reeds nurtured an artistic

Flinders Lane has the densest concentration of commercial galleries in Australia, with many more dotted throughout the city and inner suburbs. *Art Almanac* (www.art-almanac.com.au) has comprehensive listings, with good regional coverage as well.

community that included Nolan, Albert Tucker, Arthur Boyd, Joy Hester, John Perceval and Danila Vassilieff, who utilised styles incorporating elements of surrealism and expressionism. Their property has since been turned into the Heide Museum of Modern Art, which has an impressive collection of modern and contemporary Australian art exhibited in three galleries and scattered throughout the tranquil gardens.

Other well-known Melbourne painters of the 20th century include French expatriate Mirka Mora (b 1928), known for her colourful, bohemian paintings; she and her art-dealer husband Georges (founder of Tolarno Galleries) were hugely influential upon both Melbourne's art and cultural scenes. The late Howard Arkley (1955–99) is as Melbourne as they come: his airbrush technique produced fluorescent pieces that pay homage to suburbia, as well as his well-known portrait of Melbourne-raised musician Nick Cave.

Contemporary Art

Between the commercial, public and artist-run galleries there is much to discover in Melbourne's contemporary arts scene. A good place to tap in is Gertrude Contemporary Art Space, which hosts exhibitions by emerging artists and fosters innovative and challenging new works. The Australian Centre for Contemporary Art (ACCA) also hosts cutting-edge programs of exhibitions as well as developing large-scale projects with Australian (and international) artists. The Australian Centre for the Moving Image (ACMI) exhibits film and multimedia works by contemporary artists, and the Centre for Contemporary Photography has a strong photo- and film-based program.

Street Art

With its growing reputation for street art, Melbourne's urban landscape is a beacon for visitors from all around the world. Dozens of laneway walls provide an outdoor canvas for paste-up, mural and stencil art.

Local street artists of note include ghostpatrol, miso, Tai Snaith and Ha-Ha (the latter for *his* iconic Ned Kelly images – move aside, Sidney Nolan). Many of these locals are represented in the documentaries *Rash* (2005) and the more recent *Children of the Iron Snake* (2013), which get behind the scenes of Melbourne's street-art phenomenon.

Melbourne's scene was helped by the legacy of renowned international street artists such as Keith Haring (1958–1990), the New York graffiti artist who visited in 1984. He was commissioned to paint large-scale murals at NGV International and what was then the Collingwood Technical School on Johnston St; the latter work still exists today (visible next door to the Tote music club).

The city's street-art scene received further recognition through Banksy, who stencilled extensively during a visit in 2003. While several of his works remain, many have unfortunately disappeared (some accidentally painted over by unsuspecting workers). Other prominent international street artists to contribute work to Melbourne's streets include Blek le Rat (France), Shepard Fairey (USA) and Invader (France).

Literature

It may seem at first glance that in Melbourne and Victoria words and stories are relegated to the wings while sport and socialising take centre stage, but scratch the surface and you'll find they're home to writers of all descriptions, independent booksellers, a prosperous publishing industry and a thriving culture of reading and discourse on the written word. Melbourne nourishes literary types with its tempestuous weather, rich range of cultures and identities, wines bars and moody architecture.

THE ARTS LITERATURE

Regional Art Galleries

Bendigo Art Gallery

Art Gallery of Ballarat

Mornington Peninsula Regional Gallery

TarraWarra Museum of Art, Yarra Valley

Geelong Art Gallery

City Centre Street Art

Hosier/Rutledge Lane

Caledonian Lane

Blender Lane

Union Lane

Croft Lane

Melbourne's wordy reputation was formally recognised with its designation as a Unesco City of Literature (in 2008) and the birth of the Wheeler Centre (www.wheelercentre.com), Australia's first centre for 'Books, Writing and Ideas'. Located within a newly renovated wing of the State Library of Victoria (www.slv.vic.gov.au), it's home to several literary organisations and hosts a rich program of talks and events designed to 'get Melburnians thinking'.

Literary publishing companies Black Inc, Scribe, Text and Penguin are based here, and the city produces a host of magazines, journals and websites that highlight literature and intellectual life, including the *Australian Book Review, Meanjin,* Black Inc's series of 'Best' anthologies and the *Quarterly Essay,* and the short-fiction collection *Sleepers Almanac.* The City Library in Flinders Lane has an entire section dedicated to books on Melbourne.

Bookish Melbourne

State Library of Victoria

Wheeler Centre

Readings

Hill of Content

Melbourne Writers Festival

Has there been a great Victorian novel? Melbourne has certainly provided a variety of memorable backdrops for literary works, from the 19th-century cult crime fiction of *The Mystery of a Hansom Cab* (Fergus Hume; 1886) to Peter Temple's *The Broken Shore* (2005), which is also partly based in western Victoria. Christos Tsiolkas' *The Slap* (2008) is set in the backyards of the inner north, where postwar migrant families settled in Melbourne. Helen Garner's *Monkey Grip* takes readers on a journey through drugs, love and music in urban Melbourne in the 1970s, while *Utopian Man* by Lisa Lang tells the story of the late-19th-century days of 'Marvellous Melbourne' and E.W Cole's Book Arcade. Peter Carey's *True History of the Kelly Gang,* set in the central Victorian haunts of Australia's most famous bushrangers, took both the Man Booker Prize and Commonwealth Writers' Prize when it was published in 2001; despite Victoria's largely urban, multicultural population, it just may be a novel with a historical – even mythological – bush setting that can claim the 'great' title.

On the non-fiction front, Jill and Jeff Sparrow's *Radical Melbourne* (2001) looks at Melbourne's counter-culture and its secret history. Germaine Greer, another radical Melburnian, is best known for her work *The Female Eunuch* (1971), an international bestseller hailed for its contribution to feminism.

Notable books on Indigenous culture include *When the Wattle Blooms* (Shirley W Wiencke; 1984), about William Barak, a notable Wurundjeri elder; *Aboriginal Melbourne: The Lost Land of the Kulin People* (1994) by Gary Presland; and *The Melbourne Dreaming: A Guide to the Aboriginal Places of Melbourne* (1997) by Meyer Eidelson. *The Life and Adventures of William Buckley* (John Morgan; 1852) – a fascinating account of escaped convict William Buckley and the 32 years he spent living with the Wathaurung people – still offers one of the best insights to this Indigenous group's way of life.

Music

Melbourne's cultural image has involved music since the city produced two of the most enduringly fascinating talents of the 19th and early 20th centuries. Opera diva Dame Nellie Melba was an international star who lived overseas for many years, but retained a sentimental attachment to her home town (hence the name). Percy Grainger, whose innovative compositions and performances prefigured many forms of 20th-century music, was born and brought up in Melbourne. Grainger's eccentric genius extended beyond music to the design of clothing and objects; he was also known for his transgressive sex life. His life story is all on display at the Grainger Museum in Parkville.

More recently, Melbourne's live-music scene exploded in the mid-1960s with a band called the Loved Ones, which broke the imitative mould of American '50s rock 'n' roll. The early 1970s saw groups such as AC/DC, Skyhooks and Daddy Cool capture the experience of ordinary Melbourne life in their lyrics for the first time. By the end of that decade punk had descended; Melbourne's grey weather and grimy backstreets had a natural synergy with the genre, providing a more arty, post-punk sound. Nick Cave's Boys Next Door and the so-called 'Little Bands' shrieked their way through gigs at St Kilda's Crystal Ballroom (now the George Hotel), a venue whose dilapidated splendour was straight out of central casting. Bands and performers that grew out of (and beyond) this scene included the Birthday Party (evolving into Nick Cave & the Bad Seeds), Young Charlatans, Sports, the Models, Dead Can Dance, the Johnnys, X, Primitive Calculators, Sacred Cowboys, the Wreckery, Hugo Race, Crime & City Solution and the Moodists.

The '80s pub-rock scene also gave birth to Crowded House, Paul Kelly, Hunters & Collectors and Australian Crawl, while the '90s and 2000s punk/grunge era saw the likes of the Cosmic Psychos, the Meanies, Powder Monkeys, the Dirty Three, Magic Dirt and Eddy Current Suppression Ring carry the torch passed on from their late-'70s predecessors. Melbourne's other international success stories include the Seekers, Air Supply, Olivia Newton-John and Little River Band, along with Kylie Minogue, Gotye, Jet and the Temper Trap.

Melbourne's live-music scene has had a rough run of late; residents moving into new apartment buildings near established venues have certainly had their voices heard, and as a result some clubs have been forced to close, or reduce the volume. The Tote in Collingwood was an apparent victim of new liquor licensing laws requiring even small venues to have a security presence; when it closed, Melbourne's music lovers weren't happy. Around 20,000 people rallied in Melbourne's city centre, resulting in the future of live-music venues becoming an issue in the 2010 state elections. SLAM (Save Live Australia's Music), an advocate action group, successfully lobbied for numerous law changes. There was a happy ending: the Tote got new owners and the music there continues, while other venues were granted seven-day 3am licences.

Despite the liquor licence issues, Melbourne is still the live-music capital of Australia, and draws musicians from around the country. Current buzz bands include the Drones, the Twerps, UV Race and King Gizzard & the Lizard Wizard. For a city so very far away, Melbourne is also blessed with a large number of international touring acts each year – pickings are particularly rich during the summer festival season.

THE ARTS MUSIC

Melbourne Music Festivals

Big Day Out (Jan)

Laneway (Feb)

Future Music Festival (Mar)

Brunswick Music Festival (Mar)

Melbourne Music Week (Nov)

LIVE-MUSIC VENUES

In spite of the ongoing threat of music venues being closed down due to noise complaints by some inner-city residents, Melbourne still has a plethora of great venues spread throughout the city and inner suburbs. Some of the city's favourite pubs and drinking dens double as band venues: the best spots to catch a beer and a gig include the Tote in Collingwood, the Espy (Esplanade Hotel) in St Kilda, the Northcote Social Club and Richmond's Corner Hotel.

Though it prides itself as a city dedicated to smaller, independent live-music spaces, Melbourne also has its fair share of major stadiums and arenas. You'll find big-name acts selling out venues like Rod Laver Arena, Festival Hall, Sidney Myer Music Bowl and the Forum.

DOCUMENTING MELBOURNE'S PUNK SCENE

The following provide a great overview of Melbourne's punk scene:

➡ *We're Living on Dog Food* (2009) Doco directed by Richard Lowenstein

➡ *Dogs in Space* (1986) Feature film also by Richard Lowenstein, starring INXS' Michael Hutchence

➡ *The Ballroom: The Melbourne Punk & Post Punk Scene* (2011) Fantastic memoir by Dolores San Miguel recalling St Kilda's colourful punk history at the Crystal Ballroom.

The city also has a healthy club and dance music scene. The megaclubs of the '80s gave way to a more fluid dance-party culture revolving around techno and other electronic styles. The 'doof' was born: these festivals, often held in bushland settings over several days, peaked in the late '90s, though they still have their devotees. Legendary laneway club Honkytonks took its musical responsibility very seriously, nurturing local DJ talent (and a generation of club kids) through the early years of this century. Since its demise, other venues have sprung up to fill the gap. Local electronic/synthpop artists who have crossed into the mainstream include Cut Copy, the Avalanches and DJ Digital Primate.

Australian hip-hop is well represented in Victoria, with locals such as True Live and DJ Peril. Hip-hop has also proven enormously popular with young Aboriginal and Islander musicians (*All You Mob* is an excellent compilation CD of Indigenous artists). Other modern Indigenous musicians, such as Archie Roach, create unique styles by incorporating traditional instruments into modern rock and folk formats.

Jazz also has a dedicated local audience and a large number of respected musicians who are known for improvising, as well as crossing genres into world and experimental electronica. The heart of the scene is the long-running Bennetts Lane, an archetypal down-an-alley jazz club if ever there was one. Its Sunday sessions are legendary, and the venue draws a local crowd that knows its hard bop from its bebop. International and local talent also pull respectable numbers for gigs at the Melbourne International Jazz Festival and the Wangaratta Jazz & Blues Festival.

Ninety years after Nellie Melba was made a dame, classical music still has a strong presence in Melbourne. The Melbourne Symphony Orchestra, based at the Arts Centre's recently renovated Hamer Hall, performs works drawn from across the classical spectrum, from the popular to challenging contemporary composition. The all-acoustic Melbourne Recital Centre (the only venue of its type in Australia), which opened in 2009 to rave reviews, hosts around 250 concerts a year.

Music Festivals in Regional Victoria

Apollo Bay Music Festival (Feb/Mar)

Golden Plains (Mar)

Port Fairy Folk Festival (Mar)

Wangaratta Jazz & Blues Festival (Oct/Nov)

Queenscliff Music Festival (Nov)

Falls Festival (Dec)

Meredith Music Festival (Dec)

Cinema & Television

Although Sydney might be considered the centre of the Australian film industry, new production facilities at Docklands, slightly lower costs for film production and generous government subsidies have seen Melbourne wield its movie-making muscle. And Melbourne does looks gorgeous on the big screen. Film-makers tend to eschew the stately and urbane and highlight the city's complexity, from the winsomely suburban to the melancholic and gritty.

Film culture is nurtured in Victoria through local funding projects, tertiary education and exhibition. Funding for features, documentaries, shorts, digital media and game content is provided by Film Victoria (www.film.vic.gov.au), which also provides mentoring schemes. Federation Square has consolidated a big part of Melbourne's screen culture, housing the Australian Centre for the Moving Image (ACMI) and the Special Broadcasting Service (SBS) television channel.

The prominence of film in Melbourne is evident in the number of film festivals the city hosts. Apart from the main Melbourne International Film Festival (www.melbournefilmfestival.com.au), there's everything from the Melbourne Underground Film Festival (www.muff.com.au) to shorts at the St Kilda Film Festival (www.stkildafilmfestival.com.au) and the Sydney-import Tropfest (www.tropfest.com.au). Other film-festival genres include foreign-made, seniors, hip-hop, queer and documentary.

Some well-known Australian films shot in Melbourne and regional Victoria include *Mad Max*, *Picnic at Hanging Rock*, *Chopper*, *Romper Stomper*, *Animal Kingdom* and *The Man from Snowy River*, while international films include *Where the Wild Things Are*, *Ghost Rider*, *Jackie Chan's First Strike* and *Salaam Namaste*.

There's an enduring affection for police drama and comedy shows on Australian TV, and many of these have emanated from Melbourne. The barely fictionalised Melbourne-organised-crime series *Underbelly* didn't initially make it to air in the city in which it was set – not because of its tits-and-arse overload but because a court decided that its plot lines could prejudice concurrent court proceedings. Other made-in-Melbourne TV series to hit the small screen include *Prisoner*, *The Secret Life of Us*, *Rush*, *Offspring* and *Miss Fisher's Murder Mysteries*, all shot in various parts of town, such as Fitzroy, Collingwood and the city's western waterfront. Beloved local comedy includes *Kath & Kim,* a hilarious piss-take of nouveau-riche suburban habits – very much in the mould of Melbourne's favourite aunty, Dame Edna Everage from Moonee Ponds (among Barry Humphries' other alter egos). And, of course, there's the never-ending froth of soap opera *Neighbours*. In regional Victoria, TV drama *SeaChange* was filmed on location at Barwon Heads on the Bellarine Peninsula.

Theatre

Melbourne's longstanding theatrical heritage is evident in the city's legacy of Victorian-era theatres such as the Princess and Athenaeum. While the blockbusters pack out these grand dames, Melbourne's theatre scene encompasses a wide spectrum of genres.

Melbourne's most high-profile professional theatre company, the Melbourne Theatre Company (MTC; www.mtc.com.au), is also Australia's oldest, and stages up to a dozen performances year-round at both the Arts Centre and its own purpose-built theatre located nearby. Productions are usually firmly focused on satisfying the company's 20,000-strong middle-market subscriber base, though with a new director this may change. Expect works by Australians such as David Williamson, locals Hannie Rayson and Joanna Murray-Smith, and well-known international playwrights.

The Malthouse Theatre (www.malthousetheatre.com.au) is dedicated to performing contemporary Australian works and nurturing emerging writers, and is known for relevance, audacity and artistic daring under its artistic director, Marion Potts.

Victoria also has a number of thriving progressive fringe-theatre companies, including Wodonga's HotHouse, Black Lung, Mutation Theatre and Hayloft, which stage residencies in traditional theatre settings as well as popping up in unusual places.

Humble in size, Carlton's La Mama (www.lamama.com.au) has a huge place in the heart of the city's theatre scene. Founded in 1967, it is, as its

Beat Magazine (www.beat.com.au) and *Fasterlouder* (www.fasterlouder.com.au) have weekly, all-genre gig guides; Mess+Noise (ww.messandnoise.com) is a great forum for local indie/rock news and happenings. The 3MBS arts diary (www.3mbs.org.au/arts.html) is an invaluable resource for what's going on in classical music.

name might suggest, the mother of independent theatre in Melbourne, and helped forge the careers of David Williamson, Jack Hibberd, Barry Dickens and Graeme Blundell.

Dance

The Australian Ballet (www.australianballet.com.au) is the national ballet company and considered one of the finest in the world. It performs regularly at Melbourne's Arts Centre, with a program of classical and modern ballets.

Victoria's flagship contemporary dance company, Chunky Move (www.chunkymove.com), is a tidy package of bold – often confronting – choreography, pop-culture concepts, technically brilliant dancers, sleek design and smart marketing. The artistic director and choreographer who founded the company in 1995, Gideon Obarzanek, moved on in 2012, and was succeeded by acclaimed Dutch choreographer Anouk van Dijk.

Kage Physical Theatre is a modern dance company producing innovative, challenging, humorous and highly entertaining performances. The company became a resident at the Abbotsford Convent in 2010 and is a partnership between Kate Denborough and Gerard Van Dyck, who met while studying a Bachelor of Dance at the Victorian College of Arts.

Melbourne is also home to a few other acclaimed contemporary choreographers. Lucy Guerin has a small, eponymous company that has attracted high praise from the *New Yorker* magazine's Joan Acocella. Shelley Lasica locates her work in non-theatre spaces, collaborating with visual artists and architects; her works blur the lines between dance and performance art.

Melbourne is a 'must-see' destination for many British travellers primarily because it's home to the TV program *Neighbours*. Pin Oak Ct in Vermont South is the suburban street that has been the show's legendary 'Ramsay Street' for more than 20 years.

Architecture & Urban Planning

For a planned city, and a relatively youthful one, Melbourne's streetscapes are richly textured. Long considered one of the world's most lovely Victorian-era cities, Melbourne captures the confident spirit of that age, with exuberantly embellished Second Empire institutions and hulking former factories that would do Manchester proud. Flinders Street Station and the original Queen Victoria Hospital (now part of the QV shopping centre) herald in the Federation era, when a new Australian identity was being fashioned from the fetching combination of red brick and ornate wood. Look down Swanston St from Lonsdale St and you'll catch a glimpse of a mini-Manhattan – Melbourne's between-the-wars optimism is captured in its string of stunning (if somewhat stunted) art deco skyscrapers, such as the Manchester Unity Building. Walter Burley Griffin worked in the city at this time too, creating the ornate, organic Newman College in the University of Melbourne and the mesmerising ode to the metropolitan, the Capitol Theatre, now a part-time cinema and university lecture hall.

By mid-century, modernist architects sought new ways to connect with the local landscape as well as honouring the movement's internationalist roots; the most prominent, Roy Grounds, designed the Arts Centre and the original NGV Australia on St Kilda Rd. Others include Robin Boyd, Kevin Borland and Alistair Knox, but their work is mostly residential so is rarely open to the public. You can, however, visit a beautiful Boyd building anytime: Jimmy Watson's wine bar in Carlton. Melbourne also had its own mid-century furniture design stars, Grant and Mary Featherston; their iconic Contour chair of 1951 is highly prized by collectors, as are their '70s modular sofas.

The 1990s saw a flurry of public building works: Melbourne's architects fell in love with technology and designed with unorthodox shapes, vibrant colours, tactile surfaces and sleek structural features. Denton Corker Marshall's Melbourne Museum, Melbourne Exhibition & Convention Centre, Bolte Bridge, and the CityLink sound tunnel are emblematic of this period. Federation Square, one of the last of these major projects, continues to polarise opinion. Despite its detractors, its cobbled, inscribed piazza has become the city's chosen site for celebration and protest – surely the best compliment a populace can pay to an architect. Ashton Raggatt McDougall's Melbourne Recital Centre is a recent architectural prizewinner, with an interior that is, according to Melbourne University's Philip Goad, 'like a beautiful violin'.

Today, Melbourne's architectural energy most often comes not from the monumental but from what goes on in-between the new and the old, the towering and the tiny. It's also literally about energy – sustainable practice, in the inner city at least, has become all but de rigueur. Mid-careerists such as Six Degrees, Elenberg Fraser and Kerstin Thompson create witty, inventive and challenging buildings and interiors that see raw or reimagined spaces spring to life.

Sport

Cynics snicker that sport is the sum of Victoria's culture, although they're hard to hear above all that cheering, theme-song singing and applause. Victorians do take the shared spectacle of the playing field very seriously. It's undeniably the state's most dominant expression of common beliefs and behaviour, and brings people together from across all backgrounds.

The Sporting Life

Melbourne is the birthplace of Australian Rules football and hosts a disproportionate number of international sporting events, including the Australian Open tennis championship, the Australian Formula One Grand Prix car race and the Melbourne Cup horse race. The city's arenas, tracks, grounds and courts are regarded as some of the world's best developed and best situated. The rest of Victoria is home to more major events, such as the Rip Curl Pro (aka the Bells Beach Surf Classic), the Australian Motorcycle Grand Prix on Phillip Island, the Stawell Gift 120m sprint (held since 1878) and numerous country horse races, including the atmospheric Hanging Rock meet.

Australian Rules Football

Underneath the cultured chat and designer threads of your typical Melburnian, you'll find a heart that truly belongs to one thing: the footy. Understanding the basics of Australian Rules football is definitely a way to get a local engaged in conversation, especially during the winter season. Melbourne is the national centre for the sport, and the Melbourne-based Australian Football League (AFL; www.afl.com.au) administers the national competition.

During the footy season (March to September), the vast majority of Victorians become obsessed: entering tipping competitions at work, discussing hamstring injuries and suspensions over the water cooler, and devouring huge chunks of the daily newspapers devoted to mighty victories, devastating losses and the latest bad-boy behaviour (on and off the field).

The MCG, affectionately referred to as the 'G', has been the home of Australian football since 1859 and its atmosphere is unforgettable. The AFL now has teams in every mainland state, but nine of its 18 clubs are still based in Melbourne, along with regional Geelong. All Melbourne teams play their home games at either the MCG or Etihad Stadium, and matches between two local teams ensure a loud, parochial crowd. Barracking has its own lexicon and is often a one-sided 'conversation' with the umpire. One thing is certain: fans always know better. Once disparagingly referred to as 'white maggots' because of their lily-white uniforms, umpires are now decked out in bright orange, so players can spot them in the thick of the game. (With the colour switch, they are now simply called 'maggots'.)

Sporting Highlights

AFL at the MCG

Boxing Day Cricket Test, MCG

Bells Beach Surf Classic

Australian Open

Formula One Grand Prix

Stawell Gift

After the final siren blows, and the winning club theme song is played (usually several times over), it's off to the pub. Supporters of opposing teams often celebrate and commiserate together. Despite the deep tribal feelings and passionate expression of belonging that AFL engenders, violence is almost unheard of before, during or after games.

The second-tier Victorian Football League (VFL; www.victorianfootball league.com.au) fields teams in regional centres Bendigo, Ballarat and Geelong, and in various Melbourne suburbs.

Cricket

Cricket is Victoria's summer love and it's the game that truly unites the state with the rest of Australia. It has a stronghold in Victoria, given the hallowed ground of the MCG and Cricket Australia's base in Melbourne. Seeing a Test at the 'G' is a must-do-before-you-die rite of devotion for cricket fans from around the world – particularly the Boxing Day Test, which attracts crowds of 80,000-plus; for many sport-mad Melburnians, it's a bigger deal than Christmas itself. Warm days, cricket's leisurely pace and gangs of supporters who've travelled from far and wide often make for great spectator theatrics. A schedule of Tests, one-day internationals, T20 (both the national Big Bash League and international games) and the Sheffield Shield state competition keeps fans happy throughout the rest of the season.

Soccer & Rugby

What many visitors know as 'football' in their home countries is referred to as 'soccer' in Australia, despite the Football Federation's official assertion of the football tag. Considering all the competition, the game's rise in Melbourne has been spectacular. A new A-League national competition was formed in 2005, running from October to May, and with it came a large supporter base and a higher profile for the game. Australia's solid performance in the 2006 FIFA World Cup also contributed to its newfound popularity, as does its status as the 'world game'. The city's original team, the Melbourne Victory (www.melbournevictory. com.au), was joined in the competition by the Melbourne Heart (www. melbourneheartfc.com.au) in the 2010–11 season. Soccer's amazingly vocal supporters (including a British-style cheer squad) make for some atmospheric play.

Melbourne Storm (www.melbournestorm.com.au), the first and only Victorian team in the National Rugby League (NRL), enjoyed spectacular success over the last decade, winning the premiership twice. They've

Famous Victorian Athletes

Pat Cash (tennis)

Neil Fraser (tennis)

Alan Jones (Formula 1)

Andrew Bogut (NBA basketball)

Travis Blackley (MLB baseball)

Mark Philippoussis (tennis)

Shane Warne (cricket)

Lionel Rose (boxing)

Mark Viduka (soccer)

Stuart Appleby (golf)

Ben Graham (NFL American football)

FORMULA-ONE RACING

These are the kind of figures that make petrolheads swoon: 300km/h, 950bhp and 19,000rpm. The Australian Grand Prix is held at Albert Park's 5.3km street circuit, which winds around the normally tranquil park's lake and is known for its smooth, fast surface. The buzz, both on the streets and in your ears, takes over Melbourne for four days in March, attracting 110,000 spectators on race day. Since 2009 it's been a twilight race, starting at 5pm (mainly for the benefit of TV audiences in the European time zones). Visit www.grandprix.com.au for event and ticketing details.

While the first official Australian Grand Prix F1 event was held at Albert Park in 1996 (after Melbourne controversially pinched the race from Adelaide), the lake track was used for grand-prix racing during the 1950s, seeing the likes of legends Jack Brabham and Stirling Moss battle it out. Today, with the retirement of Mark Webber, the nation's attention turns to Aussie young-gun Daniel Ricciardo, who's signed with the Red Bull Racing team.

actually won four titles, but sadly for Victorian league fans, they were stripped of their 2007 and 2009 titles for salary-cap breaches.

Rugby union is also growing in popularity, with the Melbourne Rebels joining the Super Rugby (Super 15) competition in 2011. Union does draw surprisingly large, often sell-out, crowds to international tests at Etihad Stadium, which recorded its highest sporting attendance – 56,605 – during a tour for the Wallabies (the national team).

Melbourne's new purpose-built rectangular stadium, AAMI Park, on the site of Olympic Park Stadium, has a capacity of 30,000, showing the state's continued commitment to embracing 'other' football codes in the future – hosting A-League soccer matches, NRL and Super Rugby matches.

Tennis

The last two weeks of January is tennis time in Melbourne, when the city hosts the Australian Open (www.australianopen.com) championships. The world's best come to compete at Melbourne Park in the year's first of the big four Grand Slam tournaments. With daily attendance figures breaking world records – well over half a million people come through the turnstiles over the two weeks – a carnival atmosphere prevails. Visitors come from around the world to attend, but it's also a favourite with locals, who make the most of summer holiday leave or amble over to East Melbourne after work. While the entertainment and a few glasses of sparkling wine in the sun are a big part of the draw, there's a hushed respect during matches on centre court. Tensions off the court between ultra-nationalistic fans have erupted in the past, but the most disruptive element is usually the elements themselves – the chance of at least one 40°C scorcher of a day is high.

Horse Racing

The roses are in bloom, the city's aflutter, and the nerves of milliners, fashion retailers, dry cleaners, beauty therapists and caterers are beyond frayed. It's Spring Racing Carnival time in Melbourne.

The two-mile (3.2km) Melbourne Cup has been run on the first Tuesday in November at Flemington Racecourse since 1861. Watched by 700 million people in more than 170 countries, the Cup brings the whole of Australia to a standstill for its three-or-so minutes, and Melburnians have the day off as a public holiday. Once-a-year gamblers organise Cup syndicates with friends, and gather to watch the race from pubs, clubs, TAB betting shops and backyard barbecues. Punters, partiers, celebrities and the fashion-conscious (who spend an estimated $54.5 million on clothes and accessories for the event) pack the grandstands, car parks, lawns and marquees of Flemington.

The Cup's heady social whirl gets even headier at Derby Day and Oaks Day, which are considered more glamorous events than the Cup itself, while serious racegoers bet their way through the Cox Plate, the Caulfield Cup, the Dalgety, and the Mackinnon Stakes, too.

Melbourne's favourite runs include the 4km 'Tan' track (around the Royal Botanic Gardens), the 5km path around Albert Park Lake and the sweeping paths of Fitzroy Gardens. The bicycle tracks beside the Yarra River and along the bay also see a lot of well-trained traffic.

Survival Guide

DIRECTORY A–Z 338

Accommodation 338
Business Hours 340
Customs Regulations . . . 340
Electricity 340
Embassies &
Consulates 340
Gay & Lesbian
Travellers 340
Health 341
Internet Access 341
Legal Matters 341
Money 341
Post 342
Public Holidays 342
Safe Travel 342
Telephone 343
Tourist Information 343
Travellers with
Disabilities 343
Visas 344
Women Travellers 344

TRANSPORT 345

GETTING THERE
& AWAY 345
Air 345
Land 346
Sea 346
GETTING AROUND 346
Air 346
Bicycle 346
Boat 347
Bus 347
Car & Motorcycle 347
Train 348
Tours 348

Directory A–Z

Accommodation

Accommodation across the state ranges from camping and caravan parks to youth hostels, motels, boutique B&Bs, hotels and resorts. Many tourist offices offer a free accommodation booking service; check out the comprehensive *Accommodation Guide* published by the **RACV** (✆13 72 28; www.racv. com.au).

Accommodation prices tend to be seasonal, especially along the coast and the Murray River. Peak times are the Christmas school holidays (from mid-December to the end of January) and the Easter long weekend, when you'll need to book well in advance and prices skyrocket at popular beach resorts. Winter (June to August) is the cheapest time to travel around most of the state – except at the ski resorts, where July and August represent peak season. Places at popular getaways such as the Mornington Peninsula and Daylesford often charge more for weekend stays.

Accommodation prices in Melbourne are generally steady all year, but peak for major events such as the Australian Open (January), the Grand Prix (March), AFL finals (September) and the Spring Racing Carnival (November). Midrange to deluxe hotels publish 'rack rates', but always ask for current specials.

Throughout the year, prices in many regional towns (where business travellers outnumber tourists) rise from Monday to Thursday and can drop considerably for the weekends.

Camping & Caravanning

Camping holidays are experiencing a resurgence in popularity in Victoria, with some outstanding national park camping grounds and privately run caravan parks to choose from. The only place where camping or caravanning isn't viable is central Melbourne.

At commercial caravan parks, expect to pay at least $25/30 for an unpowered/powered site for two people,

PRICE RANGES

Price ranges for accommodation in our reviews are rated with a $ symbol, indicating the price of a standard double room.

➡ **$** under $100
➡ **$$** $100 to $200
➡ **$$$** over $200

and from $70 to $150 for a cabin or unit, depending on the size and facilities. These rates will almost certainly double at coastal areas and popular holiday spots during school holidays. Sites at **Parks Victoria** (www.parkweb. vic.gov.au) camping grounds range from free to $28, and you can usually have up to six people and one vehicle per site. These should be booked in advance, but often a ranger will come in and collect your money. For the most popular grounds, such as Wilsons Prom and Cape Otway, a ballot is held over the Christmas and Easter holiday periods. Free camping is available in many places, including along the Murray and Goulburn Rivers and in the High Country – check with Parks Victoria. There are also a couple of free campgrounds scattered around the Otways.

BOOK YOUR STAY ONLINE

For more accommodation reviews by Lonely Planet authors, check out http://lonelyplanet.com/hotels/. You'll find independent reviews, as well as recommendations on the best places to stay. Best of all, you can book online.

Hostels

Most of Victoria's backpacker hostels are in Melbourne and the most popular regional centres, such as Halls Gap, along the Great Ocean Road, Mildura, Bendigo and Ballarat. There are nine **YHA hostels** (www.yha.com. au) in the state, and quite a few more independent backpackers. Expect to pay $23 to $30 for a dorm bed and from $70 for a private double.

B&Bs & Guesthouses

This rapidly growing segment of the accommodation market generally means staying in someone's home or in a purpose-built addition to a home, but increasingly B&Bs are self-contained cottages. It could be a grand historic home, secluded farmhouse, restored miner's cottage or beachside bungalow. In the English tradition, a big cooked breakfast is part of the deal. Rates are usually midrange (from $80 to $180 for a double) but can be much higher depending on the location and level of luxury. In many places, a minimum two-night stay is required, and not only during peak periods – this is almost always the case on weekends, especially in places like Daylesford.

Booking can be made online through Tourism Victoria, or check these sites:

➡ **Beds & Breakfasts** (www. bedsandbreakfasts.com.au)

➡ **Bed & Breakfast** (www. bedandbreakfast.com.au)

➡ **Great Places to Stay** (www.greatplacestostay.com.au)

Hotels & Motels

Motels are the most common type of accommodation around the state and popular with travellers looking for central, no-frills, familiar accommodation. Motels usually have studios and family apartments from $100 to $200, with TV, en suite bathroom, air-conditioning,

tea- and coffee-making facilities and usually a pool and barbecue area.

In Melbourne and large provincial centres, hotels are usually aimed at business and luxury travellers – centrally located, with business centres and restaurants attached. For a standard double room in a top-end hotel, expect to pay upwards of $250, midrange around $150 and for budget doubles from $90.

In country towns, a hotel refers to the local pub, which may have refurbished rooms upstairs, usually with shared facilities down the hall. These are often a good budget option, with rooms under $90, and you're sure to rub shoulders with a few locals down in the bar.

Apartments & Holiday Rental Accommodation

Most common along the coast and at ski resorts and popular spots like the Grampians and Murray River, holiday accommodation is generally self-contained, with kitchen, one or two bedrooms and parking. Holiday houses along the coast are usually just that – an entire house that you can rent for a week or longer and is ideal for families or groups.

➡ **Holiday Great Ocean Road** (☑03-5237 1098; www. holidaygor.com.au; studios from $190, 2BR cottage from $250)

➡ **Holiday Rentals** (www. holidayrentals.com.au)

➡ **Holiday Shacks** (www. holidayshacks.com.au)

➡ **Stayz** (www.stayz.com.au)

Houseboats

One of the great ways to stay in Victoria is on a houseboat. They range from basic two-bedroom boats with a small kitchen and the simplicity of a rural cabin to luxurious 12-berth craft with deck spa and all mod cons. They're especially popular in Mildura, Echuca, Eildon, Mallacoota and around Nelson and the Lower Glenelg National Park.

LIGHTHOUSE STAYS

Lighthouse keepers in days of old notoriously endured a lonely, tough existence, but these days you can get a taste of what their lives must have been like and do so in relative comfort. Of Victoria's 20-plus lighthouses, 10 are managed by Parks Victoria, and you can stay in the refurbished keeper's cottages at five of them. Some, like Point Hicks and Gabo Island, are remote, while Cape Otway and Cape Schanck are easily accessible to families:

➡ **Cape Schanck** (☑1300 885 259; www. capeschancklighthouse.com.au; 420 Cape Schanck Rd; d from $130)

➡ **Cape Otway** (☑03-5237 9240; www.lightstation.com; d from $250)

➡ **Gabo Island** (☑03-5161 9500, Parks Victoria 13 19 63; www.parkweb.vic.gov.au; up to 8 people $148-190)

➡ **Point Hicks** (☑03-5158 4268, 03-5156 0432; www. pointhicks.com.au; bungalow $100-120, cottage $330)

➡ **Wilsons Promontory** (☑Parks Victoria 13 19 63; www. parkweb.vic.gov.au; 8-bed cottage $90-100, 20-bed $120-134)

Business Hours

BUSINESS	OPENING HOURS
Banks	9.30am-4pm Mon-Thu, to 5pm Fri
Post offices	9am-5pm Mon-Fri, 9am-noon Sat
Tourist offices	9am-5pm daily
Shopping centres	9am-5.30pm, often to 9pm Thu & Fri
Restaurants	lunch noon-3pm, dinner 6-10pm
Cafes	breakfast 8-11am (later on weekends), all-day lunch
Pubs	11am-1am
Bars & clubs	4pm-late (between 2am and 5am)

Customs Regulations

For detailed information on customs and quarantine regulations, contact the **Australian Customs & Border Protection Service** (☑02-6275 6666, 1300 363 263; www.customs.gov.au) and the **Department of Agriculture, Fisheries & Forestry** (☑02-6272 3933; www.daff.gov.au).

When entering Australia you can bring in most articles free of duty provided that customs is satisfied they are for personal use and that you'll be taking them with you when you leave. Duty-free quotas per person (note the unusually low figure for cigarettes):

➡ **Alcohol** 2.25L (over the age of 18)

➡ **Cigarettes** 50 cigarettes (over the age of 18)

➡ **Dutiable goods** Up to the value of $900 ($450 for people under 18)

Narcotics, of course, are illegal, and customs inspectors and their highly trained hounds are diligent in sniffing them out. Quarantine regulations are strict, so you *must* declare all goods of animal or vegetable origin – wooden spoons, straw hats, the lot. Fresh food (meat, cheese, fruit, vegetables etc) and flowers are prohibited. There are disposal bins located in airports where you can dump any questionable items if you don't want to bother with an inspection. You must declare currency in excess of $10,000 (including foreign currency).

Electricity

240V/50Hz

Embassies & Consulates

Most embassies are in Canberra (ACT) or Sydney, but some countries maintain consulates (or, more often, honorary consulates) in Melbourne. Check the embassy's website for more details.

The following are all in Canberra:

Canadian Embassy (☑02-6270 4000; www.australia.gc.ca; Commonwealth Ave, Yarralumla)

Dutch Embassy (☑02-6220 9400; www.netherlands.org.au; 120 Empire Circuit, Yarralumla)

French Embassy (☑02-6216 0100; www.ambafrance-au.org; 6 Perth Ave, Yarralumla)

German Embassy (☑02-6270 1911; www.canberra.diplo.de; 119 Empire Circuit, Yarralumla)

Irish Embassy (☑02-6214 0000; www.embassyofireland.au.com; 20 Arkana St, Yarralumla, ACT)

New Zealand Embassy (☑02-6270 4211; www.nzembassy.com; Commonwealth Ave, Yarralumla)

UK Embassy (☑02-6270 6666; www.ukinaustralia.fco.gov.uk; Commonwealth Ave, Yarralumla)

US Embassy (☑02-6214 5600; canberra.usembassy.gov; 1 Moonah Pl, Yarralumla)

Gay & Lesbian Travellers

Homosexuality is legal and the age of consent is 17. The straight community's attitude towards gays and lesbians is, on the whole, open-minded and accepting.

The gay scene in Victoria is squarely based in Melbourne, where there are exclusive venues and accommodation options. Around the state, places such as Daylesford and Hepburn Springs, Phillip Island and the Mornington Peninsula have a strong gay presence and accommodation catering for gays and lesbians. Melbourne's **Midsumma Festival** (www.midsumma.org.au) in January is the state's biggest GLBQT festival and incorporates the annual Pride March. Daylesford's **ChillOut Festival** (www.chilloutfestival.com.au) in March is the biggest gay and lesbian event in regional Victoria.

Health

Few travellers to Victoria will experience anything worse than a bad hangover, but if you do fall ill the standard of hospitals and health care is high. Tap water is safe to drink throughout the state.

Insurance

While the standard of health care in Australia is high and is not overly expensive by international standards, travel insurance should be considered essential for international travellers. Make sure you have appropriate coverage if you plan on doing any 'dangerous' activities such as skiing, rock climbing, diving or motorcycling.

Vaccinations

Proof of yellow-fever vaccination is required only from travellers entering Australia within six days of having stayed overnight or longer in a yellow-fever-infected country. No specific vaccinations are required to travel in Victoria.

Health Care

Australia's Medicare system (www.medicareaustralia.gov. au) covers Australian residents for some health-care costs and emergency care (with reciprocity for citizens of New Zealand, Belgium, UK, Netherlands, Sweden, Finland, Italy, Malta and Ireland). Melbourne and the major provincial centres have high-quality hospitals.

Internet Access

Melbourne has plenty of internet cafes and wi-fi access is increasingly common, both in public places as well as hotels, cafes and bars. In regional Victoria, you'll find free internet access at the local library, and sometimes at the tourist office. Most caravan parks, hotels and motels offer wi-fi these days (sometimes free).

Legal Matters

Most travellers won't have any contact with the Victorian police or any other part of the legal system. Those that do are likely to experience these while driving. There is a significant police presence on Victoria's roads, and they have the power to stop your car and ask to see your licence (you're required by law to carry it), to check your vehicle for road-worthiness, and also to insist that you take a breath test for alcohol. The blood alcohol limit is 0.05%.

If you are arrested, it's your right to telephone a friend, relative or lawyer before any formal questioning begins.

Money

The Australian dollar is made up of 100 cents. There are 5¢, 10¢, 20¢, 50¢, $1 and $2 coins, and $5, $10, $20, $50 and $100 notes.

ATMs

Most bank branches have 24-hour ATMs and will accept debit cards linked to international network systems, such as Cirrus, Maestro, Visa and MasterCard. Most banks charge a fee (around $2 or 3%) for the privilege of using their ATM if you don't have an account with them. Almost all retail outlets have Eftpos, which allows you to pay for purchases electronically without a fee.

Changing Money

Change foreign currency at most larger banks or foreign-exchange booths in the city and at Melbourne Airport's international terminal. Most large hotels will also change currency (or travellers cheques) for their guests, but the rate might not be as good as from other outlets.

Credit Cards

The most commonly accepted credit cards are Visa and MasterCard, and to a lesser extent American Express and Diners Club. For lost or stolen card services call the following:

➡ **American Express** (☎1300 132 639; www.americanexpress.com.au)

➡ **Diners Club** (☎1300 360 060)

➡ **MasterCard** (☎1800 120 113; www.mastercard.com.au)

➡ **Visa** (☎1800 450 346)

Tipping

Tipping isn't obligatory in Australia and you'll rarely be made to feel uncomfortable

PRACTICALITIES

....

➡ DVD: Region 4

➡ Emergency: ☎000

➡ Newspapers: The **Age** (www.theage.com.au), long Melbourne's broadsheet, covers local, national and international news. The **Herald Sun** (www.heraldsun. com.au) is a big-selling tabloid strong on sport, especially AFL.

➡ Radio & TV: The **Australian Broadcasting Commission** (ABC; www.abc.net.au) is the national TV and radio broadcaster; commercial TV networks Seven, Nine, Ten and SBS all have more than one digital channel.

➡ Weights & measures: Australia uses the metric system.

if you don't do so. That said, tips are always appreciated, especially where the service has been notable, in which case 5% to 10% is ample in restaurants. For hotel porters, $5 should suffice. Tipping is less common in regional or country towns in Victoria, although a little rounding up never goes astray.

Post

Australia Post (☏03-8847 9045, 13 76 78; www.auspost. com.au) divides international destinations into two zones: Asia-Pacific and the rest of the world. Airmail letters cost $1.85 and $2.60, respectively. Postage for postcards ($2.60) is the same to any country. Stamps can be purchased at post offices, newsagents and some small grocery or general stores.

Public Holidays

Victoria observes the following nine public holidays:

New Year's Day 1 January

Australia Day 26 January

Labour Day First or second Monday in March

Easter Good Friday and Easter Monday in March/April

Anzac Day 25 April

Queen's Birthday Second Monday in June

Melbourne Cup Day First Tuesday in November

Christmas Day 25 December

Boxing Day 26 December

Safe Travel

Australia is a relatively safe place to travel by world standards (crime- and war-wise at any rate) but natural disasters have been wreaking havoc of late. Bushfires, floods and cyclones regularly decimate parts of most states and territories, but if you pay attention to

warnings from local authorities and don't venture into affected areas, you should be fine.

Animal Bites & Stings
FLIES & MOSQUITOES

For four to six months of the year, you'll have to cope with those two banes of the Australian outdoors: the fly and the mosquito ('mozzie'). Flies aren't too bad in the city but they start getting out of hand in the country, and the further out you go, the more numerous and persistent they seem to be. Widely available repellents such as Aerogard and Rid may also help to deter the little bastards, but don't count on it.

Mozzies are a problem in summer, particularly for campers near water. Try to keep your arms and legs covered as soon as the sun goes down and use insect repellent liberally.

SNAKES & SPIDERS

Bushwalkers should be aware that snakes and spiders, some venomous, are quite common in the Victoria bush, but the risk of getting bitten is very low. Snakes are usually quite timid in nature, and in most instances will move away if disturbed. Wear boots and socks to cover the ankles when walking in summer.

If bitten, a pressure bandage and immobilisation is the best course of action while awaiting medical care. All snake bites can be treated with antivenom. Spiders to watch out for are the 'redback' and 'white-tail' varieties.

TICKS & LEECHES

The common bush-tick (found in the forest and scrub country all along Australia's east coast) can be dangerous if left lodged in the skin, as the toxin excreted by the tick can cause partial paralysis and, in theory, death, although this is extremely rare. Check your

body for lumps every night if you're walking in tick-infested areas. Remove the tick by dousing it with methylated spirits or kerosene and levering it out, but make sure you remove it intact.

Leeches are common, but while they will suck your blood, they are not dangerous and are easily removed by the application of salt or heat.

Environmental Hazards

Bushfires happen every year in Victoria. In hot, dry and windy weather, be extremely careful with any naked flame – cigarette butts thrown out of car windows have started many fires. On a 'total fire ban' day it's forbidden even to use a camping stove in the open. Locals will not be amused if they catch you breaking this particular law; they'll happily turn you in to the authorities, and the penalties are severe.

Bushwalkers should seek local advice before setting out – be careful if a total fire ban is in place, or delay your trip. If you're out in the bush and you see smoke, even a long way away, take it seriously – bushfires move very quickly and change direction with the wind. Go to the nearest open space, downhill if possible. A forested ridge is the most dangerous place to be.

More bushwalkers actually die of cold than in bushfires. Even in summer, temperatures can drop below freezing at night in the mountains and Victorian weather is notoriously changeable. Exposure in even moderately cool temperatures can sometimes result in hypothermia. Always take suitable spare clothing and adequate water and carbohydrates.

Swimming

Popular Victorian beaches are patrolled by surf lifesavers in summer, with patrolled areas marked off by a pair of red-

and-yellow flags. Always swim between the flags if possible.

Victoria's ocean beaches often have treacherous waves and rips. Even if you're a competent swimmer, you should exercise extreme caution and avoid the water altogether in high surf. If you happen to get caught in a rip when swimming and are being taken out to sea, try not to panic. Raise one arm until you have been spotted, and then swim parallel to the shore – *don't* try to swim back against the rip.

A number of people are also paralysed every year in rivers and lakes and from piers by diving into shallow water and hitting a sandbar or submerged log; always check the depth of the water before you leap.

Telephone

The increasingly elusive public payphone is either coin- or card-operated; local calls are unlimited and cost 50¢, calls to mobile phones are timed and attract higher charges. Some accept credit cards; many don't work at all.

➡ area code ☎03

➡ country code ☎61

➡ international access code (for dialling out) ☎0011

➡ toll-free ☎1800; ☎1300 numbers are the cost of a local call.

Mobile Phones

All Australian mobile-phone numbers have four-digit prefixes beginning with ☎04.

Australia's digital network is compatible with GSM 900 and 1800 handsets. Quad-based US phones will also work. Prepaid SIM cards are available from a range of telecommunications providers:

Dodo (☎13 36 36; www.dodo. com)

Optus (☎1800 780 219; www. optus.com.au)

Telstra (☎13 22 00; www. telstra.com.au)

Virgin (☎1300 555 100; www. virginmobile.com.au)

Vodafone (☎1300 650 410; www.vodafone.com.au)

Phonecards

There's a wide range of local and international phonecards available from most newsagents and post offices for a fixed dollar value (usually $5 to $50). These can be used with any public or private phone by dialling a toll-free access number and then the PIN on the card.

Tourist Information

Regional centres throughout the state will usually have a visitor centre or tourist information booth in a central location. These are listed throughout this book.

Tourism Victoria (☎13 28 42; www.visitvictoria.com.au) The state tourism body has a thorough website and phone service. Its online travel planner offers maps, travel ideas and a route planner.

Travellers With Disabilities

Many of the attractions in Melbourne and regional Victoria are accessible for wheelchairs. Trains and newer trams have low steps to accommodate wheelchairs and people with limited mobility. Many car parks in the city have convenient spaces allocated for disabled drivers. All pedestrian crossings feature sound cues and accessible buttons.

Travellers Aid (www.travellers aid.org.au) City (☎03-9654 2600; Level 3, 225 Bourke St); Southern Cross Station (☎03-9670 2072; Lower Concourse, Southern Cross Station); Flinders St Station (☎03-9610 2030; Main Concourse, Flinders St Station) These centres are particularly helpful to those with special needs and offer a variety of facilities to travellers, including showers, baby-change facilities, toilets, lounge area, public telephone, lockers, stroller and wheelchair hire, and ironing facilities.

City of Melbourne (www. melbourne.vic.gov.au) Online mobility map and information for people with disabilities.

National Information Communication & Awareness Network (Nican; ☎TTY 1800 806 769, TTY 02-6241 1220; www.nican.com.au) Australia-wide directory providing information on access, accommodation, sporting and recreational activities, transport and specialist tour operators.

VicDeaf (☎03-9657 8111; www.vicdeaf.com.au) Auslan interpreter service available.

VicRoads (☎13 11 71; www. vicroads.vic.gov.au) Supplies parking permits for disabled drivers.

Vision Australia (☎1300 847 466; www.visionaustralia. org.au) The Royal Victorian Institute for the Blind has become part of this national organisation.

SUNBURN & SKIN CANCER

Australia has one of the highest rates of skin cancer in the world. Don't be fooled by Victoria's variable weather and cloudy days – UV exposure here is as dangerous as anywhere in the country. If you're going out in the summer sun, particularly at the beach, use 50-plus water-resistant sunscreen and wear a hat, sunglasses and shirt as much as possible. Do the same for your kids' sensitive skin.

Visas

All visitors to Australia need a visa (only New Zealand nationals are exempt, and even they receive a 'special category' visa on arrival). Application forms for the several types of visa are available from Australian diplomatic missions overseas, travel agents or the website of the **Department of Immigration & Citizenship** (www.immi.gov.au).

If you are from a country not covered by either the eVisitor or ETA categories, or you want to stay longer than three months, you'll need to apply for a tourist visa.

eVisitor

Many European passport holders are eligible for a free eVisitor visa, allowing stays in Australia for up to three months within a 12-month period. eVisitor visas must be applied for online (www.immi.gov.au/e_visa/evisitor.htm). They are electronically stored and linked to individual passport numbers, so no stamp in your passport is required. It's advisable to apply at least 14 days prior to your proposed date of travel to Australia.

Electronic Travel Authority (ETA)

Passport holders from eight countries that aren't part of the eVisitor scheme – Brunei, Canada, Hong Kong, Japan, Malaysia, Singapore, South Korea and the USA – can apply for either a visitor or business ETA. These are valid for 12 months, with stays of up to three months on each visit. You can apply for the ETA online (www.eta.immi.gov.au), which attracts a nonrefundable service charge of $20.

Working Holiday Visas (417)

Visitors aged 18 to 30 from Belgium, Canada, Cyprus, Denmark, Estonia, Finland, France, Germany, Hong Kong, Ireland, Italy, Japan, South Korea, Malta, Netherlands, Norway, Sweden, Taiwan and the UK are eligible for a working holiday visa, which allows you to visit for up to one year and gain casual employment.

You can apply for this visa up to a year in advance. Conditions include having a return air ticket or sufficient funds for a return or onward fare. The application fee is $420.

Work & Holiday Visas (462)

Nationals from Argentina, Bangladesh, Chile, Indonesia, Malaysia, Thailand, Turkey and the USA aged between the ages of 18 and 30 can apply for a work and holiday visa prior to entry to Australia. Once granted, this visa allows the holder to enter Australia within three months of issue, stay for up to 12 months, leave and re-enter Australia any number of times within that 12 months, undertake temporary employment to supplement a trip, and study for up to four months. For details see www.immi.gov.au/visitors/working-holiday/462. The application fee is $420.

Women Travellers

Victoria is generally a safe place for women travellers, although the usual sensible precautions apply. It's best to avoid walking alone late at night, especially when no one else is around; if you're out for a big night on the town, always keep enough money aside for a taxi back to your accommodation. Alcohol-fuelled violence is becoming more common in Melbourne's city centre. The same applies to rural towns, where there are often a lot of unlit, semideserted streets. Lone women should also be wary of staying in basic pub accommodation unless it looks safe and well managed.

Like many other places, Aussie male culture does sometimes manifest itself in sexist bravado, and sexual harassment isn't uncommon, especially when alcohol is involved.

We do not recommend that women hitchhike alone.

The following organisations offer advice and services for women:

Royal Women's Hospital Health Information Service (☑03-8345 2000; www.thewomens.org.au; 20 Flemington Rd, Parkville)

Royal Women's Hospital Sexual Assault Unit (☑03-8345 3494, 1800 806 292; www.thewomens.org.au/SexualAssaultInformation; 20 Flemington Rd, Parkville)

Transport

GETTING THERE & AWAY

Air

Airlines

Qantas (☑13 13 13; www. qantas.com) Australia's main carrier, with frequent flights to/from Melbourne and regional centres.

Jetstar (☑13 15 38; www. jetstar.com) The budget subsidiary of Qantas has frequent scheduled flights to/from Melbourne and Avalon Airports.

Virgin Australia (☑13 67 89; www.virginaustralia.com) An extensive domestic network covering most major cities across the country.

Tiger (☑03-9034 3733; www. tigerairways.com) Budget flights from Melbourne to numerous destinations throughout Australia.

Regional Express Airlines (Rex; ☑13 17 13; www.rex.com.

au) Flights from Melbourne to Adelaide, Sydney and regional centres, including Mildura and Albury.

Sharp Airlines (☑1300 556 694; www.sharpairlines. com) Flights from Melbourne's **Essendon Airport** (MEB; ☑03-9948 9300; www.essendonairport.com.au) to Portland, Hamilton and Flinders Island.

Airports

Melbourne Airport (MEL; ☑03-9297 1600; www.melbourneairport.com.au), often referred to as Tullamarine or Tulla, is around 25km northwest of the city centre. All international and domestic terminals are within the same complex. There are no direct train or tram services linking it with the city, but **airport shuttle buses** (Map p50; ☑03-9335 2811; www. skybus.com.au; adult/child one-way $18/7) meet flights and taxis descend like flies.

Avalon Airport (AVV; ☑03-5227 9100, 1800 282 566; www.avalonairport.com.au) is around 55km southwest of the city centre on the way to Geelong. At the time of writing, only Jetstar flights to/from Sydney and Brisbane use the airport. **Sita Coaches** (☑03-9689 7999; www.sitacoaches.com.au) operates an airport shuttle, meeting all flights and picking up or dropping off at Southern Cross Station ($22/42 one way/return). The trip takes around 40 to 50 minutes.

REGIONAL AIRPORTS

Mildura Airport (MQL; ☑03-5055 0500; www.milduraairport.com.au) has scheduled flights to/from Melbourne and Adelaide. During the ski season, **QantasLink** (☑13 13 13; www.qantas.com) flies from Sydney to **Mt Hotham Airport** (MHU; www.mthotham. com.au).

CLIMATE CHANGE & TRAVEL

Every form of transport that relies on carbon-based fuel generates CO_2, the main cause of human-induced climate change. Modern travel is dependent on aeroplanes, which might use less fuel per kilometre per person than most cars but travel much greater distances. The altitude at which aircraft emit gases (including CO_2) and particles also contributes to their climate change impact. Many websites offer 'carbon calculators' that allow people to estimate the carbon emissions generated by their journey and, for those who wish to do so, to offset the impact of the greenhouse gases emitted with contributions to portfolios of climate-friendly initiatives throughout the world. Lonely Planet offsets the carbon footprint of all staff and author travel.

Land

Bus

Firefly (Map p50; ☑1300 730 740; www.fireflyexpress.com. au) Day and overnight buses from Melbourne to Adelaide ($60, 11 hours) and Sydney ($60, 14 hours).

Greyhound Australia (☑1300 473 946; www.grey-hound.com.au) Interstate buses between Melbourne's Southern Cross Station and Adelaide ($60, 10 hours), Sydney ($79, 14 hours) and Canberra ($70, nine hours).

Premier Motor Service (☑13 34 10; www.premierms. com.au) Interstate buses between Melbourne and Sydney via Gippsland and the New South Wales coast ($85, 18 hours), continuing to Brisbane and Cairns.

Train

NSW TrainLink (☑13 22 32; www.nswtrainlink.info) Express trains to Melbourne from Sydney ($110.70, 11 hours, two daily) via Albury (from $56.85, 3¼ hours, two daily).

Great Southern Rail (☑13 21 47; www.gsr.com.au) Operates the *Overland* service between Melbourne and Adelaide ($58-166, 10 hours, three weekly), departing Melbourne at 8.05am and Adelaide at 7.40am. Bring your car along on the Motorail.

V/Line (☑13 61 96; www. vline.com.au) No direct interstate rail services but has train and coach combinations to Adelaide, Sydney, Canberra and Mt Gambier (via the Great Ocean Road).

Sea

Spirit of Tasmania (☑1800 634 906; www.spiritoftasmania. com.au; adult/car one-way from $174/89) is a beloved vehicle and passenger ferry sailing nightly to Devonport on Tasmania's northern coast from Station Pier in Port Melbourne, with additional day sailings during summer. The crossing takes around 11 hours. A wide variety of seasonal fares are available, from basic seats to private en suite cabins. Vehicles can be taken across from $89 one-way.

GETTING AROUND

Air

QantasLink (☑13 13 13; www.qantas.com) Flies to Mildura and Mt Hotham.

Regional Express (REX; ☑13 17 13; www.rex.com.au) Rex flies to Albury and Mildura.

Bicycle

Without the vast distances of other mainland states, Victoria is perfect for cycling, whether road touring or mountain biking.

Bicycles are carried for free on the Queenscliff–Sorrento ferry and all V/Line regional train services provided you check in 30 minutes before departure – but be aware if buying a train-coach combination ticket that V/Line bus services do not carry bicycles. The system of rail trails (disused train lines adapted as cycling paths) is growing in country Victoria, and provides scenic, hassle-free cycling. Some routes connect with V/Line

....

VICTORIAN RAIL TRAILS

Victoria's rail trails are a great way to see parts of regional Victoria by bike, and more trails are being developed as funding becomes available. Some of the best:

TRAIL	START/FINISH	LENGTH
Murray to Mountains	Wangaratta/Bright	116km
East Gippsland	Bairnsdale/Orbost	94km
Great Southern	Leongatha/Foster	58km
High Country	Wodonga/Old Tallangatta	37km
Lilydale–Warburton	Lilydale/Warburton	40km
Bellarine Peninsula	Geelong/Queenscliff	32.5km
Bass Coast	Anderson/Wonthaggi	16km
O'Keefe	Bendigo/Axedale	23km
Gippsland Lakes	Colquhoun/Lakes Entrance	17km
Camperdown–Timboon	Camperdown/Timboon	40km
Ballarat–Skipton	Ballarat/Skipton	56km
Port Fairy–Warrnambool	Port Fairy/Warrnambool	37km

TOP CAR-TOURING ROUTES

Great Ocean Road (Torquay to Warrnambool)

Great Alpine Hwy (Wangaratta to Bairnsdale)

Eildon-Jamieson Rd (Eildon to Jamieson)

Grand Ridge Road (Warragul to Korumburra)

Bogong High Plains Rd (Mt Beauty to Omeo)

Grampians Tourist Rd (Halls Gap to Dunkeld; Halls Gap to Wartook)

Around the Bay (Melbourne to Melbourne via Sorrento, Queenscliff and Geelong)

Yarra Ranges (Healesville to Marysville and Warburton)

Wilderness Coast (Orbost to Mallacoota via Marlo and Cann River)

Goldfields Touring (Castlemaine, Maldon, Maryborough, Dunolly, Bendigo)

train stations. See www. railtrails.com.au for details.

Bikes can be hired in Melbourne and most towns in regional Victoria, particularly any town where there are well-established cycling paths. Typical hire costs $25 to $50 a day, depending on the quality of the bike. Melbourne also has a popular **bike-share program** (☑1300 711 590; www.melbournebikeshare.com.au) with pick-up and drop-off points around the inner city.

Boat

The only scheduled boat services are the regular daily **Queenscliff–Sorrento Car & Passenger Ferries** (☑03-5258 3244; www.searoad.com.au; adult/child/car return from $20/16/112) between Queenscliff and Sorrento, and the **Inter Island Ferries** (☑03-9585 5730; www.interislandferries.com.au; adult/child/bike return $24/12/8) from Stony Point on the Mornington Peninsula to French Island and Phillip Island.

Charter boats and cruises can get you around on the water in the Gippsland Lakes and Murray region.

Bus

Victoria's regional bus network **V/Line** (☑13 61 96; www.vline.com.au) offers both a relatively cheap and reliable service, though it can require planning if you intend to do more than straightforward city-to-city trips. The buses basically supplement the train services, so you'll often find yourself on a train and bus combination, changing services en route. For getting between smaller country towns, a bus may well be the only public-transport option and it may not even run daily. In some regions, private transport companies run bus services that often connect with V/Line trains and buses.

Car & Motorcycle

Victoria has some fantastic touring routes for cars and motorcycles, and a lack of public transport in many areas outside the metropolitan area means your own vehicle is often the best way to go.

Driving

Foreign driving licences are valid as long as they are in English or accompanied by a translation. If in doubt, pick up an International Drivers Licence from your home country's automobile association.

Driving is on the left-hand side of the road. The speed limit in residential areas is 50km/h, rising to 70km/h or 80km/h on some main roads

and dropping to 40km/h in specially designated areas such as school zones. On highways the speed limit is generally 100km/h, while on some sections of freeway it's 110km/h.

Wearing seat belts is compulsory, and children up to seven years of age must be belted into an approved safety seat. Motorcyclists must wear crash helmets at all times. The police strictly enforce Victoria's blood-alcohol limit of 0.05% with random breath testing (and drug testing) of drivers.

Toll Roads

Melbourne's **CityLink** (☑13 26 29; www.citylink.com.au) tollway road system has two main routes: the Southern Link, which runs from the southeastern suburb of Malvern to Kings Way on the southern edge of the city centre; and the Western Link, which runs from the Calder Fwy intersection with the Tullamarine Fwy south to the West Gate Fwy.

A CityLink 24-hour pass costs $14.90 and is valid for 24 hours from your first entry through a tollway. A 24-hour Tulla Pass is $5.30 and a weekend pass is $14.90. The easiest way to buy a pass is with a credit card online or by telephoning CityLink.

If you accidentally find yourself on the CityLink toll road (and it's very easy to do), don't panic – there's a three-day grace period in which you can arrange payment. Passes are not required for motorbikes.

EastLink (☑13 54 65; www.eastlink.com.au), which links the Eastern, Monash and Frankston freeways, charges $5.69 for a full-trip pass. To use CityLink and EastLink, you can start a 30-day Melbourne Pass ($5.50 start-up), which will automatically accumulate your tolls and fees.

Automobile Associations

Royal Automobile Association of Victoria (RACV; ☑13 19 55; www.racv.com.au) Provides emergency breakdown service, literature, maps and accommodation service. For roadside assistance, RACV has reciprocal agreements with automobile associations in all other states, and many other countries. Basic membership costs $95 (plus $52 joining fee).

Car Hire

The following major car hire companies are represented at the airport, at city locations and in major regional centres:

Avis (☑13 63 33; www.avis.com.au)

Budget (☑1300 362 848; www.budget.com.au)

Europcar (☑1300 131 390; www.europcar.com.au)

Hertz (☑13 30 39; www.hertz.com.au)

Thrifty (☑1300 367 227; www.thrifty.com.au)

Campervans

The following companies have offices in Melbourne and a range of van sizes:

Apollo (☑1800 777 779; www.apollocamper.com)

Aussie Campervans (☑03-9317 4991; www.aussiecampervans.com)

Britz Australia (☑1300 738 087; www.britz.com.au)

Jucy (☑1800 150 850; www.jucy.com.au)

Travellers Auto Barn (☑1800 674 374, 02-9326 3988; www.travellers-autobarn.com.au)

Wicked Campers (☑1800 246 869; www.wickedcampers.com.au)

Train

V/Line (☑13 61 96; www.vline.com.au) runs a network of trains around the state, most emanating out of Melbourne's **Southern Cross Station** (www.southerncrossstation.net.au; cnr Collins & Spencer Sts). It's a comfortable and efficient way to travel but the rail network is limited to a handful of main lines, so you will often need to rely on train-bus combinations (conveniently also operated by V/Line).

REGIONAL TRAIN LINES	MAIN STATIONS
Geelong	Melbourne, Geelong, Colac, Warrnambool
Bendigo	Melbourne, Kyneton, Bendigo, Swan Hill, Echuca
Ballarat	Melbourne, Ballarat, Ararat, Nhill
Gippsland	Melbourne, Traralgon, Bairnsdale
Seymour	Melbourne, Seymour, Wangaratta, Albury

Tours

If you want to venture further afield but don't feel like travelling solo, or are time-poor, there are literally dozens of tours through Victoria to suit all tastes and budgets. Recommended operators:

Adventure Tours Australia (☑1300 654 604; www.adventuretours.com.au) Backpacker-style bus tours between Melbourne and Adelaide, and Melbourne and Sydney, via the coast roads, plus a whole range of single- and multiday tours.

TRAIN FARES AT A GLANCE

Sample one-way V/Line fares from Melbourne:

DESTINATION	FARE ($)	DURATION (HR)
Ballarat	12.80	1½
Bendigo	19.40	2
Castlemaine	14.20	1½
Swan Hill	35.80	4
Echuca	24.60	3½
Seymour	10	1¼
Bairnsdale	31	3½
Warrnambool	31	3¼

Autopia Tours (☎03-9318 0021; www.autopiatours. com.au) Small-group tours to the Grampians, Great Ocean Road, Yarra Valley and the snow-fields, lasting one to three days.

Bunyip Tours (Map p50; ☎1300 286 947; www.bunyip-tours.com) Tours to the Great Ocean Road, Phillip Island, Mornington Peninsula and Wilsons Promontory.

Echidna Walkabout (☎03-9646 8249; www.echidna walkabout.com.au) Runs nature ecotrips (from one- to five-day expeditions) featuring bushwalking and koala spotting as far afield as east Gippsland.

Go West (☎03-9485 5290; www.gowest.com.au) Day tours to the Great Ocean Road and Phillip Island with commentary (in several languages) provided on iPods.

Groovy Grape (☎1800 661 177; www.groovygrape.com. au) Backpacker-style minibus with tours between Adelaide and Melbourne via the Great Ocean Road.

Steamrail Victoria (☎03-9844 1122; www.steamrail.com. au) For steam-train devotees, and those who are looking for an unusual day out, this not-for-profit organisation puts old trains back on the tracks for jaunts to various country destinations around the state.

Wild-Life Tours (☎1300 661 730; www.wildlifetours.com.au) One- to three-day trips to the Grampians and Phillip Island, and Melbourne to Adelaide via the Great Ocean Road.

TRANSPORT TOURS

Behind the Scenes

SEND US YOUR FEEDBACK

We love to hear from travellers – your comments keep us on our toes and help make our books better. Our well-travelled team reads every word on what you loved or loathed about this book. Although we cannot reply individually to postal submissions, we always guarantee that your feedback goes straight to the appropriate authors, in time for the next edition. Each person who sends us information is thanked in the next edition – the most useful submissions are rewarded with a selection of digital PDF chapters.

Visit **lonelyplanet.com/contact** to submit your updates and suggestions or to ask for help. Our award-winning website also features inspirational travel stories, news and discussions.

Note: We may edit, reproduce and incorporate your comments in Lonely Planet products such as guidebooks, websites and digital products, so let us know if you don't want your comments reproduced or your name acknowledged. For a copy of our privacy policy visit lonelyplanet.com/privacy.

AUTHOR THANKS

Anthony Ham

Thanks to Maryanne Netto for sending me to such wonderful places – your legacy will endure. To co-authors Trent and Kate who brought such excellence to the book. To David Andrew for so many wise wildlife tips. And to every person whom I met along the road – from knowledgeable and patient tourist-office staff to other travellers. And to Marina, Carlota and Valentina – home is wherever you are.

Trent Holden & Kate Morgan

A huge thanks to the lovely Maryanne Netto for giving us the chance to work on our hometown book – a great gig. To coordinating author, Anthony Ham, it's always such a pleasure to work with you. We'd like to thank both of our families, especially Tim and Larysa, Gary and Heather, for all of your help, not to mention a place to crash at times! Shout out to Shaun at Port Fairy Motors for your help in getting us back on the road quick smart in a time of chaos. To Linda Bosidis, Caro Cooper, Jane Ormond, Paul and Max Waycott, Alex and Mat Forsman, cheers for great insider tips and suggestions. Finally big thanks to Tasmin Waby, Glenn van der Knijff and all of the in-house staff who worked hard on this book during a tough transitional time.

ACKNOWLEDGMENTS

Climate map data adapted from Peel MC, Finlayson BL & McMahon TA (2007) 'Updated World Map of the Köppen-Geiger Climate Classification', *Hydrology and Earth System Sciences*, 11, 163344.

Cover photograph: Loch Ard Gorge, Port Campbell National Park, David South/Alamy.

THIS BOOK

This 9th edition of Lonely Planet's *Melbourne & Victoria* guidebook was researched and written by Anthony Ham, Trent Holden and Kate Morgan. The previous edition was written by Jayne D'Arcy, Paul Harding and Donna Wheeler. This guidebook was commissioned in Lonely Planet's Melbourne office and produced by the following:

Commissioning Editor
Maryanne Netto
Destination Editor
Tasmin Waby
Product Editor
Elizabeth Jones
Senior Cartographer
Julie Sheridan
Book Designer
Jessica Rose
Assisting Editors Carolyn Bain, Carolyn Boicos, Lauren Hunt, Ali Lemer, Katie O'Connell, Susan Paterson
Assisting Cartographers
Mick Garrett, Diana Von Holdt

Cover Research
Naomi Parker

Thanks to Anita Banh, Imogen Bannister, Elin Berglund, David Carroll, Brendan Dempsey, Andrew Dixon, Paul Harding, Noirin Hegarty, David Kemp, Andrea Yvonne Leber, Kate Mathews, Catherine Naghten, Victoria Nielson, Karyn Noble, Darren O'Connell, Martine Power, Matthew Riddle, Luke Savage, Angela Tinson, Anna Tyler, Glenn van der Knijff, Ilona Watkins

Index

A
Abbotsford Convent 62
Aboriginal people
  arts 70
  cultural centres 57, 65-6, 70, 154, 160, 208, 210
  food 319
  history 308-9
  rock art 208, **10**
  tours 57, 80, 154, 208, 285
accommodation 338-9, *see also individual locations*
activities 34-7, *see also individual activities*
AFL 22, 118, 334-5
air travel 345, 346
Aireys Inlet 165-6
airports 345
Albert Park 74-5
Albert Park Lake 74-5
Albury 304
Alpine National Park **276**
amusement parks 73
Anglesea 164-5
animal bites & stings 342
animals, *see individual animals*
apartments 339
Apollo Bay 170-2
aquariums 57, 157
arcades 54, 56
architecture 332-3
area codes 343
art galleries, *see museums & galleries*
arts 10, 326-33, *see also literature, music, visual arts*
Arts Centre Melbourne 58
Arthurs Seat 218
Ash Wednesday 140
ATMs 341

Map Pages **000**
Photo Pages **000**

Australian Alps Walking Track 234
Australian Centre for the Moving Image (ACMI) 113
Australian Formula One Grand Prix 335
Australian Motorcycle Grand Prix 226
Australian Open (tennis) 336
Australian Rules Football 22, 118, 334-5

B
B&Bs 339
Bairnsdale 244
Ballarat 190-5, **192**
ballet 118, 332
Balnarring 222
Bandt, Adam 307
Barmah National Park 298
Barwon Heads 160-2
Batman, John 310, 311
Baw Baw National Park 257
Baw Baw Village 257
beaches 19
  Anglesea 164
  Apollo Bay 170
  Barwon Heads 160
  Bells Beach 163-4
  Bunurong Marine & Coastal Park 236
  Cape Bridgewater 185
  Croajingolong National Park 254
  Cumberland River 169
  Elwood 74
  Fairhaven 165
  Gibson Beach 175
  Johanna Beach 174
  Lorne 166
  Mallacoota 253
  Mildura 284
  Mornington 217
  Ninety Mile Beach 243
  Phillip Island 226-7

Seaspray 243
Sorrento 220
St Kilda 71
Torquay 162
Warrnambool 177
Wilsons Promontory 239
Beech Forest 173
Beechworth 266-9
beer 108, 293, *see also breweries*
Bellarine Peninsula 41, 157-62
  accommodation 149
Bellarine Taste Trail 161
Bells Beach 163-4
Benalla 302
Bendigo 196-201, **197**
  children, travel with 198
bicycle travel, *see cycling, mountain biking*
Big Desert Wilderness Park 288
bike-sharing program 75
birdwatching 243, 254, 288
Birregurra 168
Black Saturday bushfires 139, 140
Blairgowrie 218, 220
Block Arcade 56
boat travel 77, 157, 346, 347
boating 34
books 327-8
  cooking 322
Brambuk Cultural Centre 210
breweries 17
  Beechworth 268
  Bright 273
  Forrest 171
  Geelong 155
  Gippsland 238
  High Country, the 261
  Melbourne 63, 108
  Mildura 287
Otways, the 173
Red Hill 224
Wangaratta 304

Woodend 148
Yarra Valley 139
Bright 271-4, **272**
Brunswick 97-9, 110
Buchan 249
Buchan Caves Reserve 249
Buckley, William 221
budgeting 15
Bunjil 58
Bunurong Marine & Coastal Park 236
bus travel 128, 346, 347
bushrangers 54, 302, 303, 314, 315
bushwalking, *see walking*
business hours 340

C
cafes 321
campervans 348
camping 338
canoeing 35
  Echuca 295
  Gippsland 242
  Melbourne 75
Cape Bridgewater 185
Cape Conran Coastal Park 252
Cape Duquesne 185
Cape Howe Wilderness Area 254
Cape Otway 173-4
Cape Woolamai 230, **5**
car hire 348
car travel 127-8, 347-8
caravanning 338
Carlton **66**
  accommodation 86
  drinking & nightlife 109-10
  food 97-9
  shopping 124
  sights 63-7
casinos 57
Castlemaine 202-5, **203**
cathedrals, *see churches & cathedrals*

Cave, Nick 329
caves 249
cell phones 343
children, travel with 38-9, 80, 198
Chiltern 301-2
Chinatown 52-4
churches & cathedrals
Sacred Heart Cathedral 198
Scots Church 56
St Michael's Uniting Church 56
St Patrick's Cathedral 57
St Paul's Cathedral 49
cideries 139
cinema, see film
cinemas 113-14
classical music 118, 328
climate 14, 20-3, see also individual regions
clothing, see fashion, markets, shopping
Clunes 195
coffee 321
Coldstream 134, 137, 139
Collingwood, see Fitzroy
Collingwood Children's Farm 62
comedy 115
consulates 340
contemporary art 327
Cook, Captain James 61, 255, 309
Corryong 274
costs 15
courses 79-80, 235, 238, 271, 272
Cowes 229, **228**
Craig's Hut 261
credit cards 341
cricket 335
Croajingolong National Park 254-5
cross-country skiing 141, see also skiing
Lake Mountain 141
Mt Baw Baw 257
Mt Buffalo 270
Mt Buller 263
Mt Hotham 278
culture 306-7, 326-33
Cumberland River 169
customs regulations 340
cycling 34, 35-6, 346-7, see also mountain biking
Bellarine Peninsula 159
Bendigo 198
events 36
Gippsland 237, 251

High Country, the 268, 271
Mansfield 262
Melbourne 75
Rutherglen 299
safety 36
Warrnambool 179
Yarra Valley 138
Yarrawonga 298

D
dance 118, 332
Dandenongs, the 131-3, **132**
dangers 125, 342-3
Daylesford 141-7, **145**
Dimboola 214
Dinner Plain 278-80
disabilities, travellers with 343
distilleries 176, 271, 301
diving, see also snorkelling
Apollo Bay 171
Gippsland 236, 252
Port Campbell 176
Portsea 222
Queenscliff 158
Docklands
drinking & nightlife 106
food 93
sights 57-9
dog-sled tours 279
dolphins 220, 253
drinking 321-3, see also individual locations
drinks, see beer, coffee, tea, wine
driving 127-8, 347-8
Dromana 218
Dunkeld 212
DVDs 341

E
East Gippsland Rail Trail 251
East Melbourne **60**
accommodation 85
sights 59-61
Echuca 292-7, **294**
economy 306-7
Eildon 260-1
electricity 340
embassies 340
emergencies 15, 126, 341
entertainment, see individual locations
environmental hazards 342
environmental issues 307
Errinundra National Park 250-1

Eureka Stockade 190, 191, 313-14
events, see festivals & events
exchange rates 15

F
Fairhaven 165-6
Falls Creek 275-7, **12**
Falls Festival 168
farmers 307
fashion 324-5
Fawkner, John Pascoe 311
Federation Square 45, **10**
ferry travel 77, 157, 346, 347
festivals & events 20-3, see also individual festivals & events, individual locations
film festivals 21, 22, 104, 168, 331
music festivals 168, 329, 330
sporting events 334
film 306, 330-1
festivals 21, 22, 104, 168, 331
Fish Creek 237-8
fishing 36
Gippsland 247, 253
High Country, the 275
Lake Eildon 260
Mornington Peninsula 218
Murray River 291
Port Campbell 175
Fitzroy **64**
accommodation 85-6
drinking & nightlife 107, 109
food 95-7
shopping 121-3
sights 61-3
Flinders 223-4
Flinders Street Station 48-9
food 318-23, see also individual locations
Bellarine Peninsula 161
Great Ocean Road 176
High Country, the 266
Milawa Gourmet Region 265-6
food trucks 94
football (Australian Rules) 22, 118, 334-5, see also soccer
Footscray 59
Formula One racing 335

Forrest 171
Fort Nepean 222
Fort Queenscliff 157
Foster 239, 241-2
French Island 224-5

G
galleries, see museums & galleries
Gariwerd 207-9, **209**
gay travellers 104-5, 142-3, 340
Geelong 152-7, **153**
Gippsland 42, 231-55, **232-3**
accommodation 231
climate 231
food 231
highlights 232-3
travel seasons 231
Gippsland Lakes Coastal Park 243
Glenelg River 186
Glenrowan 302, 303
glow-worms 170, 173, 271
gold rush 194, 312-13, 314-15
Golden Triangle, the 204
Goldfields region 41, 187-207, **188-9**
accommodation 187
climate 187
food 187
highlights 188-9
travel seasons 187
golf
Anglesea 164
Hepburn Springs 142
Melbourne 77
Mildura 284
Mornington Peninsula 223
Queenscliff 157
Swan Hill 290
Yarrawonga 298
Goongerah 251
Goulburn Valley 302
graffiti 327
Grainger, Percy 66-7, 328
Grampians, the 10, 41, 187, 207-14, **188-9**
accommodation 187
climate 187
food 187
highlights 188-9
travel seasons 187
Grampians National Park (Gariwerd) 207-9, **209**
Grand Ridge Road 238

INDEX G-L

Great Ocean Road 9, 41, 149-86, **150-1**
  accommodation 149
  car travel 156
  climate 149
  food 149
  highlights 150-1
  tours 163
  travel seasons 149
Great Ocean Walk 16, 172
Great South West Walk 185
Great Southern Rail Trail 237
Griffiths Island 181
guesthouses 339
Gunbower National Park 292

H
Halls Gap 210-12, **211**
hang-gliding 270
Hanging Rock 148
Harcourt 205
Harrietville 277-8
Hattah Lakes 289
Hattah-Kulkyne National Park 289
Healesville 134-7
Healesville Sanctuary 135
health 341
hedge mazes 217, 271
Heide Museum of Modern Art 62, 326-7
Heidelberg School (art movement) 326
Hepburn Bathhouse & Spa 142
Hepburn Springs 141-7, **142**
Hester, Joy 45, 327
High Country, the 12, 42, 256-80, **258-9**
  accommodation 256
  climate 256
  food 256
  highlights 258-9
  travel seasons 256
hiking, see walking
historic buildings & sites
  Abbotsford Convent 62
  Battery Hill 181
  Beechworth Historic Precinct 267
  Bonegilla 304
  Briars, the 218
  Byramine Homestead 298

Map Pages **000**
Photo Pages **000**

Carman's Tunnel 205
Central Deborah Goldmine 196
Collins Settlement Historic Site 220
Como House 70-1
Flagstaff Hill Maritime Village 177
Fort Queenscliff 157
Government House 70
Historic Port of Echuca 293
Maryborough Railway Station 206
Melbourne Town Hall 49
Old Melbourne Gaol 54
Old Mildura Homestead 284
Old Psyche Bend Pump Station 284
Parliament House 49, 52
Portland Historic Waterfront 184
Rio Vista 284
Royal Arcade 54
Royal Exhibition Building 66
Young & Jackson's 49
historic towns 19, 39
history 308-17
  books 328
  Dreamtime 308
  Eureka Stockade 190, 191, 313-14
  European settlement 309-11
  founding of Melbourne 310-11
  gold rush 194, 312-13, 314-15
  Great Depression 315
  Great Ocean Road 164
  immigration 312, 316, 320, 321
  Indigenous peoples 308-9
  Kelly, Edward (Ned) 54, 302, 303, 314, 315
  prehistory 308
HMAS Castlemaine 77
Hoddle, Robert 311
holidays 342
Hollow Mountain 207
horse racing 336
horse riding 36
  Aireys Inlet 165
  Bendigo 198
  Corryong 274
  Daylesford 142
  Echuca 295
  Falls Creek 276

Grampians, the 208
Lake Eildon 260
Mansfield 262
Mornington Peninsula 223
Mt Bogong 275
Warrnambool 179
Horsham 213
Hosier Lane 48, 56
hostels 339
hot springs 19, 218
hotels 339
houseboats 339
  Echuca 296
  Lake Eildon 260
  Mildura 286
  Swan Hill 291

I
immigration 344
Indigenous peoples, see Aboriginal people
indoor rock climbing 78, see also rock climbing
insurance 341
internet access 126, 341
internet resources 15, 126
Inverloch 235-6
itineraries 24-33

J
Jamieson 261
jazz 330
Jeparit 288
Johanna Beach 164, 174

K
Kangaroo Lake 292
Karbeethong 253
kayaking 35
  Apollo Bay 170
  Echuca 295
  Melbourne 75
  Warrnambool 179
  Yarrawonga 298
Kelly, Edward (Ned) 54, 302, 303, 314, 315
Kelly Gang, the 303, 315
Kennett River 170
Kiewa Valley 274-5
King Valley 265
Kinglake 134, 140
kiteboarding 78-9
koalas 170, 224-5, 226
Koonwarra 237
Koorie Heritage Trust 57
Korumburra 236-7
Kyneton 201-2

L
Lake Boga 292
Lake Charm 292
Lake Eildon National Park 257, 260
Lake Elizabeth 171
Lake Mountain 141
Lake Nagambie 302
Lake Nhill 214
Lake Weeroona 198
Lake Wendouree 190
Lakes District 12, 242-8
Lakes Entrance 246-8, **246-7**
Lakes National Park 244
Lalor, Peter 313, 314
laneways 9, 56
language 14
lawn bowls 78, 159
leeches 342
legal matters 341
lesbian travellers 104-5, 142-3, 340
lighthouses
  accommodation 339
  Cape Nelson Lighthouse 186
  Cape Otway Lightstation 173
  Cape Schanck Lightstation 223
  Flagstaff Hill 177
  Gabo Island Lightstation 253
  Point Hicks Lighthouse 255
  Point Lonsdale Lighthouse 160
  Split Point Lighthouse 165
  Wilsons Promontory 239
Lilydale to Warburton Rail Trail 138
Linga 288-9
literature 327-8, see also books
Little Desert National Park 213-14
live music 17-18, 115-17, 329
Loch Ard 175
Loch Ard Gorge 175
Loch Sport 244
London Bridge (Port Campbell National Park) 175
London Bridge (Portsea) 222
Lorne 166-9, **167**
Lower Glenelg National Park 186
Luna Park 73, **11**

M

Macedon Ranges 147-8
MacKillop, St Mary 184
Mahogany Ship, the 181
Maldon 205-7
Mallacoota 252-4, **12**
Mallee, the 288-9
mallee gums 289
Man from Snowy River, The 261, 274
Mansfield 261-3
markets 17, 123, 322, 325
  Apollo Bay Community Market 170
  Bright 271
  Footscray Market 59
  Geelong Vintage Market 156
  Gippsland 236
  Mansfield 261
  Prahran Market 71
  Queen Victoria Market 55
  Red Hill Market 224
  South Melbourne Market 74
Marlo 251-3
Maryborough 206-7
Marysville 139-41
mazes 217, 271
MCG 59-60, 334
measures 341
medical services 126
Melba, Dame Nellie 328
Melba Gully 173
Melbourne 40, 44-128, **46-7, 50-1, 56, 60, 64, 66, 68, 72**
  accommodation 44, 81-9
  activities 75-9
  children, travel with 80
  climate 44
  courses 79-80
  drinking & nightlife 102-13
  entertainment 113-19
  food 44, 89-102
  free attractions 74
  GLBT culture 104-5
  highlights 46-7
  internet resources 126
  itineraries 48
  shopping 119-25
  sights 45-75
  tours 80-1
  travel seasons 44
  travel to/from 126-7
  travel within 127-8
  walking tour 56

Melbourne Airport 126-127, 345
  accommodation 81
Melbourne Cricket Ground (MCG) 59-60, 334
Melbourne Cup 23, 336
Melbourne General Cemetery 74
Melbourne International Comedy Festival 21
Melbourne Museum 65-6
Melbourne Planetarium 76
Melbourne Recital Centre 58
Merricks 222
Metung 245-6
microbreweries, *see* breweries
Midsumma Festival 20
Milawa Gourmet Region 265-6
Mildura 12, 284-8, **285**
mobile phones 343
Moggs Creek 165
money 15, 126, 341-2
Mora, Mirka 327
Morgan, Dan 'Mad Dog' 303
Mornington 217-18
Mornington Peninsula 41, 215-24, **216, 219**
  accommodation 215
  climate 215
  food 215
  highlights 216
  travel seasons 215
Mornington Peninsula National Park 223
motels 339
motorcycle grand prix 226
motorcycle travel 127-8, 347-8
mountain biking 35-6, *see also* cycling
  Bright 271
  Forrest 171
  Harrietville 277
  Lake Mountain 141
  Mansfield 262
  Mt Buller 264
  Mt Hotham 278
MoVida 90
Mt Abrupt 212
Mt Arapiles State Park 213
Mt Baw Baw 257
Mt Beauty 274-5
Mt Bogong 274
Mt Buffalo 270
Mt Buffalo National Park 270-1
Mt Buller 263-5

Mt Donna Buang 138
Mt Ellery 250-1
Mt Feathertop 277, 278
Mt Franklin 146
Mt Hotham 278-80
Mt Macedon 147, 148
Mt St Phillack 257
Mt Stapylton 207
Mt Stirling 261
Mt Sturgeon 212
multiculturalism 312, 316, 320, 321
Murray cod 291
Murray River region 42, 281, **282-3**
  accommodation 281
  climate 281
  food 281
  highlights 282-3
  travel seasons 281
Murray to Mountains Rail Trail 268, 271, 303
Murray-Sunset National Park 288-9
museums & galleries 18
  Alcaston Gallery 63
  Anna Schwartz Gallery 55
  Army Museum Bandiana 304
  Art Gallery of Ballarat 190
  Australian Centre for Contemporary Art 58
  Australian Centre for the Moving Image (ACMI) 45, 48
  Benalla Art Gallery 302
  Bendigo Art Gallery 198
  Bonegilla Migrant Experience 304
  Boom Gallery 152
  Buda 202
  Burke Museum 267
  Castlemaine Art Gallery & Historical Museum 202
  Celia Rosser Gallery 237-8
  Centre for Contemporary Photography (CCP) 63
  Charles Nodrum Gallery 61
  Chinese Museum 53-4
  Collingwood Arts Precinct 63
  Convent Gallery 142
  Costume & Pioneer Museum 302
  Dunkeld Historical Society Museum 212

Echuca Historical Museum 293
Flagstaff Hill Maritime Village 177
Gallery Gabrielle Pizzi 63
Geelong Art Gallery 152
Gertrude Contemporary Art Space 63
Gippsland Regional Maritime Museum 242
Gold Dragon Museum & Gardens 196
Goldfields Historical Museum 204
Grainger Museum 66-7
Great Aussie Beer Shed 293
Great Ocean Road National Heritage Centre 166
Hadfield's Rod Museum 202
Heide Museum of Modern Art 62, 326-7
Hellenic Museum 55
History House 184
History of Motorsport Museum 226
Horsham Regional Art Gallery 213
Ian Potter Centre: NGV Australia 45
Ian Potter Museum of Art 66
Immigration Museum 57
Jewish Holocaust Centre 74
Jewish Museum of Australia 71
Johnston Collection 61
Kyneton Historical Museum 201
Linden Arts Centre & Gallery 73
Living Museum 59
Maldon & District Museum 205
Man from Snowy River Museum 274
Melbourne Museum 65-6
Melbourne Planetarium 76
Monash University Museum of Art (MUMA) 74
Mornington Peninsula Regional Gallery 217
Museo Italiano 67
Museum of Australian Democracy at Eureka 191
National Alpine Museum of Australia 263-4

museums & galleries
  continued
National Holden Museum 293
National Sports Museum 60
National Wool Museum 152
NGV International 57-8
Old Geelong Gaol 152
Old Melbourne Gaol 54
Old Treasury Building 49
Orbost Exhibition Centre 251
Polly Woodside 58
Port Fairy History Museum 181
Portland Maritime Discovery Centre 184
Qdos Art Gallery 167
Queenscliff Maritime Museum 157
RAAF Museum 79
Scienceworks 76
Sorrento Museum 220
Sovereign Hill 190
State Library of Victoria 54
Surf World Museum 162
Sutton Gallery 63
Swan Hill Pioneer Settlement 290
Swan Hill Regional Art Gallery 290
TarraWarra Museum of Art 135
Tolarno Galleries 55
Walhalla Historical Museum 234
Warrnambool Art Gallery 179
West Space 55
Williamstown Railway Museum 76-7
Worsley Cottage 206
music 306, 328-30
  classical music 118
  festivals 168, 329, 330
  live music 17-18, 115-17, 329
  opera 118
  musicals 114
MV Mary Ann 295
Myrtleford 270

N
Nagambie 302
National Gallery of Victoria (NGV) International 57

national parks
Alpine National Park **276**
Barmah National Park 298
Baw Baw National Park 257
Chiltern-Mt Pilot National Park 301
Croajingolong National Park 254-5
Dandenong Ranges National Park 131
Errinundra National Park 250-1
Grampians National Park (Gariwerd) 207-9, **209**
Gunbower National Park 292
Hattah-Kulkyne National Park 289
Lake Eildon National Park 257, 260
Lakes National Park 244
Little Desert National Park 213-14
Lower Glenelg National Park 186
Mornington Peninsula National Park 223
Mt Buffalo National Park 270-1
Murray-Sunset National Park 288-9
Port Campbell National Park 174
Port Nepean National Park 222-3
Snowy River National Park 249-50
Tarra-Bulga National Park 238
Wilsons Promontory National Park 11, 42, 231, 238-42, **240**, **11**
Wyperfeld National Park 288
Yarra Ranges National Park 138
Neighbours 332
Nelson 186
newspapers 126, 341
Nhill 214
Ninety Mile Beach 243
Nolan, Sir Sidney 45, 326
Nooramunga Marine & Coastal Park 242
Northcote, see Fitzroy

O
Ocean Grove 160
Old Melbourne Gaol 54

Olympic Games 315
Omeo 280
opening hours 340
opera 118
Orbost 251
Otway Fly 173
outdoor activities 34-7, see also individual activities
Oxley 265-6

P
paddle steamers 251, 284-5, 290, 293, 294-5
paddleboarding 78-9, 182
paragliding 271
parking 128
parks & gardens, see also national parks
Bendigo 198
Birrarung Marr 48
Castlemaine 202
Ceres 67
Cheetham Wetlands 77
Daylesford 142
Fitzroy Gardens 61
Flagstaff Gardens 55, 57
Geelong 154
Herring Island Park 71
Horsham 213
Kyneton 201
Macedon Ranges 147
Mornington 217
National Rhododendron Gardens 131
Royal Botanic Gardens 69-70
St Kilda Botanical Gardens 73
Yarra Bend Park 62-3
passports 344
Paynesville 244-5
pelicans 245
Penguin Parade (Phillip Island) 226
penguins 174, 226, 253, **11**
Phar Lap 65, 313
Phillip Island 11, 41, 215, 225-30, **216**, **227**
  accommodation 215
  climate 215
  highlights 216
  travel seasons 215
phonecards 343
Picnic at Hanging Rock 148
Pink Lakes 288
planning 14-5, see also individual regions
  budgeting 15

calendar of events 20-3
children, travel with 38-9
internet resources 15
itineraries 24-33
Melbourne & Victoria basics 14-15
outdoor activities 34-7
repeat visitors 16
travel seasons 14, 20-3
Victoria's regions 40-2
Point Cook 79
Point Gellibrand 77
Point Hicks 255
Point Lonsdale 160
Point Nepean National Park 222-3
politics 306-7, 316-17, 329
population 306, 307
Port Albert 242
Port Campbell 175-7
Port Fairy 181-4, **182**
Port Melbourne 74-5
Portland 184-5
Portsea 222
possums 55, 292, 309
postal services 126, 342
Power, Harry 265
Power's Lookout 265
Prahran **68**
  accommodation 86-7
  drinking & nightlife 110-12
  food 101
  shopping 124-5
  sights 69-71
Provenance 268
PS Adelaide 293
PS Alexander Arbuthnot 294
PS Canberra 294
PS Curlip 251
PS Emmylou 295
PS Melbourne 284
PS Pevensey 293, 295
PS Pride of the Murray 295
PS Pyap 290
public holidays 342
public transport 128
Puffing Billy 131
punk music 329, 330
PV Mundoo 284
PV Rothbury 285, **12**

Q
Queen Victoria Market 55
Queenscliff 157-9, **158**

R

radio 341
rail trails 346
Raymond Island 244-5
Red Hill 224
Reed, John & Sunday 62, 326
religion 307
rental accommodation 339
Rhyll 229-30
Richmond **60**
  drinking & nightlife 106-7
  food 94
  shopping 125
  sights 59-61
Riley, Jack 274
rock art 208, **10**
rock climbing 78, 207, 213, 270, 271
Rod Laver Arena 117
Royal Arcade 54
Royal Botanic Gardens 69-70
Royal Exhibition Building 66
Royal Mail Hotel 212
Royal Melbourne Zoo 67
rugby 335-6
running 78, 336
Rutherglen 299-302

S

safe travel 125, 342-3
sailing 78
Sale 242-3
sanctuaries, *see* wildlife sanctuaries
scenic flights
  Bright 271
  Geelong 154
  Mansfield 262
  Melbourne 80
  Mildura 286
  Phillip Island 228
  Port Campbell 175
  Torquay 162
scenic railways 39
  Bellarine Peninsula Railway 39, 158
  Daylesford Spa Country Railway 142
  Mornington Railway 39, 218
  Puffing Billy 39, 131
  South Gippsland Railway 237
  Victorian Goldfields Railway 202, 205
  Walhalla Goldfields Railway 234, **13**

Scienceworks 76
Sealers Cove Walk 241, **11**
seals 185, 226, 253
Seaspray 243
Seaworks 16, 76
Seddon 59
Serra Range 207
Shepherds Flat 146
Shipwreck Coast 175
shopping 324-5, *see also individual locations*
Shrine of Remembrance 70
Simone, Patrizia 272
skiing 12, 37, *see also cross-country skiing*
  Falls Creek 275
  Lake Mountain 141
  Mt Baw Baw 257
  Mt Buller 263-4
  Mt Hotham 278-9
skydiving 302
snakes 342
snorkelling, *see also diving*
  Gippsland 236
  Port Campbell 176
  Portsea 222
  Queenscliff 158
snowboarding 12, 37
  Falls Creek 275
  Mt Baw Baw 257
  Mt Hotham 278-9
snowshoeing 264, 275
Snowy River National Park 249-50
soccer 335
Sorrento 220-2
South Melbourne
  accommodation 88-9
  drinking & nightlife 112
  food 102
  shopping 125
  sights 74-5
South Yarra **68**
  accommodation 86-7
  drinking & nightlife 110-12
  food 101
  shopping 124-5
  sights 69-71
Southbank
  food 93
  sights 57-9
Sovereign Hill 190
spas
  Daylesford 143
  Dinner Plain 278
  Gippsland 237, 247
  Hepburn Springs 142, 143

Melbourne 75-7
Mt Buller 264
spiders 342
sport 10, 119, 334-6, *see also individual sports*
St Andrews 138
St Kilda 11, **72**
  accommodation 87-8
  drinking & nightlife 112-13
  food 99-101
  shopping 125
  sights 71-4
stand-up paddleboarding 78-9, 182
State Library of Victoria 54
street art 327
sunburn 343
superb parrot 298
surfing 37, *see also surfing lessons*
  Bells Beach 163-4
  Gippsland 236, 253
  Great Ocean Road 37
  Mornington Peninsula 222
  Phillip Island 226-7
  Torquay 162
surfing lessons, *see also surfing*
  Anglesea 164
  Apollo Bay 170
  Inverloch 235
  Lakes Entrance 247
  Lorne 168
  Mornington Peninsula 223
  Port Fairy 182
  Torquay 162
  Warrnambool 179
Swan Hill 289-91
swimming 78
  safety 342-3

T

taxis 128
tea 321
telephone services 343
television 331, 341
tennis 336
theatre 114-15, 331-2
ticks 342
Tidal River 238
Timboon 176
tipping 341-2
toll roads 128, 347-8
Torquay 162-3
tourist information 126, 343

tours 80-1, 348-9
Tower Hill Reserve 180-1
train travel 39, 128, 346, 348, *see also scenic railways*
tram travel 81, 128
transport 345-9
travel to/from Victoria 345-6
travel within Victoria 346-9
trekking, *see walking*
Trentham 147-8
True History of the Kelly Gang 303, 314, 328
Tucker, Albert 45, 62, 327
Twelve Apostles 174, **8**

V

vacations 342
vaccinations 341
vegetarian travellers 320
Victorian Alps 256-80
Victorian Football League (VFL) 335
visas 344
visual arts 55, 326-7
von Guérard, Eugene 326
Vue de Monde 92

W

Wahgunyah 301
Walhalla 13, 234-5
walking 34-5
  Bendigo 198
  Bright 271
  Cape Conran Coastal Park 252
  Chiltern-Mt Pilot National Park 301
  French Island 224-5
  Gippsland 234, 237, 244, 251
  Grampians, the 207, 208, 214
  Great Ocean Road 172, 176
  Harrietville 277
  High Country, the 257
  Lakes Entrance 247
  Lorne 166
  Mallacoota 253
  Mansfield 262
  Marysville 139
  Mt Beauty 274
  Mt Buffalo 270
  Mt Hotham 278
  Port Fairy 182
  Portland 185
  Sale 242-3

walking *continued*
Snowy River National Park 250
Warrnambool 179
Wilsons Promontory 238-9, 241
Wangaratta 302-4
Warburton 138
Warrnambool 177-80, **178**
Wartook Valley 212-13
waterfalls
Beauchamp Falls 173
Erskine Falls 168
Hopetoun Falls 173
Little River Falls 249
McKenzie Falls 207
Steavenson Falls 139
Triplet Falls 173
waterskiing 295
weather 14, 20-3, *see also individual regions*
websites 15, 126
weights 341
Welcome Stranger gold nugget 204
Werribee 79

West Melbourne 59, 76-7
Westgate Bridge 76, 77
whale watching 177, 179, 253
Wheeler Centre 54
White Night Melbourne 20
wi-fi access 341
wildlife 19, 39
wildlife sanctuaries
Ballarat Bird World 191
Jirrahlinga Koala & Wildlife Sanctuary 160
Williamstown 76-7
Wilsons Promontory 11, 42, 231, 238-42, **240**, **11**
Windsor 69, **68**
accommodation 86-7
drinking & nightlife 110-12
food 101
shopping 124-5
windsurfing 78-9
wine 322-3, *see also* wineries
wineries 17, 322-3
Bellarine Peninsula 161

Gippsland 238
Grampians, the 210
Great Ocean Road 164, 176
King Valley 265
Macedon Ranges 147
Milawa Gourmet Region 265-6
Mildura 284
Mornington Peninsula 224
Mt Beauty 275
Nagambie 302
Phillip Island 227-8
Rutherglen 300
Wahgunyah 301
Werribee 79
Yackandandah 269
Yarra Valley 137
Wodonga 304
women travellers 344
Woodend 148
Wurundjeri people 308-9, 319
Wye River 170
Wyperfeld National Park 288

Y
Yackandandah 269-70
Yanakie 239, 241-2
Yarra Ranges National Park 138
Yarra River 34, 35, 62-3, 81, 134, 138, 308
Yarra Valley 134-41, **134**
Yarra Valley Cider & Ale Trail 16, 139
Yarra Valley Railway 135
Yarraville 59
Yarrawonga 298-9

Z
ziplining 173
zoos, *see also* aquariums, wildlife sanctuaries
Ballarat Wildlife Park 191
Halls Gap Zoo 210
Mansfield Zoo 261-2
Royal Melbourne Zoo 67
Werribee Open Range Zoo 79

Map Legend

Sights

- Beach
- Bird Sanctuary
- Buddhist
- Castle/Palace
- Christian
- Confucian
- Hindu
- Islamic
- Jain
- Jewish
- Monument
- Museum/Gallery/Historic Building
- Ruin
- Sento Hot Baths/Onsen
- Shinto
- Sikh
- Taoist
- Winery/Vineyard
- Zoo/Wildlife Sanctuary
- Other Sight

Activities, Courses & Tours

- Bodysurfing
- Diving
- Canoeing/Kayaking
- Course/Tour
- Skiing
- Snorkelling
- Surfing
- Swimming/Pool
- Walking
- Windsurfing
- Other Activity

Sleeping

- Sleeping
- Camping

Eating

- Eating

Drinking & Nightlife

- Drinking & Nightlife
- Cafe

Entertainment

- Entertainment

Shopping

- Shopping

Information

- Bank
- Embassy/Consulate
- Hospital/Medical
- Internet
- Police
- Post Office
- Telephone
- Toilet
- Tourist Information
- Other Information

Geographic

- Beach
- Hut/Shelter
- Lighthouse
- Lookout
- Mountain/Volcano
- Oasis
- Park
- Pass
- Picnic Area
- Waterfall

Population

- Capital (National)
- Capital (State/Province)
- City/Large Town
- Town/Village

Transport

- Airport
- Border crossing
- Bus
- Cable car/Funicular
- Cycling
- Ferry
- Metro station
- Monorail
- Parking
- Petrol station
- Subway station
- Taxi
- Train station/Railway
- Tram
- Underground station
- Other Transport

Note: Not all symbols displayed above appear on the maps in this book

Routes

- Tollway
- Freeway
- Primary
- Secondary
- Tertiary
- Lane
- Unsealed road
- Road under construction
- Plaza/Mall
- Steps
- Tunnel
- Pedestrian overpass
- Walking Tour
- Walking Tour detour
- Path/Walking Trail

Boundaries

- International
- State/Province
- Disputed
- Regional/Suburb
- Marine Park
- Cliff
- Wall

Hydrography

- River, Creek
- Intermittent River
- Canal
- Water
- Dry/Salt/Intermittent Lake
- Reef

Areas

- Airport/Runway
- Beach/Desert
- Cemetery (Christian)
- Cemetery (Other)
- Glacier
- Mudflat
- Park/Forest
- Sight (Building)
- Sportsground
- Swamp/Mangrove

OUR STORY

A beat-up old car, a few dollars in the pocket and a sense of adventure. In 1972 that's all Tony and Maureen Wheeler needed for the trip of a lifetime – across Europe and Asia overland to Australia. It took several months, and at the end – broke but inspired – they sat at their kitchen table writing and stapling together their first travel guide, *Across Asia on the Cheap*. Within a week they'd sold 1500 copies. Lonely Planet was born.

Today, Lonely Planet has offices in Franklin, London, Melbourne, Oakland, Beijing and Delhi, with more than 600 staff and writers. We share Tony's belief that 'a great guidebook should do three things: inform, educate and amuse'.

OUR WRITERS

Anthony Ham

Coordinating Author, Goldfields & the Grampians, Mornington Peninsula & Phillip Island, Gippsland & Wilsons Promontory, The High Country, The Murray River & Around Anthony was born in Melbourne, grew up in Sydney and spent much of his adult life travelling the world. He recently returned to Australia after 10 years living in Madrid. In this coastal odyssey he found a perfect fit for his passion for wild landscapes that reminded him just how much he missed the land of his birth. He brings to the book the unique perspective of knowing the land intimately and yet seeing it anew as if through the excited eyes of an outsider. Anthony also wrote Plan Your Trip section, Melbourne & Victoria Today, History and the Survival Guide chapters.

Read more about Anthony at:
lonelyplanet.com/members/anthony_ham

Trent Holden

Melbourne, Around Melbourne, Great Ocean Road & Bellarine Peninsula, Food & Drink, Fashion & Shopping, The Arts, Sport Melbourne born and bred, Trent's a proud Victorian who's certain he lives in the best city in the world. A rabid AFL footy fan (carn the Hawks!) and cricket tragic, he's an equally passionate supporter of Melbourne's underground rock'n'roll scene. He's also spent several years living down the Great Ocean Road and has had a stint in country Victoria in Trentham. This is Trent's 15th title for Lonely Planet, covering destinations across Asia and Africa.

Kate Morgan

Melbourne, Around Melbourne, Great Ocean Road & Bellarine Peninsula, Food & Drink, Fashion & Shopping, The Arts, Sport Kate grew up in the southeastern suburb of Frankston before living for several years in the seaside suburb of St Kilda and finally crossing the river to the inner-north neighbourhood of Northcote. She's spent the past few years travelling the world writing guidebooks and has recently relocated to London as Lonely Planet's Destination Editor for Western Europe. Kate loves coming home to Melbourne for a good coffee, the great live-music scene and trips down the Great Ocean Road.

Published by Lonely Planet Publications Pty Ltd
ABN 36 005 607 983
9th edition – Jul 2014
ISBN 978 1 74220 215 0
© Lonely Planet 2014   Photographs © as indicated 2014
10 9 8 7 6 5 4 3 2 1
Printed in China

Although the authors and Lonely Planet have taken all reasonable care in preparing this book, we make no warranty about the accuracy or completeness of its content and, to the maximum extent permitted, disclaim all liability arising from its use.